SANFORD GUIDE

D0557571

THE SANFORD GUIDE
To Antimicrobial Therapy
2018

48th Edition

David N. Gilbert, M.D.
Henry F. Chambers, M.D.
George M. Eliopoulos, M.D.
Michael S. Saag, M.D.
Andrew T. Pavia, M.D.

Douglas Black, Pharm.D.
David O. Freedman, M.D.
Kami Kim, M.D.
Brian S. Schwartz, M.D.

THE SANFORD GUIDE   48th Edition
To Antimicrobial Therapy
2018

Editors

David N. Gilbert, M.D.
Chief of Infectious Diseases,
Providence Portland Medical Center, Oregon
Professor of Medicine,
Oregon Health Sciences University

George M. Eliopoulos, M.D.
Beth Israel Deaconess Hospital
Professor of Medicine,
Harvard Medical School, Boston, Massachusetts

Henry F. Chambers, M.D.
Professor of Medicine
Director, Clinical Research Services
UCSF Clinical and Translational Sciences Institute
University of California, San Francisco

Michael S. Saag, M.D.
Director, UAB Center for AIDS Research
Professor of Medicine and Director,
Division of Infectious Diseases,
University of Alabama, Birmingham

Andrew T. Pavia, M.D.
George & Esther Gross Presidential Professor
Chief, Division of Pediatric Infectious Diseases,
University of Utah, Salt Lake City

Publisher
Antimicrobial Therapy, Inc.

Contributing Editors

Douglas Black, Pharm.D.
Associate Professor of Pharmacy,
University of Washington, Seattle

Brian S. Schwartz, M.D.
Associate Professor of Medicine,
University of California at San Francisco

David O. Freedman, M.D.
Emeritus Professor of Medicine,
University of Alabama at Birmingham

Kami Kim, M.D.
Professor of Internal Medicine,
Division of Infectious Diseases
and International Medicine,
Morsani College of Medicine,
University of South Florida, Tampa

Managing Editor

Jeb C. Sanford

Memoriam

Jay P. Sanford, M.D.
1928-1996
Merle A. Sande, M.D.
1939-2007
Robert C. Moellering, Jr., M.D.
1936-2014

The GUIDE TO ANTIMICROBIAL THERAPY is updated annually and published by:

ANTIMICROBIAL THERAPY, INC.
P.O. Box 276, 11771 Lee Highway
Sperryville, VA 22740-0276 USA
Tel 540-987-9480 Fax 540-987-9486
Email: info@sanfordguide.com
www.sanfordguide.com

Acknowledgements
Thanks to Silvina Trapé and Jonatan Bohman for manuscript design and layout and to Cenveo Corp.
for printing and binding this edition of the SANFORD GUIDE.

Note to Readers
Since 1969, the SANFORD GUIDE has been independently prepared and published. Decisions regarding the content of the SANFORD GUIDE are solely those of the editors and the publisher. We welcome questions, comments and feedback concerning the SANFORD GUIDE. All of your feedback is reviewed and taken into account in updating the content of the SANFORD GUIDE.

Every effort is made to ensure accuracy of the content of this guide. However, current full prescribing information available in the package insert for each drug should be consulted before prescribing any product. The editors and publisher are not responsible for errors or omissions or for any consequences from application of the information in this book and make no warranty, express or implied, with respect to the currency, accuracy, or completeness of the contents of this publication. Application of this information in a particular situation remains the professional responsibility of the practitioner.

For the most current information, subscribe to webedition.sanfordguide.com
or Sanford Guide mobile device applications

Printed in the United States of America
ISBN 978-1-944272-06-7
Pocket Edition (English)

Antimicrobial Stewardship (AMS) and the Sanford Guide

Since 1969, The Sanford Guide to Antimicrobial Therapy has addressed the central tenets of antibiotic stewardship: administering **the right drug at the right time in the right dose.** Other facets of stewardship are addressed. For example, the application of molecular diagnostics and biomarkers can facilitate:

> Rapid identification of the presence or absence of pathogens and/or viruses or other microbes.
> With rapid identification, therapy can switch from empiricism to specific/directed therapy.
> Biomarkers can assist in customizing the duration of therapy.

We have expanded and highlighted stewardship considerations in Sanford Guide digital editions with a new section on Antimicrobial Stewardship, which can be found below Alternative Regimens on relevant pages.

Sanford Guide with Stewardship Assist is a digital solution which allows institutions to disseminate localized stewardship guidelines and recommendations through the Sanford Guide Web Edition and Sanford Guide Collection app. This product allows antimicrobial stewardship programs to:

> Display institutional resistance data in a user-friendly antibiogram similar to the Sanford Guide Spectra of Activity.
> Add localized AMS recommendations for each organism/antibiotic interaction on the Spectra of Activity.
> Develop separate antibiograms for different wards and facilities.
> Display institution-specific stewardship recommendations at the top of Sanford Guide content pages.
> Disseminate stewardship recommendations through web and mobile app platforms without the need for in-house development or IT support.

- Visit www.sanfordguide.com/stewardship for product information and to schedule a demonstration for your stewardship team.

Selected Sanford Guide Stewardship Resources In This Edition

> Suggested Duration of Therapy for Selected Bacterial Infections (Table 3)
> Dosing Adjustments for Renal Impairment (Table 17A)
> Dosing Adjustments for Obesity (Table 17C)
> Continuous or Prolonged Infusion Dosing (Table 10E)
> Pharmacology of Antimicrobial Agents (Table 9A, 9C)
> Pharmacodynamics of Antimicrobial Agents (Table 9B)
> Treatment Options for Multi-drug Resistant Bacteria (Table 5, Table 6)
> Antibacterial Activity Spectra (Table 4)

—TABLE OF CONTENTS—

ABBREVIATIONS

3TC = lamivudine
Ab,% = percent absorbed
ABC = abacavir
ABCD = amphotericin B colloidal dispersion
ABLC = ampho B lipid complex
AD = after dialysis
ADF = adefovir
AG = aminoglycoside
AIDS = Acquired Immune Deficiency Syndrome
AM-CL = amoxicillin-clavulanate
AM-CL-ER = amoxicillin-clavulanate extended release
Amox = amoxicillin
AMP = ampicillin
Ampho B = amphotericin B
AM-SB = ampicillin-sulbactam
AP = atovaquone proguanil
APAG = antipseudomonal aminoglycoside
ARDS = acute respiratory distress syndrome
ARF = acute rheumatic fever
ASA = aspirin
ATS = American Thoracic Society
ATV = atazanavir
AUC = area under the curve
Azithro = azithromycin
bid = 2x per day
BL/BLI = beta-lactam/beta-lactamase inhibitor
BSA = body surface area
BW = body weight
C&S = culture & sensitivity
C/S = culture & sensitivity
CAPD = continuous ambulatory peritoneal dialysis
CARB = carbapenems
CDC = U.S. Centers for Disease Control
Cefpodox = cefpodoxime proxetil
Ceftaz = ceftazidime
Ceph = cephalosporin
CFB = ceftobiprole
CFP = cefepime
Chloro = chloramphenicol
CIP = ciprofloxacin; CIP-ER = CIP extended release
Clarithro = clarithromycin; ER = extended release
Clav = clavulanate
Clinda = clindamycin
CLO = clofazimine
Clot = clotrimazole
CMV = cytomegalovirus
Cobi = cobicistat
CQ = chloroquine phosphate
CrCl = creatinine clearance
CrCln = CrCl normalized for BSA
CRRT = continuous renal replacement therapy
CSD = cat-scratch disease

CSF = cerebrospinal fluid
CXR = chest x-ray
Dapto = daptomycin
DBPCT = double-blind placebo-controlled trial
dc = discontinue
ddC = zalcitabine
ddI = didanosine
DIC = disseminated intravascular coagulation
Diclox = dicloxacillin
div = divided
DLV = delavirdine
DOR = doripenem
DOT = directly observed therapy
Doxy = doxycycline
DR = delayed release
DRSP = drug-resistant S. pneumoniae
DRBPCT = Double blind, randomized, placebo-controlled trial
DS = double strength
EBV = Epstein-Barr virus
EES = erythromycin ethyl succinate
EFZ = efavirenz
ELV = elvitegravir
EMB = ethambutol
EMT = ethambutol
ENT = entecavir
ER = extended release
ERTA = ertapenem
Eryth = erythromycin
ESBLs = extended spectrum β-lactamases
ESR = erythrocyte sedimentation rate
ESRD = endstage renal disease
Flu = fluconazole
Flucyt = flucytosine
FOS-APV = fosamprenavir
FQ = fluoroquinolone
FTC = emtricitabine
G = generic
GAS = Group A Strep
Gati = gatifloxacin
GC = gonorrhea
Gemi = gemifloxacin
Gent = gentamicin
gm = gram
GNB = gram-negative bacilli
Grazo = grazoprevir
Griseo = griseofulvin
Gtts = drops
H/O = history of
HEMO = hemodialysis
HHV = human herpesvirus
HIV = human immunodeficiency virus
HLR = high-level resistance
HSCT = hematopoietic stem cell transplant

HSV = herpes simplex virus
IA = injectable agent/anti-inflammatory drugs
IDV = indinavir
IFN = interferon
IM = intramuscular
IMP = imipenem-cilastatin
INH = isoniazid
Inv = investigational
IP = intraperitoneal
IT = intrathecal
Itra = itraconazole
IV = intravenous
IVDU = intravenous drug user
IVIG = intravenous immune globulin
Keto = ketoconazole
kg = kilogram
LAB = liposomal ampho B
LCM = lymphocytic choriomeningitis virus
LCR = ligase chain reaction
Levo = levofloxacin
LP/R = lopinavir/ ritonavir
mcg (or μg) = microgram
MDR = multi-drug resistant
MER = meropenem
Metro = metronidazole
Mino = minocycline
mL = milliliter
Moxi = moxifloxacin
MQ = mefloquine
MSM = men who have sex with men
MSSA/MRSA = methicillin-sensitive/resistant S. aureus
MTB = Mycobacterium tuberculosis
NAI = not FDA-approved (indication or dose)
NAF = Nafcillin
NB = name brand
NF = nitrofurantoin
NFR = nelfinavir
NNRTI = non-nucleoside reverse transcriptase inhibitor
NRTI = nucleoside reverse transcriptase inhibitor
NSAIDs = non-steroidal
NUS = not available in the U.S.
NVP = nevirapine
O Ceph = oral cephalosporins
Oflox = ofloxacin
P Ceph = parenteral cephalosporins
PCR = polymerase chain reaction
PEP = post-exposure prophylaxis
PI = protease inhibitor
PIP-TZ = piperacillin-tazobactam
PO = oral dosing
PQ = primaquine
PRCT = Prospective randomized controlled trials
PTLD = post-transplant lymphoproliferative disease

ABBREVIATIONS (2)

Pts = patients
Pyri = pyrimethamine
PZA = pyrazinamide
q wk = dose weekly
q[x]h = every [x] hours, e.g., q8h = every 8 hrs
qid = 4x per day
QS = quinine sulfate
Quinu-dalfo = Q-D = quinupristin-dalfopristin
R = resistant
RFB = rifabutin
RFP = rifapentine
Rick = Rickettsia
RIF = rifampin
RSV = respiratory syncytial virus
RTI = respiratory tract infection
RTV = ritonavir
rx = treatment
SA = Staph. aureus

sc = subcutaneous
SSPE = Subacute sclerosing panencephalitis
SD = serum drug level after single dose
Sens = sensitive (susceptible)
SM = streptomycin
Sofos = sofosbuvir
SQV = saquinavir
SS = steady state serum level
STD = sexually transmitted disease
subcut = subcutaneous
Sulb = sulbactam
Sx = symptoms
TAF = tenofovir alafenamide
Tazo = tazobactam
TBc = tuberculosis
TDF = tenofovir
TEE = transesophageal echocardiography
Telco = teicoplanin

Telithro = telithromycin
Tetra = tetracycline
tid = 3x per day
TMP-SMX = trimethoprim-sulfamethoxazole
TNF = tumor necrosis factor
Tobra = tobramycin
TPV = tipranavir
TST = tuberculin skin test
UTI = urinary tract infection
Vanco = vancomycin
Velpat = velpatasvir
VISA = vancomycin intermediately resistant S. aureus
VL = viral load
Von = voriconazole
VZV = varicella-zoster virus
ZDV = zidovudine

ABBREVIATIONS OF JOURNAL TITLES

AAC: Antimicrobial Agents & Chemotherapy
Adv PID: Advances in Pediatric Infectious Diseases
AHJ: American Heart Journal
AIDS Res Hum Retrovir: AIDS Research & Human Retroviruses
AJG: American Journal of Gastroenterology
AJM: American Journal of Medicine
AJRCCM: American Journal of Respiratory Critical Care Medicine
AJTMH: American Journal of Tropical Medicine & Hygiene
Aliment Pharmacol Ther: Alimentary Pharmacology & Therapeutics
Am J Hlth Pharm: American Journal of Health-System Pharmacy
Amer J Transpl: American Journal of Transplantation
AnEM: Annals of Emergency Medicine
AnIM: Annals of Internal Medicine
Ann Pharmacother: Annals of Pharmacotherapy
AnSurg: Annals of Surgery
Antivir Ther: Antiviral Therapy
ArDerm: Archives of Dermatology
ArIM: Archives of Internal Medicine
ARRD: American Review of Respiratory Disease
BMJ: British Medical Journal
BMT: Bone Marrow Transplantation
Brit J Derm: British Journal of Dermatology
Can JID: Canadian Journal of Infectious Diseases
Canad Med J: Canadian Medical Journal
CCM: Critical Care Medicine
CCTID: Current Clinical Topics in Infectious Disease
CDSR: Cochrane Database of Systematic Reviews
CID: Clinical Infectious Diseases
Clin Micro Inf: Clinical Microbiology and Infection
CMN: Clinical Microbiology Newsletter
Clin Micro Rev: Clinical Microbiology Reviews
CMAJ: Canadian Medical Association Journal
COID: Current Opinion in Infectious Disease

Curr Med Res Opin: Current Medical Research and Opinion
Derm Ther: Dermatologic Therapy
Dermatol Clin: Dermatologic Clinics
Dig Dis Sci: Digestive Diseases and Sciences
DMID: Diagnostic Microbiology and Infectious Disease
EID: Emerging Infectious Diseases
EJCMID: European Journal of Clin. Micro & Infectious Diseases
Eur J Neurol: European Journal of Neurology
Exp Mol Path: Experimental & Molecular Pathology
Exp Rev Anti Infect Ther: Expert Review of Anti-Infective Therapy
Gastro: Gastroenterology
Hpt: Hepatology
ICHE: Infection Control and Hospital Epidemiology
IDC No. Amer: Infectious Disease Clinics of North America
IDCP: Infectious Diseases in Clinical Practice
IJAA: International Journal of Antimicrobial Agents
Inf Dis: Infectious Diseases
JAIDS HR: Journal of AIDS and Human Retrovirology
J All Clin Immun: Journal of Allergy and Clinical Immunology
J Am Ger Soc: Journal of the American Geriatrics Society
J Chemother: Journal of Chemotherapy
J Clin Micro: Journal of Clinical Microbiology
J Clin Virol: Journal of Clinical Virology
J Derm Treat: Journal of Dermatological Treatment
J Hpt: Journal of Hepatology
J Inf: Journal of Infection
J Med Micro: Journal of Medical Microbiology
Micro Immunol Inf: Journal of Microbiology, Immunology, & Infection
J Ped: Journal of Pediatrics
J Viral Hep: Journal of Viral Hepatitis
JACC: Journal of American College of Cardiology
JAC: Journal of Antimicrobial Chemotherapy
JAIDS: Journal of Acquired Immune Deficiency Syndromes

JAMA: Journal of the American Medical Association
JAVMA: Journal of the American Veterinary Medicine Association
JCI: Journal of Clinical Investigation
JCM: Journal of Clinical Microbiology
JIC: Journal of Infection and Chemotherapy
JID: Journal of Infectious Diseases
JNS: Journal of Neurosurgery
JPIDS: Journal of Pediatric Infectious Diseases Society
JTMH: Journal of Tropical Medicine and Hygiene
Ln: Lancet
LnID: Lancet Infectious Disease
Mayo Clin Proc: Mayo Clinic Proceedings
Med Lett: Medical Letter
Med Mycol: Medical Mycology
MMWR: Morbidity & Mortality Weekly Report
NEJM: New England Journal of Medicine
Neph Dial Transpl: Nephrology Dialysis Transplantation
OFID: Open Forum Infectious Diseases
Ped Ann: Pediatric Annals
Peds: Pediatrics
Pharmacother: Pharmacotherapy
PIDJ: Pediatric Infectious Disease Journal
QJM: Quarterly Journal of Medicine
Scand J Inf Dis: Scandinavian Journal of Infectious Diseases
Sem Resp Inf: Seminars in Respiratory Infections
SGO: Surgery Gynecology and Obstetrics
SMJ: Southern Medical Journal
Surg Neurol: Surgical Neurology
Transpl Inf Dis: Transplant Infectious Diseases
Transpl: Transplantation
TRSM: Transactions of the Royal Society of Medicine

TABLE 1 – CLINICAL APPROACH TO INITIAL CHOICE OF ANTIMICROBIAL THERAPY[a]

Treatment based on presumed site or type of infection. In selected instances, treatment and prophylaxis based on identification of pathogens.
Regimens should be reevaluated based on pathogen isolated, antimicrobial susceptibility determination, and individual host characteristics. *(Abbreviations on 2)*

ANATOMIC SITE/DIAGNOSIS/ MODIFYING CIRCUMSTANCES	ETIOLOGIES (usual)	SUGGESTED REGIMENS[c]		ADJUNCT DIAGNOSTIC OR THERAPEUTIC MEASURES AND COMMENTS
		PRIMARY	ALTERNATIVE[§]	
ABDOMEN: See *Peritoneum, page 47; Gallbladder, page 12;* and *Pelvic Inflammatory Disease, page 26*				
BONE: Osteomyelitis. Microbiologic diagnosis is essential. If blood culture negative, need culture of bone (*Eur J Clin Microbiol Infect Dis 33:371, 2014*). Culture of sinus tract drainage not predictive of bone culture. For comprehensive review of antimicrobial penetration into bone, see *Clinical Pharmacokinetics 48:89, 2009.*				
Hematogenous Osteomyelitis (*see IDSA guidelines for vertebral osteo: CID July 29, 2015*)				
Empiric therapy—Collect bone and blood cultures before empiric therapy				
Newborn (<4 mos.)	S. aureus, Gm-neg. bacilli, Group B strep, Kingella kingae in children	**MRSA possible: Vanco + (Ceftaz or CFP)**	**MRSA unlikely: (Nafcillin or Oxacillin) + (Ceftaz or CFP)**	Severe allergy or toxicity: (**Linezolid[NAI]** 10 mg/kg IV/po q8h + Aztreonam).
Children (>4 mos.) – Adult: Osteo of extremity (*NEJM 370:352, 2014*)	S. aureus, Group A strep, Gm-neg. bacilli rare, Kingella kingae in children	**MRSA possible: Vanco** 40 mg/kg/day div q6h	**MRSA unlikely: (Nafcillin or Oxacillin)** 150 mg/kg/day div q6h (max. 12 gm).	Severe allergy or toxicity: **Clinda** or **TMP-SMX** or **Linezolid[NAI]**. Adults: **Ceftaz** 2 gm IV q8h. **CFP** 2 gm IV q12h. See *Table 10B* for *adverse reactions to drugs.*
		Add **Ceftaz** or **CFP** if Gm-neg. bacilli on Gram stain		
		Adult doses below.		
Adult (>21 yrs) **Vertebral osteo ± epidural abscess** (*see IDSA guidelines for vertebral osteo: CID 61:859, 2015*) **Blood & bone cultures essential.**	S. aureus most common but variety other organisms. Brucella, M. tuberculosis, Coccidioides important in regions of high endemicity for the organisms	**Vanco** 15-20 mg/kg IV q 8-12h *(vanco serum levels 15-20 µg/mL)* + (**Ceftriaxone** 2 gm q24h OR **CFP** 2 gm q8h OR **Levo** 750 mg q24h)	**Dapto** 6 mg/kg IV q24h OR **Linezolid** 600 mg q12h + (**Ceftriaxone** 2 gm q24h OR **CFP** 2 gm q24h OR **Levo** 750 mg q24h)	**Ceftriaxone** should not be used if pseudomonas suspected. **Piperacillin/Tazobactam** another option for pseudomonas or other Gram-negative coverage. **Dx:** MRI diagnostic test of choice, indicated to rule out epidural abscess. **Risk factors for recurrence:** end-stage renal disease, MRSA infection, undrained paravertebral or psoas abscess; pathogen-specific therapy for >8 wks recommended if any of these are present (*CID 62:1262, 2016*); complicated infection (*CID 62:1261, 2016 and Lancet 385-875, 2015*). Whenever possible empirical therapy should be administered after cultures are obtained.

[a] DOSAGES SUGGESTED are for adults (unless otherwise indicated) with clinically severe (often life-threatening) infections. Dosages also assume normal renal function, and not severe hepatic dysfunction.
[§] ALTERNATIVE THERAPY INCLUDES these considerations: allergy, pharmacology/pharmacokinetics, compliance, costs, local resistance profiles.

TABLE 1 (2)

ANATOMIC SITE/DIAGNOSIS/ MODIFYING CIRCUMSTANCES	ETIOLOGIES (usual)	SUGGESTED REGIMENS* PRIMARY	ALTERNATIVE§	ADJUNCT DIAGNOSTIC OR THERAPEUTIC MEASURES AND COMMENTS
BONE/Hematogenous Osteomyelitis *(continued)*				
Specific therapy—Culture and in vitro susceptibility results known. *See CID Jul 29, 2015 for IDSA Guidelines*				
	MSSA	**Nafcillin** or **Oxacillin** 2 gm IV q4h or **Cefazolin** 2 gm IV q8h	**Vanco** 15-30 mg/kg IV q 3-12h for trough of 15-20 μg/mL, OR **Dapto** 6-8 mg/kg IV q24h OR **Linezolid** 600 mg IV/po q12h	**Other options if susceptible in vitro and allergy/toxicity issues** (see *NEJM 362:11, 2010*): 1) **TMP-SMX** 8-10 mg/kg/d po/IV div q8h + **RIF** 300-450 mg bid: limited data, particularly for MRSA (see *AAC 53:2672, 2009*); 2) **Levo** 750 mg po q24h) + **RIF** 600 mg po q24h; 3) **Fusidic acid**^NUS 500 mg IV q8h + **RIF** 300 mg po bid. (*CID 42:394, 2006*); 4) **Ceftriaxone** 2 gm IV q24h *(CID 54:585, 2012)*
	MRSA—*See Table 6, page 87; IDSA Guidelines CID 52:e18-55, 2011; CID 52:285-92, 2011*	**Vanco** 15-20 mg/kg IV q 8-12h for trough of 15-20 μg/mL ± **RIF** 300-450 mg po bid	**Linezolid** 600 mg po q12h IV/po ± **RIF** 300 mg po/IV bid OR **Dapto** 6 mg/kg q24h IV ± **RIF** 300-450 mg po/IV bid	*(MSSA only):* Duration of therapy: 6 weeks, provided that epidural or paravertebral abscesses can be drained; consider longer course in those with extensive infection or abscess particularly if not amenable to drainage because of increased risk of treatment failure (*OFID Dec 5:1, 2014*) (although data are lacking that this approach improves efficacy versus a 6 wks course) and >8 weeks in patients undergoing device implantation (*CID 60:1330, 2015*).
Hemoglobinopathy: Sickle cell/thalassemia	Salmonella; other Gm-neg. bacilli	**CIP** 400 mg IV q12h OR **CIP** 750 mg po bid	**Levo** 750 mg IV/po q24h	Thalassemia: transfusion and iron chelation risk factors. Because of decreasing levels of susceptibility to fluoroquinolones among Salmonella spp. and growing resistance among other gram-negative bacilli, would add a second agent (e.g., third-generation cephalosporin) until susceptibility test results available. Alternative for salmonella is Ceftriaxone 2 gm IV q24h if nalidixic acid resistant, which is predictive of fluoroquinolone resistance.
Contiguous Osteomyelitis Without Vascular Insufficiency				
Empiric therapy: Get cultures!				
Foot bone osteo due to nail through tennis shoe	P. aeruginosa	**CIP** 750 mg po bid or **Levo** 750 mg po bid	**Ceftaz** 2 gm IV q8h or **CFP** 2 gm IV q8h	See *Skin—Nail puncture, page 58*. Need debridement to remove foreign body.
Long bone, post-internal fixation of fracture	S. aureus, Gm-neg. bacilli, P. aeruginosa	**Vanco** 15-20 mg/kg q8-12h IV for trough of 15-20 μg/mL + **[Ceftaz** or **CFP]**, See Comment	**Linezolid** 600 mg IV/po; bid^NAI + **(Ceftaz** or **CFP)**. See Comment	Often necessary to remove hardware after union to achieve eradication. May need revascularization. **Regimens listed are empiric.** Adjust after culture data available. If susceptible Gm-neg. bacillus, **CIP** 750 mg po bid or **Levo** 750 mg po q24h. For other S. aureus options: *See Hem. Osteo, Specific Therapy, page 5.*
Osteonecrosis of the jaw	Probably rare adverse reaction to bisphosphonates	Infection may be secondary to bone necrosis and loss of overlying mucosa. Treatment: minimal surgical debridement, chlorhexidine rinses, antibiotics (e.g. PIP-TZ). Evaluate for concomitant actinomycosis, for which specific long-term antibiotic treatment would be warranted.		
Prosthetic joint	*See prosthetic joint, page 33*			
Spinal implant infection	S. aureus, coag-neg staphylococci, gram-neg bacilli	Onset within 30 days: culture, treat for 3 mos.	Onset after 30 days remove imp/ant, culture & treat	See *CID 55:1481, 2012*
Sternum, post-op	S. aureus, S. epidermidis, occasionally, gram-negative bacilli	**Vanco** 15-20 mg/kg q8-12h IV for trough of 15-20 μg/mL recommended for serious infections.	**Linezolid** 600 mg po/IV^NAI bid	Sternal debridement for cultures & removal of necrotic bone. For S. aureus options: *Hem. Osteo. Specific Therapy, page 5.* If setting or gram stain suggests possibility of gram-negative bacilli, add appropriate coverage based on local antimicrobial susceptibility profiles (e.g., cefepime, PIP-TZ).

Abbreviations on page 2. ^NOTE: All dosage recommendations are for adults (unless otherwise indicated) and assume normal renal function. §Alternatives consider allergy, PK, compliance, local resistance, cost.

TABLE 1 (3)

ANATOMIC SITE/DIAGNOSIS/ MODIFYING CIRCUMSTANCES	ETIOLOGIES (usual)	SUGGESTED REGIMENS* PRIMARY	SUGGESTED REGIMENS* ALTERNATIVE§	ADJUNCT DIAGNOSTIC OR THERAPEUTIC MEASURES AND COMMENTS
BONE (continued)				
Contiguous Osteomyelitis With Vascular Insufficiency.				
Most pts are **diabetics** with peripheral neuropathy & infected skin ulcers (see *Diabetic foot, page 17*)	Polymicrobic [Gm+ cocci (to include MRSA) (aerobic & anaerobic) and Gm-neg. bacilli (aerobic & anaerobic)]	Debride overlying ulcer & submit bone for histology & culture. Select antibiotic based on culture results & treat for 6 weeks. **No empiric therapy unless acutely ill.** If acutely ill, see suggestions, *Diabetic foot, page 17*. Revascularize if possible.		**Diagnosis of osteo:** Culture bone biopsy (gold standard). Poor concordance of culture results between swab of ulcer and bone – need bone. Sampling by needle puncture inferior to biopsy (CID 49:888, 2009). Osteo likely if ulcer >2 cm², positive probe to bone, ESR >70 & abnormal plain x-ray (JAMA 299:806, 2008). **Treatment:** (1) Culture bone biopsy; (2) Revascularize if possible; (3) Specific antimicrobial(s).
Chronic Osteomyelitis: **Specific therapy** By definition, implies presence of dead bone. **Need valid cultures**	S. aureus, Enterobacteriaceae, P. aeruginosa	**Empiric rx not indicated.** Base systemic rx on results of culture, sensitivity testing. If acute exacerbation of chronic osteo, rx as acute hematogenous osteo. Surgical debridement important.		**Important adjuncts:** removal of orthopedic hardware, surgical debridement; vascularized muscle flaps, distraction osteogenesis (Ilizarov) techniques. Antibiotic-impregnated cement & hyperbaric oxygen adjunctive. **NOTE: RIF + (Vanco or β-lactam)** effective in animal model and in a clinical trial of S. aureus chronic osteo. The contribution of rifampin-containing regimens in this setting is not clear, however (AAC 53:2672, 2009).
BREAST: Mastitis—Obtain culture; need to know if MRSA present. Review with definitions: BMJ 342:d396, 2011.				
Postpartum mastitis (Recent Cochrane Review: Cochrane Database Syst Rev 2013 Feb 28:2:CD005458; see also CID 54:71, 2012)				
Mastitis without abscess	S. aureus; less often S. pyogenes (Gp A or B), E. coli, bacteroides species, maybe Corynebacterium sp. & selected coagulase-neg. staphylococci (e.g., S. lugdunensis)	**NO MRSA:** **Outpatient:** Diclo 500 mg po qid or **Cephalexin** 500 mg po qid **Inpatient: Nafcillin** or **Oxacillin** 2 gm IV q4-6h	**MRSA Possible:** **Outpatient: TMP-SMX-DS** tabs 1-2 po bid or, if susceptible, **Clinda** 300 mg po q12h. **Inpatient: Vanco** 1 gm q12h; if over 100 kg, 1.5 gm IV q12h.	If no abscess & controllable pain, ↑ freq of nursing may hasten response.
Mastitis with abscess				For painful abscess I&D is standard; needle aspiration reported successful. Resume breast feeding from affected breast as soon as pain allows. (Breastfeed Med 9:239, 2014)
Non-puerperal mastitis with abscess	S. aureus; less often Bacteroides sp., peptostreptococcus, & selected coagulase-neg. staphylococci	See regimens for Postpartum mastitis, page 6.		Smoking and diabetes may be risk factors (BMJ 342:d396, 2011). If **subareolar & odoriferous,** most likely anaerobes; need to add **Metro** 500 mg IV/po tid. If not subareolar, staph. Need pretreatment aerobic/anaerobic cultures. Surgical drainage for abscess. **I&D standard.** Corynebacterium sp. assoc. with chronic granulomatous mastitis (JCM 53:2895, 2015). Consider **TB in chronic infections.**
Breast implant infection	Acute: S. aureus, S. pyogenes, TSS reported. Chronic: Look for rapidly growing Mycobacteria	Acute: **Vanco** 15-20 mg/kg IV q8-12h.	Chronic: Await culture results. See Table 12A for mycobacteria treatment.	Risk of complications higher with late-onset infection (>30 days post implantation). Antibiotics alone may be sufficient for minor infections; explantation often required for more serious infections. Plast. Reconstr. Surg 139:20, 2017.

Abbreviations on page 2.   *NOTE: All dosage recommendations are for adults (unless otherwise indicated) and assume normal renal function. § Alternatives consider allergy, PK, compliance, local resistance, cost.

TABLE 1 (4)

ANATOMIC SITE/DIAGNOSIS/ MODIFYING CIRCUMSTANCES	ETIOLOGIES (usual)	SUGGESTED REGIMENS*		ADJUNCT DIAGNOSTIC OR THERAPEUTIC MEASURES AND COMMENTS
		PRIMARY	ALTERNATIVE$	
CENTRAL NERVOUS SYSTEM				
Brain abscess				
Primary or contiguous source Review: *NEJM 371:447, 2014.* Mild infection: *NEJM 371:150, 2014.*	Streptococci (60–70%), bacteroides (20–40%), Enterobacteriaceae (25–33%), S. aureus (10–15%), S. anginosus grp. Rare: Nocardia (*below*), Listeria. See *S. aureus Comment*	**P Ceph 3 ((Cefotaxime** 2 gm IV q4h **or Ceftriaxone** 2 gm IV q12h) **+ (Metro** 7.5 mg/kg q6h or 15 mg/kg IV q12h)) Duration of rx usually 4–6 wks or until resolution by neuroimaging (CT/MRI)	**Pen G** 3–4 million units IV q4h + **Metro** 7.5 mg/kg q6h or 15 mg/kg q12h	If CT scan suggests cerebritis or abscesses <2.5 cm and pt neurologically stable and conscious, start antibiotics and observe. Otherwise, surgical drainage necessary. If blood cultures or other clinical data do not yield a likely etiologic agent, aspirate even small abscesses for diagnosis if this can be done safely. Experience with Pen G (HD) + metro without Ceftriaxone or Nafcillin/Oxacillin has been good. We use Ceftriaxone because of frequency of isolation of Enterobacteriaceae. S. aureus rare without positive blood culture; if S. aureus, use vanco until susceptibility known. Strep. anginosus grp. esp. prone to produce abscess. Ceph/metro does not cover listeria.
Post-surgical, post-traumatic. Review: *NEJM 371:447, 2014.*	S. aureus, Enterobacteriaceae	**For MSSA: (Nafcillin** or **Oxacillin)** 2 gm IV q4h + **(Ceftriaxone** or **Cefotaxime)**	**For MRSA: Vanco** 15–20 mg/kg IV q 8-12h for trough of 15–20 mcg/mL + **(Ceftriaxone** or **Cefotaxime)**	Empiric coverage, de-escalated based on culture results. **Aspiration of abscess usually necessary for dx & rx. If P. aeruginosa suspected,** substitute (Cefepime or Ceftazidime) for (Ceftriaxone or Cefotaxime).
HIV-1 Infected (AIDS)	Toxoplasma gondii	See *Table 13A, page 160*		
Nocardia Haematogenous abscess	N. farcinica, N. asteroides & N. brasiliensis See *AAC 58:795, 2014* for other species.	**TMP-SMX:** 15 mg/kg/day of TMP & 75 mg/kg/day of SMX, IV/po div in 2-4 doses + **Imipenem** 500 mg IV q6h. If multiorgan involvement some add **Amikacin** 7.5 mg/kg q12h. After 3–6 wks of IV therapy, switch to po therapy. Immunocompetent pts: **TMP-SMX, minocycline** or **AM-CL** x 3+ months. Immunocompromised pts: Treat with 2 drugs x 1 yr.	**Linezolid** 600 mg IV or po q12h + **meropenem** 2 gm q8h	Linezolid 600 mg po bid reported effective. For in vitro susceptibility testing: Wallace (+1) 903-877-7680 or U.S. CDC (+1) 404-639-3158. **TMP-SMX** remains a drug of choice for CNS nocardia infection: in vitro resistance to TMP-SMX may be increasing (*CID 51:1445, 2010*), but whether this is associated with worse outcomes is not known and a recent study casts doubt on this with only 2.5% of 552 isolates resistant; difficulties with end-point determinations might account for discrepancies in reported rates of resistance (*JCM 50:670, 2012*). If sulfonamide resistant or sulfa-allergic, **Amikacin** plus one of: **IMP, MER, Ceftriaxone** or **Cefotaxime. N. farcinica** is resistant to third-generation cephalosporins, which should not be used for treatment of infection caused by this organism. *N. farcinica* TMP-SMX resistance reported, see *JCM 50:670, 2012* (before stopping TMP-SMX).
Subdural empyema: In adult 60–90% is extension of sinusitis or otitis media. Rx same as primary brain abscess. Surgical emergency, must drain. Review in *LnID 7:62, 2007.*				
Encephalitis/encephalopathy *IDSA Guideline: CID 47:303, 2008; CID 57:1114, 2009).* *Intl diagnosis consensus: CID 57:1114, 2013.* (For Herpes see *Table 14A, page 175* and for rabies, *Table 20B, page 243*)	H. simplex (42%), VZV (15%), M. TB (15%), Listeria (10%) arbovirus, West Nile, rabies, Lyme, Parvo B19, Cat-scratch, Mycoplasma, EBV and others.	**Start IV Acyclovir** while awaiting results of CSF PCR for H. simplex. For amebic encephalitis, see *Table 13A*. Start **Doxycycline** 100 mg q12h if setting suggests R. rickettsii, Anaplasma, Ehrlichia or Mycoplasma. **Ceftriaxone** 2 gm q24h **or Doxycycline** 100 mg q12h x 14 days for Lyme encephalitis.	Review of encephalitis: *LnID 10:835, 2010.* **Anti-NMDAR** (N-Methyl-D-Aspartate Receptor) encephalitis: an autoimmune encephalitis, more common than individual viral etiologies as a cause of encephalitis in the California Encephalitis Project cohort (*CID 54:899, 2012*). Refs: *Chest 145:174-3, 2014; J Clin Neuroscience 21:722 & 1169, 2014.*
Meningitis, "Aseptic": Pleocytosis of up to 100s of cells, CSF glucose normal, neg. culture for bacteria (See *Table 14A, page 172*) Ref: *CID 47:783, 2008*	Enteroviruses, HSV-2, LCM, HIV, VZV, other viruses, syphilis, drugs (NSAIDs, metronidazole, carbamazepine, lamotrigine TMP-SMX, IVIG, (e.g., detuximab, infliximab)), rarely leptospirosis, Lyme.	For all but leptospirosis, IV fluids and analgesics. D/C drugs that may be etiology. For lepto (**Doxy** 100 mg IV/po q12h or (**Pen G** 5 million units IV q6h) or (**AMP** 0.5–1 gm IV q6h). Repeat LP if suspect partially-treated bacterial meningitis. For VZV or HSV q8h symptoms given IV **acyclovir** 5-10 mg/kg IV q8h if severe neuro meningitis (NOTE: distinct from HSV encephalitis where early rx is mandatory).	If available, PCR of CSF for enteroviruses. VZV, HSV-2: concurrent or history of prior genital lesions often absent (*see J Neurovirol 19:166, 2013*). For lepto, possible epidemiologic history and concomitant hepatitis, conjunctival suffusion and/or other organ involvement. Etiologies by PCR (% of cases): enterovirus (26-35%), HSV (0-3%), VZV (8%), varies — CNN paloclonal bands, aseptic meningitis; *see page 60.* Etiologies: *Med 95:e2372, 2016.*

Abbreviations on page 2.   *NOTE: All dosage recommendations are for adults (unless otherwise indicated) and assume normal renal function. $ Alternatives consider allergy, PK, compliance, local resistance, cost.*

TABLE 1 (5)

ANATOMIC SITE/DIAGNOSIS/ MODIFYING CIRCUMSTANCES	ETIOLOGIES (usual)	SUGGESTED REGIMENS*		ADJUNCT DIAGNOSTIC OR THERAPEUTIC MEASURES AND COMMENTS
		PRIMARY	ALTERNATIVE§	
CENTRAL NERVOUS SYSTEM *(continued)*				
Meningitis, Bacterial, Acute: Goal is empiric therapy, then CSF exam within 30 min. If focal neurologic deficit, give empiric therapy, then head CT, then LP. For distribution of pathogens by age group, see *NEJM 364:2016, 2011.*				
Empiric Therapy—CSF Gram stain is negative—Immunocompetent				
Age: Preterm to <1 mo *LnID 10-32, 2010*	Group B strep 49%, E. coli 18%, listeria 7%, misc. Gm-neg. 10%, misc. Gm-pos. 10%	AMP 75-100 mg/kg IV q6h + Cefotaxime 75 mg/kg IV q6h + Gentamicin 2.5 mg/kg IV q8h or 5-7 mg/kg IV q24h. Intraventricular treatment not recommended.	AMP 75-100 mg/kg IV q6h + Cefotaxime 75 mg/kg IV q6h OR AMP 75-100 mg/kg IV q6h + Gent 2.5 mg/kg IV q8h	Regimens active vs. Group B strep, most coliforms, & listeria. If premature infant with long nursery stay, S. aureus, enterococci, and resistant coliforms potential pathogens. **If high risk of MRSA,** use vanco + cefotaxime. Alter regimen after culture/ sensitivity data available.
Age: 1 mo– 50 yrs *Recent review: Lancet Infect Dis 16:339, 2016.*	S. pneumo, meningococci. **H. influenzae** uncommon, **listeria unlikely if young adult & immunocompetent** (add **Ampicillin** if suspect listeria: 2 gm IV q4h)	Adult dosage: [(Cefotaxime 2 gm IV q4-6h OR Ceftriaxone 2 gm IV q12h)] + Dexamethasone + Vanco. Dexamethasone: 0.15 mg/kg IV q6h x 2-4 days. Give with, or just before, 1st dose of antibiotic to block TNF production (see Comment). See footnote¹ for Vanco Adult dosage and¹ for ped. dosage	[(MER 2 gm IV q8h) (Peds: 40 mg/kg IV q8h)] + IV Dexamethasone + Vanco¹	Value of **Dexamethasone** shown in children with H. influenzae and adults with S. pneumoniae in some studies (*NEJM 357:2437 & 2441, 2007; LnID 4:139, 2004*). In the Netherlands, adoption of dexamethasone treatment in adult pneumococcal meningitis led to reduced mortality and hearing loss compared with historical control group (*Neurology 75:1533, 2010*). For patients with severe β-lactam allergy, see below (*Empiric Therapy- positive gram stain and Specific Therapy*) for alternative therapies.
Age: >50 yrs or alcoholism or other debilitating assoc diseases or impaired cellular immunity	S. pneumo, listeria, meningo- cocci, Gm-neg. bacilli	(AMP 2 gm IV q4h) + (Ceftriaxone 2 gm IV q12h or Cefotaxime 2 gm IV q4-6h) + Vanco + IV Dexamethasone For Vanco dose, see footnote¹. Dexamethasone: 0.15 mg/kg IV q6h x 2-4 days, 1st dose before, or concomitant with, 1st dose of antibiotic.	MER 2 gm IV q8h + Vanco + IV Dexamethasone. For severe pen. Allergy, see Comment.	For patients with severe β-lactam allergy, see below (*Empiric Therapy— positive gram stain and Specific Therapy*) for alternative agents that can be substituted to cover likely pathogens. LP without CT for patients with altered level of consciousness and non-focal neurological exam associated with earlier treatment and improved outcome (*CID 60:1162, 2015*)
Post-neurosurgery Ventriculostomy/lumbar catheter; ventriculoperitoneal (atrial) shunt or Penetrating trauma w/o basilar skull fracture Shunt-related meningitis IDSA Guidelines: *CID 64:e34, 2017.*	S. epidermidis, S. aureus, P. acnes. Facultative and aerobic gram-neg bacilli, including: P. aeruginosa & A. baumannii (may be multi-drug resistant)	**Vanco** (to achieve trough level of 15-20 mg/mL) + (Cefepime or Ceftaz 2 gm IV q8h) • **If severe Pen/Ceph allergy:** substitute either: aztreonam 2 gm IV q6-8h or CIP 400 IV q8-12h. Intraventricular antibiotic dosing (lower dose for slit ventricles, intermediate dose for normal size ventricles, higher dose for enlarged ventricles): Amikacin 30 mg, Gent 4-8 mg in adults, 1-2 mg in infants, children, Polymyxin E (Colistin) 10 mg, Tobramycin 5-20 mg, Vanco 5-20 mg, Daptomycin 5 mg. Frequency of administration depends on drainage output: < 50 ml/24h: every 3rd day, 50-100 ml/24h: every second day, 100-150 ml/day: once daily, 150-200 ml/24h: increase dose of vancomycin by 1 mg, 200-250 ml/24h: increase dose of vancomycin by 5 mg, gentamicin by 1 mg	**Vanco** (to achieve trough level of 15-20 mg/mL) + (MER 2 gm IV q8h)	• Remove infected shunt and place external ventricular catheter for drainage or pressure control. • Intraventricular therapy used if the shunt cannot be removed or cultures fail to clear with systemic therapy. • **Shunt reimplantation:** If coagulase-negative staphylococci, diphtheroids, or P. acnes: no CSF abnormalities, day 3 after externalization in CSF cultures are negative at 48h; CSF cultures with S. aureus or Gram-negative organism: the last positive CSF culture. If S. aureus or Gram-negative organism: 10 days after last positive CSF culture.

¹ **Vanco adult dose:** 15-20 mg/kg IV q8 -12h to achieve level of 15-20 μg/mL

² **Dosage of drugs used to treat children age ≥1 mo:** Cefotaxime 50 mg/kg per day IV q6h; **Ceftriaxone** 50 mg/kg IV q6h; **Ceftriaxone** 50 mg/kg IV q12h; **Vanco** 15 mg/kg IV q6h to achieve trough level of 15-20 μg/mL

Abbreviations on page 2. *ᵃNOTE: All dosage recommendations are for adults (unless otherwise indicated) and assume normal renal function. § Alternatives consider allergy, PK, compliance, local resistance, cost.*

TABLE 1 (6)

ANATOMIC SITE/DIAGNOSIS/ MODIFYING CIRCUMSTANCES	ETIOLOGIES (usual)	SUGGESTED REGIMENS°		ADJUNCT DIAGNOSTIC OR THERAPEUTIC MEASURES AND COMMENTS
		PRIMARY	ALTERNATIVE§	
CENTRAL NERVOUS SYSTEM/Meningitis, Bacterial, Acute/Empiric Therapy—CSF Gram stain is negative—Immunocompetent *(continued)*				
Trauma with basilar skull fracture	S. pneumoniae, H. influenzae, S. pyogenes	Vanco (to achieve trough level of 15-20 mg/mL.) + Ceftriaxone 2 gm IV q12h or Cefotax 2 gm IV q6h) + [Dexamethasone 0.15 mg/kg IV q6h x 2-4 d (1st dose with or before 1st antibiotic dose)]. See *Clin Micro Rev 21:519, 2008.*		
Empiric Therapy—Positive CSF Gram stain				
Gram-positive diplococci	S. pneumoniae	(Ceftriaxone 2 gm IV q12h or Cefotaxime 2 gm IV q4-6h) + Vanco 15-20 mg/kg IV q8-12h (to achieve 15-20 µg/mL trough) + Dexamethasone 0.15 mg/kg IV q6h; first dose is given 15-20 minutes prior to first antibiotic dose, and then continued for 4 days for confirmed pneumococcal infection.	Alternatives: MER 2 gm IV q8h or Moxi 400 mg IV q24h.	
Gram-negative diplococci	N. meningitidis	Cefotaxime 2 gm IV q4-6h or Ceftriaxone 2 gm IV q12h)	Alternatives: Pen 6.4 mill. units IV q4h or AMP 2 gm IV q4h or chloro 1 gm IV q6h (Chloro less effective than other alternatives; see *JAC 70:979, 2015*)	
Gram-positive bacilli or coccobacilli	Listeria monocytogenes	AMP 2 gm IV q4h ± Gentamicin 2 mg/kg IV loading dose then 1.7 mg/kg IV q8h	If pen allergic use TMP/SMX 5 mg/kg (TMP component) q6-8h. Use of meropenem associated with increased 30-day mortality (*Clin Microbiol Infect 22: 725, 2016*). Data showing beneficial effect of gentamicin combination therapy are inconclusive.	
Gram-negative bacilli	H. influenzae, enterics, P. aeruginosa	(Ceftazidime or Cefepime 2 gm IV q8h) + Gentamicin 2 mg/kg IV 1st dose then 1.7 mg/kg IV q8h	Alternatives: MER 2 gm IV q8h (covers ESBLs). Aztreonam 2 gm IV q6-8h (safe in beta-lactam allergic patient). Dexamethasone not recommended for Gram-negatives other than suspected H. influenzae infection administered as 0.15 mg/kg IV q6h; first dose is given 15-20 minutes prior to first antibiotic dose, and then continued for 4 days if H. influenzae infection is confirmed.	
Specific Therapy—Positive culture of CSF with in vitro susceptibility results available				
H. influenzae Dexamethasone 0.15 mg/kg IV q6h; first dose is given 15-20 minutes prior to first antibiotic dose, and then continued for 4 days in microbiologically confirmed cases.	β-lactamase positive	Ceftriaxone 2 gm IV q12h (adult), 50 mg/kg IV q12h (peds)		Pen. allergic: Chlor = 12.5 mg/kg IV q6h (max. 4 gm/day.) (Chloro less effective than other alternatives: see *JAC 70:979, 2015*). CIP 400 mg IV q8-12h; Aztreonam 2 gm q6-8h.
Listeria monocytogenes (*CID 43:1233, 2006*)		AMP 2 gm IV q4h ± Gentamicin 2 mg/kg IV loading dose, then 1.7 mg/kg IV q8h		If pen allergic use TMP/SMX 5 mg/kg (TMP component) q6-8h. Use of meropenem associated with increased 30-day mortality (*Clin Microbiol Infect 22: 725, 2016*). Data showing beneficial effect of gentamicin combination therapy are inconclusive.
N. meningitidis		Pen G (typical adult dose 4 million units q4h) x 7 days or Ceftriaxone 2 gm IV q12h x 7 days (preferred if MIC is 0.1 to 1.0 µg/m); if β-lactam allergic, Chloro 12.5 µg/g (u.p to 1 gm) q6h (Chloro less effective than other alternatives; see *JAC 70:979, 2015*).		Other alternatives: MER 2 gm IV q8h or Moxi 400 mg q24h. Rare isolates resistant to chloro; FQ-resistant isolates encountered rarely. Increased risk of invasive meningococcal infection in recipients of eculizumab (*MMWR 66:734, 2017*).

Abbreviations on page 2.   °NOTE: All dosage recommendations are for adults (unless otherwise indicated) and assume normal renal function. § Alternatives consider allergy, PK, compliance, local resistance, cost.

TABLE 1 (7)

ANATOMIC SITE/DIAGNOSIS/MODIFYING CIRCUMSTANCES	ETIOLOGIES (usual)	SUGGESTED REGIMENS*		ADJUNCT DIAGNOSTIC OR THERAPEUTIC MEASURES AND COMMENTS
		PRIMARY	ALTERNATIVE§	
CENTRAL NERVOUS SYSTEM/Meningitis, Bacterial, Acute/Specific Therapy—Positive culture of CSF with in vitro susceptibility results available *(continued)*				
S. pneumoniae Notes: 1. Dexamethasone 0.15 mg/kg IV q6h: first dose 15-20 minutes prior to first antibiotic dose, and then continued for 4 days. 2. If MIC ≥1, repeat CSF exam after 24-48h. 3. Treat for 10-14 days	Pen G MIC <0.1 mcg/mL 0.1-1 mcg/mL ≥2 mcg/mL Ceftriaxone MIC ≥1 mcg/mL	Pen G 4 million units IV q4h or AMP 2 gm IV q4h Ceftriaxone 2 gm IV q12h or Cefotaxime 2 gm IV q4-6h Vanco 15-20 mg/kg IV q8-12h (15-20 µg/mL trough target) + (Ceftriaxone or Cefotaxime as above) Vanco 15-20 mg/kg IV q8-12h (15-20 µg/mL trough target) + (Ceftriaxone or Cefotaxime as above)		**Alternatives: Ceftriaxone** 2 gm IV q12h, **Chloro** 1 gm IV q6h (Chloro less effective than other alternatives; see JAC 70:979, 2015) **Alternatives: Cefepime** 2 gm IV q8h or **MER** 2 gm IV q8h. **Alternatives: Moxi** 400 mg IV q24h **Alternatives: Moxi** 400 mg IV q24h If MIC to Ceftriaxone >2 mcg/mL, add **RIF** 600 mg po/IV 1x/day to **Vanco** + (Ceftriaxone or Cefotaxime).
E. coli, other coliforms, or P. aeruginosa	Consultation advised— need susceptibility results			**Alternatives: MER** 2 gm IV q8h) + **CIP** 400 mg IV q8h (need to confirm susceptibility) Reculture CSF after 4-5 days of therapy. If culture is still positive, may need adjunctive intrathecal or intraventricular antibiotic therapy.
Prophylaxis for H. influenzae and N. meningitidis				
Haemophilus influenzae type B Household or close contact group defined as persons who reside with the patient or a nonresident who has spent 4 hours or more with the index patient for at least 5 of the 7 days preceding the day of hospitalization of the patient.		**RIF** 20 mg/kg (not to exceed 600 mg) once daily x 4 days for individuals ≥1 mo; 10 mg/mg once daily x 4 days for age <1 mo.		**Household or Close Contacts:** Rifampin chemoprophylaxis recommended for index patients (unless treated with cefotaxime or Ceftriaxone) and all household contacts in households with members aged <4 years who are not fully vaccinated or members aged <18 years who are immunocompromised, regardless of their vaccination status. **Child Care Contacts:** Rifampin chemoprophylaxis recommended in child care settings when two or more cases of invasive Hib disease have occurred within 60 days and unimmunized or underimmunized children attend the facility; when prophylaxis is indicated, it should be prescribed for all attendees, regardless of age or vaccine status, and for child care providers.
Prophylaxis for Neisseria meningitidis exposure (close contact)		**RIF** 10 mg/kg (max dose 600 mg) q12h x 2 days (adult or child ≥1 mo); 5 mg/kg q12h x 2 dose child <1 mo OR **Ceftriaxone** single IM dose of 250 mg (adult) or 125 mg (child age <15 years) OR **CIP** single po 500 mg dose (age ≥18; not recommended in pregnant or lactating women, or if CIP resistant isolates circulating in the local community).		**Spread by respiratory droplets**, not aerosols, hence close contact req. ↑ risk if close contact for at least 4 hrs during wk before illness onset (e.g., housemates, day care contacts, cellmates) or exposure to pt's nasopharyngeal secretions (e.g., kissing, mouth-to-mouth resuscitation, intubation, nasotracheal suctioning).
Meningitis, chronic Defined as symptoms + CSF pleocytosis for ≥4 wks	MTB cryptococcosis, other fungal, neoplastic, Lyme, syphilis, Whipple's disease	Treatment depends on etiology. No urgent need for empiric therapy, but when TB suspected treatment should be expeditious.		Long list of possibilities: bacteria, parasites, fungi, viruses, Neoplasms, vasculitis, and other miscellaneous etiologies—see Manual. Clin 28:1061, 2010. See NEJM 370:2408, 2014 for diagnosis of neuroleptospirosis by next generation sequencing technologies.
Meningitis, eosinophilic Hawaii J Med Public Health, 72(6 Suppl 2):52, 2013	Angiostrongyliasis, gnathostomiasis, baylisascaris	Anti-helminthic therapy probably not beneficial		1/3 lack peripheral eosinophilia. Need serology to confirm diagnosis. Steroid ref.: Cochrane Database Syst Rev. 2015 Feb 17;(2):CD009088
Meningitis, HIV-1 infected (AIDS) See Table 11, SANFORD GUIDE TO HIV/AIDS THERAPY	As in adults, >50 yrs: also consider cryptococci, M. tuberculosis, syphilis, HIV aseptic meningitis, Listeria monocytogenes	If etiology not identified: treat as adult >50 yrs + obtain CSF/serum cryptococcal antigen (see Comments)	For crypto rx, see Table 11A, page 130	C. neoformans most common etiology in AIDS patients. H. influenzae, pneumococci, listeria, TBc, syphilis, viral, histoplasma & coccidioides also need to be considered. Obtain blood cultures.

Abbreviations on page 2.   *NOTE: All dosage recommendations are for adults (unless otherwise indicated) and assume normal renal function. § Alternatives consider allergy, PK, compliance, local resistance, cost.*

TABLE 1 (8)

ANATOMIC SITE/DIAGNOSIS/ MODIFYING CIRCUMSTANCES	ETIOLOGIES (usual)	SUGGESTED REGIMENS* PRIMARY	SUGGESTED REGIMENS* ALTERNATIVE§	ADJUNCT DIAGNOSTIC OR THERAPEUTIC MEASURES AND COMMENTS
EAR				
External otitis				
Chronic	Usually 2° to seborrhea			Control seborrhea with dandruff shampoo containing selenium sulfide (Selsun) or [(ketoconazole shampoo) + (medium potency steroid solution, triamcinolone 0.1%)].
Fungal	Candida species	Eardrops: [(Polymyxin B + Neomycin + hydrocortisone) + selenium sulfide shampoo]	Fluconazole 200 mg po x 1 dose & then 100 mg po x 3-5 days.	
"Necrotizing (malignant) otitis externa" Risk groups: Diabetes mellitus, AIDS, chemotherapy. *See Am J Otolaryngol 37:425, 2016*	Pseudomonas aeruginosa in >95% (*Oto J & Neurotology 34:620, 2013*)	CIP 400 mg IV q8h; 750 mg po q8-12h only for early disease	PIP-TZ 3.375 gm q4h or extended infusion (3.375 gm over 4 hrs q8h) + Tobra	Very high ESRs are typical. Debridement usually required. R/O osteomyelitis: CT or MRI scans. If bone involved, treat for 6-8 wks. Other alternatives if P. aeruginosa is susceptible: IMP 0.5 gm q6h or MER 1 gm IV q8h or CFP 2 gm IV q12h or Ceftaz 2 gm IV q8h.
"Swimmer's ear", occlusive devices (earphones), contact dermatitis; psoriasis. *Otolaryngol Head Neck Surg 150:S1, 2014*	Acute infection usually 2° S. aureus (11%); other: Pseudomonas (11%), Anaerobes (2%), S. epidermidis (46%), candida (8%)	Mild: Eardrops: acetic acid + propylene glycol + HC (VoSol HCl) 5 gtts 3-4x/day until resolved. Moderate-severe: Eardrops CIP + HC (CIP HC Otic) 3 gtts bod x 7 days. Alternative: Finafloxacin 0.3% otic suspension 4 gtts q12h x 7d (for P. aeruginosa and S. aureus).	CIP HC (CIP HC Otic) 3 gtts	Rx includes gentle cleaning. Recurrences prevented (or decreased) by drying with alcohol drops (1/3 white vinegar, 2/3 rubbing alcohol) after swimming, then antibiotic drops or 2% acetic acid solution. Ointments should not be used in the ear. Do not use neomycin or other aminoglycoside drops if tympanic membrane punctured.
Otitis media—infants, children, adults (*Cochrane review: Cochrane Database Syst Rev. Jan 31;1:CD000219, 2013; American Academy of Pediatrics Guidelines: Pediatrics 131e964, 2013*)				
Acute Two RCTs indicate efficacy of antibiotic rx if age <36 mos & definite AOM (*NEJM 364:105, 116 & 168, 2011*)				
Initial empiric therapy of acute otitis media (AOM) **NOTE: Treat children <2 yrs old.** If >2 yrs old, afebrile, no ear pain, neg./questionable exam—consider adequate treatment without antimicrobials. Favorable results in mostly afebrile pts with waiting 48hrs before deciding on antibiotic use (*JAMA 296:1235, 1290, 2006*)	Overall detection in middle ear fluid: No pathogen 4% Virus 70% Bact. + virus 66% Bacteria 92% Bacterial pathogens from middle ear: S. pneumo 49%, H. influenzae 29%, M. catarrhalis 28%. Ref: CID 43:1417 & 1423, 2006. Children 6 mos–3 yrs, 2 episodes AOM/yrs & 63% are virus positive (*CID 46:815 & 824, 2008*).	**If NO antibiotics in prior month:** Amox 80-90 mg/kg/d divided q8h or q12h (preferred) AM-CL 90/6.4 mg/kg/d divided bid OR **Cefdinir** 14 mg/kg/d divided q12h or once q24h **Cefpodoxime proxetil** 10 mg/kg/d divided q12h or once q24h **Cefuroxime axetil** 30 mg/kg/d divided q12h **Duration of rx:** <2 yrs x 10 days; ≥2 yrs x 5-7 days. Appropriate duration unclear. 5 days may be inadequate for severe disease (*NEJM 347:1169, 2002*)	**Received antibiotics in prior month: AM-CL 90/6.4 mg/kg/d** OR **Ceftriaxone** 50 mg/kg IV or IM once daily x 3 days Other options include oral Cefdinir, Cefpodoxime proxetil, Cefprozil, or Cefuroxime axetil but these may be less effective for pen-non-susceptible S. pneumoniae **All doses are pediatric For adult dosages, see Sinusitis, page 51, and Table 10A**	**β-lactam allergy:** If history unclear or rash, oral ceph OK; avoid ceph if IgE-mediated allergy, e.g., anaphylaxis. **TMP-SMX:** high failure rate if etiology is DRSP or H. influenzae. **Macrolides:** limited efficacy against S. pneumo and H. influenza, use only if β-lactam not an option. **Drug resistance:** Risk ↑ if age <2 yrs, antibiotics last 3 mos, &/or daycare attendance. Selection of drug based on (1) effectiveness against S. pneumo, inc. DRSP. Cefaclor, Loracarbef & Cefibuten less active vs. S. pneumo, inc. DRSP (Pen resistant) than other β-lactams. **Otitis media with effusion:** no benefit of antibiotics (*Cochrane Database Syst Rev Sep 129:CD009163, 2012*). **Persistent otorrhea with PE tubes:** Hydrocortisone/Bacitracin/Colistin eardrops—5 drops tid x 7 d more effective than po AM-CL (*NEJM:3:70-723, 2014*). **Refractory or recurrent AOM, age 6 months to 5 years:** Levofloxacin 20 mg/kg/d in divided doses q12h if other options have failed. Tympanostomy tubes may prevent recurrent AOM.

Abbreviations on page 2.   *NOTE: All dosage recommendations are for adults (unless otherwise indicated) and assume normal renal function. § =Alternatives consider allergy, PK, compliance, local resistance, cost.

TABLE 1 (9)

ANATOMIC SITE/DIAGNOSIS/ MODIFYING CIRCUMSTANCES	ETIOLOGIES (usual)	SUGGESTED REGIMENS*		ADJUNCT DIAGNOSTIC OR THERAPEUTIC MEASURES AND COMMENTS
		PRIMARY	ALTERNATIVE§	
EAR/Otitis media—infants, children, adults *(continued)*				
Treatment for clinical failure after 3 days	Drug-resistant S. pneumoniae main concern	**NO antibiotics** in month prior to last 3 days: AM-CL HD Cefdinir or Cefpodoxime or Cefprozil or Cefuroxime Axetil or IM Ceftriaxone x 3 days. *For dosage, see footnote³* *All doses are pediatric* *Duration of rx as above*	**Antibiotics in month prior to last 3 days:** [IM Ceftriaxone) or (Clindamycin and/or tympanocentesis] *See Clindamycin Comments*	Clindamycin not active vs. H. influenzae or M. catarrhalis, S. pneumo resistant to macrolides are usually also resistant to clindamycin. Definition of failure: no change in ear pain, fever, bulging TM or otorrhea after 3 days of therapy. Tympanocentesis will allow culture. **Levo** 20 mg/kg/d in divided doses q12h if other options have failed (not FDA approved).
After >48 hrs of nasotracheal intubation	Pseudomonas sp., klebsiella, enterobacter	**Ceftazidime** or **CFP** or **IMP** or **MER** or [PIP-TZ) or **CIP**. *(For dosages, see Ear, Necrotizing (malignant) otitis externa, page 11)*		With nasotracheal intubation >48 hrs, about ½ pts will have otitis media with effusion.
Prophylaxis: acute otitis media	Pneumococci, H. influenzae, M. catarrhalis, Staph. aureus, Group A strep *(see Comments)*	Antimicrobial prophylaxis is not recommended.	**Use of antibiotics to prevent otitis media is a major contributor to emergence of antibiotic-resistant S. pneumo.** Pneumococcal protein conjugate vaccine decreases frequency of acute otitis media infections. Tympanostomy tube may prevent recurrent. AOM *(Otolaryn Head Neck Surg 156(4S):S88, 2017)*. Evidence supporting benefits of adenoidectomy are inconclusive *(Cochrane Database Syst Rev 2010:CD008282)* Avoid FQ ear drops post-T-tubes; increased risk of chronic perforation *(NEJM 2017:264-1052)*	
Mastoiditis: Complication of acute or chronic otitis media. If chronic, look for cholesteatoma (Keratoma)				
Acute				
Generally too ill for outpatient therapy.	1st episode: S. pneumoniae H. influenzae M. catarrhalis If secondary to chronic otitis media: S. aureus P. aeruginosa S. pneumoniae	Obtain cultures, then empiric therapy. 1st episode: **Ceftriaxone 2 gm** IV once daily OR **Levofloxacin** 750 mg IV once daily	Acute exacerbation of chronic otitis media: Surgical debridement of auditory canal, then [**Vanco** (dose to target trough of 15-20 mcg/mL) + **PIP-TZ** 3.375 gm IV q6h] OR [**Vanco** (dose as above) + **Ciprofloxacin** 400 mg IV q8h]	• Diagnosis: CT or MRI • Look for complications: sistectomies, suppurative lateral sinus thrombophlebitis, purulent meningitis, brain abscess • ENT consultation for possible mastoidectomy
Chronic				
Generally not ill enough for parenteral antibiotics	As per 1st episode and: S. aureus P. aeruginosa Anaerobes Fungi	Culture ear drainage. May need surgical debridement. Topical Fluoroquinolone ear drops. ENT consult.		• Diagnosis: CT or MRI

³ **Drugs & peds dosage (all po unless specified) for acute otitis media: Amoxicillin UD (usual dose)** = 40 mg/kg per day div q12h or q8h. **Amoxicillin HD (high dose)** = 90 mg/kg per day div q12h or q8h. **AM-CL HD** = 90 mg/kg per day of amox component (Augmentin ES-600) available with 600 mg AM & 42.9 mg CL 1 mL—dose: 90 mL/kg/day div bid. **Cefuroxime axetil** 30 mg/kg per day div q12h. **Ceftriaxone** 50 mg/kg IM x 3 days. **Clindamycin** 20-30 mg/kg per day div qid (may be effective vs. H. influenzae). **Cefpodoxime** 10 mg/kg per day x 5 days, then 10 mg/kg per day x 1; other FDA-approved regimens: 10 mg/kg q24h x 3 days & 30 mg/kg x 1. **Clarithro** 15 mg/kg per day div q12h; **Cefpodoxime proxetil** 10 mg/kg per day as single dose; **Cefaclor** 40 mg/kg per day div q8h; **Loracarbef** 15 mg/kg q12h. **Cefdinir** 7 mg/kg q12h or 14 mg/kg q24h.

NOTE: All dosage recommendations are for adults (unless otherwise indicated) and assume normal renal function. § Alternatives consider allergy, PK, compliance, local resistance, cost.

Abbreviations on page 2.

TABLE 1 (10)

ANATOMIC SITE/DIAGNOSIS/ MODIFYING CIRCUMSTANCES	ETIOLOGIES (usual)	SUGGESTED REGIMENS°		ADJUNCT DIAGNOSTIC OR THERAPEUTIC MEASURES AND COMMENTS
		PRIMARY	ALTERNATIVE§	
EYE				
Eyelid: (See *Cochrane Database Syst Rev 5:CD005556, 2012*)				
Blepharitis	Etiol. unclear. Factors include Staph. aureus & Staph. epidermidis, seborrhea, rosacea, & dry eye	Lid margin care with baby shampoo & warm compresses q24h. Artificial tears if assoc. dry eye (see **Comment**).		Topical ointments of uncertain benefit (*Cochrane Database Syst Rev. 2017 Feb 7;2:CD011965*). If associated rosacea, add doxy 100 mg po bid for 2 wks then tm q24h.
Hordeolum (Stye) Cochrane review of effectiveness of non-surgical interventions found no evidence for or against non-surgical interventions for treatment of acute internal hordeola (*Cochrane Database Syst Rev. 2017 Jan 9;1:CD000774*).				
External (eyelash follicle):	Staph. aureus	Hot packs only. Will drain spontaneously		Infection of superficial sebaceous gland.
Internal (Meibomian glands): Can be acute, subacute or chronic.	Staph. aureus, MSSA	Oral **Dicloxacillin** + hot packs		Also called acute meibomianitis. Rarely drain spontaneously; may need I&D
	Staph. aureus, MRSA	**TMP-SMX-DS**, tabs ii po bid		and curve. Role of fluoroquinolone eye drops is unclear. MRSA often
	Staph. aureus, MRSA (MDR)	**Linezolid** 600 mg po bid		resistant to lower conc.; may be susceptible to higher concentration of FQ in ophthalmologic solutions of gati, levo or moxi.
Conjunctiva: Review: *JAMA 310:1721, 2013*				
Conjunctivitis of the newborn (ophthalmia neonatorum): by day of onset post-delivery—all dose pediatric				
Onset 1st day	Chemical due to silver nitrate prophylaxis	None		Usual prophylaxis is erythro ointment; hence, silver nitrate irritation rare.
Onset 2-4 days	N. gonorrhoeae	**Ceftriaxone** 25–50 mg/kg IV x 1 dose (see **Comment**), not to exceed 125 mg		Treat mother and her sexual partners. Hyperpurulent. Topical rx inadequate. **Treat neonate for concomitant Chlamydia trachomatis.**
Onset 3-10 days	Chlamydia trachomatis	**Erythro** base or ethylsuccinate syrup 12.5 mg/kg q6h x 14 days. No topical rx needed.		Diagnosis by NAAT. Alternative: **Azithro** suspension 20 mg/kg po q24h x 3 days. Treat mother & sexual partner.
Onset 2-16 days	Herpes simplex types 1, 2	Topical anti-viral rx under direction of ophthalmologist.		Also give: Acyclovir 60 mg/kg/day IV x 3 doses (*Red Book online, accessed Jan 2011*).
Ophthalmia neonatorum prophylaxis: Erythro 0.5% ointment x 1 or Tetra 1% ointment§§ x 1 application; effective vs. gonococcus but not C. trachomatis				
Pink eye (viral conjunctivitis) Usually unilateral	Adenovirus (types 3 & 7 in children, 8, 11 & 19 in adults)	No treatment. If symptomatic, artificial tears may help. (some studies show 2 day reduction of symptoms with steroids; not recommended)		Highly contagious. Onset of ocular pain and photophobia in an adult suggests associated keratitis.–rare.
Inclusion conjunctivitis (adult) Usually unilateral & concomitant genital infection	Chlamydia trachomatis	**Azithro** 1 gm once	Doxy 100 mg po bid x 7 days	Oculogenital disease. Diagnosis NAAT. Urine NAAT for both GC & chlamydia. Treat sexual partner. May need to repeat dose of azithro.
Trachoma —a chronic chronic bacterial keratoconjunctivitis linked to poverty *JAMA 310:1721, 2013*	Chlamydia trachomatis	**Azithro** 20 mg/kg po single dose—78% effective in children; Adults: 1 gm po.	Doxy 100 mg po bid x minimum of 21 days or Tetracycline 250 mg po qid x 14 days.	Starts in childhood and can persist for years with subsequent: damage to cornea. Topical therapy of marginal benefit. Avoid doxy/tetracycline in young children. Mass treatment works.
Suppurative conjunctivitis, bacterial: Children and Adults (Eyedrops speed resolution of symptoms: *Cochrane Database Syst Rev. Sep 12;9:CD001211, 2012*)				
JAMA 310:1721, 2013	Staph. aureus, S. pneumoniae, H. influenzae, Viridans Strep., Moraxella sp.	FQ ophthalmic soln: CIP (generic); others expensive (Besi, Levo, Moxi) All 1-2 gtts q2h while awake 1st 2 days, then q4-8h up to 7 days.	Polymyxin B + Trimethoprim solution 1-2 gtts q3–6h x 7-10 days.	FQs best spectrum for empiric therapy. High concentrations ↑ likelihood of activity vs. S. aureus—even MRSA. TMP spectrum may include MRSA. Polymyxin B spectrum only Gm-neg. bacilli but no ophthal. prep of only TMP. Most S. pneumo resistant to Gent & Tobra.
Gonococcal (peds/adults)	N. gonorrhoeae	**Ceftriaxone** 25–50 mg/kg IV/IM (not to exceed 125 mg) as one dose in children; 1 gm IM/IV as one dose in adults		

Abbreviations on page 2.   °*NOTE: All dosage recommendations are for adults (unless otherwise indicated) and assume normal renal function.* §*Alternatives consider allergy, PK, compliance, focal resistance, cost.*

TABLE 1 (11)

EYE (continued)

Cornea (keratitis): Usually serious and often sight-threatening. Prompt ophthalmologic consultation essential for diagnosis; antimicrobial and adjunctive therapy! Herpes simplex most common etiology in developed countries; bacterial and fungal infections more common in underdeveloped countries.

ANATOMIC SITE/DIAGNOSIS/ MODIFYING CIRCUMSTANCES	ETIOLOGIES (usual)	SUGGESTED REGIMENS* PRIMARY	SUGGESTED REGIMENS* ALTERNATIVE§	ADJUNCT DIAGNOSTIC OR THERAPEUTIC MEASURES AND COMMENTS
Viral				
H. simplex (See Clin Exp Ophthalmol 44:824, 2016)	H. simplex, types 1 & 2	Trifluridine ophthalmic sol'n, one drop q2h up to 9 drops/ day until re-epithelialized, then one drop q4h up to 5x/ day, for total not to exceed 21 days. See Comment	Ganciclovir 0.15% ophthalmic gel: Indicated for acute herpetic keratitis. One drop 5 times per day while awake until corneal ulcer heals; then, one drop three times per day for 7 days.	Oral acyclovir 400 mg 5 times daily or valacyclovir 1000 mg twice daily also effective. For severe infection or immunocompromised host, consider adding oral acyclovir 400 mg po five times daily or oral valacyclovir 1000 mg bid. Topical acyclovir 3% ointment 5 times daily is a first-line treatment for HSV epithelial keratitis outside the United States. Approx 30% recurrence rate within one year; consider prophylaxis with acyclovir 400 mg bid for 12 months or valacyclovir 500 mg once daily to prevent recurrences.
Varicella-zoster ophthalmicus	Varicella-zoster virus	Famciclovir 500 mg po tid x 10 days	Acyclovir 800 mg po 5x/day x 10 days	Clinical diagnosis most common; dendritic figures with fluorescein staining in patient with varicella-zoster of ophthalmic branch of trigeminal nerve.
Bacterial		All treatment listed for bacterial, fungal, protozoan is topical unless otherwise indicated		
Acute: No comorbidity	S. aureus, S. pneumo., S. pyogenes, Haemophilus sp.	Moxi ophthalmic 0.5%: 1 drop q1h for the first 48h then taper according to response	CIP 0.3% ophthal or Levo 0.5% ophthal. 1-2 gtts/hr x 24-72 hrs, then taper OR Gatifloxacin eye drops: 1-2 gtts q2h while awake x 2 days, then q4h x 3-7 days	Regimens vary: some start rx by applying drops q5 min for 5 doses; some apply drops q15-30 min for several hours; some extend interval to q2h during sleep. In a clinical trial, drops were applied q1h for 48-72h, then q2h through day 6; then q2h during waking hours on days 7-9; then q6h until healing (Cornea 29:751, 2010). NOTE: despite high concentrations, may fail vs. MRSA. Prior use of fluoroquinolones associated with increased MICs (JAMA Ophthalmol. 131:310, 2013); high MICs associated with poorer outcome (Clin Infect Dis 54:1381, 2012).
Contact lens users	P. aeruginosa	CIP 0.3% ophthalmic solution or Levo 0.5% ophthalmic solution 1-2 gtts hourly x24-72h, taper based on response.	Gent or Tobra 0.3% ophthalmic solution 1-2 gtts hourly x24h then taper based on clinical response.	Recommend alginate swab culture and susceptibility testing; refer to ophthalmologist. Cornea abrasions treated with Tobra, Gent, or CIP gtts for 5 days; referral to ophthalmologist recommended cornea infiltrate or ulcer, visual loss, lack of improvement or worsening symptoms (Am Fam Physician. 87:114, 2013).
Dry cornea, diabetes, immunosuppression	Staph. aureus, S. epidermidis, S. pneumoniae, S. pyogenes, Enterobacteriaceae, listeria	CIP 0.3% ophthalmic solution 1-2 gtts hourly x24-72 hrs, then taper based on clinical response. See Comment.	Vanco (50 mg/mL) + Ceftaz (50 mg/mL) hourly for 24-72h, taper depending upon response. See Comment.	Specific therapy guided by results of alginate swab culture.
Fungal	Aspergillus, fusarium, candida and others.	Natamycin (5%): 1 drop every 1-2 h for several days; then q3-4h for several days; can reduce frequency depending upon response.	Amphotericin B (0.15%): 1 drop every 1-2 hours for several days; can reduce frequency depending upon response.	Obtain specimens for fungal wet mount and cultures. Numerous other treatment options (1% topical itra for 6 wks, oral itra 100 mg bid for 3 wks, topical voriconazole 1% hourly for 2 wks, topical miconazole 1% 5x a day, topical silver sulphadiazine 0.5-1.0% 5x a day) appear to have similar efficacy (Cochrane Database Syst Rev 2004241, 2012).

Abbreviations on page 2. *aNOTE: All dosage recommendations are for adults (unless otherwise indicated) and assume normal renal function. §Alternatives consider allergy; PK, compliance, local resistance, cost.*

TABLE 1 (12)

ANATOMIC SITE/DIAGNOSIS/ MODIFYING CIRCUMSTANCES	ETIOLOGIES (usual)	SUGGESTED REGIMENS*		ADJUNCT DIAGNOSTIC OR THERAPEUTIC MEASURES AND COMMENTS
		PRIMARY	ALTERNATIVE§	
EYE/Cornea (keratitis) *(continued)*				
Mycobacteria: Post-refractive eye surgery	*M. chelonae: M. abscessus*	**Gati** or **Moxi** eye drops: 1 gtt qid in conjunction with other active antimicrobial eyedrops (**Amikacin** 50 mg/L and **Clarithro** 10 mg/L).		Alternative: systemic rx: **Doxy** 100 mg po bid + **Clarithro** 500 mg po bid *(PLoS One 10:do!t6236, 2015).*
Protozoan Soft contact lens users. Ref: *CID 35:434, 2002.*	*Acanthamoeba, sp.*	Topical 0.02%–0.2% biguanide **chlorhexidine** or 0.02%–0.06% Polyhexamethylene biguanide (**PHMB**) in combination with propamidine (0.1%) or hexamidine (0.1%). Start with lower dose of PHMB and titrate to clinical response.		Initially, drops should be applied up to hourly day and night for the first 48 hours then hourly during the daytime for the first week, then with subsequent taper over 3 - 4 weeks. Debridement may also be warranted *(Am J Ophthalmol 145:130, 2008).* Uncommon. Trauma and soft contact lenses are risk factors.
Lacrimal apparatus				
Canaliculitis	Actinomyces Staph., Strept. Rarely, Arachnia, fusobacterium, nocardia, candida	Apply hot packs to punctal area 4x/day. Refer to ophthalmologist for removal of granules and local irrigation with an antibiotic solution.		Digital pressure produces exudate at punctum; Gram stain confirms diagnosis.
Dacryocystitis (lacrimal sac)	S. pneumo, S. aureus, H. influenzae, S. pyogenes, P. aeruginosa	Often consequence of obstruction of lacrimal duct. Empiric systemic antimicrobial therapy based on Gram stain of aspirate—see *Comment.*		Need ophthalmologic consultation. Surgery may be required. Can be acute or chronic. Culture to detect MRSA.
Endophthalmitis: Endogenous (secondary to bacteremia or fungemia) and exogenous (post-injection, post-operative) types Bacterial: Haziness of vitreous key to diagnosis. Needle aspirate of both vitreous and aqueous humor for culture prior to therapy. Intravitreal administration of antimicrobials essential.				
Postocular surgery (cataracts) Early, acute onset (incidence 0.05%)	S. epidermidis 60%, Staph. aureus, streptococci, & entero- cocci each 5–10%, Gm-neg. bacilli 6%	**Immediate ophthal. consult.** If only light perception or worse, immediate vitrectomy + intravitreal vanco 1 mg & intravitreal ceftazidime 2.25 mg.		
Low grade, chronic	P. epidermidis 60%, Staph. aureus. (rare).	Intraocular **Vanco.** Usually requires vitrectomy, lens removal.		
Post filtering blebs for glaucoma	Strep. species (viridans & others), H. influenzae	Referral to ophthalmologist for intravitreal **Vanco** 1 mg + **Ceftaz** 2.25 mg and a topical ophthalmic antimicrobial.		
Post-penetrating trauma	Bacillus sp., S. epiderm.	Referral to ophthalmologist for intravitreal **Vanco** 1 mg + (**Ceftaz** 2.25 mg or **Amikacin** 0.4 mg) + systemic **Vanco** 15-20 mg/kg IV q8-12h + [**Ceftaz** 1 g IV q8h or **CIP** 400 mg IV/po q12h]. Vitrectomy may be required.		
Hematogenous	S. pneumoniae, N. meningitidis, Staph. aureus, Grp B Strep, K. pneumo	[**Cefotax** 2 gm IV q4h or **Ceftriaxone** 2 gm IV q24h) + **Vanco** 30-60 mg/kg/day IV in 2-3 div doses to achieve target trough serum concentration of 15-20 mcg/mL pending cultures. Intravitreal antibiotics as with early postocular surgery. Urgent ophthalmological consultation.		
IV heroin abuse	S. aureus, Bacillus cereus, Candida sp.	Empirically, as above for hematogenous with definitive therapy based on etiology and antimicrobial susceptibility. Urgent ophthalmological consultation.		

Abbreviations on page 2.   **NOTE: All dosage recommendations are for adults (unless otherwise indicated) and assume normal renal function.* *§ Alternatives consider allergy, PK, compliance, local resistance, cost.*

TABLE 1 (13)

ANATOMIC SITE/DIAGNOSIS/ MODIFYING CIRCUMSTANCES	ETIOLOGIES (usual)	SUGGESTED REGIMENS*		ADJUNCT DIAGNOSTIC OR THERAPEUTIC MEASURES AND COMMENTS
		PRIMARY	ALTERNATIVE§	
EYE/Endophthalmitis (continued)				
Mycotic (fungal): Broad-spectrum antibiotics, often corticosteroids, indwelling venous catheters	Candida sp., Aspergillus sp.	Intravitreal **Ampho B** 0.005–0.01 mg in 0.1 mL. Also see Table 11A, page 129 for concomitant systemic therapy. See Comment.		Patients with Candida spp. chorioretinitis usually respond to systemically administered antifungals (Clin Infect Dis 52:262, 2011). Intravitreal ampho and/or vitrectomy may be necessary for those with vitritis or endophthalmitis. (IDSA guidelines CID 62:e09, 2016).
Retinitis				
Acute retinal necrosis	Varicella zoster, Herpes simplex	IV **Acyclovir** 10-12 mg/kg IV q8h x 5-7 days, then **Acyclovir** 800 mg po 5 x/day OR **Valacyclovir** 1000 mg po tid OR **Famciclovir** 500 mg po tid		Strong association of VZ virus with atypical necrotizing herpetic retinopathy. Ophthalmology consultation.
HIV+ (AIDS) CD4 usually <100/mm³	Cytomegalovirus	See Table 14A, page 174		Occurs in 5-10% of AIDS patients
Progressive outer retinal necrosis	VZV, H. simplex, CMV (rare)	**Acyclovir** 10-12 mg/kg IV q8h for 1-2 weeks, then (**Valacyclovir** 1000 mg po tid, or **Famciclovir** 500 mg po tid, or **Acyclovir** 800 mg po tid). Ophthalmology consultation imperative; approaches have also included intra-vitreal injection of anti-virals (foscarnet, ganciclovir implant). In rare cases due to CMV use **Ganciclovir/Valganciclovir** (See CMV retinitis, Table 14A).		Most patients are highly immunocompromised (HIV with low CD4 or transplantation). In contrast to Acute Retinal Necrosis, lack of intraocular inflammation or arteritis. May be able to stop oral antivirals when CD4 recovers with ART (Ocul Immunol Inflammation 15:425, 2007).
Orbital cellulitis (see page 55 for erysipelas, facial)	S. pneumoniae, H. influenzae, M. catarrhalis, S. aureus, anaerobes, group A strep, occ. Gm-neg. bacilli post-trauma	**Vancomycin** 15-20 mg/kg IV q8-12h (target **Vancomycin** trough serum concentrations of 15-20 μg/mL) + ([**Ceftriaxone** 2 gm IV q24h + **Metronidazole** 1 gm IV q12h] OR **PIP-TZ** 3.375 gm IV q6h)		If **Penicillin/Ceph allergy: Vanco + Moxi** 400 mg IV q24h. Problem is frequent inability to make microbiologic diagnosis. Image orbit (CT or MRI). Risk of cavernous sinus thrombosis. If vanco intolerant, another option for S. aureus is dapto 6 mg/kg IV q24h.

Abbreviations on page 2.   *NOTE: All dosage recommendations are for adults (unless otherwise indicated) and assume normal renal function. § Alternatives consider allergy, PK, compliance, local resistance, cost.

TABLE 1 (14)

ANATOMIC SITE/DIAGNOSIS/ MODIFYING CIRCUMSTANCES	ETIOLOGIES (usual)	SUGGESTED REGIMENS[a] PRIMARY	ALTERNATIVE[a]	ADJUNCT DIAGNOSTIC OR THERAPEUTIC MEASURES AND COMMENTS
FOOT **"Diabetic foot"**—Two thirds of patients have triad of neuropathy, deformity and pressure-induced trauma. IDSA Guidelines CID 54:e-22, 2012.				**General:** 1. Glucose control, eliminate pressure on ulcer 2. Assess for peripheral vascular disease 3. Caution in use of TMP-SMX in patients with diabetes, as many have risk factors for hyperkalemia (e.g., advanced age, reduced renal function, concomitant medications) (Arch Intern Med 170:1045, 2010). 4. improved outcomes in healing of diabetic foot ulcer with negative-pressure wound therapy (See Curr Opin Infect Dis 29:145, 2016 for review).
Ulcer without inflammation	Colonizing skin flora	No antibacterial therapy.		
Mild infection	S. aureus (assume MRSA), S. agalactiae (Gp B), S. pyogenes predominate	Oral therapy: Dicloc or Cephalexin or AM-CL (not MRSA) Doxy or TMP-SMX-DS (MRSA) Clinda (covers MSSA, MRSA, strep) *Dosages in footnote[a]*		**Principles of empiric antibacterial therapy:** 1. Obtain culture: cover for MRSA in moderate, more severe infections pending culture data, local epidemiology.
Moderate infection. Osteomyelitis See Comment.	As above, plus coliforms possible	Oral: As above Parenteral therapy: [based on prevailing susceptibilities] (AM-SB or PIP-TZ or ERTA or other carbapenem) plus (Vanco or alternative anti-MRSA drug as below) until MRSA excluded]		2. Severe limb and/or life-threatening infections require initial parenteral therapy with predictable activity vs. Gm-positive cocci including MRSA, coliforms & other aerobic Gm-neg. rods, & anaerobic Gm-neg. bacilli.
Extensive local inflammation plus systemic toxicity.	As above, plus anaerobic bacteria. Role of enterococci unclear.	Parenteral therapy: (Vanco plus β-lactam/β-lactamase inhibitor) or (vanco plus [DORI or IMP or MER]). Other alternatives: 1. Dapto or Linezolid for vanco 2. CIP or Levo or Aztreonam) plus Metronidazole for β-lactam/β-lactamase inhibitor	*Dosages in footnote[a]*	3. NOTE: The regimens listed are suggestions consistent with above principles. Other alternatives exist & may be appropriate for individual patients.
		Assess for arterial insufficiency!		Risk of associated osteomyelitis is increased if ulcer area >2 cm², positive probe to bone (CID 2016;63:944), ESR >70 and abnormal plain x-ray. Negative MRI reduces likelihood of osteomyelitis (CID 47:519 & 528, 2008). MRI is best imaging modality (CID 47:519 & 528, 2008).
Onychomycosis: See Table 11, page 133, fungal infections				See pages 4, 1–2% evolve to osteomyelitis.
Puncture wound: Nail/Toothpick	P. aeruginosa (Nail), S. aureus, Strept (Toothpick)	Cleanse. Tetanus booster. Observe.		
GALLBLADDER Cholecystitis, cholangitis, biliary sepsis, or common duct obstruction (partial: 2⁰ to tumor, stones, stricture). Cholecystitis Ref: NEJM 358:2804, 2008.	Enterobacteriaceae 68%, enterococci 14%, bacteroides 10%, Clostridium sp. 7%, rarely candida	(PIP-TZ or AM-SB) or DORI IMP or MER or DORI *Dosages in footnote on page 17.*	(P Ceph 3[b] + Metro) or (Aztreonam[b] + Metro) or (CIP[b] + Metro) or Moxi [b] Add Vanco for empiric activity vs. enterococci	In severely ill pts, antibiotic therapy complements adequate biliary drainage. 15–30% it's will require decompression: surgical, percutaneous or ERCP-placed stent. Gallbladder bile cultures positive in 40–60% (J Infect 51:128, 2005). No benefit to continuation of antibiotics after surgery in pts with acute calculous cholecystitis (JAMA 3312:145, 2014).

[a] TMP-SMX-DS 1-2 tabs po bid, **Minocycline** 100 mg po bid, **Pen VK** 500 mg po qid, (O Ceph 2, 3: **Cefprozil** 500 mg po q12h, **Cefdinir** 300 mg po q12h, **Cefdinir** 300 mg po q12h or 600 mg po q24h, **Cefuroxime axetil** 500 mg po q12h. **Cefpodoxime** 200 mg po q12h), CIP 750 mg po bid, **Levo** 750 mg po bid, **Dicloc** 500 mg qid, **Cephalexin** 500 mg po qid. AM-CL 875/125 bid, **Doxy** 100 mg bid, **Clinda** 300-450 mg tid.
AM-CL-ER 2000/125 mg po bid, **TMP-SMX-DS** 1-2 tabs po bid, CIP 750 mg po bid, **Levo** 750 mg po bid, **Moxi** 400 mg po q24h, **Linezolid** 600 mg po bid.
[b] **Parenteral β-lactam/β-lactamase inhibitors:** AM-SB 3 gm IV q6h, **PIP-TZ** 3.375 gm IV q6h or 4 hr infusion of 3.375 gm IV q8h; **carbapenems: Doripenem** 500 mg (1-hr infusion) q8h; **ERTA** 1 gm IV q24h, **IMP** 0.5 gm IV q6h, **MER** 1 gm IV q8h, **Dapto** 6 mg per kg IV q24h, **Linezolid** 600 mg IV q8h, **Aztreonam** 2 gm IV q12h, **Levo** 750 mg IV q24h, **Moxi** 400 mg IV q24h, **Metro** 1 gm IV loading dose & then 0.5 gm IV q6h or 1 gm IV q12h.

Abbreviations on page 2.

NOTE: All dosage recommendations are for adults (unless otherwise indicated) and assume normal renal function. § Alternatives consider allergy, PK, compliance, local resistance, cost.

TABLE 1 (15)

ANATOMIC SITE/DIAGNOSIS/ MODIFYING CIRCUMSTANCES	ETIOLOGIES (usual)	SUGGESTED REGIMENS*		ADJUNCT DIAGNOSTIC OR THERAPEUTIC MEASURES AND COMMENTS
		PRIMARY	ALTERNATIVE§	
GASTROINTESTINAL				
Gastroenteritis—Empiric Therapy (laboratory studies not performed or culture, microscopy, toxin results NOT AVAILABLE) *NEJM 370:016, 2014;* single dose treatment often sufficient				
Premature Infant with necrotizing enterocolitis	Associated with intestinal flora	Treatment should cover broad range of intestinal bacteria using drugs appropriate to age and local susceptibility patterns, rationale as in diverticulitis/peritonitis, page 22.		Pneumatosis intestinalis, if present on x-ray confirms diagnosis. Bacteremia-peritonitis in 30-50%. If Staph. epidermidis isolated, add vanco (IV). For review and general management, see *NEJM 364:255, 2011.*
Mild diarrhea (≤3 unformed stools/day, minimal associated symptomatology)	Bacterial (see *Severe, below*), viral (norovirus), parasitic. Viral usually causes mild to moderate disease.	Fluids only + lactose-free diet, avoid caffeine		**Rehydration:** For po fluid replacement, see *Cholera, page 20.* **Antimotility** (Do not use if fever, bloody stools, or suspicion of HUS): Loperamide (Imodium) 4 mg po, then 2 mg after each loose stool to max. of 16 mg per day, Bismuth subsalicylate (Pepto-Bismol) 2 tablets (262 mg) po qid.
Moderate diarrhea (≥4 unformed stools/day &/or systemic symptoms)	For traveler's diarrhea, see *page 21*	Antimotility agents (see *Comments*) + fluids		**Hemolytic uremic syndrome (HUS):** Risk in children infected with E. coli O157:H7 is 8-10%. Early treatment with TMP-SMX or FQs ↑ risk of HUS.
Severe diarrhea (≥6 unformed stools/day, &/or temp ≥101°F, tenesmus, blood, or fecal leukocytes). **NOTE: Severe afebrile bloody diarrhea should ↑ suspicion of Shiga-toxin E. coli O157:H7 & others** (*MMWR 58 (RR-12):1, 2009*)	Shigella, salmonella, C. jejuni, Shiga toxin + E. coli, toxin-positive C. difficile, Klebsiella oxytoca, E. histolytica. For typhoid fever, see *page 63*	**Azithro** 1000 mg po x 1 dose or 500 mg po q12h x 3 days	**CIP** 750 mg po x 1 dose, continue for 3 days if not resolved **OR** 500 mg po q12 x 3 days	**Norovirus:** Etiology of over 90% of non-bacterial diarrhea (± nausea/ vomiting). Lasts 12-60 hrs. Hydrate. No effective antiviral. **Other potential etiologies:** Cryptosporidia—no treatment in immuno-competent host. Cyclospora—usually chronic diarrhea, responds to TMP-SMX (see *Table 13A*). Klebsiella oxytoca identified as cause of antibiotic-associated hemorrhagic colitis (cytotoxin positive): *NEJM 355:2418, 2006.*
		If recent antibiotic therapy (C. difficile toxin colitis possible): promptly test stool for C. diff. toxin		
Gastroenteritis—Specific Therapy (results of culture, microscopy, toxin assay AVAILABLE) Ref.: *NEJM 370:1532, 2014;* IDSA infectious diarrhea guideline (*CID ahead of print 10/19/17*).				
If culture negative, probably **Norovirus (Norwalk)** other virus (*EID 17:1381, 2011*) — see *Norovirus, page 180*	Aeromonas/Plesiomonas	**CIP** 750 mg po bid x 3 days.	**TMP-SMX DS** tab 1 po bid x 3 days	Although no absolute proof, increasing evidence for Plesiomonas as cause of diarrheal illness (*NEJM 361:1560, 2009*). Plesiomonas susceptibilities: *PLoS One, 9; e77677, 2013.*
NOTE: WBC >15,000 suggestive of C. difficile in hospitalized patient.	Amebiasis (Entamoeba histolytica, Cyclospora, Cryptosporidium and Giardia). See *Table 13A*	**Azithro** 500 mg po q24h x 3 days **OR Azithro** 1000 mg po one dose	**Erythro stearate** 500 mg po qid x 5 days or **CIP** 500 mg po bid (FQ resistance increasing) (*CID 2017;65:1624*).	**Post-Campylobacter Guillain-Barré** assoc. 15% of cases (*Ln 366:1653, 2005*). Assoc. with small bowel lymphoproliferative disease; may respond to antimicrobials (*NEJM 350:239, 2004*). **Reactive arthritis** another potential sequelae. See *Traveler's diarrhea, page 21.*
	Campylobacter jejuni History of fever in 53-83%. Self-limited diarrhea in normal host.			
	Campylobacter fetus Diarrhea uncommon. More systemic disease in debilitated hosts	**Gentamicin** (see *Table 10D*)	**AMP** 100 mg/kg/day IV div q6h or **IMP** 500 mg IV q6h	Draw blood cultures. In bacteremic pts, 32% of C. fetus resistant to FQs (*CID 47:790, 2008*). Meropenem inhibits C. fetus at low concentrations in vitro. Clinical review: *CID 58:1579, 2014.*

Abbreviations on page 2.   *NOTE: All dosage recommendations are for adults (unless otherwise indicated) and assume normal renal function. PK, compliance, local resistance, cost. § Alternatives consider allergy, PK, compliance, local resistance, cost.

TABLE 1 (16)

ANATOMIC SITE/DIAGNOSIS/ MODIFYING CIRCUMSTANCES	ETIOLOGIES (usual)	SUGGESTED REGIMENS* PRIMARY	ALTERNATIVE*	ADJUNCT DIAGNOSTIC OR THERAPEUTIC MEASURES AND COMMENTS
GASTROINTESTINAL/Gastroenteritis—Specific Therapy (results of culture, microscopy, toxin assay AVAILABLE)* *(continued)*				
Differential diagnosis of toxin-producing diarrhea: • C. difficile • Klebsiella oxytoca • S. aureus • Shiga toxin producing E. coli (STEC) • Enterotoxigenic B. fragilis *(CID 47:797, 2008)*	C. difficile toxin positive antibiotic-associated colitis. Probiotics: (lactobacillus or saccharomyces) C. difficile: po meds okay; WBC <15,000; no increase in serum creatinine.	**Vanco** 125 mg po qid × 10 days	**Metro** 500 mg po tic × 10 days	Inconsistent results *(AnIM 157:878, 2012; Lancet 382:1249, 2013).* **D/C antibiotic if possible; avoid antimotility agents, hydration, enteric isolation.** Recent review suggests antimotility agents, tube can be used cautiously in certain pts with mild disease who are no rx *(CID 48: 598, 2009).* **Relapse in 10–20%.** Note: Metro no longer recommended as first-line therapy and should be used only if resources preclude access to Vanco or Fidaxomicin.
	po meds okay; Sicker; WBC >15,000; ≥50% increase in baseline creatinine	**Vanco** 125 mg po qid × 10 days. To use IV Vanco po, see Table 10A, page 111.	**Fidaxomicin** 200 mg po bid × 10 days	Fidaxomicin...... 10–20%, Fidaxomicin had lower rate of recurrence than Vanco for non-NAP1 strains *(N Engl J Med 364:422, 2011).* Bezlotoxumab 1 dose IV + standard rx reduced relapse rate 11–14% *(NEJM 2017, 376:305).*
More on C. difficile: *Treatment review: JAMA 313:398, 2015*	Post-treatment relapse	**Vanco** 125 mg po qid × 10-14 days, then immediately start taper *(See Comments)*	**Fidaxomicin** 200 mg po bid × 10 days	**Vanco taper** (all doses 125 mg po): week 1 - tid, week 2 - bid week 3 - q24h week4 - q48h, week 5 - q72h. Ref: CID 2007;65:1h (15/16 [93%] versus 7/26 [27%]) ► curing recurrent C. difficile infection *(New Engl J Med 365:407, 2011).* Pre-transplant Vanco taper increases success of fecal transplants *(CID 2017;65:1214).* **Bezlotoxumab,** anti Cd toxin B approved, decreases recurrence 10% but very expensive *NEJM 376-381 2017.* If Metro used or initial therapy can use standard 10-day course of Vanco. **Fecal transplant** more efficacious *(New Engl J Med 365-457, 2013).* For vanco instillation into bowel, add 500 mg vanco to 5x0 mL of saline. For vanco initial therapy, *see ICHE 31:431, 2010.* NOTE: IV vanco not effective. Indications for colectomy, *see Comment.*

	Enterohemorrhagic E. coli (EHEC): O157:H7 & O104:H4 & others. Hemolytic uremic syndrome complicates 6-9% *(see Comment)*	Treatment:
		1. If afebrile, bloody diarrhea:
		  a. Hydration
		  b. Avoid antiperistaltic drugs
		  c. No antibiotics
		2. If febrile, bloody diarrhea, risk of bacteremia:
		Azithro 500 mg IV/po once daily x 3 d.
				Risk of antibiotic therapy is HUS due to Shiga toxin production.
				HUS = renal failure, hemolytic anemia, thrombocytopenia. Risk of HUS with antibiotic use for EHEC: OR 2.24 (CI 1.45-3.46). Hence, restrict antibiotics to patients with increased risk of, or documentation of bacteremia due to EHEC.
				Refs: CID 2016;62:1251 & 1259; CID 2012;55:33; Infection 1992;20:25; IJID 2000;181:664.

	Post-op ileus; severe disease with toxic megacolon *(NEJM 359:1932, 2008; CID 61:934, 2015)*	**Metro** 500 mg IV q8h × **Vanco** 500 mg po q6h via nasogastric tube (or naso-small bowel tube) ± vanco 500 mg q6h retention enema. *See comment for dosage. No data on efficacy of Fidaxomicin in severe life-threatening disease.*		Suggested that stopping NSAIDs helps. Ref: NEJM 355:2418, 2006.
	Klebsiella oxytoca — antibiotic-associated diarrhea	Responds to stopping antibiotic		
	Listeria monocytogenes	Usually self-limited. Value of oral antibiotics (e.g., ampicillin or TMP-SMX) unknown, but their use might be reasonable in populations at risk for serious listeria infections. Those with bacteremia/meningitis require antibacterial therapy. *see pages 9 & 62.*		Recognized as a cause of food-associated febrile gastroenteritis. Not often noted in standard stool cultures. Populations at ↑ risk of severe systemic disease: pregnant women, neonates, the elderly, and immunocompromised hosts *(MMWR 57:1097, 2008).*
	Salmonella, non-typhi— For typhoid (enteric) fever, see page 63 Fever in 71–91%; history of bloody stools in 34%	If asymptomatic or illness mild, antimicrobial therapy not indicated. **Treat** if age <1 yr or >50 yrs, if immunocompromised, if hospitalized with fever and severe diarrhea *(see typhoid fever, page 63).* If resistant to TMP-SMX and chloro. Ceftriaxone, cefotaxime usually active. **CIP** 500 mg bid) or **Azithro** 500 mg po once daily x 7 days (14 days if immunocompromised). **(Levo** 500 mg q24h) x 7-10 days (14 days if immunocompromised).		↑ IV therapy required *(see footnote* on page 25, for dosage). CLSI has established new interpretive breakpoints for susceptibility to CIP: susceptible strains, MIC ≤0.06 μg/mL. *(Clin Infect Dis 55:1107, 2012).* **Primary treatment of enteritis is fluid and electrolyte replacement.**

(Continued on next page)

NOTE: All dosage recommendations are for adults (unless otherwise indicated) and assume normal renal function. ‡ Alternatives consider allergy, PK, compliance, focal resistance, cost.

Abbreviations on page 2.

TABLE 1 (7)

ANATOMIC SITE/DIAGNOSIS/ MODIFYING CIRCUMSTANCES	ETIOLOGIES (usual)	SUGGESTED REGIMENS*		ADJUNCT DIAGNOSTIC OR THERAPEUTIC MEASURES AND COMMENTS
		PRIMARY	ALTERNATIVE§ (AVAILABLE) *(continued)*	
GASTROINTESTINAL/Gastroenteritis—Specific Therapy (results of culture, microscopy, toxin assay AVAILABLE) *(continued)*				
(Continued from previous page)	**Shigella** Fever in 58%, history of bloody stools 51%	CIP 750 mg po bid x 3 days **Pockets of resistance (see Comment)** **Peds doses:** Azithro 10 mg/kg/day once daily x 3 days. For severe disease, **Ceftriaxone** 50-75 mg/kg per day x 2-5 days. CIP suspension 10 mg/kg bid x 5 days. Benefit of treatment unclear. Susceptible to **Metro**, **Ceftriaxone**, and **Moxi**.	Azithro 500 mg po once daily x 3 days	immunocompromised children & adults: Treat for 7-10 days. Pockets of resistance. *S. flexneri* resist to CIP & Ceftriaxone (*MMWR 59:1619, 2010*); *S. sonnei* resist to CIP in travelers (*MMWR 64:318, 2015*); *S. sonnei* suscept to CIP but resist to Azithro in MSM (*MMWR 64:597, 2015*). CDC recommends avoiding CIP if MIC ≥0.12 μg/mL (*CDC Health Alert Network, Apr 18, 2017*).
	Spirochetosis (Brachyspira pilosicoli)			Anaerobic intestinal spirochete that colonizes colon of domestic & wild animals plus humans. Called enigmatic disease due to uncertain status (*Digest Dis & Sci 58:202, 2013*).
	Vibrio cholerae (toxigenic - O1 & O39) Treatment decreases duration of disease, volume losses, & duration of excretion	**Primary therapy is rehydration.** Select antibiotics based on susceptibility to locally prevailing isolates. Options include: **Doxycycline** 300 mg po single dose OR **Azithromycin** 1 gm po single dose OR **Tetracycline** 500 mg po qid x 3 days OR **Erythromycin** 500 mg po qid x 3 days.	**For pregnant women:** **Azithromycin** 1 gm po single dose OR **Erythromycin** 500 mg po qid x 3 days **For children:** **Azithromycin** 20 mg/kg po as single dose; for other age-specific alternatives, see CDC website http://www.cdc.gov/haiti/cholera/hcp_goingtohaiti.htm	**Antimicrobial therapy shortens duration of illness, but rehydration is paramount.** When IV hydration is needed, use Ringer's lactate. Switch to po repletion with Oral Rehydration Salts (ORS) as soon as able to take oral fluids. ORS are commercially available for reconstitution in potable water. If not available, WHO suggests a substitute can be made by dissolving ½ teaspoon salt and 6 level teaspoons of sugar per liter of potable water (http://www.who.int/cholera/technical/en/). Haiti outbreak can be found at http://www.cdc.gov/haiti/cholera/ CDC recommendations for management developed for Haiti outbreak can be found at http://www.cdc.gov/haiti/cholera/hcp_goingtohaiti.htm Isolates from this outbreak demonstrate reduced susceptibility to ciprofloxacin and resistance to sulfisoxazole, nalidixic acid and furazolidone. Vaccine for cholera available (*Med Lett Drugs Ther. 58:113, 2016*).
	Vibrio parahaemolyticus, V. mimicus, V. fluvialis			Shellfish exposure common. Treat severe disease: **FQ, Doxy, P Ceph 3**
	Vibrio vulnificus	Antimicrobial rx does not shorten course. Hydration.		Usual presentation is skin lesions & bacteremia; life-threatening; treat early: **Ceftaz + Doxy**—see page 56; **Levo or CIP + ceftaz or Ceftriaxone.** Ref: *Epidemiol Infect. 142:878, 2014.*
	Yersinia enterocolitica Fever in 68%, bloody stools in 26%	No treatment unless severe. If severe, combine **Doxy** 100 mg IV bid + (**Tobra** or **Gent** 5 mg/kg per day once q24h). **TMP-SMX** or **FQs** are alternatives.		Mesenteric adenitis pain can mimic acute appendicitis. Lab diagnosis difficult; requires "cold enrichment" and/or yersinia selective agar. Desferrioxamine therapy increases severity, discontinue if pt on it. Iron overload states predispose to yersinia.
Gastroenteritis—Specific Risk Groups—Empiric Therapy				
Anoreceptive intercourse Proctitis (distal 15 cm only)	Herpes viruses, gonococci, chlamydia, syphilis. See *Genital Tract, page 22*			*See specific GI pathogens. Gastroenteritis, above.*
Colitis	Shigella, salmonella, campylobacter, E. histolytica *(see Table 13A)*			
HIV-1 infected (AIDS): **>10 days diarrhea**	Acid fast: Cryptosporidium parvum, Cyclospora cayetanensis Other: Isospora belli, microsporidia (Enterocytozoon bieneusi, Septata intestinalis) G. lamblia			*See Table 13A*
Neutropenic enterocolitis **or "typhlitis"** (CID 56:711, 2013) (World J Gastroenterol 23: 42, 2017)	Mucosal invasion by **Clostridium septicum** and others. Occasionally caused by C. sordellii or P. aeruginosa	Appropriate agents include PIP-TZ, IMP, MER, DORI plus bowel rest.		Tender right lower quadrant may be clue, but may be diffuse or absent in immunocompromised. Need surgical consult. Surgical resection controversial but may be necessary. **NOTE:** Resistance of clostridia to clindamycin reported. PIP-TZ, IMP, MER, DORI should cover most pathogens.

Abbreviations on page 2. *NOTE: All dosage recommendations are for adults (unless otherwise indicated) and assume normal renal function. §Alternatives consider allergy, PK, compliance, local resistance, cost.*

TABLE 1 (18)

ANATOMIC SITE/DIAGNOSIS/ MODIFYING CIRCUMSTANCES	ETIOLOGIES (usual)	SUGGESTED REGIMENS*		ADJUNCT DIAGNOSTIC OR THERAPEUTIC MEASURES AND COMMENTS
		PRIMARY	ALTERNATIVE§	
GASTROINTESTINAL/Gastroenteritis—Specific Risk Groups—Empiric Therapy *(continued)*				
Traveler's diarrhea, self-medication. Patient often afebrile **Single dose therapy** is now the recommended guideline (Am J Travel Med 2016; J Trav Med 24:S63, 2017; JAMA 2017;318-957)	**Acute:** 60% due to diarrheagenic *E. coli*; shigella, salmonella, or campylobacter. C. difficile, amebiasis (see Table 13A). **If chronic:** cyclospora, crypto-sporidia, giardia, isospora	Azithro 1000 mg po once or 500 mg po q24h for ³ days OR Cipro 750 mg po x 1 dose or 500 mg po x 3 days OR Levo 500 mg po x q24h for 1-3 days OR Oflox 300 mg po bid for 3 days OR **Rifaximin** 200 mg po bid for 3 days **For pediatrics:** Azithro 10 mg/kg/day as a single dose for 3 days or Ceftriaxone 50 mg/kg/day as single dose for 3 days. Avoid FQs. **For pregnancy:** Use Azithro. Avoid FQs. **For loperamide,** see *Comment.*		**Antimotility agent:** For non-pregnant adults with no fever or blood in stool, add **loperamide** 4 mg po x 1, then 2 mg po after each loose stool to a maximum of 16 mg per day. **Comments:** Rifaximin approved for ages 12 and older. Works only for diarrhea due to non-invasive *E. coli*; do not use if fever or bloody stool. Ref: *NEJM 361:1560, 2009; Clin Micro Inf 21:744, 2015.* **NOTE:** Self treatment with FQs associated with acquisition of resistant Gm-neg bacilli (*CID 60:837, 847, 872, 2015*). Increasing resistance of Campylobacter to FQ, particularly in Asia. Azithro now first line choice.
Advise patient: 1 dose usually sufficient, continue for 3d if not resolved after 1 dose. **Prevention of Traveler's diarrhea**		Not routinely indicated. Current recommendation is to take FQ + Imodium with 1st loose stool.		
Gastrointestinal Infections by Anatomic Site: Esophagus to Rectum				
Esophagitis	Candida albicans, HSV, CMV	See *Sanford Guide to HIV/AIDS* Therapy and *Table 11A.*		
Duodenal/Gastric ulcer gastric cancer, MALT lymphoma (not ²⁹NSAIDs) Comparative effectiveness & tolerance of treatment (Toronto Consensus Conference of *Helicobacter pylori* Infection in Adults; *Gastro 151:51, 2016;* Maastricht V/Florence Consensus Report *Gut 66:6, 2017; Overview: Med Lett 2017;59:113*)	**Helicobacter pylori** See *Comment* Prevalence of pre-treatment resistance increasing, especially clarithro (*AAC 2017:61:e02558-16*). Avoid macrolide if previous antibiotics & try to avoid prior antibiotic given. Consensus recs slightly different but rec all H. pylori should be treated. Test & treat without EGD if age <45 yrs.	**Quadruple therapy (14 days):** Bismuth subsalicylate 2 tabs qid (See footnote¹) + Tetracycline 500 mg qid + Metro 500 mg tid + PPI x 14 days.	PPI + Amox 1000 mg bid + metro 500 mg bid + Clari 500 mg bid x 14 days.	**Comments:** Any one of these **proton pump inhibitors (PPI)** may be used: omeprazole 20 mg bid, esomeprazole 30 mg bid, Lansoprazole 30 mg bid, rabeprazole 20 mg bid, pantoprazole 40 mg bid. In many locations, 20% failure rates with previously recommended *triple* regimens (**PPI + Amox + Clari-thro**). Exercise caution regarding potential interactions with other drug; contraindications in pregnancy and warnings for other special populations. **Dx: Stool antigen**—Monoclonal EIA >90% sens. & 92% specific. Other tests: if endoscoped, rapid urease &/or histology &/or culture; serology less sens & spec; urea breath test, but some office-based tests underperform. Testing ref: *BMJ 344:44, 2012.* **Test of cure:** Repeat stool antigen and/or urea breath test >8 wks post-treatment. **Treatment outcome:** Failure rate of triple therapy 20% due to clarithro resistance.
Small intestine: **Whipple's disease** (*NEJM 356:55, 2007; LnID 8:179, 2008*) Treatment: *JAC 69:219, 2014.* See *Infective endocarditis, culture-negative, page 30.*	*Tropheryma whipplei*	**(Doxy** 100 mg po bid **+ Hydroxychloroquine** 200 mg pot id) x 1 year, then **Doxy** 100 mg po bid for life Immune reconstitution inflammatory response (IRIS) reactions occur: Thalidomide therapy may be better than steroids for IRIS reaction (*J Infect 60:79, 2010*)		In vitro susceptibility testing and collected clinical experience (*JAC e5:219, 2014*). In vitro resistance to TMP-SMX plus frequent clinical failures & relapses. Frequent in vitro resistance to carbapenems. Ceftriaxone demonstrates high MICs against intracellular organisms in vitro (*AAC 48: 747, 2004*).

¹ **Bismuth preparations:** (1) In U.S. **bismuth subsalicylate (Pepto-Bismol)** 262 mg tabs; adult dose for helicobacter is 2 tabs (524 mg) qid. (2) Outside U.S., **colloidal bismuth subcitrate (De-Nol)** 120 mg chewable tablets; dose is 1 tablet qid. In the U.S., bismuth subcitrate is available in combination cap only (Pylera; each cap contains bismuth subcitrate 140 mg + Metro 125 mg + Tetracycline 125 mg).

² **Bismuth subsalicylate** dosage for prevention of traveler's diarrhea is 2 tabs chewed well qid given as 3 caps po 4x daily for 10 days **together with** a twice daily PPI

* *NOTE: All dosage recommendations are for adults (unless otherwise indicated) and assume normal renal function. §Alternatives consider allergy, PK, compliance, local resistance, cost. Abbreviations on page 2.*

TABLE 1 (19)

ANATOMIC SITE/DIAGNOSIS/ MODIFYING CIRCUMSTANCES	ETIOLOGIES (usual)	SUGGESTED REGIMENS* PRIMARY	ALTERNATIVE§	ADJUNCT DIAGNOSTIC OR THERAPEUTIC MEASURES AND COMMENTS
GASTROINTESTINAL/Gastrointestinal Infections by Anatomic Site: Esophagus to Rectum *(continued)*				
Diverticulitis, perirectal abscess, peritonitis Also see *Peritonitis, page 47* Amer. Gastroenterol. Assn Guidelines: *Gastroenterol 2015;149:1944* & Synopsis: *JAMA 2017;318:291.*	Enterobacteriaceae, occasionally P. aeruginosa, Bacteroides sp., enterococci	**Outpatient rx—mild diverticulitis, drained perirectal abscess:** [(TMP-SMX-DS bid) or CIP 750 mg bid or Levo 750 mg q8h] + **Metro 500 mg q8h.** All po x 7-10 days. **Mild–moderate disease—Inpatient—Parenteral Rx:** (e.g., focal periappendiceal peritonitis, peridiverticular abscess, endomyometritis) PIP-TZ 3.375 gm IV q6h or 4.5 gm IV q8h or ERTA 1 gm IV q24h or MOXI 400 mg IV q24h **Severe life-threatening disease, ICU patient:** IMP 500 mg IV q6h or MER 1 gm IV q8h or DORI 500 mg q8h (1-hr infusion). For **Ceftolozane-tazo** & **Ceftaz-avibactam** dosing, see *Peritonitis, page 47*. **Severe penicillin/cephalosporin allergy:** (Aztreonam 2 gm IV q6h to q8h) + [Metro (500 mg IV q6h) or (1 gm IV q12h)] OR [(CIP 400 mg IV q12h) or (Levo 750 mg IV q24h) + Metro].	AM-CL-ER 1000/62.5 mg 2 tabs po bid x 7-10 days OR Moxi 400 mg po q24h x 7-10 days. [(CIP 400 mg IV q12h) or (Levo 750 mg IV q24h)]+ (Metro 500 mg IV q6h or Moxi 400 mg IV q24h) AMP + Metro + (CIP 400 mg IV q12h or Levo 750 mg IV q24h) OR (AMP 2 gm IV q6h + Metro 500 mg IV q6h + **Aminoglycoside**^{a} (see *Table 10D, page 122*.)]	Must "cover" both Gm-neg, aerobic & Gm-neg. anaerobic bacteria. **Drugs active only vs. anaerobic Gm-neg. bacilli:** clinda, metro. **Drugs active only vs. aerobic Gm-neg. bacilli:** APAG, P Ceph 2/3/4 (see *Table 10A, page 106*), aztreonam, CIP, Levo. **Drugs active vs. both aerobic/anaerobic Gm-neg. bacteria:** cefoxitin, cefotetan, TC-CL, PIP-TZ, AM-SB, ERTA, DORI, IMP, MER, Moxi, & tigecycline. **Increasing resistance of B. fragilis group** **% Resistant:** Clinda 42-80 / Moxi 34-45 / Cefoxitin 48-60 / Cefotetan 19-35 *Ref: Anaerobe 17:147, 2011; AAC 56:1247, 2012; Surg Infect 10:111, 2009.* **Resistance (B. fragilis):** Metro, PIP-TZ rare. Resistance to FQ increased in enteric bacteria, particularly if any FQ used recently. **Ertapenem** poorly active vs. P. aeruginosa/Acinetobacter sp. Concomitant surgical management important, esp. with moderate-severe disease. Role of enterococci remains debatable. Probably need drugs active vs. enterococci in infections of biliary tract. **Tigecycline: Black Box Warning:** All cause mortality higher in pts treated with tigecycline (2.5%) than comparators (1.8%) in meta-analysis of clinical trials. Cause of mortality risk difference of 0.6% (95% CI 0.1, 1.2) not established. Tigecycline should be reserved for use in situations when alternative treatments are not suitable *(FDA MedWatch Sep 27, 2013).* AGA guidelines recommend antibiotics be used selectively in acute, uncomplicated diverticulitis *(Gastro 149: 1944, 2015).*
GENITAL TRACT: Mixture of empiric & specific treatment. Divided by sex of the patient. For sexual assault (rape), see Table 15A, page 154. *See CDC Guidelines for Sexually Transmitted Diseases: MMWR 64(RR-3):1, 2015; Med Lett 2017;59:105.*				
Both Women & Men:				
Chancroid *(Curr Op Inf Dis 29:52, 2016)* Ulcer is painful.	H. ducreyi	Ceftriaxone 250 mg IM single dose OR Azithro 1 gm po single dose	CIP 500 mg bid po x 3 days OR Erythro base 500 mg po tid x 7 days.	In HIV+ pts, failures reported with single dose azithro *(CID 21:409, 1995).* Evaluate after 7 days, ulcer should objectively improve. All patients treated for chancroid should be tested for HIV and syphilis. All sex. partners of pts with chancroid should be examined and treated if they have evidence of disease or have had sex within the last 10 days.
Non-gonococcal or post-gonococcal urethritis, cervicitis **NOTE: Assume concomitant N. gonorrhoeae** (Chlamydia conjunctivitis, see page 13)	Chlamydia 50%, Mycoplasma genitalium (30%). Other known etiologies (10–15%): trichomonas, herpes simplex virus, see *JID 206:357, 2012.* Ref: *CID 61:S74, 2015*	(Doxy 100 mg bid po x 7 days) or (Azithro 1 gm po as single dose). Evaluate & treat sex partner. In pregnancy: Azithromycin 1 gm po single dose for Amox 500 mg po tid x 7 days.	(Erythro base 500 mg qid po x 7 days) or (Ofloc 300 mg q12h po x 7 days) or (Levo 500 mg q24h x 7 days). In pregnancy: Erythro base 500 mg po qid for 7 days. Doxy & FQs contraindicated.	**Diagnosis:** NAAT for C. trachomatis & N. gonorrhoeae on urine or cervix or urethra specimens *(AnIM 142:914, 2005).* Test all urethritis/cervicitis pts for HIV & syphilis. **Evaluate & treat sex. partners.** Azithromycin 1 gm was superior to doxycycline for M. genitalium male urethritis *(CID 48:1649, 2009),* but may select resistance leading to failure of multi-dose azithromycin retreatment regimens *(CID 48:1655, 2009).*

---

^{a} **Aminoglycoside** = antipseudomonal aminoglycosidic aminoglycoside, e.g., Amikacin, Gentamicin, Tobramycin

Abbreviations on page 2. *NOTE: All dosage recommendations are for adults (unless otherwise indicated) and assume normal renal function. § Alternatives consider allergy, PK, compliance, local resistance, cost.*

TABLE 1 (20)

ANATOMIC SITE/DIAGNOSIS/ MODIFYING CIRCUMSTANCES	ETIOLOGIES (usual)	SUGGESTED REGIMENS[a]		ADJUNCT DIAGNOSTIC OR THERAPEUTIC MEASURES AND COMMENTS
		PRIMARY	**ALTERNATIVE[a]**	
GENITAL TRACT/Both Women & Men *(continued)* - CDC Guidelines: *MMWR 64(RR-3):1, 2015*				
Non-gonococcal urethritis: Mycoplasma genitalium	Mycoplasma genitalium. Ref: *CID 61:S802, 2015*.	Azithro 500 mg po x1 then 250 mg po once daily x 4 days	Moxi 400 mg once daily x 10-14 days	Diagnosis is by NAAT, but usually not available. Doxy ineffective. No cell wall so beta-lactams ineffective. Cure with single dose Azithro only 67% (*CID 61*:389, 2015). Increasing resistance may work. Pristinamycin may work. *Em Int Dis 23:809, 2017*.
Recurrent/persistent urethritis	C. trachomatis (43%), M. genitalium (30%), T. vaginalis (13%) (*CID 52:163, 2011*).	Metro 2 gm po x1 dose + Azithro 1 gm po X1	Tinidazole 2 gm po X1 + Azithromycin 1 gm po X1	High failure rate of Azithro if M. genitalium (*CID 56:934, 2013*). Can try Moxi 400 mg po once daily x 10 days if Azithro failure (*PLoS One 3:e3618, 2008*). Three FQ resistance in Japan (*JAC 69:2376, 2014*).
Rectal, proctitis MSM and increasingly in women	C. trachomatis, M. genitalium, N. gonorrhoeae, syphilis, HSV	Treat for GC and chlamydia; Doxy 100 mg bid x 7 d preferred over Azithro	If LGV suspected treat **Doxy** 100 bid 21 d	Proctitis: prefer doxy x 7 d (*Sex Trans Dis 41:79, 2014*). Higher failures with azithro (*JAC 70:961, 2015*).
Gonorrhea. FQs no longer recommended for treatment of gonococcal infections (See CDC Guidelines *MMWR 64(RR-3):1, 2015; CID 61:S205, 2015*).				
Cephalosporin resistance: *JAMA 309:163 & 185, 2013*.				
Conjunctivitis (adult).	N. gonorrhoeae	Ceftriaxone 1 gm IM or IV single dose + Azithro 1 gm po x1		Consider one-time saline lavage of eye.
Disseminated gonococcal infection (DGI, dermatitis-arthritis syndrome)	N. gonorrhoeae	Ceftriaxone 1 gm IV q24h + Azithro 1 gm po x1	(Cefotaxime 1 gm q8h IV or Ceftizoxime 1 gm q8h IV) + Azithro 1 gm po x1	Treat for a minimum of 7 days. Owing to high-level resistance to oral cephalosporins and fluoroquinolones in the community, "step-down" therapy should be avoided unless susceptibilities are known and demonstrate full activity if cephalosporin or fluoroquinolone R/O meningitis/endocarditis. Treat presumptively for concomitant C. trachomatis. Azithro now recommended to cover resistant GC (usually tetra resistant, too) and C. trachomatis
Endocarditis	N. gonorrhoeae	Ceftriaxone 1-2 gm IV q12-24 hours x 4 weeks + Azithro 1 gm po x1		GC endocarditis may occur in the absence of concomitant urogenital symptoms (*Infection 42:25, 2014*). Severe valve destruction may occur. Ceftriaxone resistance in N. gonorrhoeae has been reported (*AAC 55: 3538, 2011*); determine susceptibility of any isolate recovered.
Pharyngitis Dx: NAAT	N. gonorrhoeae	Ceftriaxone 250 mg IM x1 + Azithro 1 gm po x1).	Due to resistance concerns, do not use FQs	Pharyngeal GC more difficult to eradicate. Repeat NAAT 14 days post-rx. Spectinomycin*, cefixime, cefpodoxime & cefuroxime not effective for ALL of these approaches listed below:
Urethritis, cervicitis, proctitis (uncomplicated, std'd) For urethritis, see page 27. Diagnosis: Nucleic acid amplification test (NAAT) on vaginal swab, urine or urethral swab *MMWR 64(RR-3):1, 2015*	N. gonorrhoeae (50% of pts with urethritis, cervicitis have concomitant C. trachomatis — treat for both even if NAAT indicates single pathogen).	Ceftriaxone 250 mg IM x1 + Azithro 1 gm x1 Rx failure: Ceftriaxone 500 mg IM x1 + Azithro 2 gm po x1; treat partner, NAAT for test of cure 1 wk post-treatment Severe Pen/Ceph allergy: (Gent 240 mg IM + Azithro 2 gm po x 1 dose) OR (Gemi 320 mg + Azithro 2 gm po x 1 dose) (*CID 59:1083, 2014*) (nausea in >20%)		**Oral** cephalosporin use is no longer recommended as primary therapy owing to emergence of resistance. *MMWR 61:590, 2012*. Other single-dose cephalosporins: cefixime 400 mg po. OR ceftizoxime 500 mg IM, cefoxitin 2 gm IM + probenecid 1 gm po.
Pregnancy		Ceftriaxone 250 mg IM x1 + Azithro 1 gm po x1		Screen for syphilis.
Granuloma inguinale (Donovanosis)	Klebsiella (formerly Calymmatobacterium) granulomatis	Azithro 1 gm po q wk x 3 wks	TMP-SMX one DS tablet bid x 3 wks OR Erythro 500 mg po qid x 3 wks OR CIP 750 mg po bid x 3 wks OR Doxy 100 mg po bid x 3 wks.	Clinical response usually seen in 1 wk. Rx until all lesions healed, may take 4 wks. Treatment failures & recurrence seen with Doxy & TMP-SMX. Relapse can occur 6-18 months after apparently effective Rx. If improvement not evident in first few days, some experts add Gent 1 mg/kg IV q8h.
Herpes simplex virus		See Table 14A, page 175		
Human papilloma virus (HPV)		See Table 14A, page 180		

Abbreviations on page 2.   [a]NOTE: All dosage recommendations are for adults (unless otherwise indicated) and assume normal renal function. ⇨ Alternatives consider allergy, PK, compliance, local resistance, cost.

TABLE 1 (21)

ANATOMIC SITE/DIAGNOSIS/ MODIFYING CIRCUMSTANCES	ETIOLOGIES (usual)	SUGGESTED REGIMENS*		ADJUNCT DIAGNOSTIC OR THERAPEUTIC MEASURES AND COMMENTS
		PRIMARY	ALTERNATIVE§	
GENITAL TRACT/Both Women & Men (continued)				
Lymphogranuloma venereum Ref: CID 61:S865, 2015	Chlamydia trachomatis, serovars. L1, L2, L3	Doxy 100 mg po bid x 21 days	Erythro 0.5 gm po qid x 21 days or Tetracycline 1 gm po q.v. X 3 wks (clinical data lacking)	Dx based on serology; biopsy contraindicated because sinus tracts develop. Nucleic acid ampli tests for C. trachomatis will be positive. In MSM, presents as fever, rectal ulcer, anal discharge (CID 39:996, 2004; Dis Colon Rectum 52:507, 2009).
Pthirius pubis (**pubic lice, "crabs"**) & scabies	Pthirus pubis & Sarcoptes scabiei	See Table 134, page 166		
Syphilis Diagnosis: JAMA 312:1922, 2014; treatment: JAMA 312:1905, 2014; management: CID 61:S818, 2015. Overview: Lancet 389: 1550, 2017.				
Early: primary, secondary, or latent <1 yr. Screen with treponema-specific antibody or RPR/VDRL, see JCM 50:2 & 148, 2012; CID 58:1176, 2014. Chance is painless.	T. pallidum **NOTE:** Test all pts with syphilis for HIV; test all HIV patients for latent syphilis. Screen MSM and/or HIV pts every 3-12 mos (JAMA 315:2321 & 2328, 2016)	Benzathine pen G (Bicillin L-A) 2.4 million units IM x 1 or Azithro 2 gm po x 1 dose (See Comment)	(Doxy 100 mg po bid x 14 days) or (Tetracycline 500 mg po qid x 14 days) or (Ceftriaxone 1 gm IM/IV q24h x 10-14 days). Follow-up mandatory. Ceftriaxone efficacy (CID 2017:65:1683)	If early or congenital syphilis, quantitative VDRL at 0, 3, 6, 12 & 24 mos after rx. If 1° or 2° syphilis, VDRL should ↓ 2 tubes at 6 mos, 3 tubes 12 mos, & 4 tubes 24 mos. Update on congenital syphilis (MMWR 64(RR-3):1, 2015). Early latent: 2 tubes ↓ at 12 mos. With 1°, 50% will be RPR seronegative at 12 mos, 24% neg. FTA/ABS at 2-3 yrs (AnIM 114:1005, 1991). If titers fail to fall, examine CSF; if CSF (+), treat as neurosyphilis; if CSF is negative, retreat with benzathine Pen G 2.4 mU IM weekly x 3 wks. If no other options: Azithro 2 gm po x 1 dose (equivalent to Benzathine pen 2.4 M X 1 dose in early syphilis (J Infect Dis 201:1729, 2010). Azithro-resistant syphilis documented in California, Ireland, & elsewhere (CID 44:S130, 2007; AAC 54:583, 2010). **NOTE:** Use of benzathine procaine penicillin is inappropriate!
More than 1 yr's duration (latent of indeterminate duration, cardiovascular, late benign gumma)	For penicillin desensitization method, see Table 7, page 88 and MMWR 64(RR-3):1, 2015	Benzathine pen G (Bicillin L-A) 2.4 million units IM at week X 3 = 7.2 million units total	Doxy 100 mg po bid x 28 days or Tetracycline 500 mg po qid x 28 days; Ceftriaxone 1 gm IV or IM daily for 10-14 days MAY be an alternative (No clinical data; consult an ID specialist)	No published data on efficacy of alternatives. Indications for LP (CDC: neurologic symptoms, treatment failure, any eye or ear involvement, other evidence of active syphilis (aortitis, gumma, iritis).
Neurosyphilis—Very difficult to treat. Includes ocular (retro-bulbar neuritis) syphilis **All need CSF exam.** HIV infection (AIDS) CID 44:S130, 2007		Pen G 18-24 million units per day either as continuous infusion or as 3-4 million units IV q4h x 10-14 days. Treatment same as HIV uninfected for 10-14 days regardless of CD4 count: MMWR 59:625, 2002	Ceftriaxone 2 gm (IV or IM) q24h x 14 days. 23% failure rate reported (AJM 93:481, 1992). For penicillin allergy: either desensitize to penicillin or obtain infectious diseases consultation. Serologic criteria for response to rx: 4-fold or greater ↓ in VDRL titer over 6-12 mos. (CID 28(Suppl. 1):S21, 1999). See Syphilis discussion in CDC Guidelines MMWR 64(RR-3):1, 2015 Treat for neurosyphilis if CSF VDRL negative but >20 CSF WBCs (STD 39:291, 2012).
Pregnancy and syphilis		Same as for non-pregnant, some recommend 2nd dose (2.4 million units) Benzathine Pen G 1 wk after initial dose esp. in 3rd trimester or with 2° syphilis	Skin test for penicillin allergy. Desensitize if necessary, as parenteral Pen G is only therapy with documented efficacy!	Monthly quantitative VDRL or equivalent. If 4-fold ↑, re-treat. Doxy, tetracycline contraindicated. Erythro not recommended because of high risk of failure to cure fetus.

NOTE: All dosage recommendations are for adults (unless otherwise indicated) and assume normal renal function. § Alternatives consider allergy; PK, compliance, local resistance, cost.

Abbreviations on page 2.

NOTE: All dosage recommendations are for adults (unless otherwise indicated) and assume normal renal function. § Alternatives consider allergy; PK, compliance, local resistance, cost.

TABLE 1 (22)

ANATOMIC SITE/DIAGNOSIS/ MODIFYING CIRCUMSTANCES	ETIOLOGIES (usual)	SUGGESTED REGIMENS*		ADJUNCT DIAGNOSTIC OR THERAPEUTIC MEASURES AND COMMENTS
		PRIMARY	ALTERNATIVE§	
GENITAL TRACT/Both Women & Men/Syphilis (continued)				
Congenital syphilis (Update on Congenital Syphilis; MMWR 64(RR-3):i, 2015)	T. pallidum	**Aqueous crystalline Pen G** 50,000 units/kg per dose IV q12h x 7 days, then q8h for 10 days	**Procaine Pen G** 50,000 units/kg IM q24h for 10 days	A no rel alternative: Ceftriaxone ≤30 days old, 75 mg/kg IV/IM q24h (use with caution in infants with jaundice) or >30 days old 100 mg/kg IV/IM q24h. Treat 10-14 days. If symptomatic, ophthalmologic exam indicated. If more than 1 day of rx missed, restart entire course. **Need serologic follow-up!**
Warts, anogenital	See Table 14A, page 180			
Women:				
Amnionitis, septic abortion	Bacteroides, esp. Prevotella bivia; Group B, A streptococci; Enterobacteriaceae; C. trachomatis. Rarely U. urealyticum.	[(Cefoxitin or DORI) or IMP or MER or **AM-SB** or **ERTA** + doxy] OR **PIP-TZ**) [Clinda + (Aminoglycoside or Ceftriaxone)] *Dosage: see footnote*§ **NOTE:** in US and Europe, 1/3 of Grp B Strep resistant to clindamycin.		D&C of uterus. **In septic abortion,** Clostridium perfringens may cause fulminant intravascular hemolysis. **In postpartum patients with enigmatic** fever and/or pulmonary emboli, **consider septic pelvic vein thrombophlebitis** (see *Vascular septic pelvic vein thrombophlebitis, page 70*). After discharge: doxy or clinda for C. trachomatis.
Cervicitis, mucopurulent Treatment based on results of nucleic acid amplification test	N. gonorrhoeae	Treat for Gonorrhea, page 23		Criteria for diagnosis: 1) (muco) purulent endocervical exudate and/or 2) sustained endocervical bleeding after passage of cotton swab. >10 WBC/ hpf of vaginal fluid is suggestive. Intracellular gram-neg diplococci on
	Chlamydia trachomatis	Treat for non-gonococcal urethritis, page 23. If due to Mycoplasma genitalium, less likely to respond to doxy than azithro and emerging resistance to both azithro and -TQ.		smear but insensitive. If in doubt, send swab or urine for culture, EIA or nucleic acid amplification test and treat for both.
Endomyometritis/septic pelvic phlebitis				
Early postpartum (1st 48 hrs) (usually after C-section)	Bacteroides, esp. Prevotella bivia; Group B, A streptococci; Enterobacteriaceae; C. trachomatis; M. hominis	[(Cefoxitin or ERTA or IMP or MER or **AM-SB** or **PIP-TZ**) + doxy] or [Clinda + (Aminoglycoside or Ceftriaxone)] *Dosage: see footnote*§		See Comments under Amnionitis, septic abortion, above
Late postpartum (48 hrs to 6 wks) (usually after vaginal delivery).	Chlamydia trachomatis M. hominis	**Doxy** 100 mg IV or po q12h times 14 days		Tetracyclines not recommended in nursing mothers; discontinue nursing. M. hominis sensitive to tetra, clinda, not erythro.
Fitzhugh-Curtis syndrome	C. trachomatis N. gonorrhoeae	Treat as for pelvic inflammatory disease immediately below.	**Doxy** or Ceftriaxone or Clinda	Perihepatitis (violin-string adhesions). Sudden onset of RUQ pain. Associated with salpingitis. Transaminases elevated in <30% of cases.
Pelvic actinomycosis: usually tubo-ovarian abscess	A. Israelii most common	**AMP** 200 mg/kg/day in 3-4 divided doses x 4-6 wks then Pen VK 2-4 gm/day in 4 divided doses x 6-12 mo		Complication of intrauterine device (IUD). Remove IUD. Can use **Pen G** 10-20 million units/day IV instead of **AMP** x 4-6 wks.

* **P Ceph 2 (Cefoxitin** 2 gm IV q6-8h; **Cefotetan** 2 gm IV q12h; **Cefuroxime** 750 mg IV q8h); **AM-SB** 3 gm IV q6h; **PIP-TZ** 3.375 gm q6h or for nosocomial pneumonia: 4.5 gm IV q6h or 4-hr infusion of 3.375 gm q8h; **Clinda** 450-900 mg IV/po q12h; **Clinda** 450-900 mg IV q8h; **Aminoglycoside** (Gent, see Table 10D, page 122); **P Ceph 3 (Cefotaxime** 2 gm IV q8h; **Ceftriaxone** 2 gm IV q24h); **Dori** 500 mg IV q8h (1-hr infusion); **ERTA** 1 gm IV q24h; **Azithro** 500 mg IV q24h; **MER** 1 gm IV q8h; **IMP** 0.5 gm IV q6h; **MER** 1 gm IV q8h; **Linezolid** 600 mg IV/po q12h; **Vanc** 1 gm IV q12h

§**NOTE:** All dosage recommendations are for adults (unless otherwise indicated) and assume normal renal function. § alternatives consider allergy, PK, compliance, local resistance, cost. Abbreviations on page 2.

TABLE 1 (23)

ANATOMIC SITE/DIAGNOSIS/ MODIFYING CIRCUMSTANCES	ETIOLOGIES (usual)	SUGGESTED REGIMENS* PRIMARY	ALTERNATIVE†	ADJUNCT DIAGNOSTIC OR THERAPEUTIC MEASURES AND COMMENTS
GENITAL TRACT/Women *(continued)*				
Pelvic Inflammatory Disease (PID), salpingitis, tubo-ovarian abscess	N. gonorrhoeae, chlamydia, bacteroides, Enterobacteria-ceae, streptococci, especially S. agalactiae	**Outpatient rx:** [(**Ceftriaxone** 250 mg IM or IV x 1) (± **Metro** 500 mg po bid x 14 days) + (**Doxy** 100 mg po bid x 14 days)] **OR** (**Cefoxitin** 2 gm IM with **Probenecid** 1 gm po both as single dose) plus (**Doxy** 100 mg po bid with **Metro** 500 mg bid—both times 14 days)	**Inpatient regimens:** [(**Cefotetan** 2 gm IV q12h or **Cefoxitin** 2 gm IV q6h) + (**Doxy** 100 mg IV/po q12h)] (**Clinda** 900 mg IV q8h) + (**Gent** 2 mg/kg loading dose, then 1.5 mg/kg q8h or 4.5 mg/kg once per day), then **Doxy** 100 mg bid x 14 days	Another alternative parenteral regimen: **AM-SB** 3 gm IV q6h + **Doxy** 100 mg IV/po q12h. Recommended treatments don't cover M. genitalium so if no response after 7-10 d consider M. genitalium NAAT and treat with **Moxi** 400 mg/day x14 days. Remember: Evaluate and treat sex partner. FQs not recommended due to increasing resistance *MMWR 64(RR-3):1, 2015 & www.cdc.gov/std/ treatment).* Suggest initial inpatient evaluation/therapy for pts with tubo-ovarian abscess.
Outpatient rx: limit to pts with temp <38°C, WBC <11,000 per mm³, minimal evidence of peritonitis, active bowel sounds & able to tolerate oral nourishment *NEJM 372:2039, 2015; CDC Guidelines MMWR 64(RR-3):1, 2015*	Less commonly: G. vaginalis, Haemophilus influenzae, cytomegalovirus (CMV), M. genitalium, U. urealyticum			For inpatient regimens, continue treatment until satisfactory response for ≥24-hr before switching to outpatient regimen. Improved routine testing for chlamydia and N. gonorrhoeae among outpatients resulted in reduced hospitalization and ectopic pregnancy rates *(J Adolescent Health 51:80, 2012)*
Vaginitis— *MMWR 64(RR-3):1, 2015*				
Candidiasis	Candida albicans 80–90%. C. glabrata, C. tropicalis may be increasing—they are less susceptible to azoles	**Oral azoles: Fluconazole** 150 mg po x 1; **Itraconazole** 200 mg po bid x 1 day. For milder cases, Topical Therapy with one of the over the counter preparations usually is successful (e.g., clotrimazole, butoconazole, miconazole, or tioconazole) as creams or vaginal suppositories.	**Butoconazole, Clotrimazole, Miconazole, Tioconazole** or **Terconazole** (all intravaginal) variety of preparations from 1 dose to 7-14 days *(See Table 11A, page 128)*	Nystatin vag. tabs times 14 days less effective. Other rx for azole-resistant strains: gentian violet, boric acid. If recurrent candidiasis (4 or more episodes per yr): 6 mos. suppression with: fluconazole 150 mg po q week or itraconazole 100 mg po q24h or clotrimazole vag. suppositories 500 mg q week.
Pruritus, thick cheesy discharge, pH <4.5 *See Table 11A, page 128*				
Trichomoniasis *(CID 61:S837, 2015)*	Trichomonas vaginalis **Dx:** NAAT & POP available & most sensitive; wet mount not sensitive. *Ref: JCM 54:7, 2016.*	**Metro** 2 gm as single dose or 500 mg po bid x 7 days **OR** **Tinidazole** 2 gm po single dose **Pregnancy:** See Comment	**For rx failure:** Re-treat with metro 500 mg po bid x 7 days; if this fails, metro 2 gm po q24h x 5 days, or tinidazole 2 gm po q24h x 5 days. If still failure, **Tinidazole** 2 gm po q24h x 5 days.	**Treat male sexual partners** (**2 gm** metronidazole **as single dose).** Nearly 20% men w/NGU are infected with trichomonas *(JID 188:465, 2003).* For alternative option in refractory cases, see *CID 33:1341, 2001.* **Pregnancy:** No data indicating metro teratogenic or mutagenic. First-line drug for treatment of trichomonas, including issues in pregnancy, see *MMWR 64(RR-3):1, 2015.*
Copious foamy discharge, pH >4.5 Treat sexual partners— *see Comment*				
Bacterial vaginosis (BV)	Etiology unclear: associated with Gardnerella vaginalis, mobilluncus, Mycoplasma hominis, Prevotella sp., & Atopobium vaginae et al.	**Metro** 0.5 gm po bid x 7 days or **Metro vaginal gel[10]** (1 applicator intravaginally) 1x/day x 5 days **OR** 2% **Clinda vaginal cream** 5 gm intravaginally at bedtime x 7 days	**Clinda** 0.3 gm po bid x 7 days **or Clinda ovules** 100 mg intravaginally at bedtime x 3 days. **Secnidazole** 2 gm packet (granules in applesauce, yogurt, pudding) x 1 dose over 30 min.	Reported 50% ↑ in cure rate if abstain from sex or use condoms: *CID 44:213 & 220, 2007.* Treatment of male sex partner **not** indicated unless balanitis present. Topical lindane tabs 750 mg po q24h x 7 days available; no published data. Oral Metro & oral Clinda have similar efficacy regimens *(see CDC STD Guidelines: MMWR 64(RR-3):1, 2015).* If recurrent BV, can try adding boric acid gelatin capsule 600 mg hs x 21 days, followed by then vaginal boric acid gel 2x/week x 16 weeks *(Sex Trans Dis 36:732, 2009).*
Malodorous vaginal discharge, pH >4.5				

[10] 1 applicator contains 5 gm of gel with 37.5 mg metronidazole

Abbreviations on page 2. * *NOTE: All dosage recommendations are for adults (unless otherwise indicated) and assume normal renal function.* § *Alternatives consider allergy, PK, compliance, local resistance, cost.*

TABLE 1 (24)

ANATOMIC SITE/DIAGNOSIS/ MODIFYING CIRCUMSTANCES	ETIOLOGIES (usual)	SUGGESTED REGIMENS°		ADJUNCT DIAGNOSTIC OR THERAPEUTIC MEASURES AND COMMENTS
		PRIMARY	ALTERNATIVE°	
GENITAL TRACT *(continued)*				
Men:				
Balanitis	Candida 40%, Group B strep, gardnerella	**Metro** 2 gm po as a single dose OR **Fluconazole** 150 mg po x1 OR **Itra** 200 mg po bid x 1 day.		Occurs in 1/4 of male sex partners of women infected with candida. Exclude circinate balanitis (Reiter's syndrome); (non-infectious) responds to hydrocortisone cream.
Epididymo-orchitis *(CID 61:S770, 2015)*				
Age <35 years	N. gonorrhoeae, Chlamydia trachomatis	**Ceftriaxone** 250 mg IM x 1 + **Doxy** 100 mg po bid x 10 days.) + bed rest, scrotal elevation, analgesics.		Enterobacteriaceae occasionally encountered. Test all pts age <35 yrs for HIV and syphilis.
Age ≥35 years or MSM (insertive partners in anal intercourse)	Enterobacteriaceae (coliforms)	**Levo** 500-750 mg IV/po once daily) OR **(Oflox** 300 mg po bid) or (400 mg IV twice daily) for 10-14 days. For MSM can be mixed GC/chlamydia with enterics so treat with FQ AND **Ceftriaxone** 250 mg IM x1) Also: bed rest, scrotal elevation, analgesics.		Midstream pyuria and scrotal pain and edema. **NOTE:** Do urine NAAT (nucleic acid amplification test) to ensure absence of N. gonorrhoeae with concomitant risk of FQ-resistant gonorrhoeae or of chlamydia if using agents without reliable activity. Other causes include mumps, brucella, TB, intravesicular BCG, B. pseudomallei, coccidioides, Behçet's.
Non-gonococcal urethritis	*See page 23 (CID 61:S763, 2015)*			
Prostatitis—Review: CID 50:1641, 2010. See Guidelines 2015 http://onlinelibrary.wiley.com/doi/10.1111/bju.13170/epdf				
Acute				
Uncomplicated (with risk of STD; age <35 yrs)	N. gonorrhoeae, C. trachomatis	**Ceftriaxone** 250 mg IM x 1 then **Doxy** 100 mg po bid x 10 days.		FQs no longer recommended for gonococcal infections. Test for HIV. In AIDS pts, prostate may be the focus of Cryptococcus neoformans.
Uncomplicated with low risk of STD	Enterobacteriaceae (coliforms)	**FQ** (dosage: see *Epididymo-orchitis, >35 yrs, above*) or **TMP-SMX** 1 DS tablet (160 mg TMP) po bid x 10-14 days (minimum). Some authorities recommend 4 weeks of therapy.		Treat as acute urinary infection, 14 days (not single dose regimen). Some recommend 3-4 wks therapy. If uncertain, do NAAT for C. trachomatis and N. gonorrhoeae. If resistant enterobacteriaceae use **ERTA** 1 gm IV qd. If resistant pseudomonas, use **IMP** or **MER** (500 mg IV q6 or q8 respectively).
Chronic bacterial	Enterobacteriaceae 80%, enterococci 15%, P. aeruginosa	**CIP** 500 mg po bid x 4-6 wks OR **Levo** 750 mg po q24h x 4 wks.	**TMP-SMX-DS** 1 tab pc bid x 1-3 mos (Fosfomycin: see *Comment*)	With treatment failures consider infected prostatic calculi. FDA approved dose of Levo is 500 mg; editors prefer higher dose. Fosfomycin penetrates prosta e; case report of success with 3 gm po q24h x 12-16 wks (*CID 6:e1141, 2015*) or 3 gm q36 x 6 wks (*AAC 60:1854, 2016*).
Chronic prostatitis/chronic pain syndrome	The most common prostatitis syndrome. Etiology is unknown.	α-adrenergic blocking agents are controversial (*AnIM 133:367, 2000*).		Pt has 5x of prostatitis but negative cultures and no cells in prostatic secretions. Rev: *JAC 46:157, 2000*. In randomized double-blind study, CIP and an alpha-blocker of no benefit (*AnIM 141:581 & 639, 2004*).
HAND *(Bites: See Skin)*				
Paronychia				
Nail biting, manicuring	Staph. aureus (maybe MRSA)	Incision & drainage; culture	**TMP-SMX-DS** 1-2 tabs po bid while waiting for culture result.	See *Table 6 for alternatives*. Occasionally--candida, gram-negative rods.
Contact with saliva—dentists, anesthesiologists, wrestlers	Herpes simplex (Whitlow)	**Acyclovir** 400 mg po x 10 days	**Famciclovir** or **Valacyclovir**, see *Comment*	Gram stain and routine culture negative. Famciclovir/valacyclovir for primary genital herpes; see *Table 14A, page 175*
Dishwasher (prolonged water immersion)	Candida sp.	**Clotrimazole** (topical)		Avoid immersion of hands in water as much as possible.

Abbreviations on page 2.   °NOTE: *All dosage recommendations are for adults (unless otherwise indicated) and assume normal renal function.* ² *Alternatives consider allergy, PK, compliance, local resistance, cost.*

TABLE 1 (25)

ANATOMIC SITE/DIAGNOSIS/ MODIFYING CIRCUMSTANCES	ETIOLOGIES (usual)	SUGGESTED REGIMENS*		ADJUNCT DIAGNOSTIC OR THERAPEUTIC MEASURES AND COMMENTS
		PRIMARY	ALTERNATIVE§	
HEART				
Infective endocarditis—Native valve—empirical rx awaiting cultures—No IV illicit drugs	**NOTE:** Diagnostic criteria include evidence of continuous bacteremia (multiple positive blood cultures), new murmur (worsening of old murmur) of valvular insufficiency, definite emboli, and echocardiographic (transthoracic or transesophageal) evidence of valvular vegetations, *see Table 15C, page 213*			
Valvular or congenital heart disease but no modifying circumstances *See Table 15C, page 213 for prophylaxis*	Viridians strep 30–40%, "other" strep 15–25%, enterococci 5–18%, staphylococci 20–35% (including coag-neg staphylococci *CID 46:232, 2008*).	**Vanco** 15–20 mg/kg q8-12h (target trough conc of 15-20 μg/mL) + **Ceftriaxone** 2g 24h OR **Vanco** 15-20 mg/kg q8-12h (target trough conc of 15-20 μg/mL) + **Gent** 1 mg/kg q8h IV/IM	Substitute **Dapto** 6 mg/kg IV q24h (or q48h for CrCl <30 mL/min) for **Vanco**	If patient not acutely ill and not in heart failure, wait for blood culture results. If initial 3 blood cultures neg, after 24–48 hrs, obtain 2–3 more blood cultures before empiric therapy started. Gent dose is for CrCl of 80 mL/min or greater; even low-dose Gentamicin for only a few days carries risk of nephrotoxicity (*CID 48:713, 2009*). Gent is used for synergy; peak levels need not exceed 4 μg/mL and troughs should be <1 μg/mL. Coagulase-negative staphylococci can occasionally cause native valve endocarditis (*CID 46:232, 2008*). Modify therapy based on identification of specific pathogen as soon as possible to obtain best coverage and to avoid toxicities. **Surgery indications:** See *NEJM 368:1425, 2013*. Role of surgery in pts with left-sided endocarditis & large vegetation (*NEJM 366:2466, 2012*). No difference in 15 yr survival between bioprosthetic and mechanical valve (*JAMA 312:1323, 2014*).
Infective endocarditis—Native valve—culture positive Ref: *Circulation 132:1435, 2015.*				
Viridians strep, S. bovis (S. gallolyticus) with penicillin G MIC ≤0.12 mcg/mL	Viridians strep, S. bovis (S. gallolyticus subsp. gallolyticus)	(Pen G 12–18 million units/day IV, divided q4h x 4 wks) OR (Ceftriaxone 2 gm IV q24h x 4 wks)	[(Pen G or Ceftriaxone 2 gm IV q24h) + Gentamicin 3 mg per kg IV q24h] x 2 wks.	4-wks regimen for most patients. Avoid 2-wks regimen for patients age >65 years, those with cardiac or extracardiac abscess, creatinine clearance of <50 mL/min, impaired eighth cranial nerve function, or Abiotrophia, Granulicatella, or Gemella spp infection. Vancomycin 15 mg/kg q12h x 4 weeks, dose adjusted to achieve trough concentrations of 10-15 μg/mL for patients allergic to or intolerant of Pen or Ceftriaxone.
Viridians strep, S. bovis (S. gallolyticus) with Penicillin G MIC >0.12 to <0.5 mcg/mL	Viridians strep, S. bovis (S. gallolyticus subsp. gallolyticus)	Pen G 24 million units/day IV (divided q4h) x 4 wks + Gent 3 mg/kg IV q24h x 2 wks	Vanco 15 mg/kg q12h x 4 wks, dose adjusted to achieve trough concentrations of 10-15 μg/mL	If the isolate is Ceftriaxone susceptible (MIC <0.5 μg/mL), then Ceftriaxone x 4 wks alone is an option.
For viridans strep or S. bovis with pen G MIC ≥0.5 mcg/mL **NOTE:** Inf. Dis. consultation suggested	Viridians strep, S. bovis, nutritionally variant streptococci (new names are: Abiotrophia sp. & Granulicatella sp.)	[(Pen G 24 million units per 24h IV, divided q4h x 4 wks) + (Gent 3 mg/kg/d in 2-3 divided doses x 4 wks)] OR (AMP 12 gm/day IV, divided q4h + Gent as above x 4 wks)	Vanco 15 mg/kg q12h x 4 wks, dose adjusted to achieve trough concentrations of 10-15 μg/mL	For streptococci with Ceftriaxone MIC <0.5 μg/mL, Ceftriaxone 2 gm q24h can be substituted for ampicillin or penicillin. For gentamicin given 1 mg/kg q8h target peak serum concentration of 3-4 μg/mL, and trough serum concentration of <1 μg/mL.

Abbreviations on page 2.   *See NOTE: All dosage recommendations are for adults (unless otherwise indicated) and assume normal renal function. §Alternatives consider allergy, PK, compliance, local resistance, cost.*

TABLE 1 (26)

HEART/Infective endocarditis—Native valve—culture positive (continued) Ref: Circulation 132:1435, 2015:

ANATOMIC SITE/DIAGNOSIS/ MODIFYING CIRCUMSTANCES	ETIOLOGIES (usual)	SUGGESTED REGIMENS[a]		ADJUNCT DIAGNOSTIC OR THERAPEUTIC MEASURES AND COMMENTS
		PRIMARY	ALTERNATIVE[a]	
Enterococci, penicillin and aminoglycoside susceptible	E. faecalis	[(AMP 2 gm IV q4h or Pen G 24 million units) + Gent 3 mg/kg/d IV in 2-3 divided doses] x 4-6 wks	[(AMP 2 gm IV q4h + Ceftriaxone 2 gm IV q12h) x 6 wks] Penicillin-intolerant patient only: (Vanco 30 mg/kg/d IV in 2 divided doses + Gent 1 mg/kg IV q8h) x 4-6 wks	Native valve 4 ks Pen or AMP + Gent if symptoms <3 mo; 6 wks if symptoms >3 mo; prosthetic valve: 6 wks. Target Vanco trough of 10-20 µg/mL. Adjust dose of Gent to achieve peak serum conc. of 3-4 µg/ml and trough of <1 µg/mL. AMP+Ceftriaxone preferred for patients with creatinine clearance <50 mL/min or who develop such as gent regimen. Vanco + Gent toxic; consider pen desensitization.
Enterococci, Penicillin susceptible, Gentamicin resistant (MIC >500 µg/mL), streptomycin susceptible (MIC <500 µg/mL)	E. faecalis E. faecium	(AMP 2 gm IV q4h) + Ceftriaxone 2 gm IV q12h) x 6 wks	[(AMP 2 gm IV q4h or Pen G 24 million units) + streptomycin 15 mg/kg IV q24h] x 4-6 wks	10-25% E. faecalis and 45-50% E. faecium Gent resistant. May have to consider surgical removal of infected valve. Must confirm streptomycin MIC for synergy if strep combo used. AMP + Ceftriaxone regimen preferred, if creatinine clearance <50 mL/min, concern for impaired eighth nerve function.
Enterococci, Penicillin, aminoglycoside, Vancomycin resistant	E. faecalis E. faecium	Dapto 8-12 mg/kg IV q24h + Ampicillin 2 gm IV q4h	Linezolid 600 mg IV/po q12h	Quinupristin-Dalfopristin 7.5 mg/kg IV q8h (via central line for E. faecium, not active vs E. faecalis). Duration of therapy ≥8 weeks, expert consultation strongly advised. Valve replacement often required for cure.
Infective endocarditis, Gram-negative bacilli	Enterobacteriaceae or P. aeruginosa	Optimal therapy unknown, infectious diseases consult recommended; an aminoglycoside (Tobra if P. aeruginosa) + (Cefepime or Meropenem) is a reasonable option.		Choice of agents based on in vitro susceptibilities, fluoroquinolone an option instead of aminoglycoside, but few data.
Infective endocarditis, fungal	Candida sp. Aspergillus	Optimal therapy unknown, infectious diseases consultation recommended; an azole or echinocandin is a reasonable choice. High failure rate with medical therapy alone, consider early surgery.		
Staphylococcal endocarditis Aortic &/or mitral valve infection—MSSA Surgery indications: see Comment page 28.	Staph. aureus, methicillin-sensitive	Nafcillin (oxacillin) 2 gm IV q4h x 4-6 wks	[(Cefazolin 2 gm IV q8h x 4-6 wks) OR Vanco 30-60 mg/kg/d in 2-3 divided doses to achieve trough of 15-20 mcg/mL x 4-6 wks	If IgE-mediated penicillin allergy, 10% cross-reactivity to cephalosporins (AnIM 141:16, 2004). Cefazolin and Nafcillin probably similar in efficacy and Cefazolin better tolerated (AAC 55:5122, 2011)
Aortic and/or mitral valve—MRSA	Staph. aureus, methicillin-resistant	Vanco 30-60 mg/kg/d in 2-3 divided doses to achieve target trough concentrations of 15-20 mcg/mL recommended for serious infections	Dapto 8-10 mg/kg q24h V (NOT FDA approved for this indication or dose)	In clinical trial (NEJM 355-653, 2006), high failure rate with both vanco and dapto in small numbers of pts. For other alternatives, see Table 6, page 87. Daptomycin references: JAC 58:596 & 2921, 2013. Case reports of success with Telavancin (JAC 65:1315, 2010; AAC 54 5376, 2010; AAC 66: 2186, 2011) and ceftaroline (JAC 67:1267, 2012; J Infect Chemother 19: 42, 2013).
Tricuspid valve infection (usually IVDUs) MSSA, uncomplicated	Staph. aureus, methicillin-sensitive	Nafcillin 2 gm IV q4h x 2 wks (uncomplicated)	If penicillin allergy: Vanco 30-60 mg/kg/d in 2-3 divided doses to achieve trough of 15-20 mcg/mL x 4 wks OR Dapto 8-12 mg/kg IV q24↑ x 4 wks OR Cefazolin 2 gm IV q8h x 4 wks	2-week regimen not long enough if metastatic infection (e.g., osteo) or left-sided endocarditis. Dapto resistance can occur de novo, after or during vanco, or after/during dapto therapy.

Abbreviations on page 2.   [a]NOTE: All dosage recommendations are for adults (unless otherwise indicated) and assume normal renal function. § Alternatives consider allergy; PK, compliance, local resistance, cost.

TABLE 1 (27)

ANATOMIC SITE/DIAGNOSIS/ MODIFYING CIRCUMSTANCES	ETIOLOGIES (usual)	SUGGESTED REGIMENS*		ADJUNCT DIAGNOSTIC OR THERAPEUTIC MEASURES AND COMMENTS
		PRIMARY	ALTERNATIVE§	
HEART/Infective endocarditis—Native valve—culture positive *(continued)*				
Tricuspid valve—MRSA	Staph. aureus, methicillin-resistant	Vanco 15-20 mg/kg q8-12h to achieve target trough concentrations of 15-20 mcg/mL recommended for serious infections × 4-6 wks	Dapto 8-12 mg/kg IV q24h OR equiv to **Vanco** for rt-sided endocarditis; both vanco & dapto did poorly if lt-sided endocarditis *(See Comments & table 6, page 87).*	Dapto dose of 8-12 mg/kg IV q24h may not FDA-approved.
Slow-growing fastidious Gm-neg. bacilli—any valve	**HACEK group** *(See Comments).*	Ceftriaxone 2 gm IV q24h × 4 wks OR CIP 400 mg IV q12h × 4 wks	Dapto 8-12 mg/kg IV q24h × 4-6 wks equiv to **Vanco** for rt-sided endocarditis; both vanco & dapto did poorly if lt-sided endocarditis *(See Comments & table 6, page 87).* **AM-SB** 3 gm IV q6h × 4 wks OR **Levo** 750 mg/IV q24h × 4 wks OR **Moxi** 400 mg po/IV q24h × 4 wks	**HACEK** (acronym for Haemophilus parainfluenza, H. aphrophilus, Actinobacillus, [now Aggregatibacter aphrophilus] Aggregatibacter, Actinobacillus, Cardiobacterium, Eikenella, Kingella). **Ampicillin** 2 gm IV q4h an option if growth of isolate in vitro is sufficient for reliable determination of ampicillin susceptibility.
Bartonella species—any valve	B. henselae, B. quintana	Doxy 100 mg IV/po bid × 6 weeks + Gent 3 mg/kg/day IV divided in 3 equal doses × 2 wks	If can't use gentamicin: **Doxy** 100 mg IV/po bid × 6 wks + **Rifampin** 300 mg IV/po bid × 2 wks	**Dx:** Immunofluorescent antibody titer ≥1:800; blood cultures only occ. positive, or PCR of tissue from surgery. B. quintana transmitted by body lice among homeless.
Infective endocarditis—"culture negative"				
Fever, valvular disease, and ECHO vegetations ± emboli and neg. cultures.	Etiology in 348 cases studied by serology, culture, histopath, & molecular detection: C. burnetii 48%, Bartonella sp. 28%, and rarely (Abiotrophia elegans [nutritionally variant strep], Mycoplasma hominis, Legionella pneumophila, Tropheryma whipplei—together 1%), & rest without etiology identified (most on antibiotic). *See CID 51:131, 2010 for approach to work-up.* Chronic Q fever: *CID 2017;65:1872. AHA treatment guidelines Circulation 132:1435, 2015.* Study from Germany suggests T. whipplei *(J Clin Micro 50:216, 2012).*			
Infective endocarditis—Prosthetic valve (cultures pending)	S. aureus now most common etiology *(JAMA 297:1354, 2007)*			
Early (<2 mos post-op)	S. epidermidis, S. aureus. Rarely Enterobacteriaceae, diphtheroids, fungi	Vanco 15-20 mg/kg q8-12h + Gent 1 mg/kg IV q8h + RIF 600 mg po q24h **NOTE:** because many clinicians delay addition of rifampin until bacterial inoculum has been reduced to decrease likelihood of emerging resistance, pathogen identification and susceptibility information should generally be available before addition of rifampin is required.		Early surgical consultation advised especially if etiology is S. aureus, evidence of heart failure, presence of diabetes and/or renal failure, or concern for valve ring abscess *(JAMA 297:1354, 2007; CID 44:364, 2007).* Early valve surgery not associated with improved 1 year survival in patients with S. aureus prosthetic valve infection *(CID 60:741, 2015).*
Late (>2 mos post-op)	S. epidermidis, viridans strep, enterococci, S. aureus			
Infective endocarditis— Prosthetic valve—positive blood cultures Indications for surgery: severe heart failure, S. aureus infection, prosthetic dehiscence, resistant organism, emboli due to large vegetation. (See AHA guidelines; Circulation 132:1435, 2015.) Surgical consultation advised:	Staph. epidermidis	(Vanco 15-20 mg/kg IV q8-12h + RIF 300 mg po q8h) × 6 wks + Gent 1 mg/kg IV q8h × 2 wks	If S. epidermidis is susceptible to nafcillin/oxacillin in vitro (not common), then substitute nafcillin (or oxacillin) for vanco. Target vanco trough concentrations 15-20 μg/mL. Some clinicians prefer to wait 2-3 days after starting vanco/ gent before starting RIF, to decrease bacterial density and thus minimize risk of selecting rifampin-resistant subpopulations.	
	Staph. aureus	Methicillin sensitive: (**Nafcillin** 2 gm IV q8-12h + **RIF** 300 mg po q8h) × 6 wks + **Gentamicin** 1 mg per kg IV q8h × 2 wks. Methicillin resistant: (**Vanco** 15-20 mg/kg IV q8-12h + **RIF** 300 mg po q8h (to achieve a target trough of 15-20 mcg/mL) × 6 wks + **Gentamicin** 1 mg per kg IV q8h × 2 wks.		See infective endocarditis, native valve, culture positive, page 28. In theory, could substitute CIP for aminoglycoside, but no clinical data and resistance is common. Select definitive regimen based on susceptibility results. Can occur with native valves also.
	Viridans strep, enterococci Enterobacteriaceae or P. aeruginosa	See infective endocarditis, native valve, culture positive, page 126 Aminoglycoside (Tobra if P. aeruginosa) + (PIP-TZ or P Ceph 3 AP or P Ceph 4 or an anti-pseudomonal Pen)		
	Candida, aspergillus	*Table 11, page 126*		High mortality. Valve replacement plus antifungal therapy standard therapy but some success with antifungal therapy alone.

Abbreviations on page 2. *NOTE: All dosage recommendations are for adults (unless otherwise indicated) and assume normal renal function.* § Alternatives consider allergy, PK, compliance, local resistance, cost

TABLE 1 (28)

ANATOMIC SITE/DIAGNOSIS/ MODIFYING CIRCUMSTANCES	ETIOLOGIES (usual)	SUGGESTED REGIMENS*		ADJUNCT DIAGNOSTIC OR THERAPEUTIC MEASURES AND COMMENTS
		PRIMARY	ALTERNATIVE†	
HEART (continued)				
Infective endocarditis—Q fever *Emerg Infect Dis 21:1183, 2015 JCM 52:1637, 2014*	Coxiella burnetii	**Doxy** 100 mg po bid + **hydroxychloroquine** 600 mg/day for at least 18 mos *(Mayo Clin Proc 83:574, 2008)*. Pregnancy: Need long term **TMP-SMX** *(see CID 45:548, 2007)*.		Dx: FA > 800 phase I IgG plus evidence of endocarditis or vasculopathy or signs of chronic Q fever. Q fever positive Coxiella burnetii PCR of blood or tissue. Possible false-positive IFA > 800 phase I IgG. Treatment dura. 18 mos for native valve, 24 mos for prosthetic valve. Monitor serologically for 5 yrs.
Pacemaker/defibrillator infections	S. aureus (40%), S. epidermidis (40%), Gram-negative bacilli (5%), fungi (5%).	Device removal + **Vanco** 15-20 mg/kg IV q8-12h (methicillin-resistant strain). If methicillin-susceptible staphylococci: **Nafcillin** 2 gm IV q4h OR **Cefazolin** 2 gm IV q8h	Device removal + **Dapto** 6 mg per kg IV q24h[AU]	**Duration of rx after device removal:** For "pocket" or subcutaneous infection, 10-14 days; if lead-assoc. endocarditis, 4-6 wks depending on organism. Device removal and absence of valvular vegetation assoc. with significantly higher survival at 1 yr *(JAMA 307:1727, 2012)*. British guidelines: *JAC 70:325, 2015*.
Pericarditis, bacterial	Staph. aureus, Strep. pneumoniae, Group A strep, Enterobacteriaceae	[**Vanco** 15-20 mg/kg q8-12h + (**Ceftriaxone** 2 gm IV q24h OR **Cefepime** 2 gm IV q8h)] *(Dosage, see footnote[#])*	**Vanco** + **CIP** 400 mg q12h (see footnote[#])	Drainage required if signs of tamponade. Forced to use empiric vanco due to high prevalence of MRSA. Adjust regimen based on results of organism ID and susceptibility. Use **Nafcillin**, Oxacillin, or Cefazolin for confirmed MSSA infection.
Rheumatic fever with carditis Ref.: *Ln 366:155, 2005*	Post-infectious sequelae of Group A strep infection (usually pharyngitis)	ASA, and usually prednisone 2 mg/kg po q24h for symptomatic treatment of fever, arthritis, arthralgia. May not influence carditis.		Clinical features: Carditis, polyarthritis, chorea, subcutaneous nodules, erythema marginatum. Prophylaxis: *see page 63*. ASA dose: 80-100 mg/kg/day (pediatric), 4-8 gm/day (adult). Eradication of group A streptococcus also recommended: Child, Penicillin V, 250 mg po bid x 10 days; adult, Penicillin V 500 mg po bid x 10 days.
Ventricular assist device-related infection Manifest & mgmt: *CID 57:1488, 2013* Prevent & mgmt: *CID 64: 222, 2017*	S. aureus, S. epidermidis, aerobic gm-neg bacilli, Candida sp	After culture of blood, wounds, drive line, device pocket and maybe pump: **Vanco** 15-20 mg/kg q8-12h + (**Cefepime** 2 gm IV q12h) + **Flu** 800 mg IV q24h.		Can substitute **Daptomycin** 10 mg/kg/day[AU] for **Vanco**, (**CIP** 400 mg IV q12h or **Levo** 750 mg IV q24h) for cefepime, and (**Vori**, **Caspo**, **Micafungin** or **Anidulafungin**) for Flu. Modify regimen based on results of culture and susceptibility tests. Higher than FDA-approved Dapto dose because of potential emergence of resistance.
JOINT—*Also see Lyme Disease, page 60*				
Reactive arthritis (See Comment for definition)		Only treatment is non-steroidal anti-inflammatory drugs		Definition: Urethritis, conjunctivitis, arthritis, and sometimes uveitis and rash. Arthritis: asymmetrical oligoarthritis of ankles, knees, feet, sacroilitis. Rash: palms and soles—keratoderma blennorrhagica; circinate balanitis of glans penis. HLA-B27 positive predisposes to Reiter's.
Reiter's syndrome (See Comment for definition)	Occurs wks after infection with C. trachomatis, Campylobacter jejuni, Yersinia enterocolitica, Shigella/Salmonella sp.			
Poststreptococcal reactive arthritis (See Rheumatic fever, above)	Immune reaction after strep pharyngitis: (1) arthritis onset in <10 days, (2) lasts months, (3) unresponsive to ASA	Treat strep pharyngitis and then NSAIDs (prednisone needed in some pts)		A reactive arthritis after a β-hemolytic strep infection in absence of sufficient Jones criteria for acute rheumatic fever. Ref.: *Pediatr Emerg Care 28:1085, 2012*.

** **Aminoglycosides** (see *Table 10D, page 122;*) **IMP** 1 gm IV q6h, **MER** 1 gm IV q8h, **Nafcillin** or **Oxacillin** 2 gm IV q4h, **PIP-TZ** 3.375 gm IV q6h or 4.5 gm IV q8h, **AM-SB** 3 gm IV q6h, **P Ceph 1** (cephalothin 2 gm IV q4h or cefazolin 2 gm IV q8h), **CIP** 750 mg po bid or 400 mg IV q12h, **RIF** 600 mg po q24h, **Aztreonam** 2 gm IV q8h, **CFP** 2 gm IV q12h

Abbreviations on page 2.   *NOTE: All dosage recommendations are for adults (unless otherwise indicated) and assume normal renal function; § Alternatives consider allergy, PK, compliance, local resistance, cost.

TABLE 1 (29)

ANATOMIC SITE/DIAGNOSIS/ MODIFYING CIRCUMSTANCES	ETIOLOGIES (usual)	SUGGESTED REGIMENS*		ADJUNCT DIAGNOSTIC OR THERAPEUTIC MEASURES AND COMMENTS
		PRIMARY	ALTERNATIVE§	
JOINT (continued)				
Septic arthritis: Treatment requires both adequate drainage of purulent joint fluid and appropriate antimicrobial therapy. **There is no need to inject antimicrobials into joints.** Empiric therapy after collection of blood and joint fluid for culture; review Gram stain of joint fluid.				
Infants <3 mos (neonate)	Staph. aureus, Enterobacteriaceae, Group B strep	**If MRSA not a concern: (Nafcillin OR Cefazolin) + Cefotaxime**	**If MRSA a concern: Vanco + Cefotaxime**	Blood cultures frequently positive. Adjacent bone involved in 2/3 pts. Group B strep and gonococci most common community-acquired etiologies. Kingella kingae suspect; ceftriaxone (Ped Infect Dis J 2016, 35:340).
Children (3 nos–14 yrs)	S. aureus 27%, S. pyogenes & S. pneumo 14%, H. influ 3%, Gm-neg. bacilli 6%, other (GC, N. mening) 14%, unk 36%	**MRSA prevalence high: Vanco + Cefotaxime** **MRSA prevalence low: Cefazolin**		Marked ↓ in H. influenzae since use of conjugate vaccine. **NOTE:** Septic arthritis due to salmonella has no association with sickle cell disease, unlike salmonella osteomyelitis. 10 days of therapy as effective as a 30-day treatment course if there is a good clinical response and CRP levels normalize quickly (CID 48:1201, 2009).
Adults (review Gram stain): See page 60 for Lyme Disease and page 60 for gonococcal arthritis				
Acute monoarticular				
At risk for sexually-transmitted disease	**N. gonorrhoeae** (see page 23), S. aureus, streptococci, rarely aerobic Gm-neg. bacilli	**Gram stain negative: Ceftriaxone** 1 gm IV q24h or **Cefotaxime** 1 gm IV q8h or **Ceftizoxime** 1 gm IV q8h	If Gram stain shows Gm+ cocci in clusters: **Vanco** 15-20 mg/kg IV q8-12h.	Suspected gonococcal infections (GC): culture urethra, cervix, anal canal, throat, blood, joint fluid. For treatment comments, see Disseminated GC, page 23. Treat with Azithromycin 1 gm po or Doxycycline 100 mg twice daily for 7 days if GC proven or suspected.
Not at risk for sexually-transmitted disease	S. aureus, streptococci, Gm-neg. bacilli	Gram stain shows Gram-pos. cocci: **Vanco** 15-20 mg/kg IV q8-12h Gram stain shows Gram-neg bacilli: **Cefepime** 2 gm q8h IV OR **Meropenem** 1 gm q8h IV Gram stain neg: **Vanco** 15-20 mg/kg IV q8-12h + [**Ceftriaxone** 1 gm IV q24h OR + **Cefepime** 2 gm q8h IV q8h (preferred for possible healthcare-associated infection)] For treatment duration, see Table 3, page 74 See Table 2 & Table 12		Differential includes gout and chondrocalcinosis (pseudogout). **Look for crystals in joint fluid.** Adjust regimen based on culture and susceptibility. **NOTE:** See Table 6 for MRSA treatment.
Chronic monoarticular	Brucella, nocardia, mycobacteria, fungi			
Polyarticular, usually acute	Gonococci, B. burgdorferi (Lyme), acute rheumatic fever, viruses, e.g. hepatitis B, rubella vaccine, parvo B19, staph and strep may also cause polyarticular infections	Gram stain usually negative for GC. If sexually active, culture urethra, cervix, anal canal, throat, blood, joint fluid, and then: **Ceftriaxone** 1 gm IV q24h. No STD risk, Gram stain negative: **Vanco + Ceftriaxone** 1 gm IV q24h.		GC may be associated with pustular/hemorrhagic skin lesions and tenosynovitis; treat with **Ceftriaxone** for 7 days and with **Azithromycin** 1 gm po x1 OR **Doxycycline** 100 mg po twice daily for 7 days if GC proven or suspected. Consider Lyme disease if exposure areas known to harbor infected ticks (see page 60); usually large joint. Vanco• CIP or Levo also an option if low STD risk. Expanded differential includes gout, pseudogout, reactive arthritis. (HLA-B27 pos.).
Septic arthritis, post intra-articular injection	MSSE/MRSE 40%, MSSA/ MRSA 20%, P. aeruginosa, Propionibacteria, AFB	**NO** empiric therapy. Arthroscopy for culture/sensitivity, crystals, woshout		Treat based on culture results x 14 days (assumes no foreign body present).

Abbreviations on page 2.   *NOTE: All dosage recommendations are for adults (unless otherwise indicated) and assume normal renal function. §Alternatives consider allergy; PK, compliance, local/resistance, cost.

TABLE 1 (30)

ANATOMIC SITE/DIAGNOSIS/ MODIFYING CIRCUMSTANCES	ETIOLOGIES (usual)	SUGGESTED REGIMENS* PRIMARY	SUGGESTED REGIMENS* ALTERNATIVE*	ADJUNCT DIAGNOSTIC OR THERAPEUTIC MEASURES AND COMMENTS
JOINT *(continued)*				
Infected prosthetic joint (PJI) • Suspect infection if sinus tract or wound drainage; acutely painful prosthesis; chronically painful prosthesis; w/painful prosthesis. or high ESR/CRP assoc. w/painful prosthesis. • **Empiric therapy is NOT recommended.** Treat based on culture and sensitivity results. **3 surgical options:** 1) debridement and prosthesis retention (if sx <3 wks or implantation <30 days) 2) 1 stage, direct exchange; 3) 2 stage: debridement, removal, reimplantation **IDSA Guidelines:** *CID 56:e1, 2013.* • Data do not allow assessment of value of adding antibacterial cement to temporary joint spacers (*CID 55:474, 2012*). • Evidence of systemic absorption of Tobra from antibiotic-impregnated cement spacers (*CID 58:1783, 2014*). *(Continued on next page)*	MSSA/MSSE	**Debridement/Retention:** [(Nafcillin 2 gm IV q4h or Oxacillin 2 gm IV q4h, IV) + RIF 300 mg po bid] OR (Cefazolin 2 gm IV q8h + RIF 300 mg po bid) x 2-6 wks followed by [(CIP 750 mg po bid OR Levo 750 mg po q24h) + RIF 300 mg po bid] for 3-6 months (shorter duration for total hip arthroplasty) **1-stage exchange:** IV/po regimen as above for 3 mos **2-stage exchange:** regimen as above for 4-6 wks	(Daptomycin 6-8 mg/kg IV q24h OR Linezolid 600 mg po/IV bid) ± Rifampin 300 mg po bid	• **Confirm isolate susceptibility to fluoroquinolone and rifampin:** for fluoroquinolone-resistant isolate consider using other active highly bioavailable agent, e.g., TMP-SMX, Doxy, Minocycline, Amoxicillin-Clavulanate, Clindamycin, or Linezolid. • **Enterococcal infection:** addition of aminoglycoside optional. • **P. aeruginosa infection:** consider adding aminoglycoside if isolate is susceptible, (but if this improves outcome unclear.) • Prosthesis retention most important risk factor for treatment failure (*Clin Microbiol Infect 16:1789, 2010*). (Linezolid 600 mg + Rifampin 300 mg) may be effective as salvage therapy if device removal not possible (*Antimicrob Agents Chemother 55:4308, 2011*) • If prosthesis is retained, consider long-term, suppressive therapy, particularly for staphylococcal infections; depending on in vitro susceptibility options include TMP-SMX, Doxycycline, Minocycline, Amoxicillin, Ciprofloxacin, Cephalexin.
	MRSA/MRSE	**Debridement/Retention:** (Vanco 15-20 mg/kg IV q8-12h + RIF 300 mg po bid) x 2-6 weeks followed by [(CIP 750 mg po bid OR Levo 750 mg po q24h) + RIF 300 mg po bid] for 3-6 months (shorter duration for total hip arthroplasty) **1-stage exchange:** IV/po regimen as above for 3 mos **2-stage exchange:** regimen as above for 4-6 wks	(Daptomycin 6-8 mg/kg IV q24h OR Linezolid 600 mg po/IV bid) ± Rifampin 300 mg po bid	• Culture yield may be increased by sonication of prosthesis (*N Engl J Med 357:654, 2007*). • Other treatment consideration: Rifampin is bactericidal vs. biofilm-producing bacteria. Never use Rifampin alone due to rapid development of resistance. Rifampin 300 mg po/IV bid + Fusidic acid*** 500 mg po/IV tid is another option (*Clin Micro Inf 12(S3):93, 2006*). • Watch for toxicity if Linezolid is used for more than 2 weeks of therapy.
	Streptococci (Grps A, B, C, D, viridans, other)	**Debridement/Retention** (Poorer outcomes with retention compared with removal and exchange. *CID 64:1742, 2017*): Penicillin G 20 million units IV continuous infusion q24h or in 6 divided doses OR **Ceftriaxone** 2 gm IV q24h x 4-6 wks **1 or 2 stage exchange:** regimen as above for 4-6 wks	Vancomycin 15 mg/kg IV q12h	

Abbreviations on page 2.   *NOTE: All dosage recommendations are for adults (unless otherwise indicated) and assume normal renal function. § Alternatives consider allergy, PK, compliance, local resistance, cost.*

TABLE 1 (31)

ANATOMIC SITE/DIAGNOSIS/ MODIFYING CIRCUMSTANCES	ETIOLOGIES (usual)	SUGGESTED REGIMENS*		ADJUNCT DIAGNOSTIC OR THERAPEUTIC MEASURES AND COMMENTS
		PRIMARY	**ALTERNATIVE§**	
JOINT/Infected prosthetic joint (PJI) *(continued)*				
(Continued from previous page)	Enterococci	**Debridement/Retention:** Pen-susceptible: Ampicillin 12 gm IV OR Penicillin G 20 million units IV continuous infusion q24h or in 6 divided doses x 4-6 wks Pen-resistant: Vancomycin 15 mg/kg IV q12h x 4-6 wks **1 or 2 stage exchange:** regimen as above for 4-6 wks	Daptomycin 6-8 mg/kg IV q24h OR Linezolid 600 mg po/IV bid	*(continued from previous page)*
	Propionibacterium acnes (Hold broth cultures, especially in infections of the shoulder, for 10 days to maximize recovery of *P. acnes.* (*J Clin Microbiol* 54:3043, 2016)).	**Debridement/Retention:** Penicillin G 20 million units IV continuous infusion or in 6 divided doses OR Ceftriaxone 2 gm IV q24h x 4-6 wks **1 or 2 stage exchange:** regimen as above for 4-6 wks	Vancomycin 15 mg/kg IV q12h OR Clindamycin 300-450 mg po qid	
	Gm-neg enteric bacilli	**Debridement/Retention:** Ertapenem 1 gm q24h IV OR other beta-lactam (e.g., Ceftriaxone 2 gm IV q24h OR Cefepime 2 gm IV q12h, based on susceptibility) x 4-6 wks **1 or 2 stage exchange:** regimen as above for 4-6 wks	Ciprofloxacin 750 mg po bid	
	P. aeruginosa	**Debridement/Retention:** Cefepime 2 gm IV q12h OR MER 1 gm IV q8h + Tobra 5.1 mg/kg once daily IV **1 or 2 stage exchange:** regimen as above for 4-6 wks	Ciprofloxacin 750 mg po bid or 400 mg IV q8h	
Rheumatoid arthritis	TNF inhibitors (adalimumab, certolizumab, etanercept, golimumab, infliximab) and other anti-inflammatory biologics (tofacitinib, rituximab, tocilizumab, abatacept) ↑ risk of TBc, fungal infection, legionella, listeria, and malignancy. *See Med Lett 55:1, 2013 for full listing.*			
Septic bursitis; Olecranon bursitis; prepatellar bursitis	Staph. aureus >80%, M. tuberculosis (rare), M. marinum (rare)	**(Nafcillin or Oxacillin 2 gm IV q4h or Cefazolin 2 gm IV q8h if MSSA)**	**(Vanco 15-20 mg/kg IV q8-12h or Linezolid 600 mg po bid) if MRSA**	Empiric MRSA coverage recommended if risk factors are present and in high prevalence areas. Immunosuppression, not duration of therapy, is a risk factor for recurrence; 7 days of therapy may be sufficient for immuno-competent patients undergoing one-stage bursectomy (*JAC 65/1008, 2010*). If MSSA **Dicloxacillin** 500 mg po qid as oral step-down. If MRSA **Dapto** 6 mg/kg IV q24h.

Abbreviations on page 2. *NOTE: All dosage recommendations are for adults (unless otherwise indicated) and assume normal renal function. §Alternatives consider allergy, PK, compliance, local resistance, cost.*

TABLE 1 (32)

ANATOMIC SITE/DIAGNOSIS/ MODIFYING CIRCUMSTANCES	ETIOLOGIES (usual)	SUGGESTED REGIMENS*		ADJUNCT DIAGNOSTIC OR THERAPEUTIC MEASURES AND COMMENTS
		PRIMARY	ALTERNATIVE*	
KIDNEY & BLADDER (Reviewed in Nature Rev 13:269, 2015; IDSA Guidelines CID 52: e103, 2011)				
Acute Uncomplicated Cystitis & Pyelonephritis in Women				
Cystitis Diagnosis: dysuria, frequency, urgency, suprapubic pain & no vaginal symptoms See AAC 60:2860, 7535 & 7536, 2016	E. coli (75-95%) P. mirabilis K. pneumoniae S. saprophyticus	**Nitrofurantoin** 100 mg po bid x 5 d OR **TMP-SMX** 1 tab po bid x 3 days (Avoid TMP-SMX if 20% or more local E. coli are resistant) OR **Nitrofurantoin** 100 mg po bid x 5 days OR (**CIP** 250 mg po bid OR **CIP-ER** 500 mg po once daily) x 3 days	**Fosfomycin** 3 gm po 1 dose OR **Cefdinir** 300 mg bid x 3-7 days OR **Cefdinir** 300 mg bid x 3-7 days OR **Pivmecillinam** (NUS) 400 mg po bid x 3-7 days	• Pyridium (phenazopyridine) may hasten resolution of dysuria. • Other beta lactams are less effective. • Nitrofurantoin & Fosfomycin active vs. ESBLs; however, if early pyelonephritis, avoid these drugs due to low renal concentrations. • Other antimicrobials can limit systemic spread of cystitis. • Out-patient therapy of UTIs due to MDR bacteria: - Fosfomycin & nitrofurantoin usually active. - Increasing TMP-SMX & FQ resistance (AAC 2016;60:2680). - Beta-lactams least efficacious. - Ref: CID 2016;63:960. • In D3RPCT of women in nursing homes, compared cranberry capsules vs. placebo; no difference in bacteriuria/pyuria (JAMA 2016;316:1873 (ed) & 1879).
Pyelonephritis Diagnosis: fever, CVA, pain, nausea/vomiting	Same as for Cystitis, above. Need urine culture & sensitivity testing	**Outpatient:** **Ceftriaxone** 1 gm IV, then (**CIP** 500 mg po bid OR **CIP-ER** 1000 mg po once daily OR **Levo** 750 mg po once daily x 5 days) Culture/sens results may allow **TMP-SMX DS** 1 tab po bid	**Inpatient: Local resistance data important** **Ceftriaxone** 1 gm IV q24h OR **FEP** 400 mg IV q12h OR **Levo** 750 mg po once daily x 5 days. If ESBLs & E coli: **MER** 0.5-1 gm IV q8h	• When tolerating fluids, can transition to oral therapy; drug choice based on culture/sens results. • No need for follow-up urine cultures in pts who respond to therapy. • If symptoms do not abate quickly, imaging of urinary tract for complications, e.g., silent stone or stricture. • Avoid Fosfomycin, Moxifloxacin, Nitrofurantoin, Pivmecillinam due to low rena concentrations. • Other options: AM/CL 500/125 po bid x 7-10 days; Cefdinir 300 mg po bid x 7-13 days
Pregnancy: Asymptomatic bacteriuria & cystitis Drug choice based on culture / sensitivity results; do follow-up culture one week after last dose of antibiotic	E. coli (70%) Klebsiella sp. Enterobacter sp. Proteus sp. Grp B Streptococcus	**Nitrofurantoin** (but not in 3rd trimester at term) 1 tab po q12h x 5-7 days OR **Amox-Clav** 500 mg po q8h x 3-7 days OR **Cephalexin** 500 mg po q6h x 3-7 days	**TMP-SMX DS** (but not in 1st trimester or at term) 1 tab po q12h x 3 days OR **Cefpodoxime** 100 mg po q12h x 3-7 days	• Treatment recommended to avoid progression to cystitis or pyelonephritis. • Untreated bacteriuria associated with increased risk of low birth wt, preterm birth & increased perinatal mortality. • If post-treatment culture positive, re-treat with different drug of longer course of same drug. • Avoid nitrofurantoin in 3rd trimester due to risk of hemolytic anemia in newborn.
Pregnancy: Acute pyelonephritis Diagnosis: CVA pain, fever, nausea/vomiting in 2nd/3rd trimester. See Comment	Same as for Cystitis, above Regimens are empiric therapy (See Comment)	**Moderately ill: Ceftriaxone** 1 gm IV q24h OR **Cefepime** 1 gm IV q12h. For pen/cephalosporin allergic, **Aztreonam** 1 gm IV q8h. No activity vs. Gram-pos cocci.	**Severely ill: Pip-Tazo** 3.375 gm IV q6h OR **MER** 1 gm IV q8h OR **ERTA** 1 gm IV q24h	Differential dx includes: placental abruption & infection of amniotic fluid. • Try to avoid FQs and AGs during pregnancy. • Switch to po therapy after afebrile x 48 hrs. • Treat for 10-14 days. • If fever recurs, re-treat. Once asymptomatic continue suppressive therapy for duration of pregnancy: Nitrofurantoin 50-100 mg qhs OR Cephalexin 250-500 mg qhs.
Recurrent UTIs in Women (≥2 or more infections in 6 mos/ 3 or more infections in 1 yr). Risk factors: family history, spermicide use, presence of cystocele, elevated post-void residual urine volume	Same as for Cystitis, above Regimens are options for antimicrobial prophylaxis	**Continuous:** (**TMP-SMX SS** OR **TMP** 100 mg OR **Cephalexin** 250 mg OR **CIP** 125 mg) po once daily	**Post-coital:** (**TMP-SMX SS** OR **Cephalexin** 250 mg OR **CIP** 125 mg) 1 tab po	• No strong evidence to support use of cranberry juice. • Topical estrogen cream reduces risk of recurrent UTI in postmenopausal women. • Probiotics need more study. • In DB-RPCT of women age ≥65 yrs in nursing home, cranberry capsules resulted in no difference in bacteriuria/pyuria (JAMA 2016;316:1873 & 1879).

Abbreviations on page 2.   *NOTE: All dosage recommendations are for adults (unless otherwise indicated) and assume normal/renal function. ‡ Alternatives consider allergy, PK, compliance, local resistance, cost:

TABLE 1 (33)

ANATOMIC SITE/DIAGNOSIS/ MODIFYING CIRCUMSTANCES	ETIOLOGIES (usual)	SUGGESTED REGIMENS*		ADJUNCT DIAGNOSTIC OR THERAPEUTIC MEASURES AND COMMENTS
		PRIMARY	ALTERNATIVE§	
KIDNEY & BLADDER/Acute Uncomplicated Cystitis & Pyelonephritis in Women (continued)				
Asymptomatic Bacteriuria in Women Defined: 2 consecutive clean catch urine cultures with ≥10⁵ CFU/mL of same organism	Same as for Cystitis, above	**Treatment indicated:** pregnancy, urologic procedure causing bleeding from mucosa	**No treatment indicated:** non-pregnant premenopausal women, spinal cord injury pts, elderly women in/out of nursing home, prosthetic joint surgery	• Asymptomatic bacteriuria & pyuria are discordant. 60% of pts with pyuria have no bacteriuria and pyuria commonly accompanies asymptomatic bacteriuria.
Acute Uncomplicated Cystitis & Pyelonephritis in Men. Risk of uncomplicated UTI increased with history of insertive anal sex & lack of circumcision. *See also, Complicated UTIs in Men & Women, below*				
Cystitis	E. coli (75-95%) Rarely other enterobacteriaceae	**TMP-SMX DS** 1 tab po bid x 3 days OR **Nitrofurantoin** 100 mg po bid x 5 days	(**CIP** 500 mg po bid OR **CIP-ER** 1000 mg po once daily OR **Levo** 750 mg po once daily) x 3 days	• If recurrent, evaluate for prostatitis. • Cystitis plus symptoms of bladder outlet obstruction suggests concomitant acute bacterial prostatitis. • Consider presence of STDs. Recommend NAAT for C. trachomatis & N. gonorrhoeae.
Pyelonephritis	*Low risk of MDR-GNB:* Pockets of MDR-resistant ESBL producing E. coli (EID 2016,22:1594)	**CIP** 400 mg IV q12h OR **Levo** 750 mg IV once daily) x 7-14 days	*High risk of MDR GNB:* **MER** 0.5-1 gm IV q8h x 7-14 days	• Avoid Nitrofurantoin due to low renal concentration in prostate. • If any hint of obstructive uropathy, image collecting system asap. • Case report: Fosfomycin 3 gm daily used for MDR gm-neg bacilli (CID 61:1141, 2015).
Acute Complicated UTIs in Men & Women Defined: UTI plus co-morbid condition that increases infection severity & risk of failure, e.g., diabetes, pregnancy, late diagnosis, chronic foley catheter, suprapubic tube, obstruction secondary to stone, anatomic abnormalities, immunosuppression	E. coli or Other enterobacteriaceae plus: P. aeruginosa Enterococci S. aureus Candida sp.	*Low risk of MDR GNB:* **Levo** 750 mg IV once daily OR **Ceftriaxone** 1 gm IV once daily OR **Cefepime** 1 gm IV q12h OR **Pip-Tazo** 3.375 gm IV q6h OR **Gent** 5 mg/kg IV Once daily. If Pen-allergic: **Aztreonam** 2 gm IV q8h	*Risk of MDR GNB ≥20%:* **MER** 0.5-1 gm IV q8h OR **Ceftolozane-tazobactam** 1.5 gm IV q8h OR **Ceftazidime-avibactam** 2.5 gm IV q8h OR **MER-vaborbactam** 4 gm IV q8h	Prior to empiric therapy: urine culture and sensitivity. If hypotensive: blood cultures. If obstructive uropathy suspected, need imaging of urinary tract asap. *See Comments* • Uncontrolled infection, esp. if obstruction, can result in emphysematous pyelonephritis, renal abscess, carbuncle, papillary necrosis or perinephric abscess. • Due to co-morbidities & frequent infection, increased risk of drug-resistance pathogens. • Due to high incidence of resistance and infection severity, Nitrofurantoin, Fosfomycin & TMP-SMX should not be used for empiric therapy. • If enterococci cultured, need to adjust therapy based on in vitro susceptibility. • Duration of treatment varies with status of co-morbid conditions, need for urologic procedures & individualized pt clinical response.

*NOTE: All dosage recommendations are for adults (unless otherwise indicated) and assume normal renal function. § Alternatives consider allergy, PK, compliance, local resistance, cost.

TABLE 1 (34)

ANATOMIC SITE/DIAGNOSIS/ MODIFYING CIRCUMSTANCES	ETIOLOGIES (usual)	SUGGESTED REGIMENS*		ADJUNCT DIAGNOSTIC OR THERAPEUTIC MEASURES AND COMMENTS
		PRIMARY	ALTERNATIVE§	
LIVER (for Primary (Spontaneous) Bacterial Peritonitis (SBP), see page 47)				
Cholangitis		See Gallbladder, page 17		
Cirrhosis & variceal bleeding	Esophageal flora	(Norfloxacin 400 mg po bid OR CIP 400 mg q12h) x max. of 7 days	Ceftriaxone 1 gm IV once daily for max. of 7 days	Short term prophylactic antibiotics in cirrhotics with G-I hemorr, with or without ascites, decreases rate of bacterial infection & ↑ survival (J Hepa ol 60:1310, 2014).
Hepatic abscess Klebsiella liver abscess ref.: Ln ID 12:881, 2012	Enterobacteriaceae (esp. Klebsiella sp.), bacteroides, enterococci, Entamoeba histolytica, Yersinia entero- colitica (rare), Fusobacterium necrophorum (Lemierre's). For echinococcus, see Table 13, page 165. For cat-scratch disease (CSD), see pages 46 & 59	Metro + (Ceftriaxone OR Cefoxitin OR PIP-TZ OR AM-SB OR CIP or levo.	Metro (for amoeba) + e ther IMP, MER OR DORI	Serological tests for amebiasis should be done on all patients; if neg., surgical drainage or percutaneous aspiration. In pyogenic abscess, ½ have identifiable GI source or underlying biliary tract disease. If amoeba serology positive: treat with Metro alone without surgery. Empiric Metro included for both E. histolytica & bacteroides. Hemochromatosis associated with Yersinia enterocolitica liver abscess; regimens listed are effective for yersinia. Klebsiella pneumonia genotype K1 associated ocular & CNS Klebsiella infections.
Hepatic encephalopathy	Urease-producing gut bacteria	Rifaximin 550 mg po bid (take with lactulose)		Ref.: NEJM 375:1660, 2016.
Leptospirosis, see page 62	Leptospirosis	See page 59		
Peliosis hepatis in AIDS pts	Bartonella henselae and B. quintana			Suspect if fever & abdominal pain post-transplant. Exclude hepatic artery thrombosis. Presence of candida and/or VRE bad prognosticators.
Post-transplant infected "bioma"	Enterococci (incl. VRE), candida, Gm-neg. bacilli (P. aeruginosa 8%), anaerobes 5%	Linezolid 600 mg IV bid + PIP-TZ 4.5 gm IV q6h + Flu 400 mg IV q24h	Dapto 6 mg/kg per day + Levo 750 mg IV q24h + Flu 400 mg IV q24h	
Viral hepatitis	Hepatitis A, B, C, D, E, G	See Table 14E and Table 14F		
LUNG/BRONCHI				
Bronchiolitis/wheezy bronchitis (expiratory wheezing)				
Infants/children (≤ age 5) See RSV, Table 14A, page 181 Ref.: Ln 368-312, 2006	Respiratory syncytial virus (RSV) 50%, parainfluenza 25%, human metapneumovirus	Antibiotics not useful, mainstay of therapy is oxygen and hydration. Ribavirin not recommended for bronchiolitis except HSCT and perhaps other transplant pts		RSV most important. Rapid diagnosis with antigen detection methods. For prevention a humanized mouse monoclonal antibody, palivizumab. See Table 14A, page 181. RSV immune globulin no longer available. Guidance from the American Academy of Pediatrics recommends use of palivizumab only in newborn infants born at 29 weeks gestation (or earlier) and in special populations (e.g., those infants with significant heart disease. (Pediatrics 2014;134:415-420)
Bronchitis				
Infants/children (≤ age 5)	<Age 2: Adenovirus; age 2-5: Respiratory syncytial virus, parainfluenza 3 virus, human metapneumovirus	Antibiotics indicated only with associa ed sinusitis or heavy growth on throat culture for S. pneumo., Group A strep, H. influenzae or no improvement in 1 week. Otherwise rx is symptomatic.		
Adolescents and adults with acute tracheobronchitis (Acute bronchitis) Ref.: JAMA 312:2678, 2014	Usually viral. M. pneumoniae 5%, C. pneumoniae 5%. See Persistent cough (Pertussis).	Antibiotics not indicated. Antitussive in indicated bronchodilators. Throat swab PCR available for Dx of mycoplasma or chlamydia.		Purulent sputum alone not an indication for antibiotic therapy. Expect cough to last 2 weeks. If fever/signs, get chest x-ray. If mycoplasma documented, prefer doxy over macrolides due to increasing macrolide resistance (JAC 68:506, 2013).

Abbreviations on page 2.

Abbreviations on page 2.

§NOTE: All dosage recommendations are for adults (unless otherwise indicated, and assume norma. renal function, PK, compliance, local resistance, cost.

TABLE 1 (35)

ANATOMIC SITE/DIAGNOSIS/ MODIFYING CIRCUMSTANCES	ETIOLOGIES (usual)	SUGGESTED REGIMENS*		ADJUNCT DIAGNOSTIC OR THERAPEUTIC MEASURES AND COMMENTS
		PRIMARY	ALTERNATIVE§	
LUNG/Bronchi/Bronchitis (continued)				
Persistent cough (>14 days), afebrile during community outbreak: Pertussis (whooping cough) 10–20% adults with cough >14 days have pertussis (Review: Chest 146:205, 2014)	Bordetella pertussis & occ. Bordetella parapertussis. Also consider asthma, gastro-esophageal reflux, post-nasal drip, mycoplasma and also chlamydia.	**Peds doses: Azithro**/ **Clarithro** po OR **Erythro estolate²ª** OR **Erythro base²ª** (doses in footnote²)	**Adult doses: Azithro** po 500 mg day 1, 250 mg q24h days 2–5 OR **Erythro** 500 mg qid times 14 days OR **TMP-SMX-DS** 1 tab bid times 14 days OR (**Clarithro** 500 mg bid or 1 gm ER q24h times 7 days)	3 stages of illness: catarrhal (1–2 wks), paroxysmal coughing (2–4 wks), and convalescence (1–2 wks). Treatment may abort or eliminate pertussis in catarrhal stage, but does not shorten paroxysmal stage. **Diagnosis:** PCR on nasopharyngeal secretions or ↑ pertussis-toxin present. **Rx aimed at eradication of NP carriage.** In non-outbreak setting, likelihood of pertussis increased if post-tussive emesis or inspiratory whoop present (JAMA 304:890, 2010).
Pertussis: Prophylaxis of household contacts.	Drugs and doses as per treatment immediately above. Vaccination of newborn contacts.			Recommended by Am. Acad. Ped. Red Book 2006 for all household or close contacts; community-wide prophylaxis not recommended.
Acute bacterial exacerbation of chronic bronchitis (ABECB), adults (almost always smokers with COPD) Ref: NEJM 359-2355, 2008.	Viruses 20–50%, C. pneumoniae 5%, M. pneumoniae <1%; role of S. pneumo, H. influenzae & M. catarrhalis controversial. Tobacco use, air pollution contribute.	**Severe ABECB** = ↑ dyspnea, ↑ sputum viscosity/purulence, ↑ sputum volume. For severe ABECB: (1) consider chest x-ray, esp. if febrile &/ or low O₂, sat.; (2) inhaled anticholinergic bronchodilator; (3) oral corticosteroid for just 5 days (JAMA 309:2223, 2013); (4) D/C tobacco use; (5) non-invasive positive pressure ventilation. Role of antimicrobials is debated even for severe disease, but study of >80,000 patients shows value of antimicrobial therapy in patients hospitalized with severe disease (JAMA 303(20):2035, 2010). **For mild or moderate disease, no antimicrobial treatment** maybe **Amox, Doxy, TMP-SMX, or O Ceph. For severe disease, AM-CL, Azithro/Clarithro, or O Ceph** with enhanced activity vs. drug-resistant S. pneumo (**Gemi, Levo, Moxi** or **Pruliflox**). **Duration** varies in footnote. Range 3–10 days. Limit **Gemi** to 5 days to decrease risk of rash. **Azithro** 250 mg daily x 1 yr modestly reduced frequency of acute exacerbations in pts with milder disease (NEJM 365:689, 2011). Drugs & doses in footnote². Dosage in footnote².		Many potential etiologies: obstruction, cystic fibrosis, dyskinetic cilia, tobacco, prior severe or recurrent necrotizing bronchitis; e.g. pertussis.
Bronchiectasis Thorax 65 (Suppl 1): i1, 2010; Am J Respir Crit Care Med 188:647, 2013.	H. influ, P. aeruginosa, and rarely S. pneumo.	**Gemi, Levo,** or **Moxi** x 7-10 days. Dosage in footnote².		**Caveats:** higher rates of macrolide resistance in oropharyngeal flora; potential for increased risk of a) cardiovascular deaths from macrolide-induced QTc prolongation, b) liver toxicity, or c) hearing loss (see JAMA 309:1295, 2013).
Acute exacerbation	Not applicable	Two randomized trials of **Erythro** 250 mg bid (JAMA 309:1260, 2013) or **Azithro** 500 mg 3x/wk (JAMA 309:1251, 2013) x1year showed significant reduction in the rate of acute exacerbations, better preservation of lung function, and better quality of life versus placebo in adults with non-cystic fibrosis bronchiectasis.		**Pre-treatment screening:** baseline liver function tests, electrocardiogram; assess hearing, sputum culture to exclude mycobacterial disease.
Prevention of exacerbation				
Specific organisms	Aspergillus (see Table 11) MAI (Table 12) and P. aeruginosa (Table 5B).			

² **ADULT DOSAGE: AM-CL:** 875/125 or 500/125 mg po bid or 2000/125 mg po q8h or (JAMA 309:1260, 2013) mg po q8h or 500 mg immediate-release q12h; **Azithro** 500 mg po x 1 dose, then 250 mg q24h x 4 days or 500 mg po q24h x 3 days; Oral cephalosporins: **Cefaclor** 500 mg po q8h or 500 mg extended-release q12h; **Cefdinir** 300 mg po q12h or 600 mg po q24h; **Cefditoren** 400 mg po q12h; **Cefixime** 400 mg po q24h; **Cefpodoxime** proxetil 200 mg po q12h; **Cefprozil** 500 mg po q12h; **Ceftibuten** 400 mg po q24h; **Cefuroxime axetil** 250 or 500 mg q12h; **Clarithro** extended release 1000 mg po q24h; **Doxy** 100 mg po bid; **Erythro** 500 mg po qid; **Erythro estolate** 40 mg/kg/day po div q6h; **Erythro base** 40 mg/kg/day div q6h; **Loracarbef** 400 mg po q12h; **Levo** 500 mg po q24h; **Moxi** 400 mg po q24h; Pruliflox 600 mg po q24h (where available); **TMP-SMX** 1 DS tab po bid.

PEDS DOSAGE: Azithro 10 mg/kg/day po on day 1, then 5 mg/kg po q24h x 4 days; **Clarithro** 7.5 mg/kg po q12h; **Erythro base** 40 mg/kg/day div q6h; **Erythro estolate** 40 mg/kg/day div q6h; **TMP-SMX** 8 mg/kg/day (TMP component) div bid.

Abbreviations on page 2.   *NOTE: All dosage recommendations are for adults (unless otherwise indicated) and assume normal renal function. § Alternatives consider allergy, PK, compliance, local resistance, cost.

TABLE 1 (36)

ANATOMIC SITE/DIAGNOSIS/ MODIFYING CIRCUMSTANCES	ETIOLOGIES (usual)	SUGGESTED REGIMENS*		ADJUNCT DIAGNOSTIC OR THERAPEUTIC MEASURES AND COMMENTS
		PRIMARY	ALTERNATIVE§	
LUNG/Bronchi/Bronchus *(continued)*				
Pneumonia: CONSIDER TUBERCULOSIS IN ALL PATIENTS; ISOLATE ALL SUSPECT PATIENTS				
Neonatal: Birth to 1 month	Viruses: CMV, rubella, H. simplex Bacteria: Group B strep, listeria, coliforms, S. aureus, P. aeruginosa Other: Chlamydia trachomatis, syphilis	AMP + Gentamicin ± Cefotaxime. Add Vanco if MRSA a concern. For chlamydia therapy, Erythro 12.5 mg per kg po or IV qid times 14 days.		Blood cultures indicated. Consider C. trachomatis if afebrile pneumonia, staccato cough. IgM >18; therapy with erythro or sulfisoxazole. If MRSA documented, Vanco, Clinda, & Linezolid alternatives. Linezolid dosage from birth to age 11 yrs is 10 mg per kg q8h.
Age 1–3 months Pneumonitis syndrome. Usually afebrile	C. trachomatis, RSV, parainfluenza virus 3, human metapneumovirus, Bordetella, S. pneumoniae, S. aureus (rare)	**Outpatient: po** Amox 90-100 mg/kg/d x 10-14 days OR Azithro 10 mg/kg x 1 dose then 5 mg/kg once daily x 4 days	**Inpatient:** • If afebrile: Erythro 10 mg/kg IV q6h or Azithro 2.5 mg/kg IV q12h (see *Comment*) • If febrile: Cefotaxime 200 mg/kg per day div q8h OR Ceftriaxone 75-100 mg/kg q24h	Pneumonitis syndrome: Cough, tachypnea, dyspnea, diffuse infiltrates, afebrile. Usually requires hospital care. Reports of hypertrophic pyloric stenosis after erythro under age 6 wks; not sure about azithro; bid azithro dosing theoretically might ↓ risk of hypertrophic pyloric stenosis. If lobar pneumonia, give AMP 200-300 mg per kg per day for S. pneumoniae. No empiric coverage for S. aureus, as it is rare etiology.
		For **RSV**, see *Bronchiolitis, page 37*		
Infants and Children, age >3 months to 18 yrs (IDSA Treatment Guidelines: *CID 53:617, 2011*)				
Outpatient	RSV, human metapneumovirus, rhinovirus, influenza virus, adenovirus, parainfluenza virus, Mycoplasma, H. influenzae, S. pneumoniae, S. aureus (rare)	Amox 90 mg/kg in 2 divided doses x 5 days	Azithro 10 mg/kg x 1 dose (max 500 mg), then 5 mg/kg (max 250 mg) x 4 days OR Amox-Clav 90 mg/kg (Amox) in 2 divided doses x 5 days	Antimicrobial therapy not routinely required for preschool-aged children with CAP as most infections are viral etiologies.
Inpatient	As above	Fully immunized: AMP 50 mg/kg IV q6h Not fully immunized: Cefotaxime 150 mg/kg IV divided q8h	Fully immunized: Cefotaxime 150 mg/kg IV divided q8h	If atypical infection suspected, add Azithro 10 mg/kg x 1 dose (max 500 mg), then 5 mg/kg (max 250 mg) x 4 days. If community MRSA suspected, add Vanco 15-20 mg/kg q8-12h OR Clinda 40 mg/kg IV q6-8h. Duration of therapy: 10-14 days. Depending on clinical response, may switch to oral agents as early as 2-3 days

TABLE 1 (37)

ANATOMIC SITE/DIAGNOSIS/ MODIFYING CIRCUMSTANCES	ETIOLOGIES (usual)	SUGGESTED REGIMENS* PRIMARY	ALTERNATIVE†	ADJUNCT DIAGNOSTIC OR THERAPEUTIC MEASURES AND COMMENTS
LUNG/Bronchi/Pneumonia *(continued)*				
Community-acquired, empiric therapy for outpatient Prognosis prediction: CURB-65 *(Thorax 58:377, 2003)* C: confusion = 1 pt U: BUN >19 mg/dl = 1 pt R: RR >30/min = 1 pt B: BP <90/60 = 1 pt Age >65 yr = 1 pt Total = 1, ok to treat as out-patient; ≥2 hospitalization recommended	S. pneumo, atypicals and mycoplasma in particular, Hemophilus, Moraxella, viral pathogens: up to 30% of cases *(BMC Infect Dis 15:89, 2015)* and co-infection, often viral, in ~20% of cases *(BMC Infect Dis 15:64, 2015.)*	*IDSA/ATS Guideline for CAP in adults: CID 44 (Suppl 2): S27-S72, 2007; NEJM 370:543, 2014; NEJM 371:1619, 2014.* Azithro 500 mg po day 1 then 250 mg daily day 2-5 OR Clarithro 500 mg po bid or Clarithro-ER 1 gm po q24h OR Doxy 100 mg po bid x 5-7 days OR if Doxy unavailable Minocycline 200 mg po/IV x 1, then 100 mg po/IV bid	Levo 750 mg po q24h x 5 days OR Moxi 400 mg po q24h x 5 days OR [Amox-Clav (1000/62.5) (Augmentin-XR) 2 tabs po bid or Amox 1 g po tid] + [Azithro or Clarithro x 7 days]	**Azithro/Clarithro:** active against atypical pneumonia agents, but S. pneumo resistance as high as 20-30%; **alternative regimen (Levo or Moxi)** recommended if high prevalence of macrolide resistance or co-morbidities (e.g. COPD, alcoholism). Similar outcomes with oral versus IV fluoroquinolone therapy *(CID 63:1, 2016)* **Moxi** has anaerobic activity and may be preferred over levo for post-obstructive pneumonia or aspiration.
Community-acquired, empiric therapy for patient admitted to hospital, non-ICU (See *NEJM 370:543, 2014*)	As above + legionella, Gram-negative bacilli IVDU: S. aureus Post-influenza: S. aureus, S. pneumo. No pathogen detected in majority of patients, viruses more common than bacteria *(NEJM 373:415, 2015)*	(Ceftriaxone 1 g IV q24h or Ceftaroline 600 mg IV q12h) + Azithro 500 mg IV/po q24h	(Ceftriaxone OR Ceftaroline) + Levo 750 mg IV/po q24h OR Moxi 400 mg IV q24h OR Gati 400 mg IV q24h (not available in US) OR + Doxy 100 mg IV/po q12h	**Amox + Azithro or Clarithro** another alternative for patients with comorbidities, in setting of high prevalence of S. pneumo macrolide resistance, or if prior antibiotic in last 3 mo. Oral cephalosporins (cefdinir 300 mg q12h, cefpodoxime 200 mg q12h or cefprozil 500 mg q12h) can be substituted for Amox-Clav or Amox. Administration of antibiotic within 6h associated with improved survival in pneumonia with severe sepsis *(Eur Respir J 39:156, 2012)* Better outcome with ceftaroline than Ceftriaxone in one RCT *(Lancet ID 15:161, 2015)*. Duration of therapy 5-7 days. Improved outcome with β-lactam/macrolide combo vs β-lactam alone in hospitalized CAP of moderate- or high- but not low-severity *(Thorax 68:493, 2013)* Blood and sputum cultures recommended. Test for Influenza during influenza season. Consider urinary pneumococcal antigen and urinary legionella for sicker patients.
Community-acquired, empiric therapy for patient admitted to ICU	As above	As above +(Vanco 15-20 mg/kg IV q8-12h OR Linezolid 600 mg IV/po q12h) **Procalcitonin:** Several clinical trials and meta-analyses indicate that normalization of procalcitonin levels can be used to guide duration of antibiotic therapy. Safe to discontinue antibiotics when procalcitonin level has decreased to 0.1-0.2 mcg/mL. *(CID 55:651, 2012; JAMA 309:717, 2013).*	As above +(Vanco 15-20 mg/kg IV q8-12h OR Linezolid 600 mg IV/po q12h)	Add Vanco or Linezolid q8-12h to cover MRSA for pneumonia with concomitant or precedent influenza or for pneumonia in an IVDU. *(AJCCM 2015;24:8; AAC 2017;61:e0242-16)* **Do nasal PCR for S. aureus; if neg, safe to dc vanco** *(CID 57:1275, 2013).* **Legionella:** Not all legionella species detected by urine antigen; if suspicious perform culture or do PCR on airway secretions *(CID 52:1280, 2013)*
Hospital-acquired or Ventilator-associated pneumonia IDSA guidelines: CID 63:e61, 2016	As above + MDR Gram-negatives in 39 of 174 pts with non-ventilator HAP, respiratory virus detected *(Resp Med 2017;122:76)*	Cefepime 2 gm IV q12h OR PIP-TZ 4.5 gm q6h Per Guidelines, suggest use of adjunctive inhaled antibiotic if etiologic bacteria are susceptible to only polymyxins or AG. Proposed regimens in Table 10F.	MER 1 gm IV q8h OR Levo 750 mg IV q12h OR	Add Vanco or Linezolid if unit or hospital MRSA prevalence >10-20%, prior IV antibiotic use within 90 days, acute renal replacement therapy prior to VAP onset, septic shock or high risk of mortality, ARDS preceding VAP, unknown MRSA prevalence or presence of MRSA risk factors (e.g. IVDU, MRSA infection or colonization). For suspected Pseudomonas or high risk of mortality add CIP 400 mg IV q8h or Levo 750 mg IV q24h or Tobra 5 mg/kg IV q24h or AMK 15 mg/kg IV q24h. Aztreonam 2 gm IV q8h can substitute for other beta-lactams if there is beta-lactam hypersensitivity, but lacks coverage for S. aureus. Consider addition of Colistin if carbapenem-resistant Gram-negative is suspected.

Abbreviations on page 2. *NOTE: All dosage recommendations are for adults (unless otherwise indicated) and assume normal renal function. § Alternatives consider allergy, PK, compliance, local resistance, cost.

TABLE 1 (38)

ANATOMIC SITE/DIAGNOSIS/ MODIFYING CIRCUMSTANCES	ETIOLOGIES (usual)	SUGGESTED REGIMENS*		ADJUNCT DIAGNOSTIC OR THERAPEUTIC MEASURES AND COMMENTS
		PRIMARY	ALTERNATIVE$	

LUNG/Bronchi/Pneumonia (continued)

Pneumonia —Selected specific therapy after culture results (sputum, blood, pleural fluid, etc.) available. Also See Table 2, page 71

ANATOMIC SITE/DIAGNOSIS/ MODIFYING CIRCUMSTANCES	ETIOLOGIES (usual)	PRIMARY	ALTERNATIVE$	ADJUNCT DIAGNOSTIC OR THERAPEUTIC MEASURES AND COMMENTS
Acinetobacter baumannii (See also Table 5B); Crit Care Med 43:1194 & 1332, 2015	Patients with VAP; long ICU stay with repeated antibiotic exposure	Empiric rx: positive culture, no in vitro suscept results, prevalence of resistance < 20%: **Cefepime, Ceftazidime, Amp-Sulb.** If prevalence of resistance > 20%: (**MER or IMP**) ± (**Minocycline or a Polymyxin**). Doses in footnote[13]	Specific rx: culture & suscept results available & suscept organism: **Cefepime, Ceftazidime, Amp-Sulb.** If MDR organism & critically ill: **MER + Minocycline + Amp-Sulb + a Polymyxin.** May need adjunctive inhaled **Colistin.** Doses in footnote[13]	Subactam portion of AM-SB often active; dose: 3 gm IV q6h. Polymyxin resistance may evolve. Treatment options: CID 60:1295 & 1304, 2015. Some acid nebulized Colistin 75 mg q12h (See Table 10F). Minocycline ref: CID 59:S367, S374, S381, 2014.
Actinomycosis	A. Israelii and rarely others	**AMP** 200 mg/kg/day in 3-4 divided doses x 4-6 wks then **Pen VK** 2-4 gm/day in 4 divided doses x 6-12 mo.	**Doxy or Ceftriaxone OR Clinda** IV x 4-5 wks, then po x 6-12 mo	Can use **Pen G** instead of AMP: 10-20 million units/day IV x 4-6 wks, then Pen VK x 6-12 mo.
Anthrax Inhalation (applies to oropharyngeal & gastrointestinal forms): **Treatment** (Cutaneous: See page 52) Ref: www.bt.cdc.gov; CDC panel recommendations for adults: Emerg Infect Dis 2012; Doi: 10.3201/ eid2002130687. American Academy of Pediatrics recommendations for children: Pediatrics 133:e1411, 2014.	Bacillus anthracis To report possible bioterrorism event: 770-488-7100 Plague, tularemia: See page 43. Chest x-ray: mediastinal widening & pleural effusion	**Adults (including pregnancy): CIP** 400 mg IV q8h + (**Linezolid** 600 mg IV q12h or **Clindamycin** 900 mg IV q8h) + **Meropenem** 2 gm IV q8h (See comments) + **Children (including pregnancy): CIP** 10 mg/kg IV q8h (max 400 mg per dose) + [**Linezolid** 10 mg/kg IV q8h (age <12 yr) or **Linezolid** 15 mg/kg q12h (age >12 yr) (max 600 mg per dose)] + **Meropenem** 40 mg/kg IV q8h (max 2 gm per dose) (see comments). Switch to po after 2 wks if stable. **CIP** 15 mg/kg q12h or **Doxy** 2.2 mg/kg q12h (<45 kg) or 100 mg q12h (>45 kg) to complete 60-day regimen for oral dosage.	**Children (including pregnancy): CIP** 400 mg IV q8h + (**Linezolid** 10 mg/kg IV q12h or **Clindamycin** 40-80 mg/kg IV over 3 hrs), switch to po after 2 wks, if stable **CIP** 500 mg q12h x60-day regimen. **Children** see above for dosing) + **Doxy** 100 mg q12h x 60 days + 3-dose series of Biothrax (not FDA approved, to be made available on investigational basis)	1. Meropenem if meningitis cannot be excluded; Linezolid preferred over Clinda for meningitis. 2. Pen (≤ 4 million units IV (adults) or 67,000 units/kg (children, max 4 million units per dose) IV q4h can be substituted for Meropenem for pen-susceptible strains. 3. For children <8 years of age avoid tooth staining likely with Doxy with Doxy Clinda 10 mg/kg q8h (max dose 900 mg) or Levo 8 mg/kg (max dose 250 mg) q12h for <50 kg, 500 mg q24h for > 50 kg for pen-susceptible strains Amox 25 mg/kg/day (max dose 1 gm) q8h for Pen V 25 mg/kg/day (use 1 gm) q8h. 4. Levo and Moxi are alternatives to CIP 5. For complete recommendations see Emerg Infect Dis 20(2), doi: 10.3201/ eid2002130687 (adults) and Pediatrics 133:e1411, 2014 (children). 6. Anth ax immune globulin (Anthrasil) FDA approved for emergency use (U.S. strategic national stockpile).
Anthrax, prophylaxis: See: Emerg Infect Dis 20(2): doi: 10.3201/eid2002.130687. 60 days of antimicrobial prophylaxis + 3-dose series of Biothrax Anthrax Vaccine Adsorbed	Info: www.bt.cdc.gov	**Adults (including pregnancy): CIP** 500 mg po q12h or **Doxy** 100 mg po q12h x 60 days + 3-dose series of Biothrax Anthrax Vaccine Adsorbed	**Children (including pregnancy): CIP** 500 above for dosing) or **Doxy** 100 mg q12h x 60 days + 3-dose series of Biothrax (not FDA approved, to be made available on investigational basis)	1. Consider alternatives to Doxy for pregnant adult. 2. Alternatives include Clinda, Levo, Moxi, and for pen-susceptible strains Amox or Pen VK.

[13] Doses of antibiotics used to treat pneumonia due to Acinetobacter sp., Klebsiella sp., and Pseudomonas sp. Penicillins: **Pip-Tazo** loading dose 4.5 gm IV over 30 min, then, 4 hrs later, start 3.375 gm IV over 4 hrs & repeat q8h; **Amp-sulb** 3 gm IV q6h. Cephalosporins: **Ceftazidime** 2 gm IV q8h; **Ceftaz-avibactam** 2.5 gm IV q8h; **Ceftolozane-tazo** 1.5 gm IV q8h. **Aztreonam** 2 gm IV q8h; **FQs: CIP** 400 mg IV q8h; **Levo** 750 mg IV q24h. Carbapenems: **MER** 1-2 gm IV q8h; **MER-vaborbactam** 4 gm IV over 3 hrs q8h; **IMP** 0.5-1 gm q8h. Aminoglycosides: **Gent/Tobra** 7 mg/kg IV x 1, then 5 mg/kg IV q8h. **Polymyxin B** 2.5 mg/kg IV over 2 hrs, then 1.5 mg/kg over 1 hr & repeat q12h. Minocycline 200 mg IV x 1, then 100 mg IV q12h.

Abbreviations on page 2.   *NOTE: All dosage recommendations are for adults (unless otherwise indicated) and assume normal renal function. § Alternatives consider allergy, PK, compliance, local resistance, cost.

TABLE 1 (39)

ANATOMIC SITE/DIAGNOSIS/ MODIFYING CIRCUMSTANCES	ETIOLOGIES (usual)	SUGGESTED REGIMENS*		ADJUNCT DIAGNOSTIC OR THERAPEUTIC MEASURES AND COMMENTS
		PRIMARY	ALTERNATIVE†	
LUNG/Bronchi/Pneumonia/Selected specific therapy after culture results (sputum, blood, pleural fluid, etc.) available. *(continued)*				
Burkholderia (Pseudomonas) pseudomallei (etiology of melioidosis) can cause primary or secondary skin infection *See NEJM 367:1035, 2012*	Gram-negative	**Initial therapy rx:** Ceftazidime 30–50 mg per kg IV q8h (2 gm q8h) or TMP-SMX 8 mg/kg IV q8h, Rx minimum 10 days & improving, then po therapy	**Post-parenteral po rx:** **Adults** (see Comment for dosing): TMP-SMX 8 mg/kg (TMP component) bid + **Doxy** 2 mg/kg bid x 3 mos.	**Children ≤8 yrs old & pregnancy:** For oral regimen, use AM-CL-ER 1000/62.5, 2 tabs bid times 20 wks. Elevated organism relapse rate is 10%. Max. daily ceftazidime dose: 6 gm. Tigecycline: No clinical data but active in vitro (AAC 50:1555, 2006)
Chlamydophila pneumoniae	Chlamydophila pneumoniae	Azithro 500 mg on day one then 250 mg x 4 days OR Levo 750 mg x 5 days	Doxy 100 mg q12h x 5 days OR Clarithro 500 mg bid x 5 days.	Clinical diagnosis, rarely confirmed microbiologically.
Haemophilus influenzae	β-lactamase negative	AMP IV, Amox po, TMP-SMX, Azithro/Clarithro, Doxy.	Doxy 100 mg q12h x 5 days OR Azithro/Clarithro, Doxy, FQ	25–35% strains β-lactamase positive. ↑ resistance to both TMP-SMX and doxy. See Table 10A, page 106 for dosages.
	β-lactamase positive	AM-CL, O Ceph 2/3, P Ceph 3, FQ Dosage: Table 10A		
Klebsiella sp.—ESBL pos. & other coliforms[14]	β-lactamase positive	IMP or MER; if resistant: [Colistin + (IMP or MER)] or Ceftolo-tazo, Ceftaz-avi or MER-vabor (See footnotes for dosing)	Azithro 500 mg x1 on day 1 then 250 mg for total of 7-10 days	ESBL inactivates all cephalosporins, β-lactam/β-lactamase inhibitor drug activ not predictable; co-resistance to all FGs & often aminoglycosides.
Legionella pneumonia	Legionella pneumophila, other legionella species	(Levo 750 mg po/IV or Moxi 400 mg po/IV) x 7-10 days	Azithro 500 mg po on day 1 and then 250 mg once daily for 4 days (see Comments) OR Levo 750 po/IV x 5 days	Consider longer courses of therapy for immunocompromised hosts, severe illness. Trend for better outcomes with FQ over macrolide (AAC 69:2354, 2014). Doxy another option. See Table 10A, page 106 for dosages.
Moraxella catarrhalis	93% β-lactamase positive	AM-CL, O Ceph 2/3, P Ceph 2/3, Macrolide*, FQ, TMP-SMX, Doxy		If Doxy not available, Mino 200 g po/IV x 1 dose, then 100 mg po/IV bid.
Mycoplasma pneumoniae	Mycoplasma pneumoniae	Doxy 100 mg q12h x 7-10 days		Increasing prevalence of macrolide resistance so Doxy or Levo are preferred agents for documented mycoplasma infection.
Nocardia pneumonia Expert Help: Wallace Lab (+1) 903-877-7680; CDC (+1) 404-639-3158 Ref: Medicine 88:250, 2009.	N. asteroides, N. brasiliensis	TMP-SMX 15 mg/kg/day IV/po in 2-4 divided doses + Imipenem 500 mg IV q6h TMP-SMX 10 mg/kg/day in 2-4 divided doses x 3-6 mos. Mild, low risk of MDR GNB: Monotherapy: [TMP-SMX or (CIP or Levo)] (Dosing in footnote[b])	IMP 500 mg IV q6h + Amikacin 7.5 mg/kg IV q12h x 3-4 wks & then po TMP-SMX	**Duration:** 3 mos. if immunocompetent; 6 mos. if immunocompromised. Agree with efforts to de-escalate **Measure peak sulfonamide levels:** Target is 100-150 mcg/mL 2 hrs post po dose. Linezolid active in vitro (Ann Pharmacother 41:1694, 2007). In vitro resistance to TMP-SMX may be increasing (Clin Infect Dis 51:1445, 2010), but whether this is associated with worse outcomes is not known. Known ESBL producer: MER or Ceftolo-tazo° or Ceftaz-avi° or MER-vabor°.
Pseudomonas aeruginosa Adjunctive Colistin inhalation rx for severe pneumonia, See Table 10F MRD strain rx (Virulence 8-403, 2017)	Risk factors: cystic fibrosis, neutropenia, mechanical ventilation, tracheostomy	Ceftazidime, Cefepime, IMP, MER or Aztreonam) or CIP or Levo) (Dosing in footnote[a])	Septic & high risk for MDR GNB: Combination rx: [(Pip-tazo, Ceftazidime or Cefepime) + (Tobra or CIP or Levo) or ((CIP or Levo) + (Tobra or Gent)] (Dosing in footnote[b])	Known KPC producer: Ceftaz-avi° or MER-vabor or (MER + Polymyxin B). Known metallo-type (NDM) carbapenemase producer: Ceftaz-avi° + Aztreonam) or (MER + Polymyxin B). Dosing in footnote[a]. ° not FDA-approved indication

---

[14] Dogma on duration of therapy not possible with so many variables; i.e. certainty of diagnosis, infecting organism, severity of infection, number/severity of co-morbidities. Agree with efforts to de-escalate & shorten course. Treat at least 7-8 days. Need clinical evidence of response: fever resolution, improved oxygenation, falling WBC. Refs: AJRCCM 171:388, 2005; CID 43:S75, 2006; COID 19:185, 2006.

[15] **Macrolide** = Azithromycin, Clarithromycin and Erythromycin.

Abbreviations on page 2. *NOTE: All dosage recommendations are for adults (unless otherwise indicated) and assume normal renal/renal function. § Alternatives consider allergy; PK, compliance, local resistance, cost.*

TABLE 1 (40)

ANATOMIC SITE/DIAGNOSIS/ MODIFYING CIRCUMSTANCES	ETIOLOGIES (usual)	SUGGESTED REGIMENS*		ADJUNCT DIAGNOSTIC OR THERAPEUTIC MEASURES AND COMMENTS
		PRIMARY	ALTERNATIVE§	
LUNG/Bronchi/Pneumonia/Selected specific therapy after culture results (sputum, blood, pleural fluid, etc.) available. *(continued)*				
Q Fever Acute atypical pneumonia. See *MMWR 62 (3);1, 2013*	Coxiella burnetii	No valvular heart disease: Doxy 100 mg po bid x 14 days	Valvu ar heart disease: Doxy 100 mg po bid + hydroxychloroquine 200 mg tid x 12 months	In pregnancy: **TMP-SMX DS** 1 tab po bid throughout pregnancy. Even in absence of valvular heart disease, % of pts develop endocarditis (*CID 62:537, 2016*).
Staphylococcus aureus Duration of treatment: 2-3 wks if just pneumonia; 4-6 wks if concomitant endocarditis and/or osteomyelitis. *CID 52 (Feb 1):1, 2011.*	Nafcillin/oxacillin susceptible	Nafcillin/oxacillin 2 gm IV q4h	Doxy 100 mg po bid + Vanco 30-60 mg/kg/d iv in 2-3 divided doses or linezolid 600 mg IV q12h	Adjust dose of vancomycin to achieve target trough concentrations of 15-20 mcg/mL. Some authorities recommend a 25-30 mg/kg loading dose (actual body weight) in severely ill patients (*CID 49:325, 2009*). Prospective trial for MRSA pneumonia: cure rate with Linezolid (58%), Vanco (47%), p = 0.042; no difference in mortality (*CID 54:621, 2012*).
IDSA Guidelines.	MRSA	Vanco 15-20 mg/kg q8-12h IV in 2-3 divided doses or Linezolid 600 mg IV/po q12h	Dapti not an option; pneumonia developed during dapto rx (*CID 49:1286, 2009*). Ceftaroline 600 mg IV q8h.	Telavancin 10 mg/kg IV x 60 min q24h another option. Perhaps lower efficacy if CrCl <50mL/min (*AAC 58:2030, 2014*).
Stenotrophomonas maltophilia		TMP-SMX 15-20 mg/kg/day div q6h (TMP component)	Mino 200 mg IV qd (*AAC 2016;71:1071*).	FQ is an alternative if susceptible in vitro. Rarely may need to use polymyxin combination therapy.
Streptococcus pneumoniae	Penicillin-susceptible	AMP 2 gm IV q6h, Amox 1 gm po tid	Pen G IV*, Doxy, O Ceph 2, P Ceph 2/3; may add Azithro 500 mg IV/po qd until afebrile, (min. of 5 days) and/or until serum procalcitonin normal.	
	Penicillin-resistant, high level	FQs with enhanced activity: Gemi, Levo, Moxi; P Ceph 3 (resistance rare); high-dose IV AMP, Vanco IV—see Table 5A, page 85 for more data. If all options not possible (e.g., allergy), Ceftaroline 600 mg IV q12h superior to Ceftriaxone (*CID 51:641, 2010*).		See Table 10A, page 106 for other dosages. Treat until afebrile 3-5 days, (min. of 5 days). In CAP trial, Linezolid active: 600 mg IV or po q12h.
Tularemia Inhalational tularemia Ref: *JAMA 285:2763, 2001* & www.bt.cdc.gov	Francisella tularemia Treatment	Doxy 100 mg IV or po bid times 14-21 days or CIP 400 mg IV (or 750 mg po) bid times 14-21 days.	Streptomycin 15 mg per kg IV bid) or (Gent 5 mg per kg IV qd) times 10 days	Pregnancy: as for non-pregnant adults. Tobramycin should work.
	Postexposure prophylaxis	Doxy 100 mg po bid times 14 days	CIP 530 mg po bid times 14 days	Pregnancy: As for non-pregnant adults
Viral (interstitial) pneumonia suspected See Influenza, Table 14A, page 179. Ref: *Chest 133:1221, 2008.*	Consider: Influenza, adenovirus, coronavirus (MERS/SARS), hantavirus, metapneumovirus, parainfluenza virus, respiratory syncytial virus	Oseltamivir 75 mg po bid for 5 days or Zanamivir two 5 mg inhalations twice a day for 5 days.		No known efficacious drugs for adenovirus, coronavirus, hantavirus, meta-pneumovirus, parainfluenza or RSV. Need travel (MERS/SARS) & exposure (Hanta) history. RSV and human metapneumovirus as serious as influenza in the elderly (*NEJM 352:1749 & 1810, 2005; CID 44:1152 & 1159, 2007*).
Yersinia pestis (Plague) *EID 2017;23:553;* *MMWR 64:918, 2015*	Y. pestis if aerosolized, suspect bioterror.	(Gentamicin 5 mg/kg IV q24h) or Streptomycin 30 mg/kg/day IV in 2 div doses) x 10 days	CIP 530 mg po bid or 400 mg IV q12h	Doxy 200 mg IV q12h x 1 day, then 100 mg po bid x 7-10 days. Chloramphenicol also effective but potentially toxic. Consider if evidence of plague meningitis.

** **IV Pen G dosage: no meningitis, 2 million units IV q4h. If concomitant meningitis, 4 million units IV q4h.**

* *NOTE: All dosage recommendations are for adults (unless otherwise indicated) and assume normal* renal function. § Alternatives consider allergy, PK, compliance, local resistance, cost.

Abbreviations on page 2.

TABLE 1 (41)

ANATOMIC SITE/DIAGNOSIS/ MODIFYING CIRCUMSTANCES	ETIOLOGIES (usual)	SUGGESTED REGIMENS[a] PRIMARY	ALTERNATIVE[a]	ADJUNCT DIAGNOSTIC OR THERAPEUTIC MEASURES AND COMMENTS
LUNG—Other Specific Infections				
Aspiration pneumonia/anaerobic lung infection/lung abscess	Anaerobes and viridans group streptococci predominate.	Clindamycin 300–450 mg po tid OR Ampicillin-sulbactam 3 g IV q6h OR Ceftriaxone 1 gm IV q24h + Metro 500 mg IV q6h OR 1 gm IV q12h	Moxi 400 mg po q24h OR ERTA 1 gm IV q24h	Typically anaerobic infection of the lung aspiration pneumonitis, necrotizing pneumonia, lung abscess and empyema (REF: Anaerobe 18:235, 2012) Other treatment options: PIP-TZ 3.375 g IV q6h or Moxi 400 mg IV/po q24h or Amox/Clav 875/125 mg
Chronic pneumonia with fever, night sweats and weight loss	M. tuberculosis, coccidioidomycosis, histoplasmosis.	See Table 11 and Table 12. For risk associated with TNF inhibitors, see CID 41(Suppl 3):S187, 2005.		Risk factors: HIV+, foreign-born, alcoholism, contact with TB, travel into developing countries
Cystic fibrosis				**Cystic Fibrosis Foundation Guidelines:**
Acute exacerbation of pulmonary symptoms BMC Medicine 9:32, 2011	S. aureus or H. influenzae early in disease; P. aeruginosa later in disease Nontuberculous mycobacteria emerging as an important pathogen (Semin Respir Crit Care Med 34:124, 2013)	For P. aeruginosa: (Peds doses) Tobra 3.3 mg/kg q8h or 12 mg/kg IV q24h. Combine tobra with PIP-TZ 4.5 gm IV q6h or Ceftaz 50 mg/kg IV q8h to max of 6 gm per day, if resistant to above, CIP/ Levo used if P. aeruginosa susceptible. See footnote[b] & Comment	For S. aureus: (1) MSSA— Oxacillin/Nafcillin 2 gm IV q4h. (2) MRSA—Vanco 15–20 mg/kg (actual wt) IV q8-12h (to achieve target trough concentration of 15–20 µg/mL	1. Combination therapy for P. aeruginosa infection. 2. Once-daily dosing for aminoglycosides. 3. Need more data on continuous infusion beta-lactams. 4. Routine use of steroid not recommended. **Inhalation options** (P. aeruginosa suppression): 1) Nebulized tobra 300 mg bid x 28 days, no rx for 28 days, repeat; 2) Inhaled tobra powder-hand held: 4-28 mg cap bid x 28 days, no rx for 28 days, repeat; Nebulized aztreonam (Cayston): 75 mg bid after pre-dose bronchodilator. Ref: Med Lett 56:51, 2014.
	Burkholderia (Pseudomonas) cepacia. Mechanisms of resistance (Semin Resp Crit Care Med 36:99, 2015)	TMP-SMX 5 mg per kg (TMP) IV q6h Need culture & sens results to guide rx.	Chloro 15–20 mg per kg IV/po q6h.	B. cepacia has become a major pathogen. Patients develop progressive respiratory failure, 62% mortality at 1 yr. Fail to respond to aminoglycosides, anti-pseudomonal beta-lactams. Patients with B. cepacia should be isolated from other CF patients.
Empyema. IDSA Treatment Guidelines for Children, CID 53-617, 2011; exudative pleural effusion criteria (JAMA 311:2422, 2014).				
Neonatal	Staph. aureus.	See Pneumonia, neonatal, page 39		Drainage indicated.
Infants/children (1 month–5 yrs)	Staph. aureus, Strep. pneumoniae, H. influenzae	See Pneumonia, age 1 month–5 years, page 39		Drainage indicated.
Child >5 yrs to ADULT—Diagnostic thoracentesis; chest tube for empyema				
Acute, usually parapneumonic For dosage, see Table 10B or footnote page 25	Strep. pneumoniae, Group A strep	Cefotaxime or Ceftriaxone (Dosage, see footnote[b] page 25)	Vanco	Tissue Plasminogen Activator (10 mg) + DNase (5 mg) bid x 3 days via chest tube improves outcome (NEJM 365:518, 2011).
	Staph. aureus: Check for MRSA	Nafcillin or Oxacillin if MSSA	Vanco or Linezolid if MRSA	Usually complication of S. aureus pneumonia &/or bacteremia.
	H. influenzae	Ceftriaxone	TMP-SMX or AM-SB	
Subacute/chronic	Anaerobic strep, Strep. milleri, Bacteroides sp., Enterobacteriaceae, M. tuberculosis	Clinda 450–900 mg IV q8h + Ceftriaxone	Cefoxitin or IMP or PIP-TZ or AM-SB (Dosage, see footnote[c] page 25)	Intrapleural tissue plasminogen activator (t-PA) 10 mg + DNase 5 mg via chest tube twice daily for 3 days improved fluid drainage, reduced frequency of surgery, and reduced duration of the hospital stay; neither agent effective alone (N Engl J Med 365:518, 2011). Pro/con debate: Chest 145:14, 17, 20, 2014. Pleural biopsy with culture for mycobacteria and histology if TBc suspected.

[a] Other options: (Tobra + aztreonam 50 mg per kg IV q8h); (IMP 15–25 mg per kg IV q6h > tobra); CIP commonly used in children, e.g. CIP IV/po + ceftaz IV (LnID 3-532, 2003).

Abbreviations on page 2.

[b] NOTE: All dosage recommendations are for adults (unless otherwise indicated) and assume normal renal function. § Alternatives consider allergy, PK, compliance, local resistance, cost.

TABLE 1 (42)

ANATOMIC SITE/DIAGNOSIS/ MODIFYING CIRCUMSTANCES	ETIOLOGIES (usual)	SUGGESTED REGIMENS*		ADJUNCT DIAGNOSTIC OR THERAPEUTIC MEASURES AND COMMENTS
		PRIMARY	ALTERNATIVE§	
LUNG—Other Specific Infections (continued)				
Human immunodeficiency virus infection (HIV+): *See Sanford Guide to HIV/AIDS Therapy*				
CD4 T-lymphocytes <200 per mm³ or clinical AIDS Dry cough, progressive dyspnea, & diffuse infiltrate	Pneumocystis jirovecii (PJP or PCP) most likely; also MTB, fungi, Kaposi's sarcoma, & lymphoma **NOTE:** AIDS pts may develop pneumonia due to DRSP or other pathogens—see next box below	*Rx listed here is for severe pneumocystis; see Table 11A, page 135 for po regimens for mild disease.* **Prednisone 1** (see Comment) **TMP-SMX** (IV: 15 mg per kg per day div q8h (TMP component) or po: 2 DS tabs q8h), total of 21 days	(Clinda 600 mg IV q8h + Primaquine 30 mg po q24h) or (pentamidine isethionate 4 mg per kg per day IV) times 21 days. See Comment	Diagnosis (induced sputum or bronchial wash) for: histology or monoclonal antibody, strains or PCR. **Prednisone** 40 mg bid po times 5 days then 40 mg q24h po times 5 days then 20 mg q24h po times 11 days is indicated with PCP should be given at initiation of anti-PCP rx; don't wait until pt's condition deteriorates. If PCP studies negative, consider bacterial pneumonia, TBc, cocci, histo, crypto, Kaposi's sarcoma or lymphoma. Pentamidine not active vs. bacterial pathogens.
Prednisone first if suspect pneumocystis (see Comment)				
CD4 T-lymphocytes normal Acute onset, purulent sputum & pulmonary infiltrates ± pleuritic pain. **Isolate pt until TBc excluded: Adults**	Strep. pneumoniae, H. influenzae, aerobic Gm-neg. bacilli (including P. aeruginosa). Legionella rare, MTB.	**Ceftriaxone** 1 gm IV q24h (over age 65) **1 gm IV q24h**) + **Azithro.** (Could use **Levo.** or **Moxi** IV q24h) (see Comment)		For suspected bacterial pneumonia, other regimens for CAP also are options.
LYMPH NODES (approaches below apply to lymphadenitis without an obvious primary source)				
Lymphadenitis, acute				
Generalized	Etiologies: EBV, early HIV infection, syphilis, toxoplasma, tularemia, Lyme disease, sarcoid, lymphoma, systemic lupus erythematosus, **Kikuchi-Fujimoto** disease and others. For differential diagnosis of fever and lymphadenopathy *see NEJM 359:2333, 2913.*			
Cervical—*see cat-scratch disease (CSD) on next page*	CSD (B. henselae), Grp A strep, Staph. aureus, anaerobes, MTB (scrofula), M. avium, M. scrofulaceum, M. malmoense, toxo, tularemia	History & physical exam directs evaluation. If nodes fluctuant, aspirate and base rx on Gram & acid-fast stairs. **Kikuchi-Fujimoto** disease causes fever and benign self-limited adenopathy; the etiology is unknown *(CID 39:138, 2004).*		
Inguinal				
Sexually transmitted	HSV, chancroid, syphilis, LGV			
Not sexually transmitted	GAS, SA, tularemia, CSD, Y. pestis	Consider bubonic plague & glandular tularemia.		
Axillary	GAS, SA, CSD, tularemia, Y. pestis, sporotrichosis	Consider bubonic plague & glandular tularemia.		
Extremity, with associated nodular lymphangitis	Sporotrichosis, leishmania, Nocardia brasiliensis, Mycobacterium marinum, Mycobacterium chelonae, tularemia	Treatment varies with specific etiology		A distinctive form of lymphangitis characterized by subcutaneous swellings along inflamed lymphatic channels. Primary site of skin invasion usually present; regional adenopathy variable. **Duration:** 3 mos. if immunocompetent; 6 mos. if immunocompromised.
Nocardia lymphadenitis & skin abscesses	N. asteroides, N. brasiliensis	**TMP-SMX** 5-10 mg/kg/day based on TMP IV/po div in 2-4 doses	**Sulfisoxazole** 2 gm po qid or **Minocycline** 100-200 mg po bid.	**Linezolid:** 500 mg po bid reported effective *(Ann Pharmacother 41:1694, 2007).*

Abbreviations on page 2.   *NOTE: All dosage recommendations are for adults (unless otherwise indicated) and assume normal renal function. § Alternatives consider allergy, PK, compliance, local resistance, cost.

TABLE 1 (43)

ANATOMIC SITE/DIAGNOSIS/ MODIFYING CIRCUMSTANCES	ETIOLOGIES (usual)	SUGGESTED REGIMENS*		ADJUNCT DIAGNOSTIC OR THERAPEUTIC MEASURES AND COMMENTS
		PRIMARY	ALTERNATIVE§	
LYMPH NODES *(continued)*				
By Pathogen:				
Cat-scratch disease—immunocompetent patient Axillary/epitrochlear nodes 46%, neck 26%, inguinal 17% (*Int J Antimicrob Agts 44:16, 2014*)	Bartonella henselae	**Azithro dosage—Adults** (<45.5 kg): 500 mg po x 1, then 250 mg/day x 4 days; liquid azithro 10 mg/kg x 1, then 5 mg/kg per day x 4 days.	Adult: **Clarithro** 500 mg po bid or **RIF** 300 mg po bid + **TMP-SMX DS** 1 tab po bid or **CIP** 500 mg po bid (duration at least 10 days)	Dis: Antibody titer; PCR increasingly available. **Hepatosplenic, CNS or Retinal infection: Doxy** 100 mg po bid + **RIF** 300 mg po bid) x 4-6 wks. Needle drainage of suppurative node(s) provides patient comfort.
Bubonic plague (see also, *plague pneumonia*) Ref: *MMWR 64:918, 2015*	Yersinia pestis	(**Streptomycin** 30 mg/kg/day IV in 2 div doses or **Gentamicin** 5 mg/kg/day IV single dose) x 10 days	[**Levo** 500 mg IV/po once daily or **CIP** 500 mg po (or 400 mg IV) q12h] x 10 days or **Moxi** 400 mg IV/po q24h x 10-14 days	**Doxy** 200 mg IV/po bid x 1 day, then 100 mg IV/po bid x 10 days another option. FQs effective in animals & small case series.
MOUTH				
Aphthous stomatitis, recurrent	Etiology unknown	Topical steroids (Kenalog in Orabase) may ↓ pain and swelling; if AIDS, *see SANFORD GUIDE TO HIV/AIDS THERAPY.*		
Actinomycosis: "Lumpy jaw" after dental or jaw trauma	Actinomyces israelii	AMP 200 mg/kg/day in 3-4 divided doses x 4-6 wks then **Pen VK** 2-4 gm/day in 4 divided doses x 6-12 mo	(**Ceftriaxone** 2 gm IV q24h or **Clinda** 600-900 mg IV q8h or **Doxy** 100 mg IV/po bid) x 4-6 wks, then **Pen VK** 2-4 gm/d x 6-12 mos	**NOTE:** Metro not active vs. actinomyces. Ref: *BMJ 343:d6099, 2011.*
Buccal cellulitis Children <5 yrs	H. influenzae	**Ceftriaxone** 50 mg/kg IV q24h	AM-CL 45-90 mg/kg po div bid or **TMP-SMX** 8-12 mg/kg (TMP comp) IV/po div bid	With Hib immunization, invasive H. influenzae infections have ↓ by 95%. Now occurring in infants prior to immunization.
Candida Stomatitis ("Thrush")	C. albicans	Fluconazole	Echinocandin	*See Table 11, page 126.*
Dental (Tooth) abscess	Aerobic & anaerobic Strep sp.	Mild: **AM-CL** 875/125 mg po bid	Severe: **PIP-TZ** 3.375 gm IV q6h	Surgical drainage / debridement. If Pen-allergic: **Clinda** 600 mg IV q6-8h
Herpetic stomatitis	Herpes simplex virus 1 & 2	*See Table 14A*		
Submandibular space infection, bilateral (Ludwig's angina)	Oral anaerobes, facultative streptococci, S. aureus (rare).	**PIP-TZ** or (**Pen G** IV + **Metro** IV)	**Clinda** 600 mg IV q6-8h (for Pen-allergic pt)	Ensure **adequate airway** and **early surgical debridement.** Add Vanco IV if gram-positive cocci on gram stain. Look for dental infection.
Ulcerative gingivitis (Vincent's angina or Trench mouth)	Oral anaerobes + vitamin deficiency	**Pen G** 4 million units IV q4h or **Metro** 500 mg IV q6h	**Clinda** 600 mg IV q8h	Replete vitamins (A-D). Can mimic scurvy. Severe form is NOMA (Cancrum oris) (*Ln 368:147, 2006*)
MUSCLE				
"Gas gangrene" Contaminated traumatic wound. Can be spontaneous without trauma.	C. perfringens, other histotoxic Clostridium sp.	(**Clinda** 900 mg IV q8h) + (**Pen G** 24 million units/day div. q4-6h IV)	Vanco 15-20 mg/kg IV q8-12h	Susceptibility of C. tertium to penicillins and metronidazole is variable; resistance to clindamycin and 3GCs is common, so vanco or metro (500 mg q8h) recommended. IMP or MER expected to have activity in vitro against Clostridium spp.
Pyomyositis	Staph. aureus, Group A strep, (rarely Gm-neg. bacilli), variety of anaerobic organisms	(**Nafcillin** or **Oxacillin** 2 gm q4h) or **Cefazolin** 2 gm IV q8h if MSSA	Vanco 15-20 mg/kg/day q8-12h if MRSA	In immunocompromised or if otherwise suspected, add gram-negative and/ or anaerobic coverage. Evaluate for drainage of abscesses.

Abbreviations on page 2.   *NOTE: All dosage recommendations are for adults (unless otherwise indicated) and assume normal renal function. §Alternatives consider allergy, PK, compliance, local resistance, cost.*

TABLE I (44)

ANATOMIC SITE/DIAGNOSIS/ MODIFYING CIRCUMSTANCES	ETIOLOGIES (usual)	SUGGESTED REGIMENS°		ADJUNCT DIAGNOSTIC OR THERAPEUTIC MEASURES AND COMMENTS
		PRIMARY	ALTERNATIVE§	
PANCREAS: Review: *NEJM 354:2142, 2006.*				
Acute alcoholic (without necrosis) or **acute necrotizing (idiopathic) pancreatitis**	Not bacterial	None No necrosis on CT	1–9% become infected **but** prospective studies show no advantage of prophylactic antimicrobials. Observe for pancreatic abscesses or necrosis which require therapy.	
Post-necrotizing pancreatitis; Infected pseudocyst; pancreatic abscess	Enterobacteriaceae, enterococci, S. aureus, S. epidermidis, anaerobes, candida	Need culture of abscess/infected pseudocyst to direct therapy; **PIP-TZ** is reasonable empiric therapy.	Can often get specimen by fine-needle aspiration. **Moxi, MER, IMP, ERTA** are all options *(AAC 56:6434, 2012).*	
Antimicrobic prophylaxis, necrotizing pancreatitis	As above	If >30% pancreatic necrosis on CT scan (with contrast), initiate antibiotic therapy: **IMP** 0.5–1 gm IV q6h or **MER** 1 gm IV q8h. No need for empiric Fluconazole. If patient worsens CT guided aspiration for culture & sensitivity. Controversial: *Cochrane Database Sys Rev 2003: CD 002941; Gastroenterol 126:977, 2004; Ann Surg 245:674, 2007.*		
PAROTID GLAND				
"Hot" tender parotid swelling	S. aureus, S. pyogenes, oral flora, & aerobic Gm-neg bacilli (rare), mumps, rarely enteroviruses/ Influenza; parainfluenza; **Nafcillin** or **Oxacillin** 2 gm IV q4h or cefazolin 2 gm IV q8h if MSSA; **Vanco** if MRSA; **Metro** or **Clinda** for anaerobes		Predisposing factors: stone(s) in Stensen's duct, dehydration. Therapy depends on ID of specific etiologic organism.	
"Cold" non-tender parotid swelling	Granulomatous disease (e.g., mycobacteria, fungi, sarcoidosis, Sjögren's syndrome), drugs (iodides, et al.), diabetes, cirrhosis, tumors			History/lab results may narrow differential; may need biopsy for diagnosis
PERITONEUM/PERITONITIS:				
Primary (Spontaneous) Bacterial Peritonitis (SBP) Dx: Pos culture & ≥250 PMN/mcL of ascitic fluid Ref: *Aliment Pharmacol Ther 2015,41:1116*	E. coli 33% Other enterobacteriaceae 11% P. aeruginosa 1% Gm+ cocci 40% Strept sp 15% Staph sp 18% Enterococci 9%	**Community-acquired: low risk of MDR GNB, VRE:** PIP-TZ 3.375 gm IV q6h or **Ceftriaxone** 2 gm IV q24h or **CIP** 400 mg IV q12h *(J Hepatol 60:1310, 2014)*	**Nosocomial: high risk of MDR GNB, VRE:** Meropenem 1 gm IV q8h + **Dapto** 6 mg/kg IV q24h **Note:** In random controlled trial, combination superior to Ceftaz alone *(Hepatology 63:1299, 2015).*	Diagnosis of SBP: For microbiologic dx: inoculate 10mL of ascitic fluid into one aerobic and one anaerobic blood culture bottles; yield better if inoculate 2 aerobic and 2 anaerobic bottles *Comment:* for VRE, may need higher doses of Dapto, eg 8–10 mg/kg per day.
		Secondary prophylaxis: **Norfloxacin** 400 mg daily or **CIP** 500 mg po daily until transplantation or liver function improves to compensated state. Average duration of Rx 5 days but varies with severity of infection To protect renal function: on day 1 & day 3 give IV albumin 1.5 gm/kg		
Prophylaxis after UGI (Variceal) bleeding		Hospitalized pts: **Ceftriaxone** 1 gm, IV once daily x 7 days or **Norfloxacin** 400 mg po bid x 7 days or **CIP** 500 mg po bid x 7 days		
Prevention of SBP *(Amer J Gastro 104:993, 2009).* Cirrhosis & ascites *(Aliment Pharmacol Ther 2015,41:1116)* For prevention after UGI bleeding, see Liver, page 37		**CIP** 500 mg/day *(J Hepatol 2008; 48:774)*	**TMP-SMX** ↓ peritonitis or spontaneous bacteremia from 27% to 3% *(AnIM 122:595, 1995).* Ref. for CIP: *Hepatology 22:1171, 1995*	

Abbreviations on page 2.   °NOTE: *All dosage recommendations are for adults (unless otherwise indicated) and assume normal renal function.* §Alternatives consider allergy, PK, compliance, local resistance, cost.

TABLE 1 (45)

ANATOMIC SITE/DIAGNOSIS/ MODIFYING CIRCUMSTANCES	ETIOLOGIES (usual)	SUGGESTED REGIMENS* PRIMARY	SUGGESTED REGIMENS* ALTERNATIVE§	ADJUNCT DIAGNOSTIC OR THERAPEUTIC MEASURES AND COMMENTS
PERITONEUM/PERITONITIS *(continued)*				
Secondary (bowel perforation, ruptured appendix, ruptured diverticula) Ref: *CID 50:133, 2010 (IDSA Guidelines)* **Antifungal rx?** No need for surgery for viscus perforation. Treat for candida if: pure culture from abdomen or blood. In controlled study, no benefit from preemptive rx to prevent invasive candidiasis *(CID 61:1671, 2015).* **Pediatric appendicitis.** In retrospective review, Ceftriaxone 50 mg/kg (max 2 gm) once daily + Metro 30 mg/kg (max 1500 mg) once daily as effective as Erta *(JPIDS 2017;6:57)*	Enterobacteriaceae, Bacteroides sp., enterococci, P. aeruginosa (3–15%), C. albicans (see *Comment*) If VRE documented, dapto may work *(Int. J Antimicrob Agents 32:369, 2008).* See *Table 5A* for other options for treatment of VRE.	**Mild-moderate disease—Inpatient:** PIP-TZ 3.375 gm IV q6h or 4.5 gm IV q8h or 4-hr infusion of 3.375 gm q8h **OR** ERTA 1 gm IV q24h **OR** MOXI 400 mg IV q24h **Severe life-threatening disease—ICU patient: Surgery for source control +** IMP 500 mg IV q6h or MER 1 gm IV q8h or DOR! 500 mg IV q8h (1-hr infusion) or (Ceftolozane-tazobactam 1.5 gm IV q8h + Metro 500 mg q8h) or (Ceftazidime-avibactam 2.5 gm IV q8h + Metro 500 mg q8h) **Concomitant surgical management important.**	[(CIP 400 mg IV q12h or Levo 750 mg IV q24h) + (Metro 1 gm IV q12h)) or (CFP 2 gm q12h + Metro) **NOTE:** avoid tigecycline unless no other alternative due to increased mortality risk (FDA warning). **Surgery for source control +** [AMP + Metro + (CIP 400 mg IV q8h or Levo 750 mg IV q24h)] OR [AMP 2 gm IV q6h + Metro 500 mg IV q6h + aminoglycoside] *(see Table 10D, page 122)*	Must "cover" both Gm-neg. aerobic & Gm-neg. anaerobic bacteria. Empiric coverage of MRSA, enterococci and candida not necessary unless culture indicates infection. **Drugs active only vs. anaerobic Gm-neg. bacilli:** Metro. **Drugs active only vs. aerobic Gm-neg. bacilli:** aminoglycosides, P Ceph 2/3/4, Aztreonam, AP Pen, CIP, Levo, Ceftolozane-tazo, Ceftaz-avibactam, DORI, IMP, MER. **Drugs active vs. both aerobic/anaerobic Gm-neg. bacteria:** TC-CL, PIP-TZ, DORI, IMP, MER. Increasing resistance of Bacteroides species *(Anaerobe 17:147, 2013; AAC 56:1247, 2012)* to:

	Metro	PIP-TZ, TC-CL	Cefoxitin	Cefotetan	Clindamycin
% Resistant			5–30	17–87	19–35

Essentially no resistance of Bacteroides to: Metro, PIP-TZ, TC-CL, Carbapenems. Case report of B. fragilis resistant to all drugs except minocycline, tigecycline & linezolid *(MMWR 62:694, 2013).* Ertapenem not active vs. P. aeruginosa/ Acinetobacter species. If absence of ongoing fecal contamination, aerobic/anaerobic culture of peritoneal exudate/abscess may be of help in guiding specific therapy. Less need for aminoglycosides. **With severe pen allergy, can "cover" Gm-neg. aerobes with CIP or Aztreonam. Remember DORI/IMP/MER are β-lactams.** IMP dose, increased to 1 gm q6h if suspect P. aeruginosa and pt. is critically ill. Resistance to Moxi increasing. See *CID 59:698, 2014* (suspect. of anaerobic bacteria). Recent data suggest that short course antibiotic-Rx (approx 4 days) may be sufficient where there is adequate source control of complicated intra-abdominal infections *(NEJM 372:21, 2015).*

| Abdominal actinomycosis | A. Israelii & rarely others | AMP 200 mg/kg/day in 3–4 divided doses x 4–6 wks then Pen VK 2–4 gm/day in 4 divided doses x 6–12 mo | Doxy or Ceftriaxone or Clinda | Presents as mass +/– fistula tract after abdominal surgery, e.g., for ruptured appendix. Can use IV Pen G instead of AMP: 10–20 million units/day IV x 4–6 wks. |
| Associated with chronic ambulatory peritoneal dialysis (Abdominal pain, cloudy dialysate, dialysate WBC >100 cell/μL with >50% neutrophils; normal = <8 cells/μL. Ref: *Perit Dial Int 30:393, 2010.)* | Gm+ 45%, Gm– 15%, Multiple 1%, Fungi 2%, MTB 0.1% *(Perit Dial Int 24:424, 2004).* | Empiric therapy: Need activity vs. MRSA (Vanco) & aerobic gram-negative bacilli (Ceftaz, CFP, Carbapenem, CIP, Aztreonam, Gent). Add Fluconazole if gram stain shows yeast. Use intraperitoneal dosing, unless bacteremia (rare). For bacteremia, IV dosing. For dosing detail, see *Table 19, page 241.* | | For diagnostic: concentrate several hundred mL of removed dialysis fluid by centrifugation. Gram stain concentrate and then inject into aerobic/anaerobic blood culture bottles. A positive Gram stain with acid initial therapy. If culture shows Staph. epidermidis and no S. aureus, good chance of "saving" dialysis catheter; **If multiple Gm-neg. bacilli cultured, consider catheter-induced bowel perforation and need for catheter removal.** See *Perit Dialysis Int 29:5, 2009.* Other indications for catheter removal: relapsing/refractory peritonitis, fungal peritonitis, catheter tunnel infection. |

Abbreviations on page 2.   *NOTE: All dosage recommendations are for adults (unless otherwise indicated) and assume normal renal function. § Alternatives consider allergy, PK, compliance, local resistance, cost.*

TABLE 1 (46)

ANATOMIC SITE/DIAGNOSIS/ MODIFYING CIRCUMSTANCES	ETIOLOGIES (usual)	SUGGESTED REGIMENS* PRIMARY	SUGGESTED REGIMENS* ALTERNATIVE§	ADJUNCT DIAGNOSTIC OR THERAPEUTIC MEASURES AND COMMENTS
PHARYNX				
Pharyngitis/Tonsillitis: "Strep throat"				
Exudative or Diffuse Erythema Associated cough, rhinorrhea, hoarseness and/or oral ulcers suggest viral etiology. IDSA Guidelines on Group A Strep: CID 55:1279, 2012; CID 55:e86, 2012. Pros & cons of diagnostics (JCM 2016,54:2413) Even with rapid detection of S. pyogenes, probably still need back-up culture if rapid test is negative (AJM 2016,54:2413).	Group A, C, G Strep; EBV; Primary HIV; N. gonorrhea; Respiratory viruses. Student health clinic pts: F. necrophorum found in 20%, Grp A Strep in 10% (AnIM 162:241, 311 & 876, 2015). In another study, F. necrophorum in 15.5% (age 14-20 yrs) (JCM 2017,55:1147).	For Strep pharyngitis (adult): (Pen V OR Benzathine Pen) OR Cefdinir OR Cefpodoxime). If suspect F. necrophorum: AM-CL OR Clinda Peds: Pen V or Amox Doses in footnote**. FQs, tetracyclines & TMP-SMX not recommended due to resistance, clinical failures (JCM 2012:50:4067)	For Strep pharyngitis: Clinda OR Azithro OR Clarithro. If suspect F. necrophorum: Metro: Resistant to macrolides Doses in footnote**.	**Dx: Rapid Strep test.** If rapid test neg., do culture (CID 59:e43, 2014). No need for post-treatment rapid strep test or culture. **Complications of Strep pharyngitis:** 1. Acute rheumatic fever – follows Grp A. S. pyogenes infection, rare after 9 days of onset of symptoms. See footnote**. For prevention, start treatment within 9 days of onset of symptoms. 2. Children age <7 yrs at risk for post-streptococcal glomerulonephritis. 3. Pediatric autoimmune neuropsychiatric disorder associated with Grp A Strep (PANAS) infection. 4. Peritonsillar abscess; Suppurative phlebitis are potential complications. Not effective for pharyngeal GC: spectinomycin, cefixime, cefpodoxime and cefuroxime. Ref: MMWR 61:590, 2012. See MMWR 64(RR-03):1, 2015 for most recent CDC STD guidelines.
2 PCR assays for GpA strep FDA approved: COBAS Strept A, Alere Strept A	Gonococcal pharyngitis	Ceftriaxone 250 mg IM x 1 dose + Azithro 1 gm po x 1 dose	FQs not recommended due to resistance	Doses in footnote**. Prospective study favors AM-CL (JAC 1989,24:227)
Proven S. pyogenes recurrence or documented relapse Grp A infections: 6 in 1 yr; 4 in 2 consecutive yrs		Cefdinir OR Cefpodoxime	AM-CL OR Clinda	Hard to distinguish true Grp A Strep infection from chronic Grp A Strep carriage and/or repeat viral infections.
Peritonsillar abscess – Sometimes a serious complication of exudative pharyngitis ("Quinsy") (JAC 68:1941, 2013)	F. necrophorum (44%) Grp A Strep (33%) Grp C/G Strep (9%) Strep anginosus grp	Benefit of tonsillectomy unclear (Peds 2017,139:e20163490)	Surgical drainage plus PIP-TZ 3.375 gm IV q6h or (Metro 500 mg IV/po q6-8h+ Ceftriaxone 2 gm IV q24h)	Pen allergic: Clinda 600-900 mg IV q6-8h	**Avoid macrolides:** Fusobacterium is resistant. Reports of beta-lactamase production by oral anaerobes (Anaerobe 9:105, 2003). See jugular vein suppurative phlebitis, page 50. See JAC 68:1941, 2013. Etiologies ref: CID 57:e139:e20163490, 2009.
Other complications	See parapharyngeal space infection and jugular vein suppurative phlebitis (see next page)			

** **Treatment of Group A, C & G strep:** Treatment durations are from approved package inserts. Subsequent studies indicate efficacy of shorter treatment courses. All po unless otherwise indicated.

PEDIATRIC DOSAGE: Benzathine penicillin 25,000 units per kg IM to max. 1.2 million units; **Pen V** 250 mg bid or tid x 10d; (wt < 27kg); **Amox** 50 mg/kg po once daily (max 1000 mg) x 10 days; **AM-CL** 45 mg per kg per day div. q12h x 10 days; **Cephalexin** 20 mg/kg/dose bid (max 500 mg/dose) x 10 days; **Cefuroxime axetil** 20 mg per kg per day ÷ iv. bid x 10 days; **Cefpodoxime proxetil** 10 mg per kg div. x 10 days; **Cefdinir** 7 mg per kg q12h x 5-10 days or 14 mg per kg q24h x 10 days; **Cefprozil** 15 mg per kg per day div. bid x 10 days; **Cefadroxil** 30 mg/kg once daily (max 1 gm/day) x 10 days; **Clarithro** 15 mg per kg per day div. bid or 250 mg q8h x 10 days; **Azithro** 12 mg per kg po once daily x 5 days; many studies show efficacy of 3 day rx or 5 day rx q8H x 10 days.

ADULT DOSAGE: Benzathine penicillin 1.2 million units IM x 1; **Pen V** 500 mg bid or 250 mg qid x 10 days; **Cefdinir** 200 mg bid x 10 days; **Cefuroxime axetil** 250 mg bid x 4 days; **Cefpodoxime proxetil** 100 mg bid x 5 days; **Cefdinir** 300 mg q12h x 5-10 days or 600 mg q24h x 10 days; **Cefprozil** 500 mg q24h x 10 days; **NOTE: All O Ceph 2 drugs approved for 10-day rx of strep pharyngitis; increasing number of studies show efficacy of 4-6 days; **Clarithro** 250 mg bid x 10 days; **Azithro** 500 mg x 1 and then 250 mg q24h x 4 days or 500 mg q24h x 3 days; **Clinda** 300 mg bid x 10 days.

** Primary rationale for therapy is eradication of Group A strep (GAS) and prevention of acute rheumatic fever (ARF). Benzathine penicillin Ganas been shown in clinical trials to ↓ rate of ARF from 2.8 to 0.2%. This was associated with clearance of GAS on pharyngeal cultures (CID 19:1110, 1994). Subsequent studies have been based on cultures, not actual prevention of ARF. Treatment decreases duration of symptoms.

Abbreviations on page 2.   *NOTE: All dosage recommendations are for adults (unless otherwise indicated*) and assume normal renal function. § Alternatives consider allergy, PK, compliance, local resistance, cost.

TABLE 1 (47)

ANATOMIC SITE/DIAGNOSIS/ MODIFYING CIRCUMSTANCES	ETIOLOGIES (usual)	SUGGESTED REGIMENS*		ADJUNCT DIAGNOSTIC OR THERAPEUTIC MEASURES AND COMMENTS
		PRIMARY	ALTERNATIVE§	
PHARYNX/Pharyngitis/Tonsillitis/Exudative or Diffuse Erythema *(continued)*				
Membranous pharyngitis: due to **Diphtheria** Respiratory isolation, nasal & pharyngeal cultures (special media), obtain antitoxin. **Place pt in respiratory droplet isolation.**	C. diphtheriae (human to human), C. ulcerans and C. pseudotuberculosis (animal to human) (rare)	**Treatment: antibiotics + antitoxin** **Antibiotic therapy: Erythro** 500 mg IV qid OR **Pen G** 50,000 units/kg (max 1.2 million units) IV q12h. Can switch to **Pen VK** 250 mg po qid when able. Treat for 14 days	**Diphtheria antitoxin:** Horse serum. Obtain from CDC, +1-404-639-2889. Do scratch test before IV therapy. Dose depends on stage of illness: <48hrs: 20,000-40,000 units; <48hrs membranes: 40,000-60,000 units; >3 days & bull neck: 80,000-120,000 units	Ensure adequate airway. EKG & cardiac enzymes. F/U cultures 2 wks post-treatment to document cure. Then, diphtheria toxoid immunization. Culture contacts; treat contacts with either single dose of **Pen G** IM: 600,000 units if age <6 yrs, 1.2 million units if age ≥6 yrs. If Pen-allergic, **Erythro** 500 mg po qid x 7-10 days. Assess immunization status of dose contacts: toxoid vaccine as indicated. In vitro, C. diphtheriae suscept. to clarithro, azithro, clinda, FQs, TMP/SMX.
Vesicular, ulcerative pharyngitis (viral)	Coxsackie A9, B1-5, ECHO (multiple types), Enterovirus 71, Herpes simplex 1,2	Antibacterial agents not indicated. For HSV-1, 2: **acyclovir** 400 mg tid po x 10 days.	HSV: **Famciclovir** 250 mg po tid x 7-10 days or **Valacyclovir** 1000 mg po bid x 7-10 days	Small vesicles posterior pharynx suggests enterovirus. Viruses are most common etiology of acute pharyngitis. **Suspect viral if concurrent conjunctivitis, coryza, cough, skin rash, hoarseness.**
Epiglottitis (Supraglottis): Concern in life-threatening obstruction of the airway				
Children	H. influenzae (rare), S. pyogenes, S. pneumoniae, S. aureus (includes MRSA), viruses	Peds dosage: (**Cefotaxime** 50 mg per kg IV q8h or **Ceftriaxone** 50 mg per kg IV q24h) + **Vanco**	Peds dosage: **Levo** 10 mg/kg IV q24h + **Clinda** 7.5 mg/kg IV q6h	Have tracheostomy set "at bedside". **Levo** use in children is justified as emergency empiric therapy in pts with severe beta-lactam allergy. Ref: Ped Clin No Amer 53:215, 2006. Use of steroids is controversial; do not recommend.
Adults	Group A strep, H. influenzae (rare) & many others	Same regimens as for children. See footnote²⁰	Adult dosage: See footnote²⁰	
Paraphyngeal space infection [Spaces include: sublingual, submandibular (Ludwig's angina) *(see page 46)* lateral pharyngeal, retropharyngeal, pretracheal & descending mediastinitis]				
Poor dental hygiene, dental extractions, foreign bodies (e.g., toothpicks, fish bones) Refs: Infection 2016,44:77; Otol Head Neck Surg 2016,155:155	Polymicrobic: S. aureus, Strep sp., anaerobes, Eikenella corrodens. Anaerobes outnumber aerobes 10:1.	[(**Clinda** 600-900 mg IV q8h) or (**Pen G** 24 million units/day by cont. infusion or div. q4-6h IV)+ **Metro** 1 gm load and then 0.5 gm IV q6h]	**PIP-TZ** 3.375 gm IV q6h or 4-hr infusion of 3.375 gm q8h; **AM-SB** 3 gm IV q6h	Close observation of airway, 1/3 require intubation. MRI or CT to identify abscess; surgical drainage. **Metro** may be given 1 gm IV q12h. Complications: infection of carotid (rupture possible) & jugular vein phlebitis.
Jugular vein suppurative phlebitis (Lemierre's syndrome) LnID 12:808, 2012.	Fusobacterium necrophorum in vast majority	**PIP-TZ** 4.5 gm IV q8h or **IMP** 500 mg IV q6h or (**Metro** 500 mg po/IV q8h + **Ceftriaxone** 2 gm IV once daily)	**Clinda** 600-900 mg IV q8h. **Avoid macrolides- fusobacterium is resistant**	Emboli: pulmonary and systemic common. Erosion into carotid artery can occur. Lemierre described F. necrophorum in 1936; other anaerobes & Gm-positive cocci are less common etiologies of suppurative phlebitis post-pharyngitis.
Laryngitis (hoarseness)	Viral (90%)	Not indicated		

²⁰ Parapharyngeal space infection: **Ceftriaxone** 2 gm IV q24h; **Cefotaxime** 2 gm IV q4-8h; **PIP-TZ** 3.375 gm IV q6h or 4-hr infusion of 3.375 gm q8h (based on TMP component) div q6h, q8h, or q12h; **Clinda** 600-900 mg IV q6-8h; **Levo** 750 mg IV q24h; **Vanco** 15 mg/kg IV q12h.

Abbreviations on page 2.

* NOTE: All dosage recommendations are for adults (unless otherwise indicated) and assume normal renal function. § Alternatives consider allergy, PK, compliance, local resistance, cost.

TABLE 1 (48)

ANATOMIC SITE/DIAGNOSIS/ MODIFYING CIRCUMSTANCES	ETIOLOGIES (usual)	SUGGESTED REGIMENS*		ADJUNCT DIAGNOSTIC OR THERAPEUTIC MEASURES AND COMMENTS
		PRIMARY	ALTERNATIVE§	
SINUSES, PARANASAL				
Sinusitis, acute *Guidelines: Pediatrics 132:e262 & 284, 2013 (American Academy of Pediatrics); Otolaryngol Head Neck Surg 2015;152 (Suppl 2):S1*		Most common: obstruction of sinus ostia by inflammation from virus or allergy. Treatment: Saline irrigation		Treatment: • Clinda: Haemophilus & Moraxella sp. are resistant; may need 2nd drug (*IDSA Guidelines*)
Treatment goals: • Speed resolution • Prevent bacterial complications (*see Comment*) • Prevent chronic sinusitis • Avoid unnecessary use of antibiotics	S. pneumonia 33% H. influenza 32% M. catarrhalis 9% Anaerobes 6% Grp A strep 2% Viruses 15-18% S. aureus 10% (*see Comment*)	**Antibiotics for bacterial sinusitis if:** 1) fever, pain, puru-lent nasal discharge; 2) still symptomatic after 10 days with no antibiotic; 3) clinical failure despite antibiotic therapy		• Dura'ion of rx: 5-7 days (*IDSA Guidelines*), 10-14 days (*Amer Acad Ped Guidelines*) • Adjuvctive rx: 1) do not use topical decongestant for >3 days; 2) no definite benefit from nasal steroids and antihistamines; 3) saline irrigation may help • Avoid macrolides & TMP-SMX due to resistance
Discussion of when to start antibacterial rx (*AnIM 2017;166:201*)		*No penicillin allergy* **Peds: Amox** 90 mg/kg/day divided q12h or **Amox-Clav** (Amox comp) suspension 90 mg/kg/day divided q12h. **Adult: Amox-Clav** 1000 mg/62.5-2 tabs po bid x 5-7 days	*Penicillin allergy* **Peds (if anaphylaxis): Clinda** 30-40 mg/kg/day divided tid or qid x 10-14 days (*see Comment*) **Peds (no anaphylaxis):** **Cefpodoxime** 10 mg/kg/day po div q12h **Adult (if anaphylaxis):** **Levo** or **doxy** **Adult (no anaphylaxis):** **Cefpodoxime** 200 mg pc bid	• EmpIrc rx does not target S. aureus: incidence same in pts & controls (*CID 45:e121, 2007*) • Potential complications: transient hyposmia, orbital infection, epidural abscess, brain abscess, meningitis, cavernous sinus thrombosis. For other adult drugs and doses, *see footnote†*.
Clinical failure after 3 days	As above; consider diagnostic tap/aspirate	**Mild/Mod. Disease: AM-CL-ER** OR (**Cefpodoxime, Cefprozil, or Cefdinir**) *See Table 11, pages 125 & 134.*	**Severe Disease: Gati**bus**, Gemi, Levo, Moxi** *Adult doses in footnote‡‡*	**Severe/hospitalized: AM-SB** 3 gm IV q6h or **Ceftriaxone** 1-2 gm IV q24h or **Levo** 750 mg IV/po q24h. If no response in 48 hrs, CT sinus & surgical consult.
Diabetes mellitus with acute ketoacidosis; neutropenia; deferoxamine rx: Mucormycosis	Rhizopus sp. (mucor), aspergillus			
Hospitalized + nasotracheal or nasogastric intubation	Gm-neg. bacilli 47% (pseudomonas, acinetobacter, E. coli common), Gm+ (S. aureus) 35%, yeasts 18%. Polymicrobial in 80%	Remove nasotracheal tube: if fever persists and ENT available, recommend sinus aspiration for C/S & S. aureus PCR prior to empiric therapy	**IMP** 0.5 gm IV q6h or **MER** 1 gm IV q8h. Add vanco for MRSA if Gram stain known	After 7 days of nasotracheal or nasogastric tubes, 95% have x-ray "sinusitis" (fluid in sinuses), but on transnasal puncture only 38% culture + (*AJRCCM 150:776, 1994*). For pts requiring mechanical ventilation with nasotracheal tube for 21 wk, bacterial sinusitis occurs in <10% (*CID 27:851, 1998*). May need fluconazole if yeast on Gram stain of sinus aspirate.
Sinusitis, chronic Adults Defined: (drainage, blockage, facial pain, ↓ sense of smell) + (Polyps, purulence or abnormal endoscopy or sinus CT scan: *JAMA 314:926, 2015*)	Multifactorial inflammation of upper airways	**Standard maintenance therapy:** Saline irrigation + topical corticosteroids	**Intermittent/Rescue therapy:** For symptomatic nasal polyps: oral steroid x 1-3 wks. For polyps+ purulence: **Doxy** 20C mg po x 1 dose, then 100 mg po once daily x 20 days	Leukotriene antagonists considered allergy for pts with nasal polyps. No antihistamines unless clearly allergic sinusitis. Some suggest >12 wks of macrolide rx; data only somewhat supportive; worry about AEs.

‡‡ **Adult doses for sinusitis** (all oral): **AM-CL-ER** 2000/125 mg bid, **amox high-dose (HD)** 1 gm tid, **Clarithro** 500 mg bid or **Clarithro ext. release** 1 gm q24h, **Doxy** 100 mg bid, **respiratory FQs** (**Gati** 400 mg q24h)*bus due to hypo/hyperglycemia; **Gemi** 320 mg q24h (*not FDA indication but should work*), **Levo** 750 mg q24h x 5 days, **Moxi** 400 mg q24h); **O Ceph** (**Cefdinir** 300 mg q12h or 600 mg q24h, **Cefpodoxime** 200 mg bid, **Cefprozil** 250-500 mg bid, **Cefuroxime** 250-500 mg bid), **TMP-SMX** 1 double-strength (DS) tab bid, **TMP-SMX** 1 double-strength (strength 160 mg) bid (results a ter 3- and 10-day rx similar).

Abbreviations on page 2. *§NOTE: All dosage recommendations are for adults (unless otherwise indicated and assume normal renal function. PK compliance, local resistance, cost.*

§NOTE: All dosage recommendations are for adults (unless otherwise indicated and assume normal renal function, PK, compliance, local resistance, cost.

TABLE 1 (49)

ANATOMIC SITE/DIAGNOSIS/ MODIFYING CIRCUMSTANCES	ETIOLOGIES (usual)	SUGGESTED REGIMENS*		ADJUNCT DIAGNOSTIC OR THERAPEUTIC MEASURES AND COMMENTS
		PRIMARY	ALTERNATIVE§	
SKIN See IDSA Guideline: CID 59:147, 2014.				
Acne vulgaris (Med Lett 2016;58:13; JAMA 2016;316:1402; J Am AcadDerm 2016;74-945). BP = benzoyl peroxide; TR = topical retinoid; AB = antibiotic				
Mild (all topical therapy).		BP or TR or (BP + TR) or topical (BP + AB)	Add TR or BP if not used. Consider topical **Dapsone**	• TR as monotherapy for comedonal acne or with topical AB for mixed or inflammatory acne • Clinda & Erythro are recommended topical AB • Only use systemic AB if moderate or severe acne that is resistant to topical therapy • Try to limit systemic AB use to 3 mos • Oral isotretinoin should be restricted to severe nodular acne, recalcitrant acne or acne that causes psychosocial distress and/or scarring
Moderate (topical or combined topical + oral therapy)		Topical combination therapy: (BP + AB) + TR) OR (BP + AB) or (BP + TR) OR Oral/topical combination therapy: (Oral AB + TR + BP + topical AB)	Change combination as in Primary or (if female) add oral contraceptive or oral spironolactone to combination	
Severe (oral antibiotic + topical therapy and maybe oral retinoid)		(Oral AB + topical combination therapy: BP + AB + retinoid) OR (Oral AB + oral isotretinoin)	Consider different oral AB or (if female) add oral contraceptive or oral spironolactone.	
Acne rosacea Ref: NEJM 2017;377:1754	Skin mite: Demadex folliculorum (Arch Derm 146:896, 2010)	For Erythema stage: generic **Metro** gel or cream bid x 8-12 weeks	Papulopustular: Ivermectin (Ssoolantra) 1% cream once daily x 8-12 weeks (Expensive)	Systemic oral therapy reserved for severe disease, e.g., **Doxy** 40 mg (low dose) once daily +/- isotretinoin 0.1-0.5 mg/kg/d (low dose) x 6-8 mos. Many other therapy options, see NEJM 2017;377:1754.
Anthrax, cutaneous **To report bioterrorism event:** 770-488-7100; **For info:** www.bt.cdc.gov Treat as inhalation anthrax if systemic illness. Refs: AJRCCM 184:1333, 2011 (Review); CID 59:147, 2014 (Clinical Prac Guideline); Pediatrics 133:e1411, 2014.	B. anthracis. Spores are introduced into/ under the skin by contact with infected animals/animal products. See Lung, page 41.	**Adults: CIP** 500 mg po q12h or **Doxy** 10 mg po q12h. **Children: CIP** 15 mg/kg (max dose 500 mg) po q12h or for pen-susceptible strain **Amox** 25 mg/kg (max dose 1 gm) po q8h For bioterrorism exposure, 3-dose series of Biothrax Anthrax Vaccine Adsorbed is indicated.	**Amox** 500 mg po q12h.	1. Duration of therapy 60 days for bioterrorism event because of potential inhalational exposure and 7-10 days for naturally acquired disease. 2. Consider alternative to Doxy for pregnancy. 3. Alternatives for adults: Levo 750 mg q24h or Moxi 400 mg q24h or Clinda 600 mg q8h or for pen-susceptible strains Amox 1 gm q8h or Pen VK 500 mg q6h 4. Alternatives for children: Doxy 2.2 mg/kg (max dose 100 mg) q12h (tooth staining likely with 60-day regimen age <8 years) or Clindamycin 10 mg/kg (max dose 600 mg) q8h or Levo 8 mg/kg q12h (max dose 250 mg) if <50 kg and 500 mg q24h if >50 kg
Bacillary angiomatosis: For other Bartonella infections, see Cat-scratch disease lymphadenitis, page 46, and Bartonella systemic infections, page 59				
In immunocompromised (HIV-1, bone marrow transplant) patients Also see Sanford Guide to HIV/AIDS Therapy	Bartonella henselae and quintana	**Clarithro** 500 mg po qid or **Doxy** 100 mg po bid or **Azithro** 250 mg po bid (see Comment)	**Erythro** 500 mg po qid or **Doxy** 100 mg po bid (or **Doxy** 100 mg po bid + **RIF** 300 mg po bid)	For AIDS pts, continue suppressive therapy until HIV treated and CD >200 cells/µL for 6 mos. **Drugs to avoid:** TMP-SMX, CIP, Pen, cephalosporins.

TABLE 1 (50)

ANATOMIC SITE/DIAGNOSIS/ MODIFYING CIRCUMSTANCES	ETIOLOGIES (usual)	SUGGESTED REGIMENS[a]		ADJUNCT DIAGNOSTIC OR THERAPEUTIC MEASURES AND COMMENTS
		PRIMARY	ALTERNATIVE[s]	
SKIN *(continued)*				
Bite: Remember tetanus prophylaxis— See Table 20B, page 243 for rabies prophylaxis. Review: CMR 24:231, 2011. **Avoid primary wound closure.**				
Alligator *(Alligator mississippiensis)*	Gram negatives including Aeromonas hydrophila, Clostridia sp.	Severe wound: Surgical debridement + (**CIP 400 mg** IV q12h po bid or **Levo 750 mg** IV q24h + **Amp-Sulb** 3 gm q6h); **OR Pip-Tazo** 4.5 g m IV q8h	Severe wound: Surgical debridement + (**TMP-SMX** 8-10 mg/kg/day IV q6-8h or q8h + **Amp-Sulb** 3 gm q6h or **Cefepime 2** gm IV q8h + **Metro** 500 mg q8h)	Oral flora of American alligator isolated: Aeromonas hydrophila and other gram-negatives, and anaerobes including Clostridium spp (*S Med J 82:262, 1989*).
Bat, raccoon, skunk	Strep & staph from skin; rabies	Pip-Tazo 4.5 gm IV q8h	Doxy 100 mg po bid or 500/125 mg po bid	In America, **anti-rabies rx indicated:** rabies immune globulin + vaccine. (*See Table 20B, page 243*)
Bear	S. aureus, coagulase-negative staph, viridans streptococci, Enterobacteriaceae, Aeromonas, B. cereus, Neisseria spp. (*Clin Microbiol Rev 24: 231, 2011*)		Vanco IV (trough 15-20 mcg/ mL.) / **Cefepime 2** gm (IV OR IM q8h OR q8+12h) + **Metro** 500 mg q8h OR **AmoxiClav** 875-2 gm po bic + **CIP 500-** 750 mg po bic.	Injuries often result in hospital level care. Infection with Mycobacterium fortuitum reported (*J Clin Micro 43: 1009, 2005*). Rabies =occurs in bears (*MMWR 48: 761, 1999*).
Camel	S. aureus, Streptococcus spp, P. aeruginosa, Other Gm-neg bacilli	Pip-Tazo 4.5 gm q8h	Cephalexin 500 mg po qid + CIP 750 mg po bid	See *EJCMID 18:918, 1999.* Rabies can occur in camels (*PLoS Negl Trop Dis. 2016; 1*(9): e00048900).
Cat: 80% get infected, culture & treat empirically.	**Pasteurella multocida,** Streptococci, Staph. aureus, Moraxella	AM-CL 875/125 mg po bid or 1000/62.5 mg 2 tabs po bid	Cefuroxime axetil 0.5 gm po q12h or Doxy 100 mg po bid. Do not use cephalexin. Sens. to FQs in vitro.	**P. multocida** resistant to dicloxacillin, cephalexin, clinda; many strains resistant to erythro (most sensitive to azithro but no clinical data). P. multocida infection develops within 24 hrs. Observe for osteomyelitis. If culture + for only
Cat-scratch disease *page 46*	Toxins (pain may respond to immersion in hot water as tolerated) Evaluate for retained foreign body (spine) May become secondarily infected	Doxy 100 mg po bid + Amox-clav 8:75/125 mg po bid		P. multocida, can switch to pen G IV or pen VK po. *See Dog Bite.* Toxin inury presents as immediate pain, erythema, edema; resembles strep cellulitis. May become infected with marine organisms or staphylococci (*CID 14. 689, 1992*).
Catfish sting				
Dogs: Only 5% get infected; treat only if bite severe or bad co-morbidity (e.g. diabetes).	**Pasteurella canis,** S. aureus, Streptococci, Fusobacterium sp, Capnocytophaga caninorsus	AM-CL 875/125 mg po bid or 1000/62.5 mg 2 tabs po bid	Adult: Clinda 300 mg po q6h + FQ Child: Clinda + TMP-SMX	Consider anti-rabies prophylaxis: rabies immune globulin + vaccine (*see Table 20B*). Capnocytophaga in splenectomized pts may cause local eschar, sepsis with DIC. **P. canis resistant to diclox, cephalexin, clinda and erythro,** sensitive to Ceftriaxone, cefuroxime, cefpodoxime and FQs.
Horse	Actinobacillus, Pasteurella, Enteric Gram negative bacilli, S aureus, streptococci, anaerobes	AM-CL 875/125 mg po bid	Doxy 100 mg po bid	Debridement often needed; IV antibiotics may be needed for severe wounds; Strep. equi meningitis and brain abscess reported (*Lancet 376: 1794, 2k10*)

Abbreviations on page 2.   **NOTE: All dosage recommendations are for adults (unless otherwise indicated) and assume normal renal function. § Alternatives consider allergy; PK, compliance, local resistance, cost.*

TABLE 1 (5t)

ANATOMIC SITE/DIAGNOSIS/ MODIFYING CIRCUMSTANCES	ETIOLOGIES (usual)	SUGGESTED REGIMENS[a]		ADJUNCT DIAGNOSTIC OR THERAPEUTIC MEASURES AND COMMENTS
		PRIMARY	ALTERNATIVE[§]	
SKIN/Bite (continued)				
Human For bacteriology, see CID 37:1481, 2003	Viridans strep 100%, Staph epidermidis 53%, corynebacterium 41%, **Staph. aureus 29%, eikenella 15%,** peptostrep 26%	**Early (not yet infected): AM-CL 875/125 mg po bid times 5 days. Later:** Signs of infection (usually in 3-24 hrs): **(AM-SB** 1.5 gm IV q6h **or Cefoxitin** 2 gm IV q8h) or **(PIP-TZ** 3.375 gm IV q6h or 4.5 gm q8h or 4-hr infusion of 3.375 gm q8h).	Pen allergy: **Clinda** + (either **CIP** or **TMP-SMX**)	**Cleaning, irrigation and debridement most important.** For clenched fist injuries, x-rays should be obtained. Bites inflicted by hospitalized, consider aerobic Gm-neg. bacilli. **Eikenella** resistant to **clinda, nafcillin/oxacillin, metro, P Ceph 1, and erythro; susceptible to FQs and TMP-SMX.**
Komodo dragon	Staphylococcus spp, Bacillus spp, Aeromonas, Pseudomonas, Enterobacteriaceae, Burkholderia, anaerobes	**AM-CL** 875 mg po bid plus **CIP** 750 po bid	**PIP-TZ** 4.5 gm IV q8h	Microbiology: see CMR 24: 231, 2011. Also have toxic venom (PNAS 106: 8969, 2009).
Leech (Medicinal) (Ln 381:1606, 2013)	Aeromonas hydrophila	**CIP** (400 mg IV or 750 mg po) bid	**TMP-SMX DS** 1 tab po bid	Aeromonas found in GI tract of leeches. Some use prophylactic antibiotics when leeches used medicinally, but not universally accepted or necessary.
Pig (swine)	Polymicrobic: Gm+ cocci, Gm-neg. bacilli, anaerobes, Pasteurella sp., Actinobacillus sus	**AM-CL** 875/125 mg po bid	**P Ceph 3** or **AM-SB** or **IMP**	Information limited but infection is common and serious (Ln 348:888, 1996). Pigs may be colonized with MRSA (Clin Microbiol Rev 24: 231, 2011). Potential pathogens include Streptococcus suis leading to meningitis (NEJM 354: 1325, 2005; Rinsho Shinkeigaku 53:792, 2013)
Prairie dog	Monkeypox	See Table 14A, page 180. No rx recommended		From macaques, risk of infection with herpes B virus, rare but potentially fatal encephalitis/myelitis (CID 35: 1191, 2002). Potential risk of rabies.
Primate, Monkey, non-human See Table 14A, Herpes simiae.	Herpesvirus simiae	**Valacyclovir** (PEP) or **Acyclovir** or **Ganciclovir**		Bacteria similar to human bites (CID 24: 231, 2011); for deep bites, can use antibiotics as for human bites.
Rat	Spirillum minus & Streptobacillus moniliformis	**AM-CL** 875/125 mg po bid	**Doxy** 100 mg po bid	Anti-rabies rx not indicated. Causes rat bite fever (Streptobacillus moniliformis); Pen G or doxy, alternatively erythro or clinda.
Seal	Marine mycoplasma	**Tetracycline** or **Doxy** for 2-4 wks		Can take weeks to appear after bite. Disseminated disease reported (CID 62:491, 2016).
Snake: pit viper. (Ref.: NEJM 347:347, 2002).	Pseudomonas sp., Enterobacteriaceae, Staph. aureus and epidermidis, Clostridium sp.	**Primary therapy is antivenom.** Tetanus prophylaxis indicated. **Amox/Clav** + **CIP** for prevention. **Pip/Tazo** for empirical therapy of infected wound. Adjust per culture results.		
Spider bite: Most necrotic ulcers attributed to spiders are probably due to another cause, e.g., cutaneous anthrax (Ln 364:549, 2004) or MRSA infection (spider bite painful; anthrax not painful).				
Widow (Latrodectus)	Not infectious	None	May be confused with "acute abdomen". Diazepam or calcium gluconate helpful to control pain, muscle spasm. Tetanus prophylaxis.	
Brown recluse (Loxosceles) NEJM 352:700, 2005	Not infectious. Overdiagnosed! Spider distribution limited to S. Central & desert SW of US.	Bite usually self-limited & self-healing. No therapy of proven efficacy.	**Dapsone** 50 mg po q24h often used despite marginal supportive data	Dapsone causes hemolysis (check for G6PD deficiency). Can cause hepatitis; baseline & weekly liver panels suggested.
Swan	P. aeruginosa	**CIP** 750 mg po bid		Case report of P. aeruginosa infection (Lancet 350: 340, 1997). However, other aquatic organisms or host skin organisms have potential to cause infection.
Tasmanian devil	Pasteurella multocida (CID 14: 1266, 1992)	Treat as cat bite		15% of P. multocida from devils were TMP-SMX resistant (Lett Appl Microbiol 62: 237, 2016)

Abbreviations on page 2. [a]*NOTE: All dosage recommendations are for adults (unless otherwise indicated) and assume normal renal function.* [§]*Alternatives consider allergy, PK, compliance, local resistance, cost.*

TABLE 1 (52)

ANATOMIC SITE/DIAGNOSIS/ MODIFYING CIRCUMSTANCES	ETIOLOGIES (usual)	SUGGESTED REGIMENS[a]		ADJUNCT DIAGNOSTIC OR THERAPEUTIC MEASURES AND COMMENTS
		PRIMARY	ALTERNATIVE[§]	
SKIN *(continued)*				
Boils—Furunculosis **Active lesions** *See Table 6, page 87*	Staph. aureus, both MSSA & MRSA *IDSA Guidelines: CID 59:147, 2014*	**Boils and abscesses uncomplicated patient** (e.g., no immunosuppression) **I&D** + **TMP/SMX 1 DS** (2 DS for BMI >40) bid or **I&D** + **Clinda** 300 mg tid equally efficacious (see *JACC NEJM 372:1093, 2015, NEJM 2016;374:823, and NEJM 376:2545, 2017)*		Other options: **Doxy** 100 mg po bid or **Minocycline** 100 mg po bid for 5–10 days plus **Fusidic acid**[NUS] 250–500 mg po q8-12h ± **RIF**; **Cephalexin** 500 mg po tid-qid or **Dicloxacillin** 500 mg po tid-qid, only in low prevalence setting for MRSA. Also: **Dalbavancin** 1.5 gm IV x 1 or **Oritavancin** 1200 mg IV x 1. If dx uncertainty or assessing adequacy of I&D, ultrasound is helpful *(NEJM 370:1039, 2014)*. **NOTE: needle aspiration is inadequate.**
		Incision and Drainage mainstay of therapy!		
To lessen number of furuncle recurrences —decolonization *For surgical prophylaxis, see Table 15B, page 210.*	MSSA & MRSA. *IDSA Guidelines, CID 59:e10, 2014*	7-day therapy: **Chlorhexidine** (2%) washes daily; 2% **Mupirocin ointment** anterior nares 2x daily.	**Mupirocin ointment** in anterior nares bid x 7 days + **Chlorhexidine** (2%) washes daily x 7 days + **(TMP-SMX DS** 1 tab po bid + **RIF** 300 mg po bid) x 7 days	Optimal regimen uncertain. Can substitute bleach baths for chlorhexidine *(Inf Control Hosp Epidemiol 32:872, 2011) but only modest effect (CID 58:679, 2014).* In vitro resistance of mupirocin & retapamulin roughly 10% *(JAC 58:2878, 2014).* One review found mupirocin resistance ranging from 1-81% *(JAC 70:2681, 2015).*
Burns. Overall management: *NEJM 350:810, 2004 - step-by-step case outline*				
Initial wound care Use burn unit, if available Topical rx options *(NEJM 359:1037, 2008; Clin Plastic Surg 36:597, 2009)*	**Not infected** Prophylaxis for potential pathogens: Gm-pos cocci Gm-neg bacilli Candida	Early excision & wound closure. Variety of skin grafts/substitutes. Shower hydrotherapy. Topical antimicrobials	**Silver sulfadiazine cream** 1% applied 1-2 x daily. Minimal pain. Transient reversible neutropenia due to margination in burn - not marrow toxicity	**Mafenide** acetate cream is an alternative but painful to apply. Anti-tetanus prophylaxis indicated. Severe burn pt on ventilator: prophylactic Amp-Sulb or Cefazolin may reduce mortality *(CID 62:60 & 67, 2016).*
Burn wound sepsis Proposed standard def: *J Burn Care Res 28:776, 2007.* Need quantitative wound cultures	Strep. pyogenes, Enterobacter sp., S. aureus, S. epidermidis, E. faecalis, E. coli, P. aeruginosa. Fungi (rare). Herpesvirus (rare).	**Vanco** high dose to rapidly achieve trough concentration of 15-20 μg/mL. **(MER** 1 gm IV q8h or **Cefepime** 2 gm IV q8h) + **Fluconazole** 6 mg/kg IV qd		Vanco allergic/intolerant: **Dapto** 6-10 mg/kg IV qd IgE mediated allergy to beta lactams: **Aztreonam** 2 gm IV q6h. ESBL- or carbapenemase-producing MDR gm-neg bacilli: only option is **Polymyxin B** (preferred) or **Colistin**] + **(MER** or **IMP)**
		See **Comments for alternatives**		
Cellulitis, erysipelas: NOTE: Consider diseases that masquerade as cellulitis *(Cleve Clin J Med 79:547, 2012)*				
Extremities, non-diabetic *For diabetes, see below.* Practice guidelines: *CID 59:147, 2014.* **NOTE:** stasis dermatitis can masquerade as erysipelas *(J Am Acad Derm 2015;73:70)*	Streptococcus sp., Groups A, B, C & G. Staph. aureus, including MRSA (but rare). Strep sp: No purulence Staph sp: Purulence. Etiologic study: *JInfect (2017) doi 10.1093 OFID/OFV181)*	**Inpatients:** Elevate legs. **Pen G** 1-2 million units IV q6h or **Cefazolin** 1 gm IV q8h. **Pen-allergic: Vanco** 15 mg/kg IV q12h. When afebrile: **Pen VK** 500 mg po qid ac & hs. Total therapy: 10 days.	**Outpatient:** Elevate legs. **Pen G** 1-2 million units po q d or 6 tts x 10 days. If Pen-allergic: **Azithro** 500 mg po x 1 dose, then 250 mg po once daily x 4 days (total 5 days). Rarely, **Linezolid** 600 mg po bid or **Tedizolid** 200 mg po q24h.	• **Erysipelas:** elevation, IV antibiotic, treat T. pedis if present, if no purulence, no need for culture. • If unsure as to presence of deep abscess, bedside ultrasound can help. • If present: furunculosis (boils) • **TMP-SMX** 1 DS DR **Clinda** 300 mg tid effective for uncomplicated cellulitis in non-diabetic outpatients *(NEJM 372:2460, 2015)* • **Oritavancin** 1200 mg IV x1 OR **Dalbavancin** 1.5 gm IV x 1 also effective for outpatient therapy of more severe infections in patients who might otherwise be admitted to the hospital (see *NEJM 370:2180, 2014).* *NEJM 370:2169, 2014).*
Facial, adult (erysipelas)	Strep. sp. (Grp A, B, C & G), Staph. aureus (to include MRSA), S. pneumo	**Vanco** 15 mg/kg IV q 12h (to achieve target trough concentration of 15-20 μg/mL x 7-10 days	**Dapto** 4 mg/kg IV q 24h or **Linezolid** 600 mg IV q 12h. Treat 7-10 days if not bacteremic	• Choice of empiric therapy must have activity vs. S. aureus. S. aureus or erysipelas of face can mimic streptococcal erysipelas of an extremity. Forced to treat empirically for MRSA until in vitro susceptibilities available.

Abbreviations on page 2.   [a]NOTE: *All dosage recommendations are for adults (unless otherwise indicated) and assume normal renal function.* §*Alternatives consider allergy, PK, compliance, local resistance, cost.*

TABLE 1 (53)

ANATOMIC SITE/DIAGNOSIS/ MODIFYING CIRCUMSTANCES	ETIOLOGIES (usual)	SUGGESTED REGIMENS*		ADJUNCT DIAGNOSTIC OR THERAPEUTIC MEASURES AND COMMENTS
		PRIMARY	ALTERNATIVE§	
SKIN *(continued)*				
Diabetes mellitus and erysipelas (See *Foot, "Diabetic", page 17*)	Strep. sp. (Grp A, B, C & G), Staph. aureus, Enterobacteriaceae; Anaerobes	Early mild: **TMP-SMX-DS** 1-2 tabs po bid + (**Pen VK** 500 mg po qid or **Cephalexin** 500 mg po qid). **For severe disease: IMP, MER, ERTA** or **DORI IV** + (**Linezolid** 600 mg IV/po bid or **vanco** IV or **dapto** 4 mg/kg IV q 24h). *Dosage, page 17. Diabetic foot.*		Prompt surgical debridement indicated to rule out necrotizing fasciitis and to obtain cultures. If septic, consider x-ray of extremity to demonstrate gas. **Prognosis dependent on blood supply: assess arteries.** *See diabetic foot, page 17.* For severe disease, use regimen that targets both aerobic gram-neg bacilli & MRSA.
Erysipelas 2° to lymphedema (congenital = Milroy's disease); post-breast surgery with lymph node dissection	Streptococcus sp., Groups A, C, G	Benzathine pen G 1.2 million units IM q4 wks or Pen VK 500 mg po bid or Azithro 250 mg po qd		Indicated only if pt is having frequent episodes of cellulitis. Benefit in controlled clinical trial *(NEJM 368:1695, 2013).*
Dandruff (seborrheic dermatitis)	Malassezia species	Ketoconazole shampoo 2% or selenium sulfide 2.5% *(see page 11, chronic external otitis)*		
Erythema multiforme	H. simplex type 1, mycoplasma, Strep. pyogenes, drugs (sulfonamides, penicillins)			Treat underlying disorder / Remove offending drug; symptomatic Rx.
Erythema nodosum	Sarcoidosis, inflammatory bowel disease, MTB, coccidioidomycosis, yersinia, sulfonamides, Whipple's disease.			**Rx: NSAIDs; glucocorticoids** if refractory. Identify and treat precipitant disease if possible.
Erythrasma	Corynebacterium minutissimum	Localized infection: **Topical Clinda** 2-3 x daily x 7-14 days	Widespread infection: **Clarithro** 500 mg po bid or **Erythro** 250 mg po bid x 14 days	Dx: Coral red fluorescence with Wood's lamp. If infection recurs, prophylactic bathing with anti-bacterial soap or wash with benzyl peroxide. One-time dose of Clari 1 gm po reported to be effective *(Int J Derm 52:516, 2013; J Derm Treatm 14:70, 2013).*
Folliculitis	S. aureus, candida, P. aeruginosa common	Usually self-limited, no Rx needed. Could use topical mupirocin for Staph and topical antifungal for Candida.		
Furunculosis	Staph. aureus	See *Boils, page 55*		
Hemorrhagic bullous lesions Hx of sea water-contaminated abrasion or eating raw seafood in cirrhotic pt.	Vibrio vulnificus	**Ceftriaxone** 2 gm IV q24h + (**Doxy** or **Minocycline**) 100 mg po/IV bid	**CIP** 750 mg po bid or **Levo** 750 mg IV q24h	Wound infection in healthy hosts, but bacteremia mostly in cirrhotics or use of TNF-inhibitors. Pathogenesis: Exposure to contaminated seawater. Can cause necrotizing fasciitis. Surgical debridement needed. Ref: *NEJM 2016;375:1780.*
Herpes zoster (shingles). *See Table 14A*				

Abbreviations on page 2. *NOTE: All dosage recommendations are for adults (unless otherwise indicated) and assume normal renal function. § Alternatives consider allergy, PK, compliance, local resistance, cost.*

TABLE 1 (54)

ANATOMIC SITE/DIAGNOSIS/ MODIFYING CIRCUMSTANCES	ETIOLOGIES (usual)	SUGGESTED REGIMENS*		ADJUNCT DIAGNOSTIC OR THERAPEUTIC MEASURES AND COMMENTS
		PRIMARY	ALTERNATIVE§	
SKIN (continued)				
Impetigo—See CID 59:147, 2014.				
"Honey-crust" lesions. Ecthyma is closely related. Causes "punched out" skin lesions.	Group A strep **impetigo** (rarely Strept. sp. Groups B, C or G); crusted lesions are Staph. aureus + streptococci. Staph. aureus may be secondary colonizer.	Few lesions: (Mupirocin ointment 2% tid or fusidic acid cream^NUS 2%, OR retapamulin ointment 1% bid. Treat for 5 days	Numerous lesions: Pen VK 250-500 mg po q6h x 5 days or Benzathine Pen 600,000 units IM x 1 or TMP-SMX po x 3-5 days (Lancet 394:2132, 2014). For MRSA: Mupirocin	Topical rx: OTC ointments (bacitracin, neomycin, polymyxin B not as effective as prescription ointments. For mild disease, topical rx as good as po antibiotics (Cochrane Database Syst Rev CD003261, 2012). **Ecthyma:** Infection deeper into epidermis than impetigo. May need parenteral penicillin. Military outbreaks reported: CID 48: 1213 & 1220, 2009 (good images).
Bullous (if ruptured, thin "varnish-like" crust)	Staph. aureus MSSA & MRSA: strains that produce exfoliative toxin A.	For MSSA: po therapy with Dicloxacillin, Oxacillin, Cephalexin, AM-CL, Clinda, TMP-SMX-DS, OR Mupirocin ointment OR Retapamulin ointment	ointment OR po therapy with, TMP-SMX-DS, Minocycline, Doxy, Clinda. Treat for 7 days	
Infected wound, extremity —Post-trauma (for bites, see page 53; for post-operative, see below)—Gram stain negative		For dosages, see table 10A		
Mild to moderate; uncomplicated	Polymicrobic: S. aureus (MSSA & MRSA), aerobic & anaerobic strep, Enterobacteriaceae, C. perfringens, C. tetani; if water exposure, Pseudomonas sp., Aeromonas sp., Acinetobacter in soldiers in Iraq (see CID 47:444, 2008).	Clinda 300-450 mg po tid	Minocycline 100 mg po bid or linezolid 600 mg po bid (Vanco 15-20 mg/kg IV q8-12h OR Dapto 6 mg/kg IV q 24h OR Ceftaroline 600 mg IV q12h OR Telavancin 10 mg/kg IV q24h) + CIP 400 mg IV q12h (q8h if P. aeruginosa) OR Levo 750 mg IV q24h)	**Culture & sensitivity, check Gram stain. Tetanus toxoid if indicated.** **Mild infection.** Suggested drugs focus on S. aureus & Strep species. If suspect Gm-neg. bacilli, add **AM-CL-ER 1000/62.5 two tabs po bid.** If MRSA is erythro-resistant, assume inducible resistance to clinda. **Fever—sepsis:** Another alternative is **Linezolid** 600 mg IV/po q12h. If Gm-neg. bacilli & severe pen allergy, **CIP or Levo**
Debride wound, if necessary. Febrile with sepsis—hospitalized Debride wound, if necessary.		(PIP-TZ or DORI)^NAI OR IMP or MER or ERTA (Dosage, page 25)) + Vanco 15-20 mg/kg q8-12h		
Infected wound, post-operative—Gram stain positive cocci - see below				
Surgery not involving GI or female genital tract				
Without sepsis (mild, afebrile)	Staph. aureus, Group A, B, C or G strep sp.	Clinda 300-450 mg po tid	Dapto 6 mg per kg IV q24h or telavancin 10 mg/kg IV q24h	Check Gram stain of exudate. If Gm-neg. bacilli, **add β-lactam/β-lactamase inhibitor: AM-CL-ER po or (ERTA or PIP-TZ)** IV. Dosage on page 25.
With sepsis (severe, febrile)		Vanco 15-20 mg/kg (actual wt) IV q8-12h (to achieve target trough concentration of 15-20 µg/mL		
Surgery involving GI tract (includes oropharynx, esophagus) or female genital tract—fever, neutrophilia	MSSA/MRSA, coliforms, bacteroides & other anaerobes	(PIP-TZ or (P Ceph 3 + metro) or DORI or ERTA or IMP or MER)] + (Vanco 1 gm IV q12h or Dapto 6 mg/kg IV q 24h) Mild Infection: AM-CL-ER 1000/62.5 OR TMP-SMX-DS 1-2 tabs po bid + Dosages Table 10A & footnote 23, page 64	Dapto 6 mg per kg IV q24h or DORI or ERTA or IMF or (Dapto 6 mg/kg IV q 24h) 2 tabs po bid + Gm+ cocci on Gram stain.	For all treatment options, see Peritonitis, page 47. Most important: Drain wound & get cultures. Can sub **Linezolid** for Vanco. Can sub **CIP or Levo** for β-lactams if susceptibility permits.
Meleney's synergistic gangrene	See Necrotizing Fasciitis, page 58			

Abbreviations on page 2.   *NOTE: All dosage recommendations are for adults (unless otherwise indicated) and assume normal renal function. § Alternatives consider allergy, PK, compliance, local resistance, cost.

TABLE 1 (55)

ANATOMIC SITE/DIAGNOSIS/ MODIFYING CIRCUMSTANCES	ETIOLOGIES (usual)	SUGGESTED REGIMENS*		ADJUNCT DIAGNOSTIC OR THERAPEUTIC MEASURES AND COMMENTS
		PRIMARY	ALTERNATIVE§	
SKIN/Infected wound, post-operative—Gram stain negative *(continued)*				
Infected wound, post-op, febrile patient— **Positive gram stain:** Gram-positive cocci in clusters	S. aureus, possibly MRSA	**Do culture & drain wound** **Oral:** TMP-SMX-DS 1 tab bid or bid or Clinda 300–450 mg po tid *(see Comment)*	**IV: Vanco** 15-20 mg/kg q8-12h or **dapto** q-6 mg/kg IV q24h or **Ceftaroline** 600 mg IV q12h or **Telavancin** 10 mg/kg IV q24h	Need culture & sensitivity to verify MRSA. Other po options for CA-MRSA include minocycline 100 mg po q12h or **Doxy** 100 mg po bid (inexpensive) & linezolid 600 mg po q12h (expensive). If MRSA clinda-sensitive but erythro-resistant, watch out for inducible clinda resistance. Dalbavancin and oritavancin recently FDA approved for treatment of acute bacterial skin and skin structure infections.
Necrotizing fasciitis ("flesh-eating bacteria") Reviews: *Infect Dis Clin N Amer 2017;31:497; NEJM 2017;377:2253.*				
Post-surgery, trauma, or strepto-coccal skin infections *See Gas gangrene, page 46, & Toxic shock, page 65.* *Refs: NEJM 2017;377:2253; IDSA Guidelines: CID 2014;59:e10*	**5 types:** (1) Strep sp, Grp A, C, G; (2) Clostridia sp.; (3) polymicrobic: aerobic + anaerobic (If S. aureus + anaerobic strep = Meleney's synergistic gangrene); (4) MRSA; (5) V. vulnificus; (6) Klebsiella sp.	*For treatment of clostridia, see Muscle, gas gangrene, page 46.* Meleney's synergistic gangrene, Fournier's gangrene, necrotizing fasciitis req incision & probing of fascial plane. **Need Gram stain/culture** to determine if etiology is strep, clostridia, polymicrobial, or S. aureus. **Treatment: Pen G** if strep or clostridia. **IMP or MER** if polymicrobial, add **Vanco OR dapto** if MRSA suspected. **NOTE: If strep necrotizing fasciitis,** treat with **penicillin** and **clinda** (900 mg IV q6h); **if clostridia ± gas gangrene,** add **clinda & penicillin.** *See toxic shock syndrome, streptococcal, page 66.* IVIG not recommended.		The terminology of **polymicrobic** wound infections is not precise. All require **prompt surgical debridement + antibiotics.** Dx of necrotizing fasciitis req incision & probing of fascial plane. Hyperbaric oxygen (HBO) for necrotizing soft tissue infection adjunctive.
Puncture wound—**nail, toothpick**	Through tennis shoe: P. aeruginosa	Local debridement to remove foreign body & tetanus prophylaxis; no antibiotic therapy.		Osteomyelitis evolves in only 1–2% of plantar puncture wounds. Consider x-ray if chance of radio-opaque foreign body.
Staphylococcal scalded skin syndrome *Ref: PIDJ 19:819, 2000*	Toxin-producing S. aureus	**Nafcillin** or **Oxacillin** 2 gm q4h children: 150 mg/kg/ day div q6h) or **MRSA: Vanco** 15-20 mg/kg IV (children 40-60 mg/kg/day div. q6h) for MRSA		Toxin causes **intraepidermal** split and positive Nikolsky sign. Biopsy differentiates: drugs cause epidermal/dermal split, **called toxic epidermal necrolysis**—more serious.
Ulcerated skin lesions: Differential Dx	Consider: anthrax, tularemia, P. aeruginosa (ecthyma gangrenosum), plague, blastomycosis, spider (rarely), mucormycosis, mycobacteria, leishmania, YAWS, arterial insufficiency, venous stasis, and others.			
Ulcerated skin: venous/arterial insufficiency; pressure with secondary infection (infected decubiti) Care of non-healing, non-infected ulcers (*AnIM 159:532, 2013; AnIM 162:359, 2015).*	Polymicrobic: Streptococcus sp. (Groups A, C, G), Enterococci, anaerobic strep, Pseudomonas sp., Bacteroides sp., Staph. aureus	Severe local or possible bacteremia: **IMP** or **MER** or **DORI** or **ERTA.** If Gm-pos cocci on gram stain, add **Vanco.**	[(**CIP** or **Levo**) + **Metro**] or [(**CIP** or **Ceftaz**) + **Metro**]. If Gm-pos cocci on gram stain, add **Vanco.**	If ulcer clinically inflamed, treat IV with no topical rx. If not clinically inflamed, consider debridement, removal of foreign body, lessening direct pressure for weight-bearing limbs & leg elevation (if no arterial insufficiency). Topical rx to reduce bacterial counts: silver sulfadiazine 1% or combination antibiotic ointment. **Chlorhexidine & povidone-iodine may harm "granulation tissue"—Avoid.** If not inflamed, healing improved on air bed, protein supplement, radiant heat, electrical stimulation (*AnIM 159:39, 2013).*
		Dosages, see footnotes 4,5,6,11,13		
Whirlpool (Hot Tub) folliculitis	Pseudomonas aeruginosa	Usually self-limited, treatment not indicated		Decontaminate hot tub: drain and chlorinate. Also associated with exfoliating beauty aids (loofah sponges).
Whirlpool Nail Salon, soft tissue infection	Mycobacterium (fortuitum or chelonae)	**Minocycline, Doxy** or **CIP**		Ref: *CID 38:38, 2004.*
SPLEEN. For post-splenectomy prophylaxis, see Table 15A, page 208; for Septic Shock Post-Splenectomy, see Table 1, page 66. Vaccines: CID 58:309, 2014.				
Splenic abscess Endocarditis, bacteremia	Staph. aureus, streptococci	**Nafcillin** or **Oxacillin** 2 gm IV q4h or **Cefazolin** 2 gm IV q8h if MSSA	**Vanco** 15-20 mg/kg IV q8-12h (to achieve target trough concentration of 15-20 µg/mL).	Burkholderia (Pseudomonas) pseudomallei is common cause of splenic abscess in SE Asia. Presents with fever and LUQ pain. Usual treatment is antimicrobial therapy and splenectomy.

Abbreviations on page 2.   *NOTE: All dosage recommendations are for adults (unless otherwise indicated) and assume normal renal function § Alternatives consider allergy, PK, compliance, local resistance, cost.*

TABLE 1 (56)

ANATOMIC SITE/DIAGNOSIS/ MODIFYING CIRCUMSTANCES	ETIOLOGIES (usual)	SUGGESTED REGIMENS*		ADJUNCT DIAGNOSTIC OR THERAPEUTIC MEASURES AND COMMENTS
		PRIMARY	ALTERNATIVE*	
SPLEEN/Splenic abscess *(continued)*				
Contiguous from intra-abdominal site	Polymicrobic	*Treat as Peritonitis, secondary, page 47*		
Immunocompromised	Candida sp.	Amphotericin B *(Dosage, see Table 11, page 126)*	Fluconazole, caspofungin	
SYSTEMIC SYNDROMES (FEBRILE/NON-FEBRILE) Spread by Infected TICK, FLEA, or LICE				
Epidemiologic history crucial. Babesiosis, Lyme disease, & Anaplasma (Ehrlichiosis) have same reservoir & tick vector.				Seven diseases where pathogen visible in peripheral blood smear: African/ America/ trypanosomiasis; babesia; bartonellosis; filariasis; malaria; relapsing fever.
Babesiosis: *see JAMA 315:1767, 2016.* Do not treat if asymptomatic, young, has spleen, and immunocompetent; can be fatal in lymphoma pts.	Etiol: B. microti et al. Vector: Usually ixodes ticks Host: White-footed mouse & others	[(Atovaquone 750 mg po q12h) + (Azithro 600 mg po day 1, then 500-1000 mg per day) times 7-10 days]. If severe infection [Clinda 1.2 gm IV bid or 600 mg po bid times 7 days + Quinine 650 mg po bid times 7 days. **Ped. dosage:** Clinda 20-40 mg per kg per day and quinine 25 mg per kg per 3ay]. Exchange transfusion–See Comment.		Do Giemsa-stained blood smear: antibody test available. PCR if available. Do: Exchange transfusions successful as adjunct if used early, in severe disease. May need treatment for 6 or more wks if immunocompromised. Look for Lyme and/or Anaplasma co-infection.
Bartonella infections: Treatment review: *Int J Antimicrob Agts 44:16, 2014.*				
Bacteremia, asymptomatic	B. quintana, B. henselae	Doxy 100 mg po/IV bid x 4 wks + Gent 1 mg/kg qhs x 1st 2 wks		Can lead to endocarditis &/or trench fever: found in homeless, alcoholics, esp. if flea/leg pain. Often missed since asymptomatic.
Cat-scratch disease	B. henselae	Azithro 500 mg po x 1 dose, then 250 mg/day x 4 days. Or symptomatic only–see *Lymphadenitis, page 46:* usually lymphadenitis, hepatitis, splenitis, FUO, neuroretinitis, transverse myelitis, oculoglandular syndrome.		
Bacillary angiomatosis; Peliosis hepatis– pts with AIDS	B. henselae, B. quintana	**Uncomplicated:** Erythro 500 mg po qid or Doxy 100 mg po bid x 3 months or longer. Regardless of CD4 count, DC therapy after 3-4 mos. observe. If no relapse, no suppressive rx. If relapse, Doxy, Azithro or Erythro x 3 mos. Stop when CD4 >200 x 6 mos.	**Complicated (CNS involvement):** Doxy 100 mg IV/po bid + RIF 300 mg po bid	**Manifestations of Bartonella infections: Immunocompetent Patient:** Bacteremia/endocarditis/FUO/ encephalitis Cat scratch disease Vertebral osteo Trench fever Parinaud's oculoglandular syndrome **HIV/AIDS Patient:** Bacillary angiomatosis Bacillary peliosis Bacteremia/endocarditis/FUO
Endocarditis *(see page 28)* *Int J Antimicrob Agts 44:16, 2014*	B. henselae, B. quintana	Surgical removal of infected valve If suspect endocarditis: Ceftriaxone 2 gm IV once daily x 6 weeks + Gent 1 mg/ kg IV q8h x 14 days + Doxy 100 mg IV/po bid x 6 wks	If proven endocarditis: Doxy 100 mg IV/po bid x 6 wks + Gent 1 mg/kg IV q8h x TI days	Gentamicin toxicity: If Gent toxicity, substitute Rifampin 300 mg IV/po bod D14 days. Role of valve removal surgery to cure unclear. Presents as SBE. Diagnosis: ECHO, serology & PCR of resected heart valve. **Note:** Empiric Ceftriaxone for possible endocarditis due to Strept. sp. while awaiting blood culture results.
Oroya fever (acute) & Verruga peruana (chronic) (South American Bartonellosis)	B. bacilliformis; *AAC 48:192, 2014;* *Pediatrics 128:e1084, 2011*	**Oroya fever: (Adult)(CIP** 500 mg po bid + Ceftriaxone 1 gm IV once daily) x 14 days OR Chloro 500-750 mg/kg/day IV po in 4 div doses + Ceftriaxone 1 gm IV once daily) x 14 days.	**Verruga peruana:** (Adult) Azithro 500 mg po once daily x 7 days OR CIP 500 mg po bid x 7-10 days	Oroya fever (Pregnancy): Amox-clav 100/62.5 mg po bid. Oroya fever, severe infection (Child): (CIP or Chloro) + Ceftriaxone Verruga peruana (Child): Azithro 10/mg/kg po once daily x 7 days OR CIP 20 mg/kg po in 2 div doses x 14 days
Trench fever (FUO)	B. quintana	No endocarditis: Doxy 100 mg bid x 4 wks + Gentamicin 3 mg/kg once daily for 1st 2 wks of therapy (AAC 48:1921, 2004).		Vector is body louse. Do not use: TMP-SMX, FQs, cefazolin or Pen. If endocarditis, need longer rx. See Emerg ID 2:217, 2005).

Abbreviations on page 2.   **NOTE: All dosage recommendations are for adults (unless otherwise indicated), and assume normal renal function. §Alternatives consider allergy, PK, compliance, local resistance, cost.*

TABLE 1 (57)

ANATOMIC SITE/DIAGNOSIS/ MODIFYING CIRCUMSTANCES	ETIOLOGIES (usual)	SUGGESTED REGIMENS*		ADJUNCT DIAGNOSTIC OR THERAPEUTIC MEASURES AND COMMENTS
		PRIMARY	ALTERNATIVE§	
SYSTEMIC SYNDROMES (FEBRILE/NON-FEBRILE) Spread by infected TICK, FLEA, or LICE *(continued)*				
Ehrlichiosis.ᴬ CDC def. is one of: (1) 4x ↑ IFA antibody, (2) detection of Ehrlichia DNA in blood or CSF by PCR, (3) visible morulae in WBC, and IFA ≥1:64. New species in WI, MN *(NEJM 365:422, 2011)*.				
Human monocytic ehrlichiosis (HME) *CID 45(Suppl 1):S1, 2007*	Ehrlichia chaffeensis (Lone Star tick is vector)	**Doxy** 100 mg po/IV bid times 7–10 days	**Tetracycline** 500 mg po qid x 7–10 days. No current rec. for children or pregnancy	30 states: mostly SE of line from NJ to III. to Missouri to Oklahoma to Texas. History of outdoor activity and tick exposure. April–Sept. Fever, rash (36%), leukopenia and thrombocytopenia. Blood smears no help. PCR for early dx.
Human Anaplasmosis (formerly known as Human granulocytic ehrlichiosis) *MMWR 65:1, 2016; JAMA 315:1767, 2016*	Anaplasma (Ehrlichia) phagocytophilum (Ixodes sp. ticks are vector). Dog variant is Ehrlichia ewingii	**Doxy** 100 mg po or IV times 7–14 days	**Tetracycline** 500 mg po qid times 7–14 days. Not in children or pregnancy. **Chloro** is an alternative.	Upper Midwest, NE, West Coast & Europe. H/O tick exposure. April–Sept. Febrile flu-like illness after outdoor activity. No rash. Leukopenia/ thrombocytopenia common. Dx: PCR best; blood smear insensitive *(Am J Trop Med Hyg 93:66, 2015)*. Rx: RIF active in vitro *(IDCNA 22:433, 2008)* but worry about resistance developing. Minocycline should work if doxy not available.
Lyme Disease NOTE: Think about concomitant tick-borne disease—e.g., babesiosis, anaplasmosis and ehrlichiosis. Guidelines: *CID 51:1, 2010; NEJM 370:1724, 2014; JAMA 315:1767, 2016.*				
Bite by ixodes-infected tick in an endemic area — Postexposure prophylaxis	Borrelia burgdorferi **IDSA guidelines** *CID 51:1, 2010*	If endemic area, if nymphal partially engorged deer tick: **Doxy** 200 mg po times 1 dose	If not endemic area, not engorged, not deer tick: No treatment	Prophylaxis study in endemic area: erythema migrans developed in 3% of the control group and 0.4% doxy group *(NEJM 345:79 & 133, 2001)*. Can substitute **Minocycline** if **Doxy** is unavailable. Peds (age 28 yrs): **Doxy** 4 mg/kg (max 200 mg) po x 1.
Early (erythema migrans) *See Comment*		**Doxy** 100 mg po bid or **Amoxicillin** 500 mg po tid or **cefuroxime axetil** 500 mg po bid times for 14–21 days. (10 days as good as 20: *AnIM 138:697, 2003)*	**Doxy** 100 mg po tid or **Erythro** 250 mg po qid.	High rate of clinical failure with azithro & erythro *(Drugs 57:157, 1999)*. Peds call po for 14–21 days): **Amox** 50 mg per kg per day in 3 div. doses or **Cefuroxime axetil** 30 mg per kg per day in 2 div. doses or **Erythro** 30 mg per kg per day in 3 div. doses.
Carditis *See Comment*	See Comment for peds doses	(**Ceftriaxone** 2 gm IV q24h) or (**Cefotaxime** 2 gm IV q8h) or (**Pen G** 3 million units IV q4h) times 14–21 days	**Doxy** (see Comments) 100 mg po bid times, 14–21 days or **Amoxicillin** 500 mg po tid times 14–21 days.	Lesions usually homogeneous—not target-like *(AnIM 136:423, 2002)*. First degree AV block. Oral regimen. Generally self-limited. High degree AV block (PR >0.3 sec.): IV therapy permitted; pacemaker not necessary, but temporary pacing in 39% *(CID 59:996, 2014)*.
Facial nerve paralysis (isolated finding, early)		(**Doxy** 100 mg po bid) or **Amoxicillin** 500 mg po) tid times 14–21 days	(**Ceftriaxone** 2 gm IV q24h times 14–21 days.	LP suggested excluding central neurologic disease. If LP neg., oral regimen OK. If abnormal or not done, suggest parenteral Ceftriaxone.
Meningitis, encephalitis *For encephalopathy, see Comment*	Applicable to European cases *(CID 57:333 & 341, 2013)*. Guidance on diagnostics: *EID 22:1169, 2016*	**Ceftriaxone** 2 gm IV q24h times 14–28 days	(**Pen G** 20 million units IV q24h in div. dose) or (**Cefotaxime** 2 gm IV q8h) times 14–28 days	Encephalomyelitis: memory difficulty, depression, somnolence or headache, CSF abnormalities. 18/18 pts, 89% had objective CSF abnormalities, improved with Ceftriaxone 2 gm per day times 30 days *(JID 180:377, 1999)*. No compelling evidence that prolonged treatment has any benefit in post-Lyme syndrome *(Neurology 69:91, 2007)*.
Arthritis		(**Doxy** 100 mg po bid) or (**Amoxicillin** 500 mg po tid), both times 30–60 days	(**Ceftriaxone** 2 gm IV q24h) or (**Pen G** 20–24 million units per day IV) times 14–28 days. If pen. allergic: (**Azithro** 500 mg po q24h times 7–10 days) or (**Erythro** 500 mg po qid times 14–21 days).	Start with 1 mo of therapy; if only partial response, treat for a second mo.
Pregnancy		**Amoxicillin** 500 mg po tid times 21 days.	If pen. allergic: **Azithro** 500 mg po q24h times 14–28 days. Choice should not include doxy.	No benefit from rx *(AJM 126:S65, 2013; CID 51:1, 2010; AAC 58:6701, 2014; NEJM 345:85, 2001)*. Constructive review: *CID 56:1267, 2014.*
Post-Lyme Disease Syndromes		None indicated		

---

zz In endemic area (New York), high % of both adult ticks and nymphs were jointly infected with both Anaplasma (HGE) and B. burgdorferi *(NEJM 337:49, 1997)*.

Abbreviations on page 2.   §NOTE: All dosage recommendations are for adults (unless otherwise indicated) and assume normal renal function. § Alternatives consider allergy, PK, compliance, local resistance, cost.

TABLE 1 (58):

ANATOMIC SITE/DIAGNOSIS/ MODIFYING CIRCUMSTANCES	ETIOLOGIES (usual)	SUGGESTED REGIMENS*		ADJUNCT DIAGNOSTIC OR THERAPEUTIC MEASURES AND COMMENTS
		PRIMARY	ALTERNATIVE§	
SYSTEMIC SYNDROMES (FEBRILE/NON-FEBRILE)/Spread by Infected TICK, FLEA, or LICE (continued)				
Plague, bacteremic (see also Bubonic plague and plague pneumonia)	Yersinia pestis	**(Streptomycin** 30 mg/kg/day IV in 2 div doses OR **Gentamicin** 5 mg/kg/day IV single dose) x 10 days	**(Levo** 500 mg IV/po once da Iv (or **CIP** 590 mg po or 400 mg IV) q12h) x 10 days or **Moxi** 400 mg IV/po q24-h x 10-14 days	**Doxy** 200 mg IV/po bid x 1 day, then 100 mg IV/po bid x 7-10 days another option. FQs effective in animals & small case series (EID 2017;23-533).
Relapsing fever				
Louse-borne (LBRF)	Borrelia recurrentis Reservoir: human Vector: Louse pediculus humanus	**Tetracycline** 500 mg IV/po x 1 dose or **Doxy** 100 mg IV/po x 1 dose	**Erythro** 500 mg IV/po x 1 dose	Jarisch-Herxheimer (fever, ↑ pulse, ↑ resp., ↓ blood pressure) in most patients (occurs in ~2 hrs). Not prevented by prior steroids. **Dx: Examine peripheral blood smear during fever for spirochetes.** Can relapse up to 10 times.
Tick-borne (TBRF)	No Amer: B. hermsii, B. turicata; Africa: B. hispanica, B. crocidurae, B. duttonii; Russia: B. miyamoto (see Comment)	**Doxy** 100 mg po bid x 7-10 days	**Erythro** 500 mg po qid x 7-10 days	Jarisch-Herxheimer reaction may occur. Postexposure **Doxy** pre-emptive therapy highly effective (NEJM 355:148, 2006). B. miyamoto: Dx by ref lab serum PCR. Fever, headache, thrombocytopenia & tick exposure (NE USA). Seems to respond to Doxy, Amox, Ceftriaxone (AnIM 163-91 & 141, 2015; NEJM 373-468, 2015).
Rickettsial diseases (MMWR 65(RR-2):1, 2016).				
Spotted fevers (NOTE: Rickettsial pox not included)				
Rocky Mountain spotted fever (RMSF) (LnID 8:143, 2008 and MMWR 55 (RR-4), 2007)	R. rickettsii (Dermacentor tick vector)	**Doxy** 100 mg po/IV bid times 7 days (or for 2 days after temp. normal. Do not use in pregnancy. Some suggest loading dose: 200 mg IV/po q 12h x 3 days, then 100 mg po bid)	**Pregnancy:** Chloro 50 mg/kg/ day in 4 div doses. If can not obtain Chloro, no choice but Doxy despite risks (fetal bone & teeth malformation; maternal toxicity).	Fever, rash (88%), petechiae 40–50%. **Rash spreads from distal extremities to trunk.** Rash spreads centrifugally—opposite of RMSF. Onset 1st to 72 hrs. Dx: Immunohistology on skin biopsy; confirmation with in 1st 72 hrs. Dx: Immunohistology on skin biopsy; confirmation with in 1st 72 hrs. No good early diagnostic test. Highest incidence in SE and South Central states; also seen in Oklahoma, S. Dakota, Montana. Cases reported from 42 U.S. states. **NOTE: Only 3–18% of pts present with fever, rash, and hx of tick exposure; many early deaths in children & empiric doxy reasonable** (MMWR 49: 885, 2000).
NOTE: Can mimic ehrlichiosis. Pattern of rash important—see Comment				
Other spotted fevers, e.g., Rickettsial pox, African tick bite fever, R. parkeri	At least 8 species on 6 continents (CID 45 (Suppl 1) S39, 2007).	**Doxy** 100 mg po bid times 7 days	**Chloro** 500 mg po/IV qid times 7 days or s.c. **Azithro** or **Clarithro** (if mild disease)	Clinical diagnosis suggested by: 1) fever, intense myalgia, headache; 2) exposure to mites or ticks; 3) localized eschar (tache noire) or rash. Definitive Dx: PCR of blood, skin biopsy or sequential antibody tests.
Typhus group—Consider in returning travelers with fever				
Louse-borne: epidemic typhus Ref: LnID 8-417, 2008.	R. prowazekii (vector is body or head louse)	**Doxy** 100 mg IV/po bid times 7 days; single 200 mg dose 95% effective.	**Chloro** 500 mg IV/po qid 5 days	**Brill-Zinsser disease** (Ln 357:1198, 2001) is a relapse of typhus acquired during WWII. Truncal rash (64%) spreads centrifugally—opposite of RMSF. Louse borne typhus is a wintertime disease. Diagnosis by serology. R. prowazekii found in flying squirrels in SE US. Delouse clothing of infected pt.
Murine typhus (cat flea reservoir); EID 14:1019, 2008.	R. typhi (rat reservoir and flea vector): CID 46:913, 2008	**Doxy** 100 mg IV/po bid times 7 days	**Chloro** 500 mg IV/po qic times 5 days	Rash in 20-54%, onset diagnostic. Most treatment most pts recover in 2 wks. Faster recovery with treatment. Dx based on suspicion; confirmed serologically.
Scrub typhus (World J Crit Care 4:244, 2015)	O. tsutsugamushi [rodent reservoir; vector is larval stage of mites (chiggers)].	**Doxy** 100 mg po/IV bid x 7 days. In pregnancy: **Azithro** 500 mg po x one dose	**Chloro** 500 mg po x 7 days	Asian rim of Pacific. Confirm with serology. If Doxy resistance suspected, alternatives are **RIF** 300 or 450 mg po bid x 7 days or **Azithro** 500 mg q24h (AAC 58:1488, 2014).

Abbreviations on page 2. *NOTE: All dosage recommendations are for adults (unless otherwise indicated) and assume normal renal function. §Alternatives consider allergy, PK, compliance, local resistance, cost.

TABLE 1 (59)

ANATOMIC SITE/DIAGNOSIS/ MODIFYING CIRCUMSTANCES	ETIOLOGIES (usual)	SUGGESTED REGIMENS*		ADJUNCT DIAGNOSTIC OR THERAPEUTIC MEASURES AND COMMENTS
		PRIMARY	ALTERNATIVE*	
SYSTEMIC SYNDROMES (FEBRILE/NON-FEBRILE)/Spread by Infected TICK, FLEA, or LICE (continued)				
Tularemia, typhoidal type Ref: bioterrorism, see JAMA 285:2763, 2001; ID Clin No Amer 22:489, 2008; MMWR 58:744, 2009.	Francisella tularensis. (Vector depends on geography: ticks, biting flies, mosquitoes identified). Direct inoculation of wounds.	Moderate/severe: ((Gent or Tobra 5 mg per kg per day div. q8h IV) or (Streptomycin 10 mg/kg IV/IM q12h)) x 10 days	Mild: [CIP 400 mg IV (or 750 mg po) bid or Doxy 100 mg IV/po bid] x 14-21 days	Diagnosis: Culture on cysteine-enriched media & serology. Dangerous in the lab. Hematogenous meningitis is a complication: treatment is **Streptomycin** + **Chlor** 50-100 mg/kg/day IV in 4 divided doses (Arch Neurol 66:523, 2009).
Other Zoonotic Systemic Bacterial Febrile Illnesses (not spread by fleas, lice or ticks: Obtain careful epidemiologic history				
Brucellosis Refs: NEJM 352:2325, 2005; CID 6:e1426, 2008; MMWR 25:693, 2008; BMJ 336:701, 2008; PLoS One 7:e32090, 2012.	B. abortus—cattle B. suis—swine B. melitensis—goats B. canis—dogs	**Non focal disease:** [Doxy 100 mg po bid x 6 wks + Gent 5 mg/kg once daily for 1st 7 days	[Doxy 100 mg po bid + RIF (600-900 mg po once daily) x 6 wks. Less optimal: CIP 500 mg po bid + (Doxy or RIF) x 6 wks	Bone involvement, esp. sacroiliitis in 20-30%. Neurobrucellosis: Usually meningitis. 1% of all pts with brucellosis. Role of corticosteroids unclear; not recommended. Endocarditis: Rare but most common cause of death. Need surgery + antimicrobials. Pregnancy: TMP-SMX may cause kernicterus if given during last week of pregnancy.
		Spondylitis, Sacroiliitis: [Doxy + Gent (as above) + RIF] x min 3 mos	[CIP 750 mg po bid + RIF (600-900 mg po once daily) x min 3 mos	
		Neurobrucellosis: [Doxy + RIF (as above) + Ceftriaxone 2 gm IV q12h until CSF returned to normal (AAC 56:1523, 2012)		
		Endocarditis: Surgery + [(RIF + Doxy + TMP-SMX) x 1-1/2 to 6 mos + Gent] x 2-4 wks (CID 56:e1407, 2013)		
		Pregnancy: Not much data. RIF 900 mg po once daily x 6 wks	RIF 900 mg po once daily + TMP-SMX 5 mg/kg (TMP comp) po bid x 4 wks	
Leptospirosis (Curr Topics Micro Immunol 387:65, 2015)	Leptospira—in urine of domestic livestock, dogs, small rodents	**Severe illness:** Pen G 1.5 million units IV q6h or Ceftriaxone 2 gm IV q24h. Duration: 7 days	**Mild illness:** Doxy 100 mg IV/po q12h or Amoxicillin 500 mg po tid x 7 days or 500 mg po once daily x 2 days	Severity varies. Varies from mild anicteric illness to severe icteric disease (Weil's disease) with renal failure and myocarditis. AST/ALT do not exceed 5x normal. Jarisch-Herxheimer reaction can occur post-Pen therapy.
Salmonella bacteremia other than S. typhi-non-typhoidal	Salmonella enteritidis—a variety of serotypes from animal sources	If NOT acquired in Asia: Ceftriaxone 2 gm IV q24h or Azithro x 7 days or CIP 400 mg IV q12h or Levo 750 mg po once daily x 14 days (See Comment)	If acquired in Asia: Ceftriaxone 2 gm IV q24h or Azithro 1 gm po once daily x 5-7 days. Do NOT use FQs until susceptibility determined. (See Comment)	In vitro resistance to nalidixic acid indicates relative resistance to FQs. Bacteremia can infect any organ/tissue. Look for infection of atherosclerotic aorta, osteomyelitis, sickle cell cells, etc. Duration range 1-4 days (immunocompetent) to ≥6 wks if mycotic aneurism or endocarditis. Alternative, if susceptible: **TMP-SMX** 8-10 mg/kg/day divided q8h. CLSI has established new interpretive breakpoints for susceptibility to Ciprofloxacin: susceptible strains, MIC <0.06 μg/mL (CID 55:1107, 2012).

Abbreviations on page 2.   *NOTE: All dosage recommendations are for adults (unless otherwise indicated) and assume normal renal function. § Alternatives consider allergy, PK, compliance, local resistance, cost.

TABLE 1 (60)

ANATOMIC SITE/DIAGNOSIS/ MODIFYING CIRCUMSTANCES	ETIOLOGIES (usual)	SUGGESTED REGIMENS* PRIMARY	ALTERNATIVE§	ADJUNCT DIAGNOSTIC OR THERAPEUTIC MEASURES AND COMMENTS
SYSTEMIC SYNDROMES (FEBRILE/NON-FEBRILE) *(continued)*				
Miscellaneous Systemic Febrile Syndromes				
Fever in Returning Travelers Etiology by geographic exposure & clinical syndrome (*AnIM 158:456, 2013*).	Dengue (Flavivirus) Malaria (*Plasmodia* sp). Typhoid (*Salmonella* sp)	Supportive care; see *Table 14A, page 172* Diagnosis: peripheral blood smear See *Table 1, page 62*.		Average incubation period 4 days: serodiagnosis. See *Table 13A, page 157* Average incubation 7-14 days; diarrhea in 45%.
Kawasaki syndrome 6 weeks to 12 yrs of age, peak at 1 yr of age; 85% below age 5. *Pediatrics 124:1, 2009.* Tongue image (*NEJM 373:467, 2015*)	Self-limited vasculitis with ↑ temp, rash, conjunctivitis, strawberry tongue, cervical adenitis, red hands/feet & coronary artery aneurysms	IVIG 2 gm per kg over 8-12 hrs x 1 + **ASA** 20-25 mg per kg qid THEN **ASA** 3-5 mg per kg per day po q24h times 6-8 wks	If still febrile after 1st dose of IVIG, some give 2nd dose. In Japan: **IVIG** + prednisolone 2 mg/kg/day. Continue steroid until CRP normal for 15 days (*Lancet 379:1571, 2012*)	IV gamma globulin (2 gm per kg over 10 hrs) in pts rx before 10th day of illness ↓ coronary artery lesions. See *Table 14A, page 187* for IVIG adverse effects. In children, wait until 11+ months after IVIG before giving live virus vaccines.
Rheumatic Fever, acute Ref.: *Ln 366:155, 2005*	Post-Group A strep pharyngitis (not Group B, C, or G). (See *Pharyngitis, page 49*)	(1) Symptom relief: **ASA** 80-100 mg per kg per day in children; 4-8 gm per day in adults. (2) Eradicate Group A strep: **Pen** times 10 days (3) Start prophylaxis: see below		
Prophylaxis Primary prophylaxis: Treat S. pyogenes pharyngitis		**Benzathine pen G** 1.2 million units IM (see *Pharyngitis, page 49*)	**Penicillin** for 10 days prevents rheumatic fever even when started 7–9 days after onset of illness **Alternative: Penicillin V** 250 mg po bid or **Sulfadiazine** (sulfisoxazole) 1 gm po q24h or **Erythro** 250 mg po bic.	
Secondary prophylaxis (previous documented rheumatic fever)		**Benzathine pen G** 1.2 million units IM q3-4 wks	Duration? No carditis: 5 *yrs or until age 21, whichever is longer; carditis without residual heart disease: 10 since last attack; carditis with residual valvular disease: 10 yrs since last episode or until age 40 whichever is longer	
Typhoidal syndrome (typhoid fever, enteric fever) FQ resistance increasing in infected travelers (*BMC Infect Dis 15:212, 2015*)	*Salmonella typhi, S. paratyphi* A, B, C & S. choleraesuis. **NOTE: In vitro resistance to nalidixic acid predicts clinical failure of CIP (FQs). Do not use empiric FQs if Asia-acquired infection. Need susceptibility results.**	If NOT acquired in Asia: (CIP 400 mg IV q12h or Levo 750 mg po/IV q24h) x 7-14 days (See Comment) In children, azithro 10 mg/kg once daily x 7 days	If acquired in Asia: (Ceftriaxone 2 gm IV daily x 7-14 d) or (Azithro 1 gm po x 1 dose, then 500 mg po daily x 7 days) or (Chlora 500 mg po/IV q6h x 14 d) (See Comment)	**Dexamethasone:** Use in severely ill pts: 1st dose just prior to antibiotic, 3 mg/kg IV, then 1 mg/kg q6h x 8 doses. **Complications:** perforation of terminal ileum 6/or cecum, osteo, septic arthritis, mycotic aneurysm, meningitis, hematogenous pneumonia. Failure of MER in pt with S. *enterica* strain producing ESBLs and resistant to FQs & azithro responded to addition of fosfomycin IV (*CID 2017;65:1754*)
Sepsis: Following suggested empiric therapy assumes pt is bacteremic; mimicked by viral, fungal, rickettsial infections and pancreatitis (*Intensive Care Medicine 34:17, 2008; IDC Nor Amer 22:1, 2008*).				
Neonatal—early onset Age <7 days	Group B strep, E. coli, klebsiella, enterobacter, Staph. aureus (uncommon), listeria (rare in U.S.)	**AMP** 150 mg/kg/day IV div q8h + **Cefotaxime** 100 mg/kg/day div q12h +/- **Gent** 5 mg/kg q 24 h or 2.5 mg/kg/day q8h IV or IM (If meningitis, consider increasing to **AMP** 200 mg/kg/day IV div q6h and **Cefotaxime** 150 mg/kg/day q8h)		Blood cultures are key but only 5-10% +. Discontinue antibiotics after 72 hrs if cultures and course do not support diagnosis. In Spain, listeria predominates; in S. America, salmonella. If Grp B Strep infection + severe beta-lactam allergy, alternatives include: erythro & clinda; report of clinda resistance at 38% & erythro resistance at 51% (*AAC 56:739, 2012*).

Abbreviations on page 2.   *NOTE: All dosage recommendations are for adults (unless otherwise indicated) and assume normal renal function. §Alternatives consider allergy, PK, compliance, local resistance, cost.

TABLE 1 (61)

ANATOMIC SITE/DIAGNOSIS/ MODIFYING CIRCUMSTANCES	ETIOLOGIES (usual)	SUGGESTED REGIMENS*		ADJUNCT DIAGNOSTIC OR THERAPEUTIC MEASURES AND COMMENTS
		PRIMARY	ALTERNATIVE§	
SYSTEMIC SYNDROMES (FEBRILE/NON-FEBRILE)/Sepsis (continued)				
Neonatal—late onset Age >7 days	As above + H. influenzae & S. epidermidis	AMP 200-300 mg/kg/day IV div q6h + Cefotaxime 75 mg/kg q8h +/- Gent 5 mg/kg q24h IV or IM	(AMP 200 mg/kg/day IV div q6h + Ceftriaxone 75-100 mg/kg IV q24h) or AMP 200 mg/kg/day IV div q6h + Gent 5 mg/kg/day div once daily or q8h IV or IM	If MRSA is a concern, add Vanco 15 mg/kg IV q12h (Wt < 2000 gm). See also Comment (early onset).
Child; not neutropenic	Strep. pneumoniae, meningococci, Staph. aureus (MSSA & MRSA), H. influenzae now rare	(Cefotaxime 50 mg/kg IV q8h or Ceftriaxone 100 mg/kg q24h) + Vanco 15 mg/kg q6h	Aztreonam 7.5 mg/kg IV q6h + Linezolid	Major concerns are S. pneumoniae & community-associated MRSA. Coverage for Gm-neg. bacilli included but H. influenzae infection now rare. Meningococcemia mortality remains high (Ln 355:961, 2000).
Adult not neutropenic **NO HYPOTENSION but LIFE-THREATENING**	Aerobic Gm-neg. bacilli; S. aureus; streptococci; others	[(IMP or MER) + Vanco] OR (PIP-TZ + Vanco)	(Dapto 6 mg/kg IV q24h) + (Cefepime or PIP-TZ)	Systemic inflammatory response syndrome (SIRS): 2 or more of the following: 1. Temperature >38°C or <36°C 2. Heart rate >90 beats per min. 3. Respiratory rate >20 breaths per min. 4. WBC >12,000 per mcL or >10% bands **Sepsis:** SIRS + a documented infection (+ culture) **Severe sepsis:** Sepsis + organ dysfunction; hypotension or hypoperfusion abnormalities (lactic acidosis, oliguria, ↓ mental status) **Septic shock:** sepsis-induced hypotension (systolic BP >90 mmHg) not responsive to 500 mL IV fluid challenge + peripheral hypoperfusion.
Source unclear—consider primary bacteremia, intra-abdominal or skin source. May be **Life-threatening**. Survival greater with quicker, effective empiric antibiotic Rx (CCM 38:1045 & 1211, 2010).		**NO HYPOTENSION**—For Septic shock, see page 66 If ESBL and/or carbapenemase-producing GNB. Empiric options pending clarification of clinical syndrome/culture results: **Low prevalence:** Vanco + PIP-TZ **High prevalence:** Colistin + (MER or IMP) (See Table 5B, page 86) *Dosages in footnote[23]*	For Colistin combination dosing, see Table 10A, page 116.	
If suspect biliary source (see Gallbladder page 17)	Enterococci + aerobic Gm-neg. bacilli	PIP-TZ or TC-CL	Ceftriaxone + Metro or (CIP or Levo) + Metro *Dosages—footnote[23]*	If enterococci a concern, add ampicillin or vanco to metro regimens
If community-acquired pneumonia (see page 40 and following pages)	S. pneumoniae; MRSA; Legionella, Gm-neg. bacillus, others	(Levo or Moxi) + (PIP-TZ) + Vanco	Aztreonam + (Levo or Moxi) + Linezolid	Many categories of CAP, see material beginning at page 40. Suggestions based on most severe CAP, e.g., MRSA after influenza or Klebsiella pneumonia in an alcoholic.
If illicit use IV drugs	S. aureus	Vanco if high prevalence of MRSA. Do NOT use empiric Vanco + Oxacillin pending organism ID.	Vanco + PIP-TZ *Dosages in footnote[23]*	If CA-MRSA (JID 195:202, 2007). In vitro nafcillin increased production of toxins by CA-MRSA (JID 195:202, 2007). Dosages in footnote[23]
If suspect intra-abdominal source	Mixture aerobic & anaerobic Gm-neg. bacilli	See secondary peritonitis, page 48.		
If petechial rash	Meningococcemia	Ceftriaxone 2 gm IV q12h (until sure no meningitis); consider Rocky Mountain spotted fever—see page 61		
If suspect urinary source, e.g. pyelonephritis	Aerobic Gm-neg. bacilli & enterococci	See pyelonephritis, page 35		

[23] P Ceph 3 [Cefotaxime 2 gm IV q8h, use q4h if life-threatening; Ceftizoxime 2 gm IV q4h; Ceftriaxone 2 gm IV q12h); PIP-TZ 3.375 gm IV q4h or 4-hr infusion of 3.375 gm q8h, **Aminoglycosides** (See Table 10D, page 122), AMP 200 mg/kg/day divided q6h, **Clinda** 900 mg q8h, IMP 0.5 gm IV q6h, MER 1 gm IV q8h, ERTA 1 gm IV q24h, DORI 500 mg IV q8h (1-hr infusion), **Nafcillin** or **Oxacillin** 2 gm IV q4h, **Aztreonam** 2 gm IV q8h, **Metro** 1 gm loading dose then 0.5 gm q6h or 1 gm IV q12h, **Vanco** loading dose 25-30 mg/kg IV, then 15-20 mg/kg IV q8-12h (dose in obese pt, see Table 7C, page 239), **Ceftazidime** 2 gm IV q8h, [Cefepime 2 gm IV q12h (q8h if neutropenic), Cefpirome*** 2 gm IV q12h), CIP 400 mg IV q12h), Levo 750 mg q24h, Linezolid 600 mg IV q12h.

*NOTE: All dosage recommendations are for adults (unless otherwise indicated) and assume normal renal function. § Alternatives consider allergy; PK, compliance, local resistance, cost.

Abbreviations on page 2.

TABLE 1 (62)

ANATOMIC SITE/DIAGNOSIS/ MODIFYING CIRCUMSTANCES	ETIOLOGIES (usual)	SUGGESTED REGIMENS[a]		ADJUNCT DIAGNOSTIC OR THERAPEUTIC MEASURES AND COMMENTS
		PRIMARY	ALTERNATIVE§	
SYSTEMIC SYNDROMES (FEBRILE/NON-FEBRILE)/Sepsis *(continued)*				
Neutropenia: Child or Adult (absolute PMN count <500 per mm³) in cancer and transplant patients. Guideline: *CID 52:427, 2011[1] (inpatients); J Clin Oncol 31:794, 2013 (outpatients)*				
Prophylaxis *(J Clin Oncol 31:794, 2013)*				
Post-chemotherapy—impending neutropenia	Pneumocystis (PCP), Viridans strep			In patients expected to have PMN <100 for >7 days consider: Levo 500-750 mg po q24h. Acute leukemics undergoing intensive induction consider addition of Fluc 400 mg q24h. In patients with AML or MDS who have prolonged neutropenia, consider Posa instead at 200 mg TID *(N Engl J Med 356:348, 2007)*. Safe & effective during induction rx for acute lymphoblastic leukemia (ALL) *(CID 2017;65:1790)*.
Post allogeneic stem cell transplant	Aerobic Gm-neg bacilli; ↑ risk pneumocystis, herpes viruses, candida aspergillus	TMP-SMX (vs. PCP) + Acyclovir (vs. HSV/VZV)+ pre-emptive monitoring for CMV + Posa (vs. mold)		In autologous HCT, not active prophylaxis nor CMV screening is recommended. Fluc OK with TMP-SMX and acyclovir.
Empiric therapy—febrile neutropenia (≥38.3°C for >1 hr or sustained >38°C and absolute neutrophil count <500 cells/µL) *(IDSA Guidelines: CID 52:427, 2012). (Outpatients: J Clin Oncol 31:794, 2013).*				
Low-risk adults Anticipate <7 days neutropenia, no co-morb, can take po meds	Aerobic Gm-neg bacilli, Viridans strep	CIP 750 mg po bid + AM-CL 875 /125 mg po bid. Treat until absolute neutrophil count >1000 cells/µL.	Treat as outpatients with 24/7 access to 1patient care if: no focal findings, no hypotension, no COPD, no fungal infection, age range 16-60 yrs; motivated and compliant pts and family. If pen allergy: can substitute clinda 300 mg po qid for AM-CL	
High-risk adults and children (Anticipate >7 days profound neutropenia, active co-morbidities)	Aerobic Gm-neg. bacilli; to include P. aeruginosa; cephalosporin-resistant viridans strep; MRSA	**Empiric therapy:** CFP, IMP, MERO, DORI, or PIP-TZ. Consider addition of Vanco as below. *Dosages: See footnote on page 64 and Table 10B* Include empiric Vanco if: Suspected CLABSI, severe mucositis, SSTI, PNA, or hypotension	**Combination therapy:** If pt has severe sepsis/shock, consider add Tobra AND Vanco AND Echinocandin	Increasing resistance of viridans streptococci to penicillins, cephalosporins & FQs *(CID 34:1469 & 1524, 2002)*. What if severe IgE-mediated β-lactam allergy? Aztreonam plus Tobra. Work-up should include blood, urine, CXR with additional testing based on symptoms. Low threshold for CT scan. If cultures remain neg, but pt afebrile, treat until absolute neutrophil count ≥500 cells/µL.
Persistent fever and neutropenia after 5 days of empiric antibacterial therapy—see *CID 52:427, 2011.*	Candida species, aspergillus, VRE, resistant GNB	Add either (Caspofungin 70 mg IV day 1, then 50 mg IV q24h or Micafungin 100 mg IV q24h) or (Anidulafungin 200 mg IV x 1 dose, then 100 mg IV q24h) OR Voriconazole 6 mg per kg IV q12h times 2 doses, then 4 mg per kg IV q12h		Conventional Ampho B causes more fever & nephrotoxicity & lower efficacy than lipic-based ampho B; both Caspofungin & Voriconazole better tolerated; & perhaps more efficacious than lipid-based Ampho B *(NEJM 346:225, 2002 & 351:1391 & 1445, 2005)*.

Abbreviations on page 2.   *NOTE: All dosage recommendations are for adults (unless otherwise indicated) and assume normal renal function. § Alternatives consider allergy; PK; compliance, local resistance, cost.

TABLE 1 (63)

ANATOMIC SITE/DIAGNOSIS/ MODIFYING CIRCUMSTANCES	ETIOLOGIES (usual)	SUGGESTED REGIMENS*		ADJUNCT DIAGNOSTIC OR THERAPEUTIC MEASURES AND COMMENTS
		PRIMARY	ALTERNATIVE§	
SYSTEMIC SYNDROMES (FEBRILE/NON-FEBRILE)/Sepsis *(continued)*				
Shock syndromes **Septic shock: Fever & hypotension** **Bacteremic shock, endotoxin shock** Goals: 1. Effective antibiotics 2. Fluid resuscitation 3. Vasoactive drugs, if needed 4. Source control Refs: Chest 145:1407, 2014; NEJM 369:840, 2013; CCM 188:77, 2013	Bacteremia with aerobic Gm-neg. bacteria or Gm+ cocci	Lower mortality with sepsis treatment "bundle" (NEJM 2017;376-2223, 2235, 2282) • Blood cultures & serum lactate • Initiate effective antibiotic therapy: ○ No clear source but high prevalence of MDR GNB: **PIP-TZ + Vanco** ○ No clear source but high prevalence of K. pneumoniae: **[Polymyxin B** (preferred) **or Colistin + (MER or IMP)]** • IV crystalloid: 20-40 mL/kg for hypotension or elevated lactate; prefer lactated Ringers (AnIM 161:347 & 372, 2014) • If hypotensive after fluids, nor-epinephrine • Attempt to identify & correct source of bacteremia • Monitor lactate & central venous O$_2$ sat (target ≥70%) (NEJM 369:2126, 2013) • Transfuse if hematocrit <30% (NEJM 371:1381, 2014) • See Comment for continuation.		• Hydrocortisone in stress dose: 100 mg IV q8h if BP still low after fluids and one vasopressor. Benefit in pts with severe shock (CCM 2017:45-2078). • Insulin Rx: Current target is glucose level of 140-180 mg/dL. Attempts at tight control (80-110 mg/dL) resulted in excessive hypoglycemia (NEJM 363:2540, 2010). • Impact of early effective antibiotic therapy (CCM 38:1045 & 1211, 2010) • Bacteremia due to carbapenemase-producing K. pneumoniae: lowest mortality with combination rx: carbapenem + Polymyxin B (preferred over Colistin unless urinary tract source) (AAC 58:2322, 2014). • Number of pts needed to treat with appropriate antimicrobial rx to prevent one pt death reported as 4 (CCM 42:2342 & 2444, 2014). • Shock associated with leaky capillaries which results in increased volume of drug distribution. Hence, need loading dose of antibiotics and, early in treatment, larger maintenance doses (AAC 59:22995, 2015).
Septic shock: post-splenectomy or functional asplenia Asplenic pt care: Chest 2016; 150:1394	S. pneumoniae, N. meningitidis, H. influenzae, Capnocytophaga (DF-2)	No dog bite: **Ceftriaxone 2 gm** IV q24h (↑ to 2 gm q12h if meningitis) Post-dog bite: **(PIP-TZ 3.375 gm** IV q6h OR **MER 1 gm** IV q8h) **+ Clinda 900 mg** IV q8h	No dog bite: **(Levo 750 mg** or **Moxi 400 mg)** one IV q24h	Howell-Jolly bodies in peripheral blood smear confirm absence of functional spleen. Often results in symmetrical peripheral gangrene of digits due to severe DIC. For prophylaxis, see Table 15A, page 208. Vaccines: CID 58:309, 2014.
Toxic shock syndrome. Clostridium sordellii Clinical picture: shock, capillary leak, hypoconcentration, leukemoid reaction, afebrile Ref. CID 43:1436 & 1447, 2006.	Clostridium sordellii; hemorrhagic & lethal toxins	Fluids, aq. **Penicillin G** 18-20 million units per day div. q4-6h + **Clindamycin 900 mg** IV q8h. Surgical debridement is key.		Occurs in variety of settings that produce anaerobic tissue, e.g., post-partum. Several deaths reported after use of abortifacient regimen of mifepristone (RU486) & misoprostol. Since 2006, switch to po mifepristone & then vaginal misoprostol, instead of vaginal misoprostol. 2001-2006 standard medical abortion: po mifepristone, plus prophylactic Doxy resulted in dramatic decrease in clostridial TSS (NEJM 361:145, 2009). Mortality nearly 100% if WBC >50,000/µL.
Toxic shock syndrome, staphylococcal. Review: LnID 9:281, 1009 Colonization by toxin-producing Staph. aureus of vagina (tampon-assoc.), surgical/ traumatic wounds, endometrium, burns	Staph. aureus (toxic shock toxin-mediated)	**(Nafcillin** or **Oxacillin 2 gm** IV q4h) or (if MRSA, **Vanco** 15-20 mg/kg q8-12h) + **Clinda** 600-900 mg IV q8h + IVIG (Dose in Comment)	**(Cefazolin** 1-2 gm IV q8h) or (if MRSA, **Vanco** 15-20 mg/kg q8-12h OR **Dapto** 6 mg/kg IV q24h) **Clinda** 600-900 mg IV q8h+ **IVIG** (Dose in Comment)	**IVIG reasonable** (see Streptococcal TSS) – dose 1 gm per kg on day 1, then 0.5 gm per kg days 2 & 3 – antitoxin antibodies present. If suspect TSS, "turn off" toxin production with clinda: report of success with Linezolid (CID 195:202, 2007). Exposure of MRSA to nafcillin increased toxin production in vitro. JID 195:202, 2007.

Abbreviations on page 2.   *NOTE: All dosage recommendations are for adults (unless otherwise indicated) and assume normal renal function. § Alternatives consider allergy, PK, compliance, local resistance, cost.

TABLE 1 (64)

ANATOMIC SITE/DIAGNOSIS/ MODIFYING CIRCUMSTANCES	ETIOLOGIES (usual)	SUGGESTED REGIMENS*		ADJUNCT DIAGNOSTIC OR THERAPEUTIC MEASURES AND COMMENTS
		PRIMARY	ALTERNATIVE§	
SYSTEMIC SYNDROMES (FEBRILE/NON-FEBRILE)/SEPSIS/SHOCK syndromes				
Toxic shock syndrome, streptococcal. NOTE: For Necrotizing fasciitis without fever shock, *see page 58.* Ref: *LnID 9:281, 2009.*				
Associated with **invasive disease,** i.e., erysipelas, necro-tizing fasciitis; secondary strep infection of varicella. Secondary household contact TSS cases reported (*NEJM 335:547 & 590, 1996; CID 27:150, 1998*).	Group A, B, C, & G Strep. pyogenes, Group B strep ref: *EID 15:223, 2009.*	(**Pen G** 24 million units per day IV in div. doses) plus (**Clinda** 900 mg IV q8h).	**Ceftriaxone** 2 gm IV q24h + **Clinda** 900 mg IV q8h.	**Definition:** isolation of Group A strep, hypotension and ≥2 of: renal impairment, coagulopathy, liver involvement, ARDS, generalized rash, soft tissue necrosis. Associated with invasive disease. **Surgery usually required.** Mortality 30-50%, myositis 80% even with early rx (*CID 14:2, 1992*). Clinda: ↓ toxin production. Use of NSAID may predispose to TSS. For reasons pen G may fail in fulminant S. pyogenes infections (*see JID 167:1401, 1993*).
		Prospective observational study (*CID 59:358, 366 & 851, 2014*) indicates:		
		• Clinda decreases mortality		
		• IVIG perhaps of benefit: 1 gm/kg on day 1, then 0.5 gm/kg days 2, 3		
		• High incidence of secondary cases in household contacts		
Toxin-Mediated Syndromes—no fever unless complicated				
Botulism (*CID 41:1167, 2005. As biologic weapon: JAMA 285:1059, 2001; www.bt.cdc.gov*)				
	Clostridium botulinum	For all types: Follow vital capacity; other supportive care	Heptavalent equine serum antitoxin—CDC (*see Comment*)	Equine **antitoxin.** Heptavalent currently only antitoxin available (U.S.) for non-infant botulism: CDC (+1 404-639-2206 M-F OR +1 404-639-2888 evenings/weekends). For infants, *use Baby BIG (human botulism immune globulin): California Infant Botulism Treat & Prevent Program.*
Food-borne Dyspnea at presentation bad sign (*CID 43:1247, 2006*).	Less common: C. barati, C. butyricum	If no ileus, purge GI tract		
			No antibiotics; may lyse C. botulinum in gut and ↑ load of toxin	**Antimicrobials:** May make infant botulism worse. Untested in wound botulism. When used, pen G 10-20 million units per day usual dose. If complications (pneumonia, UTI) occur, avoid antimicrobials with assoc. neuromuscular blockade, i.e., aminoglycosides, tetracycline, polymyxins. **Differential dx:** Guillain-Barré, myasthenia gravis, tick paralysis, organo-phosphate toxicity, West Nile virus. EMG can help.
Infant (Adult intestinal botulism is rare variant: EIN 18:1, 2012).		Human botulinum immunoglobulin (BIG) IV, single dose. Call (+1) 510-540-2646. Do not use equine antitoxin.		
Wound		Debridement & anaerobic cultures. No proven value of local antitoxin. Role of antibiotics untested.	Trivalent equine antitoxin (*see Comment*)	Wound botulism can result from spore contamination of tar heroin. Ref: *CID 31:1018, 2000.* Mouse bioassay failed to detect toxin in 1/3 of patients (*CID 48:1669, 2009*).
Tetanus: Trismus, generalized muscle rigidity, muscle spasm Ref: *AnIM 154:329, 2011.*	C. tetani-production of tetanospasmin toxin	Six treatment steps: 1. Urgent endotracheal intubation to protect the airway. Laryngeal spasm is common. Early tracheostomy. 2. Eliminate reflex spasms with diazepam, 20 mg/day IV or midazolam. Worst cases: need neuromuscular blockade with vecuronium. 3. Neutralize toxin: Human hyperimmune globulin IM; start tetanus immunization—Human immunity from clinical tetanus. 4. Surgically debride infected source tissue. Start antibiotic: (**Pen G** 3 million units IV q4h or **Doxy** 100 mg IV q12h or **Metro** 1000 mg IV q12h) x 7-10 days. 5. Avoid light as may precipitate muscle spasms. 6. Use beta blockers, e.g., short acting esmolol, to control sympathetic hyperactivity.		Reports of benefit: combining diazepam with magnesium sulfate (*Ln 368:1436, 2006*).

Abbreviations on page 2.   *NOTE: All dosage recommendations are for adults (unless otherwise indicated) and assume normal renal function. § Alternatives consider allergy, PK, compliance, local resistance, cost.*

TABLE 1 (65)

ANATOMIC SITE/DIAGNOSIS/ MODIFYING CIRCUMSTANCES	ETIOLOGIES (usual)	SUGGESTED REGIMENS*		ADJUNCT DIAGNOSTIC OR THERAPEUTIC MEASURES AND COMMENTS
		PRIMARY	ALTERNATIVE§	
VASCULAR				
IV line infection (See IDSA Guidelines CID 49:1, 2009).				
Heparin lock, midline catheter, **non-tunneled** central venous catheter (subclavian, internal jugular), peripherally inserted central catheter (PICC). 2008 study found ↑ infection risk/thrombosis if femoral vein used, esp. if BMI >28.4 (JAMA 299:2413, 2008). **See Comment**	Staph. epidermidis, Staph. aureus (MSSA/MRSA). **Diagnosis:** Fever & either + blood cult from line & peripheral vein OR >15 colonies on tip of removed line OR culture from catheter positive 2 hrs earlier than peripheral vein culture.	**Vanco** 15-20 mg/kg q8-12h. **Other alternatives—See Comment.** Other rx and duration: **(1)** If **S. aureus**, remove catheter. Can use TEE result to determine if 2 or 4 wks of therapy (JAC 57:1172, 2006). **(2)** If **S. epidermidis**, can try to "save" catheter. 80% cure after 7-10 days of therapy. With only systemic antibiotics, high rate of recurrence (CID 49:1187, 2009). If **leuconostoc** or **lactobacillus**, which are Vanco resistant, need **Pen G, Amp** or **Clinda**.	For documented MSSA **Nafcillin** or **Oxacillin** 2 gm IV q4h or **Cefazolin** 2 gm IV q8h. If no response to, or intolerant of, **Vanco**: switch to **Daptomycin** 6 mg per kg IV q24h. Culture removed catheter. With "roll" method, >15 colonies (NEJM 312:1142, 1985) suggests infection. Lines do not require "routine" changing when not infected. When infected, do not insert new catheter over a wire. Antimicrobial-impregnated catheters may ↓ infection risk; the debate is lively (CID 37:65, 2003 & 38:1287, 2004 & 39:1829, 2004). Are femoral lines more prone to infection than subclavian or internal jugular lines? Meta-analysis: no difference (CCM 40:2479, 2012). In random vein study, subclavian site had lowest risk of infection & thrombosis (NEJM 373:1220, 2015).
Tunnel type indwelling venous catheters and ports (Browiac, Hickman, Groshong, Quinton), dual lumen hemodialysis catheters (Permacath). For **prevention, see below.**	Staph. epidermidis, Staph. aureus, (Candida sp.). Rarely: leuconostoc or lactobacillus—both resistant to vanco (see Table 2, page 71) (Dx, see above)	If neutropenic or burn pt, add anti-pseudomonas drug, e.g., **PIP-TZ.** If pt receiving hyperalimentation, add **Micafungin** as empiric therapy for Candida sp.		If subcutaneous tunnel infected, very low cure rates; need to remove catheter. Beware of silent infection in clotted hemodialysis catheters. Indium scans detect (Am J Kid Dis 40:832, 2002). Etiologic bacteria & antibiotic resistance in central IV lines of oncology pts (CID 62:1203, 2016).
Impaired host (burn, neutropenic)	As above + Pseudomonas sp., Enterobacteriaceae, Corynebacterium jeikeium, aspergillus, rhizopus	[**Vanco** + (**Cefepime** or **Ceftaz**)] or (**Vanco** + **PIP-TZ**) or **IMP** or [(**Cefepime** or **Ceftaz**) + **Aminoglycoside**]. (Dosage in footnotes, page 64).		Usually have associated septic thrombophlebitis: biopsy of vein to rule out fungi. If fungal, surgical excision + amphotericin B. Surgical drainage, ligation or removal often indicated.
Hyperalimentation	With tunnel: Candida sp. common (see Table 11, resistant Candida species)	If candida, **Voriconazole** or an echinocandin (**Anidulafungin, Micafungin, Caspofungin**) if clinically stable. Dosage: see Table 11B, page 137.		Remove venous catheter and discontinue antimicrobial agents if possible. Ophthalmologic consultation recommended. **Rx all patients with + blood cultures.** Table 11A, Candidiasis, page 126
Intravenous lipid emulsion	Staph. epidermidis, Malassezia furfur	**Vanco** 1 gm IV q12h. **Fluconazole** 400 mg IV q24h		Discontinue intralipid
Prevention of Infection of Long-Term IV Lines CID 52:1087, 2011	To minimize risk of infection: Hand washing and **1.** Maximal sterile barrier precautions during catheter insertion **2.** Use >0.5% chlorhexidine prep with alcohol for skin antisepsis **3.** If infection rate high despite #1 & 2, use either chlorhexidine/silver sulfadiazine or minocycline/rifampin-impregnated catheters or "lock" solutions (see Comment). **4.** If possible, use subclavian vein, avoid femoral vessels. Lower infection risk in jugular vs. femoral vein if BMI >28.4 (JAMA 299:2413, 2008).			IV line "lock" solutions under study. No FDA-approved product. Reports of the combination of TMP, EDTA & ethanol (AAC 55:4430, 2011). Trials to begin in Europe. Another report: lock soln of sodium citrate, methylene blue, methylparabens (CCM 39:613, 2011). Recent meeting abstracts support 70% ethanol.

Abbreviations on page 2.   *NOTE: All dosage recommendations are for adults (unless otherwise indicated) and assume normal renal function. § Alternatives consider allergy, PK, compliance, local resistance, cost.

TABLE 1 (66)

ANATOMIC SITE/DIAGNOSIS/ MODIFYING CIRCUMSTANCES	ETIOLOGIES (usual)	SUGGESTED REGIMENS*		ADJUNCT DIAGNOSTIC OR THERAPEUTIC MEASURES AND COMMENTS
		PRIMARY	ALTERNATIVE§	
VASCULAR/IV line Infection *(continued)*				
Mycotic aneurysm	S. aureus (28-71%), S. epidermidis, Salmonella sp. (15-24%), M.TBc, S. pneumonia, many others	**Vanco** (dose sufficient to achieve trough level of 15-20 µg/mL.) + (**Ceftriaxone or CIP**)	**Dapto** could be substituted for Vanco. For GNB: **Cefepime** or **Carbapenems**. For MDR-GNB, [**Polymyxin B** (preferred) or **Colistin**] + **MER**	No data for cefaroline or telavancin. Best diagnostic imaging: CT angiogram. Blood cultures positive in 50-85%. **De-escalate to specific therapy when culture results known**. Treatment duration varies but usually 6 wks from date of definitive surgery.
		Treatment is combination of antibiotic + surgical resection with revascularization.		
Suppurative (Septic) Thrombophlebitis				
Cranial dural sinus:				
Cavernous Sinus CN III, IV, V (branches V1/V2), VI at risk (Note: VI and V2, numbers are subscript)	S. aureus (70%) Streptococcus sp. Anaerobes (rare) Mucormycosis (diabetes)	[**Vanco** (dose for trough conc of 15-20 µg/mL.) + **Ceftriaxone** 2 gm IV q12h], add **Metro** 500 mg IV q8h if dental/sinus source	(**Dapto** 8-12 mg/kg IV q24h OR **Linezolid** 600 mg IV q12h), add **Metro** 500 mg IV q8h if dental/sinus source	• Diagnosis: CT & MRI • Treatment: 1) obtain specimen for culture; 2) empiric antibiotics; 3) may need adjunctive surgery; 4) heparin until afebrile, then coumadin for severa weeks
Lateral Sinus: Complication of otitis media/mastoiditis (pathogens similar to otitis media)	Polymicrobial (often) Aerobes, e.g., Proteus sp, E. coli S. aureus P. aeruginosa B. fragilis Other GNB	**Cefepime** 2 gm IV q8h + **Metro** 500 mg IV q8h + **Vanco** (dose for trough conc of 15-20 µg/mL.)	**Meropenem** 2 gm IV q8h + **Linezolid** 600 mg IV q12h	• Diagnosis: CT & MRI • Treatmeat: 1) consider radical mastoidectomy; 2) obtain cultures; 3) antibiotics; 2) anticoagulation controversial • Prognosis: favorable
Superior Sagittal Sinus: Complication of bacterial meningitis or bacterial frontal sinusitis	S. pneumoniae N. meningitides H. influenzae (rare) S. aureus (very rare)	As for meningitis: **Ceftriaxone** 2 gm IV q12h + **Vanco** (dose for trough conc of 15-20 µg/mL.) + **Dexamethasone**	As for meningitis: **Meropenem** 2 gm IV q8h + **Vanco** (dose for trough conc of 15-20 µg/mL.) + **Dexamethasone**	• Diagnosis: MRI • Prognosis: bad; causes cortical vein thrombosis, hemorrhagic infarcts and brainstem herniation. Anticoagulants not recommended

Abbreviations on page 2. *§NOTE: All dosage recommendations are for adults (unless otherwise indicated) and assume normal renal function. § Alternatives consider allergy, PK, compliance, local resistance, cost.*

TABLE 1 (67)

ANATOMIC SITE/DIAGNOSIS/ MODIFYING CIRCUMSTANCES	ETIOLOGIES (usual)	SUGGESTED REGIMENS* PRIMARY	SUGGESTED REGIMENS* ALTERNATIVE§	ADJUNCT DIAGNOSTIC OR THERAPEUTIC MEASURES AND COMMENTS
VASCULAR/Suppurative (Septic) Thrombophlebitis *(continued)*				
Jugular Vein, Lemierre's Syndrome: Complication of pharyngitis, tonsillitis, dental infection, EBV. Ref: *NEJM 371:2018, 2015.*	Fusobacterium necrophorum (anaerobe) Less often: Other Fusobacterium S. pyogenes Bacteroides sp.	(**PIP-TZ** 3.375 gm IV q6h OR **Amp-Sulb** 3 gm IV q6h) x 4 weeks	[**Imipenem** 500 mg IV q6h OR (**Metro** 500 mg IV q8h + **Ceftriaxone** 2 gm IV once daily)] x 4 weeks. Another option: **Clinda** 600-900 mg IV q8h	• Diagnosis: Preceding pharyngitis and antibiotics therapy, persistent fever and pulmonary emboli • Imaging: Hi-res CT scan • Role of anticoagulants unclear
Pelvic Vein: Includes ovarian vein and deep pelvic vein phlebitis	Aerobic gram-neg bacilli Streptococcus sp. Anaerobes	Antibiotics + anticoagulation (heparin, then coumadin). *Low prevalence of MDR GNB:* **PIP-TZ** 3.375 gm IV q6h OR 4.5 gm IV q6h OR (**Ceftriaxone** 2 gm IV once daily + **Metro** 500 mg IV q8h)	*High prevalence of MDR GNB:* **Meropenem** 1 gm IV q8h. If severe beta-lactam allergy: **CIP** 400 mg IV q12h + **Metro** 500 mg IV q8h)	• Diagnosis: ovarian vein infection presents 1 week post-partum with fever & local pain; deep pelvic vein presents 3-5 days post-delivery with fever but no local pain. CT or MRI may help. • Treat until afebrile for 48 hrs & WBC normal • Coumadin for 6 weeks
Portal Vein (Pylephlebitis): Complication of diverticulitis, appendicitis and (rarely) other intra-abdominal infection	Aerobic gram-neg bacilli: E. coli, Klebsiella & Proteus most common. Other: aerobic/anaerobic streptococci, B. fragilis, Clostridia	*Low prevalence of MDR GNB (<20%):* **PIP-TZ** 4.5 gm IV q8h OR (**CIP** 400 mg IV q12h + **Metro** 500 mg IV q8h)	*High prevalence of MDR GNB (≥20%):* If ESBL producer: **Meropenem** 1 gm IV q8h; If carbapenemase producer: (**Polymyxin B** (preferred) or **Colistin**) + **MER**	• Diagnosis: Pain, fever, neutrophilia in pt with intra-abdominal infection. • Abdominal CT scan • Pyogenic liver abscess is a complication • No anticoagulants unless hypercoagulable disease (neoplasm) • Surgery on vein not indicated

*NOTE: All dosage recommendations are for adults (unless otherwise indicated) and assume normal renal function. §Alternatives consider allergy; PK, compliance, local resistance, cost.

TABLE 2 – RECOMMENDED ANTIMICROBIAL AGENTS AGAINST SELECTED BACTERIA

BACTERIAL SPECIES	ANTIMICROBIAL AGENT (See page 2 for abbreviations)		
	RECOMMENDED	ALTERNATIVE	ALSO EFFECTIVE[1] (COMMENTS)
Achromobacter xylosoxidans spp xylosoxidans (formerly Alcaligenes)	IMP, MER, DORI (no DORI for pneumonia)	TMP-SMX. Some strains susc. to ceftaz, PIP-TZ	Resistant to aminoglycosides, most cephalosporins & FQs. Ref: *Ann Amer Thor Soc 12:252, 2015*
Acinetobacter calcoaceticus– baumannii complex	If suscept: IMP or MER or DORI. For MDR strains: (Polymyxin B or Colistin) + (IMP or MER)	AM-SB used for activity of sulbactam (CID 51:79, 2010). Perhaps Minocycline IV	Resistant to aminoglycosides, FQs. Minocycline, effective against many strains (CID 51:79, 2010) (See Table 5B, page 86)
Actinomyces israelii	AMP or Pen G	Doxy, Ceftriaxone	Clindamycin, Erythro
Aeromonas hydrophila & other sp.	CIP or Levo	TMP-SMX or (P Ceph 3, 4)	See AAC 56:1110, 2012.
Arcanobacterium haemolyticum	Azithro	Pen G, Ceftriaxone, Vancomycin, and many other agents	Resistance to TMP-SMX (AAC 38: 142, 1994). Resistance to Levofloxacin, Clindamycin reported (J Med Microbiol 64: 369, 2015)
Bacillus anthracis (anthrax): inhalation	See Table 1, page 41.		
Bacillus cereus, B. subtilis	Vancomycin, Clinda	FQ, IMP	
Bacteroides sp., B. fragilis & others	Metronidazole or PIP-TZ	DORI, ERTA, IMP, MER, AM-CL	Increasing resistance to: Clinda, Cefoxitin, Cefotetan, Moxi. Ref: CID 59:698, 2014.
Bartonella henselae, quintana See Table 1, pages 30, 46, 52, 59	Varies with disease entity & immune status. Active: Azithro, Clarithro, Erythro, Doxy & in combination: RIF, Gent, Ceftriaxone. Not active: CIP, TMP-SMX, Pen, most cephalosporins, Aztreonam.		
Bordetella pertussis	Azithro or clarithro	TMP-SMX	See PIDJ 31:78, 2012.
Borrelia burgdorferi, B. afzelii, B. garinii (Lyme & relapsing fever)	See specific disease entity		
Brucella sp.	Drugs & duration vary with localization or non-localization. See specific disease entities. PLoS One 7:e32090, 2012.		
Burkholderia cepacia	TMP-SMX or MER or CIP	Minocycline or chloramphenicol	Multiple mechanisms of resistance. Need culture & sensitivity to guide therapy (Sem Resp Crit Care Med 36:99, 2015)
Burkholderia pseudomallei Curr Opin Infect Dis 23:554, 2010; CID 41:1105, 2005	Initially, IV Ceftaz or IMP or MER, then po (TMP-SMX + Doxy x 3 mos) (AAC 49:4010, 2005). One study showed TMP-SMX alone was non-inferior to combination with Doxy (Lancet 383: 807, 2014)		(Thai, 12–80% strains resist to TMP-SMX). FQ not very active in vitro. AM-CL possible alternative to TMP-SMX (Int J Antimicrob Agents 43: 310, 2014).
Campylobacter jejuni	Azithro	Erythro or CIP	TMP-SMX, Pen & cephalosporins not active.
Campylobacter fetus	Gentamicin	IMP or Ceftriaxone	AMP, Chloramphenicol
Capnocytophaga ochracea (DF-1)	Dog bite: Clinda or AM-CL	Septic shock, post-splenectomy: PIP-TZ, Clinda, IMP, DORI, MER	FQ activity variable; aminoglycosides, TMP-SMX & Polymyxins have limited activity. LN ID 9:439, 2009.
Capnocytophaga canimorsus (DF-2)	Dog bite: AM-CL, PIP-TZ, CFP		
Chlamydophila pneumoniae	Doxy	Azithro, FQ	Clarithro
Chlamydia trachomatis	Doxy or Azithro	Erythro	
Citrobacter diversus (koseri), C. freundii	Life threatening illness: IMP, MER, DORI	Non-life threatening illness: CIP or Gent	Emergence of resistance: AAC 52:995, 2007.
Clostridium difficile	Mild illness: Metronidazole (po)	Moderate/severe illness: Vancomycin (po) or Fidaxomicin (CID 51:1306, 2010).	See also Table 1, page 19 re severity of disease.
Clostridium perfringens	Pen G ± clindamycin	Doxy	Erythro, Chloramphenicol, Cefazolin, Cefoxitin, PIP-TZ, Carbapenems
Clostridium tetani	Metronidazole	Doxy	Role of antibiotics unclear.
Corynebacterium diphtheriae	Erythro + antitoxin	Pen G + antitoxin	RIF reported effective (CID 27:845, 1998)
Corynebacterium jeikeium	Vancomycin	Daptomycin	Most strains are resistant to pen and Erythro (Clin Microbiol Inf 2: 209, 1996)
Corynebacterium minutissimum	Clinda 1% lotion	Clarithro or Erythro	Causes erythrasma
Coxiella burnetii (Q fever) acute disease (CID 52:1431, 2011).	Doxy, FQ (see Table 1, page 31)	Erythro, Azithro, Clarithro	Endocarditis: Doxy + hydroxychloroquine (JID 188:1322, 2003; LnID 3:709, 2003; LnID 10:527, 2010).
chronic disease, e.g., endocarditis	Doxy + hydroxy chloroquine	TMP-SMX, Chloro	
Ehrlichia chaffeensis Ehrlichia ewingii Anaplasma phagocytophila	Doxy	Rifampin (no large studies)	Chloro not effective. In severe infections, consider doxycycline desensitization if allergic (MMWR 65(2): 1, 2016).
Eikenella corrodens	AM-CL, IV Pen G	TMP-SMX, FQ	Resistant to Clinda, Cephalexin, Erythro, Metro, Diclox

TABLE 2 (2)

BACTERIAL SPECIES	ANTIMICROBIAL AGENT (See page 2 for abbreviations)		
	RECOMMENDED	ALTERNATIVE	ALSO EFFECTIVE[1] (COMMENTS)
Elizabethkingia meningoseptica (formerly Chryseobacterium)	Levo or TMP-SMX	CIP, Minocycline	Resistant to Pen, cephalosporins, carbapenems, aminoglycosides, Vanco (JCM 44:1181, 2006)
Enterobacter species	Recommended agents vary with clinical setting and degree and mechanism of resistance.		
Enterococcus faecalis	Highly resistant. See Table 5A, page 85		
Enterococcus faecium	Highly resistant. See Table 5A, page 85		
Erysipelothrix rhusiopathiae	Penicillin G or amox	P Ceph 3, FQ	IMP, PIP-TZ (vancomycin, APAG, TMP-SMX resistant)
Escherichia coli	Can be highly resistant. Treatment varies with degree & mechanism of resistance, see Table 5B.		
Francisella tularensis (tularemia) See Table 1, page 43	Gentamicin, Tobramycin, or Streptomycin	Mild infection: Doxy or CIP	Chloramphenicol, RIF. Doxy/chloro bacteriostatic → relapses CID 53:e133, 2011.
Gardnerella vaginalis (bacterial vaginosis)	Metronidazole or Tinidazole	Clindamycin	See Table 1, page 26 for dosage
Helicobacter pylori	See Table 1, page 21		Drugs effective in vitro often fail in vivo.
Haemophilus aphrophilus (Aggregatibacter aphrophilus)	[(Penicillin or AMP) ± Gentamicin] or [AM- SB ± Gent]	(Ceftriaxone ± Gent) or CIP or Levo	Resistant to Vanco, Clinda, Methicillin
Haemophilus ducreyi (chancroid)	Azithro or Ceftriaxone	Erythro, CIP	Most strains resistant to Tetracycline, Amox, TMP-SMX
Haemophilus influenzae Meningitis, epiglottitis & other life-threatening illness	Cefotaxime, Ceftriaxone	AMP if susceptible and β-lactamase neg, FQs	Chloramphenicol rarely used due to hematotoxicity.
non-life threatening illness	AM-CL, O Ceph 2/3		Azithro, Clarithro, Telithro
Klebsiella ozaenae/ rhinoscleromatis	CIP		Acta Otolaryngol 131:440, 2010.
Klebsiella species	Treatment varies with degree & mechanism of resistance, see Table 5B.		
Lactobacillus species	Pen G or AMP	Clindamycin	**May be resistant to vancomycin**
Legionella sp.	Levo or Moxi	Azithro	Telithro active in vitro.
Leptospira interrogans	Mild: Doxy or Amox	Severe: Pen G or ceftriaxone	
Leuconostoc	Pen G or AMP	Clinda	**NOTE: Resistant to vancomycin**
Listeria monocytogenes	AMP ± Gent for synergy	TMP-SMX	Erythro, penicillin G (high dose); APAG may be synergistic with β-lactams. Meropenem active in vitro. **Cephalosporin-resistant!**
Moraxella (Branhamella) catarrhalis	AM-CL or O Ceph 2/3, TMP-SMX	Azithro, Clarithro, Dirithromycin, Telithro	Erythro, Doxy, FQs
Mycoplasma pneumoniae	Doxy	Azithro, Minocycline	Clindamycin & ß lactams NOT effective. Increasing macrolide resistance (JAC 68:506, 2013; AAC 58:1034, 2014).
Neisseria gonorrhoeae (gonococcus)	Ceftriaxone,	Azithro (high dose)	FQs and oral cephalosporins no longer recommended: high levels of resistance.
Neisseria meningitidis (meningococcus)	Ceftriaxone	Chloro, MER	(Chloro less effective than other alternatives: see JAC 70:979, 2015)
Nocardia asteroides or **Nocardia brasiliensis**	TMP-SMX + IMP	Linezolid	Amikacin + (IMP or ceftriaxone or Cefotaxime) (AAC 58:795, 2014).
Pasteurella multocida	Pen G, AMP, Amox, AM-CL, Cefuroxime, Cefpodoxime	Doxy, Levo, Moxi, TMP-SMX	Resistant to Cephalexin, Oxacillin, Clindamycin, Erythro, Vanco. Rare beta-lactamase-producing isolates have been reported (EJCMID 20: 210, 2001).
Plesiomonas shigelloides	CIP	TMP-SMX	AM-CL, Ceftriaxone & Chloro active. Resistant to: Amp, Tetra, aminoglycosides
Propionibacterium acnes (not acne)	Penicillin, Ceftriaxone	Vanco, Dapto, Linezolid	May be resistant to Metro.
Proteus sp, Providencia sp, Morganella sp. (Need in vitro susceptibility)	Recommended drugs vary with clinical setting and frequency & mechanism of resistance.		
Pseudomonas aeruginosa (ID Clin No Amer 23:277, 2009). Combination therapy? See Clin Micro Rev 25:450, 2012.	No in vitro resistance: PIP-TZ, AP Ceph 3, DORI, IMP, MER, Tobra, CIP, Aztreonam. For serious inf., use AP β-lactam + (Tobra or CIP)	For UTI, if no in vitro resistance, single drugs effective: PIP-TZ, AP Ceph 3, Cefepime, IMP, MER, aminoglycoside, CIP, Aztreonam	If resistant to all beta lactams, FQs, aminoglycosides: Colistin + MER or IMP. Do not use DORI for pneumonia. Suggest consult for extensively resistant strains.
Rhodococcus (C. equi)	Customary to use combination Rx. Choose 2 from: Azithro, Levo, or Rif (Lancet ID 10:350, 2010).	(Vanco or IMP) + (Azithro, Levo or RIF)	Vancomycin active in vitro; intracellular location may impair efficacy (CID 34:1379, 2002). Avoid Pen, Cephalosporins, Clinda, Tetra, TMP-SMX.
Rickettsia species (includes spotted fevers)	Doxy	Chloramphenicol (in pregnancy)	See specific infections (Table 1). (MMWR 65(RR-2):1, 2016)

TABLE 2 (3)

BACTERIAL SPECIES	ANTIMICROBIAL AGENT (See page 2 for abbreviations)		
	RECOMMENDED	**ALTERNATIVE**	**ALSO EFFECTIVE[1] (COMMENTS)**
Salmonella typhi (CID 50:241, 2010; AAC 54:5201, 2010; BMC ID 51:37, 2005)	If FQ & nalidixic acid susceptible: CIP	Ceftriaxone, Cefixime, Azithro, Chloro	Concomitant steroids in severely ill. Watch for relapse (1-6%) & ileal perforation. FQ resistance reported with treatment failures (AAC 52:1278, 2008). Chloro less effective than other alternatives: see JAC 70:979, 2015).
Serratia marcescens	If no in vitro resistance: PIP-TZ, LEVO, Gent	If in vitro resistance due to ESBL: Carbapenem	Avoid extended spectrum Ceph if possible. See specific syndrome if MDR documented.
Shigella sp.	FQ or azithro	Ceftriaxone is alternative; TMP-SMX depends on susceptibility.	
Staph. aureus, methicillin-susceptible	Oxacillin/Nafcillin	P Ceph 1, Vanco, Teicoplanin[NUS], Clinda, Ceftaroline	ERTA, IMP, MER, AM-CL, FQ, PIP-TZ, Linezolid, Dapto, Telavancin.
Staph. aureus, methicillin-resistant (health-care associated) IDSA Guidelines: CID 52 (Feb 1):1, 2011.	Vancomycin	Teicoplanin[NUS], TMP-SMX (some strains resistant), Linezolid, Daptomycin, Telavancin, Ceftaroline	Fusidic acid[NUS], >60% CIP-resistant in U.S. (Fosfomycin + RIF). Partially Vanco-resistant strains (GISA, VISA) & highly resistant strains now described—see Table 6, page 87.
Staph. aureus, methicillin-resistant [community- associated (CA-MRSA)]	(TMP-SMX or Doxy or Mino)	Clinda (if D-test neg— see Table 5A & 6).	CA-MRSA usually multi-resistant. Oft resist. to Erythro & Variably to FQ. Vanco, Teico[NUS], Telavancin, Dapto, Ceftaroline can be used in pts requiring hospitalization (see Table 6, page 87).
	Vanco or Teico[NUS]	Linezolid or Dapto	
Staph. epidermidis	If Oxa-susceptible: oxacillin, nafcillin, cefazolin If Oxa-resistant: Vancomycin	Dapto, linezolid	Rifampin (if Susceptible) often used with (FQ or TMP-SMX) for infections assoc with prostheses.
Staph. haemolyticus	If Oxa-susceptible: oxacillin, nafcillin, cefazolin If Oxa-resistant: Vancomycin	Dapto, linezolid	For UTI: TMP-SMX, nitrofurantoin, oral ceph, FQ may be active.
Staph. lugdunensis	If Oxa-susceptible: oxacillin, nafcillin, cefazolin If Oxa-resistant: Vancomycin	PenG if pen-susceptible. Daptomycin, linezolid. If Oxa-susc: oral ceph or AM-CL.	Approx 52% susceptible to penG and 95% to oxacillin; high rates of susc to doxy or TMP-SMX (JCM 55: 585, 2017).
Staph. saprophyticus (UTI)	Oral cephalosporin or AM-CL	FQ	Almost always methicillin-susceptible
Stenotrophomonas (Xanthomonas, Pseudomonas) maltophilia	TMP-SMX	Minocycline (Diag Micro Infect Dis 85:352, 2016; JAC 2016,71:1071)	FQ (if in vitro suscept)(AAC 2014,58:176)
Streptobacillus moniliformis	Penicillin G	Doxy	Maybe Erythro, Clinda, Ceftriaxone
Streptococcus, anaerobic (Peptostreptococcus)	Penicillin G	Clindamycin	Doxy, vancomycin, linezolid, ERTA (AAC 51:2205, 2007).
Streptococcus anginosus group	Penicillin	Vanco or Ceftriaxone	Avoid FQs; macrolide resistance emerging
Streptococcus pneumoniae penicillin-susceptible	Penicillin G, Amox	Multiple agents effective, e.g., Ceph 2/3, Clinda	If meningitis, higher dose, see Table 1, page 10.
penicillin-resistant (MIC ≥2.0)	Vanco, Levo, Ceftriaxone, Ceftaroline, Amox (HD), Linezolid		
Streptococcus pyogenes, (Grp A), **Streptococcus sp** (Grp B, C, G). Erysipelas, bacteremia, TSS	Penicillin G, cephalosporin	Clinda, vanco, dapto, linezolid	For TSS, necrotizing fasciitis: Pen G+Clinda. Avoid FQ, TMP-SMX, tetracyclines. Pockets of macrolide/clinda resistance (JCM 49: 439, 2011).
Tropheryma whipplei	Doxy + Hydroxychloroquine	Ceftriaxone or Mero, then TMP-SMX	Clinical failures with TMP-SMX
Vibrio cholerae	Azithro	CIP, Doxy	Rehydration salts primary therapy. Vaccine available.
Vibrio parahaemolyticus	Doxy	Azithro, CIP	If bacteremic, treat as for V. vulnificus
Vibrio vulnificus, alginolyticus, damsela	Doxy + Ceftriaxone	Levo	CID 52:788, 2011
Yersinia enterocolitica	Ceftriaxone if bacteremic, CIP otherwise	TMP-SMX	CIP resistance (JAC 53: 1068, 2004); also resistance to Pen, Amp, 1st gen Cephs, Erythro.
Yersinia pestis (plague)	Streptomycin or Gent	Doxy or CIP	Levo, Moxi. CDC advice for treatment and prevention (https://www.cdc.gov/plague/healthcare/clinicians.html).

[1] Agents are more variable in effectiveness than "Recommended" or "Alternative". Selection of "Alternative" or "Also Effective" based on in vitro susceptibility testing, pharmacokinetics, host factors such as auditory, renal, hepatic function, & cost.

**TABLE 3 - SUGGESTED DURATION OF ANTIBIOTIC THERAPY FOR SELECTED
CLINICAL SYNDROMES IN IMMUNOCOMPETENT PATIENTS**

Overview of variables affecting duration of therapy

Variables involved in duration of therapy are summarized in Curr Opin Infect Dis 2015,28:170 and include:

- PK/PD of antibiotic used, e.g., long tissue half-life of Azithro
- Identified pathogen (etiology)
- Host factors, e.g., neutropenic, HIV
- Severity of infection, e.g., cystitis vs. bacteremia
- Severity of host inflammatory response as measured by biomarkers, e.g., serum procalcitonin

Due to these many variables, it is usually not possible to recommend a definite duration except where there is a single pathogen in a healthy person, e.g., E. coli cystitis or Legionella pneumonia. For most situations, need to individualize duration until the patient is clinically stable and biomarkers have normalized.

CLINICAL SITUATION		DURATION OF THERAPY (Days)
SITE	**CLINICAL DIAGNOSIS**	
Bacteremia	Bacteremia with removable focus (no endocarditis)	10-14 *(See Table 1)*
Bone	Osteomyelitis, adult; acute	42 *(Ln 385:875, 2015)*
	adult; chronic	Until ESR normal (often >3 months)
	child; acute; staph. and enterobacteriaceae	21
	child; acute; strep, meningococci, haemophilus	14
		Can shorten **14/21** to **7** days if resolution of S&S and biomarkers normalize
Ear	Otitis media with effusion	<2 yrs: 10; ≥2 yrs: 5-7
Endocardium	Infective endocarditis, native valve: Viridans strep	14 or 28 *(See Table 1, page 28)*
	Enterococci	28 or 42 *(See Table 1, page 29)*
	Staph. aureus	14 (R-sided only) or 28 *(See Table 1, page 29)*
GI *Also see Table 1*	Bacillary dysentery (shigellosis)/traveler's diarrhea	single dose, up to 3 days if no response
	Typhoid fever (S. typhi): Azithro	5-7 (children/adolescents)
	Ceftriaxone	7-14 [Short course ↑ effective *(AAC 44:450, 2000)*]
	FQ	7-10
	Chloramphenicol	14
	Helicobacter pylori	14 days now preferred
	Pseudomembranous enterocolitis (C. difficile)	10
Genital	Non-gonococcal urethritis or mucopurulent cervicitis	7 days doxy or single dose azithro
	Pelvic inflammatory disease	14
Heart	Pericarditis (purulent)	28 or until resolution of S&S and biomarkers normalize
Joint	Septic arthritis (non-gonococcal): Adult	14-28
	Infant/child	10-14 (Response varies, stop when resolution of S&S and biomarkers normalize).
	Gonococcal arthritis/disseminated GC infection	7 *(See Table 1, page 23)*
Kidney	Cystitis, acute	3
	Pyelonephritis *(Ln 380:484, 2012)*	7 (7 days if CIP used; 5 days if levo 750 mg)
Lung *(Curr Op ID 28:177, 2015)*	Pneumonia, pneumococcal Community-acquired pneumonia	Fall of serum procalcitonin by 80% or ≤0.25 ng/mL
	Pneumonia, enterobacteriaceae or pseudomonal	21, often up to 42 (variable, until biomarkers normalize)
	Pneumonia, staphylococcal	21-28 (variable, until biomarkers normalize)
	Pneumocystis pneumonia (PCP) in AIDS	21
	Other immunocompromised	14
	Legionella, mycoplasma, chlamydia	5
		(Curr Med Res Opin 2004,20:555; Chest 2004,125:2135)
	Lung abscess	Usually **28-42**, but variable
Meninges	N. meningitidis	7
	H. influenzae	7
	S. pneumoniae	10-14
	Listeria meningoencephalitis, gp B strep, coliforms	21 (longer in immunocompromised)
	Child: relapses seldom occur until 3 or more days post-rx.	
Multiple systems	Brucellosis *(See Table 1, page 62)*	42 (depends on site of infection)
	Tularemia *(See Table 1, pages 45, 62)*	7-21 depending on severity
Muscle	Gas gangrene (clostridial)	10 but depends on severity
Pharynx	Group A strep pharyngitis *Also see Pharyngitis, Table 1, page 49*	10 (Pen VK), 5 (O Ceph 2/3, Azithro) *(PIDJ 36:507, 2017)*
	Diphtheria (membranous)	14 (Pen G, Erythro)
	Carrier	1 dose (Pen G), 7-10 (Erythro)
Prostate	Chronic prostatitis	30-90 (TMP-SMX), 28-42 (FQ)
Sinuses	Acute bacterial sinusitis (usually viral etiology)	5
Skin	Cellulitis, erysipelas	Until 3 days after acute inflamm disappears
Systemic	Lyme disease	*See Table 1, page 60.*
	Rocky Mountain spotted fever *(See Table 1, page 61)*	Until afebrile 2 days

TABLE 4A - ANTIBACTERIAL ACTIVITY SPECTRA

The data are intended to serve as a general guide to antibacterial usefulness based on treatment guidelines and recommendations, in vitro activity, predominant patterns of susceptibility or resistance and/or demonstrated clinical effectiveness. **Variability in resistance patterns due to regional differences or as a consequent of clinical setting (e.g., community-onset vs. ICU-acquired infection) should be taken into account when using this table because activities of certain agents can differ significantly from what is shown in the table**, which are by necessity based on aggregate information. We have revised and expanded the color / symbol key to provide a more descriptive categorization of the table data.

++ = Recommended: Agent is a first line therapy; reliably active in vitro, clinically effective.

+ = Active: Agent is a potential alternative agent (active in vitro, clinically comparable to known effective agents or a therapeutically interchangeable agents and hence likely to be clinically effective, but second line due to overly broad spectrum, toxicity, limited clinical experience, or paucity of direct evidence of effectiveness)

± = Variable: Variable activity such that the agent, although clinically effective in some settings or types of infections is not reliably effective in others, or should be used in combination with another agent, and/or its efficacy is limited by resistance which has been associated with treatment failure

0 = Not recommended: Agent is a poor alternative to other agents because resistance is likely to be present or occur, due to poor drug penetration to site of infection or an unfavorable toxicity profile, or limited or anecdotal clinical data to support effectiveness

? = Insufficient Data to recommend use

NA = No activity: Agent has no activity against this pathogen

Aerobic gram-pos cocci — Penicillins

Organism	Penicillin G	Penicillin VK	Nafcillin	Oxacillin	Cloxacillin	Flucloxacillin	Dicloxacillin	Ampicillin	Amoxicillin	Amox-Clav	Amp-Sulb	Pip-Tazo
E. faecalis (S)	±	0	0	0	0	0	0	++	++	±	±	+
E. faecium (S)	±	0	0	0	0	0	0	±	±	±	±	±
E. faecalis (VRE)	±	0	0	0	0	0	0	±	±	0	0	0
E. faecium (VRE)	±	0	0	0	0	0	0	0	0	0	0	0
S. aureus MSSA	0	0	++	++	++	++	++	0	0	+	+	+
S. aureus HA-MRSA	0	0	0	0	0	0	0	0	0	0	0	0
S. aureus CA-MRSA	0	0	0	0	0	0	0	0	0	0	0	0
Staph coag-neg (S)	±	0	++	++	++	++	++	±	±	+	+	+
Staph coag-neg (R)	0	0	0	0	0	0	0	0	0	0	0	0
S. epidermidis (R)	0	0	0	0	0	0	0	0	0	0	0	0
S. epidermidis (S)	±	0	++	++	++	++	++	±	±	+	+	+
S. lugdunensis	±	+	±	±	±	±	±	±	±	+	+	+
S. saprophyticus	0	+	0	0	0	0	0	+	+	+	+	+
Strep. anginosis gp	++	++	+	+	+	+	+	+	+	+	+	+
Strep. pyogenes (A)	++	++	+	+	+	+	+	++	++	++	++	++
Strep. agalactae (B)	++	++	+	+	+	+	+	++	++	++	++	++

Aerobic gram-pos cocci — Carbapenems / Aztreonam

Organism	Doripenem	Ertapenem	Imipenem	Meropenem	Mero-Vabor	Aztreonam
E. faecalis (S)	±	0	+	±	±	0
E. faecium (S)	0	0	0	0	0	0
E. faecalis (VRE)	0	0	0	0	0	0
E. faecium (VRE)	0	0	0	0	0	0
S. aureus MSSA	+	+	+	+	+	0
S. aureus HA-MRSA	0	0	0	0	0	0
S. aureus CA-MRSA	0	0	0	0	0	0
Staph coag-neg (S)	+	+	+	+	+	0
Staph coag-neg (R)	0	0	0	0	0	0
S. epidermidis (R)	0	0	0	0	0	0
S. epidermidis (S)	+	+	+	+	+	0
S. lugdunensis	+	+	+	+	+	0
S. saprophyticus	+	+	+	+	+	0
Strep. anginosis gp	+	+	+	+	+	0
Strep. pyogenes (A)	+	+	+	+	+	0
Strep. agalactae (B)	+	+	+	+	+	0

Aerobic gram-pos cocci — Fluoroquinolone

Organism	Ciprofloxacin	Delafloxacin	Ofloxacin	Levofloxacin	Moxifloxacin	Norfloxacin	Prulifloxacin	Gemifloxacin	Gatifloxacin
E. faecalis (S)	±	+	±	±	±	+	±	+	+
E. faecium (S)	0	0	0	0	0	0	0	0	0
E. faecalis (VRE)	0	0	0	0	0	0	0	0	0
E. faecium (VRE)	0	0	0	0	0	0	0	0	0
S. aureus MSSA	0	+	0	±	±	0	0	+	+
S. aureus HA-MRSA	0	+	0	0	0	0	0	0	±
S. aureus CA-MRSA	0	+	0	±	±	0	0	±	±
Staph coag-neg (S)	0	+	0	±	±	0	0	±	±
Staph coag-neg (R)	0	+	0	0	0	0	0	0	0
S. epidermidis (R)	0	+	0	0	0	0	0	0	0
S. epidermidis (S)	0	+	0	±	±	0	0	±	±
S. lugdunensis	+	+	+	+	+	+	+	+	+
S. saprophyticus	0	+	0	+	+	0	0	+	+
Strep. anginosis gp	+	+	+	+	+	0	+	+	+
Strep. pyogenes (A)	±	+	±	+	+	0	±	+	+
Strep. agalactae (B)	±	+	±	+	+	0	±	+	+

Aerobic gram-pos cocci — Parenteral Cephalosporins

Organism	Cefazolin	Cefotetan	Cefoxitin	Cefuroxime	Cefotaxime	Ceftizoxime	Ceftriaxone	Ceftazidime	Cefepime	Ceftaz-Avibac	Ceftaroline	Ceftol-Tazo
E. faecalis (S)	0	0	0	0	0	0	±	0	0	0	0	0
E. faecium (S)	0	0	0	0	0	0	0	0	0	0	0	0
E. faecalis (VRE)	0	0	0	0	0	0	0	0	0	0	0	0
E. faecium (VRE)	0	0	0	0	0	0	0	0	0	0	0	?
S. aureus MSSA	++	+	+	+	+	+	+	±	+	±	+	0
S. aureus HA-MRSA	0	0	0	0	0	0	0	0	0	0	+	0
S. aureus CA-MRSA	0	0	0	0	0	0	0	0	0	0	+	0
Staph coag-neg (S)	++	+	+	+	+	+	+	±	+	±	+	?
Staph coag-neg (R)	0	0	0	0	0	0	0	0	0	0	+	0
S. epidermidis (R)	0	0	0	0	0	0	0	0	0	0	+	?
S. epidermidis (S)	++	+	+	+	+	+	+	±	+	±	+	0
S. lugdunensis	++	+	+	+	+	+	+	±	+	±	+	?
S. saprophyticus	+	+	+	+	+	+	+	±	+	±	+	+
Strep. anginosis gp	+	+	+	+	+	+	+	±	+	±	+	+
Strep. pyogenes (A)	++	+	+	+	+	+	+	±	+	±	+	+
Strep. agalactae (B)	++	+	+	+	+	+	+	±	+	±	+	+

TABLE 4A (2)

Organism	Penicillin G	Penicillin VK	Nafcillin	Oxacillin	Cloxacillin	Flucloxacillin	Dicloxacillin	Ampicillin	Amoxicillin	Amox-Clav	Amp-Sulb	Pip-Tazo	Doripenem	Ertapenem	Imipenem	Meropenem	Mero-Vabor	Aztreonam	Ciprofloxacin	Delafloxacin	Ofloxacin	Levofloxacin	Moxifloxacin	Norfloxacin	Prulifloxacin	Gemifloxacin	Gatifloxacin	Cefazolin	Cefotetan	Cefoxitin	Cefuroxime	Cefotaxime	Ceftizoxime	Ceftriaxone	Ceftazidime	Cefepime	Ceftaz-Avibac	Ceftaroline	Ceftol-Tazo
Aerobic gram-pos cocci *(continued)*																																							
Strep. gp. C,F,G	++	++	+	+	+	+	+	+	+	+	+	+	+	+	+	+	+	O	+I	+	+I	+I	+I	O	+I	+I	+I	+	+	+	+	+	+	+	+	+	+	+	+
Strep. pneumoniae	++	++	+	+	+	+	+	+	+	+	+	+	+	+	+	+	+	O	+I	+	+I	+	+	O	+I	+I	+I	+	+	+	+	+	+	+	+	+	+	+	+
Viridans Strep.	+I	+I	+	+I	+	+	+	+	+	+	+I	+	+	+	+	+	+	O	O	+	O	+	+	O	O	+	+	+	+	+	+	+	+	++	+I	+	+I	+	+
Aerobic gram-pos bacilli																																							
Arcanobacter. sp	+	+	?	?	+	+	?	+	+	+	+	+	+	+	+	+	+	O	+	?	+	+	+	O	+	+	+	?	?	?	?	?	?	?	+	+	+	?	?
C. diphtheriae	++	++	O	O	O	O	O	+	+	+	+	+	+	?	?	?	?	O	?	?	?	?	?	O	+	+I	+	?	?	?	?	?	?	?	?	?	?	?	?
C. jeikeium	+	O	O	O	O	O	O	O	O	O	O	O	?	?	?	?	?	O	O	?	O	O	+I	O	O	+I	?	O	O	O	?	O	O	O	O	O	O	O	O
L. monocytogenes	+	+	O	O	O	O	O	++	+	+	+	+	+	O	+	+I	+	O	O	?	O	+	+I	O	O	O	+	O	O	O	?	O	O	O	O	O	+I	O	O
Nocardia sp.	O	O	O	O	O	O	O	O	O	O	+I	?	?	?	+I	+	+	O	O	?	O	+	+	O	O	O	O	O	O	O	?	O	O	+I	O	O	O	?	?
Aerobic GNB-Enteric																																							
Aeromonas sp.	O	O	O	O	O	O	O	O	O	O	+I	+	+	+	+	+	+	+	+	?	+	+	+	+	+	+	+	O	+	O	?	+	+	+	+	+	+	+	+
C. jejuni	O	O	O	O	O	O	O	O	O	O	O	O	?	?	+	+	+I	O	O	?	+	+	+	+	+	+	+	O	O	O	O	+	+	+	+	+	+	O	O
C. freundii	O	O	O	O	O	O	O	O	O	O	O	++	+	+	+	++	++	+I	+	+	+	+	+	+	+	+	+	O	O	O	O	+	+	+	+	+	+	O	+
C. koseri	O	O	O	O	O	O	O	O	O	O	O	+I	+	+	+	++	++	+I	+	+	+	+	+	+	+	+	+	O	O	O	O	+	+	+	+	+	+	O	+
E. aerogenes	O	O	O	O	O	O	O	O	O	O	O	?	+	+	+	+	+	+	+	+	+	+	+	+	+	+	+	O	O	O	O	+	+	+	+	+	+	O	+
E. cloacae	O	O	O	O	O	O	O	O	O	O	O	?	+	+	+	+	+	+	+	+	+	+	+	+	+	+	+	O	O	O	O	+	+	+	+	+	+	O	+
E. coli (S)	O	O	O	O	O	O	O	+I	+I	+	+I	+	+	+	+	+	+	+	+	+	+	+	+	+	+	+	+	+	+	+	+	+	+	+	+	+	+	+	+
E. coli, Klebs ESBL	O	O	O	O	O	O	O	O	O	O	O	+I	+	+	+	+	+	O	O	O	O	O	O	O	O	O	O	O	O	O	O	O	O	O	O	O	+	O	+
E. coli, Klebs KPC	O	O	O	O	O	O	O	O	O	O	O	O	O	O	O	O	+I	O	O	O	O	O	O	O	O	O	O	O	O	O	O	O	O	O	O	O	+I	O	O
E. coli, Klebs MBL	O	O	O	O	O	O	O	O	O	O	O	O	O	O	O	O	O	+I	O	O	O	O	O	O	O	O	O	O	O	O	O	O	O	O	O	O	O	O	O
Enterics CRE, NOS	O	O	O	O	O	O	O	O	O	O	O	O	O	?	O	O	O	O	O	?	O	O	O	O	O	O	O	O	O	O	O	O	O	O	O	O	+I	O	O
K. oxytoca	O	O	O	O	O	O	O	O	O	O	+I	+	+	+	+	+	+	+	+	+	+	+	+	+	+	+	+	O	+	O	+	+	+	+	+	+	+	+	+
K. pneumoniae (S)	O	O	O	O	O	O	O	O	+	+	+	+	+	+	+	+	+	+	+	+	+	+	+	+	+	+	+	+	+	+	+	+	+	+	+	+	+	+	+
Morganella sp.	O	O	O	O	O	O	O	O	O	O	O	+	+	+I	+I	+	+	+	+	+	+	+	?	+	+	+	+	O	+	+	+O	+	+	+	+	++	+	+	+
P. mirabilis	O	O	O	O	O	O	O	+	+	+	+	+	+	+	+I	+	+	+	+	+	+	+	?	+	+	+	+	O	+	+	+	+	+	+	+	+	+	+	+
P. vulgaris	O	O	O	O	O	O	O	O	O	+	+	+	+	+	+I	+	+	+	+	+	+	+	+	+	+	+	+	O	+	+	+	+	+	+	+	+	+	+	+
Providencia sp.	O	O	O	O	O	O	O	O	O	+	+	+	+	+	+I	++	++	+	+	+	+	+	+	+	+	+	+	O	+	O	O	+	+	+	+	+	+	?	?

TABLE 4A (3)

	Penicillin G	Penicillin VK	Nafcillin	Oxacillin	Cloxacillin	Flucloxacillin	Dicloxacillin	Ampicillin	Amoxicillin	Amox-Clav	Amp-Sulb	Pip-Tazo	Doripenem	Ertapenem	Imipenem	Meropenem	Mero-Vabor	Aztreonam	Ciprofloxacin	Delafloxacin	Ofloxacin	Levofloxacin	Moxifloxacin	Norfloxacin	Prulifloxacin	Gemifloxacin	Gatifloxacin	Cefazolin	Cefotetan	Cefoxitin	Cefuroxime	Cefotaxime	Ceftizoxime	Ceftriaxone	Ceftazidime	Cefepime	Ceftaz-Avibac	Ceftaroline	Ceftol-Tazo
Aerobic GNB – Enteric (continued)																																							
Salmonella sp.	0	0	0	0	0	0	0	+l	+l	+	+	+	+	+	+	+	+	+	+	+	+	+	+	0	+	+	+	0	?	?	?	+	+	+	+	+	+	?	?
Serratia sp.	0	0	0	0	0	0	0	0	0	0	0	+	+	+	+	+	+	+	+	+	+	+	+	0	+	+	+	0	+	?	0	+	+	+	+	+	+	?	?
Shigella sp.	0	0	0	0	0	0	0	?	0	0	0	+	+	+	+	+	+	+	‡	+	+	‡	+	0	‡	+	+	0	?	?	0	+	+	+	+	+	+	?	?
Y. enterolitica	0	0	0	0	0	0	0	0	0	+l	+l	+	?	?	+	+	+	+	‡	+	+	‡	+	0	‡	?	+	0	+l	+l	+l	+	+	+	+	+	+	?	+
Aerobic GNB – Non-enteric																																							
Bartonella sp.	0	0	0	0	0	0	0	0	0	0	0	0	0	0	0	0	0	0	0	0	0	0	0	0	0	0	0	0	0	0	0	0	0	0	0	0	0	0	0
B. pertussis	0	0	0	0	0	0	0	0	0	0	0	0	0	0	0	0	0	0	?	?	?	?	?	0	?	?	?	0	0	0	+	0	0	0	0	‡	0	0	0
B. burgdorferi	+	0	0	0	0	0	0	‡	‡	+	+	0	0	0	‡	0	0	0	0	?	?	0	?	0	0	?	?	0	0	0	+	‡	0	‡	0	+	0	?	0
Brucella sp.	0	0	0	0	0	0	0	0	0	0	0	0	+	?	0	?	0	0	+	?	+	+	?	0	+	+	+	+	+	+	0	0	0	+	0	+	0	+	0
Capnocytophaga	+l	0	0	0	0	0	0	+l	+l	‡	‡	‡	0	?	‡	+	0	+	‡	?	?	+	?	0	+	?	+	+	+	+	0	+	0	+	0	+	+	?	0
C. burnetii	0	0	0	0	0	0	0	0	0	0	0	0	+	0	0	0	0	0	+	?	+	+	+	0	+	+	+	0	0	0	0	0	0	0	0	0	0	?	0
Ehrlichia, Anaplas	0	0	0	0	0	0	0	0	0	0	0	0	0	0	0	0	0	0	?	?	?	+	?	0	+	?	?	0	0	0	0	0	0	0	0	0	0	0	0
Eikenella sp	+l	0	0	0	0	0	0	+l	+l	‡	‡	+	+	+	+	+	+	+	+	+	+	+	+	0	+	+	+	0	0	0	+	+	+	+	+	+	+	+	0
F. tularensis	0	0	0	0	0	0	0	0	0	0	0	0	0	0	0	0	0	0	+	?	+	+	?	0	+	+	+	0	0	0	0	+	‡	+	+	+	+	+	0
H. ducreyi	0	0	0	0	0	0	0	0	0	‡	+	+	+	+	+	+	+	+	+	+	+	+	+	0	+	+	+	0	+	+	+	+	+	+	+	+	+	+	0
H. influenzae	0	0	0	0	0	0	0	‡	‡	‡	‡	+	+	+	+	+	+	+	‡	‡	+	‡	+	0	‡	+	+	0	+l	+l	0	+	+	+	+	+	+	+l	+
Kingella sp	0	0	0	0	0	0	0	0	0	0	0	+	+	+	+	+	+	+	+	+	+	+	+	0	+	+	+	+	+l	+l	+	+	+	+	+	+	+	+	0
K. granulomatis	+	0	0	0	0	0	0	+	+	+	+	0	0	0	0	0	0	0	+	?	+	+	+	0	+	+	+	0	0	0	0	+	+	+	+	+	+	?	?
Legionella sp.	0	0	0	0	0	0	0	0	0	0	0	0	+	0	0	0	0	0	+	?	+	+	+	0	+	+	+	0	0	0	0	0	0	0	0	0	0	?	0
Leptospira sp.	‡	0	0	0	0	0	0	0	0	0	0	0	0	+	+	+	0	0	+	?	+	+	+	0	+	+	+	0	0	0	0	+	+	+	0	0	0	?	0
M. catarrhalis	0	0	0	0	0	0	0	0	0	+	+	+	+	+	+	+	+	+	+	+	+	+	+	0	+	+	+	+	+	+	+	+	+	+	+	+	+	+	+
N. gonorrhoeae	0	0	0	0	0	0	0	0	0	‡	+	+	+	+	+	+	+	+	+	+	+	+	+	0	+	+	+	0	+l	+l	+l	+	+	+	+	+	+	+	+
N. meningitidis	+	0	0	0	0	0	0	‡	‡	+	+	+	+	+	+	+	+	+	+	+	+	+	+	0	+	+	+	0	0	0	‡	+	+	+	+	+	+	+	+
P. multocida	‡	0	0	0	0	0	0	‡	‡	+	+	+	+	+	+	+	+	+	+	+	+	+	+	0	+	+	+	0	0	0	+	+	+	+	0	+	+	0	?
R. rickettsii	0	0	0	0	0	0	0	0	0	0	0	0	0	0	0	0	0	0	+l	?	+l	+l	+l	0	+l	+	?	0	0	0	0	0	0	0	0	0	0	?	0
T. pallidum	+	+	0	0	0	0	0	‡	‡	0	0	0	0	0	0	0	0	0	0	?	+	+	+	0	+	+	+	0	0	0	0	+	+	+	0	0	0	0	0
V. cholera	0	0	0	0	0	0	0	+	+	‡	‡	0	+	+	+	+	+	+	+	+	+	+	+	0	+	+	+	0	?	?	0	+	+	+	+	+	0	0	0
V. parahaemolyticus	0	0	0	0	0	0	0	0	0	0	0	0	?	?	?	?	?	?	+	?	+	+	?	0	+	?	?	0	?	?	0	+	+	+	+	+	+	?	?

TABLE 4A (4)

Organism	Penicillin G	Penicillin VK	Nafcillin	Oxacillin	Cloxacillin	Flucloxacillin	Dicloxacillin	Ampicillin	Amoxicillin	Amox-Clav	Amp-Sulb	Pip-Tazo	Doripenem	Ertapenem	Imipenem	Meropenem	Mero-Vabor	Aztreonam	Ciprofloxacin	Delafloxacin	Ofloxacin	Levofloxacin	Moxifloxacin	Norfloxacin	Prulifloxacin	Gemifloxacin	Gatifloxacin	Cefazolin	Cefotetan	Cefoxitin	Cefuroxime	Cefotaxime	Ceftizoxime	Ceftriaxone	Ceftazidime	Cefepime	Ceftaz-Avibac	Ceftaroline	Ceftol-Tazo
Aerobic GNB - Non-enteric (continued)																																							
V. vulnificus	O	O	O	O	O	O	O	O	O	O	O	O	?	?	?	?	?	?	+	?	+	?	?	O	+	?	?	O	O	O	O	+	+	+	+|	+	+	?	?
Y. pestis	D	O	O	O	O	O	O	O	O	O	O	O	?	?	?	?	?	?	+	?	?	?	?	O	+	?	?	O	O	O	O	+	?	+	+|	+	O	O	O
Aerobic GNB non-fermenter																																							
A. baumannii	O	O	O	O	O	O	O	O	+|	+|	+|	+|	+	O	+‡	+|	+|	?	+|	?	+|	+|	O	+|	?	?	O	O	O	O	+|	O	+|	+|	+|	?	?	+|
B. cepacia	O	O	O	O	O	O	O	O	O	O	O	O	+|	O	+|	+|	+|	?	+	?	O	+	O	O	O	O	O	O	O	O	O	O	O	O	+|	+|	+	O	+
P. aeruginosa	O	O	O	O	O	O	O	O	O	O	O	+	+|	O	+	+	+	O	+	+	+	+	O	O	O	O	O	O	O	O	O	O	O	O	+|	+	+	O	+
S. maltophilia	O	O	O	O	O	O	O	O	O	O	O	+|	O	O	O	O	O	O	O	+	+|	+|	‡	O	+	?	?	O	O	O	O	O	O	O	+|	O	+|	O	O
Aerobic - cell wall-deficient																																							
C. trachomatis	O	O	O	O	O	O	O	O	O	O	O	O	O	?	O	O	?	O	O	?	‡	‡	+	O	O	+	+	O	O	O	O	O	O	O	O	O	O	O	O
Chlamydophila sp.	O	O	O	O	O	O	O	+|	O	O	O	O	O	?	O	O	?	O	O	?	+	+	+	O	+	?	+	O	O	O	O	O	O	O	O	O	O	O	O
M. genitalium	O	O	O	O	O	O	O	O	O	O	O	O	O	?	O	O	?	O	O	?	O	+|	+‡	O	O	?	+	O	O	O	O	O	O	O	O	O	O	O	O
M. pneumoniae	O	O	O	O	O	O	O	O	O	O	O	O	O	?	O	O	?	O	O	?	+	‡	‡	O	+	?	+	O	O	O	O	O	O	O	O	O	O	O	O
U. urealyticum	O	O	O	O	O	O	O	O	O	O	O	O	O	?	O	O	?	O	O	?	+	+	+	O	+	+	+	O	O	O	O	O	O	O	O	O	O	O	O
Anaerobic GNB																																							
B. fragilis	O	O	O	O	O	O	O	O	O	+	+	‡	+	‡	+	+	‡	O	O	+	‡	‡	+	O	O	+	+	O	?	+|	O	O	O	O	O	O	O	O	O
F. necrophorum	++	+|	O	O	O	O	O	+|	+|	+	+	+	+	+	+	+	+	O	O	+	+	+	+|	O	O	?	?	O	+	+	?	+	O	+	O	O	O	?	+
P. melaninogenica	+	+|	O	O	O	O	O	+|	+|	+	+	+	+	+	+	+	+	O	O	+	O	O	?	O	O	?	?	O	+	+	?	O	O	+	O	O	O	?	?
Anaerobic gram-positive																																							
Actinomyces sp.	++	++	O	O	O	O	O	++	++	+	+	‡	+	‡	+	+	+	O	O	+	O	O	?	O	O	?	O	O	?	+	O	+	O	+	O	O	O	O	O
C. difficile	++	O	O	O	O	O	O	+	O	O	O	O	+	O	+	+|	+|	O	O	+	O	O	+|	O	O	O	O	O	+	+	?	O	O	O	O	O	O	O	O
Clostridium sp.	++	+	O	O	O	O	O	+	+	+	+	+	+	+	+	+	+	O	O	+	O	O	+|	O	O	?	O	?	+	+	?	+	?	+	?	?	?	?	?
P. acnes	++	++	?	?	?	?	?	+	+	+	+	+	+	+	+	+	+	O	O	+	O	+|	+|	O	+|	?	O	+	+	+	O	+	+	+	+	+	+	+	+
Peptostreptococci	++	++	O	O	O	O	O	++	++	+	+	+	+	+	+	+	+	O	O	O	O	+|	+	O	O	?	+	+	+	+	+	+	+	+	+	+	+	+	+

TABLE 4A (5)

	Oral Cephalosporins										Aminoglyco			Macrolides						Tetracyclines				Glyco/Lipo						Ox-lid		Poly		Other								
	Cefadroxil	Cephalexin	Cefaclor	Cefprozil	Cefurox-Axe	Cefixime	Ceftibuten	Cefpodoxime	Cefdinir	Cefditoren	Gentamicin	Tobramycin	Amikacin	Chloramphen	Clindamycin	Erythromycin	Azithromycin	Clarithromycin	Telithromycin	Doxycycline	Minocycline	Tetracycline	Tigecycline	Daptomycin	Vancomycin	Teicoplanin	Telavancin	Oritavancin	Dalbavancin	Linezolid	Tedizolid	Polymyxin B	Colistin	Fusidic Acid	Rif (comb)	TMP-SMX	Nitrofurantoin	Fosfomycin (IV)	Fosfomycin (po)	Metronidazole	Quinu-Dalfo
Aerobic gram-pos cocci																																									
E. faecalis (S)	o	o	o	o	o	o	o	o	o	o	+l	o	o	+l	o	o	o	o	o	+l	+l	+l	+	+	‡	‡	+	+	+l	+	+	o	o	+l	+l	o	+	+l	+l	o	o
E. faecium (S)	o	o	o	o	o	o	o	o	o	o	+l	o	o	+l	o	o	o	o	o	+l	+l	+l	+	+	+l	+l	+l	+	+l	‡	+	o	o	+l	+l	o	+	+l	+l	o	+
E. faecalis (VRE)	o	o	o	o	o	o	o	o	o	o	+l	o	NA	+l	o	o	o	o	o	+l	+l	+l	+l	+	o	o	+l	+l	o	+	+	o	o	o	+l	o	+	+l	+l	o	o
E. faecium (VRE)	o	o	o	o	o	o	o	o	o	o	+l	o	o	+l	o	o	o	o	o	+l	+l	+l	+l	+	o	o	+l	+	o	‡	+	o	o	o	+l	o	+	+l	+l	o	+
S. aureus MSSA	+	+	+	+	+	o	o	o	+	+	+l	o	o	+	+	+l	o	+l	+	+	+	+	+	+l	+	+l	+	+	+	+	+	o	o	+	+l	+	o	+	o	o	+
S. aureus HA-MRSA	o	o	o	o	o	o	o	o	o	o	+l	o	o	+	+l	o	o	o	+l	+l	+	+l	+	‡	+l	+l	+	+	+	+	+	o	o	+	+l	+	o	+	o	o	+
S. aureus CA-MRSA	o	o	o	o	+	o	o	o	o	o	+l	o	o	+	+l	o	o	o	+	+l	+	+l	+	+	+	+	+	+	+	+	+	o	o	+	+l	+	o	+	o	o	+
Staph coag-neg (S)	o	+l	+l	o	+	o	o	o	+	+	+l	o	o	+	+l	+l	o	+l	+	+l	+	+l	+	+l	+	+l	+	+	+	+	+	o	o	+	+l	+	o	+l	+	o	+
Staph coag-neg (R)	o	o	o	o	o	o	o	o	o	o	+l	o	o	+	+	o	o	o	+	+l	+	+l	+	‡	+l	+l	+	+	+l	+	+	o	o	o	+l	+	o	+	o	o	+
S. epidermidis (R)	o	o	o	o	o	?	?	?	?	+	+l	?	?	+	+l	+l	+l	+l	?	+l	+	+l	+	‡	+	+	+	?	+	+	+	o	o	?	o	+l	o	+l	o	o	+
S. epidermidis (S)	o	o	o	o	+	o	o	o	+	+	+l	?	?	+	+	+l	o	o	+	+l	+	+l	+	+	+	+	+	+	+	+	+	o	o	?	o	+l	o	+l	o	o	+
S. lugdunensis	+	++	++	+	++	?	?	?	?	?	o	?	?	+	+	+l	o	o	?	+	+	+	+	+	+	+	+	?	+	+	+	o	o	?	o	+l	o	+l	o	o	+
Strep. anginosis gp	+	+	+	+	+	o	o	+	+	+	+l	?	?	+	+	o	+l	o	+	+l	+	+l	+	+	+	+	+	?	+	+	+	o	o	?	o	+l	o	+	o	o	+
Strep. pyogenes (A)	+	+	+	+	+	o	o	o	o	+	+l	?	?	+	+l	+l	+l	o	+l	+l	+	+l	+	+	+	+	+	+	+	+	+	o	o	?	o	+l	o	+	o	o	+
Strep. agalactiae (B)	+	+	+	+	+	o	o	+	+	+	+l	?	?	+	+l	+l	+l	+l	+	+l	+	+l	+	+	+	+	+	?	+	+	+	o	o	?	o	+l	o	+	o	o	+
Step. gp. C,F,G	+	+	+	+	+	?	?	+	+	+	+l	?	?	+	+l	+l	+l	+l	+	+l	+	+l	+	+	+	+	+	?	+	+	+	o	o	?	o	+l	o	+	o	o	+
Strep. pneumoniae	+	+	+	+	+	?	?	+	+	+	o	o	o	+	+	+l	+l	+l	+	+l	+	+l	+	+l	+	+	+	+	+	+	+	o	o	?	o	+l	o	+	o	o	+
Viridans Strep.	+	+	+	+	+	?	?	?	+	+	+l	o	o	+	+l	+l	+l	+l	+	+l	+	+l	+	+	+	+	+	+	+	+	+	o	o	?	o	+l	o	+	o	o	+
Aerobic gram-pos bacilli																																									
Arcanobacter. sp	+	+	?	+	+	?	?	?	+	+	?	?	?	+	‡	++	‡	+	+	?	?	?	‡	+	‡	+	+	+	?	+	?	o	o	o	++	o	o	o	o	o	+
C. diphtheriae	?	o	?	?	?	o	o	o	o	o	?	o	o	o	+	o	o	o	+	?	?	?	o	o	o	o	+	?	o	+	o	o	o	?	o	o	o	o	o	o	?
C. jeikeium	o	o	o	o	o	o	o	o	o	o	o	o	o	o	o	o	o	o	o	?	?	?	+	o	+	+	+	o	o	+	?	o	o	?	+	o	o	o	o	o	?
L. monocytogenes	o	o	+	o	+	o	o	?	o	o	+l	+l	?	o	o	o	o	o	o	?	o	o	+	o	‡	+	+	o	o	+	+	o	o	o	o	+	o	o	o	o	o
Nocardia sp.	o	o	o	o	+	o	o	o	o	o	+l	o	‡	+	o	o	o	o	o	+	+l	?	?	o	o	o	o	+	o	+	?	o	o	o	o	‡	o	o	o	o	o

TABLE 4A (6)

Class	Antibiotic	Aeromonas sp.	C. jejuni	C. freundii	C. koseri	E. aerogenes	E. cloacae	E. coli (S)	E. coli, Klebs ESBL	E. coli, Klebs KPC	E. coli, Klebs MBL	Enteric CRE, NOS	K. oxytoca	K. pneumoniae (S)	Morganella sp.	P. mirabilis	P. vulgaris	Providencia sp.	Salmonella sp.	Serratia sp.	Shigella sp.	Y. enterolitica	Bartonella sp.	B. pertussis	B. burgdorferi	Brucella sp.	Capnocytophaga
Other	Quinu-Dalfo	o	o	o	o	o	o	o	o	o	o	o	o	o	o	o	o	o	o	o	o	o	o	o	o	o	o
Other	Metronidazole	o	o	o	o	o	o	o	o	o	o	o	o	o	o	o	o	o	o	o	o	o	o	o	o	o	o
Other	Fosfomycin (po)	o	o	+	+	+l	+l	+	+	+l	+l	+l	+l	o	+	+l	o	+	+l	o	o	o	o	o	o	o	o
Other	Fosfomycin (IV)	?	o	+	+	+l	+l	+	+	+l	+l	+l	+l	o	+	+l	o	+	+l	o	o	o	o	o	o	o	o
Other	Nitrofurantoin	o	o	o	+l	+l	+l	+	+l	o	+l	+l	+l	+l	o	o	o	o	o	o	+l	o	o	o	o	o	o
Other	TMP-SMX	+	o	+l	+l	+	+	+l	+l	o	+l	+l	+l	+l	+l	+l	+l	+l	+	+l	+	+	o	+	o	+	+l
Other	Rif (comb)	o	o	o	o	o	o	o	o	o	o	o	o	o	o	o	o	o	o	o	o	o	+l	o	o	+l	o
Other	Fusidic Acid	o	o	o	o	o	o	o	o	o	o	o	o	o	o	o	o	o	o	o	o	o	o	o	o	o	o
Poly	Colistin	+	o	+	+	+	+	+	+	+	+	+	+	+	o	o	o	o	+	+	+	+	o	o	o	o	o
Poly	Polymyxin B	+	o	+	+	+	+	+	+	+	+	+	+	+	o	o	o	o	+	+	+	+	o	o	o	o	o
Ox-lid	Tedizolid	o	o	o	o	o	o	o	o	o	o	o	o	o	o	o	o	o	o	o	o	o	o	o	o	o	o
Ox-lid	Linezolid	o	o	o	o	o	o	o	o	o	o	o	o	o	o	o	o	o	o	o	o	o	o	o	o	o	o
Glyco/Lipo	Dalbavancin	o	o	o	o	o	o	o	o	o	o	o	o	o	o	o	o	o	o	o	o	o	o	o	o	o	o
Glyco/Lipo	Oritavancin	o	o	o	o	o	o	o	o	o	o	o	o	o	o	o	o	o	o	o	o	o	o	o	o	o	o
Glyco/Lipo	Telavancin	o	o	o	o	o	o	o	o	o	o	o	o	o	o	o	o	o	o	o	o	o	o	o	o	o	o
Glyco/Lipo	Teicoplanin	o	o	o	o	o	o	o	o	o	o	o	o	o	o	o	o	o	o	o	o	o	o	o	o	o	o
Glyco/Lipo	Vancomycin	o	o	o	o	o	o	o	o	o	o	o	o	o	o	o	o	o	o	o	o	o	o	o	o	o	o
Glyco/Lipo	Daptomycin	o	o	o	o	o	o	o	o	o	o	o	o	o	o	o	o	o	o	o	o	o	o	o	o	o	o
Tetracyclines	Tigecycline	+	?	+	+	+	+	+	+	+	+	+	+	+	?	+	o	?	+	+	+	?	?	o	?	?	?
Tetracyclines	Tetracycline	o	+l	o	o	o	o	+l	o	o	o	o	o	o	o	o	o	o	o	o	o	?	+	+	+	+	+
Tetracyclines	Minocycline	+	+l	o	o	o	o	+l	o	o	o	+l	+l	o	+l	o	o	+l	o	+l	o	?	+	?	+	+	+
Tetracyclines	Doxycycline	+	+l	o	o	o	o	+l	o	o	o	o	o	o	o	o	o	+l	o	+l	o	?	‡	?	‡	+	+
Macrolides	Telithromycin	o	o	o	o	o	o	o	o	o	o	o	o	o	o	o	o	o	o	o	o	o	?	?	?	?	?
Macrolides	Clarithromycin	o	+	o	o	o	o	o	o	o	o	o	o	o	o	o	o	o	o	o	o	o	‡	‡	+	o	?
Macrolides	Azithromycin	o	‡	o	o	o	o	+l	o	o	o	o	o	o	o	+	o	o	+	o	+	o	‡	‡	+	+	?
Macrolides	Erythromycin	o	‡	o	o	o	o	o	o	o	o	o	o	o	o	o	o	o	o	o	o	o	+	+	+	+	?
Macrolides	Clindamycin	o	?	o	o	o	o	o	o	o	o	o	o	o	o	o	o	o	o	o	o	o	o	o	o	o	‡
Macrolides	Chloramphen	+	?	o	?	o	o	+	+l	o	o	o	+	+	?	+l	?	+	+	o	+	o	+	o	o	+	+
Aminoglyco	Amikacin	+	+	+	+	+	+	+	+l	+l	+l	+l	+	+	+	+	+	+	+	+	+	+	o	o	o	?	+l
Aminoglyco	Tobramycin	+	+	+	+	+	+	+	+l	+l	+l	+	+	+	+	+	+	+	+l	+	+	+	o	o	o	?	?
Aminoglyco	Gentamicin	+	+	+	+	+	+	+	+l	+l	+l	+	+	+	+l	+	+	+	+	+	+	+	‡	o	o	o	+l
Oral Cephalosporins	Cefditoren	?	o	+	?	o	o	?	o	o	o	o	?	o	?	?	?	?	o	?	o	?	o	o	o	o	o
Oral Cephalosporins	Cefdinir	?	o	+	+	o	o	+	o	o	o	o	+	o	+	+	?	?	o	?	?	?	o	o	o	o	o
Oral Cephalosporins	Cefpodoxime	?	o	+	+	o	o	+	o	o	o	o	+	o	+	+	+	+	+	o	+	?	o	o	o	o	o
Oral Cephalosporins	Ceftibuten	?	o	+	+	o	o	+	o	o	o	o	+	o	+	+	+	+	+	o	+	+	o	o	o	o	o
Oral Cephalosporins	Cefixime	?	o	+	+	o	o	+	o	o	o	o	+	o	+	+	+	+	+	o	+	+	o	o	o	o	o
Oral Cephalosporins	Cefurox-Axe	?	o	o	o	o	o	+	o	o	o	o	+	o	o	o	o	o	o	o	o	o	o	o	o	+l	o
Oral Cephalosporins	Cefprozil	?	?	o	o	o	o	+	o	o	o	o	+	o	+	o	o	o	o	o	o	o	o	o	o	o	o
Oral Cephalosporins	Cefaclor	?	?	o	o	o	o	+l	o	o	o	o	+	+l	o	+	o	o	o	o	o	o	o	o	o	o	o
Oral Cephalosporins	Cephalexin	o	o	o	o	o	o	+l	o	o	o	o	+l	+l	o	+	o	o	o	o	o	o	o	o	o	o	o
Oral Cephalosporins	Cefadroxil	?	o	o	o	o	o	+l	o	o	o	o	+l	+l	o	+	o	o	o	o	o	o	o	o	o	o	o

Aerobic GNB - Enteric: Aeromonas sp., C. jejuni, C. freundii, C. koseri, E. aerogenes, E. cloacae, E. coli (S), E. coli, Klebs ESBL, E. coli, Klebs KPC, E. coli, Klebs MBL, Enteric CRE, NOS, K. oxytoca, K. pneumoniae (S), Morganella sp., P. mirabilis, P. vulgaris, Providencia sp., Salmonella sp., Serratia sp., Shigella sp., Y. enterolitica

Aerobic GNB - Non-enteric: Bartonella sp., B. pertussis, B. burgdorferi, Brucella sp., Capnocytophaga

TABLE 4A (7)

Aerobic GNB - Non-enteric *(continued)* / Aerobic GNB non-fermenter

Drug	C. burnetii	Ehrlichia, Anaplas	Eikenella sp.	F. tularensis	H. ducreyi	H. influenzae	Kingella sp.	K. granulomatis	Legionella sp.	Leptospira sp.	M. catarrhalis	N. gonorrhoeae	N. meningitidis	P. multocida	R. rickettsii	T. pallidum	V. cholera	V. parahaemolyticus	V. vulnificus	Y. pestis	A. baumannii	B. cepacia	P. aeruginosa	S. maltophilia
Quinu-Dalfo	o	o	o	o	o	o	o	o	o	o	o	o	o	o	o	o	o	o	o	o	o	o	o	o
Metronidazole	o	o	o	o	o	o	o	o	o	o	o	o	o	o	o	o	o	o	o	o	o	o	o	o
Fosfomycin (po)	o	o	o	o	o	o	o	o	o	o	o	o	o	o	o	o	o	o	o	o	o	o	+|	o
Fosfomycin (IV)	o	o	o	o	o	o	o	o	o	o	o	o	o	o	o	o	o	o	o	o	o	o	+|	o
Nitrofurantoin	o	o	o	o	o	o	o	o	o	o	o	o	o	o	o	o	o	o	o	o	o	o	o	o
TMP-SMX	+	o	o	o	o	+	+	‡	+	+	o	+	o	+	o	o	o	?	?	+	+|	+|	o	‡
Rif (comb)	+|	+|	o	o	o	o	o	o	o	+|	o	o	o	o	o	o	o	o	o	o	o	o	o	o
Fusidic Acid	o	o	o	o	o	o	o	o	o	o	o	o	o	o	o	o	o	o	o	o	o	o	o	o
Colistin	o	o	o	o	o	o	o	o	o	o	o	o	o	o	o	o	o	o	o	o	+	o	+	+
Polymyxin B	o	o	o	o	o	o	o	o	o	o	o	o	o	o	o	o	o	o	o	o	+	o	+	+
Tedizolid	o	o	o	o	o	o	o	o	o	o	o	o	o	o	o	o	o	o	o	o	o	o	o	o
Linezolid	o	o	o	o	o	o	o	o	o	o	o	o	o	o	o	o	o	o	o	o	o	o	o	o
Dalbavancin	o	o	o	o	o	o	o	o	o	o	o	o	o	o	o	o	o	o	o	o	o	o	o	o
Oritavancin	o	o	o	o	o	o	o	o	o	o	o	o	o	o	o	o	o	o	o	o	o	o	o	o
Telavancin	o	o	o	o	o	o	o	o	o	o	o	o	o	o	o	o	o	o	o	o	o	o	o	o
Teicoplanin	o	o	o	o	o	o	o	o	o	o	o	o	o	o	o	o	o	o	o	o	o	o	o	o
Vancomycin	o	o	o	o	o	o	o	o	o	o	o	o	o	o	o	o	o	o	o	o	o	o	o	o
Daptomycin	o	o	o	o	o	o	o	o	o	o	o	o	o	o	o	o	o	o	o	o	o	o	o	o
Tigecycline	?	?	?	?	o	+	+	?	+	?	+	?	o	?	?	?	?	?	?	?	+	o	?	-
Tetracycline	+	+	+	+	o	+	+	+	+	+	+|	o	+	+	+	+	+	+	+	+	+|	+|	o	o
Minocycline	+	+	+	+	o	+	+	+	+	+	+	o	+	+	?	+	?	+	+	+	+|	+|	o	o
Doxycycline	‡	‡	+	‡	o	+	+	‡	+	‡	+	+|	o	+	‡	+	‡	+	+	+	o	o	o	+
Telithromycin	?	o	o	o	?	?	?	?	+	+	+	?	o	o	o	o	o	o	o	o	o	o	o	o
Clarithromycin	+	o	o	o	?	?	?	?	‡	+	+	o	o	o	o	o	+|	o	?	o	o	o	o	o
Azithromycin	+	o	o	o	‡	?	?	‡	?	?	‡	‡	‡	+	o	o	+	+	?	o	o	o	o	o
Erythromycin	+	o	o	o	‡	+	o	o	‡	?	o	?	+	o	+	o	?	?	?	o	o	o	o	o
Clindamycin	o	o	o	o	o	o	o	o	o	o	o	o	o	o	o	o	o	o	o	o	o	o	o	o
Chloramphen	+	+|	+	+	o	+	o	+	o	o	+	+	+	o	+	o	+	o	+	+	o	o	o	+
Amikacin	o	o	o	?	o	o	o	?	o	o	o	+|	o	o	o	o	?	?	?	?	+|	o	+	o
Tobramycin	o	o	o	+	+	o	o	?	o	o	o	o	o	o	o	o	?	?	?	?	+|	o	+	o
Gentamicin	o	o	+|	‡	o	o	+	o	o	o	o	+|	o	o	o	o	?	+	+	+	o	o	+	o
Cefditoren	o	o	?	o	o	+	+	o	?	o	+	+	+	o	o	o	o	o	o	o	o	o	o	o
Cefdinir	o	o	?	o	o	+	+	o	?	o	+	+	+	o	o	o	o	o	o	o	o	o	o	o
Cefpodoxime	o	o	?	o	o	+	+	o	?	o	+	+	+	o	o	o	o	o	o	o	o	o	o	o
Ceftibuten	o	o	o	o	o	+	+	o	o	o	+	+	+	o	o	o	o	o	o	o	o	o	o	o
Cefixime	o	o	o	o	o	+	+	o	o	o	+	+	+	o	o	o	o	o	o	o	o	o	o	o
Cefurox-Axe	o	o	o	o	o	+	o	o	o	o	+	o	+	o	o	o	o	o	o	o	o	o	o	o
Cefprozil	o	o	?	o	o	+	o	o	o	o	+	o	?	o	o	o	o	o	o	o	o	o	o	o
Cefaclor	o	o	o	?	o	o	o	o	o	o	+|	o	?	o	o	o	o	o	o	o	o	o	o	o
Cephalexin	o	o	o	o	o	o	o	o	o	o	o	o	o	o	o	o	o	o	o	o	o	o	o	o
Cefadroxil	o	o	o	o	o	o	o	o	o	o	o	o	o	o	o	o	o	o	o	o	o	o	o	o

TABLE 4A (8)

Drug	C. trachomatis	Chlamydophila sp.	M. genitalium	M. pneumoniae	U. urealyticum	B. fragilis	F. necrophorum	P. melaninogenica	Actinomyces sp.	C. difficile	Clostridium sp.	P. acnes	Peptostreptococci
Oral Cephalosporins	*Aerobic – cell wall-deficient*					*Anaerobic GNB*			*Anaerobic gram-positive*				
Cefadroxil	o	o	o	o	o	?	?	?	?	o	?	+	+
Cephalexin	o	o	o	o	o	?	?	?	?	o	?	o	+
Cefaclor	o	o	o	o	o	?	?	?	?	o	?	+	+
Cefprozil	o	o	o	o	o	?	?	?	?	o	?	+	+
Cefurox-Axe	o	o	o	o	o	?	?	?	?	o	+	+	+
Cefixime	o	o	o	o	o	?	?	?	?	o	?	+	+
Ceftibuten	o	o	o	o	o	?	?	?	?	o	?	+	+
Cefpodoxime	o	o	o	o	o	o	o	?	o	o	?	?	?
Cefdinir	o	o	o	o	o	o	o	?	?	o	?	?	?
Cefditoren	o	o	o	o	o	o	o	?	o	o	?	?	?
Aminoglyco Gentamicin	o	o	o	o	o	o	o	o	o	o	+	?	o
Tobramycin	o	o	o	o	o	o	o	o	o	o	o	?	o
Amikacin	o	o	o	o	o	o	o	o	o	o	o	?	o
Chloramphen	o	+	o	o	o	+	+	+	+	+	+	+	+
Macrolides Clindamycin	o	o	o	o	o	+|	+	+	‡	o	+|	+|	+
Erythromycin	+	+	?	+|	‡	o	o	+|	‡	o	+|	+|	+|
Azithromycin	‡	+	‡	+|	‡	o	o	+|	?	o	+|	+|	+|
Clarithromycin	+	+	?	+|	+	o	o	+|	?	o	+	?	+|
Telithromycin	?	+	?	+|	?	o	o	o	?	o	?	?	?
Tetracyclines Doxycycline	‡	‡	+|	+|	‡	+|	+	+	o	+	+	+	+
Minocycline	+	+	+	+|	+	+|	+	+	o	+	+	+	+
Tetracycline	+	+	+	+|	+	+|	+	+	o	+	+	+	+
Tigecycline	o	+	+	?	+	+	+	+	?	o	+	+	+
Daptomycin	o	o	o	o	o	o	o	o	o	o	+|	+	+
Glyco/Lipo Vancomycin	o	o	o	o	o	o	o	o	?	‡	+	+	+
Teicoplanin	o	o	o	o	o	o	o	o	o	o	+	+	+
Telavancin	o	o	o	o	o	o	o	o	?	o	+	+	+
Oritavancin	o	o	o	o	o	o	o	o	o	o	+	+	+
Dalbavancin	o	o	o	o	o	o	o	o	o	o	+	+	+
Ox-lid Linezolid	o	o	o	o	o	o	o	o	+	o	+	o	+
Tedizolid	o	o	o	o	o	o	o	o	?	o	o	o	?
Poly Polymyxin B	o	o	o	o	o	o	o	o	o	o	o	o	o
Colistin	o	o	o	o	o	o	o	o	o	o	o	o	o
Other Fusidic Acid	o	o	o	o	o	o	o	o	o	o	o	o	o
Rif (comb)	o	+|	o	o	o	o	o	o	o	o	o	o	o
TMP-SMX	o	o	o	o	o	o	o	o	o	o	o	+|	o
Nitrofurantoin	o	o	o	o	o	o	o	o	o	o	o	o	o
Fosfomycin (IV)	o	o	o	o	o	o	o	o	o	o	o	o	+
Fosfomycin (po)	o	o	o	o	o	o	o	o	o	o	o	o	o
Metronidazole	o	o	o	o	o	‡	‡	‡	o	‡	+	o	+|
Quinu-Dalfo	o	o	o	o	o	o	o	o	+	o	+	o	?

TABLE 4B - ANTIFUNGAL ACTIVITY SPECTRA

	Antifungal Drugs								
	Fluconazole	Itraconazole	Voriconazole	Posaconazole	Isavuconazonium sulfate	Anidulafungin	Caspofungin	Micafungin	Amphotericin B
Fungi									
Aspergillus fumigatus	0	±	++	+	++	±	±	±	+
Aspergillus terreus	0	±	++	+	++	±	±	±	0
Aspergillus flavus	0	±	++	+	++	±	±	±	+
Candida albicans	++	+	+	+	+	++	++	++	+
Candida dubliniensis	++	+	+	+	+	++	++	++	++
Candida glabrata	±	±	±	±	±	++	++	++	++
Candida guilliermondii	++	++	++	++	+	++	++	++	++
Candida krusei	0	0	+	+	+	++	++	++	0
Candida lusitaniae	++	+	+	+	+	++	++	++	0
Candida parapsilosis	++	+	+	+	+	+	+	+	++
Candida tropicalis	++	+	+	+	+	++	++	++	++
Cryptococcus sp.	++	+	+	+	+	0	0	0	++
Dematiaceous molds	0	++	++	+	+	±	±	±	++
Fusarium sp.	0	±	±	±	±	0	0	0	±
Mucormycosis	0	0	0	+	+	0	0	0	++
Scedo apiospermum	0	0	+	±	±	0	0	0	0
Scedo (Lomentospora) prolificans	0	0	0	0	0	0	0	0	0
Trichosporon spp.	±	+	+	+	+	0	0	0	+
Dimorphic Fungi									
Blastomyces	±	++	+	+	?	0	0	0	++
Coccidioides	++	++	+	+	?	0	0	0	++
Histoplasma	±	++	+	+	?	0	0	0	++
Sporothrix	±	++	+	+	?	0	0	0	++

TABLE 4C - ANTIVIRAL ACTIVITY SPECTRA

	Adenovirus	BK Virus	Cytomegalovirus	Hepatitis B	Hepatitis C	Herpes simplex	HPV	Influenza A	Influenza B	JC Virus / PML	RSV	Varicella-zoster
Hepatitis B												
Adefovir	NA	NA	NA	++	NA	NA	NA	NA	NA	NA	NA	NA
Emtricitabine	NA	NA	NA	±	NA	NA	NA	NA	NA	NA	NA	NA
Entecavir	NA	NA	NA	++	NA	NA	NA	NA	NA	NA	NA	NA
Lamivudine	NA	NA	NA	±	NA	NA	NA	NA	NA	NA	NA	NA
Telbivudine	NA	NA	NA	±	NA	NA	NA	NA	NA	NA	NA	NA
Tenofovir (TDF and TAF)	NA	NA	NA	++	NA	±	NA	NA	NA	NA	NA	NA
Hepatitis C												
Daclatasvir	NA	NA	NA	NA	++	NA	NA	NA	NA	NA	NA	NA
Dasabuvir	NA	NA	NA	NA	++	NA	NA	NA	NA	NA	NA	NA
Elbasvir	NA	NA	NA	NA	++	NA	NA	NA	NA	NA	NA	NA
Grazoprevir	NA	NA	NA	NA	++	NA	NA	NA	NA	NA	NA	NA
Interferon alfa, peg	NA	NA	NA	++	+	NA	NA	NA	NA	NA	NA	NA
Ledipasvir	NA	NA	NA	NA	++	NA	NA	NA	NA	NA	NA	NA
Ombitasvir	NA	NA	NA	NA	++	NA	NA	NA	NA	NA	NA	NA
Paritaprevir	NA	NA	NA	NA	++	NA	NA	NA	NA	NA	NA	NA
Ribavirin	±	NA	NA	NA	0	±	NA	NA	NA	NA	±	NA
Simeprevir	NA	NA	NA	NA	+	NA	NA	NA	NA	NA	NA	NA
Sofosbuvir	NA	NA	NA	NA	++	NA	NA	NA	NA	NA	NA	NA
Velpatasvir	NA	NA	NA	NA	++	NA	NA	NA	NA	NA	NA	NA
Voxilaprevir	NA	NA	NA	NA	++	NA	NA	NA	NA	NA	NA	NA
Influenza												
Amantadine	NA	NA	NA	NA	NA	NA	NA	±	±	NA	NA	NA
Oseltamivir	NA	NA	NA	NA	NA	NA	NA	++	+	NA	NA	NA
Peramivir	NA	NA	NA	NA	NA	NA	NA	+	+	NA	NA	NA
Rimantadine	NA	NA	NA	NA	NA	NA	NA	±	±	NA	NA	NA
Zanamivir	NA	NA	NA	NA	NA	NA	NA	++	+	NA	NA	NA
Herpes, CMV, VZV, misc.												
Acyclovir	NA	NA	0	NA	NA	++	NA	NA	NA	NA	NA	+
Cidofovir	+	+	++	NA	NA	+	NA	NA	NA	+	NA	+
Famciclovir	NA	NA	0	NA	NA	++	NA	NA	NA	NA	NA	+
Foscarnet	NA	NA	++	NA	NA	+	NA	NA	NA	NA	NA	+
Ganciclovir	±	NA	++	NA	NA	+	NA	NA	NA	NA	NA	+
Letermovir	NA	NA	++	NA	NA	NA	NA	NA	NA	NA	NA	NA
Valacyclovir	NA	NA	0	NA	NA	++	NA	NA	NA	NA	NA	++
Valganciclovir	±	NA	++	NA	NA	+	NA	NA	NA	NA	NA	+
Topical Agents												
Imiquimod	NA	NA	NA	NA	NA	NA	++	NA	NA	NA	NA	NA
Penciclovir	NA	NA	0	NA	NA	+	NA	NA	NA	NA	NA	0
Podofilox	NA	NA	NA	NA	NA	NA	++	NA	NA	NA	NA	NA
Sinecatechins	NA	NA	NA	NA	NA	NA	+	NA	NA	NA	NA	NA
Trifluridine	NA	NA	NA	NA	NA	+	NA	NA	NA	NA	NA	NA

TABLE 5A – TREATMENT OPTIONS FOR SYSTEMIC INFECTION DUE TO MULTI-DRUG RESISTANT GRAM-POSITIVE BACTERIA

ORGANISM	RESISTANT TO	PRIMARY TREATMENT OPTIONS	ALTERNATIVE TREATMENT* OPTIONS	COMMENTS
Enterococcus faecium; Enterococcus faecalis (Consultation suggested) For review of VRE treatment: *Infect Dis Clin North Am 30:415, 2016.*	Vancomycin (VRE), Ampicillin, Penicillin G, Gentamicin (high level resistance)	**E. faecium, systemic infection, bacteremia: Dapto** 10-12 mg/kg IV q24h + **AMP** 2 gm IV q4h **OR Ceftaroline** 600 mg IV q8h). Less desirable alternatives: **[Linezolid** 600 mg po/IV q12h **OR Quinupristin-Dalfopristin** 7.5 mg/kg IV (central line).] ± **AM-SB AMP** 2 gm IV q4h	E. faecalis: Resistance to AMP or Pen rare. If no resistance: **AMP** 2 gm IV q4h + **Ceftriaxone** 2 gm IV q12h. If Pen-resistant due to beta-lactamase: **Dapto** 8-12 mg/kg IV q12h + **AM-SB** 3 gm IV q6h.	**Addition of a beta lactam to Dapto reverses Dapto resistance & impedes development of resistance.** E. faecalis rarely resistance to penicillins. Linezolid 600 mg IV/po bid an alternative to Dapto for the treatment of VRE bacteremia, systemic infection, but data are conflicting as to which is better (*CID 61:871, 2015 and CID 61:879, 2015*). Dapto dose > 9 mg/kg is associated with lower mortality in treatment of VRE bacteremia (*CID 64:1026, 2017*). Linezolid should be used for treatment of VRE infections if Dapto MIC > 4 μg/ml.
Staphylococcus aureus (See *Table 6* for more details)	Vancomycin (VISA or VRSA) and all beta lactams (except Ceftaroline)	**Daptomycin** 6-12 mg/kg IV q24h or (**Daptomycin** 6-12 mg/kg IV q24h + **Ceftaroline** 600 mg IV q8h) (*AAC 56:5296, 2012*).	**Telavancin** 10 mg/kg IV q24h or **Linezolid** 600 mg IV/po q12h	Confirm dapto susceptibility as VISA strains may be non-susceptible. If prior vanco therapy (or persistent infection on vanco) there is significant chance of developing resistance to dapto (*JAC 66:1696, 2011*). Addition of an anti-staphylococcal beta-lactam (nafcillin or oxacillin) may restore susceptibility against Dapto-resistant MRSA (*AAC 54:3161, 2010*). Combination of Dapto + Oxacillin has been successful in clearing refractory MRSA bacteremia (*CID 53:158, 2011*). Dapto + Ceftaroline may also be effective.
Streptococcus pneumoniae	Penicillin G (MIC ≥4 μg/mL)	If no meningitis: **Ceftriaxone** 2 gm IV once daily OR **Ceftaroline** 600 mg IV q12h OR **Linezolid** 600 mg IV/po q12h	Meningitis: **Vancomycin** 15 mg/kg IV q8h OR **Meropenem** 2 gm IV q8h	Ceftriaxone 2 gm IV q12h should also work for meningitis.

TABLE 5B: TREATMENT OPTIONS FOR SYSTEMIC INFECTION DUE TO SELECTED MULTI-DRUG RESISTANT GRAM-NEGATIVE BACILLI

Many of the treatment options extensively drug-resistant GNB are not FDA approved indications (NAI). Suggested options are based on a combination of in vitro data, animal models, observational studies or clinical trials. For dosing, see specific topics in *Table 1* or drug listings in *Table 10A*.

ORGANISM	RESISTANT TO	PRIMARY TREATMENT OPTIONS	ALTERNATIVE TREATMENT OPTIONS	COMMENTS
Acinetobacter baumannii	All beta-lactams (except Sulbactam), AG, FQ, TMP-SMX	*If susceptible:* Cefepime, Ceftazidime, Amp-sulb. *If MDR:* MER or IMP	*If critically ill:* MER + Amp-sulb + Minocycline + Polymyxin B (Colistin if UTI)	For pneumonia, add nebulized Colistin 50-75 mg bid. Colistin + Rif failed in clinical trial (CID 57:349, 2013). Multiple mechanisms of resistance.
Extended spectrum beta lactamase (ESBL) produced by E. coli, K. pneumoniae, Enterobacteriaceae, P. aeruginosa	All cephalosporins, FQ, AG, TMP-SMX	MER or IMP	Ceftolozane-tazobactam[a], Ceftazidime-avibactam[a], Meropenem-vaborbactam[a]	Pip-tazo discordance: even in sensitive in vitro, may fail clinically. For UTI: Nitrofurantoin, Fosfomycin.
OXA-48 producing Enterobacteriaceae	All penicillins, FQ, AG, TMP-SMX	*If sensitive:* Cefepime, Ceftazidime	*If critically ill:* Ceftazidime-avibactam + Aztreonam	More common in areas bordering the Mediterranean Sea
KPC (serine carbapenemase) producing Enterobacteriaceae	All penicillins, cephalosporins, Aztreonam, carbapenems, FQ, AG, TMP-SMX	Ceftazidime-avibactam[a], Meropenem-vaborbactam	MER + Polymyxin B (Colistin if UTI)	For pneumonia, add nebulized Colistin 50-75 mg bid. Success with ERTA + MER (JAC 69:1718, 2014).
Metallo-carbapenemase producing GNB	All beta lactams (except Aztreonam), FQ, AG, TMP-SMX	Ceftazidime-avibactam[a] + Aztreonam	MER + Polymyxin B	For pneumonia, add nebulized Colistin 50-75 mg bid.
Stenotrophomonas maltophilia	All beta lactams, FQ, AG	TMP-SMX	*If susceptible in vitro:* FQ	Ticar-clav no longer available. Ref: Sem Resp CCM 36:99, 2015

[a] Not FDA-approved indication

TABLE 6 – SUGGESTED MANAGEMENT OF SUSPECTED OR CULTURE-POSITIVE COMMUNITY-ASSOCIATED METHICILLIN-RESISTANT S. AUREUS INFECTIONS

IDSA Guidelines: CID 52 (Feb 1):1, 2011. With the magnitude of the clinical problem and a number of new drugs, it is likely new data will require frequent revisions of the regimens suggested. (See page 2 for abbreviations).

NOTE: Distinction between community and hospital strains of MRSA blurring.

CLINICAL ILLNESS	ABSCESS, NO IMMUNOSUPPRESSION, OUT-PATIENT CARE	PNEUMONIA	BACTEREMIA OR POSSIBLE ENDOCARDITIS OR BACTEREMIC SHOCK	TREATMENT FAILURE (See footnote[2])
Management *Drug doses in footnote[1].*	**TMP/SMX** 1 DS (2 DS if BMI >40) po bid OR **Clinda** 300 mg (450 mg for BMI >40) po tid (NEJM 372:2093, 2015). For large abscesses, multiple lesions or systemic inflammatory response: **I&D + (Oritavancin** 1500 mg x 1 or **Dalbavancin** 1000 mg x 1 than 500 mg x 1 a wk later)** an option for outpatient management of sicker patients with more extensive infection who might otherwise be admitted (See NEJM 370:2180, 2014; NEJM 370:2169, 2014).	**Vanco** IV or **Linezolid** IV	**Vanco** 15–20 mg/kg IV q8-12h. Confirm adequate vanco troughs of 15-20 μg/mL. Switch to alternative regimen if **Vanco** MIC >2 μg/mL. If patient has slow response to vanco and isolate has MIC = 2, consider alternative therapy. **Dapto** 5 mg/kg IV q24h (FDA-approved dose but some authorities recommend 8-12 mg/kg for MRSA bacteremia).	**Dapto** 8-12 mg/kg IV q24h; confirm in vitro susceptibility as prior vanco therapy may select for daptomycin non-susceptibility (MIC >1 μg/mL) & some VISA strains are daptomycin non-susceptible. **Use combination therapy for bacteremia or endocarditis:** dapto + beta-lactam combination therapy [**Dapto** 8-12 mg/kg IV q24h + (**Nafcillin** 2 gm IV q4h OR **Oxacillin** 2 gm IV q4h OR **Ceftaroline** 600 mg IV q8h)] appears effective against MRSA strains as salvage therapy even if non-susceptible to dapto (Int J Antimicrob Agents, 42:450, 2013; AAC 54:3161, 2010; AAC 56:6192, 2013). **Ceftaroline** 600 mg IV q8h (J Antimicrob Chemother 67:1267, 2012; J Infect Chemother 19:42, 2013; Int J Antimicrob Agents 42:450, 2013; AAC 58:2541, 2014). **Linezolid** 600 mg IV/po q12h (Linezolid is bacteriostatic and should not be used as a single agent in suspected endovascular infection). **Telavancin** 10 mg/kg q24h IV (CID 52:31, 2011; AAC 58:2030, 2014).
Comments	**Fusidic acid** 500 mg tid (not available in the US). **Rifampin** also an option; do not use rifampin alone as resistance rapidly emerges.	Patients not responding after 2-3 days should be evaluated for complicated infection and switched to **Vancomycin**. Prospective study of Linezolid vs Vanco showed slightly higher cure rate with Linezolid, no difference in mortality (CID 54:621, 2012).	TMP-SMX NOT recommended in bacteremic pts: inferior to Vanco (BMJ 350:2219, 2015)	

[1] **Clindamycin:** 300 mg po tid. **Daptomycin:** 6 mg/kg IV q24h is the standard. FDA-approved dose for bacteremia and endocarditis but 8-12 mg/kg IV q24h is recommended by some and for treatment failures. **Doxycycline** or **Minocycline:** 100 mg po bid. **Linezolid:** 600 mg IV/po bid. **Quinupristin-Dalfopristin (Q-D):** 7.5 mg per /kg IV q8h via central line. **Rifampin:** Long serum half-life justifies dosing 600 mg po q24h; however, frequent GI upset. Do not use as a single drug because resistance develops rapidly. **TMP-SMX-DS:** Standard dose 8-10 mg per kg per day. For 70 kg person = 700 mg TMP component per day. **TMP-SMX** contains 160 mg TMP and 800 mg SMX; some dose for treatment of CA-MRSA skin and soft tissue infections (SSTI) is 1 DS tablet twice daily. **Vancomycin:** 1 gm IV q12h; up to 45-60 mg/kg/day in divided doses may be required to achieve target trough concentrations of 15-20 mcg/mL recommended for serious infections.

[2] The median duration of bacteremia in endocarditis is 7-9 days in patients treated with vancomycin (AnIM 115:674, 1991). Longer duration of bacteremia, greater likelihood of endocarditis (JID 190:1140, 2004). Definition of failure unclear. Clinical response should be factored in. **Unsatisfactory clinical response especially if blood cultures remain positive >4 days.**

TABLE 7 - ANTIBIOTIC HYPERSENSITIVITY REACTIONS & DRUG DESENSITIZATION METHODS

Penicillin. Oral route (Pen-VK) preferred. 1/3 pts develop transient reaction, usually mild. Perform in ICU setting. **Discontinue β-blockers. Have IV line, epinephrine, ECG, spirometer available.** Desensitization works as long as it is receiving Pen; allergy returns after discontinuance. History of Steven-Johnson, exfoliative dermatitis, erythroderma are contraindications. Skin testing for evaluation of Pen allergy: Testing with major determinant (benzyl Pen polylysine) and minor determinants has negative predictive value (97-99%). Risk of systemic reaction to skin testing <1% (*Ann Allergy Asth Immunol 106:1, 2011*). General refs: CID 58:1140, 2014.

- **Method:** Prepare dilutions using **Pen-VK** oral soln, 250 mg/5mL. Administer each dose @ 15 min intervals in 30 mL water/flavored bev. After Step 14 observe pt for 30 min, then give full therapeutic dose by route of choice. Ref: *Allergy, Prin & Prac, Mosby, 1993, pg. 1726.*

Step	Dilution (mg/mL)	mL Administered	Dose/Step mg	Dose/Step units	Cumulative Dose Given mg	Cumulative Dose Given units
1	0.5	0.1	0.05	80	0.05	80
2	0.5	0.2	0.1	160	0.15	240
3	0.5	0.4	0.2	320	0.35	560
4	0.5	0.8	0.4	640	0.75	1,200
5	0.5	1.6	0.8	1,280	1.55	2,480
6	0.5	3.2	1.6	2,560	3.15	5,040
7	0.5	6.4	3.2	5,120	6.35	10,160
8	5	1.2	6	9,600	12.35	19,760
9	5	2.4	12	19,200	24.35	38,960
10	5	4.8	24	38,400	48.35	77,360
11	50	1	50	80,000	98.35	157,360
12	50	2	100	160,000	198.35	317,360
13	50	4	200	320,000	398.35	637,360
14	50	8	400	640,000	798.35	1,277,360

TMP-SMX. Perform in hospital/clinic. Refs: *CID 20:849, 1995; AIDS 5:311, 1991.*

- **Method:** Use **TMP-SMX** oral susp, (40 mg TMP/200 mg SMX)/5 mL. Take with 6 oz water after each dose. Corticosteroids, antihistaminics NOT used.

Hour	Dose (TMP/SMX) (mg)
0	0.004/0.02
1	0.04/0.2
2	0.4/2
3	4/20
4	40/200
5	160/800

Penicillin. Parenteral (Pen G) route. Follow procedures/notes under Oral (Pen-VK) route. Ref: Allergy, Prin & Prac, Mosby, 1993, pg. 1726.

- **Method: Administer Pen G** IM, IV or sc as follows:

Step	Dilution (units/mL)	mL Administered	Dose/Step (units)	Cumulative Dose Given (units)
1	100	0.2	20	20
2	100	0.4	40	60
3	100	0.8	80	140
4	1,000	0.2	200	340
5	1,000	0.4	400	740
6	1,000	0.8	800	1,540
7	10,000	0.2	2,000	3,540
8	10,000	0.4	4,000	7,540
9	10,000	0.8	8,000	15,540
10	100,000	0.2	20,000	35,540
11	100,000	0.4	40,000	75,540
12	100,000	0.8	80,000	155,540
13	1,000,000	0.2	200,000	355,540
14	1,000,000	0.4	400,000	755,540
15	1,000,000	0.8	800,000	1,555,540

Ceftriaxone. Ref: *Allergol Immunopathol (Madr) 37:105, 2009.*

- **Method: Infuse Ceftriaxone IV** @ 20 min intervals as follows:

Day	Dose (mg)
1	0.001, then 0.01, then 0.1, then 1
2	1, then 5, then 10, then 50
3	100, then 250, then 500
4	1000

Desensitization Methods for Other Drugs (References)

- **Imipenem-Cilastatin.** *Ann Pharmacother 37:513, 2003.*
- **Meropenem.** *Ann Pharmacother 37:1424, 2003.*
- **Metronidazole.** *Allergy Rhinol 5:1, 2014.*
- **Daptomycin.** *Ann All Asthma Immun 100:87, 2008.*
- **Ceftazidime.** *Curr Opin All Clin Immunol 6(6): 476, 2006.*
- **Liposomal Amphotericin B.** *J Allergy Clin Immunol Pract 5:181, 2017.*
- **Vancomycin.** *Intern Med 45:317, 2006.*
- **General review,** including desensitization protocols for Amp, CFP, CIP, Clarithro, Clinda, Dapto, Linezolid, Tobra (*CID 58:1140, 2014*).

TABLE 7 (2)

Ceftaroline. 12-step IV desensitization protocol. Ref: *Open Forum Infect Dis 2:1, 2015.*

- Method: Cumulative drug infused: 600 mg. Total time required for all 12 steps: 318 minutes.

Step	Conc (mg/mL)	Vol infused (mL)	Infusion duration (min)	Drug infused this step (mg)	Cumulative drug infused (mg)
1	0.0002	5	15	0.001	0.001
2	0.0002	15	15	0.003	0.004
3	0.002	5	15	0.01	0.014
4	0.002	15	15	0.03	0.04
5	0.02	5	15	0.1	0.14
6	0.02	15	15	0.3	0.4
7	0.2	5	15	1	1.4
8	0.2	15	15	3	4.4
9	2	5	15	10	14.4
10	2	15	15	30	44.4
11	2	25	15	50	94.4
12	2	255	153	510	504.4

Valganciclovir. 12-step oral desensitization protocol. Ref: *Transplantation 98:e50, 2014.*

- Method: Administer doses at 15-minute intervals; entire protocol takes 165 minutes. Cumulative dose administered: 453.6 mg

Step	Drug administered this step (mg)	Cumulative drug administered (mg)
1	0.1	0.1
2	0.2	0.3
3	0.4	0.7
4	0.8	1.5
5	1.6	3.1
6	3.5	6.6
7	7	13.6
8	14	27.6
9	28	55.6
10	58	113.6
11	115	228.6
12	225	453.6

TABLE 8 – PREGNANCY RISK AND SAFETY IN LACTATION

Drug	Risk Category (Old)	Use during Lactation
Antibacterials		
Amikacin	D	Probably safe, monitor infant for GI toxicity
Azithromycin	B	Safe, monitor infant for GI toxicity
Aztreonam	B	Safe, monitor infant for GI toxicity
Cephalosporins	B	Safe, monitor infant for GI toxicity
Chloramphenicol	C	Avoid use
Ciprofloxacin	C	Avoid breastfeeding for 3-4 hrs after a dose, monitor infant for GI toxicity
Clarithromycin	C	Safe, monitor for GI toxicity
Clindamycin	B	Avoid use if possible, otherwise monitor infant for GI toxicity
Colistin (polymyxin E)	C	Probably safe with monitoring, but data limited
Dalbavancin	C	Probably safe with monitoring, but no data available
Daptomycin	B	Probably safe with monitoring, but data limited
Delafloxacin	No human data	No data
Doripenem	B	Probably safe with monitoring, but no data available
Doxycycline	D	Short-term use safe, monitor infant for GI toxicity
Ertapenem	B	Safe
Erythromycin	B	Safe
Fidaxomicin	B	Probably safe
Fosfomycin	B	Probably safe with monitoring
Fusidic acid	-	Safety not established
Gatifloxacin	C	Short-term use safe
Gemifloxacin	C	Short-term use safe
Gentamicin	D	Probably safe
Imipenem	C	Safe, monitor infant for GI toxicity
Isepamicin	D	Safety not established, avoid use
Levofloxacin	C	Avoid breastfeeding for 4-6 hrs after a dose, monitor infant for GI toxicity
Linezolid	C	Probably safe with monitoring, but no data available; avoid if possible
Meropenem	B	Probably safe with monitoring, but no data available
Metronidazole	B	Data and opinions conflict; best to avoid
Minocycline	D	Short-term use safe, monitor infant for GI toxicity
Moxifloxacin	C	Short-term use safe, monitor infant for GI toxicity; avoid if possible
Netilmicin	D	Safety not established
Nitrofurantoin	B	Avoid if infant <8 days of age
Ofloxacin	C	Avoid breastfeeding for 4-6 hrs after a dose, monitor infant for GI toxicity
Oritavancin	C	Probably safe with monitoring, but no data available; avoid if possible
Penicillins	B	Safe, monitor infant for GI toxicity
Polymyxin B	C	Topical administration safe (no data with systemic use)
Quinupristin/ Dalfopristin	B	Probably safe with monitoring, but no data available; avoid if possible
Rifaximin	C	Probably safe with monitoring, but no data available; avoid if possible
Streptomycin	D	Probably safe, monitor infant for GI toxicity
Tedizolid	C	Probably safe with monitoring, but no data available; avoid if possible
Telavancin	C	Probably safe with monitoring, but no data available; avoid if possible
Telithromycin	C	Probably safe with monitoring, but no data available; avoid if possible
Tetracycline	D	Short-term use safe, monitor infant for GI toxicity
Tigecycline	D	Safety not established, avoid use
TMP-SMX	C	Risk of kernicterus in premature infants; avoid if infant G6PD-deficient
Tobramycin	D	Probably safe, monitor infant for GI toxicity
Vancomycin	C	Safe with monitoring
Antifungals		
Amphotericin B (all products)	B	Probably safe, but no data available
Anidulafungin	B	Safety not established, avoid use
Caspofungin	C	Probably safe with monitoring, but no data available; avoid if possible
Fluconazole (other regimens)	D	Safe with monitoring
Fluconazole (single dose)	C	Safe with monitoring
Flucytosine	C	Safety not established, avoid use
Griseofulvin	C	Safety not established, avoid use
Isavuconazonium sulfate	C	Avoid use
Itraconazole	C	Little data available, avoid if possible
Ketoconazole	C	Little data available, avoid if possible
Micafungin	C	Safety not established, avoid use
Posaconazole	C	Safety not established, avoid use
Terbinafine	B	Little data available, avoid if possible
Voriconazole	D	Safety not established, avoid use

TABLE 8 (2)

Drug	Risk Category (Old)	Use during Lactation
Antimycobacterials		
Amikacin	D	Probably safe, monitor infant for GI toxicity
Bedaquiline	B	Safety not established, avoid use
Capreomycin	C	Probably safe, monitor infant for GI toxicity
Clofazimine	C	May color breast milk pink; probably safe but avoid if possible
Cycloserine	C	Probably safe
Dapsone	C	Safe
Ethambutol	"safe"	Probably safe
Ethionamide	C	Probably safe with monitoring
Isoniazid	C	Safe
Para-aminosalicylic acid	C	Probably safe
Pyrazinamide	C	Probably safe
Rifabutin	B	Probably safe
Rifampin	C	Probably safe
Rifapentine	C	Probably safe
Streptomycin	D	Probably safe
Thalidomide	X	Safety not established
Antiparasitics		
Albendazole	C	Data limited; one-time dose considered safe by WHO
Artemether/ Lumefantrine	C	Data limited; probably safe, particularly if infant weighs at least 5 kg
Atovaquone	C	Data limited; probably safe, particularly if infant weighs at least 5 kg
Atovaquone/Proguanil	C	Data limited; probably safe, particularly if infant weighs at least 5 kg
Benznidazole	avoid	Safe with monitoring
Chloroquine	C	Probably safe with monitoring, but data limited; avoid if possible
Dapsone	C	Safe, but avoid if infant G6PD-deficient
Eflornithine	C	Probably safe, monitor infant for toxicity
Ivermectin	C	Probably safe, monitor infant for toxicity
Mebendazole	C	Probably safe, monitor infant for toxicity
Mefloquine	B	Probably safe, monitor infant for toxicity
Miltefosine	D	Safety not established, avoid use
Nitazoxanide	B	Probably safe with monitoring, but data limited; avoid if possible
Pentamidine	C	Safety not established, avoid use
Praziquantel	B	Probably safe, monitor infant for toxicity
Pyrimethamine	C	Safe with monitoring
Quinidine	C	Probably safe, monitor infant for toxicity
Quinine	X	Probably safe, but avoid if infant G6PD-deficient
Sulfadoxine/ Pyrimethamine	C	Little data available, avoid use if possible
Tinidazole	C	Safety not established, avoid use
Antivirals		
Acyclovir	B	Safe with monitoring
Adefovir	C	Safety not established, avoid use if possible
Amantadine	C	Avoid use
Cidofovir	C	Avoid use
Daclatasvir	No human data	Safety not established, avoid use if possible
Entecavir	C	Safety not established, avoid use if possible
Famciclovir	B	Safety not established, avoid use
Foscarnet	C	Safety not established, avoid use
Ganciclovir	C	Safety not established, avoid use
Interferons	C	Probably safe, monitor infant for toxicity
Letermovir	Humans ND, toxic in animals	Safety not established, avoid use
Oseltamivir	C	Probably safe, monitor infant for toxicity
Peramivir	C	Safety not established, avoid use if possible
Ribavirin	X	No data, but probably safe with monitoring
Rimantadine	C	Avoid use
Simeprevir	C (X w/ribavirin)	Safety not established, avoid use if possible
Sofosbuvir	B (X w/ribavirin)	Safety not established, avoid use if possible
Telbivudine	B	Safety not established, avoid use if possible
Valacyclovir	B	Safe with monitoring
Valganciclovir	C	Safety not established, avoid use
Zanamivir	C	Probably safe, but no data

TABLE 8 (3)

Drug	Risk Category (Old)	Use during Lactation
Antivirals (hep C combinations)		
Epclusa	No human data, safe in animals	Safety not established, avoid if possible
Harvoni	B	Safety not established
Technivie	B	Safety not established
Viekira Pak	B	Safety not established
Zepatier	No human data, safe in animals	Safety not established, avoid if possible
Antiretrovirals		
Abacavir	C	*See general statement about antiretrovirals below*
Atazanavir	B	*See general statement about antiretrovirals below*
Darunavir	C	*See general statement about antiretrovirals below*
Delavirdine	C	*See general statement about antiretrovirals below*
Didanosine	B	*See general statement about antiretrovirals below*
Dolutegravir	B	*See general statement about antiretrovirals below*
Efavirenz	D	*See general statement about antiretrovirals below*
Elvitegravir	B	*See general statement about antiretrovirals below*
Emtricitabine	B	*See general statement about antiretrovirals below*
Enfuvirtide	B	*See general statement about antiretrovirals below*
Etravirine	B	*See general statement about antiretrovirals below*
Fosamprenavir	C	*See general statement about antiretrovirals below*
Indinavir	C	*See general statement about antiretrovirals below*
Lamivudine	C	*See general statement about antiretrovirals below*
Lopinavir/r	C	*See general statement about antiretrovirals below*
Maraviroc	B	*See general statement about antiretrovirals below*
Nelfinavir	B	*See general statement about antiretrovirals below*
Nevirapine	B	*See general statement about antiretrovirals below*
Raltegravir	C	*See general statement about antiretrovirals below*
Rilpivirine	B	*See general statement about antiretrovirals below*
Ritonavir	B	*See general statement about antiretrovirals below*
Saquinavir	B	*See general statement about antiretrovirals below*
Stavudine	C	*See general statement about antiretrovirals below*
Tenofovir alafenamide (TAF)	No human data, safe in animals	Safety not established, avoid if possible
Tenofovir disoproxil (TDF)	B	*See general statement about antiretrovirals below*
Tipranavir	C	*See general statement about antiretrovirals below*
Zalcitabine	C	*See general statement about antiretrovirals below*
Zidovudine	C	*See general statement about antiretrovirals below*

GENERAL STATEMENT ABOUT ANTIRETROVIRALS
1) HIV-infected mothers are generally discouraged from breastfeeding their infants
2) In settings where breastfeeding is required, country-specific recommendations should be followed.

TABLE 9A - SELECTED PHARMACOLOGIC FEATURES OF ANTIMICROBIAL AGENTS

For pharmacodynamics, see Table 9B; for Cytochrome P450 interactions, see Table 9C. Table terminology key at bottom of each page. Additional footnotes at end of Table 9A, page 102.

DRUG	REFERENCE DOSE (SINGLE OR MULTIPLE)	FOOD REC (PO DRUGS)[1]	ORAL ABS (%)	PEAK SERUM CONC[2] (µg/mL)	PROTEIN BINDING (%)	VOLUME OF DISTRIBUTION (Vd)[3]	AVG SERUM T½ (hr)[4]	BILE PEN (%)[5]	CSF/BLOOD[6] (%)	CSF PENETRATION[7]	AUC[8] (µg·hr/mL)	Tmax (hr)
ANTIBACTERIALS												
Aminoglycosides												
Amik, Gent, Kana, Tobra	See Table 10D			See Table 10D								ND
Neomycin	po	Tab/soln ± food	<3	0	ND	ND	ND				ND	ND
Carbapenems												
Doripenem	500 mg IV			23 (SD)	8,?	16.8 L Vss	1	117 (0-611)	0-30	No	36.3	
Ertapenem	1 gm IV			154 (SD)	95	0.12 L/kg Vss	4	10	ND	ND	572.1	
Imipenem	500 mg IV			40 (SD)	15-25	0.27 L/kg	1	minimal	8.5	Possibly[a]	42.2	
Meropenem	1 gm IV			49 (SD)	2	0.29 L/kg	1	3-300	≈ 2	Possibly[a]	72.5	
Meropenem/ Vaborbactam	Mer 2 gm/ Vab 2 gm IV q8h			Mer 43.4, Vab 55.6 (SS)	Mer 2, Vab 33	Mer 20.2L, Vab 18.6 L (Vss)	Mer 1.2, Vab 1.7	ND	ND	ND	Mer 138, Vab 196 (8 hr, SS)	
Cephalosporins (IV)												
Cefazolin	1 gm IV			188 (SD)	73-87	0.19 L/kg	1.9	29-300	1-4	No	236	
Cefotetan	1 gm IV			158 (SD)	78-91	10.3 L	4.2	2-21	ND	ND	504	
Cefoxitin	1 gm IV			110 (SD)	65-79	16.1 L Vss	0.8	280	3	No	150	
Cefuroxime	1.5 gm IV			100 (SD)	33-50	0.19 L/kg Vss	1.5	35-80	17-88	Marginal	70	
Cefotaxime	1 gm IV			100 (SD)	30-51	0.28 L/kg	1.5	15-75	10	Yes	85	
Cefizoxime	1 gm IV			60 (SD)	30	0.34 L/kg	1.7	34-82	ND	Yes	1006	
Ceftriaxone	1 gm IV			150 (SD)	85-95	5.8-13.5 L	8	200-500	8-16	Yes	284.8	
Cefepime	2 gm IV			164 (SD)	20	18 L Vss	2	10-20	10	Yes	127	
Ceftazidime	1 gm IV			69 (SD)	<10	0.24 L/kg Vss	1.9	13-54	20-40	ND	ND	
Ceftazidime/ Avibactam	2.5 gm IV q8h			Ceftaz 90.4, Avi 14.6 (SS)	Ceftaz <10, Avi 5.7-3.2	Ceftaz 17 L, Avi 22.2 L (Vss)	Ceftaz 2.8, Avi 2.7	ND	ND	ND	Ceftaz 291, Avi 33.2 (8 hr)	
Ceftolozane/ Tazobactam	1.5 gm IV q8h			Ceftolo 74.4, Tazo 18 (SS)	Ceftolo 16-21, Tazo 30	Ceftolo 13.5, Tazo 18.2 (Vss)	Ceftolo 3.1, Tazo 1.0	ND	ND	ND	Ceftolo 182, Tazo 25 (8 hr)	
Ceftaroline[avis]	600 mg IV q12h			21.3 (SS)	20	20.3 L Vss	2.7	ND	ND	ND	56.3 (12 hr)	
Ceftobiprole[avis]	500 mg IV			33-34.2 (SD)	16	18 L Vss	2.9-3.3	ND	ND	ND	116	
Cephalosporins (po)												
Cefadroxil	500 mg po	Cap/tab/susp ± food	90	16 (SD)	20	0.31 L/kg V/F	1.5	22	ND	ND	47.4	ND
Cephalexin	500 mg po	Cap/tab/susp ± food	90	18 (SD)	5-15	0.38 L/kg V/F	1	216	ND	ND	29	1
Cefaclor	500 mg po	Cap/susp ± food	93	13 (SD)	22-25	0.33 L/kg V/F	0.8	≥60	ND	ND	20.5	0.5-1.0

Food Effect (po dosing): + food = take with food, **no food** = take without food; **± food** = take with or without food; **Ora % AB** = % absorbed; **Peak Serum Level: SD** = after single dose, **SS** = steady state after multiple doses; **Volume of Distribution (Vd): V/F** = Vd/oral bioavailability, **Vss** = Vd at steady state/oral bioavailability; **CSF Penetration:** therapeutic efficacy comment based on dose, usual susceptibility or target organism & penetration into CSF; **AUC** = area under drug concentration curve; **24hr** = AUC 0-24; **Tmax** = time to max plasma concentration.

TABLE 9A (2) (Footnotes at the end of table)

DRUG	REFERENCE DOSE (SINGLE OR MULTIPLE)	FOOD REC (PO DRUGS)	ORAL ABS (%)	PEAK SERUM CONC (μg/mL)	PROTEIN BINDING (%)	VOLUME OF DISTRIBUTION (Vd)	AVG SERUM T½ (hr)	BILE PEN (%)	CSF/BLOOD (%)	CSF PENETRATION	AUC (μg•hr/mL)	Tmax (hr)
Cephalosporins (po) (continued)												
Cefaclor ER	500 mg po	Tab + food		8.4 (SD)	22-25		0.8	≥60			18.1	2.5
Cefprozil	500 mg po	Tab/susp ± food	95	10.5 (SD)	36	0.23 L/kg Vss/F	1.5				25.7	1.5
Cefuroxime axetil	250 mg tab po	Susp + food, tab ± food	52	4.1 (SD)	50	0.66 L/kg V/F	1.5				12.9	2.5
Cefdinir	300 mg po	Cap/susp ± food	25	1.6 (SD)	60-70	0.35 L/kg V/F	1.7				7.1	2.9
Cefditoren pivoxil	400 mg po	Tab + food	16	4 (SD)	88	9.3 L Vss/F	1.6				20	1.5-3.0
Cefixime	400 mg po	Tab/susp ± food	50	3-5 (SD)	65	0.93 L/kg V/F	3.1	800			25.8	4
Cefpodoxime proxetil	200 mg po	Tab ± food, Susp ± food	46	2.3 (SD)	40	0.7 L/kg V/F	2.3	115			14.5	2-3
Ceftibuten	400 mg po	Cap/susp no food	80	15 (SD)	65	0.21 L/kg V/F	2.4				73.7	2.6
Monobactams												
Aztreonam	1 gm IV			90 (SD)	56	12.6 L Vss	2	115-405	3-52	ND	271	
Penicillins												
Benzathine Penicillin G	1.2 million units IM			0.15 (SD)								
Penicillin G	2 million units IV			20 (SD)	65	0.35 L/kg	0.5	500	5-10	Yes: Pen-sens S pneumo		
Penicillin V	500 mg po	Tab/soln no food	60-73	5-6 (SD)	65	0.36 L/kg	0.5					
Amoxicillin	500 mg po	Cap/tab/susp ± food	80	5.5-7.5 (SD)	17	0.36 L/kg	1.2	100-3000	13-14	Yes (IV only)	22	1-2
Amoxicillin ER	775 mg po	Tab + food		6.6 (SD)	20		1.2-1.5				29.8	3.1
Amox/Clav	875/125 mg po	Cap/tab/susp ± food	80/30-98	11.6/2.2 (SD)	18/25	0.36/0.21 (both /kg)	1.4/1.0	amox 100-3000	ND	ND	26.8/5.1 (0-∞)	ND
Amox/Clav ER	2 tabs [total 2000/125 mg]	Tab + food	ND	17/2.1 (SD)	18/25	0.36/0.21 (both /kg)	1.4/1.0	amox 100-3000	ND	ND	71.6/5.3 (0-∞)	1.5/1.03
Ampicillin	2 gm IV			100 (SD)	18-22	0.29 L/kg	1.2	amp 100-3000	13-14	Yes	120/71 (0-∞)	
Amp/Sulb	3 gm IV			109-150/ 48-88 (SD)	28/38	0.29/0.3 (both L/kg)	1.4/1.7	amp 100-3000	ND	ND		
Cloxacillin^NUS	500 mg po	Cap no food	50	7.5-14 (SD)	95	0.1 L/kg	0.5					1-1.5
Dicloxacillin	500 mg po	Cap no food	37	10-17 (SD)	98	0.1 L/kg	0.7	5-8	9-20	Yes w/ high doses	ND	1-1.5
Nafcillin	500 mg IV			30 (SD)	90-94	271.1 Vss	0.5-1	>100	ND	ND	18.1 (0-∞)	
Oxacillin	500 mg IV	Cap no food	50	43 (SD)	90-94	0.4 L/kg	0.5-0.7	25	10-15	Yes	ND	
Pip/Tazo	3.375 gm IV			242/24 (SD)	16/48	0.24/0.4 (both L/kg)	1/1	>100	ND	ND	242/25	

Food Effect (po dosing): + food = take with or without food, **no food** = take without food, **± food** = take with or without food; **Oral % AB** = % absorbed; **Peak Serum Level: SD** = after single dose, **SS** = steady state after multiple doses; **Volume of Distribution (Vd): V/F** = Vd/oral bioavailability, **Vss** = Vd at steady state, **Vss/F** = Vd at steady state/oral bioavailability; **CSF Penetration:** therapeutic efficacy comment based on dose, usual susceptibility of target organism & penetration into CSF; **AUC** = area under drug concentration curve; **24hr** = AUC 0-24; **Tmax** = time to max plasma concentration.

TABLE 9A (3) (Footnotes at the end of table)

DRUG	REFERENCE DOSE (SINGLE OR MULTIPLE)	FOOD REC (PO DRUGS)[1]	ORAL ABS (%)	PEAK SERUM CONC[2] (µg/mL)	PROTEIN BINDING (%)	VOLUME OF DISTRIBUTION (Vd)[3]	AVG SERUM T½ (hr)[4]	BILE PEN (%)[5]	CSF/ BLOOD[6] (%)	CSF PENETRATION[7]	AUC[8] (µg*hr/mL)	Tmax (hr)
Fluoroquinolones[10]												
Ciprofloxacin	750 mg po q12h	Tab/susp ± food	70	3.6 (SS)	20-40	2.4 L/kg	4	2800-4500			31.6 (24 hr)	1-2
Ciprofloxacin	400 mg IV q12h			4.6 (SS)	20-40	2.4 L/kg	4	2800-4500	26	Inadequate for Strep	25.4 (24 hr)	
Ciprofloxacin ER	500 mg ER po q24h	Tab ± food	59	1.6 (SS)	20-40	2.4 L/kg	6.6			ND	8 (24 hr)	1-4
Delafloxacin	300 mg IV or 450 mg po q12h	Tab ± food		po 7.45, IV 9.3 (SS)	84	30-48 L Vss	4.2-8.5				po 30.8, IV 23.4 (12 hr)	1
Gemifloxacin	320 mg po q24h	Tab ± food	71	1.6 (SS)	55-73	2-12 L/kg Vss/F	7				9.9 (24 hr)	0.5-2.0
Levofloxacin	750 mg po/IV q24h	Tab ± food, soln no food	99	po 8.6, IV 12.1 (SS)	24-38	244 L Vss	7		>50		po 90.7, IV 108 (24 hr)	po 1.6
Moxifloxacin	400 mg po/IV q24h	Tab ± food	89	4.2-4.6 (SS)	30-50	2.2 L/kg	10-14		>50	Yes (CID 49:1080, 2009)	pc 48, IV 38 (24 hr)	po 1-3
Norfloxacin	400 mg po q12h	Tab no food	30-40	1.5 (400 mg SD)	10-15	1.7 L/kg	3-4	700	ND	No	6.4 (400 mg)	1
Ofloxacin	400 mg po q12h	Tab ± food	98	4.6-6.2 (SS)	32	1-2.5 L/kg	7	ND	negligible		82.4 (24 hr)	1-2
Prulifloxacin[NUS]	600 mg po	Tab ± food	ND	1.6 (SD)	45	1231 L	10.6-12.1				7.3	1
GLYCOPEPTIDES, LIPOGLYCOPEPTIDES, LIPOPEPTIDES												
Dalbavancin	1 gm IV			280-300 (SD)	93-98	0.11 L/kg	147-258	ND	ND	ND	23,443	
Daptomycin	4-6 mg/kg IV q24h			58-99 (SS)	92	0.1 L/kg Vss	8-9	ND	0-8	ND	494-632 (24 hr)	
Oritavancin	1200 mg IV			138 (SD)	85	87.6 L	245 (terminal)	ND	ND	ND	2800 (0-∞)	
Teicoplanin	6 mg/kg IV	-		40-50 (SS)	90-95	0.9-1.6 L/kg Vss	70-100	ND	negligible	No	500-600 (0-∞)	-
Telavancin	10 mg/kg IV q24h			108 (SS)	90	0.13 L/kg	8.1	Low	7-14	Need high doses	780 (24 hr)	
Vancomycin	1 gm IV q12h			20-50 (SS)	<10-55	0.7 L/kg	4-6	ND	negligible	No	500-600 if trough 20 (24 hr)	
MACROLIDES, AZALIDES, LINCOSAMIDES, KETOLIDES												
Azithromycin	500 mg po	Tab/susp ± food	37	0.4 (SD)	7-51	31.1 L/kg	68	High			4.3	2.5
Azithromycin	500 mg IV			3.6 (SD)	7-51	33.3 L/kg	68	High			9.6 (24 hr, pre SS)	
Azithromycin ER	2 gm po	Susp no food	≈ 30	0.8 (SD)	7-51	31.1 L/kg	59	High			20	5
Clarithromycin	500 mg po q12h	Tab/susp ± food	50	3-4 (SS)	65-70	4 L/kg	5-7	7000			20 (24 hr)	2.0-2.5
Clarithromycin ER	1 gm ER po q24h	Tab + food	≈ 50	2-3 (SS)	65-70		5-8				ND	5-8
Clindamycin	150 mg po	Cap ± food	90	2.5 (SD)	85-94	1.1 L/kg	2.4	250-300		No	ND	0.75

Food Effect (po dosing): + food = take with food, **no food** = take without food, **± food** = take with or without food. **Oral % AB** = % absorbed. **Peak Serum Level: SD** = after single dose, **SS** = steady state after multiple doses; **Volume of Distribution (Vd): V/F** = Vd/oral bioavailability, **Vss** = Vd at steady state, **Vss/F** = Vd at steady state/oral bioavailability. **CSF Penetration:** therapeutic efficacy comment based on dose, usual susceptibility or target organism & penetration into CSF; **AUC** = area under drug concentration curve; **24hr** = AUC 0-24; **Tmax** = time to max plasma concentration.

TABLE 9A (4) *(Footnotes at the end of the table)*

DRUG	REFERENCE DOSE (SINGLE OR MULTIPLE)	FOOD REC. (PO DRUGS)	ORAL ABS (%)	PEAK SERUM CONC (μg/mL)	PROTEIN BINDING (%)	VOLUME OF DISTRIBUTION (Vd)	AVG SERUM T½ (hr)	BILE PEN (%)	CSF/BLOOD (%)	CSF PENETRATION	AUC (μg•hr/mL)	Tmax (hr)
MACROLIDES, AZALIDES, LINCOSAMIDES, KETOLIDES *(continued)*												
Clindamycin	900 mg IV q8h	Cap ± food	High	14.1 (SS)	85-94	1.1 L/kg	2.4	250-300		No	ND	
Erythromycin base, esters	500 mg q6h	Tab/susp no food, DR caps ± food	18-45	0.1-2 (SD)	70-74	0.6 L/kg	2-4		2-13	No		delay rel: 3
Erythromycin lactobionate	500 mg IV			3-4 (SD)	70-74	0.6 L/kg	2-4					
Telithromycin	800 mg po q24h	Tab ± food	57	2.3 (SS)	60-70	2.9 L/kg	10	7			12.5 (24 hr)	1
MISCELLANEOUS ANTIBACTERIALS												
Chloramphenicol	1 gm po q6h	Cap ± food	High	18 (SS)	25-50	0.8 L/kg	4.1		45-89	Yes	ND	
Fosfomycin	3 gm po	Sachet ± food	91	26 (SD)	<10	136.1 L Vss/F	5.7			ND	150	2
Fusidic acid^NUS	500 mg po	Tab ± food	91	30 (SD)	95-99	0.3 L/kg	15	100-200	ND	ND	442 (0-∞)	2-4
Metronidazole	500 mg IV/po q6h	ER tab no food, tab/cap ± food	100	20-25 (SS)	20	0.6-0.85 L/kg	6-14	100	45-89	ND	560 (24 hr)	ER 6,8, regular 1,6
Quinupristin-dalfopristin	7.5 mg/kg IV q8h			Q 3.2/D 8 (SS)	ND	Q 0.45/D 0.24 (L/kg) VSS	Q 0.85/D 0.7	ND	ND	ND	Q 7.2/D 10.6 (24 hr)	
Rifampin	600 mg po	Cap no food	70-90	7 (SD)	80	0.65 L/kg Vss	1.5-5	10,000	7-56	Yes	40-60 (24 hr)	1.5-2
Rifaximin	200 mg po tid	Tab ± food	<0.4	0.0007-0.002 (SS)	67,5	ND	2-5		ND	No	0,008	1
Trimethoprim	100 mg po	Tab ± food	80	1 (SD)	44	100-120 L V/F	8-15		50/40		ND	1-4
TMP/SMX	160/800 mg po q12h	Tab/susp ± food	85	1-2/40-60 (SS)	44/70	100-120 L 12-18 L	11/9	100-200			ND	1-4
TMP/SMX	160/800 mg IV q8h		100	9/105 (SS)	44/70	100-120 L 12-18 L	11/9	40-70			ND	
OXAZOLIDINONES												
Linezolid	600 mg po/IV q12h	Tab/susp ± food	100	15-20 (SS)	31	40-50 L Vss	5		60-70	Yes (AUC 503/397, 2006)	po 276, IV 179 (24 hr)	po 1,3
Tedizolid	200 mg po/IV q24h	Tab ± food	91	po 2.2, IV 3.0 (SS)	70-90	67-80 L Vss	12		ND	ND	po 25.6, IV 29.2 (24 hr)	po 3, IV 1.1
POLYMYXINS												
Colistin (Polymyxin E)	150 mg IV		≈ 50	5-7.5 (SD)	≈ 50	0.34 L/kg	colistimethate 1.5-2, Colistin >4	0		No		
Polymyxin B	1.5 mg/kg IV q12h			2.8 (avg conc at SS)	60	ND	4.5-6 (old data)	ND	ND	No	66.9 (24 hr)	

Food Effect (po dosing): + food = take with food. no food = take without food. ± food = take with or without food; **Oral % AB** = % absorbed; **Peak Serum Level: SD** = after single dose, **SS** = steady state after multiple doses; **Volume of Distribution (Vd): V/F** = Vd/oral bioavailability, **Vss** = Vd at steady state, **Vss/F** = Vd at steady state/oral bioavailability; **CSF Penetration:** therapeutic efficacy comment based on dose, usual susceptibility or target organism & penetration into CSF; **AUC** = area under drug concentration curve; **24hr** = AUC 0-24; **Tmax** = time to max plasma concentration.

TABLE 9A (5) (Footnotes at the end of table)

DRUG	REFERENCE DOSE SINGLE OR MULTIPLE	FOOD REC (PO DRUGS)[1]	ORAL ABS (%)	PEAK SERUM CONC (µg/mL)	PROTEIN BINDING (%)	VOLUME OF DISTRIBUTION (Vd)[2]	AVG SERUM T½ (hr)[3]	BILE PEN (%)[4]	CSF/ BLOOD (%)	CSF PENETRATION[5]	AUC[6] (µg·hr/mL)	Tmax (hr)
TETRACYCLINES, GLYCYLCYCLINES												
Doxycycline	100 mg po	Tab/cap/susp + food		1.5-2.1 (SD)	93	53-134 L Vss	18	200-3200	26	No	31.7 (0-∞)	2
Minocycline	200 mg po	Cap/tab ± food	ND	2.0-3.5 (SD)	76	80-114 L Vss	16	200-3200	ND	ND	48.3 (0-∞)	2.1
Tetracycline	250 mg po	Cap no food	ND	1.5-2.2 (SD)	20-65	1.3 L/kg	6-12	200-3200	Poor	No	30 (0-∞)	2-4
Tigecycline	50 mg IV q12h			0.63 (SS)	71-89	7-9 L/kg	42	138	5.9-10.6	No	4.7 (24 hr)	
ANTIFUNGALS												
Benzofuran												
Griseofulvin (ultramicrosize)	250 mg po	Tab + food (high fat)	27-72	0.6-0.67 (SD)	ND	ND	9-24	ND	ND	ND	8.6-9.0 (0-∞)	4
Polyenes												
Ampho B deoxycholate	0.4-0.7 mg/kg IV q24h			0.5-3.5 (SS)		4 L/kg	24		0		17 (24 hr)	
Ampho B lipid complex (ABLC)	5 mg/kg IV q24h			1-2.5 (SS)		131 L/kg	173				14 (24 hr)	
Ampho B liposomal	5 mg/kg IV q24h			83 (SS)		0.1-0.4 L/kg Vss	6.8				555 (24 hr)	
Antimetabolites												
Flucytosine	2.5 gm po	Cap ± food	78-90	30-40 (SD)	ND	0.6 L/kg	3-5	ND	60-100	Yes	ND	2
Azoles												
Fluconazole	400-800 mg po/IV	Tab/susp ± food	90	6.7-14 (SD)	10	50 L V/F	20-50	ND	50-94	Yes	140 (8 hr) after 3 mg/kg SD	po: 1-2
Isavuconazonium sulfate (Isavuconazole)	372 mg po/IV q24h (maint)	Cap ± food	98	7.5 (SS)	99	450 L Vss	130	ND	ND	ND	121.4 (24 hr)	2-3
Itraconazole	200 mg oral soln po q24h	Cap/tab + food, soln no food	55+	Itra 2.0, OH-Itra 2.0 (SS)	99.8	796 L	35	ND	0	No	Itra 29.3, OH-Itra 45.2 (24 hr)	Itra 2.5, OH-Itra 5.3
Ketoconazole	200 mg po	Tab ± food	variable	3.5 (SD)	99	1.2 L/kg	8	ND	<10	No	12	1-2
Posaconazole oral susp	400 mg po bid	Susp ± food	ND	0.2-1.0 (200 mg SD)	98-99	226-295 L	20-66	ND	ND	Yes (JAC 56:745, 2005)	9.1 (12 hr)	3-5
Posaconazole tab	300 mg tab po q24h	Tab + food	54	2.1-2.9 (SS)	98-99	226-295 L	20-66	ND	ND	Yes (JAC 56:745, 2005)	37.9 (24 hr)	3-5
Posaconazole injection	300 mg IV q24h	-	-	3.3 (SS)	98-99	226-295 L	20-66	ND	ND	Yes (JAC 56:745, 2005)	36.1 (24 hr)	1.5
Voriconazole	200 mg po q12h	Tab/susp no food	96	3 (SS)	58	4.6 L/kg Vss	variable	ND	22-100	Yes (CID 37:728, 2003)	39.8 (24 hr)	1-2

Food Effect (po dosing): + food = take with food, no food = take without food, ± food = take with or without food; **Oral % AB** = % absorbed; **Peak Serum Level: SD** = after single dose, **SS** = steady state after multiple doses; **Volume of Distribution (Vd): V/F** = Vd/oral bioavailability, **Vss** = Vd at steady state, **Vss/F** = Vd at steady state/oral bioavailability; **CSF Penetration:** therapeutic efficacy comment based on dose, usual susceptibility or target organism & penetration into CSF; **AUC** = area under drug concentration curve; **24hr** = AUC 0-24; **'max** = time to max plasma concentration.

TABLE 9A (6) *(Footnotes at the end of table)*

DRUG	REFERENCE DOSE (SINGLE OR MULTIPLE)	FOOD REC (PO DRUGS)[1]	ORAL ABS (%)	PEAK SERUM CONC[2] (μg/mL)	PROTEIN BINDING (%)	VOLUME OF DISTRIBUTION (Vd)[3]	AVG SERUM T½ (hr)[4]	BILE PEN (%)[5]	CSF/ BLOOD[6] (%)	CSF PENETRATION[7]	AUC[8] (μg•hr/mL)	Tmax (hr)
Echinocandins												
Anidulafungin	100 mg IV q24h			7.2 (SS)	>99	30-50 L	26.5			No	112 (24 hr)	
Caspofungin	50 mg IV q24h			8.7 (SS)	97	9.7 L Vss	13	ND		No	87.3 (24 hr)	
Micafungin	100 mg IV q24h			10.1 (SS)	>99	0.39 L/kg	15-17			No	97 (24 hr)	
ANTIMYCOBACTERIALS												
First line, tuberculosis												
Ethambutol	25 mg/kg po	Tab + food	80	2-6 (SD)	10-30	6 L/kg Vss/F	4		10-50	No	29.6	2-4
Isoniazid (INH)	300 mg po	Tab/syrup no food	100	3-5 (SD)	<10	0.6-1.2 L/kg	0.7-4		up to 90	Yes	20.1	1-2
Pyrazinamide	20-25 mg/kg po	Tab ± food	95	30-50 (SD)	5-10		10-16		100	Yes	500	2
Rifabutin	300 mg po	Cap + food	20	0.2-0.6 (SD)	85	9.3 L/kg Vss	32-67	300-500	30-70	ND	4.0 (24 hr)	2.5-4.0
Rifampin	600 mg po	Cap no food	70-90	4-8 (SD)	80	0.65 L/kg Vss	1.5-5	10,000	7-56	Yes	40-60 (24 hr)	1.5-2
Rifapentine	600 mg po q72h	Tab + food	ND	15 (SS)	98	70 L	13-14	ND	ND	ND	320 (72 hr)	4,8
Streptomycin	15 mg/kg IM			25-50 (SD)	0-10	0.26 L/kg	2.5	10-60	0-30	No		
Second line, tuberculosis												
Amikacin	15 mg/kg IM			25-50 (SD)	0-10	0.26 L/kg	2.5	10-60	0-30	No		
Bedaquiline	400 mg po qd	ND		3.3 (week 2)	>99	≈ 60 x total body water Vss	24-30 (terminal 4-5 mo)	ND	≈ 0	No	22 (24 hr) after 8 wks	5
Capreomycin	1 gm IM			30 (SD)	ND	0.41/kg	2-5	ND	<10	No	ND	1-2
Cycloserine	250 mg po	Cap no food	70-90	4-8 (SD)	<20	0.47 L/kg	10	ND	54-79	Yes	110	1-2
Ethionamide	250 mg po	Tab ± food	near 100	2.2 (SD)	30	93.5 L	1.9	ND	≈ 100	Yes	7.7	1,5
Kanamycin	15 mg/kg IM			25-50 (SD)	0-10	0.26 L/kg	2.5	10-60	0-30	No		
Para-aminosalicylic acid (PAS)	4 g (granules)po	Granules + food	ND	9-35 (SD)	50-60	0.9-1.4 L/kg V/F	0.75-1.0	ND	10-50	Marginal	108 (4 gm SD, 0-∞)	8
ANTIPARASITICS												
Antimalarials												
Artemether/ lumefantrine	4 tabs (80 mg/480 mg)	Tab + food	ND	Art 0.06-0.08, DHA 0.09-01, Lum 7.4-9.8 (SD)	Art 95.4, DHA 47-76, Lum 99.7	ND	Art 1.6-2.2, DHA 1.6-2.2, Lum 101-119				Art 0.15-0.26, DHA 0.29, Lum 158-243	Art 1.5-2, Lum 6-8
Artesunate (AS)	120 mg IV	-	-	DHA 2.4 (SD)	AS 62-75, DHA 66-82	AS 0.1-0.3, DHA 0.5-1 L/kg	AS 2-4 min, DHA 0.5-1 hr	ND		ND	DHA 2.1 (SD, 0-∞)	25 min (to DHA)
Atovaquone	750 po bid	Susp + food	47	24 (SS)	99.9	0.6 L/kg Vss	67	ND	<1	No	801 (750 mg x1)	ND
Chloroquine phosphate	300 mg base	Tab + food	90	0.06-0.09 (SD)	55	100-1000 L/kg	45-55 days (terminal)	ND	ND	ND	ND	1-6

Food Effect (po dosing): + food = take with food, **no food** = take without food, **± food** = take with or without food; **Oral % AB** = % absorbed; **Peak Serum Level: SD** = after single dose, **SS** = steady state after multiple doses; **Volume of Distribution (Vd): V/F** = Vd/oral bioavailability, **Vss** = Vd at steady state, **Vss/F** = Vd/oral bioavailability; **CSF Penetration:** therapeutic efficacy comment based on dose, usual susceptibility or target organism & penetration into CSF; **24hr²** = AUC 0-24; **Tmax** = time to max plasma concentration.

TABLE 9A (7) (Footnotes at the end of table)

DRUG	REFERENCE DOSE (SINGLE OR MULTIPLE)	FOOD REC (PO DRUGS)[1]	ORAL ABS (%)	PEAK SERUM CONC (µg/mL)	PROTEIN BINDING (%)	VOLUME OF DISTRIBUTION (Vd)[3]	AVG SERUM T½ (hr)[4]	BILE PEN (%)[5]	CSF/ BLOOD (%)[6]	CSF PENETRATION[7]	AUC (µg•hr/mL)	Tmax (hr)
Antimalarials (continued)												
Mefloquine	1.25 gm po	Tab + food		0.5-1.2 (SD)	98	20 L/kg	13-24 days	ND	ND	ND	ND	17
Proguanil[11]	100 mg po	Tab + food	ND	ND	75	1600-2600 L V/F	12-?	ND	ND	ND	ND	
Quinine sulfate	648 mg po	Cap + food	76-88	3.2 (SD)	69-92	2.5-7.1 L/kg V/F	9.7-12.5	ND	2-7	No	28 (12 hr)	2.8
ANTIPARASITICS, Other												
Albendazole	400 mg po	Tab + food	Poor	0.5-1.6 (sulfoxide)	70	ND	8-12	ND	ND	ND	ND	2-5 (sulfoxide)
Benznidazole	100 mg po	Tab + food	92	2.2	44	39.2 L V/F	13.3	ND	ND	ND	51.3 (0-Inf)	2.9
Dapsone	100 mg po q24h	Tab ± food	70-100	1.1 (SS)	70	1.5 L/kg	10-50	ND	ND	ND	52.6 (24 hr)	2-6
Diethylcarbamazine	6 mg/kg po	Tab ± food	80-85	1.93 (SD)	ND	182 L V/F	9	ND	ND	ND	23.8 (0-∞)	1-2
Ivermectin	12 mg po	Tab no food	60	0.05-0.08 (SD)	93	3-3.5 L/kg	20	ND	ND	No	ND	4
Miltefosine	50 mg po tid	Cap + food	ND	76 (after 23 days)	95	ND	7-31 days	ND	ND	ND	486 (8hr)	2-8
Nitazoxanide	500 mg po	Tab/susp + food	Susp 70% of tab	Nitazox 2-9-11, gluc: 3.3-10.5 (SD)	Nitazox 99	ND	Nitazox 1.3-1.8	ND	ND	ND	Nitazox 40, gluc 46.5-63.0	Nitazox 40, gluc:1-4
Praziquantel	20 mg/kg po	Tab + food	80	0.2-2.0 (SD)		8000 L V/F	0.8-1.5	ND	ND	ND	1.51	1-3
Pyrimethamine	25 mg po	Tab ± food	High	0.1-0.3 (SD)	87	3 L/kg	96	ND	ND	ND		2-6
Tinidazole	2 gm po	Tab + food	48	48 (SD)	12	50 L	13	ND	ND	ND	902	1.6
ANTIVIRALS (non-HIV)												
Hepatitis B												
Adefovir	10 mg po	Tab ± food	59	0.02 (SD)	≤4	0.37 L/kg Vss	7.5	ND	ND	ND	0.22	1.75
Entecavir	0.5 mg po q24h	Tab/soln no food	100	4.2 ng/mL (SS)	13	>0.6 L/kg V/F	128-149 (terminal)	ND	ND	ND	0.014 (24 hr)	0.5-1.5
Telbivudine	600 mg po q24h	Tab/soln ± food		3.7 (SS)	3.3	>0.6 L/kg V/F	40-49	ND	ND	ND	26.1 (24 hr)	2
Hepatitis C												
Daclatasvir	60 mg po q24h	Tab ± food	67	0.18 (Cmin, SS)	99	47 Vss	12-15	ND	ND	ND	11 (24 hr)	2
Dasabuvir	250 mg po q12h	Tab + food	ND	0.03-3.1 (10-1200 mg SD)	ND	ND	5-8	ND	ND	ND		3
Elbasvir/ Grazoprevir	(Elba 50 + Grazo 100 mg) q24h	Tab ± food	ND	Elba 0.121, Grazo 0.165 (SS)	Elba >99.9, Grazo >98.8	ND	Elba 24, Grazo 31	ND	ND	ND	Elba 1.92, Grazo 1.42 (24 hr)	Elba 3, Grazo 2
Ledipasvir/ Sofosbuvir	90 mg + Sofos 400 g po q24h	Tab ± food	ND	Ledip: 0.3 (SS)	Ledip: >99.8	ND	Ledip: 47	ND	ND	ND	Ledip: 7.3 (24hr)	Ledip: 4-4.5

Food Effect (po dosing): + food = take with food, **no food** = take without food, **± food** = take with or without food; **Oral % AB** = % absorbed; **Peak Serum Level: SD** = after single dose, **SS** = steady state after multiple doses; **Volume of Distribution (Vd): V/F** = Vd/oral bioavailability, **Vss** = Vd at steady state, **Vss/F** = Vd steady state/oral bioavailability; **CSF Penetration:** therapeutic efficacy comment based on dose, usual susceptibility of target organism & penetration into CSF; **AUC** = area under drug concentration curve; **24hr** = AUC 0-24; **Tmax** = time to max plasma concentration.

TABLE 9A (B) (Footnotes at the end of the table)

DRUG	REFERENCE DOSE (SINGLE OR MULTIPLE)	FOOD REC (PO DRUGS)	ORAL ABS (%)	PEAK SERUM CONC (μg/mL)	PROTEIN BINDING (%)	VOLUME OF DISTRIBUTION (Vd)	AVG SERUM T½ (hr)	BILE PEN (%)	CSF/ BLOOD (%)	CSF PENETRATION	AUC (μg*hr/mL)	Tmax (hr)
Hepatitis C (cont'd)												
Ombitasvir (with Paritaprevir/RTV)	25 mg po q24h	Tab + food	ND	0.56 (SS)	ND	ND	28-34	ND	ND	ND	0.53 (24 hr)	4-5
Paritaprevir/RTV (with Ombitasvir)	150 mg (+ RTV 100 mg) po q24h	Tab + food	ND	ND	ND	ND	5,8	ND	ND	ND	4,3	
Ribavirin	600 mg po	Tab/cap/soln + food	64	3.7 (SS)	minimal	2825 L V/F	44 (terminal 298)	ND	ND	ND	228 (12 hr)	2
Simeprevir	150 mg po	Cap + food	ND	Sofos: 0.6 (SS)	>99.9	ND	41	ND	ND	ND	57.5 (24 hr)	4-6
Sofosbuvir	400 mg po q24h	Tab ± food	ND		Sofos; 61-65	ND	Sofos; 0.5-0.75	ND	ND	ND	Sofos; 0.9 (24 hr)	0.5-2
Velpatasvir/ Sofosbuvir	100 mg (+ Sofos 400 mg) po q24h	Tab ± food	ND	Velpat: 0.26 (SS)	Velpat: >99.5	ND	Velpat: 15	ND	ND	ND	Velpat: 2.98 (24 hr)	Velpat: 3
Voxilaprevir/ Velpatasvir/ Sofosbuvir (Vosevi)	100 + Vel 100 + Sof 400 mg q24h	Tab ± food	ND	Vox 0.19, Vel 0.31, Sof 0.68 (SS)	Vox >99, Vel >99, Sof 61-65	ND	Vox 33, Vel 17, Sof 0.5	ND	ND	ND	Vox 2.6, Vel 4.0, Sof 1.7 (24 hr)	Vox 4, Vel 4, Sof 2
Herpesvirus												
Acyclovir	400 mg po bid	Tab/cap/susp ± food	10-20	1.21 (SS)	9-33	0.7 L/kg	2.5-3.5	ND	ND	ND	7.4 (24 hr)	1.5-2
Cidofovir (w/ probenecid)	5 mg/kg IV	Probenecid: ± food		19.6 (SD)	<6	0.41 L/kg Vss	2.6 (diphosphate: 17-65)	ND	0	No	40.8	1,1
Famciclovir	500 mg po	Tab ± food	77	3-4 (SD)	<20	1.1 L/kg (Penciclovir)	2-3 (Penciclovir)				8.9 (Penciclovir)	0.9 (Penciclovir)
Foscarnet	60 mg/kg IV			155 (SD)	4	0.46 L/kg	3 (terminal 18-88)	No			2195 μM*hr	
Ganciclovir	5 mg/kg IV			8.3 (SD)	1-2	0.7 L/kg Vss	3,5				24.5	
Letermovir	480 mg po/IV q24h	Tab ± food	35-94	13 (po, SS)	99	45.5 L Vss	12	ND	ND	ND	71.5 (po, 24 hr)	0.75-2.25
Valacyclovir	1 gm po	Tab ± food	55	5.6 (SD)	13-18	0.7 L/kg	3				19.5 (Acyclovir)	
Valganciclovir	900 mg po q24h	Tab/soln + food	59	5.6 (SS)	1-2	0.7 L/kg	4				29.1 (Ganciclovir)	1-3 (Ganciclovir)
Influenza												
Laninamivir (octanoate=prodrug)	40 mg (prodrug) inhaled x1	-		Lan: 0.024 (SD)	Lan: <0.01	ND	Lan 64.7; Lan octanoate 1.8	ND	ND	ND	Lan: 0.745 (0-∞)	Lan: 4
Oseltamivir	75 mg po bid	Cap/susp ± food	75	carboxylate 0.35 (SS)	3	carboxylate 23-26 L	carboxylate 6-10	ND	ND	ND	carboxylate 5.4 (24 hr)	
Peramivir	600 mg IV			46.8 (SD)	<30	12.56 L	20	ND	ND	ND	102.7 (0-∞)	
Rimantadine	100 mg po q12h	Tab ± food	75-93	0.4-0.5 (SS)	40	17-19 L/kg	25	ND	ND	ND	3,5	6

Food Effect (po dosing): + food = take with food, **no food** = take without food, **± food** = take with or without food; **Oral % AB** = % absorbed; **Peak Serum Level: SD** = after single dose, **SS** = steady state after multiple doses; **Volume of Distribution (Vd): V/F** = Vd/oral bioavailability, **Vss** = Vd at steady state, **Vss/F** = Vd at steady state/oral bioavailability, **CSF Penetration:** therapeutic efficacy comment based on dose, usual susceptibility or target organism & penetration into CSF; **AUC** = area under drug concentration curve; **24hr** = AUC 0-24; **Tmax** = time to max plasma concentration.

TABLE 9A (¶) *(Footnotes at the end of table)*

DRUG	REFERENCE DOSE (SINGLE OR MULTIPLE)	FOOD REC (PO DRUGS)¹	ORAL ABS (%)	PEAK SERUM CONC² (µg/mL)	PROTEIN BINDING (%)	VOLUME OF DISTRIBUTION (Vd)³	AVG SERUM T½ (hr)⁴	BILE PEN (%)⁵	CSF/ BLOOD⁶ (%)	CSF PENETRATION⁷	AUC² (µg•hr/mL)	Tmax (hr)
ANTIRETROVIRALS												
NRTIs												
Abacavir (ABC)	600 mg po q24h	Tab/soln ± food	83	4.3 (SS)	50	0.86 L/kg	1.5	20.6	3	36	12 (24 hr)	1,3
Didanosine enteric coated (ddI)	400 mg po q24h (pt ≥60 kg)	Cap/soln no food	30-40	ND	<5	308-363 L	1.6	25-40	2	ND	2.6(24 hr)	2
Emtricitabine (FTC)	200 mg po q24h	Cap/soln ± food	cap 93, soln 75	1.8 (SS)	<4	ND	10	39	3	ND	10 (24 hr)	1-2
Lamivudine (3TC)	300 mg po q24h	Tab/soln ± food	86	2.6 (SS)	<36	1.3 L/kg	5-7	18	2	ND	11 (300 mg x1)	ND
Stavudine (d4T)	40 mg po bid (pt ≥60 kg)	Cap/soln ± food	86	0.54 (SS)	<5	46 L	1.2-1.6	3.5	2	20	2.6 (24 hr)	1
Tenofovir alafenamide (TAF)	25 mg po q24h	Tab ± food	ND	0.16 (SS)	80	ND	0.51	ND	ND	ND	0.21 (24hr)	1
Tenofovir disoproxil (TDF)	300 mg po q24h	Tab ± food	39 w/food	0.3 (300 mg x1)	<7	1.2-1.3 L/kg Vss	17	>60	1	ND	2.3 (300 mg x1)	1
Zidovudine (ZDV)	300 mg po bid	Tab/cap/syrup ± food	60	1-2 (300 mg x1)	<38	1.6 L/kg	0.5-3	11	4	2	2.1 (300 mg x1)	0.5-1.5
NNRTIs												
Delavirdine (DLV)	400 mg po tid	Tab ± food	85	19 (SS)	98	ND	5.8	ND	3	ND	180 µM•hr (24 hr)	1
Efavirenz (EFV)	600 mg po q24h	Cap/tab no food	42	4.1 (SS)	99	252 L WF	40-55	ND	3	ND	184 µM•hr (24 hr)	3-5
Etravirine (ETR)	200 mg po bid	Tab ± food	ND	0.3 (SS)	99.9	ND	41	ND	2	ND	9 (24 hr)	2.5-4.0
Nevirapine (NVP)	200 mg po bid	Tab/susp ± food	>90	2 (200 mg x1)	60	1.21 L/kg Vss	25-30	ND	4	63	110 (24 hr)	4
Rilpivirine (RPV)	25 mg po qd	Tab + food	ND	0.1-0.2 (25 mg x1)	99.7	152 L	45-50	ND	ND	ND	2.4 (24 hr)	4-5
PIs												
Atazanavir (ATV)	400 mg po q24h	Cap/powder + food	85	2.3 (SS)	85	88.3 L V/F	7	ND	2	ND	22.3 (24 hr)	2.5
Cobicistat	150 mg po q24h	Take with food	ND	0.99 (SS)	97-98	ND	4-Mar	ND	ND	ND	7.6 (24 hr)	3.5
Darunavir (DRV)	600 mg (+ RTV 100 mg) po bid	Tab/susp + food	82	3.5 (SS)	95	2 L/kg	15	ND	3	ND	116.8 (24 hr)	2.5-4.0
Fosamprenavir (FPV)	700 mg (+RTV 100 mg) po bid	Tab ± food; susp; adult no, peds ±	ND	6 (SS)	90	ND	7.7	ND	3	ND	79.2 (24 hr)	2.5
Indinavir (IDV)	800 mg (+ RTV 100 mg) po bid	Boosted cap + food	65	20.2 µM (SS)	60	ND	1.2-2.0	ND	4	11	249 µM•hr (24 hr)	0.8 (fasting)

Food Effect (po dosing): + food = take with food, no food = take without food, ± food = take with or without food; ‡ food = take with food after multiple doses; **Oral % AB** = % absorbed; **Peak Serum Level**; **SD** = single dose, **SS** = steady state after multiple doses; **V/F** = Vd/oral bioavailability; **Vss** = Vd at steady state/oral bioavailability; **CSF Penetration:** therapeutic efficacy comment based on dose, usual susceptibility or target organism & penetration into CSF; **24hr** = AUC 0-24; **Tmax** = time to max plasma concentration.

TABLE 9A (10) *(Footnotes at the end of table)*

DRUG	REFERENCE DOSE (SINGLE OR MULTIPLE)	FOOD REC (PO DRUGS)[1]	ORAL ABS (%)	PEAK SERUM CONC[2] (µg/mL)	PROTEIN BINDING (%)	VOLUME OF DISTRIBUTION (Vd)[3]	AVG SERUM T½ (hr)[4]	BILE PEN (%)[5]	CSF/BLOOD[6] (%)	CSF PENETRATION[7]	AUC[8] (µg*hr/mL)	Tmax (hr)
PIs *(continued)*												
Lopinavir/RTV (LPV/r)	400 mg/100 mg po bid	Tab ± food, soln + food	ND	9.6 (SS)	98-99	ND	LPV 5-6	ND	3	ND	LPV 186 (24 hr)	LPV 4
Nelfinavir (NFV)	1250 mg po bid	Tab/powder + food	20-80	3-4 (SS)	98	2-7 L/kg V/F	3.5-5	ND	1	0	53 (24 hr)	ND
Ritonavir (RTV)	Boosting dose varies	Cap/soln + food	65	11.2 (600 mg bid SS)	98-99	0.41 L/kg V/F	3-5	ND	1	ND	121.7 (600 mg soln SD)	soln 2-4
Saquinavir (SQV)	1 gm (+RTV 100 mg) po bid	Tab/cap + food	4 (SQV alone)	0.37 (SS)	97	700 L Vss	1-2	ND	1	ND	29.2 (24 hr)	ND
Tipranavir (TPV)	500 mg (+RTV 200 mg) po bid	Cap/soln + food	Low	47-57 (SS)	99.9	7.7-10 L	5.5-6	ND	1	ND	1600 µM*hr (24 hr)	3
INSTIs												
Dolutegravir (DTG)	50 mg po q24h	Tab ± food	ND	3.67 (SS)	>99	17.4 L V/F	14	ND	4	ND	53.6 (24 hr)	2-3
Elvitegravir (EVG)	85-150 mg po q24h	Tab + food	ND	1.2-1.5 (SS)	98-99	ND	8.7 (w/RTV)	ND	ND	ND	18 (24 hr)	4
Raltegravir (RAL)	400 mg po bid	Tab/susp ± food	ND	11.2 µM (SS)	83	287 L Vss/F	9	ND	3	1-53.5	28.7 µM*hr (12 hr)	3
Fusion, Entry Inhibitors												
Enfuvirtide (ENF T20)	90 mg sc bid		84 (sc %ab)	5 (SS)	92	5.5 L Vss	3.8	ND	1	ND	97.4 (24 hr)	4-8
Maraviroc (MVC)	300 mg po bid	Tab ± food	33	0.3-0.9 (SS)	76	194 L	14-18	ND	3	ND	3 (24 hr)	0.5-4.0

1 Refers to adult oral preparations unless otherwise noted; + food = take with food, no food = take without food, ± food = take with or without food
2 SD = after a single dose, SS = at steady state
3 V/F = Vd/oral bioavailability; Vss = Vd at steady state; Vss/F = Vd at steady state/oral bioavailability
4 Assumes CrCl >80 mL/min
5 (Peak concentration in bile/peak concentration in serum) x 100. If blank, no data
6 CSF concentrations with inflammation
7 Judgment based on drug dose and organism susceptibility. CSF concentration ideally ≥10x MIC.
8 AUC = area under serum concentration vs. time curve; 12 hr = AUC 0-12, 24 hr = AUC 0-24
9 Concern over seizure potential (see Table 10B)
10 Take all oral FQs 2-4 hours before sucralfate or any multivalent cation (calcium, iron, zinc)
11 Given with Atovaquone as Malarone for malaria prophylaxis

Food Effect (po dosing): + food = take with food, **no food** = take without food, **± food** = take with or without food; **Oral % AB** = % absorbed; **Peak Serum Level: SD** = steady state after multiple doses; **Volume of Distribution (Vd): V/F** = Vd/oral bioavailability; **Vss** = Vd at steady state/oral bioavailability, **Vss/F** = Vd at steady state/oral bioavailability; **CSF Penetration:** therapeutic efficacy comment based on dose, usual susceptibility or target organism & penetration into CSF; **AUC** = area under drug concentration curve; **24hr** = AUC 0-24; **Tmax** = time to max plasma concentration.

TABLE 9B – PHARMACODYNAMICS OF ANTIBACTERIALS[a]

BACTERIAL KILLING/PERSISTENT EFFECT	DRUGS	THERAPY GOAL	PK/PD MEASUREMENT
Concentration-dependent/Prolonged persistent effect	Aminoglycosides; daptomycin; ketolides; quinolones; metro	High peak serum concentration	24-hr AUC/MIC
Time-dependent/No persistent effect	Penicillins; cephalosporins; carbapenems	Long duration of exposure	Time above MIC
Time-dependent/Moderate to long persistent effect	Clindamycin; erythro/azithro/clarithro; linezolid; tetracyclines; vancomycin	Enhanced amount of drug	24-hr AUC/MIC

[a] Adapted from Craig, WA: IDC No. Amer 17:479, 2003 & Drusano, G.L.: CID 44:79, 2007

TABLE 9C – ENZYME -AND TRANSPORTER-MEDIATED INTERACTIONS OF ANTIMICROBIALS

>50% of all drugs are metabolized by one or more members of the CYP450 enzyme system. The metabolism of a drug that is a substrate of a particular CYP enzyme may be induced (accelerated) by another drug, resulting in under dosing and therapeutic failure. Conversely the metabolism of a drug may be inhibited (slowed) by another drug, resulting in overdosing and toxicity. A drug may act as a substrate for more than one enzyme, or it may inhibit or induce multiple enzymes. Inhibition tends to be a relatively quick process related to the dose of the inhibitor, whereas induction occurs more slowly. Risk is amplified when two or more drugs that are enzyme inhibitors or inducers are administered. CYP450 enzymes commonly involved in drug interactions include CYP3A4, CYP2C9/19, CYP1A2, and CYP2D6.

Drug transporter systems may also be involved in drug interactions. Transporters are found in many tissues, such as the kidney and GI tract, and they work to pump drugs into cells (influx) or out of cells (efflux). Examples of important drug transporters systems include P-glycoprotein (PGP), organic anion transporter (OAT), and organic cation transporter (OCT).

Knowledge of these enzymes is useful in understanding clinically relevant drug interactions and can also assist in predicting previously unrecognized interactions. With respect to specific antimicrobials, always check for drug-drug interactions when ordering these inhibitors that may cause elevated serum concentrations: macrolides, ciprofloxacin, metronidazole, TMP-SMX, isoniazid, azole antifungals, antiretrovirals, and anti-HCV drugs. Nafcillin, rifampcins, and certain antiretrovirals are known to induce metabolism and lead to treatment failure. If a drug interaction is recognized and no suitable alternative regimen exists, check serum concentration of the affected drug (if available), adjust dose, and monitor for toxicity.

See Table 22A for common drug-drug interactions.

DRUG	ISOZYME/TRANSPORTER THAT DRUG IS A SUBSTRATE OF	INHIBITED BY DRUG	INDUCED BY DRUG	IMPACT ON SERUM DRUG CONCENTRATIONS[a]
Antibacterials				
Azithromycin		PGP (weak)		mild ↑
Chloramphenicol		2C19, 3A4		↑
Ciprofloxacin		1A2, 3A4 (minor)		↑
Clarithromycin	3A4	3A4, PGP, OAT		↑
Clindamycin	3A4			↑
Erythromycin	3A4, PGP	3A4, PGP, OAT		↑
Levofloxacin		OCT		↑
Metronidazole		2C9		↑
Nafcillin			2C9 (?), 3A4	↓
Norfloxacin		1A2 (weak)		mild ↑
Oritavancin			2D6 (weak), 3A4 (weak)	mild ↑ or ↓
Quinupristin–Dalfopristin		3A4		↓
Rifampin	PGP	OAT	1A2, 2B6, 2C8, 2C9, 2C19, 2D6 (weak), 3A4, PGP	↓
Rifaximin	3A4, PGP, OATIA2, OATP1B1/3	PGP		-
Telithromycin		3A4; PGP (?)		↑
TMP/SMX	SMX: 2C9 (major), 3A4	TMP: 2C8; SMX: 2C9		↑
Trimethoprim		2C8		↑

TABLE 9C (2)

DRUG	Substrate	Inhibits	Induces	Impact
Antifungals				
Fluconazole		2C9, 2C19, 3A4		↑
Isavuconazonium sulfate (isavuconazole)	3A4	3A4, PGP, OCT2		↑
Itraconazole	3A4	3A4, PGP		↑
Ketoconazole	3A4	3A4, PGP		↑
Posaconazole	PGP	3A4, PGP		↑
Terbinafine		2D6		↑
Voriconazole	2C9, 2C19, 3A4	2C9, 2C19, 3A4		↑
Antimycobacterials (Rifampin listed above)				
Bedaquiline	3A4			
Isoniazid (INH)	2E1	2C19, 3A4		↑
Rifabutin	3A4		3A4	↓
Rifapentine			2C9, 3A4	↓
Thalidomide	2C19			↓
Antiparasitics				
Artemether/Lumefantrine	3A4 (Art, Lum)	2D6 (Lum)	3A4 (Art)	↑ or ↓
Chloroquine	2C8, 2D6	2D6		↑
Dapsone	3A4			
Halofantrine	3A4	2D6		↑
Mefloquine	3A4, PGP	PGP		↑
Praziquantel	3A4			
Primaquine	2D6, others?			
Proguanil	2C19 (→cycloguanil)			
Quinine sulfate	main 3A4, also 1A2, 2C9, 2D6	2D6		↑
Tinidazole	3A4			
Antivirals (Hepatitis C)				
Daclatasvir	3A4, PGP	2C8, UGT1A1, OATP1B1, OATP1B3		-
Dasabuvir	3A4, PGP, OATP1B1	BCRP		↑
Elbasvir	CYP3A4, PGP			
Glecaprevir	PGP, BCRP, OATP1/3	1A2 (weak), 3A4 (weak), PGP, BCRP, OATP1B1/3, UGT1A1 (weak)		↑
Grazoprevir	CYP3A4, PGP, OATP1B1/3	CYP3A4 (weak), BCRP		
Ledipasvir	PGP, BCRP	PGP, BCRP		↑
Ombitasvir	3A4, PGP	2C8, UGT1A1		↑
Paritaprevir	2C8, 2D6, 3A4, PGP	UGT1A1, OATP1B1		↑
Pibrentasvir	PGP, BCRP	1A2 (weak), 3A4 (weak), PGP, BCRP, OATP1B1/3, UGT1A1 (weak)		↑
Simeprevir	3A4, PGP, OAT	1A2 (weak), 3A4, PGP, OAT		↑

TABLE 9C (3)

DRUG	Substrate	Inhibits	Induces	Impact
Antivirals (Hepatitis C) *(continued)*				
Sofosbuvir	PGP, BCRP			
Velpatasvir	2B6, 2C8, 3A4, PGP, BCRP, OATP1B1/3	PGP, BCRP, OATP1B1/3, OATP2B1		
Antivirals (Herpesvirus)				
Cidofovir	OAT1, OAT3			↑ or ↓
Letermovir	2D6, 3A4, OATP1B1/3	2C8, 3A4, OATP1B1/3	2C9, 2C19, 3A4	
Antiretrovirals				
Atazanavir	3A4, PGP	1A2, 2C8, 3A4, UGT1A1		↑
Cobicistat (part of Stribild)	2D6, 3A4	2D6, 3A4, PGP, BCRP, OATP1B1, OATP1B3		↑
Darunavir	3A4	3A4		↑
Delavirdine	2D6, 3A4	2C9, 2C19, 3A4		↑
Dolutegravir	3A4, UGT1A1			↑
Efavirenz	2B6, 3A4	2B6, 2C9, 2C19	2C19, 3A4	↑ or ↓
Elvitegravir (part of Stribild)	CYP3A4, UGT1A1/3	PGP (weak)	2C9 (weak)	mild ↑ or ↓
Etravirine	2C9, 2C19, 3A4	2C9, 2C19 (weak)	3A4	↑ or ↓
Fosamprenavir	3A4	3A4		↑
Indinavir	3A4, PGP	3A4, PGP		↑
Lopinavir	3A4	3A4		↑
Maraviroc	3A4, PGP	2D6		↑
Nelfinavir	2C19, 3A4, PGP	3A4, PGP	3A4 (?)	↑ or ↓
Nevirapine	2B6, 3A4		3A4	↓
Raltegravir	UGT			
Rilpivirine	3A4			
Ritonavir	3A4, PGP	2D6, 3A4, PGP	1A2, 2B6, 2C9, 3A4 (long term), PGP (long term), UGT	↑ or ↓
Saquinavir	3A4, PGP	3A4, PGP?		↑
Tenofovir alafenamide (TAF)	PGP, BCRP, OATP1B1/3			
Tipranavir	3A4, PGP	OAT	PGP (weak)	↑ or ↓

*Refers to serum concentrations of companion drugs that may be affected by the listed antimicrobial. ↑=increase, ↓=decrease, blank=no drugs should be affected

TERMINOLOGY:
BCRP = breast cancer resistance protein
CYP450 nomenclature, e.g. 3A4: 3 = family, A = subfamily, 4 = gene
OAT = organic anion transporter
OATP = organic anion transporter polypeptide
OCT = organic cation transporter
PGP = p-glycoprotein
UGT = uridine diphosphate glucuronosyltransferase

REFERENCES:
Hansten PD, Horn JR. The Top 100 Drug Interactions: A Guide to Patient Management. Freeland (WA): H&H Publications, 2014; primary literature; package inserts.

TABLE 10A – ANTIBIOTIC DOSAGE* AND SIDE-EFFECTS

CLASS, AGENT, GENERIC NAME (TRADE NAME)	USUAL ADULT DOSAGE*	ADVERSE REACTIONS, COMMENTS (See Table 10B for Summary)
NATURAL PENICILLINS		**Allergic reactions a major issue.** 10% of all hospital admissions give history of pen allergy; but only 10% have allergic reaction if given ampicillin. Why? Possible reasons: inaccurate history, waning immunity with age, aberrant response during viral illness. If given, Bicillin C-R IM (procaine Pen + benzathine Pen) could be reaction to procaine. **Most serious reaction is immediate IgE-mediated anaphylaxis;** incidence only 0.05%; but 5-10% fatal. Other IgE-mediated reactions: urticaria, angioedema, laryngeal edema, bronchospasm, abdominal pain with emesis, or hypotension. All appear within 4 hrs. Can form IgE antibody against either the beta-lactam ring or the R-group side chain. **Morbilliform rash after 72 hrs is not IgE-mediated and not serious.**
Benzathine penicillin G (Bicillin L-A)	600,000-1.2 million units IM q2-4 wks	
Penicillin G	Low: 600,000-1.2 million units IM per day	
	High 20 million units IV q24h(=12 gm) div q4h	**Serious late allergic reactions:** Coombs-positive hemolytic anemia, neutropenia, thrombocytopenia, serum sickness, interstitial nephritis, hepatitis, eosinophilia, drug fever.
Penicillin V (250 & 500 mg caps)	0.25-0.5 gm po bid, tid, qid before meals & at bedtime. Pen V preferred over Pen G for oral therapy due to greater acid stability.	**Cross-allergy to cephalosporins and carbapenems** varies from 0-11%. One factor is similarity, or lack of similarity, of side chains. For pen desensitization, see Table 7. For skin testing, suggest referral to allergist. High CSF concentrations cause seizures. Reduce dosage with renal impairment, see Table 17A. Allergy: CID 59:1113, 2014; JAC 69:20-43, 2014; CID 58:1140, 2014.
PENICILLINASE-RESISTANT PENICILLINS		
Dicloxacillin (Dynapen) (250 & 500 mg caps)	0.125-0.5 gm po q6h before meals	Blood levels ~2 times greater than cloxacillin so preferred for po therapy. Hemorrhagic cystitis reported. Acute abdominal pain with GI bleeding without antibiotic-associated colitis also reported. Can impede warfarin.
Flucloxacillin (Floxapen, Lutropin, Staphcil)	0.25-0.5 gm po q6h 1-2 gm IV q4h	Cholestatic hepatitis occurs in 1:15,000 exposures: more frequently in age >55 yrs, females and therapy >2 wks duration. Can appear wks after end of therapy and take wks to resolve (JAC 66:1431, 2011). **Recommendation: use only in severe infection.**
Nafcillin (Unipen, Nafcil)	1-2 gm IV/IM q4h. Due to >90% protein binding, need 12 gm/day for bacteremia.	Extravasation can result in tissue necrosis. With 200-300 mg per kg per day hypokalemia may occur. **Reversible neutropenia** (over 10%) **with ≥21-day rx, occasionally WBC <1000 per mm³).** Can impede warfarin effect.
Oxacillin (Prostaphlin)	1-2 gm IV/IM q4h. Due to >90% protein binding, need 12 gm/day for bacteremia.	**Hepatic dysfunction with ≥12 gm per day** LFTs usually ↑ 2-24 days after start of rx, reversible. In children, more rash and liver toxicity with oxacillin as compared to nafcillin (CID 34:50, 2002).
AMINOPENICILLINS		
Amoxicillin (Amoxil, Polymox)	250 mg-1 gm po tid	IV available in UK & Europe. IV amoxicillin rapidly converted to ampicillin. Rash with infectious mono– see Ampicillin.
Amoxicillin extended release (Moxatag)	One 775 mg tab po once daily	Increased risk of cross-allergenicity with oral cephalosporins with identical side-chains: cefadroxil, cefprozil. Allergic reactions, C. difficile associated diarrhea, false positive test for urine glucose with clinitest.
Amoxicillin-clavulanate (Augmentin)	See Comment for adult products	With bid regimen, less clavulanate & less diarrhea. In pts with immediate allergic reaction to AM-CL, ↓ is due to Clav component (J Allergy Clin Immunol 125:502, 2010). Positive blood tests for 1,3-beta D-glucan with IV AM-CL (NEJM 354:2834, 2006). Hepatotoxicity linked to clavulanic acid; AM-CL causes 13-23% of drug-induced liver injury. Onset delayed. Usually mild; rare liver Failure (JAC 66:1431, 2011).
AM-CL extra-strength peds suspension (ES-600)	Peds Extra-Strength susp: 600/42.9 per 5 mL Dose: 90/6.4 mg/kg div bid.	
AM-CL-ER–extended release adult tabs	For adult formulations, see Comments IV amox-clav available in Europe	**Comparison adult Augmentin dosage regimens:**
		Augmentin 500/125 1 tab po tid
		Augmentin 875/125 1 tab po bid
		Augmentin 1000/62.5 2 tabs po bid
		Augmentin-XR
Ampicillin (Principen) (250 & 500 mg caps)	0.25-0.5 gm po q6h. 50-200 mg/kg IV/day.	A maculopapular rash occurs (not urticarial), **not true penicillin allergy.** In 65-100% pts with infectious mono, 90% with chronic lymphocytic leukemia, and 15-20% in pts taking allopurinol. EBV-associated rash does not indicate permanent allergy; post-EBV no rash when challenged. Increased risk of true cross-allergenicity with oral cephalosporins with identical side chains: cefaclor, cephalexin, loracarbef.

*NOTE: all dosage recommendations are for adults (unless otherwise indicated) & assume normal renal function.

*NOTE: all dosage recommendations are for adults (unless otherwise indicated) & assume normal renal function.
(See page 2 for abbreviations)

TABLE 10A (2)

CLASS, AGENT, GENERIC NAME (TRADE NAME)	USUAL ADULT DOSAGE*	ADVERSE REACTIONS, COMMENTS (See Table 10B for Summary)
AMINOPENICILLINS (continued)		
Ampicillin-sulbactam (Unasyn)	**1.5–3 gm IV q6h; for Acinetobacter:** 3 gm (Amp 2 gm/Sulb 1 gm) IV q4h	Supplied in vials: ampicillin 1 gm, subactam 0.5 gm or amp 2 gm, subactam 1 gm. AM-SB is not active vs pseudomonas. Total daily dose subactam ≤4 gm. Increasing resistance of aerobic gram-negative bacilli. Subactam doses up to 9–12 gm/day evaluated (J Infect 56:432, 2008). See also CID 50:133, 2010.
ANTIPSEUDOMONAL PENICILLINS		
Piperacillin-tazobactam (PIP/TZ) (Zosyn) Prolonged infusion dosing, see Comment and Table 10E. Obesity dosing, see Table 17C.	Favor prolonged infusion: load with 4.5 gm IV over 30 min, then 4 hrs later start 3.375 gm IV q4h (over 4 hr). Old dose (except P. aeruginosa): 3.375 gm IV q6h or 4.5 gm q8h. Old P. aeruginosa dose: 3.375 gm q4h or 4.5 gm q6h.	Prolonged infusion references (CID 44:357, 2007; AAC 54:460, 2010). • Micro: False-pos P. aeruginosa infection: 350–450 mg/kg/day plus q4h. For obesity dosing adjustment see Table 17C, page 239. Documented drug-induced thrombocytopenia (J Thrombo Haemostasis 11:169, 2012). Retrospective matched cohort studies have reported significantly greater risk of nephrotoxicity from PIP/TZ + Vancomycin compared with Cefepime + Vancomycin (AAC 61: e02089-16, 2017; CID 64: 116, 2017).
Temocillin^{NUS}	2 gm IV q12h.	Semi-synthetic penicillin: stable in presence of classical & ESBLs & AmpC beta-lactamases. Source: www.eumedica.be
CARBAPENEMS. Review: AAC 55:4943, 2011. **NOTE: Cross allergenicity: In studies of pts with history of Pen-allergy but no confirmatory skin testing, 0-11% had allergic reactions with cephalosporin therapy** (JAC 54:1155, 2004). In better studies, pts with positive skin tests for Pen allergy were given 1 Carbapenem: no reaction in 99% (J Allergy Clin Immunol 124:167, 2009). Of 112 pts with IgE-mediated reaction to ceph., 1 (0.9%) reacted when given a Carbapenem (CID 59:1113, 2014). Incidence of carbapenem-resistant GNB highest in Georgia, Maryland & New York (JAMA 314:1455 & 1479, 2015).		
Doripenem (Doribax) Ref: CID 49:291, 2009. For prolonged infusion dosing, see Table 10E.	Intra-abdominal & complicated UTI: **500 mg IV q8h (1-hr infusion).** For prolonged infusion, see Table 10E, page 123. Do not use for pneumonia	Most common adverse reactions (≥5%): Headache, nausea, diarrhea, rash & phlebitis. Seizure reported in post-marketing surveillance. Can lower serum valproic acid levels. Adjust dose if renal impairment. Somewhat more stable in solution than IMP or **MER** (AAC 65:1023, 2010; CID 49:291, 2009). FDA safety announcement (01/05/12): Trial of DORI for the treatment of VAP stopped early due to excess mortality and poorer cure rate. **NOTE: DORI is not approved to treat any type of pneumonia; DORI is not approved for doses greater than 500 mg q8h.**
Ertapenem (Invanz)	1 gm IV/IM q24h.	Lidocaine diluent for IM use: ask about lidocaine allergy. Standard dosage may be inadequate in obesity (BMI ≥40). Reports of DRESS (drug rash eosinophilia systemic symptoms) Syndrome. Visual hallucinations reported (NZ Med J 122:76, 2009). No predictable activity vs. P. aeruginosa.
Imipenem + cilastatin (Primaxin) Ref: JAC 58:916, 2006	**0.5 gm IV q6h;** for P. aeruginosa: 1 gm IV q6–8h (See Comment).	For P. aeruginosa, increase dosage to 3 or 4 gm per day div. q6h or q8h. Continuous infusion of carbapenems more effective (CID 49:1881, 2005). Seizures: risk of seizure low but greatest with carbapenems. No diff between IMP and MER (JAC 69:2043, 2014). Cilastatin blocks enzymatic degradation of imipenem in lumen of renal proximal tubule & also prevents tubular toxicity. Compared to MER, more in vitro resistance to IMP vs. Proteus sp., Providencia sp., Morganella sp. (Can J Med Micro 2014;25:285).
Meropenem (Merrem)	**0.5–1 gm IV q8h. Up to 2 gm IV q8h for meningitis.** Prolonged infusion in critically ill: If CrCl ≥50: 2 gm (over 3 hr) q8h If CrCl 30-49: 1 gm (over 3 hr) q8h If CrCl 10-29: 1 gm (over 3 hr) q12h (Inten Care Med 37:632, 2011)	Seizures: in meta-analysis, risk of seizure low but greatest with carbapenems. No diff between IMP and MER (JAC 69:2043, 2014). Comments: Does not require a dehydropeptidase inhibitor (cilastatin). Activity vs aerobic gm-neg. slightly 1 over IMP, activity vs staph & strep slightly ↓; anaerobes: B. ovatus, B. distasonis more resistant to meropenem.
Meropenem-vaborbactam (Vabomere)	**4 gm (2 gm meropenem + 2 gm vaborbactam)** IV q8h infused over 3 hrs (with estimated eGFR >50 mL/min).	Combination of Meropenem with vaborbactam, and ArpuC but not metalo-beta-lactamases or oxacillinases with carbapenemase activity. Approved for the treatment of complicated urinary tract infections in patients age ≥18 years caused by E. coli, K. pneumoniae, E. cloacae and other susceptible aerobic gram-negative bacilli. Contra-indicated: if known hypersensitivity to meropenem or beta lactams. AEs: hypersensitivity reactions, seizure potential, C.diff-associated diarrhea, thrombocytopenia, neuromotor impairment, phlebitis (infusion site), diarrhea, headache. Major interactions: valproic acid (concomitant use not recommended), probenecid.

(See page 2 for abbreviations) *NOTE: all dosage recommendations are for adults (unless otherwise indicated) & assume normal renal function.

TABLE 10A (3)

CLASS, AGENT, GENERIC NAME (TRADE NAME)	USUAL ADULT DOSAGE[a]	ADVERSE REACTIONS, COMMENTS (See Table 10B for Summary)
MONOBACTAMS		
Aztreonam (Azactam)	1 gm q8h–2 gm IV q6h.	Can be used in pts with allergy to penicillins/cephalosporins with exception of Ceftazidime as side-chains of Aztreonam and **Ceftazidime are identical.** PK/PD (JAC 2016;71:2704).
Aztreonam for Inhalation (Cayston)	75 mg inhaled tid x 28 days. Use bronchodilator before each inhalation.	Improves respiratory symptoms in CF pts colonized with P. aeruginosa. Alternative to inhaled Tobra. AEs: bronchospasm, cough, wheezing. So far, no emergence of other resistant pathogens. Ref: Chest 135:1223, 2009.
CEPHALOSPORINS (1st parenteral, then oral drugs). NOTE: Prospective data demonstrate correlation between use of cephalosporins (esp. 3rd generation) and ↑ risk of C. difficile toxin-induced diarrhea. May also ↑ risk of colonization with vancomycin-resistant enterococci. See Oral Cephalosporins, page 110, for important note on cross-allergenicity.		
1st Generation, Parenteral		
Cefazolin (Ancef, Kefzol)	1–1.5 gm IV/IM q8h, occasionally 2 gm IV q8h for serious infections, e.g., MSSA bacteremia (max. 12 gm/day)	Do not give into lateral ventricles—seizures! No activity vs. MRSA.
2nd Generation, Parenteral (Cephamycins): May be active in vitro vs. ESBL-producing aerobic gram-negative bacilli. Do not use as there are no clinical data for efficacy.		
Cefotetan (Cefotan)	1–3 gm IV/IM q12h. (max. dose not >6 gm q24h.)	Increasing resistance of B. fragilis, Prevotella bivia, Prevotella disiens (most common in pelvic infections); do not use for intra-abdominal infections. Methylthiotetrazole (MTT) side chain can inhibit vitamin K activation. Avoid alcohol-disulfiram reaction.
Cefoxitin (Mefoxin)	1 gm q8h–2 gm IV/IM q6-8h.	Increasing resistance of B. fragilis isolates.
Cefuroxime (Kefurox, Ceftin, Zinacef)	0.75–1.5 gm IV/IM q8h.	Improved activity against H. influenzae compared with 1st generation cephalosporins. See Cefuroxime axetil for oral preparation.
3rd Generation, Parenteral – Use correlates with incidence of C. difficile toxin diarrhea; most are inactivated by ESBLs and amp C cephalosporinase from aerobic gram-negative bacilli.		
Cefoperazone-Sulbactam[NUS] (Sulperazon)	(Usual max. daily dose (Cefoperazone combo) 1+2 gm IV q12h.) If larger doses, do not exceed 4 gm/day of sulbactam.	In SE Asia & elsewhere, used to treat intra-abdominal, biliary, & gyn. infections. Other uses due to broad spectrum of activity. Possible clotting problem due to side-chain.
Cefotaxime (Claforan)	1 gm q8-12h to 2 gm IV q4h.	Maximum daily dose: 12 gm; give as 4 gm IV q8h. Similar to ceftriaxone but, unlike ceftriaxone, but requires multiple daily doses.
Ceftazidime (Ceftaz, Ceptaz, Fortaz, Tazicef)	From 1–2 gm IV q8-12h up to 2 gm IV q6h.	Maximum daily dose: 12 gm; can give as 4 gm IV q8h.
Ceftobiprole[NUS] Similar activity to ceftaroline, incl MRSA	0.5 gm IV over 2 hrs q8h for mixed gm- neg & gm-pos infections. 0.5 gm IV over 1 hr. q12h for gm-pos infections	Associated with caramel-like taste disturbance. Ref: Clin Microbiol Infections 13(Suppl 2):17 & 25, 2007. Hydrolyzed by ESBL & AmpC cephalosporinase. Found inferior to Ceftaz + Linezolid for HAP (CID 2014;59:51)
Ceftriaxone (Rocephin)	Commonly used IV dosage in adults: 1–2 gm once daily Purulent meningitis: 2 gm q12h. Can give IM in 1% lidocaine.	"Pseudocholelithiasis" 2° to sludge in gallbladder by ultrasound (50%), symptomatic (9%) (NEJM 322:1821, 1990). More likely with ≥2 gm per day with pt on total parenteral nutrition and not eating (AnIM 115:712, 1991). Has led to cholecystectomy (CID 17:356, 1995) and gallstone pancreatitis (Ln 17:662, 1998). Can cause drug-induced thrombocytopenia (J Thrombo Q Thrombo & Haemo 2012;11:169). Combination of Ceftriaxone & Lansoprazole led to 1.4 x increased risk of increased QTc to >500 msec (J Am Coll Cardio 2016;68:1756). For Ceftriaxone Desensitization, see Table 7, page 88.

(See page 2 for abbreviations)   [a]NOTE: all dosage recommendations are for adults (unless otherwise indicated) & assume normal renal function.

TABLE 10A (4)

CLASS, AGENT, GENERIC NAME (TRADE NAME)	USUAL ADULT DOSAGE*	ADVERSE REACTIONS, COMMENTS (See Table 10B for Summary)
CEPHALOSPORINS (continued)		
Antipseudomonal		
Cefepime (Maxipime) For obesity dosing, see Table 17C	**Usual dose: 1-2 gm IV q8-12h. Prolonged infusion dosing:** Initial dose: 15 mg/kg over 30 min, then immediately begin: If CrCl >60: 6 gm (over 24 hr) daily If CrCl 30-60: 4 gm (over 24 hr) daily If CrCl 11-29: 2 gm (over 24 hr) daily	Active vs P. aeruginosa and many strains of Enterobacter, Serratia, C. freundii resistant to Ceftazidime, Cefotaxime, Aztreonam. More active vs MSSA than 3rd generation cephalosporins. Not "porin-dependent". Neutropenia after 14 days rx (Scand J Infect Dis 42:156, 2010). Failures vs. E. cloacae bacteremia with MIC of 4-8 mcg/mL (AAC 2015;59:7558). **FDA Safety warning (June 2012):** risk of non-convulsive status epilepticus, especially in pts with renal insufficiency when doses not adjusted. Seizure activity resolved after drug discontinuation and/or hemodialysis in the majority of pts. Postulated mechanism: binding to GABA receptors (Scand J Infect Dis 46:272, 2014; Crit Care 17:R264, 2013.
Cefpirome[NUS] (HR 810)	1-2 gm IV q12h	Similar to cefepime; ↑ activity vs enterobacteriaceae, P. aeruginosa, Gm + organisms. Anaerobes: less active than cefoxitin, more active than Cefotax or Ceftaz.
Ceftazidime (Fortaz, Tazicef)	**Usual dose: 1-2 gm IV/IM q8-12h. Prolonged infusion dosing:** Initial dose: 15 mg/kg over 30 min, then immediately begin: If CrCl >50: 6 gm (over 24 hr) daily If CrCl 31-50: 4 gm (over 24 hr) daily If CrCl 10-30: 2 gm (over 24 hr) daily (AAC 49:3550, 2005; Infect 37:418, 2009).	Often used in healthcare-associated infections, where P. aeruginosa is a consideration. Use may result in ↑ incidence of C. difficile-assoc. diarrhea and/or selection of vancomycin-resistant E. faecium. Risk of cross-allergenicity with aztreonam (same side chain).
Anti-staphylococcal (MRSA)		
Ceftaroline fosamil (Teflaro)	**600 mg IV q12h (5-60 min infusion)** Pneumonia/bacteremia 600 mg IV q8h[NUS]. See Comment	Avid binding to PBP 2a; active vs. MRSA. Inactivated by Amp C & ESBL enzymes. Approved for MRSA skin and skin structure infections and used for MRSA pneumonia and bacteremia, but not approved indications (J Infect Chemother 19:42, 2013). Active in vitro vs. VISA, VRSA. Refs: CID 52:1156, 2011. Used successfully for bacteremia and bone/joint infections, but NAI (AAC 58:2541, 2014). Risk of neutropenia (JAC 71:2010, 2016; AAC 60: 264, 2016).
ESBL resistant		
Ceftolozane-tazobactam (Zerbaxa) Ref: CID 2016;63:234:	1.5 gm (1/0.5 gm) IV q8h for gm-neg complicated UTI & complicated intra-abdominal (add Metro 500 mg IV q8h) infection	Infuse over 1 hr. Active vs. P. aeruginosa (MAC 2017;61:e0046517) and many gm-neg bacteria producing beta-lactamases. Cross-reaction in pts with w/ CrCl 30-50 mL/min.
ESBL and Serine-carbapenemase resistant		
Ceftazidime-avibactam (Avycaz) Ref: CID 2016;63:234; JAC 2016;71:2713 .	2.5 gm (2 gm Ceftazidime/0.5 gm avibactam) IV over 2 hrs q8h for gram-negative complicated UTI & add metronidazole 500 mg IV q8h for complicated intra-abdominal infection	Active against ESBL- & KPC-producing aerobic gm-neg bacilli. No activity vs. GNB-producing metallo-carbapenemases. Decreased efficacy in pts with w/ CrCl 30-50 mL/min (in clinical trials).

(See page 2 for abbreviations)

*NOTE: all dosage recommendations are for adults (unless otherwise indicated) & assume normal renal function.

TABLE 10A (5)

CLASS, AGENT, GENERIC NAME (TRADE NAME)	USUAL ADULT DOSAGE^a	ADVERSE REACTIONS, COMMENTS (See Table 10B for Summary)
CEPHALOSPORINS *(continued)*		
Oral Cephalosporins		
1st Generation, Oral		**Cross-Allergenicity:** Patients with a history of IgE-mediated allergic reactions to penicillin (e.g., bronchospasm, anaphylaxis, angioneurotic edema, immediate urticaria) should not receive a cephalosporin. If the history is a "measles-like" rash to penicillin, available data suggest a 5–10% risk of rash in such patients; there is no enhanced risk of anaphylaxis.
Cefadroxil (Duricef) (500 mg caps, 1 gm tabs)	0.5–1 gm po q12h.	In pts with positive Pen G skin test, only 2% given a cephalosporin will react. Can predict with cephalosporin skin testing, but not easily available *(An IM 141:16, 2004; AJM 125:572, 2008).*
Cephalexin (Keflex) (250 & 500 mg tabs)	0.25–1 gm po q6h (max 4 gm/day).	IgE antibodies against either ring structure or side chains; 80% pts lose IgE over 10 yrs post-reaction *(J Aller Clin Immunol 103:908, 1999).* Amox, Cefadroxil, Cefprozil have similar side chains; Amp, Cefaclor, Cephalexin, Cefadrine have similar side chains.
2nd Generation, Oral		
Cefaclor (Ceclor, Raniclor) (250 & 500 mg caps)	0.25–0.5 gm po q8h.	• If Pen/Ceph skin testing not available or clinically no time, proceed with cephalosporin if history does not suggest IgE-mediated reaction, prior reaction more than 10 yrs ago or cephalosporin side chain differs from implicated Pen.
Cefprozil (Cefzil) (250 & 500 mg tabs)	0.25–0.5 gm po q12h.	Any oral cephalosporin can result in C. difficile toxin-mediated diarrhea/enterocolitis.
Cefuroxime axetil po (Ceftin)	0.125–0.5 gm po q12h.	There are few drug-specific adverse effects, e.g.:
		Cefaclor: Serum sickness-like reaction 0.1–0.5%—arthralgia, rash, erythema multiforme but no adenopathy, proteinuria or demonstrable immune complexes.
3rd Generation, Oral		
Cefdinir (Omnicef) (300 mg cap)	300 mg po q12h or 600 mg q24h.	**Cefdinir:** Drug-iron complex causes red stools in roughly 1% of pts.
Cefditoren pivoxil (Spectracef)	400 mg po bid.	**Cefditoren pivoxil:** Hydrolysis yields pivalate. Pivalate (70%) & becomes pivaloylcarnitine which is renally excreted; 39–63% ↓ **in serum carnitine concentrations.** Carnitine involved in fatty acid (FA) metabolism & FA transport
Cefixime (Suprax) (400 mg tab)	0.4 gm po q12–24h.	into mitochondria. Effect transient & reversible. Contraindicated in patients with carnitine deficiency or those in whom inborn errors of metabolism might result in clinically significant carnitine deficiency. Also contains caseinate
Cefpodoxime proxetil (Vantin)	0.1–0.2 gm po q12h.	(milk protein); **avoid if milk allergy** (not same as lactose intolerance). Need gastric acid for optimal absorption.
Ceftibuten (Cedax) (400 mg tab)	0.4 gm po q24h.	**Cefpodoxime:** There are rare reports of acute liver injury, bloody diarrhea, pulmonary infiltrates with eosinophilia.
		Cephalexin: Can cause false-neg. urine dipstick test for leukocytes.

AMINOGLYCOSIDES AND RELATED ANTIBIOTICS – See Table 10D, page 122, and Table 17A, page 225

CLASS, AGENT, GENERIC NAME (TRADE NAME)	USUAL ADULT DOSAGE^a	ADVERSE REACTIONS, COMMENTS (See Table 10B for Summary)
GLYCOPEPTIDES, LIPOGLYCOPEPTIDES		
Dalbavancin (Dalvance)	1000 mg IV over 30 min; one week later, 500 mg IV over 30 min or 1500 mg IV over 30 min x 1 dose. Avoid use with saline, drug may precipitate out of solution.	If CrCl<30: 750 mg IV initial dose, then one week later 375 mg IV. **Hemodialysis:** Dose as for normal renal function. Red man syndrome can occur with rapid infusion. Potential cross-reaction in those with hypersensitivity to other glycopeptides. No activity vs. VRE. No drug-drug interactions.
Daptomycin (Cubicin) (Ref on resistance: CID 50:S10, 2010). Case series success in treating right- & left-sided endocarditis with higher dose at 8-10 mg/kg/day *(JAC 68:936 & 2921, 2013).* In retrospective study, better survival in VRE bacteremia if dosed at ≥ 10 mg/kg/day *(CID 2017;64:605).*	**Skin/soft tissue:** 4 mg per kg IV over 2 or 30 minutes q24h **Bacteremia/right-sided endocarditis:** 6 mg per kg IV over 2 or 30 minutes q24h; up to 12 mg/kg IV q24h under study **Morbid obesity:** base dose on total body weight *(AAC 51:2741, 2007).* For other dosing recommendations, see Table 17C, page 239. Dapto + ceftaroline may work as salvage therapy in pts with refractory MRSA bacteremia *(AAC 57:66, 2013; AAC 56:5296, 2012).*	**Pneumonia:** Dapto should not be used to treat pneumonia unless hematogenous in origin and is FDA approved for right-sided endocarditis with or without septic embolization/hematogenous pneumonia due to S. aureus. **Dapto Resistance** Can occur de novo, after or during Vanco therapy, or after or during Dapto therapy *(CID 50(Suppl 1):S10, 2010).* As Dapto MIC increases, MRSA more susceptible to TMP-SMX, nafcillin, oxacillin *(AAC 54:5187, 2010; CID 53:158, 2011).* **Potential muscle toxicity:** Suggest weekly CPK; DC dapto if CPK exceeds 10x normal level or if symptoms of myopathy and CPK >1,000. Package insert: stop statins during dapto rx. Dapto interferes with protime reagents & artificially prolongs the PT. *(Blood Coag & Fibrinolysis 19:32, 2008).* **NOTE:** Dapto well-tolerated at doses up to 12 mg/kg q24h x 14d *(AAC 50:3245, 2006).* Immune thrombocytopenia reported *(CID 56:1353, 2013).* Reversible neutropenia with long-term use reported *(CID 50:737, 2010; CID 50:e63, 2010).* Eosinophilic pneumonia/chronic steroid-dep pneumonia reported *(CID 50:737, 2010).*

(See page 2 for abbreviations)

^a NOTE: all dosage recommendations are for adults (unless otherwise indicated) & assume normal renal function.

TABLE 10A (6)

CLASS, AGENT, GENERIC NAME (TRADE NAME)	USUAL ADULT DOSAGE[a]	ADVERSE REACTIONS, COMMENTS (See Table 10B for Summary)
GLYCOPEPTIDES, LIPOGLYCOPEPTIDES, LIPOPEPTIDES *(continued)*		
Oritavancin (Orbactiv) Review: CID 61:627, 2015	1200 mg IV over 3 hr x 1 dose. Dilute in D5W; do not use saline	Artificially increases PT ≈ INR x 24 hr&aPTT x 48 hr. **Drug-drug interactions** with **warfarin**; ↑ warfarin serum levels. Acute urticarial has occurred. No dose adjustment for renal or hepatic insuff. Not removed by hemodialysis. In vitro activity vs. VRE (AAC 56:639, 2012).
Telavancin[NEW] (Targocid)	For septic arthritis—maintenance dose 12 mg/kg per day; S. aureus endocarditis— trough serum levels >20 mcg/mL required (12 mg/kg q12h) times 3 loading dose, then 12 mg/kg q24h)	Hypersensitivity: fever (≥3 mg/kg 2.2%, at 24 mg per kg 8.2%), skin reactions 2.4%. Marked ↓ platelets (high dose ≥15 mg/kg per day). Red neck syndrome less common than with vancomycin.
Televancin (Vibativ) Lipoglycopeptide Ref: JID 60:787, 2015; CID 61(Suppl.2), 2015	10 mg/kg IV q24h if CrCl >50 mL/min. Infuse each dose over 1 hr.	**Avoid during pregnancy; teratogenic in animals.** Do pregnancy test before therapy. Adverse events: **dysgeusia (taste)** 33% nausea 27%; vomiting 14%; headache 14%; ↑ creatinine (3.1%); foamy urine (13%); flushing if infused rapidly. Hypersensitivity: fever (≥3 mg/kg 2.2%, evidence of **renal injury** in 3% telavancin vs. 1% vanco. In practice, renal injury reported in 1/3 of 21 complicated pts (AAC 67:723, 2012). Interferes with PT, aPTT & INR for 18 hrs post-infusion.
Vancomycin (Vancocin) AAC 26:01, 2016 See Comments for dosing. Continuous infusion dosing, see Table 10E	Initial doses based on actual wt, including for obese pts. Subsequent doses adjusted based on measured trough serum levels. **For critically ill pts, give loading dose of 25-30 mg/kg IV then 15-20 mg/kg IV q8-12h.** Target trough level is 15-20 mg/mL. For individual doses over 1 gm, infuse over 1.5-2 hrs. **Dosing for morbid obesity (BMI ≥40 kg/m2):** If CrCl ≥50 mL/min & pt not critically ill: 30 mg/kg/day divided q8-12h—no dose over 2 gm. Infuse doses of 1 gm or more over 1.5-2 hrs. Check trough levels. **Morbid obesity & critically ill:** Loading dose of 25-30 mg/kg (based on actual wt), then 15-20 mg/kg (actual wt) IV q8-12h. Infuse over 1.5-2 hrs. Limit maximal single dose to 2 gm. Oral tabs for C. difficile: 125 mg po q6h Generic drug now available	Vanco treatment failure of MRSA bacteremia associated with Vanco trough concentration <15 μg/mL & MIC >1 μg/mL (CID 52:975, 2011). IDSA Guideline supports target trough of 15-20 μg/mL. (CID 52:e18, 2011). Pertinent issues: • Max Vanco effect vs. MRSA when ratio of AUC/MIC >400 (CID 52:975, 2011). • MIC values vary with method used, so hard to be sure/compare (JCM 49:269, 2011). • With MRSA Vanco MIC = 1 & Vanco dose >3 gm/day IV, AUC/MIC >400 in 80% with est. risk of nephrotoxicity of 25%. With MIC = 2 & 4 gm/day IV, AUC/MIC >400 in only 57% (nephrotoxicity risk 35%) (CID 52:969, 2011). • Higher Vanco doses assoc with nephrotoxicity; causal relation unproven; other factors: renal disease, other nephrotoxic drugs, shock/vasopressors, radiographic contrast (AAC 55:3278, 2011). • If pt clinically failing Vanco (regardless of MIC or AUC/MIC), consider other drugs active vs. MRSA: Ceftaroline, Daptomycin, Linezolid, Televancin. (See Table 5A.) **po only, C. difficile colitis: 125 mg po q6h.** Commercial po formulation very expensive. Can compound po vanco from IV formulation: 5 g. IV vanco powder + 47.5 mL sterile H2O, 0.2 gm saccharin, 0.05 gm stevia powder, 0.05 gm cherry syrup to yield 100 mL = 50 mg vanco/mL. Oral dose = 2.5 mL q6h po. **Intrathecal dose:** 5-10 mg/day IV (infants); 10-20 mg/day (children & adults) to target CSF concentration of 10-20 mg/mL. **Nephrotoxicity:** Risk increases with dose and duration; reversible (AAC 57:734, 2013). **Red Neck Syndrome:** consequence of rapid infusion with non-specific histamine release. **Other adverse effects:** rash, immune thrombocytopenia, Thrombo fibrosis (18Ay 2012); fever, neutropenia, IgA bullous dermatitis (CID 38:1425, 2004). **Obesity dosing:** Frequent under-dosing. For obesity dosing adjustments, see Table 17C, page 239. For CrCl calculation for morbidly obese patient see Table 10D or Am J Health Sys Pharm 66:642, 2009.
CHLORAMPHENICOL, CLINDAMYCIN(S), ERYTHROMYCIN GROUP, KETOLIDES, OXAZOLIDINONES, QUINUPRISTIN-DALFOPRISTIN		
Chloramphenicol (Chloromycetin)	50-100 mg/kg/day po/IV div q6h (max 4 gm/day)	No oral drug studies in U.S. Hematological (↓ RBC–1/3 pts, aplastic anemia 1:21,600 courses). Gray baby syndrome in premature infants, anaphylactoid reactions, optic atrophy or neuropathy (very rare), digital paresthesias, minor disulfiram-like reactions. Recent review suggests Chloro is probably less effective than current alternatives for serious infection: respiratory tract, enteric, meningitis (JAC 70:979, 2015).
Clindamycin (Cleocin)	0.15-0.45 gm po q6h. 600-900 mg IV/IM q8h. In obese child, calc dose based on total body wt (AAC 2017;61:e02014f6)	Based on a number of exposed pts, these drugs are the most frequent cause of **C. difficile toxin-mediated diarrhea.** In most severe form can cause pseudomembranous colitis/toxic megacolon. Available as caps, IV 'sol'n, topical (for acne) & intravaginal suppositories & cream. **Used to inhibit synthesis of toxic shock syndrome toxins.**
Lincomycin (Lincocin)	0.6 gm IV/IM q8h.	Risk of C. difficile colitis. Rarely used.

(See page 2 for abbreviations)

[a]NOTE: all dosage recommendations are for adults (unless otherwise indicated) & assume normal renal function.

TABLE 10A (7)

CHLORAMPHENICOL, CLINDAMYCIN(S), ERYTHROMYCIN GROUP, KETOLIDES, OXAZOLIDINONES, QUINUPRISTIN-DALFOPRISTIN (continued)

CLASS, AGENT, GENERIC NAME (TRADE NAME)	USUAL ADULT DOSAGE[a]	ADVERSE REACTIONS, COMMENTS (See Table 10B for Summary)
Erythromycin Group (Review drug interactions before use) Azithromycin (Zithromax) Azithromycin ER (Zmax)	po preps: Tabs 250 & 600 mg. Peds suspension: 100 & 200 mg per 5 mL. Adult ER suspension: 2 gm. Dose varies with indication, see Table 1, Acute otitis media (page 11), acute exac. chronic bronchitis (page 38), Comm-acq. pneumonia (pages 40–41), & sinusitis (page 51). IV: 0.5 gm per day.	Gastroparesis: Erythro is alt drug for tx of gastroparesis. Initiates peristalsis by binding to motilin receptors & improves gastric emptying for approx 2 wks; then effect lost due to tachyphylaxis. Erythro dose: 1.5-3 mg/kg IV over 45 min q6h or 250 mg po liquid susp bid. Ref: Gastro Clin NA 2015,44:97. Frequent drug-drug interactions: see Table 22A page 345. Major concern is on EKG. Prolonged QTc: Erythro, clarithro & azithro all increase risk of ventricular tachycardia via increase in QTc interval. Can be congenital or acquired (NEJM 358:169, 2008). Caution if positive family history of sudden cardiac death, electrolyte abnormalities or concomitant drugs that prolong QTc.
Erythromycin Base and esters (Erythrocin) IV name; E. lactobionate Clarithromycin (Biaxin) or clarithro extended release (Biaxin XL)	0.25 gm q6h–0.5 gm po/IV q6h: 15–20 mg/kg up to 4 gm q24h. Infuse over 30+ min. 0.5 gm po q12h. Extended release: Two 0.5 gm tabs po per day.	↑ risk QTc >500 msec Risk amplified by other drugs (macrolides, antiarrhythmics, & drug-drug interactions (see FDs page 114 for list)). www.qtdrugs.org & www.torsades.org. Ref: Am J Med 128:1362, 2015. Cholestatic hepatitis in approx. 1:1000 adults (not children) given E. estolate. Drug-drug interactions of note: Erythro & clarithro decrease (both statin levels, rhabdomyolysis (Ann Int Med 158:869, 2013); concomitant clarithro & colchicine (gut) can cause fatal colchicine toxicity (pancytopenia, renal failure) (CID 41:291, 2005). Concomitant clarithro & Ca++ channel blockers increase risk of hypotension, kidney injury (JAMA 310:2544, 2013). Hypoglycemia with concomitant sulfonylureas (JAMA Int Med 174:1605, 2014). Transient reversible tinnitus or deafness with 24 gm per day of erythro IV in pts with renal or hepatic impairment. Reversible sensorineural hearing loss with Azithro (J Otolaryngol 36:257, 2007). Dosages of oral erythro preparations expressed as base equivalents. Variable amounts of erythro esters required to achieve same free erythro serum level. Azithromycin reported to exacerbate symptoms of myasthenia gravis. Approved for C. difficile toxin-mediated diarrhea, including hypervirulent NAP1/B1/027 strains. Minimal GI absorption; high fecal concentrations. Limited activity vs. normal bowel flora. In trial vs. Vanco, lower relapse rate vs. non-NAP1 strains than Vanco (NEJM 364:422, 2011). Despite absence of GI absorption, 12 pts developed allergic reactions; known macrolide allergy in 3 of 12 (CID 58:537, 2014).
Fidaxomicin (Dificid) (200 mg tab)	One 200 mg tab po bid x 10 days with or without food	
Ketolide: Telithromycin (Ketek) (Med Lett 46:66, 2004; Drug Safety 31:561, 2008)	Two 400 mg tabs po q24h. 300 mg tabs available.	Drug warnings: acute liver failure & serious liver injury post treatment. (AnIM 144:415, 447, 2006). Uncommon: blurred vision 2° slow accommodation; may cause exacerbation of myasthenia gravis (Black Box Warning: Contraindicated in this disorder). Liver, eye and myasthenia complications may be due to inhibition of nicotinic acetylcholine receptor at neuromuscular junction (AAC 54:5399, 2010). Potential QTc prolongation. Several drug-drug interactions (Table 22A, page 345) (NEJM 355:2260, 2006).
Tedizolid phosphate (Sivextro) Ref: AAC 61:1315, 2015.	200 mg IV/po once daily. Infuse IV over 1 hr.	IV dose reconstituted in 250 mL of normal saline; incompatible with lactated ringers as non-soluble in presence of divalent cations. SST clinical trial result (JAMA 309:559 & 609, 2013). Excreted by liver. No adjustment for renal insufficiency. Weak inhibitor of monoamine oxidase, hence risk of serotonin syndrome, but low risk (AAC 57:3060, 2013). Low risk of thrombocytopenia at therapeutic doses (AAC 2016,71:2553).
Linezolid (Zyvox) (600 mg tab) Review: JAC 66[Suppl 4]:3, 2011	po or IV dose: 600 mg q12h. Available as 600 mg tabs, oral suspension (100 mg per 5 mL,) & IV solution. Special populations Refs: Renal insufficiency (J Infect Chemother 17:70, 2011); Liver transplant (CID 42:434, 2006); Cystic fibrosis (AAC 48:281, 2004); Burns (J Burn Care Res 31:207, 2010). Obesity: clinical failure with standard dose in 265 kg patient (Ann Pharmacother 47:e25, 2013).	Reversible myelosuppression: thrombocytopenia, anemia, & neutropenia reported. Most often after >2 wks of therapy. Increased risk on hemodialysis or peritoneal dialysis (Int J Antimicrob Ag 36:179, 2010; AAC doi:10.1093/ac (MvI84) Lactic acidosis; peripheral neuropathy, optic neuropathy: After 4 or more wks of therapy. Data consistent with time and dose-dependent inhibition of intramitochondrial protein synthesis (Pharmacotherapy 27:771, 2007). Neuropathy, not reversible. Mitochondrial toxicity (AAC 2017;61:e00542-17). Inhibitor of monoamine oxidase: risk of severe hypertension if taken with foods rich in tyramine. Avoid concomitant pseudoephedrine, phenylpropanolamine, and caution with SSRIs[1]. Serotonin syndrome (fever, agitation, mental status changes, tremors). Risk with concomitant SSRIs: (CID 42:1578 and 43:180, 2006). Incidence low (AAC 57:5901, 2013). Other: black hairy tongue, acute interstitial nephritis (IDCP 17:61, 2009); teeth staining (CID 2016,62:617). Rhabdomyolysis case probably related to linezolid in a patient receiving linezolid as a component of multi-drug therapy for XDR tuberculosis (CID 54:1624, 2012). Resistance: linezolid resistant S. epidermidis and MRSA due to mutation of the 23S rRNA binding site (JAC 68:4, 2013).

[1] SSRI = selective serotonin reuptake inhibitors, e.g., fluoxetine (Prozac).

[a]NOTE: all dosage recommendations are for adults (unless otherwise indicated) & assume normal renal function.

(See page 2 for abbreviations)

TABLE 10A (8)

CLASS, AGENT, GENERIC NAME (TRADE NAME)	USUAL ADULT DOSAGE[a]	ADVERSE REACTIONS, COMMENTS (See Table 10B for Summary)
CHLORAMPHENICOL, CLINDAMYCIN(S), ERYTHROMYCIN GROUP, KETOLIDES, OXAZOLIDINONES, QUINUPRISTIN-DALFOPRISTIN (continued)		
Quinupristin + Dalfopristin (Synercid) (CID 36:473, 2003)	7.5 mg per kg IV q12h for skin/skin structure infections, infused over 1 hour. [For previous indication of VRE infection, dose used was 7.5 mg per kg IV q(8h).] Give by central line.	Venous irritation (5%); none with central venous line. Asymptomatic ↑ in unconjugated bilirubin. **Arthralgia 2%–50%** (CID 36:476, 2003). **Note:** E. faecium susceptible, E. faecalis resistant. **Drug-drug interactions:** Cyclosporine, nifedipine, midazolam, many more—see Table 22A.
TETRACYCLINES		
Doxycycline (Vibramycin, Doryx, Monodox, Adoxa, Periostat) (20, 50, 75, 100 mg tab)	0.1 gm po/IV q12h	Similar to other tetracyclines. ↑ nausea on empty stomach. Erosive esophagitis, esp. if taken at bedtime; **take with lots of water.** Phototoxicity & photo-onycholysis occur but less than with tetracycline. Deposition in teeth less than with tetracycline (AAC 22(7):752:2887). Can be used in patients with renal failure. Pseudotumor cerebri (intracranial hypertension) can occur. Comments: Effective in treatment and prophylaxis for malaria, leptospirosis, typhus fevers.
Minocycline (Minocin, Dynacin) (50, 75, 100 mg cap; 45, 90, 135 mg ext rel tab). (IV + tab.) Contains Mg++. Monitor serum Mg++ levels if renal impairment.	200 mg po/IV loading dose, then 100 mg po/IV q12h IV minocycline available.	**Vestibular symptoms** (30–90% in some groups, none in others): vertigo 33%, ataxia 43%, nausea 50%, vomiting 3%; women more frequent than men. Hypersensitivity pneumonitis, reversible, ~34 cases reported (BMJ 310:1520, 1995). Can cause slate-grey discoloration of the skin and other tissues with long-term use. **Intracranial hypertension** can occur. Comments: More effective than other tetracyclines vs staph and in prophylaxis of meningococcal disease. P. acnes: many resistant to other tetracyclines, not to mino. Induced autoimmunity reported in children treated for acne (J Ped 153:314, 2008). Active vs Nocardia, Mycobacterium marinum and many acinetobacter isolates.
Tetracycline, Oxytetracycline (Sumycin) (250, 500 mg cap) (CID 36:462, 2003)	0.25–0.5 gm po q6h, 0.5–1 gm IV q12h	GI (oxy 19%, tetra 4%), anaphylactoid reaction (rare), deposition in teeth, negative N balance, hepatotoxicity, enamel agenesis, pseudotumor cerebri/encephalopathy. Outdated drug: Fanconi syndrome. See drug-drug interactions, Table 22A. **Contraindicated in pregnancy, hepatotoxicity in mother, transplacental to fetus.** Comments: **Pregnancy:** IV dosage over 2 gm per day may be associated with fatal hepatotoxicity. (Ref: JAC 66:1431, 2011).
Tigecycline (Tygacil) Meta-analysis & editorial: Ln ID 11:804 & 834, 2011. Also CID 54:1699 & 1710, 2012.	100 mg IV initially, then 50 mg po/IV q12h, with po possible to decrease risk of nausea. **If severe liver dis. (Child Pugh C):** 100 mg IV initially, then 25 mg IV q12h	Derivative of tetracycline. High incidence of nausea (29%) & vomiting (20%) but only % of pts discontinued therapy. Pregnancy Category D. Do not use in children under age 18. Like other tetracyclines, may cause photosensitivity, pseudotumor cerebri, pancreatitis, a catabolic state (elevated BUN) and maybe hyperpigmentation (CID 45:136, 2007). Decreases serum fibrinogen (AAC 59:1650, 2015). Tetracycline, minocycline & tigecycline associated with acute pancreatitis (Ann Pharmacother Agents, 34:766, 2009). **Black Box Warning:** In meta-analysis of clinical trials, all cause mortality higher in pts treated with tigecycline (2.5%) vs. 1.8% in comparators. Cause of mortality risk difference of 0.6% (95% CI 0.1, 1.2) not established. Tigecycline should be reserved for use in situations when alternative treatments are not suitable (FDA MedWatch Sep 27, 2013). Poor result due to low serum levels (AAC 56:1065 & 1466, 2012); high doses superior to low doses for HAP (AAC 57:1756, 2013).

NOTE: all dosage recommendations are for adults (unless otherwise indicated) & assume normal renal function.

[a]NOTE: all dosage recommendations are for adults (unless otherwise indicated) & assume normal renal function.

(See page 2 for abbreviations)

TABLE 10A (9)

CLASS, AGENT, GENERIC NAME (TRADE NAME)	USUAL ADULT DOSAGE*	ADVERSE REACTIONS, COMMENTS (See Table 10B for Summary)
FLUOROQUINOLONES (FQs): All can cause false-positive urine drug screen for opiates		
Ciprofloxacin (CIP) and Ciprofloxacin-extended release (CIP XR, Proquin XR) (100, 250, 500, 750 mg tab; 500 mg ext rel tab)	Usual Parenteral Dose: 400 mg IV q12h. For P. aeruginosa: 400 mg IV q8h. Uncomplicated Urinary Cystitis (Oral): 250 mg po bid. Other Indications (Oral): 500-750 mg po bid.	FQs are a common precipitant of C. difficile toxin-mediated diarrhea. (Pharmacother 26:435, 2006). Toxicity review: Drugs Aging 27:193, 2010. FQs (other than Moxi) avoided for use under age 16 based on joint cartilage injury in immature animals. Articular SEs in children est. 1.2-3% (LnID 3:537, 2003). The exception is anthrax. Pathogenesis believed to involve FQ chelation of Mg++ and damaging chondrites (AAC 57:1022, 2007; Int J Antimicrob Agents 33:194, 2009). No evidence of cartilage damage with Levo in children (Pediatrics 134:e146, 2014).
Delafloxacin (Baxdela) 450 mg tablets . IV for injection	300 mg IV q12h infused over 1 hr x 5-14 days 450 mg po q12h x 5-14 days	**CNS toxicity:** Poorly understood. Varies: lightheadedness, confusion, seizures. May be aggravated by NSAIDs. Peripheral neuropathy occurs: rapid onset, potentially permanent injury. **Gemi skin rash:** Macular rash after 8-10 days of rx. Incidence of rash with ≤5 days of therapy only 1.5%. Frequency highest females, < age 40, treated 14 days (22.6%). In men, < age 40, treated 14 days, frequency 7.7%. Mechanism
Gatifloxacin (Tequin)[NUS] See comments	Can switch from IV to po during course of rx. 200-400 mg IV/po q24h. (See comment)	unclear. Indication to DC therapy. Ref: Diag Micro Infect Dis 68:140, 2010. **Hypoglycemia/hyperglycemia (Dysglycemia):** Increased risk, esp. of hypoglycemia in diabetic pts from any of the
Gemifloxacin (Factive) (320 mg tab)	Ophthalmic solution (Zymar) 320 mg po q24h.	marketed FQs (Ann Pharmacotherapy 38:1525, 2004). **Thrombocytopenia** in critically ill (J Thrombo Haemostasis 11:169, 2012). **Opiate screen false-positives:** FQs can cause false-positive urine assay for opiates See Table 10C, page 121. **QT, (corrected QT) interval prolongation:** ↑ QT (>500 msec or >60 msec from baseline) is considered possible with any FQ. ↑ QT can lead to torsades de pointes and ventricular fibrillation. Overall risk is 4.7/10,000 person yrs (CID 45:1457, 2012). Risk low with current marketed drugs. Risk ↑ women, ↓ K, ↓ mg++, bradycardia. (Refs.: CID 43:1603, 2006). Major problem is ↑ risk with concomitant drugs.
		Avoid concomitant drugs with potential to prolong QTc such as (see www.qtdrugs.org; www.torsades.org.):
Levofloxacin (Levaquin) (250, 500, 750 mg tab)	250-750 mg po/IV q24h. For most indications, 750 mg is preferred dose. po therapy; avoid concurrent dairy products, multivitamins, iron, antacids due to chelation by multivalent cations & interference with absorption. No dose adjustment for morbid obesity.	**Tendinopathy:** Over age 60, approx. 2-6% of all Achilles tendon ruptures attributable to use of FQ (ArIM 163:1801, 2003). ↑ risk with concomitant steroid, renal disease or post-transplant (heart, lung, kidney) (CID 36:1404, 2003). **Chelation:** Risk of chelation of oral FQs by multivalent cations (Ca++, Mg++, Fe++, Zn++). Avoid dairy products, multivitamins Clin Pharmacol/her 40 (Suppl 1) 33-2007).
Moxifloxacin (Avelox)	400 mg po/IV q24h. Note: no need to increase dose for morbid obesity (JAC 66:2330, 2011). Ophthalmic solution (Vigamox)	**Allergic Reactions:** Rare (1/50,000), IgE-mediated: urticaria, anaphylaxis. 3 pts with Moxi had immediate reactions but tolerated CIP (Ann Pharmacother 44:740, 2010). **Retinal detachment:** Inconsistent data. **Myasthenia gravis:** Any of the FQs may exacerbate muscle weakness in pts. with myasthenia gravis.
Ofloxacin (Floxin)	200-400 mg po bid. Ophthalmic solution (Ocuflox)	**Carpal tunnel syndrome:** Pharmacoepidemiological study found increased risk of CTS with FQ use (CID 65: 684, 2017). **Pseudotumor cerebri:** Significant risk ratio (4-6) reported (Neurology 2017:89:892).

Concomitant drug columns:

Antiarrhythmics:	Anti-infectives:	Anti-Hypertensives:	CNS Drugs:	Misc:
Amiodarone	Azoles (not Posa)	Bepridil	Dolasetron	Methadone
Disopyramide	Clarithro/erythro	Isradipine	Droperidol	Naratriptan
Dofetilide	FQs (not CIP)	Nicardipine	Fosphenytoin	Ondansetron
Flecainide	Halofantrine	Moexipril	Indapamide	Salmeterol
Ibutilide	NNRTIs		Fluoxetine	Sumatriptan
Procainamide	Protease Inhibitors		Haloperidol	Tamoxifen
Quinidine, quinine	Pentamidine		Phenothiazines	Tizanidine
Sotalol	Televancin		Pimozide	
	Telithromycin		Quetiapine	
			Risperidone	
			Sertraline	
			Tricyclics	
			Venlafaxine	
			Ziprasidone	

*NOTE: all dosage recommendations are for adults (unless otherwise indicated) & assume normal renal function.

(See page 2 for abbreviations)

TABLE 10A (10)

CLASS, AGENT, GENERIC NAME (TRADE NAME)	USUAL ADULT DOSAGE*	ADVERSE REACTIONS, COMMENTS (See Table 10B for Summary)
FLUOROQUINOLONES (FQs) (continued)		
Prulifloxacin Ref: Drugs 64:2221, 2004.	Tablets: 250 and 600 mg. Usual dose: 600 mg po once daily	**Contraindications:** persons with celiac disease, pregnancy, nursing mothers, persons with seizure disorder AEs: similar to other FQs.
POLYMYXINS (POLYPEPTIDES) Note: Proteus sp., Providencia sp., Serratia sp., B. cepacia are intrinsically resistant to polymyxins. Review: CID 59:88, 2014.		
Polymyxin B (Poly-Rx) 1 mg = 10,000 international units Where available, Polymyxin B preferred over Colistin.	Doses based on actual body weight. *LOADING DOSE:* 2.5 mg/kg IV over 2 hrs. *MAINTENANCE DOSE:* 1.5 mg/kg IV 1.5 mg/kg over 1 hr, then repeat q12h. Combination therapy with carbapenem suggested to increase efficacy and reduce risk of resistance. No dose reduction for renal insufficiency. **Intrathecal therapy for meningitis:** 5 mg/day into CSF x 3-4 days, then 5 mg every other day x 2 or more weeks.	**Adverse effects: Neurologic:** rare, but serious, is neuromuscular blockade; other, circumoral paresthesias, extremity numbness, blurred vision, drowsy, irritable, ataxia; can manifest as respiratory arrest (Chest 141:515, 2012). **Renal:** reversible acute tubular necrosis. Renal Injury in 42% (Polymyxin B) vs. 60% (Colistin) (CID 57:1300, 2013). **Skin:** hyperpigmentation in 8% of 249 pts (J Clin Pharm Ther 2017;42:573). PK study showed no need to reduce dose for renal insufficiency (CID 57:524, 2013). **Polymyxin B preferred over Colistin** (See Comment under Colistin for rationale). In retrospective study, lower mortality from P. aeruginosa & A. baumannii with Polymyxin B + carbapenem vs. polymyxin monotherapy (AAC 59:6575, 2015).

*NOTE: all dosage recommendations are for adults (unless otherwise indicated) & assume normal renal function.

(See page 2 for abbreviations.)

TABLE 10A (11)

CLASS, AGENT, GENERIC NAME (TRADE NAME)	USUAL ADULT DOSAGE*	ADVERSE REACTIONS, COMMENTS (See Table 10B for Summary)
POLYMYXINS (POLYPEPTIDES)		

Colistin, Polymyxin E (Colymycin) *(continued)*

USUAL ADULT DOSAGE:

Formulation and conversion: Colistin is formulated as a prodrug, colistimethate. Product vials may be labeled as international units (IU) or mg of prodrug or the **colistin base activity (CBA)** of active drug. **Always dose based on the CBA.** *To avoid dosing errors read product labels carefully!* Conversions (CID 2014, 58:139): 1 mg CBA = 30,000 IU CBA; 33 mg CBA = 1,000,000 IU CBA; 1 mg CBA = 2.4 mg colistimethate (prodrug).

Dosing recommendations continue to evolve. At present, there are 3 sets of dosing guidance: **PK Study Group:** creatinine clearance (CrCl)-based dosing (CID 2017:64=565); **European Medicines Agency (EMA):** CrCl-based dosing (CID 2016, 62:552); **U.S. FDA:** weight- and CrCl-based dosing, as per the package insert (June 2016). Complicated calculation-based dosing has been replaced by simpler PK-based dosing using CrCl levels as benchmarks. The PK Study Group recommendations are broader divisions between CrCl levels; the EMA recommendations use finer divisions between CrCl divisions. See Comments.

For severe systemic infection and patients not on dialysis of any kind (Note: for dosing in patients on intermittent hemodialysis or CRRT, see Table 17A):

1. **Combination therapy:** Colistin + (Imipenem or Meropenem).
2. **Loading Dose:** Administer a Colistin loading dose IV, then begin daily maintenance dosing 12 hours later. Loading dose formula: 4 x body weight in kg. Use lower of ideal or actual weight. May result in loading dose > 300 mg CBA. Start daily maintenance dose 12 hrs. later.
3. **Maintenance Dose: Then, Total Daily maintenance dose: Divide daily dose to bid or bid** (from Total Daily maintenance dose table (Comments)). Editors prefer MV (Study Group). Once daily dosing not recommended due to potential for toxicity and lack of efficacy data.

Other adult dosing:
Inhaled therapy: 50-75 mg CBA in 3-4 mL saline via vibrating mesh nebulize 2-3 times/day; concentration in lung epithelial lining is 100-1000x greater with inhaled dosing vs. IV dosing alone

Meningitis (intraventricular or intrathecal dose): 10 mg/day x several weeks; intrathecal dose often combined with IV dosing

Pediatric dosing:
Systemic Infection: 2.5-5 mg/kg/day in 2-4 divided doses (based on ideal body weight).
Cystic Fibrosis: 3-8 mg/kg/day in 3 divided doses (based on ideal body weight).

Note: Resistance and allergy issues. The plasmid-encoded colistin resistance gene, mcr-1, has been found in E. coli and Klebsiella sp. Resistance is due to modification of the lipid A target of the polymyxins. Strains may also produce metallo-carbapenemases, resulting in pan-resistance (See LnID 2016,16:161; LnID 2016, 16:287; AAC 2016, 60:4420). For carbapenem-allergic patients, no clear alternatives for a companion drug with colistin. Combination therapy with Rifampin did not improve clinical response or 30-day mortality in patients with Acinetobacter infections (CID 2013, 57:349; Epidemio Infect 2013, 141:1214). In vitro and in vivo exposure to polymyxins results in rapid selection of resistant subpopulations. In vitro, minocycline prevented emergence of resistance and augmented Colistin activity but no clinical trial data. Tigecycline may function similarly, but no data.

ADVERSE REACTIONS, COMMENTS:

Nephrotoxicity (Pharmacotherapy 35:28, 2015): Reversible acute tubular necrosis due to localization of drug in proximal tubular cells; (AAC 2017; 61:e02319-16. Depending on criteria, incidence of toxicity varies, average around 25%. Risk factors: length of therapy, daily dose, and cumulative dose; exposure to concomitant nephrotoxics; obesity, diabetes mellitus, age and hypertension. In animal models, high dose ascorbic acid and melatonin prevented toxicity. In critically ill, the benefit of patient salvage may exceed the risk of nephrotoxicity.

Neurotoxicity: Frequent vertigo, facial paresthesias, abnormal vision, confusion, ataxia. Rarely, neuromuscular blockade results in respiratory failure; may unmask or exacerbate myasthenia gravis. In cystic fibrosis patients, 29% experienced paresthesias, ataxia may exceed the risk of nephrotoxicity.

Other: Maybe hyper-pigmentation (CID 45:136, 2007).

Discussion and critiques of current dosing recommendations. The PK Study Group favors the EMA recommendations over the current (June 2016) U.S. FDA approved dosing (CID 2016, 62:552). The weight- and CrCl-based approach in the FDA approved dosing is more complicated than either the PK Study Group or EMA recommendations. The PK Study Group recommendations are based on PK study of 214 critically ill patients (CID 2017; 64:565). FDA recommended doses failed to achieve target serum concentration in 66% of patients versus less than 10% in patients with CrCl < 80 mL/min (CID 2016, 62:552) due to rapid renal clearance of colistimethate prodrug with less time for conversion of prodrug to active colistin.

Total Daily maintenance dose:

CrCl (mL/min)	PK Study Group (doses div bid or tid)*	EMA (doses div bid or tid)*	U.S. FDA (Wt - IBW)*
≥90	360 mg/day		2.5-5 mg/kg/day div 2-4 doses
80 to <90	340 mg/day		
70 to <80	300 mg/day	300 mg/day	2.5-3.8 mg/kg/day div 2 doses
60 to <70	275 mg/day		
50 to <60	245 mg/day		
40 to <50	220 mg/day	183-250 mg/day	2.5 mg/kg once daily or div bid
30 to <40	195 mg/day		
20 to <30	175 mg/day	150-183 mg/day	1.5 mg/kg q36h
10 to <20	160 mg/day		
5 to <10	145 mg/day	117 mg/day	N/R
<5	130 mg/day		

* All doses are stated as colistin base activity (CBA) in mg.
IBW = ideal body weight

CLASS, AGENT (left column):

Colistin, Polymyxin E (Colymycin)

Polymyxin E (Colistin) and Polymyxin B are polymyxin class parenteral antibiotics active against multi-drug resistant (MDR) gram negative bacteria, e.g., A. baumannii, P. aeruginosa, E. coli, K. pneumoniae. Combination therapy with a carbapenem (Imipenem or Meropenem) is recommended for all patients prescribed Colistin.

Resistance issues:
Serratia sp, Proteus sp., Providencia sp., Morganella sp., and B. cepacia are intrinsically resistant to polymyxins. Pan-resistant strains of Enterobacteriaceae, including resistance to colistin mediated by plasmid-encoded gene mcr-1 (AAC 60:2443, 2016) have been identified worldwide.

Colistin is the preferred polymyxin for:
Urinary tract infections (UTIs) & Adjunctive inhalation therapy for pneumonia caused by MDR gram-negative bacilli.

For all other indications, Polymyxin B is equivalent efficacy, faster attainment of target serum conc., less inter-patient variability in PK, no dose adjustment for renal impairment and lower risk of renal toxicity (AAC 60: 2443, 2016; and AAC 2017:61: e02319-16).

(See page 2 for abbreviations)

*NOTE: all dosage recommendations are for adults (unless otherwise indicated) & assume normal renal function.

TABLE 10A (12)

CLASS, AGENT, GENERIC NAME (TRADE NAME)	USUAL ADULT DOSAGE[a]	ADVERSE REACTIONS, COMMENTS (See Table 10B for Summary)
MISCELLANEOUS AGENTS		
Fosfomycin (Monurol) (3 gm packet)	3 gm with water po times 1 dose. For emergency use: single patient IND for IV use. From FDA: 1-888-463-6332.	Diarrhea in 9% compared to 6% of pts given nitrofurantoin and 2.3% given TMP-SMX. Available outside U.S., IV & po, for treatment of multi-drug resistant bacteria. For MDR-GNB: 6-12 gm/day IV divided q6-8h. Ref: *Int J Antimicrob Ag* 37:415, 2011.
Fusidic acid™ (Fucidin, Taksta)	500 mg po/IV tid (Denmark & Canada) US: loading dose of 1500 mg po bid x 1 day, then 600 mg po bid	Activity vs. MRSA of importance. Approved outside the US; currently in U.S. clinical trials. Ref for proposed US regimen: *CID 52 (Suppl 7):S520, 2011*.
Methenamine hippurate (Hiprex, Urex)	1 gm po bid	Nausea and vomiting, skin rash or dysuria. Overall ~3%. Methenamine requires (pH ≤5.5) urine to liberate formaldehyde. Useful in suppressive therapy after infecting organisms cleared; do not use for Rx of active UTI. *Comment:* Do not force
Methenamine mandelate (Mandelamine)	1 gm po qid	fluids; may dilute formaldehyde. Of no value in pts with chronic Foley. If urine pH >5.5, co-administer ascorbic acid (1-2 gm q4h) to acidify the urine; cranberry juice (1200-4000 mL per day) has been used, results ±. Do not use concomitantly with sulfonamides (precipitate), or in presence of renal or severe hepatic dysfunction
Metronidazole (Flagyl) (250, 375, 500 mg tab/cap) Ref: *Activity vs. B. fragilis:* Still drug of choice *(CID 50 (Suppl 1):S16, 2010).*	Anaerobic infections: usually IV, 7.5 mg per kg (≤500 mg) q6h (not to exceed 4 gm q24h). With long T1/2, can use IV at 15 mg per kg q12h. If life-threatening, use loading dose of IV 15 mg per kg. Oral dose: 500 mg qid; extended release tabs available 750 mg	Common AEs: nausea (12%), metallic taste, "furry" tongue. **Avoid alcohol during 48 hrs after last dose to avoid disulfiram reaction** (N/V, flushing, tachycardia, dyspnea). Neurologic AEs with high dose/long Rx: peripheral, autonomic and optic neuropathy, **Aseptic meningitis, encephalopathy, seizures & reversible cerebellar lesion** reported *(NEJM 374:1465, 2016);* *CID 2017;64:525.* Risk of hypoglycemia with concomitant sulfonylureas. Can use IV so'n as enema for *C. difficile*. **Resistant anaerobic organisms:** Actinomycetes. Peptostreptococci. **Once-daily IV dosing of** 1,500 mg: rational based on long serum T1/2; standard in Europe; supportive retrospective studies in adults with intra-abdominal infections *(AAC 59:410, 2007).*
Nitazoxanide	*See Table 13B, page 167*	Absorption ↑ with meals. increased activity in acid urine, much reduced at pH 8 or over. Nausea and vomiting
Nitrofurantoin macrocrystals (Macrobid, Macrodantin, Furadantin (25, 50, 100 mg caps) Systematic rev: *JAC70:2456, 2015*	Active UTI: Furadantin/Macrodantin 50-100 mg po qid x 5-7 days OR Macrobid 100 mg po bid x 5-7 days Dose for long-term UTI suppression: 50-100 mg at bedtime	peripheral neuropathy, pancreatitis. **Pulmonary reactions** (with chronic rx): acute ARDS type, chronic desquamative **interstitial pneumonia with fibrosis.** Intrahepatic cholestasis & hepatocellular hepatitis. Hemolytic anemia in G6PD deficiency. Drug rash, eosinophilia, systemic symptoms (DRESS) hypersensitivity syndrome reported *(Meth J Med 67:342, 2009).* Concern that efficacy may be reduced and AEs increased with CrCl under 40 mL/min. Should not be used in infants <1 month of age. **Birth defects:** increased risk reported *(Arch Ped Adolesc Med 163:978, 2009).*
Rifampin (Rimactane, Rifadin) (150, 300 mg cap)	300 mg po bid or 600 mg po/IV qd. Rapid selection of resistant bacteria if used as monotherapy	Causes orange-brown discoloration of sweat, urine, tears, contact lens. **Many important drug-drug interactions,** *see Table 22A.* Immune complex flu-like syndrome: fever, headache, myalgias, arthralgia—especially with intermittent rx. Drug induced immune thrombocytopenia *(J Thrombosis & Haemostasis 2012;11:169).* Can cause interstitial nephritis. Risk-benefit of adding RIF to standard therapies for S. aureus endocarditis *(AAC 52:2463, 2008).* *See also, Antimycobacterial Agents, Table 12B, page 151.*
Rifaximin (Xifaxan) (200, 550 mg tab)	Traveler's diarrhea: 200 mg tab po tid times 3 days. Hepatic encephalopathy: 550 mg po bid. *C. diff* diarrhea as "chaser:" 400 mg po bid	For traveler's diarrhea and hepatic encephalopathy *(AAC 54:3618, 2010; NEJM 362:1071, 2010).* In general, adverse events equal to or less than placebo.
Secnidazole (Solosec)	2 gm packet (granules): sprinkle on applesauce, yogurt or pudding and consume mixture within 30 min without chewing granules. Follow with glass of water to aid swallowing	Nitroim-dazole for treatment of bacterial vaginosis in adults. Vulvo-vaginal candidiasis may develop requiring antifungal therapy. Potential carcinogenicity seen in rodent studies. Avoid chronic use. **AEs:** Vulvo-vaginal candidiasis (≥2%), headache, nausea, dysgeusia, vomiting, diarrhea, abdominal pain, vulvovaginal pruritus.
Sulfonamides [e.g., sulfisoxazole (Gantrisin), sulfamethoxazole (Gantanol), (Truxazole), sulfadiazine]	Dose varies with indications. *See Nocardia & Toxoplasmosis*	**CNS:** fever, headache, dizziness; **Derm:** mild rash to life threatening Stevens-Johnson syndrome, toxic epidermal necrolysis *(Brit J Derm 2016;174:1194),* photosensitivity; **Hem:** agranulocytosis, aplastic anemia; **Cross-allergenicity:** other sulfa drugs, sulfonylureas, diuretics, crystalluria (esp. sulfadiazine-need ≥1500 mL po fluid/day); **Other:** serum sickness, hemolysis if G6PD def, polyarteritis, SLE reported.

(See page 2 for abbreviations)

[a]NOTE: all dosage recommendations are for adults (unless otherwise indicated); & assume normal renal function.

TABLE 10A (13)

CLASS, AGENT, GENERIC NAME (TRADE NAME)	USUAL ADULT DOSAGE*	ADVERSE REACTIONS, COMMENTS (See Table 10B for Summary)
MISCELLANEOUS AGENTS (continued)		
Tinidazole (Tindamax)	Tabs 250, 500 mg. Dose for giardiasis: 2 gm po times 1 with food.	**Adverse reactions:** metallic taste 3.7%, nausea 3.2%, anorexia/vomiting 1.5%. All higher with multi-day dosing. Avoid alcohol during & for 3 days after last dose; cause disulfiram reaction, flushing, N/V, tachycardia.
Trimethoprim (Trimpex, Proloprim, and others) (100, 200 mg tab)	100 mg po q12h or 200 mg po q24h.	**CNS:** drug fever, aseptic meningitis; **Derm:** rash (3–7% at 200 mg/day), phototoxicity, Stevens-Johnson syndrome (rare), toxic epidermal necrolysis (rare); **Renal:** ↑ K+, ↓ Na+, ↑ Cr; Hem: neutropenia, thrombocytopenia, methemoglobinemia. ACE inhibitors & aldactone increase serum K+. Higher incidence & severity when combined. Increased risk of death. *JAMA 2015;314:2406.* Mechanism: *BMJ 2014, 349:g6196.*
Trimethoprim (TMP)– Sulfamethoxazole (SMX) (Bactrim, Septra, Sulfatrin, Cotrimoxazole) Single-strength (SS) is 80 TMP/400 SMX, double-strength (DS) 160 TMP/800 SMX	**Standard po rx:** 1 DS tab bid. P. jirovecii IV rx (base on TMP component): standard 8–10 mg per kg IV per day divided q6h, q8h, or q12h. For shigellosis: 2.5 mg per kg IV q6h.	Adverse reactions in 10%: GI: nausea, vomiting, anorexia. Skin: Rash, urticaria, photosensitivity. More serious (1–10%): TMP, ACE inhibitors & aldactone increase serum K+. Higher incidence of severity when combined. Increased risk of death (*BMJ 349:g6196, 2014*). **Stevens-Johnson syndrome & toxic epidermal necrolysis.** Skin reactions may represent toxic metabolites of SMX rather than allergy (*Ann Pharmacotherapy 32-381, 1998*). Daily ascorbic acid 0.5–1.0 gm may promote detoxification (*AIDS 36:1041, 2004*). Risk of **hypoglycemia** with concomitant sulfonylureas. **Sweet's Syndrome** can occur. Hyperkalemia: Both TMP & ACE inhibitors can block renal tubular secretions of K+ & lead to dangerous hyperkalemia (*BMJ 349:g6196, 2014*). TMP one etiology of **aseptic meningitis.** Report of psychosis during treatment of PCP (*JAC 66:1117, 2011*). TMP-SMX contains sulfites and may trigger asthma in sulfite-sensitive pts. Frequent drug cause of thrombocytopenia. No cross allergenicity with other sulfonamide non-antibiotic drugs (*NEJM 349:1628, 2003*). For TMP-SMX **desensitization,** see Table 7, page 88.
Topical Antimicrobial Agents Active vs. S. aureus & Strap. pyogenes (*CID 49:1541, 2009*). Review of topical antiseptics, antibiotics (*CID 49:1541, 2009*).		
Bacitracin (Baciguent)	20% bacitracin ointment, apply 1-5 x/day.	Active vs. staph, strep & clostridium. Contact dermatitis occurs. Available without prescription.
Fusidic acid[NUS] ointment	2% ointment, apply tid	Available in Canada and Europe (*Leo Laboratories*). Active vs. S. aureus & S. pyogenes.
Mupirocin (Bactroban)	Skin cream or ointment 2% Apply tid times 10 days. Nasal ointment 2% apply bid times 5 days.	Skin cream: itch, burning, stinging 1–1.5%; Nasal: headache 9%, rhinitis 6%, respiratory congestion 5%. Not active vs. enterococci or gm-neg bacteria. Summary of resistance: *JAC 70-2681, 2015.* If large amounts used in azotemic pts, can accumulate polyethylene glycol (*CID 49:1541, 2009*).
Polymyxin B—Bacitracin (Polysporin)	5000 units/gm; 400 units/gm. Apply 1-4x/day	Polymyxin active vs. some gm-neg bacteria but not Proteus sp., Serratia sp. or gm-pos bacteria. See *Bacitracin* comment above. Available without prescription.
Polymyxin B—Bacitracin—Neomycin (Neosporin), triple antibiotic ointment, (TAO)	5000 units/gm; 400 units/gm; 3.5 mg/gm. Apply 1-3x/day.	See *Bacitracin and polymyxin B comments above.* Neomycin active vs. gm-neg bacteria and staphylococci; not active vs. streptococci. Contact dermatitis incidence 1%; risk of nephro- & oto-toxicity if absorbed. TAO spectrum broader than mupirocin and active mupirocin-resistant strains. (*DMID 54:53, 2006*). Available without prescription.
Retapamulin (Altabax)	1% ointment; apply bid. 5, 10 & 15 gm tubes.	Microbiologic success in 90% S. aureus infections and 97% of S. pyogenes infections (*J Am Acad Derm 55:1003, 2006*). Package insert says for MSSA only (not enough MRSA pts in clinical trials). Active vs. some mupirocin-resistant S. aureus strains.
Silver sulfadiazine	1% cream, apply once or twice daily.	1 sulfonamide but the active ingredient is released silver ions. Activity vs. gram-neg & gram-neg bacteria (including P. aeruginosa). Often used to prevent infection in pts with 2nd/3rd degree burns. Rarely, may stain into the skin.

(See page 2 for abbreviations)

*NOTE: all dosage recommendations are for adults (unless otherwise indicated) & assume normal renal function.

TABLE 10B – SELECTED ANTIBACTERIAL AGENTS–ADVERSE REACTIONS–OVERVIEW

Adverse reactions in individual patients represent all-or-none occurrences, even if rare. After selection of an agent, the physicians should read the manufacturer's package insert (statements in the product labeling (package insert) must be approved by the FDA). For unique reactions, see the individual drug (Table 10A). For drug-drug interactions, see Table 22A.
Numbers = frequency of occurrence (%); + = occurs, incidence not available; ++ = significant adverse reaction; 0 = not reported; R= rare, defined as <1%.
NOTE: Important reactions in bold print. A blank means no data found. Any antibacterial can precipitate C. difficile colitis.

Column groups: Penicillinase-resistant anti-staph. penicillins (Dicloxacillin, Nafcillin, Oxacillin); Aminopenicillins (Amoxicillin, Amox-Clav, Ampicillin, Amp-Sulb); AP Pens (Pip-Taz); Carbapenems (Doripenem, Ertapenem, Imipenem, Meropenem); Monobactam (Aztreonam); Aminoglycosides (Amikacin, Gentamicin, Kanamycin, Netilmicin, Tobramycin); Misc (Linezolid, Tedizolid).

ADVERSE REACTIONS (AR) — For unique ARs, see Individual drug, Table 10A	Penicillin G, V	Dicloxacillin	Nafcillin	Oxacillin	Amoxicillin	Amox-Clav	Ampicillin	Amp-Sulb	Pip-Taz	Doripenem	Ertapenem	Imipenem	Meropenem	Aztreonam	Aminoglycosides	Linezolid	Tedizolid
Rx stopped due to AR	3				2-4.4				3.2	3.4			1,2	<1			0.5
Rash	3	4	4	4	5	3	5	2	4	1-5	+	+	+	2		2	
↑ Coombs	3	0	R	R	+	0	+	0	+	+	+	1	+	R			
Neutropenia	R	0	+	R	2	+	+	+	+	R	+	2	+	+		1.1	0.5
Eosinophilia[1]	+	+	22	22	2	+	22	22	+	+	+	+	+	8			
Thrombocytopenia	R	+	0	R	R	R	R	+	+	+	+	+	+	R		3	2.3
Nausea/vomiting		+	0	0	2	3	2	2	7	4-12	3	2	4	R		6/4	8/3
Diarrhea		0	0	0	5	9	10	2	11	6-11	6	2	5	R		8.3	10
↑ LFTs	R	+	0	+	R	+	R	R	+	+	6	4	4	2		5-10	6
↑ BUN, Cr	R	R	0	0	0	R	R	R	+	+	R	R	R	0	5-25		
Seizures	R	0	0	+	0	R	R	0	R	see footnote[2]			0	0			
Ototoxicity	0	0	0	0	0	0	0	0	0	R		R		0	3-14		
Vestibular	0	0	0	0	0	0	0	0	0	0			0	0	4-6		

[1] Eosinophilia in 25% of pts; of those 30% have clinical event (rash 30%, DRESS in 0.8%, liver injury 15%, renal injury 6%, DRESS in 0.8% (J Allergy Clin Immunol doi 10.1076/j.jaci.2015.04.005).

[2] All β-lactams in high concentration can cause seizures. In rabbit, IMP 10x more neurotoxic than benzyl penicillin (JAC 22:687, 1989). In clinical trial of IMP for pediatric meningitis, trial stopped due to seizures in 7/25 IMP recipients; hard to interpret as purulent meningitis causes seizures (PIDJ 10:122, 1991). Risk with IMP ↓ with careful attention to dosage (Epilepsia 42:1590, 2001).
Postulated mechanism: drug binding to GABAA receptor. IMP binds with greater affinity than MER.
Package insert, percent seizures: ERTA 0.5, IMP 0.4, MER 0.7. However, in 3 clinical trials of MER for bacterial meningitis, no drug-related seizures (Scand J Inf Dis 31:3, 1999; Drug Safety 22:191, 2000). In meta-analysis, seizure risk low but greatest with carbapenems vs. other beta-lactams. No difference in incidence between IMP & MER (JAC 69:2043, 2014).

TABLE 10B (2)

CEPHALOSPORINS / CEPHAMYCINS

Adverse Reactions (AR) — for unique ARs, see individual drug, Table 10A.

Drug	Rx stopped due to AR	Rash	+ Coombs	Neutropenia	Eosinophilia	Thrombocytopenia	↑PT/PTT	Nausea/vomiting	Diarrhea	↑LFTs	Hepatic failure	↑BUN, Cr	Headache
Cephalexin	+	1	–							+		+	+
Cefuroxime axetil	2.2	R	R	R				1				R	R
Cefditoren pivoxil	2	R	R	R	R				6/1	1.4	R	R	R
Ceftibuten	2	R	R			5	R		2	3		R	R
Cefprozil	2	1	R	R	3	R		4	3	2	+	R	R
Cefpodoxime	2.7	1	R	R	3	R		4	7	4		R	R
Cefixime	2	1	R	R	R	R		7	16	R		R	R
Cefdinir	3	R	R	R				15	1		R	2	R
Cefadroxil		+	+					2					
Cefaclor/Cef.ER/Loracarbef[NUS]	R	+				2		2	1–4	3	+		3
Ceftolo-tazo	2	2	<1					3/1	1–4	1.7		1.5	6
Ceftobiprole[NUS]	2.7	+				+	+	9.1/4.8	<2			R	4.5
Ceftaroline	2.7	3	9.8			+	+	4/2	5	2		R	1.5
Cefepime	1.5	2	14	1		+	+	1	1	+		1	2
Ceftriaxone	2	2	R		6	R	+	R	3	0			R
Ceftizoxime	2	2	+		4	+	+	3	4	0			
Ceftaz-avi		<5				<5		2	4	1.5			10
Ceftazidime	2	2	1		8	+	+	1	6	3		R	
Cefotaxime	2	2	+		1	+	+	+	1	+			+
Cefuroxime	R	R			7		R	R	3	4	0	0	3
Cefoxitin	+	+			3		+	1	4	0	0	0	
Cefotetan	++	+			4				1	6		R	1
Cefazolin	+	3	+					4	3	0	0	0	3

MACROLIDES / FLUOROQUINOLONES

Adverse Reaction (AR)	Erythromycin	Clarithromycin, Reg. & ER	Azithromycin, Reg. & ER	Ciprofloxacin/CIP XR	Gatifloxacin[NUS]	Gemifloxacin	Levofloxacin	Moxifloxacin	Ofloxacin
Rx stopped due to AR	1	3	+	3.5	2.9	2.2	4.3	3.8	4
Rash	R	+	–	3	2	1–22[a]	2	2	2
Nausea/vomiting	3	3	25	3	8/<3	2.7	7/2	7/2	7
Diarrhea	5	3–6	8	5	4	3.6	5	5	4
↑LFTs	R	R	+	2	R	1.5	0.1–1	2	2
↑BUN, Cr	+	R	R	R	R				R
Dizziness, light headedness			+	R	3	0.8	3	2	3
Headache	R	2		1	4	1.2	6	2	2

OTHER AGENTS

Adverse Reaction (AR)	Vancomycin	TMP-SMX	Tigecycline	Tetracycline/Doxy/Mino	Telavancin	Rifampin	Quinupristin-Dalfopristin	Metronidazole	Daptomycin	Oritavancin	Dalbavancin	Polymyxin B & E (Colistin)	Clindamycin	Chloramphenicol
Rx stopped due to AR			5						2.8	3.8	3			
Rash	3	2.4			4	R			<1.5	4	4		0	+
Nausea/vomiting		+	30/20	13	27/14		2	12	6.3	9.9/4.6	6/3		+	+
Diarrhea		+		7	7			+	5	3.7	4.4			
↑LFTs		+		+	3	+			R	2.8	0.8	R		+
↑BUN, Cr	+								R	R		++		
Dizziness, light headedness										2.7				
Headache	3	+	5	+	3	+		5	+	7.1	4.7		+	+

[a] Highest frequency: females <40 years of age after 14 days of rx; with 5 days or less of Gemi, incidence of rash <1.5%.

TABLE 10C – ANTIMICROBIAL AGENTS ASSOCIATED WITH PHOTOSENSITIVITY

The following drugs (listed alphabetically) are known to cause photosensitivity in some individuals. Note that photosensitivity lasts for several days after the last dose of the drug, at least for tetracyclines. There is no intent to indicate relative frequency or severity of reactions. *Rxr Drug Saf 34-821, 2011.*

DRUG OR CLASS	COMMENT
Antiparasitic drugs	Pyrimethamine (one report), Quinine (may cross-react with quinidine)
Azole antifungals	Voriconazole, Itraconazole, Ketoconazole, but not Fluconazole
Cefotaxime	Manifested as photodistributed telangiectasia
Ceftazidime	Increased susceptibility to sunburn observed
Dapsone	Confirmed by rechallenge
Efavirenz	Three reports
Flucytosine	Two reports
Fluoroquinclones	Worst offenders have halogen atom at position 8
Griseofulvin	Not thought to be a potent photosensitizer
Isoniazid	Confirmed by rechallenge
Pyrazinamide	Confirmed by rechallenge
Saquinavir	One report
Tetracyclines	Least common with Minocycline; common with Doxycycline
Trimethoprim	Alone and in combination with Sulfamethoxazole

TABLE 10D – AMINOGLYCOSIDE ONCE-DAILY AND MULTIPLE DAILY DOSING REGIMENS
(See Table 17A, page 225, if estimated creatinine clearance <90 mL per min.)

- General Note: dosages are given as once daily dose (OD) and multiple daily doses (MDD).

- For calculation of dosing weight in non-obese patients use Ideal Body Weight (IBW):

  Female: 45.5 kg + 2.3 kg per inch over 60 inch height = dosing weight in kg:

  Male: 50 kg + 2.3 kg per inch over 60 inch height = dosing weight in kg.

- Adjustment for calculation of dosing weight in obese patients (actual body weight (ABW) is ≥ 30% above IBW): IBW + 0.4 (ABW minus IBW) = adjusted weight (*Pharmacotherapy 27:1081, 2007; CID 25:112, 1997*).

- If CrCl >90 mL/min, use doses in this table. If CrCl <90, use doses in Table 17A, page 225.

- For non-obese patients, calculate estimated creatinine clearance (CrCl) as follows:

$$\frac{(140 \text{ minus age})(\text{IBW in kg})}{72 \times \text{serum creatinine}} = \frac{\text{CrCl in mL/min for men.}}{\text{Multiply answer by 0.85 for women (estimated)}}$$

- For morbidly obese patients, calculate estimated creatinine clearance (CrCl) as follows (*AJM 84:1053, 1988*):

$$\frac{(137 \text{ minus age}) \times [(0.285 \times \text{wt in kg}) + (12.1 \times \text{ht in meters}^2)]}{51 \times \text{serum creatinine}} = \text{CrCl (obese male)}$$

$$\frac{(146 \text{ minus age}) \times [(0.287 \times \text{wt in kg}) + (9.74 \times \text{ht in meters}^2)]}{60 \times \text{serum creatinine}} = \text{CrCl (obese female)}$$

DRUG	MDD AND OD IV REGIMENS/ TARGETED PEAK (P) AND TROUGH (T) SERUM LEVELS	COMMENTS For more data on once-daily dosing, see AAC 55:2528, 2011 and Table 17A, page 225
Gentamicin (Garamycin), Tobramycin (Nebcin)	MDD: 2 mg per kg load, then 1.7 mg per kg q8h P 4–10 mcg/mL, T 1–2 mcg per mL OD: 5.1 (7 if critically ill) mg per kg q24h P 16–24 mcg per mL, T <1 mcg per mL	**All aminoglycosides have potential to cause tubular necrosis and renal failure, deafness due to cochlear toxicity, vertigo due to damage to vestibular organs, and rarely neuromuscular blockade.** Risk minimal with oral or topical application due to small % absorption unless tissues altered by disease. Risk of nephrotoxicity ↑ with concomitant administration of cyclosporine, vancomycin, ampho B, radiocontrast.
Kanamycin (Kantrex), Amikacin (Amikin), Streptomycin	MDD: 7.5 mg per kg q12h P 15–30 mcg per mL, T 5–10 mcg per mL OD: 15 mg per kg q24h: P 56–64 mcg per mL, T <1 mcg per mL	Risk of nephrotoxicity ↓ by once-daily dosing method (especially if baseline renal function normal). In general, same factors influence risk of ototoxicity.
Netilmicin[NUS]	MDD: 2 mg per kg q8h P 4–10 mcg per mL, T 1–2 mcg per mL OD: 6.5 mg per kg q24h P 22–30 mcg per mL, T <1 mcg per mL	**NOTE: There is no known method to eliminate risk of aminoglycoside nephro/ototoxicity. Proper rx attempts to ↓ the % risk.** The clinical trial data of OD aminoglycosides have been reviewed extensively by meta-analysis (*CID 24:816, 1997*).
Isepamicin[NUS]	Only OD: Severe infections 15 mg per kg q24h, less severe 8 mg per kg q24h	Serum levels: Collect peak serum level (PSL) exactly 1 hr after the start of the infusion of the 3rd dose. In critically ill pts, PSL after the 1st dose as volume of distribution and renal function may change rapidly.
Spectinomycin (Trobicin)[NUS]	2 gm IM times 1–gonococcal infections	Other dosing methods and references: For once-daily 7 mg per kg per day of gentamicin–Hartford Hospital method (may under dose if <7 mg/Kg/day dose), see AAC 39:650, 1995.
Neomycin–oral	Prophylaxis GI surgery: 1 gm po times 3 with erythro, see Table 15B, page 210 For hepatic coma: 4–12 gm per day po	One in 500 patients (Europe) have mitochondrial mutation that predicts cochlear toxicity (*NEJM 360:642, 2009*). Aspirin supplement (3 gm/day) attenuated risk of cochlear injury from gentamicin (*NEJM 354:1856, 2006*).
Tobramycin–inhaled (Tobi): See Table 1, page 44 & Table 10F, page 124. Adverse effects few: transient voice alteration (13%) and transient tinnitus (3%).		Vestibular injury usually bilateral & hence no vertigo but imbalance & oscillopsia (*Med J Aust 196:701, 2012*).
Paromomycin–oral: See Entamoeba and Cryptosporidia, Table 13A, page 154.		

TABLE 10E - PROLONGED OR CONTINUOUS INFUSION DOSING OF SELECTED ANTIBIOTICS

Based on current and rapidly changing data, it appears that **prolonged or continuous infusion of beta-lactams is at least as successful as intermittent dosing**. Hence, this approach can be part of stewardship programs as supported by recent publications.

Antibiotic stability is a concern. Factors influencing stability include drug concentration, IV infusion diluent (e.g. NS vs. D5W), type of infusion device, and storage temperature (Ref: P&T 36:723, 2011). Portable pumps worn close to the body expose antibiotics to temperatures closer to body temperature (37°C) than to room temperature (around 25°C). Carbapenems are particularly unstable and may require wrapping of infusion pumps in cold packs or frequent changes of infusion bags or cartridges.

A meta-analysis of observational studies found reduced mortality among patients treated with extended or continuous infusion of carbapenems or piperacillin-tazobactam (pooled data) as compared to standard intermittent regimens. The results were similar for extended and continuous regimens when considered separately. There was a mortality benefit with piperacillin-tazobactam but not carbapenems (CID 56:272, 2013). The lower mortality could, at least in part, be due to closer professional supervision engendered by a study environment. On the other hand, a small prospective randomized controlled study of continuous vs. intermittent Pip-Tazo, and meropenem found a higher clinical cure race and a trend toward lower mortality in the continuous infusion patients (CID 56:236, 2013).

DRUG/METHOD	MINIMUM STABILITY	RECOMMENDED DOSE	COMMENTS
Cefepime (Continuous)	@ 37°C: 8 hours @ 25°C: 24 hours @ 49°C: ≥24 hours	Initial dose: 15 mg/kg over 30 min, then immediately begin: • If CrCl >60: 6 gm (over 24 hr) daily • If CrCl 30-60: 4 gm (over 24 hr) daily • If CrCl 11-29: 2 gm (over 4 hr) daily	CrCl adjustments extrapolated from prescribing information, not clinical data. Refs: AJHP 57:1017, 2006; Am. J. Health Syst. Pharm. 68:319, 2011.
Ceftazidime (Continuous)	@ 37°C: 8 hours @ 25°C: 24 hours @ 49°C: ≥24 hours	Initial dose: 15 mg/kg over 30 min, then immediately begin: • If CrCl >50: 6 gm (over 24 hr) daily • If CrCl 31-50: 4 gm (over 24 hr) daily • If CrCl 10-30: 2 gm (over 4 hr) daily	CrCl adjustments extrapolated from prescribing information, not clinical data. Refs: Br J Clin Pharmacol 50:184, 2000; IJAA 17:497, 2001; AAC 49:3550, 2005; Infect 37: 418, 2009; JAC 65:900, 2013.
Doripenem (Prolonged)	@ 37°C: 8 hours (in NS) @ 25°C: 24 hours (in NS) @ 49°C: 24 hours (in NS)	• If CrCl ≥50: 500 mg (over 4 hr) q8h • If CrCl 30-49: 250 mg (over 4 hr) q8h • If CrCl 10-29: 250 mg (over 4 hr) q12h	Based on a single study (Crit Care Med 36:1089, 2008).
Meropenem (Prolonged)	@ 37°C: <4 hours @ 25°C: 4 hours @ 49°C: no data	• If CrCl ≥50: 2 gm (over 3 hr) q8h • If CrCl 30-49: 1 gm (over 3 hr) q8h • If CrCl 10-29: 1 gm (over 3 hr) q12h	Initial 1 gm dose reasonable but not used by most investigators. Ref: Intens Care Med 37:632, 2011.
Pip-TZ (Prolonged)	@ 37°C: 24 hours @ 25°C: 24 hours @ 49°C: no data	Initial dose: 4.5 gm over 30 min, then 4 hrs later start: • If CrCl ≥20: 3.375 gm (over 4 hr) q8h • If CrCl <20: 3.375 gm (over 4 hr) q12h	Reasonable to begin first infusion 4 hrs after initial dose. Refs: CID 44:357, 2007; AAC 54:460, 2010. See CID 56:236, 245 & 272, 2013. In obese patients (>120 kg), may need higher doses: 6.75 gm or even 9 gm (over 4 hrs) q8h to achieve adequate serum levels of tazobactam (Int J Antimicrob Agts 41:52, 2013).
Temocillin	@ 37°C: 24 hours @ 25°C: 24 hours These apply to Temocillin 4 gm/48 mL dilution (JAC 61:382, 2009).	Initial dose: 2 gm over 30 min, then immediately begin: • If CrCl >50: 9 gm (over 24 hr) daily • If CrCl 31-50: 6 gm (over 24 hr) daily • If CrCl 10-30: 1.5 gm (over 24 hr) daily • If CrCl <10: 750 mg (over 24 hr) daily CVVH: 750 mg (over 24 hr) daily	Offers higher probability of reaching desired PK/PD target than conventional q8h dosing. This study not designed to assess clinical efficacy (JAC 70:691, 2015).
Vancomycin (Continuous)	@ 37°C: 48 hours @ 25°C: 48 hours @ 49°C: 58 days (at conc 10 μg/mL)	Loading dose of 15-20 mg/kg over 30-60 minutes, then 30 mg/kg by continuous infusion over 24 hrs. No data on pts with renal impairment.	Adjust dose to target plateau concentration of 20-25 μg/mL. Higher plateau concentrations (30-40 μg/mL) achieved with more aggressive dosing increase the risk of nephrotoxicity (Ref: Clin Micro Inf 19:E98, 2013). Continuous infusion may reduce risk of Vanco nephrotoxicity (CCM 42:2527 & 2635, 2014).

TABLE 10F – INHALATION ANTIBIOTICS

There are many reasons to consider inhaled antibiotics as an adjunct to parenteral therapy: • spectrum of activity that includes MDR GNB • documented high drug concentration in lung epithelial alveolar lining fluid • benefit in animal models of pneumonia • improved drug delivery (nebulizer) systems • Low risk of serious AEs. Refs: *Adv Drug Del Rev 2015;85–65* (review); *Chest 2017; 151:737* (clinical debate). The FDA has approved 3 products for inhalation therapy: Aztreonam, Tobramycin sol'n; Tobramycin powder. The European Medicines Agency (EMA) has approved Colistin dry powder for inhalation.

INHALED DRUG	DELIVERY SYSTEM	DOSE	COMMENT
Amikacin + Ceftazidime	Vibrating plate nebulizer	AMK: 25 mg/kg once daily x 3 days Ceftaz: 15 mg/kg q3h x 8 days	Radiographic and clinical cure of *P. aeruginosa* ventilator-associated pneumonia (VAP) similar to IV AMK/Ceftaz, including strains with intermediate resistance (*AJRCCM 184:106, 2011*).
Aztreonam (Cayston)	Altera vibrating mesh nebulizer	75 mg tid x 28 days (every other month)	Improves pulmonary function, reduces bacterial load, reduces frequency of exacerbations, and improves symptoms in cystic fibrosis (CF) pts (*Exp Opin Pharmacother 14:2115, 2013*). Cost per treatment cycle about $6070.
Colistin (colistimethate) dry powder (EMA approved) Note: Polymyxin B is not used for inhalation due to toxicity to lung epithelial cells (*AAC 2017;61:e02690-16*)	Vibrating mesh (*AAC 2014;58:7331*)	50–75 mg CBA in 3-4 mL saline via vibrating mesh nebulizer 2-3 times/day; concentration in lung epithelial lining is 100–1000x greater with inhaled dosing vs. IV dosing alone. See *AAC 2014, 58:7331.*	• Efficacious vs. *P. aeruginosa* pneumonia in mouse model (*AAC 2017;61:e02025-16*) • Favorable PK in 6 cystic fibrosis pts (*AAC 2014;58:2570*) and 12 ICU pneumonia pts (*AAC 2014;58:7331*) • Recommended by IDSA HAP/VAP Guidelines as adjunctive rx for GNB susceptible to only polymyxins and AG (*CID 2016;63:e61*)
Fosfomycin + Tobramycin (FTI) 4:1 wt/wt	eFlow vibrating mesh nebulizer	FTI 160/40 or 80/20 bid x 28 days	Both doses maintained improvements in FEV1 following a 28-day inhaled aztreonam run-in (vs. placebo) in CF patients with *P. aeruginosa*; FTI 80/20 better tolerated than 160/40 (*AJRCCM 185:171, 2012*).
Levofloxacin	eFlow vibrating mesh nebulizer	240 mg bid x 28 days	Reduced sputum density of *P. aeruginosa*, need for other antibiotics, and improved pulmonary function compared to placebo in CF pts (*AJRCCM 183:1510, 2011*).
Liposomal Amikacin	PARI LC STAR jet nebulizer	500 mg qd x 28 days (every other month)	Company reports Phase 3 study in CF pts with *P. aeruginosa* has met primary endpoint of non-inferiority compared to TOBI for FEV1 improvement. Insmed website: *http://investor.insmed.com/releasedetail.cfm?ReleaseID=774638* Accessed November 30, 2013.
Tobramycin (TOBI, Bethkis)	PARI LC PLUS jet nebulizer	300 mg bid x 28 days (every other month)	Cost: about $6700 for one treatment cycle (*Med Lett 56:51, 2014*). Major AEs: bronchospasm, voice alteration, transient tinnitus.
Tobramycin (TOBI Podhaler)	28 mg dry powder caps	4 caps (112 mg) bid x 28 days (every other month)	Improvement in FEV1 similar to Tobra inhaled solution in CF patients with chronic *P. aeruginosa* but more airway irritation with the powder. Cost of one month treatment cycle about $6700 (*Med Lett 56:51, 2014*).

TABLE 11A – TREATMENT OF FUNGAL INFECTIONS—ANTIMICROBIAL AGENTS OF CHOICE*
For Antifungal Activity Spectra, see *Table 4B, page 83*

TYPE OF INFECTION/ORGANISM/ SITE OF INFECTION	ANTIMICROBIAL AGENTS OF CHOICE		COMMENTS
	PRIMARY	ALTERNATIVE	
Aspergillosis (A. fumigatus most common, also A. flavus and others.) (See *NEJM 360:1870, 2009; Chest 146:1358, 2014*).			
Allergic bronchopulmonary aspergillosis (ABPA) Clinical manifestations: wheezing, pulmonary infiltrates, bronchiectasis & fibrosis. Airway colonization assoc. with ↑ blood eosinophils, ↑ serum IgE, ↑ specific serum antibodies.	Acute asthma attacks associated with ABPA: **Corticosteroids**	Rx of ABPA: **itraconazole** oral sol'n 200 mg po bid times 16 wks or longer	Itra decreases number of exacerbations requiring corticosteroids with improved immunological markers, improved lung function & exercise tolerance (*CID 63:433, 2016*).
Allergic fungal sinusitis: relapsing chronic sinusitis, nasal polyps without bony invasion; asthma, eczema or allergic rhinitis; ↑ IgE levels and isolation of Aspergillus sp. or other dematiaceous sp. (Alternaria, Cladosporium, etc.)	Rx controversial: systemic corticosteroids + surgical debridement (relapse common).	For failures try **Itra** 200 mg po bid times 12 mos or **Flu** nasal spray.	Controversial area.
Aspergilloma (fungus ball)	No therapy or surgical resection. Efficacy of antimicrobial agents not proven.		Aspergillus may complicate pulmonary sequestration.
Invasive, pulmonary (IPA) or extrapulmonary: Post-transplantation and post-chemotherapy in neutropenic pts (PMN <500 per mm³) but may also present with neutrophil recovery. Common pneumonia in transplant recipients. Usually a rare (≥100 days) complication in allogeneic bone marrow & liver transplantation. High mortality (*CID 44:573, 2007*). **Typical x-ray/CT lung lesions** (halo sign), cavitation, or macronodules) (*CID 44:373, 2007*). **Galactomannan antigen immunoassay:** Detects aspergillus cell wall polysaccharide. Adjunct to diagnosis in neutropenic pts. Serum sens/spec. varies from 21-86% sens/80-92% spec. BAL fluid 60-100% sens/68-100% spec. False pos. if receiving antifungals. False pos. if colonized by aspergillus or infected by fusobacterium, histo or blasto (*JAMA 2017;318:1175*). **Better diagnostic strategy:** combination of serum galactomannan & aspergillus PCR (not routinely available) (*LnID 13:519, 2013*). **Beta D-Glucan:** in fungal cell wall. Can detect invasive fungal infections with immunoassay. Many false positives + low sensitivity (*JCM 51:3478, 2013*).	Primary therapy (See *CID 63:433, 2016*): **Voriconazole** 6 mg/kg IV q12h on day 1; then either (4 mg/kg IV q12h) or (200 mg po q12h for body weight ≥40 kg, but 100 mg po q12h for body weight <40 kg) (use actual wt). Goal trough (day 4): 1.0–5.5 mg/L associated with improved response rates and reduced adverse effects (*Clin Infect Dis 55:1080, 2012*). OR Alternative therapies: **Isavuconazonium sulfate** loading dose of 372 mg (equivalent to isavuconazole 200 mg) IV/po q8 x 6 doses then 372 mg IV/po daily OR **Liposomal Ampho B** (L-AmB) 3-5 mg/kg/day IV; OR **Ampho B lipid complex** (ABLC) 5 mg/kg/day IV; OR **Caspofungin** 70 mg/day IV day 1, then 50 mg/day thereafter; OR **Micafungin^ᴺᴺ** 100 mg bid (*JAC 64:840, 2009– based on PK/PD study*); OR **Posaconazole^ᴺᴺ** 200 mg qid, then 400 mg bid after stabilization of disease. In documented azole-resistant invasive aspergillosis, most experts suggest change to either **Liposomal Ampho B** or combination of **Voriconazole + echinocandin** (*JID 2017;216(S3):S436*)	**Voriconazole:** More effective than Ampho B. Vori, both a substrate and an inhibitor of CYP2C9, CYP2C9, and CYP3A4, has potential for deleterious drug interactions (e.g., with protease inhibitors). Review concomitant medications. Measure serum level with prolonged therapy or for patients with possible drug-drug interactions. In patients with CrCl <50 mL/min, po may be preferred due to concerns for nephrotoxicity of IV vehicle in renal dysfunction. (*Clin Infect Dis 54:933, 2012*). **Isavuconazole** (prodrug ISAV-isavuconazonium sulfate): A randomized control trial of isavuconazole vs. Voriconazole for invasive aspergillosis demonstrated that isavuconazole is non-inferior to voriconazole for the treatment of invasive aspergillosis (*Ln 2016;387:760*). **Ampho B: not recommended except as a lipid formulation**, either L-AMB or ABLC. 10 mg/kg and 3 mg/kg doses of L-AMB are equally efficacious with greater toxicity of higher dose (*CID 2007; 44:1289–97*). One comparative trial found greater toxicity with ABLC than with L-AMB: 34.6% vs 9.4% adverse events and 21.2% vs 2.8% nephrotoxicity (*Cancer 112:1282, 2008*). Vori preferred as primary therapy. **Posaconazole:** 42% response rate in open-label trial of patients refractory/ intolerant to conventional therapy (*CID 44:2, 2007*). Concern for cross-resistance with azole-non-responders. Measurement of serum concentrations advisable. **Caspofungin:** ~50% response rate in IPA. Licensed for salvage therapy. **Micafungin:** Favorable responses to micafungin as a single agent in 6/12 patients with primary therapy group and 9/22 in the salvage therapy group (*Clin Infect Dis 53:1060, 2006*). **Combination therapy:** A RCT of Voriconazole plus Anidulafungin vs. Vo iconazole alone showed a trend towards reduced mortality in all patients with invasive aspergillosis in the combination therapy arm (*Ann Intern Med 162:81, 2015*). Subgroup of patients with invasive aspergillosis whose diagnosis was established by radiographic findings and GM positivity had lower mortality with combination therapy. Combination therapy should be strongly considered although further data is needed to determine which patients would benefit the most. Some experts would recommend addition of echinocandin to amphotericin-based regimen or other azoles as well.

See page 2 for abbreviations. All dosage recommendations are for adults (unless otherwise indicated) and assume normal renal function.

TABLE 11A (2)

TYPE OF INFECTION/ORGANISM/ SITE OF INFECTION	ANTIMICROBIAL AGENTS OF CHOICE		COMMENTS
	PRIMARY	ALTERNATIVE	
Blastomycosis *(CID 46:1801, 2008)* (Blastomyces dermatitidis) Cutaneous, pulmonary or extrapulmonary.	**LAB**, 3-5 mg/kg per day; OR **Ampho B**, 0.7-1 mg/kg per day, for 1-2 weeks, **then Itra** oral sol'n 200 mg tid for 3 days followed by Itra 200 mg bid for 6-12 months	Itra oral sol'n 200 mg tid for 3 days then once or twice per day for 6-12 months for mild to moderate disease; OR **Flu** 400-800 mg per day for those intolerant to Itra	Serum levels of Itra should be determined after 2 weeks to ensure adequate drug exposure. Flu less effective than Itra; role of Vori or Posa unclear but active in vitro. Can look for Blastomyces in antigen in urine as an aid to diagnosis.
Blastomycosis: CNS disease *(CID 50:797, 2010)*	**LAB** 5 mg/kg per day for 4-6 weeks, followed by **Flu** 800 mg per day	Itra oral sol'n 200 mg bid or tid; OR **Vori** 200-400 mg q12h	Flu and Vori have excellent CNS penetration, to counterbalance their slightly reduced activity compared to Itra. Treat for at least 12 months and until CSF has normalized. Monitor serum Itra levels to assure adequate drug concentrations. More favorable outcome with Voriconazole *(CID 50:797, 2010)*.
Candidiasis: Candida is a common cause of nosocomial bloodstream infection. C. albicans & non-albicans species show ↓ susceptibility to antifungal agents (esp. fluconazole). In immunocompromised pts where antifungal prophylaxis (esp. fluconazole) is widely used. Oral, esophageal, or vaginal candidiasis is a major manifestation of advanced HIV & represents common AIDS-defining diagnosis. *See CID 62:el, 2016 for updated IDSA Guidelines.*			
Candidiasis: Bloodstream infection (C. albicans & C. glabrata)			
Bloodstream: non-neutropenic patient Remove all intravascular catheters if possible; replace catheters at a new site (not over a wire). Higher mortality associated with delay in therapy *(CID 43:25, 2006)*. **Candida auris:** This is an emerging **multi-drug resistant** Candida species able to cause a wide-range of infections. It can mis-identified as *Candida haemulonii* or *Sacharomyces cerevisiae*. Molecular methods are needed to confirm species. Often resistant to azoles and amphotericin, some are echinocandin resistant too. Multi-drug resistant Candida species *(JID 2017;216(S3):S445)*.	**Caspofungin** 70 mg IV loading dose, then 50 mg IV daily; OR **Micafungin** 100 mg IV daily; OR **Anidulafungin** 200 mg IV loading dose then 100 mg IV daily. Note: Reduce **Caspo** dose for renal impairment	**Fluconazole** 800 mg (12 mg/kg) loading dose, then 400 mg daily IV OR **Lipid-based Ampho B** 3-5 mg/kg IV daily; OR **Ampho B** 0.7 mg/kg IV daily; OR **Voriconazole** 400 mg (6 mg/kg) IV twice daily for 2 doses then 200 mg q12h. Funduscopic examination within first week of therapy to exclude ocular involvement. Ocular disease present in ~15% of patients with candidemia, but endophthalmitis is uncommon (~2%) *(CID 53:262, 2011)*. Intraocular injections of Ampho B required for endophthalmitis as echinocandins have poor penetration into the eye. For septic thrombophlebitis, catheter removal and incision and drainage and resection of the vein, as needed, are recommended; duration of therapy at least 2 weeks after last positive blood culture.	**Echinocandin** is recommended for empiric therapy, particularly for patients with recent azole exposure or with moderately severe or severe illness, hemodynamic instability. **An echinocandin should be used for treatment of** *Candida glabrata* **unless susceptibility to fluconazole or voriconazole has been confirmed.** Echinocandin preferred empiric therapy with high prevalence of non-albicans candida species. Echinocandin vs. polyenes or azole associated with better survival *(Clin Infect Dis 54:1110, 2012).* A double-blind randomized trial of anidulafungin (n=127) and fluconazole (n=118) showed an 88% microbiologic response rate (119/135 candida species) with anidulafungin vs a 76% (99/130 candida species) with fluconazole (p=0.02) *(NEJM 356: 2472, 2007).* **Fluconazole** is not recommended for empiric therapy but could be considered recommended for patients with mild-to-moderate illness, hemodynamically stable, with no recent azole exposure. **Fluconazole not recommended for treatment of documented** *C. krusei***: use an echinocandin or voriconazole or posaconazole (note: echinocandins have better in vitro activity than either Vori or Posa against** *C. glabrata***).** **Fluconazole recommended** for treatment of *Candida parapsilosis* because of reduced susceptibility of this species to echinocandins. Transition from echinocandin to fluconazole for stable patients with *Candida albicans* or other azole-susceptible species. **Voriconazole** with little advantage over fluconazole (more drug-drug interactions) except for oral step-down therapy of *Candida krusei* or voriconazole-susceptible *Candida glabrata*. Recommended **duration** of therapy is 14 days after last positive blood culture. Duration of systemic therapy should be extended to 4-6 weeks for eye involvement.

See page 2 for abbreviations. All dosage recommendations are for adults (unless otherwise indicated) and assume normal renal function.

TABLE 11A (3)

TYPE OF INFECTION/ORGANISM/ SITE OF INFECTION	ANTIMICROBIAL AGENTS OF CHOICE		COMMENTS
	PRIMARY	ALTERNATIVE	
Candidiasis: Bloodstream Infection (continued)			
Bloodstream: neutropenic patient Remove all intravascular catheters if possible; replace catheters at a new site (not over a wire).	**Caspofungin** 70 mg IV loading dose, then 50 mg IV daily, 35 mg for moderate hepatic insufficiency; OR **Micafungin** 100 mg IV daily; OR **Anidulafungin** 200 mg IV loading dose then 100 mg IV daily; OR Lipid-based **Ampho B** 3-5 mg/kg IV daily.	**Fluconazole** 800 mg (12 mg/kg) loading dose, then 400 mg daily IV or po; OR **Voriconazole** 400 mg (6 mg/kg) IV twice daily for 2 doses then 200 mg (3 mg/kg) IV q12h.	**Duration of therapy** in absence of metastatic complications is for 2 weeks after last positive blood culture, resolution of signs, and resolution of neutropenia. Perform funduscopic examination after recovery of white count as signs of ophthalmic involvement may not be seen during neutropenia. See comments above for recommendations concerning choice of specific agents.
Candidiasis: Bone and Joint Infections			
Osteomyelitis	**Fluconazole** 400 mg (6 mg/kg) daily IV or po; OR **Lipid-based Ampho B** 3-5 mg/kg daily for several weeks, then oral fluconazole.	Caspo, **Mica** or **Anidula** or **Ampho B** 0.5-1 mg/kg IV daily for several weeks then oral **Fluconazole**.	Treat for a total of 6-12 months. **Surgical debridement** often necessary; **remove hardware** whenever possible.
Septic arthritis	**Fluconazole** 400 mg (6 mg/kg) daily IV or po; OR **Lipid-based Ampho B** 3-5 mg/kg IV daily for several weeks, then oral fluconazole.	Caspo, **Mica** or **Anidela** or **Ampho B** 0.5-1 mg/kg IV daily for several weeks then oral **Fluconazole**.	**Surgical debridement** in all cases; removal of prosthetic joints whenever possible. Treat for at least 6 weeks and indefinitely if retained hardware.
Candidiasis: Cardiovascular **Endocarditis, Myocarditis, Pericarditis** (See Eur J Clin Microbiol Infect Dis 27:519, 2008)	**Caspofungin** 50-150 mg/day IV; OR **Micafungin** 100-150 mg/day IV; OR **Anidulafungin** 100-200 mg/day IV; OR Lipid-based **Ampho B** 3-5 mg/kg IV daily + **5-FC** 25 mg/kg IV daily.	**Ampho B** 0.6-1 mg/kg IV daily + **5-FC** 25 mg/kg po qid	Consider use of higher doses of echinocandins for endocarditis or other endovascular infections. Can switch to **fluconazole 400-800 mg** orally in **stable patients** with negative blood cultures and fluconazole susceptible organism. See Med 90:237, 2011. Valve replacement strongly recommended, particularly if prosthetic valve endocarditis. Duration of therapy not well defined, but treat for at least 6 weeks after valve replacement and longer in those with complications (e.g., perivalvular or myocardial abscess, extensive disease, delayed resolution of candidemia). Pericarditis: Pericardial window or pericardiectomy also is recommended. Long-term (life-long?) suppression with Fluconazole 400-800 mg daily for native valve endocarditis and no valve replacement; life-long suppression for prosthetic valve endocarditis if no valve replacement.
Candidiasis: Mucosal, esophageal, and oropharyngeal **Candida esophagitis** Primarily encountered in HIV-positive patients Dysphagia or odynophagia predictive of esophageal candidiasis.	**Fluconazole** 200-400 (3-6 mg/kg) mg IV/po daily; OR **Echinocandin** (**Caspofungin** 150 mg IV daily; OR **Micafungin** 150 mg IV daily; OR **Anidulafungin** 200 mg IV loading dose then 100 mg IV daily); OR **Ampho B** 0.5 mg/kg IV daily.	An azole (**Itraconazole** solution 200 mg daily; or **Posaconazole** suspension 400 mg bid for 3 days then 400 mg daily or **Voriconazole** IV/po 200 mg q12h.	**Duration of therapy** 14-21 days. IV Echinocandin or Ampho B for patients unable to tolerate oral therapy. For Fluconazole refractory disease, Itra (80% will respond), Posa, Vori, an Echinocandin, or Ampho B. Echinocandins associated with higher relapse rate than fluconazole. ART recommended. Suppressive therapy with fluconazole 200 mg 3x/wk until CD4 >200/mm[3].

See page 2 for abbreviations. All dosage recommendations are for adults (unless otherwise indicated) and assume normal renal function.

TABLE 11A (4)

TYPE OF INFECTION/ORGANISM/ SITE OF INFECTION	ANTIMICROBIAL AGENTS OF CHOICE		COMMENTS
	PRIMARY	ALTERNATIVE	
Candidiasis: Mucosal, esophageal, and oropharyngeal *(continued)*			
Oropharyngeal candidiasis			
Non-AIDS patient	Clotrimazole troches 10 mg 5 times daily; OR Nystatin suspension or pastilles po qid; OR Fluconazole 100-200 mg daily.	Itraconazole solution 200 mg daily; OR Posaconazole suspension 400 mg bid for 3 days then 400 mg daily; or Voriconazole 200 mg q12h; OR an Echinocandin (Caspofungin 70 mg loading dose then 50 mg IV daily; or Micafungin 100 mg IV daily; or Anidulafungin 200 mg IV loading dose then 100 mg IV daily; OR Ampho B 0.3 mg/kg daily.	**Duration of therapy** 7-14 days. Clotrimazole or nystatin recommended for mild disease; Fluconazole preferred for moderate-to-severe disease. Alternative agents reserved for refractory disease.
AIDS patient	Fluconazole 100-200 mg daily for 7-14 days.	Same as for non-AIDS patient for 7-14 days.	ART in HIV-positive patients. Suppressive therapy until CD4 >200/mm³, but if required fluconazole 100 mg po thrice weekly. Oral Itra, Posa, or Vori for 28 days for Fluconazole-refractory disease. IV echinocandin also an option. Dysphagia or odynophagia predictive of esophageal candidiasis.
Vulvovaginitis			
Non-AIDS Patient	**Topical azole therapy:** Butoconazole 2% cream (5 gm) at bedtime x 3 days or 2% cream SR 5 gm x 1; OR Clotrimazole 100 mg vaginal tabs (2 at bedtime x 3 days) or 1% cream (5 gm) at bedtime times 7 days (14 days may t cure rate) or 100 mg vaginal tab x 7 days or 500 mg vaginal tab x 1; OR Miconazole 200 mg vaginal suppos (1 at bedtime x 3 days) or 100 mg vaginal suppos. q24h x 7 days or 2% cream (5 gm) at bedtime x 7 days; OR Terconazole 80 mg vaginal tab (1 at bedtime x 3 days) or 0.4% cream (5 gm) at bedtime x 7 days or 0.8% cream 5 gm intravaginal q24h x 3 days; or Tioconazole 6.5% vag. ointment x 1 dose. **Oral therapy:** Fluconazole 150 mg po x 1; OR Itraconazole 200 mg po bid x 1 day.	Recurrent vulvovaginal candidiasis: Fluconazole 150 mg weekly for 6 months.	
AIDS Patient	Topical azoles (clotrimazole, buto, mico, tico, or tercon) x3-7d; OR Topical Nystatin 100,000 units/day as vaginal tablet x14d; OR Oral Flu 150 mg x1 dose.	Fluconazole 400-800 mg (6-12 mg/kg) IV or po.	For recurrent disease 10-14 days of topical azole or oral Flu 150 mg, then Flu 150 mg po weekly for 6 mos.
Candidiasis: Other infections			
CNS Infection	Lipid-based Ampho B 3-5 mg/kg IV daily + 5-FC 25 mg/kg po qid.	Fluconazole 400-800 mg	Removal of intraventricular devices recommended. Flu 400-800 mg as step-down therapy in the stable patient and in patient intolerant of Ampho B. Experience too limited to recommend echinocandins at this time. **Treatment duration** for several weeks until resolution of CSF, radiographic, and clinical abnormalities.
Cutaneous *(including paronychia, Table 1, page 27)*	Apply topical Ampho B, Clotrimazole, Econazole, Miconazole, or Nystatin 3-4 x daily for 7-14 days or ketoconazole 400 mg po once daily x 14 days. Ciclopirox olamine 1% cream/lotion; apply topically bid x 7-14 days.		

See page 2 for abbreviations. All dosage recommendations are for adults (unless otherwise indicated) and assume normal renal function.

TABLE 11A (5)

TYPE OF INFECTION/ORGANISM/ SITE OF INFECTION	ANTIMICROBIAL AGENTS OF CHOICE		COMMENTS
	PRIMARY	ALTERNATIVE	
Candidiasis: Other infections *(continued)*			
Endophthalmitis /Chorioretinitis • Occurs in 10% of candidemia, thus ophthalmological consult for all pts • Diagnosis: typical white lesions on retinal exam and/or positive vitrectomy culture • Chorioretinitis accounts for 85% of ocular disease while endophthalmitis occurs in only 15% *(Clin Infect Dis 53:262, 2011).*	Chorioretinitis or Endophthalmitis: Lipid-based **Amphotericin B** 3-5 mg/kg daily-plus-flucytosine 25 mg/kg qid; OR **Voriconazole** 6 mg/kg po/IV q12 x 2 doses and then 4 mg/kg po/IV q12. Consider intravitreal **Amphotericin B** 5-10 mcg in 0.1 mL or intravitreal **Voriconazole** 100 mcg in 0.1 mL for sight threatening disease.	Chorioretinitis or Endophthalmitis: **Fluconazole** 6-12 mg/kg IV daily (400-800 mg/day) except for data on *C. krusei* and/or consider intravitreal **Amphotericin B** 5-10 mcg in 0.1 mL for sight-threatening disease. *Clin Infect Dis. 52:648, 2011.*	**Duration of therapy:** 4-6 weeks or longer, based on resolution determined by repeated examinations. Vitrectomy may be necessary for those with vitritis or endophthalmitis *(Br J Ophthalmol 92:466, 2008; Pharmacotherapy 27:1711, 2007).*
Neonatal candidiasis	**Ampho B** 1 mg/kg IV daily; OR **Fluconazole** 12 mg/kg IV daily.	**Lipid-based Ampho B** 3-5 mg/kg IV daily.	**Lumbar puncture** to rule out CNS disease, **dilated retinal examination,** and **intravascular catheter removal** strongly recommended. Lipid-based Ampho B used only if there is no renal involvement. Echinocandins considered 3rd line therapy. **Duration of therapy is at least 3 weeks.**
Peritonitis (Chronic Ambulatory Peritoneal Dialysis) *See Table 19, page 241.*	**Fluconazole** 400 mg po q24h x 2-3 wks; or **Caspofungin** 70 mg IV on day 1 followed by 50 mg IV q24h for 14 days; or **Micafungin** 100 mg IV q24h for 14 days.	**Ampho B,** continuous intraperitoneal dosing at 1.5 mg/L of dialysis fluid times 4-6 wks.	Remove cath immediately or if no clinical improvement in 4-7 days.
Candidiasis: Urinary tract infections			
Cystitis **Asymptomatic** *See CID 52:s427, 2011; CID 52:s452, 2011.*	If possible, remove catheter or stent. No therapy indicated except in patients at high risk for dissemination or undergoing a urologic procedure.		**High risk patients** (neonates and neutropenic patients) should be managed as outlined for treatment of bloodstream infection. For patients undergoing urologic procedures. Flu 200 mg (3 mg/kg) IV/po daily or Ampho B 0.5 mg/kg IV daily (for flu-resistant organisms) for several days pre- and post-procedure.
Symptomatic	**Fluconazole** 200 mg (3 mg/kg) IV/po daily for 14 days.	**Ampho B** 0.5 mg/kg IV daily (for fluconazole resistant organisms) for 7-10 days.	Concentration of echinocandins is low; case reports of efficacy versus azole resistant organisms *(Can J Infect Dis Med Microbiol 18:149, 2007; CID 44:e46, 2007).* Persistent candiduria in immunocompromised pt warrants ultrasound or CT of kidneys to rule out fungus ball.
Pyelonephritis	**Fluconazole** 200-400 mg (3-6 mg/kg) once daily orally.	**Ampho B** 0.5 mg/kg daily IV + 5-FC 25 mg/kg po qid.	**Treat for 2 weeks.** For suspected disseminated disease treat as if bloodstream infection is present.
Chromoblastomycosis *(Clin Exp Dermatol. 34:849, 2009).* (Cladophialophora, Phialophora, or Fonsecaea); Cutaneous (usually feet, legs); raised scaly lesions, most common in tropical areas	If lesions small & few, **surgical excision or cryosurgery with liquid nitrogen** or lesions small, chronic, extensive, burrowing: **Itraconazole.**	**Itraconazole:** 200-400 mg daily or, if no response, daily once q24h or 400 mg pulse therapy once daily for 1 week of each month for 6-12 months (or until response)[NR].	**Terbinafine**[NR] 500-1000 mg once daily alone or in combination with **Itraconazole** 200-400 oral soln's mg; or **Posaconazole** (800 mg/d) po may be effective. Anecdotal report of efficacy of topical imiquimod 5%; 5x/wk *(CID 58:1734, 2014).*

See page 2 for abbreviations. All dosage recommendations are for adults (unless otherwise indicated) and assume normal renal function.

TABLE 11A (6)

TYPE OF INFECTION/ORGANISM/ SITE OF INFECTION	ANTIMICROBIAL AGENTS OF CHOICE		COMMENTS
	PRIMARY	ALTERNATIVE	
Coccidioidomycosis (Coccidioides immitis) (IDSA Guidelines: CID 63: e112, 2016; see also Mayo Clin Proc 83:343, 2008)			
Primary pulmonary (San Joaquin or Valley Fever): For pts at low risk of persistence/complication	Antifungal rx not generally indicated. Treat if fever, wt loss and/or fatigue that does not resolve within 4-8 wks		Uncomplicated pulmonary in normal host common in endemic areas (Emerg Infect Dis 12:958, 2006). Influenza-like illness of 1-2 wks duration.
Primary pulmonary in pts with ↑ risk for complications or dissemination. Rx indicated: • immunosuppressive disease, post-transplantation, hematological malignancies or therapies (steroids, TNF-α antagonists) • Diabetes • Pregnancy in 3rd trimester. • CF antibody >1:16 • Pulmonary infiltrates • Dissemination (identification of spherules or culture of organism from ulcer, joint effusion, pus from subcutaneous abscess or bone biopsy, etc.)	**Mild to moderate severity** (EID 20:983, 2014): Itraconazole solution 200 mg po or IV bid; OR Fluconazole 400 mg po q24h for 3-12 mos		**Ampho B cure rate 50-70%. Responses to azoles are similar. Itra may have slight advantage esp. in soft tissue infection. Relapse rates after rx 40%.** Relapse rate ↑ if CF titer ≥1:256. Following CF titers after completion of rx important; rising titers warrant retreatment.
	Locally severe or disseminated disease Ampho B 0.6-1 mg/kg per day x 7 days then 0.8 mg/kg every other day or liposomal Ampho B 3-5 mg/kg IV or ABLC 5 mg/kg IV, until clinical improvement (usually several wks or longer in disseminated disease), followed by Itra or Flu for at least 1 year. Some use combination of Ampho B & Flu for progressive severe disease; controlled series lacking.	Itraconazole 400-1,000 mg po q24h indefinitely	**Posaconazole** reported successful in 73% of pts with refractory non-meningeal cocci (Chest 132:952, 2007). Not frontline therapy. Treatment of pediatric cocci to include salvage therapy with Vori & Caspo (CID 56:1573, 1579 & 1587, 2013). Can detect delayed hypersensitivity with skin test antigen called Spherusol; helpful if history of Valley Fever.
Meningitis occurs in 1/3 to 1/2 of pts with disseminated coccidioidomycosis			
Adult (CID 42:103, 2006)	Fluconazole 400-1,000 mg po q24h indefinitely	Ampho B IV as for pulmonary (above) + 0.1-0.3 mg daily intra-thecal (intraventricular) via reservoir device. OR Itra oral sol'n 400-800 mg q24h OR Voriconazole (see Comment)	**80% relapse rate, continue flucon indefinitely. Voriconazole** successful in high doses (6 mg/kg IV q12h) then oral suppression (200 mg po q12h). For practical spects of intrathecal amp B, see CID 2017;64:519. Small retrospective study suggests benefit from adjunctive corticosteroids (CID 2017;65:338).
Child (C. gattii)	Fluconazole (po) (Pediatric dose not established, 6 mg per kg q24h used)		
Cryptococcosis IDSA Guideline: CID 50:291, 2010.			
Non-meningeal (non-AIDS). Risk 57% in organ transplant & those receiving other forms of immunosuppressive agents (EID 13:953, 2007)	**Non-meningeal, non-AIDS:** Fluconazole 400 mg/day IV or po for 8 wks to 6 mos **For more severe disease:** Ampho B 0.5-0.8 mg/kg per day IV till response then change to Fluconazole 400 mg po q24h for 8-10 wks course	Itraconazole 200-400 mg solution q24h for 6-12 mos. OR (Ampho B 0.3 mg/kg per day IV + Flucytosine 37.5 mg/kg po qid) times 6 wks (use ideal body wt)	**Flucon alone 90% effective for meningeal and non-meningeal forms.** Flucon-azole as effective as Ampho B. Addition of **Interferon-g** (IFN+Ih) 50 mcg per M² subcut. 3x per wk x 9 wks) to liposomal Ampho B assoc. with response in pt failing antifungal rx (CID 38: 910, 2004). Posaconazole 400-800 mg also effective in a small series of patients (CID 45:562, 2007; Chest 132:952, 2007)
Meningitis (non-AIDS)	Ampho B 0.5-0.8 mg/kg per day IV + Flucytosine 37.5 mg/kg (some use 25 mg/kg) po q6h until pt afebrile & cultures neg (~6 wks) (NEJM 301:126, 1979), then stop Ampho B/flucyt, start Fluconazole 200 mg po q24h (AnIM 113:183, 1990); OR Fluconazole 400 mg q24h x 8-10 wks (less severely ill pt). Some recommend Flu for 2 yrs to reduce relapse rate (CID 28:297, 1999). Some recommend Ampho B plus fluconazole as induction Rx. Studies underway.	Itraconazole 37.5 mg/kg (some use 25 mg/kg), then Fluconazole 400 mg po q24h x 8-10 wks	**If CSF opening pressure ≥25 cm H₂O, repeat LP to drain fluid to control pressure.** C. gattii meningitis reported in the Pacific Northwest with response in C. neoformans; severity of disease and prognosis appear to be worse than with C. neoformans; initial therapy with **Ampho B + Flucytosine** recommended. C. gattii less susceptible to flucon than C. neoformans (Clin Microbiol Inf 14:722, 2008). Outcomes in both AIDS and non-AIDS cryptococcal meningitis improved with Ampho B + 5-FC induction therapy for 14 days in those with neurological abnormalities or high organism burden (PLoS ONE 3:e2870, 2008).

See page 2 for abbreviations. All dosage recommendations are for adults (unless otherwise indicated) and assume normal renal function.

TABLE 11A (7)

TYPE OF INFECTION/ORGANISM/ SITE OF INFECTION	ANTIMICROBIAL AGENTS OF CHOICE		COMMENTS
	PRIMARY	ALTERNATIVE	

Cryptococcosis (continued)

TYPE OF INFECTION/ORGANISM/ SITE OF INFECTION	PRIMARY	ALTERNATIVE	COMMENTS
HIV/AIDS: Cryptococcemia and/or Meningitis			
Treatment See Clin Infect Dis 50:291, 2010 (IDSA Guidelines). ↓ with ARV but still common presenting OI in newly diagnosed AIDS pts. Cryptococcal infection may be manifested by positive blood culture or positive serum cryptococcal antigen (CRAG: >95% sens). CRAG no help in monitoring response to therapy. With ARV, symptoms of acute meningitis may return: immune reconstitution inflammatory syndrome (IRIS). ↑ CSF pressure (>250 mm H2O) associated with high mortality: lower with CSF removal. If frequent LPs not possible, ventriculoperitoneal shunts an option (Surg Neurol 63:529 & 531, 2005).	Ampho B 0.7 mg/kg IV q24H + Flucytosine 25 mg/kg po q6h for at least two weeks or longer until LP is sterilized. *See Comment.* **Then** **Consolidation therapy:** Fluconazole 400–800 mg po q24h to complete a 10-wks course then suppression (see below). Deferring ART for 5 wks after initiation cryptococcal meningitis therapy significantly improved survival as compared to starting ART during the first 2 wks (NEJM 370:2487, 2014).	Amphotericin B IV or Liposomal Ampho B IV+ Fluconazole 400 mg po or IV daily; OR Amphotericin B 0.7 mg/kg or liposomal Ampho B 4 mg/kg IV q24h alone; OR Fluconazole ≥800 mg/day (1200 mg preferred) (po or IV) plus Flucytosine 25 mg/kg po q6h for 4–6 weeks.	• Outcome of treatment: treatment failure associated with dissemination of infection & high serum antigen titer, indicative of high burden of organisms and lack of 5FC use during inductive Rx, abnormal neurological evaluation & underlying hematological malignancy. Mortality rates still high, particularly in those with concomitant pneumonia (Postgrad Med 121:107, 2009). Early Dx essential for improved outcome (PLOS Medicine 4:e47, 2007). • Ampho B +5FC treated <1 cryptococcal CFUs more rapidly fungicidal than ampho + Flu or Ampho + 5FC + Flu. Ampho B 1 mg/kg/d alone much more rapidly fungicidal in vivo than Flu 400 mg/d (CID 45:76681, 2007). Use of lipid-based Ampho B associated with lower mortality compared to Ampho B deoxycholate in solid organ transplant recipients (CID 48:1566, 2009). • Monitor 5-FC levels: peak 70-80 mg/L, trough 30-40 mg/L. Higher levels assoc. with bone marrow toxicity. No difference in outcome if given IV or po (AAC 51:1038, 2007). • Failure of Flu may rarely be due to resistant organism, especially if burden of organism high at initiation of Rx. Although 200 mg qd = 400 mg qd of Flu: median survival 76 & 82 days respectively, authors prefer 400 mg po qd (BMC Infect Dis 6:118, 2006). • Trend toward improved outcomes with fluconazole 400-800 mg combined with Ampho B versus Ampho B alone in AIDS patients (CID 48:1775, 2009). Role of other azoles uncertain: successful outcomes were observed in 14/29 (48%) subjects with cryptococcal meningitis treated with posaconazole (JAC 56:745, 2005). Voriconazole also may be effective. • **When to initiate antiretroviral therapy (ART)?** Defer ART to allow for 2 weeks of anti-fungal treatment. When ART was started 1-2 weeks after diagnosis of cryptococcal meningitis mortality was increased when compared to initiation of ART >5 weeks after diagnosis (NEJM 370:2487, 2014).
Suppression (chronic maintenance therapy) Discontinuation of antifungal rx can be considered among pts who remain asymptomatic, with CD4 >100-200/mm³ for ≥6 months. Some perform a lumbar puncture before discontinuation of maintenance rx. Reappearance of pos. serum CRAG may predict relapse	Fluconazole 200 mg/day po [If CD4 count rises to >100/mm³ with effective antiretroviral rx, some authorities recommend dc suppressive rx. See www.hivatis.org. Authors would only dc if LP culture negative.]	Itraconazole 200 mg po q12h if Flu intolerant or failure. No data on Vori for maintenance.	• Itraconazole less effective than fluconazole & not recommended because of higher relapse rate (23% vs 4%). • Recurrence rate of 0.4 to 3.9 per 100 patient-years with discontinuation of suppressive therapy in 100 patients on ARV with CD4 >100 cells/mm³.

See page 2 for abbreviations. All dosage recommendations are for adults (unless otherwise indicated) and assume normal renal function.

132

TABLE 11A (8)

TYPE OF INFECTION/ORGANISM/ SITE OF INFECTION	ANTIMICROBIAL AGENTS OF CHOICE		COMMENTS
	PRIMARY	ALTERNATIVE	
Dermatophytosis			
Onychomycosis (Tinea unguium) (primarily cosmetic) Laser rx FDA approved: modestly effective, expensive (Med Lett 55:15, 2013). (NEJM 360:2108, 2009) Ref: Am J Clin Derm 15:17, 2014; BMJ 348:g1800, 2014; Clinics Derm 31:544, 2013	**Fingernail Rx Options:** **Terbinafine**[TM] 250 mg po q24h (children <20 kg: 62.5 mg/day, 20–40 kg: 125 mg/day, >40 kg: 250 mg/day) x 6 wks (79% effective) OR **Itraconazole**[T] 200 mg po q24h x 3 mos.[TM] OR **Fluconazole** 150–300 mg po q wk x 3–6 mos.[T]		**Toenail Rx Options:** **Terbinafine**[TM] 250 mg po q24h (children <20 kg: 62.5 mg/day, 20–40 kg: 125 mg/day, >40 kg: 250 mg/day) x 12 wks (76% effective) OR **Itra** 200 mg po q24h x 3 mos (59% effective) OR **Efinaconazole** 10% solution applied to nail once daily for 48 wks OR **Flu** 150–300 mg po q wk x 6-12 mos (48% effective)[TM] OR topical **Tavaborole** (Kerydin) OR topical **Efinaconazole** (Jublia)
Tinea capitis ("ringworm") (Trichophyton tonsurans, Microsporum canis, other sp. elsewhere) (PIDJ 18:191, 1999)	**Terbinafine**[TM] 250 mg po q24h x 2–4 wks (adults); 4–6 mg/kg/day (children) 10–20 kgs: 62.5 mg q24h x 2 weeks 20–40 kgs: 125 mg q24h x 2 weeks >40 kg: 250 mg q24h x 2 weeks	**Itra**[T] 5 mg/kg per day x 4 wks[TM/TA] OR **Fluc** 6 mg/kg q wk x 8-12 wks.[T,M] OR **Griseo:** adults 500 mg po q24h x 6–8 wks; children age >2 years: Micro susp: 20-25 mg/kg/day; Ultramicro tabs: 10–15 mg/kg/day Dur: at least 6 wks, continue until clear	Durations of therapy are for T. tonsurans; treat for approx. twice as long for M. canis. All agents with similar cure rates (60–100%) in clinical studies. Addition of topical ketoconazole or selenium sulfate shampoo reduces transmissibility (Int J Dermatol 39:261, 2000)
Tinea corporis, cruris, or pedis (Trichophyton rubrum, T. mentagrophytes, Epidermophyton floccosum) "Athlete's foot, jock itch", and ringworm	**Topical rx:** Generally applied 2x/day. Available as creams, ointments, sprays, by prescription & "over the counter". Apply 2x/day for 2-3 wks. Recommend: Lotrimin Ultra or Lamisil AT; contain butenafine & terbinafine—both are fungicidal	**Terbinafine** 250 mg po q24h x 2 wks[TM] OR **Ketoconazole** 200 mg po q24h x 4 wks OR **Fluconazole** 150 mg po 1x/wk for 2-4 wks[TM] OR **Griseofulvin:** adults 500 mg po q24h times 4–6 wks, children 10–20 mg/kg/day. Duration: 2-4 wks for corporis, 4-8 wks for pedis.	**Keto** po often effective in severe recalcitrant infection. Follow for hepatotoxicity; many drug-drug interactions.
Tinea versicolor (Malassezia furfur or Pityrosporum orbiculare) Rule out erythrasma—see Table I, page 56	**Ketoconazole** (400 mg po single dose)[TM] or (200 mg po q24h x 7 days) or (2% cream 1x q24h x 2 wks)	**Fluconazole** 400 mg po single dose or **Itraconazole** 400 mg po q24h x 3–7 days	**Keto** (po) times 1 dose was 97% effective in 1 study. Another alternative: **Selenium sulfide** (Selsun), 2.5% lotion, apply as lather, leave on 10 min then wash off. 1/day x 7 day or 3-5/wk times 2-4 wks
Fusariosis			

Third most common cause of invasive mold infections, after Aspergillus and Mucorales and related molds, in patients with hematologic malignancies (Mycoses 52:197, 2009). Pneumonia, skin infections, bone and joint infections, and disseminated disease occur in severely immunocompromised patients. In contrast to other molds, blood cultures are frequently positive. Fusarium solani, F. oxysporum, F. verticillioides and F. moniliforme account for approx. 90% of isolates (Clin Micro Rev 20: 695, 2007). Frequently fatal; outcome depends on decreasing the level of immunosuppression.

| | **Lipid-based Ampho B** 5–10 mg/kg/d IV; OR **Ampho B** 1–1.5 mg/kg/d IV. | **Posaconazole** 400 mg po bid with meals (if not meals, 200 mg qid); OR **Voriconazole** IV: 6 mg per kg q12h times 1 day, then 4 mg per kg q12h; po: 400 mg q12h x 1 day, then 200 mg q12h. See comments. | **Surgical debridement** for localized disease. Fusarium spp. resistance to most antifungal agents, including echinocandins. F. solani and F. verticillioides typically are resistant to azoles; F. oxysporum & F. moniliforme may be susceptible to voriconazole and posaconazole. Role of combination therapy with Vori and Ampho B awaiting speciation. (Mycoses 50: 227, 2007). Given variability in susceptibilities can consider combination therapy with Vori and Ampho B. Outcome dependent on reduction or discontinuation of immuno-suppression. Duration of therapy depends on response; long-term suppressive therapy for patients remaining on immunosuppressive therapy. |

[1] **Serious but rare cases of hepatic failure** have been reported in pts receiving Terbinafine & should not be used in those with chronic or active liver disease (see Table 11B, page 139).
[2] Use of Itraconazole has been associated with myocardial dysfunction and with onset of congestive heart failure.

See page 2 for abbreviations. All dosage recommendations are for adults (unless otherwise indicated) and assume normal renal function.

TABLE 11A (9)

TYPE OF INFECTION/ORGANISM/ SITE OF INFECTION	ANTIMICROBIAL AGENTS OF CHOICE		COMMENTS
	PRIMARY	ALTERNATIVE	
Histoplasmosis (Histoplasma capsulatum): See IDSA Guideline: CID 45:807, 2007. Best diagnostic test is urinary, serum, or CSF histoplasma antigen: MiraVista Diagnostics (1-866-647-2847)			
Acute pulmonary histoplasmosis	**Mild to moderate disease, symptoms <4 wks:** No rx: If symptoms last over one month; Itraconazole oral soln 200 mg po tid for 3 days then once or twice daily for 6-12 wks. **Moderately severe or severe: Liposomal Ampho B,** 3-5 mg/kg/d IV or **ABLC** 5 mg/kg/d IV or Ampho B 0.7-1.0 mg/kg/d for 1-2 wks, then Itra 200 mg tid for 3 days, then bid for 12 wks. **+ methylprednisolone** 0.5-1 mg/kg/d for 1-2 wks.		Ampho B for patients at low risk of nephrotoxicity. Check for Itra drug-drug interactions.
Chronic cavitary pulmonary histoplasmosis	Itra oral soln 200 mg po tid for 3 days then once or twice daily for at least 12 mos (some prefer 18-24 mos).		Document therapeutic itraconazole blood levels at 2 wks. Relapses occur in 9-15% of patients.
Mediastinal lymphadenitis, mediastinal granuloma, pericarditis; and rheumatologic syndromes	**Mild cases:** Antifungal therapy not indicated. Nonsteroidal anti-inflammatory drug for pericarditis or rheumatologic syndromes. If no response to non-steroidals, **Prednisone** 0.5-1.0 mg/kg/d tapered over 1-2 weeks for 1) pericarditis with hemodynamic compromise. 2) lymphadenitis with obstruction or compression syndromes, or 3) severe rheumatologic syndromes. Itra 200 oral soln mg po once or twice daily for 6-12 wks for moderately severe to severe cases, or if prednisone is administered.		
Progressive disseminated histoplasmosis	**Mild to moderate disease:** Itra 200 mg po tid for 3 days then bid for at least 12 mos. **Moderately severe to severe disease: Liposomal Ampho B,** 3 mg/kg/d or **ABLC** 5 mg/kg/d for 1-2 weeks then **Itra** 200 mg tid for 3 days, then bid for at least 12 mos.		Check Itra blood levels to document therapeutic concentrations. Check for Itra drug-drug interactions. **Ampho B** 0.7-1.0 mg/kg/d may be used for patients at low risk of nephrotoxicity. Confirm therapeutic Itra blood levels. Azoles are teratogenic; Itra should be avoided in pregnancy; use a lipid ampho formulation. Urinary antigen levels useful for monitoring response to therapy and relapse.
CNS histoplasmosis	**Liposomal Ampho B,** 5 mg/kg/d. for a total of 175 mg/kg over 4-6 wks, then **Itra** 200 mg 2-3x a day for at least 12 mos. Vori likely effective for CNS disease or Itra failures. (Arch neurology 65: 666, 2008; J Antimicro Chemo 57:1235, 2006).		Monitor CNS histo antigen, monitor Itra blood levels. PCR may be better for Dx than histo antigen. Absorption of Itra (check levels) and CNS penetration may be an issue; case reports of success with Fluconazole (Braz J Infect Dis 12:555, 2008) and Posaconazole (Drugs 65:1553, 2005) following Ampho B therapy.
Prophylaxis (immunocompromised patients)	Itra 200 mg po daily. Check for Itra drug-drug interactions.		Consider primary **prophylaxis in HIV-infected patients with <150 CD4 cells/mm³** in high prevalence areas. Secondary prophylaxis (i.e, suppressive therapy) indicated in HIV-infected patients with <150 CD4 cells/mm³ and other immunocompromised patients in whom immunosuppression cannot be reversed

See page 2 for abbreviations. All dosage recommendations are for adults (unless otherwise indicated) and assume normal renal function.

TABLE 11A (10)

TYPE OF INFECTION/ORGANISM/ SITE OF INFECTION	ANTIMICROBIAL AGENTS OF CHOICE		COMMENTS
	PRIMARY	ALTERNATIVE	
Madura foot (See *Nocardia & Scedosporium*)			
Mucormycosis & other related species—*Rhizopus, Rhizomucor, Lichtheimia* (CID 54:1629, 2012). Rhinocerebral, pulmonary due to angioinvasion with tissue necrosis. Key to successful rx: early rx with symptoms suggestive of sinusitis (or lateral facial pain or numbness): think mucor with palatal ulcers, &/or black eschars, onset unilateral blindness in immunocompromised or diabetic pt. Rapidly fatal without rx. Dx by culture of tissue or stain: wide ribbon-like, non-septated with variation in diameter & right angle branching. Diabetics are predisposed to mucormycosis due to microangiopathy & ketoacidosis. Iron overload also predisposes: iron stimulates fungal growth.	Liposomal Ampho B 5-10 mg/kg/day. OR Ampho B 1-1.5 mg/kg/day.	Posaconazole 400 mg bid with meals (if not taking meals, 200 mg po qid). OR Posaconazole delayed-release tablet: loading dose of 372 mg (equivalent to isavuconazole 200 mg) IV/po q8 x 6 doses then 372 mg daily	**Ampho B** (ABLC) monotherapy relatively ineffective with 20% success rate vs 69% for other polyenes (CID 47:364, 2008). Complete or partial response rates of 60-80% in isavuconazole salvage protocols (JAC 61, Suppl 1, I35, 2008). Isavuconazole: Approved for treatment of invasive mucor infection based on historical controls (Ln 2016;387:760). **Combination therapy:** Adjunctive echinocandin to liposomal Amphotericin B is promising given safety profile, synergy in murine models, and observational clinical data (Clin Infect Dis 54(S1):S73, 2012). Adjunctive Deferasirox therapy to liposomal Amphotericin B failed to demonstrate benefit (J Antimicrob Chemother. 67:715, 2012). Resistant to **Voriconazole:** prolonged use of voriconazole prophylaxis predisposes to mucormycosis infections. Total duration of therapy based on response: continue therapy until 1) resolution of clinical signs and symptoms of infection, 2) resolution or stabilization of radiographic abnormalities; and 3) resolution of underlying immunosuppression. Posaconazole for secondary prophylaxis for those on immunosuppressive therapy (CID 48:1743, 2009).
Paracoccidioidomycosis (South American blastomycosis) *P. brasiliensis* (Dermatol Clin 26:257, 2008; Expert Rev Anti Infect Ther 6:251, 2008). Important cause of death from fungal infection in HIV-infected patients in Brazil (Mem Inst Oswaldo Cruz 104:513, 2009).	Mild-moderate disease: Itra 200 mg po daily for 6-9 months for mild and for 12-18 months for moderate disease. Severe disease: Ampho B 0.7-1 mg/kg IV daily to a cumulative total of 30 mg/kg followed by Itra 200 mg po daily for at least 12 months	Ketoconazole 200-400 mg daily for 6-18 months; OR Ampho B total dose >30 mg/kg OR TMP/SMX 800/160 mg bid-tid for 30 days, then 400/80 mg/day indefinitely (up to 3-5 years)	Improvement in >90% pts on Itra or Keto. ᴺᴬᴵ Ampho B reserved for severe cases and for those intolerant to other agents. TMP-SMX suppression life-long in HIV+. Check for Itra or Keto drug-drug interactions.
Lobomycosis (keloidal blastomycosis)/ *P. loboi*	Surgical excision, clofazimine or itraconazole.		
Penicilliosis (*Talaromyces marneffei*, formerly *Penicillium marneffei*): disseminated fungal infection in AIDS pts in Asia (esp. Thailand & Vietnam).	Ampho B 0.5-1 mg/kg po per day times 2 wks followed by Itraconazole 400 mg/day for 10 wks followed by 200 mg/day po indefinitely for HIV-infected pts.	For less sick patients Itra oral sol'n 200 mg po tid x 3 days, then 200 mg po bid x 12 wks, then 200 mg po q24h. (IV if unable to po) (Oral sol'n better absorbed)	3ʳᵈ most common OI in AIDS pts in SE Asia following TBc and cryptococcal meningitis. Prolonged fever, lymphadenopathy, hepatomegaly. Skin nodules are umbilicated (mimic cryptococcal or molluscum contagiosum). Preliminary data suggests Vori effective: CID 43:1060, 2006.
Pheohyphomycosis, Black molds, Dematiaceous fungi (See Clin Microbiol Rev 27:527, 2014). Opportunistic infection in immunocompromised hosts (e.g., HIV/AIDS, transplants). Often presents with skin and soft tissue infection or mycetoma but can cause disease in bone and joint, brain abscess, endocarditis, and disseminated disease. Most clinically relevant species are within the genera of *Exophiala, Cladophialophora, Coniosporium, Cyphellophora, Fonsecaea, Phialophora*, and *Rhinocladiella*.	Surgery + Itraconazole oral sol'n 400 mg/day po, duration not defined, probably 6 moᴺᴬᴵ	Voriconazole 6 mg/kg po bid x 1 day and then 4 mg/kg po bid or Posaconazole (suspension) 400 mg bid	Both Vori and Posa have demonstrated efficacy (Med Mycol 48:769, 2010; Med Mycol 43:91, 2005) often in addition to surgical therapy. Consider obtaining anti-fungal susceptibility testing.

See page 2 for abbreviations. All dosage recommendations are for adults (unless otherwise indicated) and assume normal renal function.

TABLE 11A (1T)

TYPE OF INFECTION/ORGANISM/ SITE OF INFECTION	ANTIMICROBIAL AGENTS OF CHOICE		COMMENTS
	PRIMARY	**ALTERNATIVE**	
Pneumocystis pneumonia (PJP) caused by Pneumocystis jiroveci. Ref: *JAMA 301:2578, 2009.*			
Not acutely ill, able to take po meds. PaO₂ >70 mmHg Diagnosis: sputum PCR. Serum Beta-D Glucan may help; reasonable sensitivity & specificity, but also many false positives *(JCM 51:3478, 2013).*	(TMP-SMX-DS, 2 tabs po q8h x 21 days) OR (Dapsone 100 mg po q24h + Trimethoprim 5 mg/kg po tid x 21 days) NOTE: Concomitant use of corticosteroids usually reserved for sicker pts with PaO₂ <70 (see below)	[Clindamycin 300-450 mg po q6h + Primaquine 15 mg base po q24h] x 21 days OR Atovaquone suspension 750 mg po bid with food x 21 days	Mutations in gene of the enzyme target (dihydropteroate synthetase) of sulfamethoxazole identified. Unclear whether mutations result in resist to TMP-SMX or dapsone + TMP *(EID 10:1721, 2004).* Dapsone ref: *CID 27:191, 1998.* **After 21 days, chronic suppression in AIDS pts (see below—post-treatment suppression).**
Acutely ill, po rx not possible. PaO₂ <70 mmHg. Still unclear whether antiretroviral therapy (ART) should be started during treatment of PCP *(CID 46: 634, 2008).*	[Prednisone (15-30 min. before TMP-SMX): 40 mg po bid times 5 days, then 40 mg po q24h times 5 days, then 20 mg po q24h times 11 days) + TMP-SMX (15 mg of TMP component per kg per day) IV div. q6-q8h times 21 days]. Can substitute IV prednisolone (reduce dose 25%) for po prednisone	Prednisone as in primary rx + [(Clinda 600 mg IV q8h) + (Primaquine 30 mg base po q24h)] times 21 days OR Pentamidine 4 mg per kg per day IV times 21 days. Caspofungin active in animal models: *CID 53:61445, 2003.*	**After 21 days, chronic suppression in AIDS pts** (see post-treatment suppression). **PCP can occur in absence of HIV infection & steroids** *(CID 25:215 & 219, 1997).* Wait 4–8 days before declaring treatment failure& switching to clinda + primaquine or pentamidine in AIDS pts. *(JAIDS 48:63, 2008),* or adding caspofungin *(Transplant 84:685, 2007).*
Primary prophylaxis and post-treatment suppression	(TMP-SMX-DS or -SS, 1 tab po q24h or 1 DS 3x/wk) OR (Dapsone 100 mg po q24h). DC when CD4 >200 x/3 mos *(NEJM 344:159, 2001).*	(Pentamidine 300 mg in 6 mL sterile water by aerosol q4 wks) OR (Dapsone 200 mg po + Pyrimethamine 75 mg po + folinic acid 25 mg po —all once a week) or Atovaquone 1500 mg q24h with food.	MP-SMX-DS regimen provides cross-protection vs Toxo and other bacterial infections. Dapsone + pyrimethamine protects vs Toxo. Atovaquone suspension 1500 mg once daily as effective as daily dapsone *(NEJM 339:1889, 2998)* or inhaled pentamidine *(JID 180:369, 1999).*
Scedosporium species (Scedosporium apiospermum [Pseudallescheria boydii] and Scedosporium prolificans [new Lomentospora prolificans]) Infection occurs via inhalation or inoculation of skin. Normal hosts often have cutaneous disease. Immunocompromised hosts can have pulmonary colonization → invasive disease in lung or skin → disseminated disease.	*Scedosporium apiospermum:* Vori 6 mg/kg IV/po q12h on day 1, then 4 mg/kg IV/po q12h. *Scedosporium prolificans:* Surgical debridement and reduction of immunosuppression, consider addition of Vori as above although usually resistant.	Posa 400 mg po bid with meals (may be less active)	Surgical debridement should be considered in most cases. S. apiospermum is resistant Amphotericin B and Scedosporium prolificans is resistant to all antifungal agents. Synergy with Terbinafine and echinocandins has been reported in vitro although clinical data is limited *(AAC 48:2635, 2012).* S. prolificans osteomyelitis responded to miltefosine *(CID 61:1257, 2009)* in a case report. Consider susceptibility testing. Treatment guidelines/review: *Clin Microbiol Infect 3-27, 2014. Clin Microbiol Rev 21:157, 2008.*

See page 2 for abbreviations. All dosage recommendations are for adults (unless otherwise indicated) and assume normal renal function.

TABLE 11A (12)

TYPE OF INFECTION/ORGANISM/ SITE OF INFECTION	ANTIMICROBIAL AGENTS OF CHOICE		COMMENTS
	PRIMARY	ALTERNATIVE	
Sporotrichosis (IDSA Guideline: CID 45:1255, 2007.			
Cutaneous/Lymphocutaneous	**Itraconazole** oral sol'n po 200 mg/day for 2-4 wks after all lesions resolved, usually 3-6 mos.	If no response, **Itra** 200 mg po bid or **Terbinafine** 500 mg po bid or **SSKI** 5 drops (eye drops) tid & increase to 40-50 drops tid	Fluconazole 400-800 mg daily only if no response to primary or alternative suggestions. Pregnancy or nursing: local hyperthermia (see below).
Osteoarticular	Itra oral sol'n 200 mg po bid x 12 mos.	**Liposomal Ampho B** 3-5 mg/kg/d IV or **ABLC** 5 mg/kg/d IV or **Ampho B Deoxycholate** 0.7-1 mg/kg IV daily; if response, change to **Itra** oral sol'n 200 mg po bid x total 12 mos.	After 2 wks of therapy, document adequate serum levels of Itraconazole.
Pulmonary	If severe, **Lipid Ampho B** 3-5 mg/kg IV or **standard Ampho B** 0.7-1 mg/kg IV once daily until response, then **Itra** 200 mg po bid. Total of 12 mos.	Less severe: **Itraconazole** 200 mg po bid x 12 mos.	After 2 weeks of therapy document adequate serum levels of Itra. Surgical resection plus Ampho B for localized pulmonary disease.
Meningeal or Disseminated	**Lipid Ampho B** 5 mg/kg IV once daily x 4-6 wks, then—if better—**Itra** 200 mg po bid for total of 12 mos.	AIDS/other immunosuppressed pts: chronic therapy with **Itra** oral sol'n 200 mg po once daily.	After 2 weeks, document adequate serum levels of Itra.
Pregnancy and children	Pregnancy: cutaneous—local hyperthermia. Severe: **Lipid Ampho B** 3-5 mg/kg IV once daily. **Avoid Itraconazole.**	**Children:** Cutaneous: **Itra** 6-10 mg/kg (max of 400 mg) daily. Alternative is **SSKI** 1 drop tid increasing to max of 1 drop/kg or 40-50 drops tid/day, whichever is lowest.	For children with disseminated sporotrichosis: Standard Ampho B 0.7 mg/kg IV once daily & after response, Itra 6-10 mg/kg (max 400 mg) once daily.

See page 2 for abbreviations. All dosage recommendations are for adults (unless otherwise indicated) and assume normal renal function.

TABLE 11B – ANTIFUNGAL DRUGS: DOSAGE, ADVERSE EFFECTS, COMMENTS

DRUG NAME, GENERIC (TRADE)/ USUAL DOSAGE	ADVERSE EFFECTS/COMMENTS
Non-lipid Amphotericin B deoxycholate (Fungizone): 0.5-0.7 mg/kg IV per day as single infusion **Ampho B predictably not active vs. Scedosporium, Candida lusitaniae & Aspergillus terreus**	**Admin:** Ampho B is a colloidal suspension that must be prepared in electrolyte-free D5W at 0.1 mg/mL to avoid precipitation. No need to protect suspensions from light. Infusions cause chills/fever, myalgia, anorexia, nausea, rarely hemodynamic collapse/hypotension. Postulated due to proinflammatory cytokines, doesn't appear to be histamine release (*Pharmacol 23:966, 2003*). Infusion duration usu. **4+ hrs.** No difference found in 1 vs 4 hr infus. except chills/fever occurred sooner with 1 hr infus. Febrile reactions ↓ with repeat doses. Rare pulmonary reactions (severe dyspnea & focal infiltrates suggest pulmonary edema) assoc with rapid infus. **Severe rigors respond to meperidine (25-50 mg IV).** Premedication with acetaminophen, diphenhydramine, hydrocortisone (25-50 mg), and heparin (1000 units) had no influence on toxicity, rate, or outcome (*J Infect Dis 135:480*). NSAIDs or high-dose steroids may prove efficacious but their use may risk worsening infection under rx or age. **Toxicity:** Major concern is nephrotoxicity (↑ serum creatinine, ↓ K+, ↓ Mg++), **clinical azotemia, manifest initially by kaliuresis and hypokalemia**, then fall in serum bicarbonate (may proceed to renal tubular acidosis), ↓ in renal erythropoietin and anemia, and rising BUN/serum creatinine. Hypomagnesemia may occur. Can reduce risk of renal injury by **(a) pre- & post-infusion hydration with 500 mL saline (if clinical status allows salt load), (b)** avoidance of other nephrotoxins, eg, radiocontrast, aminoglycosides, cis-platinum, **(2)** use of lipid prep of Ampho B.
Lipid-based Ampho B products: **Amphotericin B lipid complex** (ABLC) (Abelcet): ≤5 mg/kg per day as single infusion	**Admin:** Consists of Ampho B complexed with 2 lipid bilayer: ribbons. Compared to standard Ampho B, larger volume of distribution, rapid blood clearance and high tissue concentrations (liver, spleen, lung). **Dosage: 5 mg/kg once daily:** infuse at 2.5 mg/kg per hr; adult and ped. dose the same. Saline pre- and post-dose lessens toxicity. Do NOT dilute with saline or mix with other drugs or electrolytes.[2] Do not use an in-line filter. **Toxicity:** Fever and chills 14-18%; nausea 9%, vomiting 8%; serum creatinine ↑ in 11%; renal failure 5%; anemia 4%; ↓ K 5%; rash 4%. A fatal fat embolism following ABLC infusion (*Exp Mol Path 177:246, 2004*). Majority of pts intolerant of liposomal Ampho B can tolerate ABLC (*CID 56:701, 2013*).
Liposomal Amphotericin B (LAB, AmBisome): 3-5 mg/kg IV per day as single infusion. If intolerant, majority OK with lipid form (*CID 56:701, 2013*).	**Admin:** Consists of vesicular bilayer liposome with Ampho B intercalated within the membrane. Dosage: **3-5 mg/kg per day** IV as single dose infused over a period of approx. 120 min. If tolerated, infusion time reduced to 60 min. (See footnote[2].) Saline pre- and post-dose lessens toxicity. **Major toxicity:** Gen less than Ampho B. Nephrotoxic: ↑ 18.7% vs 33.7% for Ampho. Chills 47% vs 75%, nausea 39.7% vs 38.7%, vomiting 31.8% vs 43.9%, rash 24% for both, ↓ Ca 18.4% vs 20.9%, ↓ K 20.4% vs 25.6%, ↓ mg 20.4% vs 25.6%. 86% occur within 5 min of infusion. 20– 40%, 86% occur within 5 min of infusion, incl chest pain, dyspnea, hypoxia or severe abd pain. 14% flushing & urticaria near end of 4 hr infusion. All responded to diphenhydramine (1 mg/kg) & interruption of infusion. Reactions may be due to complement activation by liposome (*CID 36:1213, 2003*).
Caspofungin (Cancidas) 70 mg IV on day 1 followed by 50 mg IV q24h (reduce to 35 mg IV q24h with moderate hepatic insufficiency)	An echinocandin which inhibits synthesis of β-(1,3)-D-glucan. Fungicidal against candida (MIC <2 mcg/mL) including those resistant to other antifungals & active against aspergillus (MIC 0.4–2.7 mcg/mL). Approved indications: empirical rx for febrile, neutropenic pts; rx of candidemia, candida intraabdominal abscesses, peritonitis, & pleural space infections; esophageal candidiasis; & invasive aspergillosis in pts refractory to or intolerant of other therapies. Serum levels on rec. dosages = peak 12, trough 1.3 (24 hrs) mcg/mL. **Toxicity:** remarkably non-toxic. Most common adverse effect: pruritus at infusion site & headache, fever, chills, vomiting, & diarrhea assoc with infusion. ↑ serum creatinine in 8% on caspo vs 21% short-course Ampho B in 422 pts with candidemia (*Ln, Oct. 12, 2005, online*). Drug metab in liver & dosage ↓ to 35 mg in moderate to severe hepatic failure. Class C for preg (embryotoxic in rats & rabbits). See *Table 22A, page 245 for drug-drug interactions, esp. cyclosporine (hepatic toxicity) & tacrolimus (drug level monitoring recommended).* Reversible thrombocytopenia reported (*Pharmacother 24:1408, 2004*). **No drug in CSF, urine or vitreous humor of the eye.**
Micafungin (Mycamine) 50 mg IV q24h for prophylaxis post-bone marrow stem cell trans; 100 mg IV q24h candidemia, 150 mg IV q24h candida esophagitis.	Approved for rx of esophageal candidiasis & prophylaxis against candida infections in HSCT recipients. Active against most strains of candida sp. & aspergillus sp. incl those resist to fluconazole such as C. glabrata & C. krusei. No antagonism seen when combo with other antifungal drugs. No dosage adjust for severe renal failure or moderate hepatic impairment. Watch for drug-drug interactions with sirolimus or nifedipine. Micafungin well tolerated & common adverse events incl nausea 2.8%, vomiting 2.4%, & headache 2.4%. Transient ↑ LFTs, BUN, creatinine reported; rare cases of significant hepatitis & renal insufficiency. **No drug in CSF or urine.**

[1] Published data from patients intolerant of or refractory to conventional Ampho B deoxycholate. **None of the lipid Ampho B preps has shown superior efficacy compared to Ampho B in prospective trials (except liposomal Ampho B was more effective vs Ampho B in rx of disseminated histoplasmosis at 2 wks).** Dosage equivalency has not been established (*CID 36:1500, 2003*).
Nephrotoxicity ↓ with all lipid Ampho B preps.
[2] Comparisons between Abelcet & AmBisome suggest higher infusion-assoc. toxicity (rigors) with Abelcet (70% vs 36%) but higher frequency of mild hepatic toxicity with AmBisome (59% vs 38%, p=0.05). Mild elevations in serum creatinine were observed in 1/3 of both (*BJ Hemat 103:198, 1998; Focus on Fungal Inf #9, 1999; Bone Marrow Tx 20:39, 1997; CID 26:1383, 1998*).
[3] HSCT = hematopoietic stem cell transplant.

See page 2 for abbreviations. All dosage recommendations are for adults (unless otherwise indicated) and assume normal renal function.

TABLE 11B (2)

DRUG NAME, GENERIC (TRADE)/ USUAL DOSAGE	ADVERSE EFFECTS/COMMENTS
Anidulafungin (Eraxis) For Candidemia: 200 mg IV on day 1 followed by 100 mg/day IV. Esophageal candida: 100 mg IV x 1, then 50 mg IV once/d.	An echinocandin with antifungal activity (cidal) against candida sp. & aspergillus sp. including Ampho B- & triazole-resistant strains. FDA approved for treatment of esophageal candidiasis (EC), candidemia, and other complicated Candida infections. Effective in clinical trials of esophageal candidiasis & in 1 trial was superior to fluconazole in rx of invasive candidiasis/candidemia in 245 pts (75.6% vs 60.2%). Like other echinocandins, remarkably non-toxic; most common side-effects: nausea, vomiting, ↓ mg, ↓ K, & headache in 11–13% of pts. No dose adjustments for renal or hepatic insufficiency. *See CID 43:215, 2006.* **No drug in CSF or urine.**
Fluconazole (Diflucan) 100 mg tabs 150 mg tabs 200 mg tabs 400 mg IV Oral suspension: 50 mg per 5 mL	IV-oral dose because of excellent bioavailability. **Pharmacology:** absorbed po, water solubility enables IV. For peak serum levels *(see Table 9A, page 99)*, T½ 30hr (range 20–50 hr). 12% protein bound. **CSF levels 50–90% of serum in normals,** ↑ in meningitis. No effect on mammalian steroid metabolism. **Drug-drug interactions common,** *see Table 22A.* Side-effects overall 16% [more common in HIV pts (21%)]. Nausea 3.7%, headache 1.9%, skin rash 1.8%, abdominal pain 1.7%, vomiting 1.7%, diarrhea 1.5%, ↑ SGOT 20%. Alopecia (scalp, pubic crest) in 12–20% pts on ≥400 mg q24h after median of 3 mos (reversible in approx. 6mo). Rare: severe hepatotoxicity *(CID 41:301, 2005),* exfoliative dermatitis. **Note: Candida krusei and Candida glabrata resistant to Flu.**
Flucytosine (Ancobon, 5-FC) 500 mg cap **Expensive:** $11,000 for 100 capsules (Sep 2015 US price)	AEs: Overall 30%. GI 6% (diarrhea, anorexia, nausea, vomiting): hematologic 22% [leukopenia, thrombocytopenia, when serum level >100 mcg/ml. (esp. in azotemic pts)]: hepatotoxicity (asymptomatic ↑ SGOT, reversible); skin rash 7%; aplastic anemia (rare—2 or 3 cases). False ↑ in serum creatinine on EKTACHEM analyzer. Bioavailability 100%. Good levels in CSF, eye & urine.
Griseofulvin (Fulvicin, Grifulvin, Grisactin) 500 mg, susp 125 mg/mL	Photosensitivity, urticaria, GI upset, fatigue, leukopenia (rare). Interferes with warfarin drugs. Increases blood and urine porphyrins, should not be used in patients with porphyria. Minor disulfiram-like reactions. Exacerbation of systemic lupus erythematosus.
Imidazoles, topical For vaginal and/or skin use	Not recommended in 1ˢᵗ trimester of pregnancy. Local reactions: 0.5–1.5% dyspareunia, mild vaginal or vulvar erythema, burning, pruritus, urticaria, rash. Rarely similar symptoms in sexual partner.
Isavuconazonium sulfate (prodrug isavuconazole) (Cresemba) po: 186 mg caps IV: 372 mg vials No drug in CSF. Ref: *Med Lett 2016;58:33*	An azole antifungal agent for treatment of invasive aspergillosis and invasive mucormycosis in adults. **Contraindications:** Coadministration with strong CYP3A4 inhibitors, e.g., Ketoconazole or high-dose Ritonavir; or strong CYP3A4 inducers, e.g., Rifampin, carbamazepine, St. John's wort, or long-acting barbiturates is contraindicated. Do not use in patients with shortened QT interval. **Dosing: Isavuconazonium sulfate** loading dose of 372 mg (equivalent to Isavuconazole 200 mg) IV/po q8 x 6 doses then 372 mg IV/po daily. **AEs:** most common: nausea, vomiting, diarrhea, headache, elevated liver chemistry tests, hypokalemia, constipation, dyspnea, cough, peripheral edema, and back pain. Hepatic: increased ALT, AST. **Teratogenic.**
Itraconazole (Sporanox) 100 mg cap. - 10 mg/mL oral solution - IV usual dose 200 mg bid x 4 doses followed by 200 mg q24h for a max of 14 days	**Itraconazole tablet & oral solution forms not interchangeable, solution preferred.** Many authorities recommend measuring drug serum concentration after 2 wks to ensure satisfactory absorption. To obtain highest plasma concentration, tablet is given with food & acidic drinks (e.g., cola) while solution is taken in fasted state; under these conditions, the peak conc. of capsule is approx. 3 mcg/ml. & of solution 5.4 mcg/ml. Peak conc. reached faster (2.2 vs 5 hrs) with solution. **Peak plasma concentrations after IV injection (200 mg) compared to oral capsule (200 mg): 2.8 mcg/ml. (on day 7 of IV) vs 2 mcg/ml. (on day 36 of po).** Protein-binding for both preparations is over 99%, which explains virtual absence of penetration into CSF **(do not use to treat meningitis).** Adverse effects: dose-related nausea 10%, diarrhea 8%, vomiting 6%, & abdominal discomfort 5.7%. Allergic rash 8.6%, ↑ bilirubin 6%, edema 3.5%, & hepatitis 2.7% reported. ↑ doses may produce hypokalemia 8% & ↑ blood pressure 3.2%. Delirium, peripheral neuropathy & tremor reported (*J Neur Neurosurg Psych 81:327, 2010*). **Reported to produce impairment in cardiac function.** Severe liver failure req transplant in pts receiving pulse rx for onychomycosis: FDA reports 24 cases with 11 deaths out of 50 mill people who received the drug prior to 2001. Other concern, as with fluconazole and ketoconazole, is **drug-drug interactions** (see *Table 22A*). Some can be life-threatening.
Ketoconazole (Nizoral) 200 mg tab	**Gastric acid required for absorption**—cimetidine, omeprazole, antacids block absorption. In achlorhydria, dissolve tablet in 4 mL 0.2N HCl, drink with a straw. Coca-Cola ↑ absorption by 65%. CSF levels "none". **Drug-drug interactions important,** *see Table 22A.* **Some interactions can be life-threatening.** Dose-dependent nausea and vomiting. Liver toxicity of hepatocellular type reported in about 1:10,000 exposed pts—usually after several days to weeks of exposure. At doses of ≥800 mg per day serum testosterone and plasma cortisol levels fall. With high doses, adrenal (Addisonian) crisis reported.
Miconazole (Monistat IV) 200 mg—*not available in U.S.*	IV miconazole indicated in patient critically ill with Scedosporium (Pseudallescheria boydii) infection. Very toxic due to vehicle needed to get drug into solution.

See page 2 for abbreviations. All dosage recommendations are for adults (unless otherwise indicated) and assume normal renal function.

TABLE 11B (3)

DRUG NAME: GENERIC (TRADE)/ USUAL DOSAGE	ADVERSE EFFECTS/COMMENTS
Nystatin (Mycostatin) 30 gm cream 500,000 units oral tab	Topical: virtually no adverse effects. Less effective than imidazoles and triazoles. po: large doses give occasional GI distress and diarrhea.
Posaconazole (Noxafil) Suspension (40 mg/mL): 400 mg po bid with meals (if not taking meals, 200 mg qid). 200 mg po tid (with food) for prophylaxis. Delayed-release tablets (100 mg): 300 mg bid x 1 day and then 300 mg daily for prophylaxis. Intravenous formulation: 300 mg IV bid x 1 day then 300 mg daily (prophylaxis). Takes 7-10 days to achieve steady state. No IV formulation.	**Suspension is dosed differently than delayed-release tablets (not interchangeable) – check dose carefully.** An oral triazole with activity against a wide range of fungi refractory to other antifungal including aspergillosis, invasive aspergillosis (variability in species), fusariosis, Scedosporium (Pseudallescheria), phaeohyphomycosis, histoplasmosis, refractory coccidioidomycosis, refractory cryptococcosis, & refractory chromoblastomycosis. Approved for prophylaxis of invasive aspergillosis & candidiasis. Clinical response in 75% of 176 AIDS pts with azole-refractory oral/esophageal candidiasis. Posaconazole has similar toxicities as other triazoles: nausea 9%, vomiting 6%, abd. pain 5%, headache 5%, diarrhea. ↑ ALT, AST, & rash (3% each). In pts rx for >6 mos, serious side-effects have included adrenal insufficiency, nephrotoxicity & QTc interval prolongation. Inhibits CYP3A4 (see Table 22A). Consider monitoring serum concentrations (AAC 53:24, 2009). **100 mg delayed-release tablets:** loading dose of 300 mg (three 100 mg delayed-release tablets) starting on the second day of therapy. Approved for prophylaxis only and not treatment. Tablets allow patients to achieve better levels than the suspension. Treatment dose unknown but prophylactic dose often achieves therapeutic levels. **The tablet and solution are not interchangeable.** Intravenous formulation approved for prophylaxis at 300 mg IV daily after a loading dose of 300 mg bid x 1 day. Consider therapeutic drug monitoring with a goal trough of >0.7 for prophylaxis and >1.0 for treatment. JAC 69:1162, 2014.
Terbinafine (Lamisil) 250 mg tab Discontinued in U.S. in May 2017.	In pts given terbinafine for onychomycosis, rare cases (8) of idiosyncratic & symptomatic hepatic injury & more rarely liver failure leading to death or liver transplant. The drug is not recommended for pts with chronic or active liver disease; hepatotoxicity may occur in pts with or without pre-existing disease. Pretreatment serum transaminases (ALT & AST) advised & alternate rx used for those with abnormal levels. Pts started on terbinafine should be warned about symptoms suggesting liver dysfunction (persistent nausea, anorexia, fatigue, vomiting, RUQ pain, jaundice, dark urine or pale stools). If symptoms develop, drug should be discontinued & liver function immediately evaluated. In controlled trials, changes in ocular lens and retina reported—clinical significance unknown. Major drug-drug interaction is 100% ↑ in rate of clearance by rifampin. AEs: usually mild, transient and rarely caused discontinuation of rx, % with AE, terbinafine vs placebo: nausea/diarrhea 2.6–5.6 vs 2.9; rash 5.6 vs 2.2; taste disturbance 2.8 vs 0.7. Inhibits CYP2D6 enzymes (see Table 22A). An acute generalized exanthematous pustulosis and subacute cutaneous lupus erythematosus reported.
Voriconazole (Vfend) IV: Loading dose 6 mg per kg q12h times 1 day, then 4 mg per kg q12h IV for invasive aspergillus & serious mold infections; 3 mg per kg IV q12h for serious candida infections. Oral: >40 kg body weight: 400 mg po q12h, then 200 mg po q12h. **<40 kg body weight:** 200 mg po q12h, then 100 mg po q12h Take oral dose 1 hour before or 1 hour after eating. Oral suspension (40 mg per mL). Same as for oral tabs. Reduce to ½ maintenance dose for moderate hepatic insufficiency	A triazole with activity against Aspergillus sp., including Ampho resistant strains of A. terreus. Active vs A. terreus, Fusarium sp., & various molds. Steady state serum levels reach 2.5–4 mcg per mL. Up to 20% of patients with subtherapeutic levels with oral administration; check levels for suspected treatment failure, life threatening infections. 300 mg bid oral dose or 8 mg/kg/d IV dose may be required to achieve target steady-state drug concentrations of 1-5 mcg/mL. Toxicity similar to other azoles/triazoles including uncommon serious hepatic toxicity (hepatitis, cholestasis & fulminant hepatic failure. Liver function tests should be monitored during rx & drug dc'd if abnormalities develop. Photosensitivity is common and can be severe. Many reports of associated skin cancers. Strongly recommend sun protective measures. CID 58:997, 2014 & Mycoses 54:e657, 2014. Anaphylactoid infusion reactions with fever and hypertension. 1 case of QT prolongation with ventricular tachycardia in a 15 y/o pt with nephroblastoma. **21% experience a transient visual disturbance** following IV or po ("altered/enhanced visual perception", blurred or colored visual change or photophobia) within 30–60 minutes. Visual changes resolve within 30–60 minutes after administration & are attenuated with repeated doses (do not attribute to drug concentrations). Persistent visual disturbance occur rarely. Cause unknown. In patients with ClCr <50 mL per min, the intravenous vehicle (SBECD-sulfobutylether-B cyclodextrin) may accumulate but not be obviously toxic. (CID 54:913, 2012). Hallucinations, hypoglycemia, electrolyte disturbance & pneumonitis attributed to drug-drug interactions high—see Table 22A. **With prolonged use, fluoride in drug can cause a painful periostitis.** (CID 59:1237, 2014) **NOTE:** Not in urine in active form. No activity vs. mucormycosis.

See page 2 for abbreviations. All dosage recommendations are for adults (unless otherwise indicated) and assume normal renal function.

TABLE 12A – TREATMENT OF MYCOBACTERIAL INFECTIONS*

Diagnosis of M. tuberculosis, Updated Guidelines *(IDSA, ATS, CDC): CID 64;e1, 2016.*

Tuberculin skin test (TST). Same as PPD *[Chest 138:1456, 2010]* Criteria for positive TST after 5 tuberculin units (intermediate PPD) read at 48–72 hours:

- ≥5 mm induration: + HIV, immunosuppressed, ≥15 mg prednisone per day, healed TBc on chest x-ray, recent close contact
- ≥10 mm induration: foreign-born, countries with high prevalence; IVD Users; low income; NH residents; chronic illness; silicosis
- ≥15 mm induration: otherwise healthy

Two-stage test to detect sluggish positivity: if 1st PPD + but <10 mm, repeat intermediate PPD in 1 wk. Response to 2nd PPD can also happen if pt received BCG in childhood.

BCG vaccine as child: if ≥10 mm induration, & from country with TBc, should be attributed to MTB. Prior BCG may result in booster effect in 2-stage TST.

Routine anergy testing not recommended.

Interferon Gamma Release Assays (IGRAs): IGRAs detect sensitivities to MTB by measuring IFN-γ release in response to MTB antigens. May be used in place of TST in all situations in which TST may be used *(MMWR 59 (RR-5), 2010)*. FDA approved tests available in the U.S.:

- QuantiFERON-TB Gold (QFT-G) (approved 2005)
- QuantiFERON-TB Gold In-Tube Test (QFT-GIT) (approved 2007)
- T-Spot (approved 2008)

IGRAs are relatively specific for MTB and do not cross-react with BCG or most nontuberculous mycobacteria. CDC recommends IGRA over TST for persons unlikely to return for reading TST & for persons who have received BCG. TST is preferred in children age <5 yrs (but IGRA is acceptable). IGRA or TST may be used without preference for recent contacts of TB with special utility for follow-up testing since IGRAs do not produce "booster effect". May also be used without preference over TBc for occupational exposures. As with TST, testing with IGRAs in low prevalence populations will result in false-positive results *(CID 53:234, 2011)*. Manufacturer's IFN-gamma cutoff ≥0.35 IU/mL for QFT-GIT may be too low for low prevalence settings, inflating positivity and conversion rates, and a higher cut-off may be more appropriate *(Am J Respir Crit Care Med 188:1005, 2013)*. For detailed discussion of IGRAs, see *MMWR 59 (RR-5), 2010 and JAMA 308:241, 2012.* False positive IGRA *(JCM 54:845, 2016)*.

Rapid (24-hr or less) diagnostic tests for MTB: (1) The Amplified Mycobacterium tuberculosis Direct Test amplifies and detects MTB ribosomal RNA; (2) the AMPLICOR Mycobacterium tuberculosis Test amplifies and detects MTB DNA. Both tests have sensitivities & specificities >95% in sputum samples that are AFB-positive. In negative smears, specificity remains >95% but sensitivity is 40–77% *(MMWR 58:7, 2009; CID 49:46, 2009)* to 60–90% *(see: http://www.cdc.gov/tb/publications/guidelines/amplification_tests/default.htm)* (3) COBAS TaqMan MTB Test: real-time PCR test for detection of M. tuberculosis in respiratory specimens (not available in the U.S.) with performance characteristics similar to other rapid tests *(J Clin Microbiol 51:3225, 2013)*.

Xpert MTB/RIF is a rapid test (2 hrs) for MTB in sputum samples which also detects RIF resistance with specificity of 99.2% and sensitivity of 72.5% in smear negative patients *(NEJM 363:1005, 2010)*. Current antibody-based and ELISA-based rapid tests for TBc not recommended by WHO because they are less accurate than microscopy ± culture *(Lancet ID 11:736, 2011).*

CAUSATIVE AGENT/ DISEASE	MODIFYING CIRCUMSTANCES	SUGGESTED REGIMENS		
		INITIAL THERAPY	CONTINUATION PHASE OF THERAPY	
I. **Mycobacterium tuberculosis exposure baseline TST/IGRA negative** (household members & other close contacts of potentially infectious cases)	Neonate– Rx essential NOTE: If fever, abnormal CXR (pleural effusion), hilar adenopathy, infiltrate) at baseline, treat for active TBc and not with INH alone.	INH (10 mg/kg/ day for 8–10 wks)	Repeat tuberculin skin test (TST) in 8–12 wks: if TST neg & CXR normal & infant age at exposure >6 mos, stop INH; if TST (≥5 mm) or age ≤6 mos, treat with INH for total of 9 mos. If follow-up CXR abnormal, treat for active TBc.	
	Children <5 years of age– Rx indicated	As for neonate for 1st 8–10 wks.	If repeat TST at 8–10 wks is negative, stop. If repeat TST ≥5 mm, continue INH for total of 9 mos. *(see Category II below).*	
	Older children & adults– Risk 2–4% 1st yr		If repeat TST at 8–10 wks is negative, repeat TST at 3 mos; if TST is positive, treat with INH for 9 mos. *(see Category II below).* Pts at high risk of progression (e.g., HIV+, immunosuppressed or on immunosuppressive therapy) and no evidence of active infection should be treated for LTBI *(see below).* For others repeat TST/IGRA at 8–10 wks: no rx if repeat TST/IGRA neg.	

See page 2 for abbreviations   * Dosages are for adults (unless otherwise indicated) and assume normal renal function   † **DOT** = directly observed therapy

TABLE 12A (2)

CAUSATIVE AGENT/ DISEASE	MODIFYING CIRCUMSTANCES	SUGGESTED REGIMENS	
		INITIAL THERAPY	ALTERNATIVE
II. Tuberculosis (LTBI, positive TST or IGRA as above, active TB ruled out) See FIGURE 1 for treatment algorithm for pt with abnormal baseline CXR (e.g., upper lobe fibronodular disease) suspected active TBc.) Review: NEJM 372:2127, 2015 Estimating risk of active MTBc in pts with positive TST or IGRA (www.tst3d.com)	Age no longer an exclusion, all persons with LTBI should be offered therapy. If pre-anti-TNF therapy, recommend at least one month of treatment for LBTI prior to start of anti-TNF therapy (Arth Care & Res 64:625, 2012). Overall, regimens containing a rifamycin (RIF, RFB or RFP) are most effective at preventing active tuberculosis (AnJM 161:419 & 449, 2014). For patients on **Isoniazid (INH)** educate and monitor clinically for signs and symptoms of hepatitis. Baseline lab testing of liver function at start of therapy not routinely indicated but is indicated for patients with HIV infection, pregnant women, and women within 3 mo of delivery, persons with a history of chronic liver disease, persons who use alcohol regularly, and persons at risk for chronic liver disease. Lab monitoring of liver function during therapy is indicated if baseline liver function tests are abnormal, if risk factors for hepatic disease are present, or to evaluate for possible adverse effects.	**INH** po once daily (adult: 5 mg/kg/day, max 300 mg/day; child: 10-15 mg/kg/day not to exceed 300 mg/day) x 9 mos. For current recommendations for monitoring hepatotoxicity on INH see MMWR 59:227, 2010. Supplemental pyridoxine 50 mg/day for HIV+ patients. A 12 dose once weekly DOT† **INH + Rifapentine** (RFP): **INH** po 15 mg/kg (max dose 900 mg); **RFP** po (wt-based dose): 10-14 kg: 300 mg; 14.1-25 kg: 450 mg; 25.1-32 kg: 600 mg; 32.1-49.9 kg: 750 mg; ≥50 kg: 900 mg. Not recommended for children age <2 yrs, pts with HIV/AIDS on ART; pregnant women; or pts presumed inferted with INH- or RIF-resistant MTB (MMWR 60:1650, 2011, NEJM 365:2155, 2011).	**INH** 300 mg once daily for 6 mo (but sligtly less effective than 9 mos; not recommended children, HIV+ persons, or those with fibrotic lesis on chest film). **INH** 2x/wk (adult: 15 mg/kg, max 900 mg; hild: 20-30 mg/kg, max dose 900 mg) x 9 mo. **RIF** once daily po (adult: 10 mg/kg/day, max ose 600 mg/day; child: 10-20 mg/kg/day, max dose 600 mg/day) for 4 mos. **INH + RIF** once daily x 3 mos (AnIM 2017;167: 8). Rates of flu-like symptoms, cutaneous reactions, and severe drug reactions (rare, 0.3%) higher wth 3 mo INH+RFP than with 9 mo INH (CID 61:527, 15), but hepatotoxicity higher with 9 mo INH (1.8% vs. 0.4) (Int. J Tuberc Lung Dis 19:1039, 2015).
	Pregnancy	Regimens as above. Once active disease is excluded may delay initiation of therapy until after delivery unless patient is recent contact to an active case, HIV+. Supplemental pyridoxine 10-25 mg/d	
LTBI, suspected INH-resistant organism		**RIF** once daily po (adult: 10 mg/kg/day, max dose 600 mg/day; child: 10-20 mg/kg/day, max dose 600 mg/day) for 4 mos.	**RFB** 300 mg once daily po may be substituted for R (in HIV+ patient on anti-retrovirals, dose may need be adjusted for drug interactions).
LTBI, suspected INH and RIF resistant organism		**Moxi** 400 mg or **EMB** 15 mg/kg once daily x 12 months	**Levo** 500 mg once daily + (**EMB** 15 mg/kg or **PZA** 25 mg/kg) once daily x 12 months. **NOTE:** PZA combo regimen, although perhaps most efficacious, poorly tolerated and may be overall less effective than FQ + EMB (CID 64:1670, 2017)

See page 2 for abbreviations   ° Dosages are for adults (unless otherwise indicated) and assume normal renal function   † **DCT** = directly observed therapy

TABLE 12A-(3)

Dose in mg per kg (max. q24h dose) (COMMENTS)

Regimen Q24h:	INH	RIF	PZA	EMB	SM	RFB
Child	10-20 (300)	10-20 (600)	15-30 (2000)	15-25	20-40 (1000)	10-20 (300)
Adult	5 (300)	10 (600)	15-30 (2000)	15-25	15 (1000)	5 (300)
2 times per wk (DOT):						
Child	20-40 (900)	10-20 (600)	50-70 (4000)	50	25-30 (1500)	10-20 (300)
Adult	15 (900)	10 (600)	50-70 (3000)	50	25-30 (1500)	5 (300)
3 times per wk (DOT):						
Child	20-40 (900)	10-20 (600)	50-70 (3000)	25-30	25-30 (1500)	10-20 (300)
Adult	15 (900)	10 (600)	50-70 (3000)	25-30	25-30 (1500)	N.a.

Second-line anti-TB agents can be dosed as follows to facilitate DOT: Cycloserine 500-750 mg po q24h (5 times per wk), Ethionamide 500-750 mg po q24h (5 times per wk), Kanamycin or capreomycin 15 mg per kg IM/IV q24h (3-5 times per wk), Ciprofloxacin 750 mg po q24h (5 times per wk), Ofloxacin 600-800 mg po q24h (5 times per wk), Levofloxacin 750 mg po q24h (5 times per wk) (CID 21:1245, 1995)

Risk factors for drug-resistant (MDR) TB: Recent immigration from Latin America or Asia or living in area of ↑ resistance (≥4%) or previous rx without RIF; exposure to known MDR TB. Incidence of MDR TB in US steady at 0.7%. Incidence of primary drug resistance is particularly high (>25%) in parts of China, Thailand, Russia, Estonia & Latvia; ~80% of US MDR cases in foreign born.

NOTE: Thrice weekly therapy for both the initial and continuation phase and twice weekly therapy in the continuation phase have higher rates of relapse and microbiological failure; acquired drug resistance compared to daily therapy (CID 64:1211, 2017).

SUGGESTED REGIMENS (in vitro susceptibility known)

SEE COMMENTS FOR DOSAGE AND DIRECTLY OBSERVED THERAPY (DOT) REGIMENS

CAUSATIVE AGENT/DISEASE	MODIFYING CIRCUMSTANCES	INITIAL THERAPY — Drugs	Interval/Doses (min. duration)	Regimen	Drugs	CONTINUATION PHASE — Interval/Doses (min. duration)	Range of Total Doses (min. duration)
III. Mycobacterium tuberculosis **A. Pulmonary TB** General reference on rx in adults & children: MMWR 52 (RR-11):1, 2003. In pts with newly diagnosed HIV and TB, Rx for both should be started as soon as possible (NEJM 362-697, 2010).	Rate of INH resistance known to be <4% (drug-susceptible organisms)	**1** (Regimen in order of preference) (See Figure 2 page 146) INH RIF PZA EMB	7 days per wk times 56 doses (8 wks) or 5 days per wk (DOT) times 40 doses (8 wks)	1a	INH/RIF†	7 days per wk times 126 doses (18 wks) or 5 days per wk (DOT) times 90 doses (18 wks). If cavitary disease, treat for 9 mos. Fixed dose combination of INH, RIF, PZA & EMB currently being evaluated (JAMA 305:1415, 2011).	182-130 (26 wks)
				1b	INH/RIF	2 times per wk times 36 doses (18 wks)	92-76 (26 wks)
				1c	INH/RFP	1 time per wk times 18 doses (18 wks) (only if HIV-neg)	74-58 (26 wks) (Not AIDS pts.)
Isolation essential! Hospitalized pts with suspected or documented active TB should be isolated in single rooms using airborne precautions until deemed non-infectious. DC isolation if 3 negative AFB smears or 1-2 neg NAAT (Xpert MTB/RIF) (CID 55:1353 & 1361, 2014).		**2** (See Figure 2 page 146) INH RIF PZA EMB	7 days per wk times 14 doses (2 wks), then 2 times per wk times 12 doses (6 wks) or 5 days per wk (DOT) times 10 doses (2 wks) then 2 times per wk times 12 doses (6 wks)	2a	INH/RIF	2 times per wk times 36 doses (18 wks)	62-58 (26 wks) (Not AIDS pts.)
				2b*	INH/RFP	1 time per wk times 18 doses (18 wks) (only if HIV-neg)	44-40 (26 wks)
		3 (See Figure 2 page 146) INH RIF PZA EMB	3 times per wk times 24 doses (8 wks)	3a	INH/RIF	3 times per wk times 54 doses (18 wks)	78 (26 wks)
USE DOT REGIMENS IF POSSIBLE (continued on next page)		**4** (See Figure 2 page 146) INH RIF PZA EMB	7 days per wk times 56 doses (8 wks) or 5 days per wk (DOT) times 40 doses (8 wks)	4a	INH/RIF	7 days per wk times 217 doses (31 wks) or 5 days per wk (DOT) times 155 doses (31 wks)	273-195 (39 wks)
				4b	INH/RIF	2 times per wk times 62 doses (31 wks)	118-102 (39 wks)

° Dosages are for adults (unless otherwise indicated) and assume normal renal function   † DOT = directly observed therapy

See page 2 for abbreviations

(continued on next page)

TABLE 12A (4)

CAUSATIVE AGENT/ DISEASE	MODIFYING CIRCUM-STANCES	SUGGESTED REGIMEN[a]	DURATION OF TREATMENT (mos.)[#]	SPECIFIC COMMENTS[a]	COMMENTS
III. Mycobacterium tuberculosis	INH (± SM) resistance	RIF, PZA, EMB (a FQ may strengthen the regimen for pts with extensive disease)	6	INH should be stopped in cases of INH resistance. Outcome similar for drug susceptible and INH-mono-resistant strains *(CID 48:179, 2009).*	*(continued from previous page)*
A. Pulmonary TB *(continued from previous page)*			WHO (2016) recommends 7 drugs pending results: INH, PZA, EMB, Moxi, SM, ETH, CLO x 9-11 mos. *(CID 2017;65:1206 & 1212)*		Alternatives for resistant strains: Moxi and levo are FQs of choice, not CIP. FQ resistance may be seen in pts previously treated with FQ. WHO recommends using moxi (if MIC ≤ 2) if resistant to earlier generation FQs *(AAC 54:4765, 2010).*
	Resistance to INH & RIF (± SM)	FQ, PZA, EMB, AMK or capreomycin (SM only if confirmed susceptible) see Comment	24	Extended rx is needed to ↓ the risk of relapse. In cases with extensive disease, the use of an additional agent (alternative agents) may be prudent to ↓ the risk of failure & additional acquired drug resistance. Resectional surgery may be appropriate.	Linezolid 600 mg once daily has excellent in vitro activity, including MDR strains and effective in selected cases of MDR TB and XDR TB but watch for toxicity *(NEJM 367:1508, 2012).*
Multidrug-Resistant Tuberculosis (MDR TB): Defined as resistant to at least 2 drugs including INH & RIF, Pt clusters with high mortality *(NEJM 363:1050, 2010).* **Extensively Drug-Resistant TB** (XDR-TB): Defined as resistant to INH & RIF plus any FQ and at least 1 of the 3 second-line drugs: capreomycin, kanamycin or amikacin *(MMWR 56:250, 2007; CID 51:379, 2010).*	Resistance to INH, RIF (± SM), & EMB or PZA	FQ (EMB or PZA if active), AMK or capreomycin (SM only if confirmed susceptible), see Comment		Use the first-line agents to which there is susceptibility. Add 2 or more alternative agents in case of extensive disease. Surgery should be considered. Survival ↑ in pts receiving active FQ & surgical intervention *(AJRCCM 169:1103, 2004).*	Clofazimine 100 mg as one component of a multiple drug regimen may improve outcome *(CID 67:1361, 2015).* Bedaquiline recently FDA approved for treatment of MDR TB based on efficacy in Phase 2 trials *(NEJM 360:2397, 2009; AAC 56:3271, 2012; NEJM 371:689, 723, 2014).* Dose is 400 mg once daily for 2 weeks then 200 mg tiw for 22 weeks administered as directly observed therapy (DOT), taken with food, and always in combination with other anti-TB meds.
	Resistance to RIF	INH, EMB, FQ, supplemented with PZA for the first 2 mos (an IA may be included for the first 2-3 mos for pts with extensive disease)	12-16	Extended use of an IA may not be feasible. An all-oral regimen times 12-18 mos. should be effective but for more extensive disease &/or to shorten duration (e.g., ≤ 12 mos.), an IA may be added in the initial 2 mos. of rx.	The investigational agent, **delamanid** *(NEJM 366:2151, 2012; Eur Respir J 45:1493, 2015)* at a dose of 100 mg bid, granted conditional approval for treatment of MDR-TB as one component of an optimized background regimen by the European Medicines Agency. **Consultation with an expert in MDR-TB management** strongly advised before use of this agent. For MDR-TB and XDR-TB, do drug susceptibility testing for ethambutol, PZA & other 2nd line drugs if possible *(CID 59:1364, 2014)*
	XDR-TB	Expert consultation strongly advised. See comments	18-24	Therapy requires administration of 4-6 drugs to which infecting organism is susceptible, including multiple second-line drugs *(MMWR 56:250, 2007).* Increased mortality seen primarily in HIV+ patients. Cure with out-patient therapy likely in non-HIV+ patients when regimens of 4 or 5 or more drugs to which organism is susceptible are employed *(NEJM 359:563, 2008; CID 47:496, 2008).* Successful sputum culture conversion correlates to initial susceptibility to FQs and kanamycin *(CID 46:42, 2008).* Bedaquiline *(CID 60:188, 2015)* and Linezolid are options.	

See page 2 for abbreviations   * Dosages are for adults (unless otherwise indicated) and assume normal renal function   † DOT = directly observed therapy

TABLE 12A (5)

CAUSATIVE AGENT/DISEASE; MODIFYING CIRCUMSTANCES	SUGGESTED REGIMENS		COMMENTS
	INITIAL THERAPY	CONTINUATION PHASE OF THERAPY (in vitro susceptibility known)	

III. Mycobacterium tuberculosis (continued)

CAUSATIVE AGENT/DISEASE; MODIFYING CIRCUMSTANCES	INITIAL THERAPY	CONTINUATION PHASE OF THERAPY (in vitro susceptibility known)	COMMENTS
B. Extrapulmonary TB Steroids: see Comment	INH + RIF (or RFB) + PZA + EMB q24h times 2 months. Some add pyridoxine 25–50 mg q24h	INH + RIF (or RFB)	IDSA recommends 6 mos for lymph node, pleural, pericardis, disseminated disease, genitourinary & peritoneal TBc; 6–9 mos for bone & joint; 9-12 mos for CNS (including meningeal) TBc. Corticosteroids "strongly rec" only for meningeal TBc [MMWR 52(RR-11):1, 2003]. Steroids not recommended for pericarditis (NEJM 371:1121 & 1155, 2014).
C. Tuberculous meningitis Excellent summary of clinical aspects and therapy (IDSA guidelines: Clin Infect Dis, Aug 10 pii: ciw376. [Epub ahead of print], 2016)	(INH + RIF + EMB + PZA) + prednisone 60 mg/day x 4 wks, then 30 mg/day x 4 wks, then 15 mg/day x 2 wks, then 5 mg/day x 1 wk	May omit EMB when susceptibility to INH and RIF established. Can D/C PZA after 2 months. Treat for total of 12 months. See Table 9, page 98; for CSF drug penetration. Initial reg of INH + RIF + SM + PZA also effective, even in patients with INH resistant organisms.	3 drugs often rec for initial rx: we prefer 4 (J Infect 59:167, 2009). Infection with MDR TB ↑ mortality & morbidity. Adjunctive corticosteroids improve survival (Cochrane Database Syst Rev, Apr 28;4:CD002244, 2016) and strongly recommended; Adult - dexamethasone 0.4 mg/kg/day week 1, 0.3 mg/kg/day week 2, 0.2 mg/kg/day week 3, 0.1 mg/kg/day week 4, then tapered to stop over 3-4 weeks; Child - dexamethasone 0.6 mg/kg/day or prednisolone 4 mg/kg/day for 4 weeks then tapered to stop over 4 weeks.
D. Tuberculosis during pregnancy	INH + RIF + EMB for 9 mos		SM should not be substituted for EMB due to toxicity. AMK, capreomycin, kanamycin, FQs also contraindicated. PZA is recommended for routine use in pregnant women by the WHO but has not been recommended for general use in U.S. due to lack of safety data, although PZA has been used in some US health jurisdictions without reported adverse events. Breast-feeding should not be discouraged. If PZA is not included in the initial treatment regimen, the minimum duration of therapy is 9 months. Pyridoxine, 25 mg/day, should be administered.
E. Treatment failure or relapse Usually due to poor compliance or resistant organisms, or subtherapeutic drug levels (CID 55:769, 2012).	Directly observed therapy (DOT). Check susceptibilities. (See section III. A, page 142 & above)	Pts whose sputum is culture-positive after 5–6 mos. = treatment failures. Failures may be due to non-compliance or resistant organisms. Confirm susceptibilities of original isolates and obtain new isolate for susceptibility to first and second line agents on current isolates. If isolates show resistance, modify regimen to include at least 2 (preferably 3) new active agents, ones that the patient has not previously received if at all possible. Patients with MDR-TB usually convert sputum within 12 weeks of successful therapy.	
F. HIV infection or AIDS— pulmonary or extrapulmonary All HIV infected patients with TB should be treated with ARVs. If CD4 <50, initiation of ARVs within 2 weeks of starting TB meds associated with improved survival (Ann Intern Med 163:32, 2015). If CD4 ≥50 no proven survival benefit with early ARVs; initiate ARVs at 2-4 weeks of TB meds for moderately severe or severe TB, 8-12 weeks for less severe TB.	INH + RIF (or RFB) + PZA INH x 2 mos Add pyridoxine 50 mg q24h	INH + RIF (or RFB) q24h times 4 months (total 6 mos.). Treat up to 9 mos. in pts with delayed response, cavitary disease.	1. Co-administration of RIF not recommended for these anti-retroviral drugs: nevirapine, etravirine, rilpivirine; maraviroc, elvitegravir (integrase inhibitor in four drug combination Stribild*), all HIV protease inhibitors. Use RFB instead. 2. Coadministration of RIF with raltegravir best avoided (use RFB instead) but if necessary increase raltegravir dose to 800 mg q12h; RIF + dolutegravir OK at 50 mg bid of latter. RIF may be coadministered with efavirenz; nucleoside reverse transcriptase inhibitors. 3. Because of possibility of developing resistance to RIF or RFB in pts with low CD4 counts who receive wkly or biwkly (2x/wk) therapy, daily dosing (preferred), or at a min 3x/wk dosing (failure rate likely higher) recommended for initial or continuation phase of rx. 4. Clinical & microbiologic response similar to that of HIV-neg patient 5. Post-treatment suppression not necessary for drug-susceptible strains. 6. Immune reconstitution inflammatory syndrome occurs in 10-20% of TB patients after initiation of ARVs.
Concomitant protease inhibitor (PI) therapy	INH 300 mg q24h + RFB (150 mg q24h or 300 mg tiw) + EMB 15 mg/kg q24h + PZA 25 mg/kg q24h x 2 mos; then INH + RFB times 4 mos. (up to 7 mos.)	INH + RFB x 4 mos. (7 mos. in slow responders, cavitary disease)	Rifamycins induce cytochrome CYP450 (RIF > RFP > RFB) & reduce serum levels of concomitantly administered PIs. Conversely, PIs inhibit CYP450 & cause ↑ serum levels of RFP & RFB. If dose of RFB is not reduced, toxicity ↑.

See page 2 for abbreviations   * Dosages are for adults (unless otherwise indicated) and assume normal renal function   † DOT = directly observed therapy

TABLE 12A (6)
FIGURE 1 ALGORITHM FOR MANAGEMENT OF AT-RISK PATIENT WITH LOW OR HIGH SUSPICION
OF ACTIVE TUBERCULOSIS WHILE CULTURES ARE PENDING *(modified from MMWR 52(RR-11):1, 2003).*

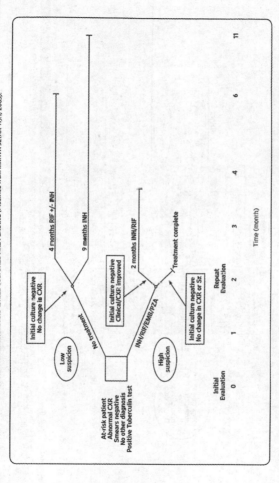

Patients at high clinical suspicion of active TB should be started on 4-drug therapy, pending results of cultures. If cultures are negative and there is no change in symptoms or CXR, the 4-drug regimen can be stopped and no further therapy is required. If cultures are negative and there is clinical or CXR improvement, continue INH-RIF for 2 additional months. For patients at low suspicion for active TB, treat for LTBI once cultures are negative.

See page 2 for abbreviations   ° Dosages are for adults (unless otherwise indicated) and assume normal renal function   ⁱ **DOT** = directly observed therapy

146

TABLE 12A (7)
FIGURE 2 [Modified from MMWR 52(RR-11):1, 2003]

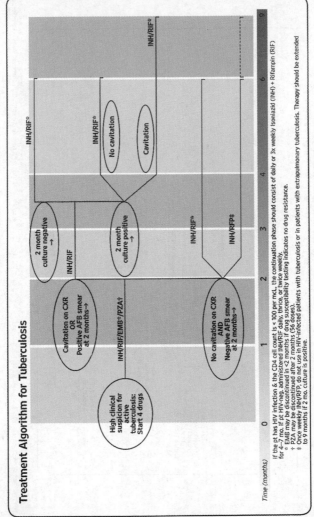

Treatment Algorithm for Tuberculosis

If the pt has HIV infection & the CD4 cell count is < 100 per mcL, the continuation phase should consist of daily or 3x weekly Isoniazid (INH) + Rifampin (RIF)
for 4–7 mo. If pt HIV-neg. administered INH/RIF daily, thrice, or twice weekly.
⬦ EMB may be discontinued in <2 months if drug susceptibility testing indicates no drug resistance.
† PZA may be discontinued after 2 months (56 doses).
‡ Once weekly INH/RFP. Do not use in HIV-infected patients with tuberculosis or in patients with extrapulmonary tuberculosis. Therapy should be extended
  to 9 months if 2 mo. culture is positive.

See page 2 for abbreviations   ⬦ Dosages are for adults (unless otherwise indicated) and assume normal renal function   † DOT = directly observed therapy

TABLE 12A (8)

CAUSATIVE AGENT/DISEASE	MODIFYING CIRCUMSTANCES	SUGGESTED REGIMENS PRIMARY/ALTERNATIVE		COMMENTS
IV. Nontuberculous Mycobacteria (NTM) (See ATS Consensus: AJRCCM 175:367, 2007; EID 17:506, 2011)				
A. Mycobacterium bovis		**INH + RIF + EMB** for 2 months then **INH + RIF** for 7 months		The M. tuberculosis complex includes M. bovis, and regimens effective for MTB (except PZA based) also likely to be effective for M. bovis. **All isolates resistant to PZA.** Isolation not required. Increased prevalence of extrapulmonary disease in U.S. born Hispanic populations and elsewhere (CID 47:168, 2008; EID 14:909, 2008; EID 17:457, 2011).
B. Bacillus Calmette-Guerin (BCG) (derived from M. bovis)	Only fever (>38.5°C) for 12–24 hrs	**INH 300 mg** q24h times 3 months		Intravesical BCG effective in superficial bladder tumors and carcinoma in situ. With sepsis, consider initial adjunctive prednisolone. Also susceptible to RFB, CIP, oflox, levo, moxi, streptomycin, amikacin, capreomycin (AAC 53:316, 2009). BCG may cause regional adenitis or pulmonary disease in HIV-infected children (CID 37:1226, 2003). **Resistant to PZA.**
	Systemic illness or sepsis	Same as for M. bovis.		
C. Mycobacterium avium-intracellulare complex (MAC, MAI, or Battey bacillus) ATS/IDSA Consensus Statement: AJRCCM 175:367, 2007; See http://aidsinfo.nih.gov/guidelines/html/4/adult-and-adolescent-oi-prevention-and-treatment-guidelines/0 for updated CDC recommendations for AIDS patients.	**Immunocompetent patients**			See AJRCCM 175:367, 2007 for details of dosing and duration of therapy, intermittent (tiw) therapy not recommended for patients with cavitary disease, patients who have been previously treated or patients with moderate or severe disease. Intermittent therapy may be an option in "nodular bronchiectatic form of the disease (Am J Respir Crit Care Med 191:96, 2015). The primary microbiological goal of therapy is 12 months of negative sputum cultures on therapy.
	Nodular/Bronchiectatic disease	[**Clarithro** 1000 mg or **Azithro** 500 mg] tiw + **EMB** 25 mg/kg tiw + **RIF** 600 mg or **RFB** 300 mg] tiw		**"Classic" pulmonary MAC:** Men 50–75, smokers, COPD. May be associated with tub use (Clin Chest Med 23:675, 2002).
	Cavitary disease or severe nodular/bronchiectatic disease	[**Clarithro** 500–1000 mg (lower dose for wt <50 kg) or **Azithro** 250 mg/day] + **EMB** 15 mg/kg/day + [RIF 600 mg/day or RFB 150–300 mg/day] ± [**Strep** or **AMK**]		**"New" pulmonary MAC:** Women 30–70, scoliosis, COPD, mitral valve prolapse, (bronchiectasis), pectus excavatum ("Lady Windermere syndrome") and fibronodular disease in elderly women (EID 16:1576, 2010). May also be associated with interferon gamma deficiency (AJM 113:756, 2002). For cervicofacial lymphadenitis (localized) in immunocompetent children, surgical excision is as effective as chemotherapy (CID 44:1057, 2007).
	HIV infection:			Moxifloxacin and gatifloxacin, active in vitro & in vivo (AAC 51:4071, 2007).
	Primary prophylaxis—Pt's CD4 count <50–100 per mm³ Discontinue when CD4 count >100 per mm³ in response to ART	**Azithro** 1200 mg po weekly OR **Clarithro** 500 mg po bid	**RFB** 300 mg po q24h OR **Azithro** 1200 mg po weekly + RiF 300 mg po q24h	Drug-resistant MAI disease seen in Table 22A, page 248. Drug-resistant MAI disease seen in 29–58% of pts in whom disease develops while taking clarithro prophylaxis & in 11% of those on azithro but has not been observed with RFB prophylaxis. Clarithro resistance more likely in pts with extremely low CD4 counts at initiation. Need to be sure no active MTB; RFB used for prophylaxis may promote selection of rifamycin-resistant MTB.
	Treatment Either presumptive dx or after + culture of blood, bone marrow, or usually, sterile body fluids, eg liver	[**Clarithro** 500 mg po bid + **EMB** 15 mg/kg/day ± **RFB** 300 mg po q24h (adjust dose) of Clari 1000 mg po bid) may be associated with ↑ mortality] OR **Azithro** 500 mg po/day + **EMB** 15 mg/kg/day +/- RFB 300–450 mg po/day		Many drug-drug interactions, see Table 22A, page 248. Adjust RFB dose as needed for drug-drug interactions. *(continued on next page)*

* Dosages are for adults (unless otherwise indicated) and assume normal renal function   † **DOT** = directly observed therapy

See page 2 for abbreviations   * Dosages are for adults (unless otherwise indicated) and assume normal renal function   † **DOT** = directly observed therapy

TABLE 12A (9)

CAUSATIVE AGENT/DISEASE	MODIFYING CIRCUMSTANCES	SUGGESTED REGIMENS PRIMARY/ALTERNATIVE		COMMENTS
IV. Nontuberculous Mycobacteria (NTM) (continued)				
C. Mycobacterium avium-intracellulare complex (continued)				(continued from previous page)
				Addition of a third or fourth drug should be considered for patients with advanced immunosuppression (CD4+ count <50 cells/µL), high mycobacterial loads (>2 log CFU/mL of blood), or in the absence of effective ART. AMK 10–15 mg/kg IV daily; Strep 1 gm IV or IM daily; CIP 400–750 mg po bid or Mox 400 mg po daily.
				Testing of susceptibility to clarithromycin and azithromycin is recommended.
				Short term (4–8 weeks) of systemic corticosteroid (equivalent to 20–40 mg of prednisone) can be used for IRIS.
	Chronic post-treatment suppression—secondary prophylaxis	**Always necessary.** [Clarithro or azithro] + EMB 15 mg/kg/day (dosage above)	**Clarithro or Azithro** + or RFB (dosage above)	Recurrences almost universal without chronic suppression. Can discontinue if no signs and symptoms of MAC disease and sustained (>6 months) CD4 count >100 cells/µL in response to ART.
D. Mycobacterium celatum	Treatment: optimal regimen not defined	May be susceptible to clarithro, FQ. Treat as if MAC.		Isolated from pulmonary lesions and blood in AIDS patients. Easily confused with M. xenopi (and MAC).
E. Mycobacterium abscessus **Mycobacterium chelonae**	Treatment: Surgical excision may facilitate clarithro rx in subcutaneous abscess and is important adjunct to rx. For role of surgery in M. abscessus pulmonary disease, see CID 52:565, 2011.	**Cutaneous infection:** Surgical debridement + **Clarithro** 500 mg po bid x 4–6 months OR **Clarithro** 500 mg po bid + **Moxifloxacin** 400 mg po once daily x 4–6 months **Pulmonary or disseminated disease:** (**Imipenem** 500 mg IV q6–12 h or 1 g IV q8h or **Cefoxitin** 8–12 gm/day in 2–3 divided doses) + **Clarithro** 1000 mg/d or **azithro** 250 mg/day IV/IM three times a week for 12 months after sputum cultures convert to negative + Surgical resection of involved lung if possible (see Comments)		M. abscessus actually a complex of 3 species: M. abscessus, M. massiliense, M bolletii. Treatment outcomes poor with half or more of patients remaining culture-positive or relapsing with infection due to strains with inducible macrolide resistance, i.e., M. abscessus subspecies abscessus (Clin Infect Dis 64:309, 2017; 2017). Inducible resistance to macrolides seen in M. abscessus subspecies massiliense due to non-functional macrolide resistance gene. Outcomes of medical therapy are better with infection from this species, compared to other members of the complex (Int J Tuberc Lung Dis 18:1141, 2014, Clin Infect Dis 64:301, 2017). 2–4 week regimen of IV **amikacin** + IV **cefoxitin** (or **IMP**) + an oral macrolide administered for 12–15 months after culture conversion for M. massiliense pulmonary infection highly effective (98% culture conversion at end of treatment) in one study (Chest 150:1211, 2016). Because of concern for inducible resistance to Clarithromycin, consider adding another drug, particularly in extensive disease with M. abscessus, limited surgical excision: options are Tigecycline 50 mg once daily IV, Linezolid 600 mg once daily PO, Clofazimine 50–100 mg once daily. M. abscessus complex susceptible in vitro to AMK (70%), clarithro (93%) (but resistance may be inducible), cefoxitin (70%), clofazimine, rifabutin, imipenem, cipro, Doxy, Mino, tigecycline (CID 42:1756, 2006). Culture-conversion may not be achievable in M. abscessus pulmonary infection; suppressive therapy may be required to control disease progression. **M. chelonae** susceptible to AMK (80%), clarithro, azithro, tobramycin (100%), IMP (60%), moxifloxacin, CIP, Mino, Doxy, linezolid (94%) (CID 42:1756, 2006). Resistant to cefoxitin, FQ. Tigecycline highly active in vitro and successfully used as salvage for M. chelonae infection in combination regimens (J Antimicrob Chemother 69:1945, 2014).
F. Mycobacterium fortuitum	Treatment: optimal regimen not defined; surgical excision of infected areas.	**AMK** + **Cefoxitin** + **Probenecid** 2–6 wks, then po **TMP-SMX**, or **doxy** 2–6 mos. Usually responds to 6–12 mos of oral rx with 2 drugs to which it is susceptible.		Resistant to all standard anti-TBc drugs. Sensitive in vitro to doxycycline, minocycline, cefoxitin, IMP, AMK, TMP-SMX, CIP, oflox, azithro, clarithro, linezolid, tmeoxifal, but some strains resistant to azithromycin, rifabutin. For M. fortuitum pulmonary disease treat with at least 2 agents active in vitro until sputum cultures negative for 12 months (AJRCCM 175:367, 2007). Disseminated disease associated with interferon-γ auto-antibodies to interferon-γ (Intern Med 53:1361, 2014).

See page 2 for abbreviations

TABLE 12A (10)

CAUSATIVE AGENT/DISEASE	MODIFYING CIRCUMSTANCES	SUGGESTED REGIMENS PRIMARY/ALTERNATIVE	COMMENTS
IV. Nontuberculous Mycobacteria (NTM) *(continued)*			
G. Mycobacterium haemophilum	Regimen(s) not defined. In animal model, Clarithro + Rifabutin effective. Combination of CIP + RFB + Clarithro reported effective but clinical experience limited *(CID 52:488, 2011)*. Surgical debridement may be necessary.		Clinical: Ulcerating skin lesions, synovitis, osteomyelitis, *cervicofacial lymphadenitis* in children. Associated with permanent eye makeup *(CID 52:488, 2011)*. Lab: Requires supplemented media to isolate. Sensitive in vitro to.: CIP, cycloserine, rifabutin, moxifloxacin. Over ½ resistant to: INH, RIF, EMB, PZA. For localized cervicofacial lymphadenitis in immunocompetent children, surgical excision as effective as chemotherapy *(CID 44:1057, 2007)* or "watchful waiting" *(CID 52:180, 2011)*.
H. Mycobacterium genavense	2 or more drugs: Clarithro, EMB, RFB, CLO, Amikacin, Moxifloxacin as alternatives.		Seen in AIDS patients with CD4 <50 and in non-HIV severely immunocompromised hosts. *For review see Clin Microbiol Infect 19:432, 2013.*
I. Mycobacterium gordonae	Rarely a true pathogen.		Frequent colonizer, not associated with disease. In vitro: sensitive to EMB, RIF, AMK, CIP, clarithro, linezolid. Resistant to INH. Surgical excision.
J. Mycobacterium kansasii	[(Azithro 500 mg or Clarithro 1000 mg) + RIF 600 mg + EMB 15 mg/kg] po q24h	INH 300 mg + Pyridoxine 50 mg + RIF 600 mg + EMB 15 mg/kg) po q24h For Rifampin resistant organism: [INH 900 mg + Pyridoxine 50 mg + EME 15 mg/kg + (Moxi 400 mg or Azithro 500 mg or Clarithro 1000 mo)] po q24h	All isolates are resistant to PZA. Treat until sputum cultures have been negative for 12 mo. For HIV+ patients on a protease inhibitor, substitute Rifabutin (150 mg/day) for Rifampin
K. Mycobacterium marinum	Two active agents for 1-2 months after surgical incision: Clarithro 500 mg bid + EMB 25 mg/kg q24h or RIF 600 mg q24h + EMB 25 mg/kg q24h Surgical excision.		For deep tissue involvement a three drug combination therapy with Rifampin 600 mg q24h + [Minocycline 100-200 mg q24h or Doxycycline 100-200 mg q24h] + Clarithromycin 500 mg bid. Monotherapy may be considered for minimal disease: Minocycline 100-200 mg q24h or Doxycycline 100-200 mg q24h or TMP-SMX 160/800 mg po bid.
L. Mycobacterium scrofulaceum	Surgical excision. Chemotherapy seldom indicated. Although regimens not defined, Clarithro + CLO with or without EMB, INH, RIF, strep + cycloserine have also been used.		In vitro resistant to INH, RIF, EMB, PZA, AMK, CIP. Susceptible to clarithro, strep, erythromycin.
M. Mycobacterium simiae	Regimen(s) not defined. Start 4 drugs as for disseminated MAC		Most isolates resistant to all 1°-line anti-TBc drugs. Isolates often not clinically significant.
N. Mycobacterium ulcerans (Buruli ulcer)	WHO recommends RIF + SM for 8 weeks. RIF + CIP recommended as alternatives by WHO *(CMM 31:19, 2009)*.		Susceptible in vitro to RIF, strep, CLO, clarithro, CIP, oflox, amikacin, moxi, linezolid. Australian guidelines *(MJA 200:267, 2014)* recommend oral combination of RIF + Clarithro or RIF + a FQ (moxifloxacin or CIP). Surgery not required for cure and reserved for those declining or intolerant of antibiotic, debridement of necrotic tissue, large defects.
O. Mycobacterium xenopi	Regimen(s) not defined. Clarithro 500 mg bid + RIF 600 mg or Rifabutin 300 mg + EMB 15 mg/kg once daily + INH 300 mg once daily.		In vitro: sensitive to clarithro and many standard antimycobacterial drugs. MOXI active in vitro and may be an alternative.
P. Mycobacterium leprae (leprosy) Classification: *CID 44:1096, 2007; Overview: Lancet ID 11:464, 2011.*	There are 2 sets of therapeutic recommendations here: one from USA (National Hansen's Disease Program [NHDP], Baton Rouge, LA) and one from WHO. Both are based on expert recommendations and neither has been subjected to controlled clinical trial.		

*See page 2 for abbreviations   * Dosages are for adults (unless otherwise indicated) and assume normal renal function   † DOT = directly observed therapy*

TABLE 12A (11)

Type of Disease	NHDP Regimen	WHO Regimen	COMMENTS
Mycobacterium leprae (leprosy) *(continued)*			
Paucibacillary Forms: (Intermediate, Tuberculoid, Borderline tuberculoid)	(Dapsone 100 mg/day + RIF 600 mg po/day) for 12 months	(Dapsone 100 mg/day (unsupervised) + RIF 600 mg 1x/mo (supervised)) for 6 mos	Side effects overall 0.4%
Single lesion paucibacillary leprosy	Treat as paucibacillary leprosy for 12 months.	Single-dose ROM therapy: (RIF 600 mg + **Oflox** 400 mg + **Mino** 100 mg) (*Ln 353:655, 1999*)	
Multibacillary forms: Borderline Borderline-lepromatous Lepromatous *See Comment for erythema nodosum leprosum (ENL)* Rev: *Lancet 363:1209, 2004*	(Dapsone 100 mg/day + **CLO** 50 mg/day + **RIF** 600 mg/day) for 24 mos **Alternative regimen:** (Dapsone 100 mg/day + RIF 600 mg/day + **Minocycline** 100 mg/day) for 24 mos if **CLO** is refused or unavailable.	(Dapsone 100 mg/day + **CLO** 50 mg/day (both unsupervised) + **RIF** 600 mg + **CLO** 300 mg once monthly (supervised)). Continue regimen for 12 months.	Side-effects overall 5%. For **erythema nodosum leprosum:** prednisone 60–80 mg/day or thalidomide 100–400 mg/day. Thalidomide available in US at 1-800-4-CELGENE. Altho thalidomide effective, WHO no longer rec because of potential toxicity however the majority of leprosy experts feel thalidomide remains drug of choice for ENL under strict supervision. **CLO (Clofazimine)** available from NHDP under IND protocol; contact at 1-800-642-2477. **Ethionamide** (250 mg q24h) or prothionamide (375 mg q24h) may be subbed for CLO. Etanercept effective in one case refractory to above standard therapy (*CID 52:e133, 2011*). Regimens incorporating clarithro, minocycline, dapsone monotherapy have been abandoned due to emergence of resistance (*CID 52:e127, 2011*), but older patients previously treated with dapsone monotherapy may remain on lifelong maintenance therapy. Moxi highly active in vitro and produces rapid clinical response (*AAC 52:3113, 2009*).

TABLE 12B – DOSAGE AND ADVERSE EFFECTS OF ANTIMYCOBACTERIAL DRUGS

AGENT (TRADE NAME)[1]	USUAL DOSAGE[a]	ROUTE/[§] DRUG RESISTANCE (RES) US[2]	SIDE-EFFECTS, TOXICITY AND PRECAUTIONS	SURVEILLANCE
FIRST LINE DRUGS				
Ethambutol (Myambutol) (100, 400 mg tab)	25 mg/kg/day for 2 mos then 15 mg/kg/day q24h as 1 dose [<10% protein binding] [Bacteriostatic to both extra-cellular & intracellular organisms]	RES: 0.3% (0–0.7%) po 400 mg tab	Optic neuritis (with decreased visual acuity, central scotomata, and loss of green and red perception; peripheral neuropathy and headache (~1%), rashes (rare), arthralgia (rare) & hyperuricemia (rare). Anaphylactoid reaction (rare). **Comment:** Primarily used to inhibit resistance. Disrupts outer cell membrane in M. avium with ↑ activity to other drugs.	Monthly visual acuity & red/green with dose >15 mg/kg /day. ≥10% loss considered significant. Usually reversible if drug discontinued.
Isoniazid (INH) (Nydrazid, Laniazid, Teebaconin) (50, 100, 300 mg tab)	Q24h dosage: 5–10 mg/kg/day up to 300 mg/day max dose: 15 mg/kg (900 mg max dose) (<10% protein binding) [Bactericidal to both extracellular and intracellular organisms] Add pyridoxine in alcoholic, pregnant, or malnourished pts.	RES: 4.1% (2.6–8.5%) po 300 mg tab IM 100 mg/ml in 10 ml (IV route not FDA-approved but has been used, esp. in AIDS)	Overall ~1%. **Liver:** Hep (children 10% mild ↑ SGOT, normalizes with continued rx, age <20 yrs rare, 20–34 yrs ~.2%, ≥50 yrs 2.3%) [also ↑ with q24h alcohol & previous exposure to Hep C (usually asymptomatic–CID 36:293, 2003)]. May be fatal. With prodromal sx, dark urine do LFTs; discontinue if SGOT >3–5x normal. **Peripheral neuropathy** (17% on 6 mg/kg per day, less on 300 mg, incidence ↑ in slow acetylators); **pyridoxine 10 mg q24h will decrease incidence;** other neurologic sequelae, convulsions, optic neuritis, toxic encephalopathy, psychosis, muscle twitching, dizziness, coma (all rare), allergic skin rashes, fever, minor disulfiram-like reaction, flushing after Swiss cheese; blood dyscrasias (rare); ↑ antinuclear (20%). **Drug-drug interactions common, see Table 22A.**	Pre-rx liver functions. Repeat if symptoms (fatigue, weakness, malaise, anorexia, nausea or vomiting) >3 days (AJRCCM 152: 1705, 1995). Some recommend SGOT at 2, 4, 6 mos esp. if age >50 yrs. Clinical evaluation every mo.
Pyrazinamide (500 mg tab)	25 mg per kg per day (maximum 2.5 gm per day) q24h as 1 dose [Bactericidal for intracellular organisms]	po 500 mg tab	Arthralgia; **hyperuricemia** (with or without symptoms): hepatitis (not over 2% if recommended dose not exceeded); gastric irritation; photosensitivity (rare).	Pre-rx liver functions. Monthly SGOT, uric acid. Measure serum uric acid if symptomatic gouty attack occurs.
Rifamate[*]– combination tablet	2 tablets single dose q24h	po (1 hr before meal)	1 tablet contains 150 mg INH, 300 mg RIF	As with individual drugs
Rifampin (Rifadin, Rimactane, Rifamate, Rifater) (100, 300, 450, 600 cap)	10.0 mg per kg per day up to 600 mg per day q24h as 1 dose [60–90% protein binding] [Bactericidal to all populations of organisms]	RES: 0.2% (0–0.3%) po 300 mg cap (IV available, Merrell-Dow)	INH/RIF d<1d = 3% for toxicity; gastrointestinal irritation, antibiotic-associated colitis, drug fever (1%), pruritus with or without skin rash (1%), anaphylactoid reactions in HIV+ pts, mental confusion, thrombocytopenia (1%), leukopenia (1%), hemolytic anemia, transient abnormalities in liver function. **"Flu syndrome"** (fever, chills, headache, bone pain, shortness of breath) seen if RIF taken irregularly or if q24h dose restarted after an interval of no rx. Discolors urine, tears, sweat, contact lens orange-brownish color. May cause drug-induced lupus erythematosus (Ln 349: 1521, 1977).	Pre-rx liver function. Repeat if symptoms. **Multiple significant drug-drug interactions, see Table 22A.**
Rifater[*]– combination tablet (See Side-effects)	Wt ≥55 kg, 6 tablets single dose q24h	po (1 hr before meal)	1 tablet contains 50 mg INH, 120 mg RIF, 300 mg PZA. Used in 1st 2 months of rx (PZA 25 mg per kg). Purpose is convenience in dosing, ↑ compliance but cost 1.38 more. Side-effects = individual drugs.	As with individual drugs, PZA 25 mg per kg
Streptomycin (IV/IM sol'n)	15 mg per kg IM q24h, 0.75–1.0 gm per day initially for 60–90 days, then 1.0 gm 2–3 times per week (15 mg per kg per day) q24h as 1 dose	RES: 3.9% (2.7–7.6%) IM (or IV)	Overall 8%. **Ototoxicity:** vestibular dysfunction (vertigo); paresthesias; dizziness & nausea (all less in pts receiving 2–3 doses per week); tinnitus and high frequency loss (1%); nephrotoxicity (rare); peripheral neuropathy (rare); allergic skin rashes (4–5%); drug fever. Available from X-Gen Pharmaceuticals, 607-732-4411. Ref. IV—CID 19:1150, 1994. Toxicity similar with qd vs tid dosing (CID 38:1538, 2004).	Monthly audiogram. In older pts, serum creatinine or BUN at start of rx and weekly if pt stable

[1] Note: Malabsorption of antimycobacterial drugs may occur in patients with AIDS enteropathy. For review of adverse effects, see AJRCCM 167:1472, 2003.
[2] **RES** = % resistance of M. tuberculosis

See page 2 for abbreviations   [a] Dosages are for adults (unless otherwise indicated) and assume normal renal function   † (higher in Hispanics, Asians, and patients <10 years old)

[§] Mean (range) (higher in Hispanics, Asians, and patients <10 years old)   † **DOT** = directly observed therapy

TABLE 12B (2)

AGENT (TRADE NAME)[1]	USUAL DOSAGE*	ROUTE/1° DRUG RESISTANCE (RES) US*§	SIDE-EFFECTS, TOXICITY AND PRECAUTIONS	SURVEILLANCE
SECOND LINE DRUGS (more difficult to use and/or less effective than first line drugs)				
Amikacin (Amikin) (IV sol'n)	7.5–10.0 mg per kg q24h [Bactericidal for extracellular organisms]	RES: (est. 0.1%) IM/IV 500 mg vial	*See Table 10B, page 119 & Table 10D, page 122*	Monthly audiogram. Serum creatinine or BUN weekly if pt stable
Bedaquiline (Sirturo) (100 mg tab) Ref: *JAC 69:2310, 2014; NEJM 371:723, 2014; CID 60:188, 2015.*	Directly observed therapy (DOT): 400 mg once daily for 2 weeks, then 200 mg 3 times weekly for 22 weeks, taken in combination with other anti-TB medications.	Does not exhibit cross-resistance to other TB drugs; always use in combination with other TB drugs to prevent selection of resistant mutants	Toxicity similar with qd vs tid dosing (*CID 38:1538, 2004*). Most common: nausea, vomiting, arthralgia, headache, hyperuricemia. Elevated transaminases. Bedaquiline in clinical trials was administered as one component of a multiple drug regimen, so side-effects were common, yet difficult to assign to a particular drug.	Moderate QTc increases (average of 10-16 ms over the 24 weeks of therapy. Potential risks of pancreatitis, myopathy, myocardial injury, severe hepatotoxicity.
Capreomycin sulfate (Capastat sulfate)	1 gm daily (15 mg per kg per day) q24h as 1 dose	RES: 0.1% (0–0.9%) IM/IV	Nephrotoxicity (36%), ototoxicity (auditory 11%), eosinophilia, leukopenia, skin rash, fever, hypokalemia, neuromuscular blockade.	Monthly audiogram, biweekly serum creatinine or BUN
Ciprofloxacin (Cipro) (250, 500, 750 mg tab)	750 mg bid	500 mg or 750 mg tab IV 200-400 mg vial	TB not a FDA-approved indication for CIP. Desired CIP serum levels 4–6 mcg per mL. *See Table 10A, page 114 & Table 10B, page 120 for adverse effects.*	None
Clofazimine (Lamprene) (50, 100 mg cap)	50 mg per day (unsupervised) + 300 mg 1 once per month supervised or 100 mg per day	50 mg (with meals)	Skin: **pigmentation (pink-brownish black)** 75–100%, dryness 20%, pruritus 5% GI: abdominal pain 50% (rarely severe leading to exploratory laparoscopy), splenic infarction (VR), bowel obstruction (VR), GI bleeding (VR). Eye: conjunctival irritation, retinal crystal deposits.	None
Cycloserine (Seromycin) (250 mg tab)	750–1000 mg per day (15 mg per kg per day) [Bacteriostatic for both extracellular & intracellular organisms]	RES: 0.1% (0–0.3%) 250 mg cap	Convulsions, **psychoses** (5–10% of those receiving 1.0 gm per day); headache; somnolence; hyperreflexia; increased CSF protein and pressure, **peripheral neuropathy.** 100 mg pyridoxine per day q24h should be given concomitantly. Contraindicated in epileptics.	None
Dapsone (25, 100 mg tab)	100 mg per day	100 mg tab	Blood: ↓ hemoglobin (1-2 gm) & ↑ retics (2-12%), in most pts. Hemolysis in G6PD deficiency. ↑ hemolysis due to concomitant atazanavir (*AAC 56:1081, 2012*). **Methemoglobinemia.** CNS: peripheral neuropathy (rare). GI: nausea, vomiting. Renal: albuminuria, nephrotic syndrome. Erythema nodosum leprosum in pts rx for leprosy (½ pts 1st year). Hypersensitivity syndrome in 0.5-3.6% (*See Surveillance*).	Hypersensitivity syndrome: fever, rash, eosinophilia, lymphadenopathy, hepatitis, pneumonitis. Genetic marker identified (*NEJM 369:1620, 2013*).
Ethionamide (Trecator-SC) (120, 250 mg tab)	500–1000 mg per day (15-20 mg per kg per day) divided 1-3 doses per day [Bacteriostatic for extracellular organisms only]	RES: 0.8% (0-1.5%) 250 mg tab	**Gastrointestinal irritation** (up to 50% on large dose); goiter; peripheral neuropathy (rare); convulsions (rare); changes in affect (rare); difficulty in diabetes control; rashes; hepatitis; purpura; stomatitis; gynecomastia; menstrual irregularity. Give drug with meals or antacids; SGOT monthly. Possibly teratogenic.	

See page 2 for abbreviations   * Dosages are for adults (unless otherwise indicated) and assume normal renal function   † **DOT** = directly observed therapy

§ Mean (range) (higher in Hispanics, Asians, and patients <10 years old)

TABLE T2B (3)

AGENT (TRADE NAME)[y]	USUAL DOSAGE[z]	ROUTE/[z] DRUG RESISTANCE (RES) US[z,§]	SIDE-EFFECTS, TOXICITY AND PRECAUTIONS	SURVEILLANCE
SECOND LINE DRUGS (continued)				
Linezolid (Zyvox) (600 mg tab, oral suspension 100 mg/mL)	600 mg once daily	PO or IV	Not FDA-approved indication. High rate of adverse events (>80% with 4 months or longer of therapy: myelosuppression, peripheral neuropathy, optic neuropathy. Avoid tyramine-containing foods, soy products, adrenergic agents (e.g., pseudoephedrine, phenylpropanol-amine) MAO inhibitors, SSRIs. 500 mg >300 mg dose for toxicity; consider reducing dose to 300 mg for toxicity or after 4 mos of therapy or culture-conversion to reduce toxicity.	Baseline and monthly complete blood count, visual acuity checks, screen for symptoms of peripheral neuropathy, neurologic examination.
Moxifloxacin (Avelox) (400 mg tab)	400 mg qd	400 mg cap	Not FDA-approved indication. Concomitant administration of rifampin reduces serum levels of moxi (CID 45:1001, 2007).	None
Ofloxacin (Floxin) (200, 300, 400 mg tab)	400 mg bid	400 mg cap	Not FDA-approved indication. Overall adverse effects 11%, 4% discontinued due to side-effects. GI: nausea 3%, diarrhea 1%. **CNS:** insomnia 3%, headache 1%, dizziness 1%	
Para-aminosalicylic acid (PAS, Paser) (Na⁺ or K⁺ salt) (4 gm cap)	4–6 gm bid (200 mg per kg per day) [Bacteriostatic for extracellular organisms only]	RES: 0.8% (0–1.5%) 450 mg tab (See Comment.)	**Gastrointestinal irritation** (10–15%); goitrogenic action (rare); depressed prothrombin activity (rare); G6PD-mediated hemolytic anemia (rare), drug fever, rashes, hepatitis, myalgia, arthralgia. Retards hepatic enzyme induction, may ↓ INH hepatotoxicity. Available from CDC, (404) 639-3670, Jacobus Pharm. Co. (609) 921-7447.	None
Rifabutin (Mycobutin) (150 mg cap)	300 mg per day (prophylaxis or treatment)	150 mg tab	Polymyalgia, polyarthralgia, granulocytopenia. Uveitis seen with 300 mg/day but increases to 8-38% if higher dose or combined with clarithro, PI or azole antifungal. Reddish urine, orange skin (pseudojaundice.	None
Rifapentine (Priftin) (150 mg tab)	600 mg twice weekly for 1st 2 mos., then 600 mg q week	150 mg tab	Similar to other rifabutins. (See RIF, RFB). Hyperuricemia seen in 21%. Causes red-orange discoloration of body fluids. Flu-like illness in pts given weekly Rifapentine + INH for latent MTB (CID 61:527, 2015).	None
Thalidomide (Thalomid) (50, 100, 200 mg cap)	100–300 mg po q24h (may use up to 400 mg po q24h for severe erythema nodosum leprosum)	50 mg tab	**Contraindicated in pregnancy. Causes severe life-threatening birth defects. Both male and female patients must use barrier contraceptive methods (Pregnancy Category X).** Frequently causes drowsiness or somnolence. May cause peripheral neuropathy. (AJM 108:487, 2000) For review, see Ln 363:1209, 2004.	In US: contact Celgene (800-4-CELGENE)

See page 2 for abbreviations   [z] Dosages are for adults (unless otherwise indicated) and assume normal renal function   † **D0T** = directly observed therapy

§ Mean (range) (higher in Hispanics, Asians, and patients <10 years old)

TABLE 13A – TREATMENT OF PARASITIC INFECTIONS

- **See Table 13D for sources for antiparasitic drugs not otherwise commercially available.**
- The following resources are available through the Centers for Disease Control and Prevention (CDC) in Atlanta. Website is www.cdc.gov. General advice for parasitic diseases other than malaria: (+1) (404) 718-4745 (days); (+1) (770) 488-7100 (after hours). For CDC Drug Service 8:00 a.m. – 4:30 p.m. EST: (+1) (404) 639-3670; fax: (+1) (404) 639-3717. See www.cdc.gov/laboratory/drugservice/index.html
- For malaria: Prophylaxis advice (+1) (770) 488-7788; treatment: (+1) (770) 488-7788; or after hours (+1) (770) 488-7100; toll-free (US) 1-855-856-4713; website: www.cdc.gov/malaria
- **NOTE: All dosage regimens are for adults with normal renal function unless otherwise stated.** Many of the suggested regimens are not FDA approved.
- For licensed drugs, suggest checking package inserts to verify dosage and side-effects. Occasionally, post-licensure data may alter dosage as compared to approved.

INFECTING ORGANISM	SUGGESTED REGIMENS		COMMENTS
	PRIMARY	**ALTERNATIVE**	
PROTOZOA—INTESTINAL (non-pathogenic: E. hartmanni, E. dispar, E. moshkovskii, E. coli, Iodamoeba bütschlii, Endolimax nana, Chilomastix mesnili)			
Balantidium coli	Tetracycline 500 mg po qid x 10 days	Metronidazole 750 mg po tid x 5 days	Another alternative: Iodoquinol 650 mg po tid x 20 days.
Blastocystis hominis Ref.: Trends Parasitol 28:305, 2012; Parasitol Int. 2016 May 28. pii: S1383-5769(16)30154-4	Metronidazole 1.5 gm po 1x/day x 10 days or 750 mg po tid x 10 days (need to treat is dubious).	Alternatives: **Iodoquinol** 650 mg po tid x 20 days or **TMP-SMX-DS**, one bid x 7 days or **Nitazoxanide** 500 mg po bid x 3 days	Role as pathogen unclear; may serve as marker of exposure to contaminated food/water. Some genotypes may be more virulent.
Cryptosporidium parvum & hominis Treatment is unsatisfactory Ref.: Curr Opin Infect Dis 23:494, 2010	**Immunocompetent—No HIV: Nitazoxanide** 500 mg po bid x 3 days (expensive)	**HIV with immunodeficiency:** Effective antiretroviral therapy best therapy. **Nitazoxanide** no clinical or parasite response compared to placebo.	**Nitazoxanide:** Approved in liquid formulation for rx of children & 500 mg tabs for adults who are immunocompetent. Ref.: CID 40:1173, 2005. **C. hominis** assoc. with ↑ in post-infection eye & joint pain, recurrent headache, & dizzy spells (CID 39:504, 2004).
Cyclospora cayetanensis; cyclosporiasis (Clin Micro Rev 23:218, 2010)	**Immunocompetent pts: TMP-SMX-DS** tab 1 po bid x 7–10 days. Other options: see Comments.	**AIDS pts: TMP-SMX-DS** tab 1 po bid for up to 3-4 wks. Immunocompromised pts: may require suppressive rx with **TMP-SMX DS 1 tab 3x/wk**	If sulfa-allergic: **CIP** 500 mg po bid x 7 days but results inconsistent. Biliary disease described in HIV pts.
Dientamoeba fragilis See AJTMH 82:614, 2010; J Clin Microbiol pii: JCM.00400-16, 2016	**Iodoquinol**[a] 650 mg po tid x 20 days or **Paromomycin**[a] 25–35 mg/kg/day po in 3 div doses x 7 days or **Metronidazole** 750 mg tid x 10 days.	For treatment failures: **Tetracycline** 500 mg po qid x 10 days + **iodoquinol**[a] 650 mg po tid x 20 days OR (**Iodoquinol**[a] + **Paromomycin**[a]) May try second course of iodoquinol	**Metronidazole** failed in prospective random placebo-control DB study (CID 58:1692, 2014). In vitro tinidazole, metronidazole most active. AAC 56:487, 2012
Entamoeba histolytica; amebiasis. If available, use stool PCR for diagnosis.			
Asymptomatic cyst passer	**Paromomycin**[a] 25-35 mg/kg/day po in 3 divided doses x 7 days OR **Iodoquinol**[a] 650 mg po tid x 20 days.	**Diloxanide furoate**[a] (Furamide) 500 mg po tid x 10 days	Colitis can mimic ulcerative colitis; ameboma can mimic adenocarcinoma of colon.
Patient with diarrhea/dysentery; mild/moderate disease. Oral therapy possible	**Metronidazole** 500–750 mg po tid x 7–10 days or **Tinidazole** 2 gm po daily x 3 days, followed by: Either (**Paromomycin**[a] 25–35 mg/kg/day or divided in 3 doses x 7 days or **Iodoquinol**[a] 650 mg po tid x 20 days) to clear intestinal cysts. See Comments.		**Nitazoxanide** 500 mg po bid x 3 days may be effective (JID 184:381, 2001 & Tran R Soc Trop Med & Hyg 101:1025, 2007).
Severe or extraintestinal infection, e.g., hepatic abscess	(**Metronidazole** 750 mg **IV to po** tid x 10 days or **Tinidazole** 2 gm 1x/day x 5 days) followed by **Paromomycin**[a] 25–35 mg/kg/day po divided in 3 doses x 7 days or **Iodoquinol**[a] 650 mg po tid x 20 days.		Serology positive (antibody present) with extraintestinal disease.
Giardia duodenalis also known as **Giardia lamblia, Giardia intestinalis.**	**Tinidazole** 2 gm po x 1	**Metronidazole** 250 mg po tid x 5 days; **Nitazoxanide** 500 mg po bid x 3 days; **Albendazole** 400 mg po once daily po x 5 days. Cochrane Database Syst Rev.2012 Dec 12: 12:CD007787.	**Refractory pts:** Quinacrine 100 mg po tid x 5 days or (**metro 750 mg po + quinacrine 100 mg po**) or (**Paromomycin** 10 mg/kg po) 3x/day x 3 wks (CID 33:22, 2001) giardia genetically heterogeneous (J Clin Invest 123:2346, 2013). **Pregnancy: Paromomycin**[a] 25–35 mg/kg/day po in 3 divided doses x 5-10 days.

[a] For source of drug, see Table 13D, page 171.

TABLE 13A (2)

INFECTING ORGANISM	SUGGESTED REGIMENS		COMMENTS
	PRIMARY	ALTERNATIVE	
PROTOZOA—INTESTINAL *(continued)*			
Cystoisospora belli **(formerly Isospora belli)** Diagnosis requires special order: AFB stain of stool	**Immunocompetent: TMP-SMX-DS** tab 1 po bid x 7-10 days; **Immunocompromised: TMP-SMX-DS** tab 1 po bid for up to 4 wks. If CD4>200 may not respond; need ART.	CIP 500 mg po tid x 7 days is second-line alternative *(AnIM 132:885, 2000)* OR Pyrimethamine 50-75 mg/day + **Folinic acid** 10-25 mg/day (po).	**Chronic suppression in AIDS pts:** either **TMP-SMX-DS** 1 tab po 3x/wk OR tab 1 po daily OR **(Pyrimethamine** 25 mg/day po + **Folinic acid** 10 mg/day po) OR as 2nd-line alternative: CIP 500 mg po 3x/wk.
Microsporidiosis	*For HIV pts: antiretroviral therapy key*		
Ocular: Encephalitozoon hellum or cuniculi, Vittaforma (Nosema) corneae, Nosema ocularum	**Albendazole** 400 mg po bid x 3 wks plus fumagillin eye drops *(see Comment).*	In HIV+ pts, reports of response of E. hellum to **Fumagillin** eyedrops *(see Comment)*. For V. corneae, may need keratoplasty	To obtain fumagillin: 800-292-6773 or *www.leiterrx.com*. Neutropenia & thrombocytopenia with adverse events.
Intestinal (diarrhea): Enterocytozoon bieneusi (HIV), Encephalitozoon (Septata) intestinalis	**Albendazole** 400 mg po bid x 3 wks; peds dose: 15 mg/kg per day div. into 2 daily doses x 7 days for **E. intestinalis.** Fumagillin equally effective.	Oral **Fumagillin** 20 mg po tid reported effective for **E. bieneusi** *(NEJM 346:1963, 2002)*. *(See Comment).* Albendazole not effective.	Dx: Most labs use modified trichrome stain. Need electron micrographs for species identification. FA and PCR methods in development. Peds dose ref.: *PIDJ 23:915, 2004*
Disseminated: E. hellum, cuniculi or intestinalis; Pleistophora sp., *others in Comment. Ref: JCM 52:3839, 2014.*	**Albendazole** 400 mg po bid x 3 wks. Fumagillin 20 mg po tid (not available in US)	No established rx for Pleistophora sp.	For Trachipleistophora sp., try Itraconazole + albendazole *(NEJM 351:42, 2004)*. Other pathogens: Brachiola vesicularum & algerae *(NEJM 351:42, 2004)*.
PROTOZOA—EXTRAINTESTINAL			
Amebic meningoencephalitis *(Clin Infect Dis 51:e7, 2010 (Balamuthia))*. CDC has free living ameba program (+1 770-488-7100)			
Acanthamoeba sp.— no proven rx Rev.: *FEMS Immunol Med Micro 50:1, 2007*	Adult IV therapy: **(Pentamidine + Fluconazole) + Miltefosine** [a] 50 mg po tid. May add **TMP-SMX, Metronidazole, and Azithromycin**		For Acanthamoeba keratitis: miltefosine or voriconazole. Need brain tissue for dx.
Balamuthia mandrillaris	**Albendazole + (Fluconazole or Itraconazole) + Miltefosine**[a] 50 mg po tid.± **penicamidine** (poorly tolerated)		Need brain tissue for dx.
Naegleria fowleri. >95% mortality. Ref. *MMWR 57:573, 2008.*	**Amphotericin** B 1.5 mg/kg/day ± intrathecal + **Rifampin** 10 mg/kg/day + **Fluconazole** 10 mg/kg/day IV/po + **Miltefosine**[a] 50 mg po tid + **Azithromycin** 500 mg IV/po. Duration of therapy is empiric as there are few survivors		
Babesia microti (US) and **Babesia divergens** (EU) *(NEJM 366:366-2397, 2012)*	**For mild/moderate disease: Atovaquone** 750 mg po bid + **Azithro** 500 mg po on day 1, then 250-1000 mg po daily for total of 7-10 days. If relapse, treat x 6 wks & until blood smear neg x 2 wks.	**For severe babesiosis: (Clindamycin** 600 mg po tid) + **(Quinine** 550 mg po tid) ≤ 7-10 days For adults, can give **Clinda** IV x 1.2 gm tid.	Overwhelming infection in asplenic patients. In immunocompromised patients, treat for 6 or more weeks *(CID 46:370, 2008)*. Transfusion related cases occur.

[a] For source of drug, see *Table 13D, page 171.*

TABLE 13A (3)

INFECTING ORGANISM	SUGGESTED REGIMENS		COMMENTS
	PRIMARY	ALTERNATIVE	

PROTOZOA—EXTRAINTESTINAL *(continued)*

Leishmaniasis *(Suggest consultation – CDC (+1) 404-718-4745).* Therapy needs individualization according to species and many options for each manifestation. **Note: Miltefosine available directly from Profounda, Inc. (+1 407-270-7790), www.impavido.com.** Definitive guidelines from IDSA/ASTMH http://cid.oxfordjournals.org/content/early/2016/11/03/cid.ciw670.full and include geographic distribution maps for each species. Diagnosis of cutaneous disease: Sample full depth punch biopsy from raised edge of ulcer. PCR mandatory to speciate; culture and histology also available. Rapid diagnosis often possible using needle aspirate, slit skin smear, brushings, or scraping of lesion edge with giemsa staining. Serology not useful.

Cutaneous: Mild Disease 4 or less lesions (<1 cm or more), none > or = to 5 cm in diameter; no lesions in cosmetically sensitive areas, no lesions over joints or genitalia; may observe. Otherwise, consider Complex Disease which includes failure of previous treatment, or substantial local or lymphatic nodules, or large regional lymphadenopathy.	**Mild Disease** in travelers frequently responds to observation or local therapy and is preferred approach if patient agrees. **Paromomycin**[a] 15% paromomycin and 12% MBCL ointment bid x 10 days rest for 10 days and then 10 more days; intralesional Antimony up to 5 mL into lesions weekly x 8-10 wks with cryotherapy at end of each treatment. CDC antimony IND does not cover intralesional use, common outside US. **Alternative: Miltefosine** (w/food) 50 mg tid (wt 30-44 kg); 50 mg tid (wt ≥45 kg). Treat for 28 days.	**Moderate Disease:** **Sodium stibogluconate**[a] (Pentostam) or **Meglumine antimoniate** (Glucantime) 20 mg/kg/day Sb IV x 20 days. Dilute in 120 mL of D5W and infuse over 1-2 hrs OR Liposomal **Amphotericin B** (3 mg/kg IV once daily days 1-5 and 10. Alternatives: **Fluconazole** 200 mg po daily x 6 weeks (for L. mexicana, L. panamensis, L. major) or **Ketoconazole** 600 mg po daily x 30 days (L. mexicana) or **Miltefosine** (dose as for mild disease). Some experts use Ampho B 0.5-1 mg/kg IV daily or qod to total dose of 15-30 mg/kg	Observation, oral therapy, topical paromomycin[a] only when low potential for mucosal spread; never use for lesions of any severity which are or may be L. braziliensis, L. panamensis or L. guyanensis which always require therapy as per mucosal leishmaniasis below. Generic pentavalent antimony varies in quality and safety. Mild disease in travelers frequently responds to observation (CID 57:370, 2013) and is acceptable per IDSA/ASTMH guidelines. Monitor for gradual healing. Miltefosine is preg cat D (do not use in pregnancy).
	Response in about 70% of pts.		
Leishmaniasis, Mucosal (Espundia) All cutaneous lesions due to L. braziliensis, L. guyanensis, or L. panamensis is proven or possible.	**Cutaneous L. braziliensis of any severity:** ○ **[Sodium Stibogluconate** (Pentostam) or **Meglumine antimoniate** (Glucantime)] 20 mg/kg/ day IV/IM x 20 days ○ **Liposomal Ampho B** 3 (mg/kg) IV once daily days 1-5 and days 14, 21 or days 1-5 and 10. ○ **Mucosal: Pentavalent antimony (Sb)**[a] 20 mg/kg/day Sb IV x 28 days for mucosal disease, or **Liposomal Amphotericin B** (regimens vary) with total cumulative dose of 20-60 mg/kg or **Amphotericin B** 0.5-1 mg/kg IV daily or qod to total dose of 20.45 mg/kg.	**Miltefosine**[a] (w/food) 50 mg po bid (wt 30-44 kg); 50 mg tid x 28 days (wt ≥45 kg). Treat for 28 days. Complete resolution in 62% of pts.	Antimony available from CDC drug service. *See Table 13D for contact information.* Miltefosine has variable activity against mucosal disease according to geographic location. Expert consultation needed.
Visceral leishmaniasis (Kala-Azar) *New World & Old World* L. donovani: India, Africa L. infantum: Mediterranean L. chagasi: New World (identical to L. infantum)	*Immunocompetent:* Liposomal Ampho B 3 mg/kg once daily days 1-5 & days 14, 21 (increase to 40 mg/kg total dose for East African VL) HIV/AIDS: Liposomal Ampho B 4 mg/kg qd on days 1-5, 10, 17, 24, 31, 38 (Curr Opin Infect Dis 26:1, 2013).	**Standard Ampho B** 1 mg/kg IV daily x 15-20 days or qod x 8 wks (to total of 15-20 mg/kg) OR **pentavalent antimony**[a] 20 mg/kg/day IV x 28 days OR **Miltefosine**[a] (w/food) 50 mg po bid (wt 30-44 kg); 50 mg tid (wt ≥45 kg).	In HIV patients, need suppression with Amphotericin B q 2-4 wks. While CD4 remains <200, VL from South Asia is resistant to antimony. Miltefosine may be less effective against L. infantum-chagasi and less efficacy data for L. donovani in Africa.

* For source of drug, see *Table 13D, page 171.*

TABLE 13A (4)

PROTOZOA—EXTRAINTESTINAL *(continued)*

Malaria (Plasmodia species) —NOTE: CDC Malaria info— prophylaxis/treatment (770) 488-7788. After hours: 770-488-7100, US toll-free 1-855-856-4713. CDC offers species confirmation and drug resistance testing. Refs: JAMA 297:2251, 2264 & 2285, 2007. See: www.cdc.gov/malaria Review of rapid diagnostic tests: CID 54:1637, 2012.

Prophylaxis—Drugs plus personal protection: screens, nets, 30-35% DEET skin repellent (avoid >50% DEET) (JAMA 2016;316:766), permethrin spray on clothing and mosquito nets. Country risk in CDC Yellow Book.

INFECTING ORGANISM	SUGGESTED REGIMENS		COMMENTS
	PRIMARY	ALTERNATIVE	
For areas free of chloroquine (CQ)-resistant P. falciparum: Central America (west of Panama Canal), Caribbean, Korea, Middle East (most).	CQ phosphate 500 mg (300 mg base) po per wk starting 1-2 wks before travel, during travel, & 4 wks post-travel, **or Atovaquone-Proguanil (AP)** 1 adult tab per day (1 day prior to, during, & 7 days post-travel). Another option for P. vivax only countries: **Primaquine (PQ)** 30 mg base po daily in non-pregnant. G6PD-normal travelers: >92% effective vs P. vivax (CID 33:1990, 2001). Note: **CQ** may exacerbate psoriasis.	**CQ Peds dose:** 8.3 mg/kg (5 mg/kg of base) po 1x/wk up to 300 mg (base) max. dose or **AP** by weight (peds tabs): 5-8 kg ½ tab, 9-10 kg ¾ tab, 11-20 kg, 1 tab; 21-30 kg, 2 tabs; 31-40 kg, 3 tabs; >40 kg, 1 adult tab per day. **Adults: Doxy** or **MQ** as below.	**AP** must be taken with food for adequate absorption CQ safe during pregnancy. **The areas free of CQ-resistant falciparum malaria continue to shrink** See CDC or WHO maps for most current information on CQ resistance. **Doxy** AEs: photosensitivity, candida vaginitis, gastritis.
For areas with CQ-resistant P. falciparum Details on considerations for malaria prophylaxis: N Engl J Med. 2016; 375:247.	Atovaquone 250 mg—Proguanil 100 mg **(Malarone)** comb. tablet, 1 per day with food 1-2 days prior to, during, & 7 days post-travel. **Not** in pregnancy. Malarone preferred for trips of a week or less; expense may preclude use for longer trips. Native population: intermittent pregnancy prophylaxis/treatment programs in a few countries. Fansidar 1 tab po 3 times during pregnancy (Expert Rev Anti Infect Ther 8:589, 2010).	Doxycycline 100 mg po daily for adults & children >8 yrs of age. Take 1-2 days before, during, & for 4 wks after travel. OR **Mefloquine (MQ)** 250 mg (228 mg base) po once per wk, 1-2 wks before, during, & for 4 wks after travel (see Comment). **Doxy:** 2.2 mg/kg po per day,(max 100 mg/day **MFQ:** ≤9 kg: 5 mg/kg weekly (4.6 mg/kg base) 10-19 kg: ¼ adult tab weekly 20-30 kg: ½ tab weekly 31-45 kg: ¾ tab weekly >45 kg: 1 tab weekly **Doxy** AEs: photosensitivity, candida vaginitis, gastritis.	**Pregnancy: MQ** current best option. Insufficient data with **Malarone.** Avoid **doxycycline** and **primaquine.** **Primaquine.** Can cause hemolytic anemia **if** G6PD deficiency present. **MQ** not recommended if cardiac conduction abnormalities, seizures, or psychiatric disorders, e.g., depression, psychosis. If used, can start 3 wks before travel to assure tolerability. Children: Weekly dosing may make MFQ preferable. For children under 10 kg, liquid is available. For children under 10 kg. MFQ needs to be compounded but AP pediatric tablets can be cut.

ᵃ For source of drug, see Table 13D, page 171.

TABLE 13A (5)

INFECTING ORGANISM	SUGGESTED REGIMENS		COMMENTS
	PRIMARY	ALTERNATIVE	

PROTOZOA—EXTRAINTESTINAL/Malaria (Plasmodium species) (continued)

Treatment of Malaria. Diagnosis is by microscopy. Alternative: rapid antigen detection test (Binax NOW); detects 96-100% of P. falciparum and 50% of other plasmodia (CID 49:908, 2009; CID 54:1637, 2012). Need microscopy to speciate. Can stay positive for over a month after successful treatment.

Uncomplicated P. falciparum (or species unidentified) Treatment for adults (except in pregnancy) for all malaria species. E.g., Artemether-Lumefantrine. 2015 WHO Guidelines suggest artemisinin combination therapy for all malaria species. E.g., Artemether-Lumefantrine.

INFECTING ORGANISM	PRIMARY	ALTERNATIVE	COMMENTS
Acquired in Cen. Amer., west of Panama Canal; Haiti, Dom. Repub., & most of Mid-East CQ sensitive	**Adults:** CQ phosphate 1 gm salt (600 mg base) po, then 0.5 gm in 6 hrs, then 0.5 gm daily x 2 days. Total: 2500 mg salt	**Peds:** CQ 10 mg/kg of base po; then 5 mg/kg of base at 6, 24, & 48 hrs. Total: 25 mg/kg base	Other chloroquine salts available in some countries, total dose may differ. **Peds: dose should never exceed adult dose. CQ + MQ prolong QTc. Doses >2x recommended may be fatal.**

CQ-resistant or unknown resistance. Note: If >5% parasitemia or Hb <7, treat as severe malaria regardless of clinical findings or lack thereof.	**Adults: Atovaquone-Proguanil** 1 gm =400 mg (4 adult tabs) po 1x/day x 3 days w/ food OR
	
	[QS 650 mg po tid x 3 days (7 days if SE Asia)] + ([Doxy 100 mg po bid) or (Tetra 250 mg po qid) or Clinda 20 mg/kg/d divided tid) x 7 days] OR
	
	Artemether-Lumefantrine° tabs 20/120 mg: 4 tabs po (at 0, 8 hrs) then bid x 2 days (total 6 doses); take with food OR
	
	a less desirable adult alternative, **Mefloquine** 750 mg po x 1 dose, then 500 mg po x 1 dose 6-12 hr later. **MQ** is 2nd line alternative due to resistance. Clinda or Tetra only if doxy not available.
	
	Available in Europe and endemic countries, WHO pre-qualified and EMA approved, **Dihydroartemisinin-piperaquine**
	5 to <7 kg PPQ 80 mg/DHA 10 mg po q24h x3 days
	7 to <13 kg PPQ 160 mg/DHA 20 mg po q24h x3 days
	13 to <24 kg PPQ 320 mg/DHA 40 mg po q24h x3 days
	24 to <36 kg PPQ 640 mg/DHA 80 mg po q24h x3 days
	36 to <75 kg PPQ 960 mg/DHA 160 mg po q24h
	                x3 days
	75 to 100 kg PPQ 1280 mg/DHA 160 mg po q24h
	                x3 days
	>100 kg no data
	
	Available in many endemic countries, and WHO qualified and EMA approved ACT is **Pyronaridine/ Artesunate** 2 tablets (180 mg/60 mg) as a single dose each day for 3 days for 24 to >45 kg or 1 tablet if 20 to <24 kg.
	Pediatric granule formulation for oral suspension (60 mg/20 mg)
	• 5 – <8 kg 1 sachet Daily for 3 days
	• 8 – <15 kg 2 sachets Daily for 3 days
	• 15 – <20 kg 3 sachets Daily for 3 days
		Peds: (QS 10 mg/kg po tid x 3 days) + (Clinda 20 mg/kg per day div. tid) —both x 7 days.
		Use **Doxy** >8 yrs of age 2.2 mg/kg bid up to 100 mg per dose OR **Atovaquone-Proguanil** (all once daily x 3 d) by weight:
		• 5-8 kg: 2 peds tabs;
		• 9-10 kg: 3 peds tabs;
		• 11-20 kg: 1 adult tab;
		• 21-30 kg: 2 adult tabs;
		• 31-40 kg: 3 adult tabs.
		• >40 kg: 4 adult tabs.
		OR **MQ** 15 mg/kg x 1, then 6-12 hrs later, 10 mg/kg ALL po.
		
		OR **Artemether-Lumefantrine°**
		• 5 kg to <15 kg: 1 tablet (20 mg/120 mg) as a single dose, then 1 tablet again after 8 hours, then 1 tablet every 12 hours for 2 days
		• 15 kg to <25 kg: 2 tablets (40 mg/240 mg) as a single dose, then 2 tablets again after 8 hours, then 2 tablets every 12 hours for 2 days
		• 25 kg to <35 kg: 3 tablets (60 mg/360 mg) as a single dose, then 3 tablets again after 8 hours, then 3 tablets every 12 hours for 2 days
		• ≥35 kg: as per adult dose
			Pregnancy:
			• **Artemether-Lumefantrine** 4 tablets (80 mg/ 480 mg) as a single dose, then 4 tablets again after 8 hours, then 4 tablets every 12 hours for 2 days (take with food)). Drug of choice in 2nd/3rd trimester. Artemether-Lumefantrine is safer than quinine in the first trimester of pregnancy (Malar. J. 13:192, 2014). Lumefantrine appears safe (Malar J 14:77, 2015) and is safer than quinine in the first trimester of pregnancy (Malaria J 13:192 2014) and PLoS Med. 2017;14(5):e1002290 and is recommended by experts in the list trimester but not yet in official guidelines
			OR
			• **Quinine sulfate** 10 mg/kg po tid x 3 days (7 days if SE Asia)+ clindamycin 20 mg/kg/day divided tid x 7 days
			Do not delay therapy if quinine available and Artemether-Lumefantrine is not in U.S.. QS is only available as quinine 324 mg capsule, thus hard to use to treat children.
			Note: Oral Artemether-Lumefantrine tabs FDA-approved but not widely stocked.
			Call 1-800-COARTEM to obtain.
			Wt <20 kg: 3 mg/kg; Wt >20 kg: 2.4 mg/kg.

° For source of drug, see Table 13D, page 171.

TABLE 13A (6)

PROTOZOA—EXTRAINTESTINAL/Malaria (Plasmodia species)/Treatment of Malaria *(continued)*

INFECTING ORGANISM	SUGGESTED REGIMENS		COMMENTS
	PRIMARY	ALTERNATIVE	
Uncomplicated/P. malariae or P. knowlesi *(JID 199: 1107 & 1143, 2009).* All regions – CQ-sensitive	CQ as above for adults & peds. In South Pacific, beware of P. knowlesi: looks like P. malariae, but behaves like P. falciparum *(CID 46:165, 2007).*	**Artemether-Lumefantrine**[a] *(20/120 mg tab)* 4 tabs po x 1 dose, repeat 1r 8 hrs, then repeat q12h x 2 days (take with food) OR **Atovaquone-Proguanil** *(1000/ 400 mg)* 4 adult tabs po daily x 3 days or DHA-PPQ or **Pyronaridine-artesunate**	PQ added to eradicate latent parasites in liver. **Screen for G6PD def. before starting PQ:** If G6PD deficient dose PQ as 45 mg once weekly x 8 wks. **Note: rare severe reactions.** CQ safe in pregnancy. Avoid PQ in pregnancy.
Uncomplicated/P. vivax or P. ovale **CQ-sensitive** (except Papua New Guinea, Indonesia which are CQ-resistant–*see below*)	**Adults:** CQ as above + **PQ base:** 30 mg po once daily x 14 days Each primaquine phosphate tab is 26.3 mg of salt and 15 mg of base. 30 mg of base = 2 26.3 mg tabs prim. phos.	**Adults:** CQ as above + **PQ base:** 0.5 mg po once daily x 14 days or **Artemether-Lumefantrine** or DHA-PPQ or **Pyronaridine-artesunate** as above + PQ base 0.5 mg po once daily x 14 days	If P. vivax or P. ovale, after pregnancy check for G6PD deficiency & give PQ 30 mg po daily times 14 days.
Uncomplicated/P. vivax **CQ-resistant:** Papua, New Guinea & Indonesia	**Adults: [QS + (doxy or tetra) + PQ]** as above or **Artemether-Lumefantrine** or DHA-PPQ (same dose as for P. falciparum)	**Adults: MQ + PQ** as above. **Peds:** <8 yrs old): **QS** alone x 7 days or **MQ** alone. If latter fail, add **Doxr** or **Tetra**	Rarely acute. Lung injury and other serious complications. *LnID 8:449, 2008.* If pregnant treat as for uncomplicated P. falciparum in pregnancy.
Severe malaria, i.e., impaired consciousness, severe anemia, renal failure, pulmonary edema, ARDS, DIC, jaundice, acidosis, seizures, parasitemia >5%. One or more of latter. **Almost always P. falciparum.** *Ref: NEJM 358:1829, 2008; Science 320-30, 2008.* **All regions** **Note:** • IV Artesunate is drug of choice but not FDA-approved. Available from CDC Drug Service under specific conditions, need to state quinidine not available or not tolerated. • IV quinidine uncommonly available. Possible emergency availability from Eli Lilly.	**Adults:** Quinidine gluconate in normal saline: 10 mg/kg (salt) IV over 1 hr then 0.02 mg/ kg/min by constant Infusion OR 24 mg/kg IV over 4 hrs & then 12 mg/kg over 4 hrs q8h. Continue until parasite density <1% & can take po QS. QS 650 mg po tid x 3 days (7 days if SE Asia) OR **Artesunate**[a] 2.4 mg/kg IV at 0, 12, 24, 48 hrs, and **Doxy** 100 mg IV q12h x 7 days). IV quinine dihydrochloride still available in many endemic countries but second line only to be used if no IV artemisinin is available. Dosing is complicated and don't think we need to include.	**Peds:** Quinidine gluconate IV—same mg/mg dose as for adults **PLUS** (**Doxy:** if <45 kg, 4 mg per kg IV q12h; if >45 kg, dose as for adults) OR (**Clinda**, **Clindamycin** 10 mg/kg IV loading dose, then 5 mg/kg IV or po (as tolerated) q8h x 7 days Follow IV **Artesunate** with a complete oral (course of one of: **Atovaquone/Proguanil**, **Artemether/Lumefantrine**, **Dihydroartemisinin/piperaquine** (not available in US). **Docy** 100 mg q12h is less preferred alternative	During quinidine IV: monitor BP, EKG (prolongation of QTc), & blood glucose (hypoglycemia). Exchange transfusion no longer recommended. Switch to QS po (Doxy, Clinda) when patient able to take oral drugs. **Steroids not recommended for cerebral malaria.** IV Artesunate from CDC (8 hr transport time post-approval), *see Table 13D (Ref: CID 44:1067 & 1075, 2007).* Can cause non-life threatening, but transfusion requiring, hemolytic anemia up to 15 days post-therapy *(AnIM 163:498, 2015).*
Malaria–self-initiated treatment: Only for people at high risk. Carry a reliable supply of recommended treatment (to avoid counterfeit meds). Use only if malaria is lab-diagnosed and no available reliable meds.	**Artemether-Lumefantrine** *(20/120 mg tab)* 4 tabs po x 1 dose, repeat 1r 8 hrs, then repeat q12h x 2 days (take with food) OR **Atovaquone-proguanil (AP)** 4 adult tabs (1 gm/400 mg) po daily x 3 days	**Peds:** Using: adult AP tabs for 3 consecutive days: 11-20 kg, 1 tab; 21-30 kg, 2 tabs; 31-40 kg, 3 tabs; >41 kg, 4 tabs. For Peds dosing of Artemether-Lumefantrine, see *Uncomplicated/P. falciparum, page 158.*	Do not use for renal insufficiency pts. Do not use if weight <11 kg, pregnant, or breast-feeding. **Artemether-Lumefantrine:** sold as Rialmet (EU) and Coartem (US & elsewhere).

[a] For source of drug, see *Table 13D, page 171.*

TABLE 13A (7)

INFECTING ORGANISM	SUGGESTED REGIMENS		COMMENTS
	PRIMARY	ALTERNATIVE	
PROTOZOA—EXTRAINTESTINAL *(continued)*			
Toxoplasma gondii (Toxoplasmosis) (Reference: *Ln 363:1965, 2004*)			
Immunologically normal patients *(For pediatric doses, see reference)*			
Acute illness w/ lymphadenopathy	No specific rx unless severe/persistent symptoms or evidence of vital organ damage.		
Acq. via transfusion (lab accident)	Treat as for active chorioretinitis.		
Active chorioretinitis; meningitis; lowered resistance due to steroids or cytotoxic drugs	[Pyrimethamine (pyri) 200 mg po once on 1st day, then 50–75 mg po q24h] + [Sulfadiazine (see footnote) S 1–1.5 gm po qid) + [Leucovorin (folinic acid) 5–20 mg 3x/wk)—see Comment] Treat 1–2 wks beyond resolution of signs/symptoms; continue leucovorin 1 wk after stopping pyri.		For congenital Toxo, Toxo meningitis in adults, & chorioretinitis, add prednisone 1 mg/kg/day in 2 div. doses until CSF protein conc. falls or vision-threatening inflammation subsides. Adjust folinic acid dose by following CBC results. Screen patients with IgG/IgM serology at commercial lab. IgG+ /IgM neg = remote past infection; IgG+/IgM+ = seroconversion. For Spiramycin, consult with Palo Alto Medical Foundation Toxoplasma Serology Lab: 650-853-4828 or toxlab@pamf.org. Details in *Ln 363:1965, 2004*. Consultation advisable.
Acute in pregnant women. Ref: *CID 47:554, 2008.*	If <18 wks gestation at diagnosis: Spiramycin¹ 1 gm po q8h until 16–18 wks; dc if amniotic fluid PCR is negative. Positive PCR: treat as below. If >18 wks gestation & documented fetal infection by positive amniotic fluid PCR: (Pyrimethamine 50 mg po q12h x 2 days, then 50 mg/day + Sulfadiazine 75 mg/kg po x 1 dose, then 50 mg/kg q12h (max 4 gm/day) + Folinic acid 10–20 mg po daily) for minimum of 4 wks or for duration of pregnancy.		
Fetal/congenital	Mgmt complex. Combo rx with pyrimethamine + sulfadiazine + leucovorin—see Comment		
AIDS			
Cerebral toxoplasmosis Ref: *MMWR 58(RR-4) 1, 2009.*	[Pyrimethamine (pyri) 200 mg x 1 po, then 75 mg/day po] + (Sulfadiazine [Wt based dose: 1 gm if <60 kg, 1.5 gm if ≥60 kg] po q6h) + (Folinic acid 10–25 mg/day po) for minimum of 6 wks after resolution of signs/ symptoms, and then suppressive rx (see below) OR TMP-SMX 10/50 mg/kg per day po or IV div q12h x 30 days (AAC 42:1346, 1998)	[Pyri + Folinic acid (as in primary regimen) + 1 of the following: (1) Clinda 600 mg po/IV q6h or (2) TMP-SMX 5/25 /Kg/day po or IV bid or (3) Atovaquone 750 mg po q6h. Treat 4–6 wks after resolution of signs/symptoms, then suppression.	Use alternative regimen for pts with severe sulfa allergy. If multiple ring-enhancing brain lesions (CT or MRI), >85% of pts respond to 7–10 days of empiric rx; if no response, suggest brain biopsy. Pyri penetrates brain even if no inflammation; folinic acid prevents pyrimethamine hematologic toxicity.
Primary prophylaxis, AIDS pts—IgG Toxo antibody + CD4 count <100) per mcL	(TMP-SMX-DS, 1 tab po q24h or 3x/wk) or (TMP-SMX-SS, 1 tab po q24h)	(Dapsone 50 mg po q24h) + (Pyri 50 mg po q wk) + (Folinic acid 25 mg po q wk) OR Atovaquone 1500 mg po q24h	Prophylaxis for pneumocystis also effective vs Toxo. Ref: *MMWR 58(RR-4):1, 2009.* Another alternative: (Dapsone 200 mg po + pyrimethamine 75 mg po + folinic acid 25 mg po) once weekly.
Suppression after rx of cerebral Toxo	(Sulfadiazine 2–4 gm po divided in 2–4 doses/day) + (Pyri 25–50 mg po q24h) + (Folinic acid 10–25 mg po q24h). DC if CD4 count >200 x 3 mos	((Clinda 600 mg po q8h) + (Pyri 25–75 mg po q24h)) OR Atovaquone 750 mg po q6–12h	(Pyri + sulfa) prevents PCP and Toxo; (clinda + pyri) prevents Toxo only. Additional drug needed to prevent PCP.
Trichomonas vaginalis	*See Vaginitis, Table 1, page 26.*		

¹ Sulfonamides for Toxo. Sulfadiazine now commercially available. Sulfisoxazole much less effective.

* For source of drug, see *Table 13D, page 171.*

TABLE 13A (8)

INFECTING ORGANISM	SUGGESTED REGIMENS		COMMENTS
	PRIMARY	ALTERNATIVE	
PROTOZOA—EXTRAINTESTINAL (continued)			
Trypanosomiasis, Ref: *Ln 362:1469, 2003.* Note: Drugs for African trypanosomiasis may be obtained free from WHO or CDC. See *Table 13D, page 171,* for source information.			
West African sleeping sickness (T. brucei gambiense)			
Early: Blood/lymphatic—CNS OK	Pentamidine 4 mg/kg IV/IM daily x 7-10 days		Suramin effective but avoid if possible due to possible co-infection with O. volvulus in W. Africa.
		In US, free from CDC drug service: **Suramin**[a] 100 mg IV (test dose), then 1 gm IV on days 1, 3, 7, 14, & 21. Peds dose is 20 mg/kg.	
Late: Encephalitis	Combination of IV **Eflornithine**[a] 400 mg/kg/day divided q12h x 7 days, plus **Nifurtimox**[a] 15 mg/kg/day po, divided q8h x 10 days (abbreviated NECT, now WHO standard of care. (*Lancet 374:56, 2009; CID 56:195 2013*)	**Melarsoprol**[a] 2.2 mg/kg/day IV x 10 days; toxic arsenical now superseded by NECT	
East African sleeping sickness (T. brucei rhodesiense)			
Early: Blood/lymphatic	**Suramin**[a] 100 mg IV (test dose), then 1 gm IV on days 1, 3, 7, 14, & 21	Peds: **Suramin**[a] 2 mg/kg test dose, then 20 mg/kg IV on days 1, 3, 7, 14 & 21	Suramin & Melarsoprol: CDC Drug Service or WHO (at no charge). (*See Table 13D*).
Late: Encephalitis (prednisolone may prevent encephalitis) Pre-treatment with Suramin advised by some.	**Melarsoprol**[a] 2.2 mg/kg/day IV x 10 days (*PLoS NTD 6:e1695, 2012*)		Early illness: patient waiting for Suramin, use pentamidine 4 mg/kg/day IV/IM x 1-2 doses. Does not enter CSF.
T. cruzi–Chagas disease or acute American trypanosomiasis Ref: *NEJM 373:456, 2015.* For chronic disease: no benefit in established cardiomyopathy (*NEJM 373:1295, 2015*)	*Adult (Age ≥12 years):* **Benznidazole**[a] 5-7 mg kg/day po in 2 doses (q12h) *Pediatric (Age <12 years):* **Benznidazole**[a] 7.5 mg/kg/day po in 2 doses (q12h) x 60 days. New pediatric tablet formulator (LAFEPE and ELEA) not widely available.	**Nifurtimox**[a] 8-10 mg/kg per day po div. 4x/day after meals x 120 days; Ages 11-16 yrs: 12.5-15 mg/kg per day div. qid po x 90 days; Children <11yrs: 15-20 mg/kg per day div. qid po x 90 days. For AEs: *Table 13B* Ref: *CID 2016:63-1056*	Due to adverse effects may give Benznidazole 300 mg per day for 60 days, regardless of body weight OR give 300 mg per day but prolong treatment to complete the total dose corresponding to 5 mg/kg per day for 60 days. *N Engl J Med 373:456, 2015.* Immunosuppression for heart transplant can reactivate chronic Chagas disease. Can transmit by organ/transfusions. Do not use benznidazole in pregnancy.
NEMATODES—INTESTINAL (Roundworms). Eosinophilia? Think Strongyloides, toxocariasis and filariasis: *CID 54:407, 2005; 4:1781 & 1655, 2006— See Table 13C.*			
Anisakis simplex (anisakiasis) Anisakiasis differentiated from Anisakidosis (*CID 51:806, 2010*). Other: A. physalary, Pseudoterranova decipiens.	Physical removal: endoscope or surgery. IgE antibody test vs A. simplex may help diagnosis. No antimicrobial therapy.	Anecdotal reports of possible treatment benefit from albendazole (*Ln 360:54, 2002; CID 41:1825, 2005*)	Anisakiasis acquired by eating raw fish: herring, salmon, mackerel, cod, squid. Similar illness due to Pseudoterranova species acquired from cod, halibut, red snapper.
Ascaris lumbricoides (ascariasis) *Ln 367:1521, 2006*	**Albendazole** 400 mg po x 1 dose OR **Mebendazole** 100 mg po bid X 3 days or 500 mg po x 1 dose	**Ivermectin** 150-200 mcg/kg po x 1 dose	Review of efficacy of single dose: *JAMA 299:1937, 2008.* Mebendazole 500 mg tabs not widely available.
Capillaria philippinensis (capillariasis)	**Mebendazole** 400 mg po bid x 10 days	**Albendazole** 500 mg po daily x 20 days	Albendazole preferred.
Enterobius vermicularis (pinworm)	**Mebendazole** 500 mg po x 1 dose, repeat in 2 weeks OR **Pyrantel pamoate** 11 mg/kg base (to max. dose of 1 gm) po x 1 dose; repeat in 2 wks	**Albendazole** 400 mg po x 1 dose, repeat in 2 wks.	Side-effects in *Table 13B, page 169.* Treat whole household.
Gnathostomiasis (adult worms in oral mucosa)	Surgical removal	**Albendazole** 400 mg/day po x 3 days	Ref: *CID 32:1378, 2001; J Helminth 80:425, 2005.*

[a] For source of drug, see *Table 13D, page 171.*

TABLE 13A (9)

INFECTING ORGANISM	SUGGESTED REGIMENS		COMMENTS
	PRIMARY	ALTERNATIVE	
NEMATODES—INTESTINAL (Roundworms) *(continued)*			
Hookworm (Necator americanus and Ancylostoma duodenale)	Albendazole 400 mg po daily x 3 days	Mebendazole 500 mg po daily x 3 days OR **Pyrantel pamoate** 11 mg/kg (to max. dose of 1 gm) po daily x 3 days	**NOTE:** Ivermectin not effective. Single dose therapy as used in public health programs has lower cure rates and 3-day albendazole superior to 3-day mebendazole, *PLoS One 6:e25003, 2011.*
Strongyloides stercoralis (strongyloidiasis) *(Hyperinfection, See Comment)*	Ivermectin 200 mcg/kg per day po x 2 days	Albendazole 400 mg po bid x 7 days ; less effective	**For hyperinfections,** repeat at 15 days. For hyperinfection: veterinary ivermectin given subcutaneously or rectally *(CID 49:1411, 2009).*
Strongylus orientalis, T. colubriformis	Pyrantel pamoate 11 mg/kg (maximum 1 gm) po x 1 dose OR Albendazole 400 mg po daily x 10 doses OR Mebendazole 500 mg po qd x 10 days	Albendazole 400 mg po x 1 dose	
Trichuris trichiura (whipworm) *NEJM 370:610, 2014; PLoS One 6:e25003, 2011*	Mebendazole 100 mg po twice daily x 3 days	Albendazole 400 mg po qd x 3 days or **Ivermectin** 200 mcg/kg po qd x 3 days	Mebendazole clearly superior for trichurs *(PLoS One,6:e25003, 2011; N Engl J Med 370:610, 2014).* Single dose Mebendazole 500 mg tab significantly less effective than 3 days (the references quoted currently support this).
NEMATODES—EXTRAINTESTINAL (Roundworms)			
Ancylostoma braziliense & caninum: causes **cutaneous larva migrans**	Albendazole 400 mg po bid x 3-7 days *(Ln ID 8:302, 2008).*	Ivermectin 200 mcg/kg po x 1 dose/day x 1–2 days (not in children if <15 kg)	Also called "creeping eruption", dog and cat hookworm. Ivermectin cure rate 81–100% (1 dose) to 97% (2–3 doses) *(CID 31:493, 2000).*
Angiostrongylus cantonensis (Angiostrongyliasis); causes eosinophilic meningitis	Mild/moderate disease: Analgesics; serial LPs (if necessary). Prednisone 60 mg/day x 14 days reduces headache & need for LPs.	Adding **Albendazole** 15 mg/kg/day to prednisone 60 mg/day both for 14 days may reduce duration of headaches and need for repeat LPs.	**Do not use Albendazole without prednisone,** see *TRSMH 102:990, 2008.* Gnathostoma and Baylisascaris also cause eosinophilic meningitis.
Baylisascariasis (Raccoon roundworm); eosinophilic meningitis	No drug proven efficacious. Try po **Albendazole,** Peds: 25–50 mg/kg/day po; Adults: 400 mg po bid with corticosteroids. Treat for one month.		*Clin Microbiol Rev. 29:375, 2016.* Other causes of eosinophilic meningitis: Gnathostoma & Angiostrongylus.
Dracunculus medinensis: Guinea worm *(Trans R Soc Trop Med Hyg 108:249, 2014)*	Slow extraction of pre-emergent worm over several days	No drugs effective. Oral analgesics, anti-inflammatory drugs, topical antiseptics/antibiotic ointments to alleviate symptoms and facilitate worm removal by gentle manual traction over several days.	
Filariasis: Determine if co-infection with either Loa loa or Onchocerca			
Lymphatic filariasis (Elephantiasis): Etiologies: Wuchereria bancrofti Brugia malayi, Brugia timori	*Mono-infection:* **Diethylcarbamazine" (DEC)*** 6 mg/kg/day po in 3 divided doses x 12 days + **Doxy** 200 mg/day po x 6 wks	*Dual infection with Onchocerciasis:* Treat Onchocerciasis first: **Ivermectin** 150 mcg/kg po x 1 dose, wait 1 month, then start **DEC** as for mono-infection *Dual infection with Loa:* DEC drug of choice for both but can cause severe encephalopathy if >2500 Loa Loa microfilaria/mL in blood. Refer to expert center for apheresis pre-DEC or prednisone + small doses of DEC. If <2500 microfilaria/mL, start regular dose of DEC	**Doxy x 6 wks may improve mild/moderate lymphedema independent of parasite infection** *(CID 55:621, 2012).* **Note: DEC can cause irreversible eye damage if concomitant Onchocerciasis.**

² May need antihistamine or corticosteroid for allergic reaction from disintegrating organisms.

* For source of drug, see *Table 13D, page 171.*

TABLE 13A (10)

INFECTING ORGANISM	SUGGESTED REGIMENS		COMMENTS
	PRIMARY	ALTERNATIVE	
NEMATODES—EXTRAINTESTINAL (Roundworms)/Filariasis (continued)			
Loiasis, Loa loa, eye worm disease: Look for dual infection with either Onchocerciasis or Lymphatic Filariasis			
	Mono-infection with <2500 L. loa microfilaria/mL: DEC 8-10 mg/kg/day po in 3 divided doses x 21 days *Mono-infection with >2500 L. loa microfilaria/mL:* Refer to expert center for apheresis prior to DEC therapy; alternatively: Albendazole 200 mg bid x 21 days	*Dual infection with Lymphatic Filariasis:* See Lymphatic filariasis, above *Dual infection with Onchocerciasis:* Treat Onchocerciasis first with ivermectin, then treat L. loa with DEC	If >5000 L. loa microfilaria/mL in blood & given ivermectin for Onchocerciasis, can facilitate entry of L. loa into CNS with severe encephalopathy. May require multiple 21 day courses of DEC to clear mono-infection
Onchocerca volvulus (Onchocerciasis), river blindness: Look for dual infection with either Loa loa or Lymphatic Filariasis			
	Mono-infection: Ivermectin 150 mcg/kg x 1 dose, then repeat every 3-6 months until asymptomatic + Doxy 200 mg/day x 6 wks. No accepted alternative therapy.	*Dual infection with Lymphatic filariasis:* See Lymphatic filariasis, above *Dual infection with L. loa:* Treat Onchocerciasis first with ivermectin, then treat L. loa with DEC. If >5000 L. Loa microfilaria/mL in blood. Refer to expert center for apheresis before starting DEC	Onchocerciasis and Loa loa are mildly co-endemic in West and Central Africa.
Body cavity			
Mansonella perstans	In randomized trial, doxy 200 mg po once daily x 6 weeks cleared microfilaria from blood in 67 of 69 patients (NEJM 361:1448, 2009). Doxy may not work outside Mali and Cameroon due to strain variation.	Albendazole in high dose x 3 weeks. Doxy may not work outside Mali and Cameroon due to strain variation.	Efficacy of doxy believed to be due to inhibition of endosymbiont wolbachia. Ivermectin has no activity. Ref: Trans R Soc Trop Med Hyg 100:458, 2006.
Mansonella streptocerca	Ivermectin 150 μg/kg x 1 dose.	Diethylcarbamazine 6 mg/kg x 12 days kills microfilaria in adults but causes transient exacerbation of clinical symptoms and may cause vision loss and hypotension if co-infected with O. volvulus.	May need antihistamine or corticosteroid for allergic reaction from disintegrating organisms. Chronic pruritic hypopigmented lesions that may be confused with leprosy. Can be asymptomatic.
Mansonella ozzardi	Ivermectin 200 μ/kg x 1 dose may be effective. Limited data but no other option. Am J Trop Med Hyg 90:1170, 2014	Usually asymptomatic. Articular pain, pruritus, lymphadenopathy reported. May have allergic reaction from dying organisms.	
Dirofilariasis: Heartworms			
D. immitis, dog heartworm	No effective drugs; surgical removal only option		Can lodge in pulmonary artery → coin lesion. Eosinophilia rare.
D. tenuis (raccoon), D. ursi (bear), D. repens (dogs, cats)	No effective drugs	Worms migrate to conjunctivae, subcutaneous tissue, scrotum, breasts, extremities. D. repens emerging throughout Europe Clin Microbiol Rev 25:507, 2012	
Gnathostoma spingerum			
Cutaneous larva migrans	Albendazole 400 mg po q24h or bid times 21 days	Ivermectin 200 μg/kg/day po x 2 days.	Other etiology of larva migrans: Ancylostoma sp., see page 162
Eosinophilic meningitis	Supportive care; monitor for cerebral hemorrhage	Case reports of steroid use: both benefit and harm from Albendazole or ivermectin (EIN 17:1174, 2011).	Other causes of eosinophilic meningitis: Angiostrongylus (see page 162) & Baylisascaris (see page 162)

^a For source of drug, see *Table 13D, page 171.*

TABLE 13A (11)

INFECTING ORGANISM	SUGGESTED REGIMENS		COMMENTS
	PRIMARY	ALTERNATIVE	
NEMATODES—EXTRAINTESTINAL (Roundworms) (continued)			
Rx directed at relief of symptoms as infection self-limited; use of anthelmintics controversial.			
Toxocariasis (Ann Trop Med Parasit 103:3, 2010)	Albendazole 400 mg po bid x 5 days ± **Prednisone** 60 mg/day	Mebendazole 100–200 mg po bid times 5 days	Severe lung, heart or CNS disease may warrant steroids (Clin Micro Rev 16:265, 2003). Differential dx of larval migrans syndromes: Toxocara canis & catis, Ancylostoma spp., Gnathostoma spp., Spirometra spp.
Visceral larval migrans			
Ocular larval migrans	First 4 wks of illness: (Oral **Prednisone** 30–60 mg po q24h + subtenon **Triamcinolone** 40 mg/wk) x 2 wks (Surgery is sometimes necessary)		No added benefit of anthelmintic drugs. Rx of little effect after 4 wks. Some use steroids (Clin Micro Rev 16:265, 2003).
Trichinella spiralis (**Trichinellosis**) — muscle infection (Review: Clin Micro Rev 22:127, 2009).	Albendazole 400 mg po bid x 8–14 days	Mebendazole 500 mg po tid x 10 days (still with concomitant prednisone)	Use albendazole/mebendazole with caution during pregnancy. ↑ IgE, ↑ CPK, ESR 0, massive eosinophilia: >5000/µL.
	Concomitant **prednisone** 40–60 mg po q24h.		
TREMATODES (Flukes) — Liver, Lung, Intestinal. All flukes have snail intermediate hosts; transmitted by ingestion of metacercariae on plants, fish or crustaceans.			
Liver flukes: Clonorchis sinensis, Metorchis conjunctus, Opisthorchis viverrini	Praziquantel 25 mg/kg po tid x 2 days	Albendazole 10 mg/kg per day po x 7 days	Same dose in children
Fasciola hepatica (sheep liver fluke), Fasciola gigantica	Triclabendazole[a] once, may repeat after 12–24 hrs. 10 mg/kg po x 1 dose. Single 20 mg/kg po dose effective in treatment failures.		
Intestinal flukes: Fasciola buski Heterophyes heterophyes; Metagonimus yokogawai, Nanophyetus salmincola	Praziquantel 25 mg/kg po tid x 1 days		Same dose in children
Lung fluke: Paragonimus sp.	Praziquantel 25 mg/kg po tid x 2 days	Triclabendazole[a] 10 mg/kg po x 2 doses over 12–24 hrs.	Same dose in children

Schistosoma sp.	• Travelers and temporary residents lightly infected with no chronic disease.
	  ○ Light infection detected by serology, eggs not usually present in stool or urine.
	  ○ Uncommon CNS involvement including spinal cord.
	  ○ Almost all travel related cases are from Africa.		

Schistosoma haematobium; GU bilharziasis.	Praziquantel 40 mg/kg po on the same day (one dose of 40 mg/kg or two doses of 20 mg/kg)		Same dose in children. (this applies to all schisto species) Some clinicians use 60 mg/kg praziquantel for travelers and temporary residents not expecting re-exposure.
Schistosoma intercalatum	Praziquantel 20 mg/kg po on the same day in 1 or 2 doses		Same dose in children.
Schistosoma japonicum; Oriental schisto.	Praziquantel 60 mg/kg po on the same day (3 doses of 20 mg/kg)		Same dose in children. Cures 60–90% pts.
Schistosoma mansoni (intestinal bilharziasis)	Praziquantel 40 mg/kg po on the same day in (one dose of 40 mg/kg or two doses of 20 mg/kg)		Praziquantel: Same dose for children and adults. Cures 60–90% pts. No advantage to splitting dose in 2 Cochrane database Syst Rev. 8:CD000053, 2014.
Schistosoma mekongi	Praziquantel 60 mg per kg po on the same day (3 doses of 20 mg/kg)		Same dose for children
Toxemic schisto; Katayama fever	Praziquantel 20 mg per kg po bid with short course of high dose prednisone. Repeat Praziquantel in 4–6 wks (Clin Micro Rev 16:225, 2010).		Reaction to onset of egg laying 4–6 wks after infection exposure in fresh water.

[a] For source of drug, see Table 13D, page 171.

TABLE 13A (12)

INFECTING ORGANISM	SUGGESTED REGIMENS		COMMENTS
	PRIMARY	**ALTERNATIVE**	
CESTODES (Tapeworms)			
Echinococcus granulosus (hydatid disease) (LnID 12:871, 2012; Inf Dis Clin No Amer 26:421, 2012) Dead or calcified cysts as determined by experienced radiologist require no therapy.	**Liver cysts:** Meta-analysis supports percutaneous aspiration-injection-reaspiration (PAIR) + albendazole for uncomplicated single liver cysts. Before & after drainage: **albendazole** ≥60 kg, 400 mg po bid or <60 kg, 15 mg/kg per day div. bid, with meals. After 1-2 days puncture (P) & needle aspirate (A) cyst content. Instill (I) hypertonic saline (15–30%) or absolute alcohol, wait 20-30 min, then re-aspirate (R) with final irrigation. **Continue albendazole for at least 30 days.** Cure in 96% as comp to 90% pts with surgical resection. Albendazole re: Acta Tropica 114:1, 2010. Complicated or multi vesicular cysts almost always require surgical intervention. Consider watch and wait for asymptomatic or non-compromising cysts.		
Lung cysts	Surgical resection. Avoid pre-operative Albendazole. May give Albendazole 400 mg po bid at least 28 days post-operatively. Ruptured or complicated cysts may require longer therapy. **Note:** Brain, cardiac, splenic, renal, bone locations uncommonly occur requiring surgical intervention. Metastatic spread into body cavities with spontaneous or iatrogenic (during surgery) cyst rupture require Albendazole. Albendazole 400 mg po bid indefinitely until clinical response with periodic surgical debulking if feasible.		
Echinococcus multilocularis (alveolar cyst disease) (COID 16:437, 2003)	**Albendazole** efficacy not clearly demonstrated, can try in dosages used for hydatid disease. Wide surgical resection only reliable rx; technique evolving. Post-surgical resection or if inoperable. Albendazole for several years (Acta Tropic 114:1, 2010).		
Intestinal tapeworms Diphyllobothrium latum (fish), Dipylidium caninum (dog), Taenia saginata (beef), & Taenia solium (pork)	**Praziquantel** 5-10 mg/kg po x 1 dose for children and adults.	**Niclosamide[a]** 2 gm po x 1 dose	Niclosamide from Expert Compounding Pharm, see Table 13D.
Hymenolepis diminuta (rats) and H. nana (humans)	**Praziquantel** 25 mg/kg po x 1 dose for children and adults.	**Niclosamide[a]** 2 gm po daily x 7 days	
Neurocysticercosis (NCC). Larval form of T. solium IDSA treatment guidelines, Clin Infect Dis 62:1375, 2016	**NOTE: Treat concomitant T. solium intestinal tapeworms,** if present, with **praziquantel** 5-10 mg/kg po x 1 dose after starting steroid. Both CT and MRI should be performed. Immunoblot preferred: ELISA lacks specificity. Serology insensitive for single lesions, calcified lesions. For multiple parenchymal lesions, subarachnoid NCC, intraventricular NCC, serology almost 100% sensitive; CSF testing no advantage over CSF testing. Parenchymal scolex on imaging is diagnostic, serology not necessary. In non-endemic areas, check stools of household contacts of confirmed cases for tapeworm eggs.		
Parenchymal NCC 1-20 "viable" or degenerating cysts by CT/MRI. Meta-analysis: Treatment assoc with cyst resolution, ↓ seizures, and ↓ seizure recurrence.	**Albendazole** 15 mg/kg/d po (max 800 mg) + **Praziquantel** 50 mg/kg/d po + **Dexamethasone** 0.1 mg/kg/d po. Start steroid 1 day before anti-parasitics. Treat for 10 days. Continue seizure meds for 1 yr. Slow steroid taper after 10 days increasing back if seizures develop. Albendazole alone adequate if only 1-2 cysts on MRI.	**Albendazole** alone 80C mg per day plus **Dexamethasone** 0.1 mg/kg per day ± Anti-seizure medica ion). See Comzaent. Limited data indicates that increasing dexamethasone to 8 mg/day X 28 days with 2-week taper decreases seizures but prolongs steroid taper. Epilepsia 55:1452, 2014	Retreat after 6 months if any viable cysts remain. Methotrexate at ≤20 mg/wk allows a reduction in steroid use (CID 44:449, 2007). Some recommend longer courses of albendazole (even 30 days) if large number of parenchymal cysticercai.
Dead calcified cysts	No treatment indicated		
Subarachnoid NCC	**Albendazole** 15 mg/kg per day (max. 1200 mg/day) + **Dexamethasone** (doses as above with very slow taper) + v-p shunt prior to therapy. 30 day course, may need to repeat multiple times or give continuously for months according to clinical and MRI evolution. Expert Rev Anti Infect Ther 9:123, 2011); continue until radiologic resolution. Intracranial pressure must be monitored and managed by an experienced clinician. If diffuse cerebral edema or raised ICP, control with steroids or shunting prior to any anti-parasitic therapy.	Long courses of combination therapy with Albendazole/praziquantale combination therapy for refractory disease.	

[a] For source of drug, see Table 13D, page 171.

TABLE 13A (13)

INFECTING ORGANISM	SUGGESTED REGIMENS		COMMENTS
	PRIMARY	ALTERNATIVE	

CESTODES (Tapeworms)/Neurocysticercosis (continued)

INFECTING ORGANISM	PRIMARY	ALTERNATIVE	COMMENTS
Intraventricular NCC	Neuroendoscopic removal is treatment of choice with or without obstruction. If surgery not possible, **Albendazole + Dexamethasone; observe closely for evidence of obstruction of flow of CSF.**	**Albendazole + Dexamethasone** (as above); place v-p shunt prior to therapy when no access to neuroendoscopy.	
Sparganosis (Spirometra mansonoides) Larval cysts: source—frogs/snakes	Surgical resection. No antiparasitic therapy. Can inject alcohol into subcutaneous masses.		

ECTOPARASITES. Refs: CID 36:1355, 2003; Ln 363:889, 2004. **NOTE: Due to potential neurotoxicity and risk of aplastic anemia, lindane not recommended.**

DISEASE	INFECTING ORGANISM	PRIMARY	ALTERNATIVE	COMMENTS
Head lice Med Lett 54:61, 2012.	Pediculus humanus, var. capitis. Re-treatment often necessary as current drugs do not kill eggs.	**Permethrin** 1% lotion: Apply to shampooed dried hair for 10 min.; repeat in 9-10 days. **OR Malathion** 0.5% lotion (Ovide): Apply to dry hair for 8-12 hrs, then shampoo. 2 doses 7-9 days apart. **OR Spinosad** 0.9% suspension; wash off after 10 min (85% effective). Repeat in 7 days, if needed.	**Ivermectin** 200-400 μg/kg po once; 3 doses at 7 day intervals effective in 95% (JID 193:474, 2006). Topical ivermectin 0.5% lotion, 75% effective. **Malathion**: Report that 1-2 20-min. applications 98% effective (Ped Derm 21:670, 2004). In alcohol—potentially flammable.	**Permethrin** success in 78%. Resistance increasing. No advantage to 5% permethrin. **Spinosad** is effective, but expensive. Wash hats, scarves, coats & bedding in hot water, then dry in hot dryer for 20+ minutes.
Pubic lice (crabs)	Phthirus pubis	Pubic hair: **Permethrin OR Malathion** as for head lice. Shave pubic hair.	Eyelids: Petroleum jelly applied qid x 10 days **OR yellow oxide of mercury** 1% qid x 14 days	Do not use lindane. Treat sex partners of the last 30 days.
Body lice	Pediculus humanus, var. corporis	No drugs for the patient. Organism lives in & deposits eggs in seams of clothing. Discard clothing; if not possible, treat clothing with 1% malathion powder or 0.5% permethrin powder. Success with ivermectin in homeless shelter. 12 mg on days 0, 7, & 14. (JID 193:474, 2006)	**Benzyl alcohol:** 76% effective.	
Myiasis Due to larvae of flies		Usually cutaneous/subcutaneous nodule with central punctum. Treatment: Occlude punctum to prevent gas exchange with petrolatum, fingernail polish, makeup cream or bacon. When larva migrates, manually remove. Ref: Clin Microbiol Rev 25:79, 2012.		
Scabies Refs: MMWR 64(RR-3):1, 2015; NEJM 362:717, 2010.	Sarcoptes scabiei	**Permethrin** 5% cream (ELIMITE) under nails (finger and toe). Apply entire skin from chin down to and including under fingernails and toenails. Leave on 8-14 hrs. Repeat in 1-2 wks. Safe for children age >2 mos.	**Ivermectin** 200 μg/kg po with food x 1, then second dose in 2 wks. Less effective: **Crotamiton** 10% cream, apply x 24 hr, rinse off, then reapply x 24 hr.	Trim fingernails. Reapply cream to hands after handwashing. Treat close contacts; wash and heat dry linens. Pruritus may persist times 2 wks after mites gone.
	Immunocompetent patients			
	AIDS and HTLV-infected patients (CD4 <150 per mm³), debilitated or developmentally disabled patients (**Norwegian scabies**—see Comments)	For Norwegian crusted scabies: **Permethrin** 5% cream daily x 7 days, then twice weekly until cured. Add **Ivermectin** po (dose in Alternative)	**Ivermectin** 200 mcg/kg po on days 1, 2, 8, 9 & 15+ **Permethrin** cream. May need add'tl doses of ivermectin on days 22 & 29.	**Norwegian scabies** in AIDS pts: Extensive, crusted. Can mimic psoriasis. Not pruritic. Highly contagious—isolate!

ᵃ For source of drug, see Table 13D, page 171.

TABLE 13B – DOSAGE AND SELECTED ADVERSE EFFECTS OF ANTIPARASITIC DRUGS

Doses vary with indication. For convenience, drugs divided by type of parasite; some drugs used for multiple types of parasites, e.g., albendazole.

CLASS, AGENT, GENERIC NAME (TRADE NAME)	USUAL ADULT DOSAGE	ADVERSE REACTIONS/COMMENTS
Antiprotozoan Drugs		
Intestinal Parasites		
Diloxanide furoate[NUS] (Furamide)	500 mg po tid x 10 days.	Source: *See Table 13D, page 171.* Flatulence, N/V, diarrhea.
Iodoquinol (Yodoxin)	Adults: 650 mg po tid or (for 30-40 mg/kg/day div. tid); children: 640 mg/kg per day div. tid.	Rarely causes nausea, abdominal cramps, rash, acne. **Contraindicated if iodine intolerance** (contains 64% bound iodine). Can cause iododerma (papular or pustular rash) and/or thyroid enlargement.
Metronidazole	Side-effects similar for all. *See metronidazole in Table 10B, page 120, & Table 10A, page 117.*	
Nitazoxanide (Alinia)	Adults: 500 mg po q12h. Children 4-11: 200 mg susp. po q12h. Take with food. Expensive.	Abdominal pain 7.8%, diarrhea 2.1%. Rev.: *CID 40:1173, 2005; Expert Opin Pharmacother 7:953, 2006.* Headaches; rarely yellow sclera (resolves after treatment).
Paromomycin (Humatin)	15-35 mg/kg/day po in 3 divided doses x 5-10 days (250 mg tabs). Source: *See Table 13D.*	**Aminoglycoside** similar to neomycin; if absorbed due to concomitant inflammatory bowel disease can result in oto/nephrotoxicity. Doses >3 gm daily are associated with nausea, abdominal cramps, diarrhea.
Aminosidine IV in U.K.		
Quinacrine	100 mg po tid x 5 days. No longer available in U.S.; www.expertpharmacy.com	**Contraindicated for pts with history of psychosis or psoriasis.** Yellow staining of skin. Dizziness, headache, vomiting, toxic psychosis (1.5%), hemolytic anemia, leukopenia, thrombocytopenia. Urticaria, rash, fever, minor disulfiram-like reactions.
Tinidazole (Tindamax)	250-500 mg tabs, with food. Regimen varies with indication.	**Chemical structure** similar to metronidazole but better tolerated. Seizures/peripheral neuropathy reported. **Adverse effects:** Metallic taste 4-6%, nausea 3-5%, anorexia 2-3%.
Antiprotozoan Drugs: Non-Intestinal Protozoa		
Extraintestinal Parasites		
Antimony compounds[NUS] Stibogluconate sodium (Pentostam) from CDC or Meglumine antimoniate (Glucantime)–French trade name	For IV use: vials with 100 mg antimony/mL. Dilute selected dose in 50 mL of D5W shortly before use. Infuse over at least 10 minutes. Intralesional injection used in many countries; 20 mg/kg qwk X 5-10 weeks.	**AEs in 1st 10 days:** headache, fatigue, elevated lipase/amylase, clinical pancreatitis. After 10 days: elevated AST/ALT/ALK/PHOS. CBC, biochemistry weekly, EKG q2 weeks if prolonged therapy. **NOTE: Reversible T wave changes in 30-60%. Risk of QTc prolongation.** Renal excretion; modify dose if renal insufficiency. Metabolized in liver; lower dose if hepatic insufficiency. Generic drug may have increased toxicity due to antimony complex formation.
Artemether-Lumefantrine, po (Coartem), FDA-approved)	4 (20 mg Artemether and 120 mg Lumefantrine) combination tablets X 6 doses over 3 days for adults. Take with food. Can be crushed and mixed with a few teaspoons of water	**Can prolong QT** – avoid in patients with congenital long QT, QTc, or need for drugs known to prolong QT. *(see list under fluoroquinolones, Table 10A,page 114).* Artemether induces CYP3A4 and both Artemether & Lumefantrine are metabolized by CYP3A4 *(see drug-drug interactions, Table 22A, page 245).* Adverse effects experienced by >30% of adults: headache, anorexia, dizziness, arthralgia and myalgia. Non-life threatening, but transfusion requiring, hemolytic anemia can occur up to 15 days post-therapy *(AnIM 163:498, 2015).*
Artesunate, IV Ref.: *NEJM 358:1829, 2008*	Available from CDC Malaria Branch. 2.4 mg/kg IV at 0, 12, 24, & 48 hrs.	**More effective than quinine & safer than quinidine.** Contact CDC at 770-488-7758 or 770-488-7100 after hours. No dosage adjustment for hepatic or renal insufficiency. No known drug interactions.
Atovaquone (Mepron) Ref.: *AAC 46:1163, 2002*	Suspension: 1 tsp (750 mg) po bid 750 mg/5 mL.	No. pts. stopping rx due to side-effects was 9%, rash 22%, GI 20%, headache 16%, insomnia 10%, fever 14%
Atovaquone and Proguanil (Malarone) For prophylaxis of P. falciparum; little data on P. vivax. Generic available in U.S.	**Prophylaxis:** 1 tab po (250 mg + 100 mg) q24h with food **Treatment:** 4 tabs po (1000 mg + 400 mg) once daily with food Adult X 3 days. Adult tab: 250/100 mg; Peds tab 62.5/25 mg. *Treatment see comment, page 158.*	Adverse effects in rx trials: Adults—abd. pain 17%, N/V 12%, headache 10%, dizziness 5%. Rx stopped in 1%. Asymptomatic mild ↑ in ALT/AST. Children cough, headache, anorexia, vomiting, rash, pruritus. *See Table 16, page 195, drug interactions, Table 22A.* Safe in G6PD-deficient pts. Can crush tabs for children and give with milk or other liquid nutrients. Renal insufficiency: contraindicated if CrCl <30 mL per min.

[a] For source of drug, see *Table 13D, page 171.*

TABLE 13B (2)

CLASS, AGENT, GENERIC NAME (TRADE NAME)	USUAL ADULT DOSAGE	ADVERSE REACTIONS/COMMENTS
Antiprotozoan Drugs: Non-Intestinal Protozoa/Extraintestinal Parasites *(continued)*		
Benznidazole* (CDC Drug Service and expected US commercial availability of FDA-approved 100 mg tab in 2018; commercial tab for that age <12 yrs, may use off-label in adults)	5 mg/kg per day po. 100 mg tabs. May use 300 mg per day for 60 days, regardless of body weight OR give 300 mg per day but prolong treatment to complete the total dose corresponding to 5 mg/kg per day for 60 days.	**Photosensitivity in 50% of pts.** GI: abdominal pain, nausea/vomiting/anorexia. Dermatitis including Stevens-Johnson. CNS: disorientation, insomnia, twitching/seizures, paresthesias, polyneuritis. Discontinue if leucopenia or thrombocytopenia. **Contraindicated in pregnancy.** Recommended dose range 5-7.5 mg/kg/day but more than 5 mg/kg has unacceptable side effects in adults, higher doses better tolerated in children.
Chloroquine phosphate (Aralen)	Dose varies—see *Malaria Prophylaxis and rx, pages 157-158.*	Minor: anorexia/nausea/vomiting, headache, dizziness, blurred vision, pruritus in dark-skinned pts. Major: protracted rx in rheumatoid arthritis can lead to retinopathy. Can exacerbate psoriasis. Can block response to intradermally administered rabies vaccine. **Contraindicated in pts with epilepsy.**
Dapsone *See Comment re methemoglobinemia*	100 mg po q24h	Usually tolerated by pts with rash after TMP-SMX. **Dapsone is common etiology of acquired methemoglobinemia** *(NEJM 364:957, 2011).* Metabolite of dapsone converts heme iron to +3 charge (no O2 transport) from normal +2. Normal blood level 1%; cyanosis at 10%; headache, fatigue, tachycardia, dizziness at 30-40%, acidosis & coma at 60%, death at 70-80%. Low G6PD is a risk factor. Treatment: methylene blue 1-2 mg/kg IV over 5 min x 1 dose.
Eflornithine (Ornidyl) (WHO or CDC drug service)	400 mg/kg/day IV divided q12h x 7 days in combination with Nifurtimox for West African Trypanosomiasis	Diarrhea in ½ pts, vomiting, abdominal pain, anemia/leukopenia in ½ pts, seizures, alopecia, jaundice, ↓ hearing. Contraindicated in pregnancy.
Fumagillin	Eyedrops + po. 20 mg bid. Leiter's: 800-292-6772.	Adverse events: Neutropenia & thrombocytopenia
Mefloquine	One 250 mg tab/wk for **malaria prophylaxis;** for rx, 1250 mg x 1 or 750 mg & then 500 mg in 6-8 hrs. In U.S.: 250 mg tab = 228 mg base; outside U.S.: 275 mg tab = 250 mg base	Side-effects in roughly 3%. Minor: headache, irritability, insomnia, weakness, diarrhea. **Toxic psychosis, seizures can occur.** Do not use with quinine, quinidine, or halofantrine. Rare: Prolonged QT interval and toxic epidermal necrolysis *(Ln 349:101, 1997).* **Not used for self-rx due to neuropsychiatric side-effects.** FDA black box for possible prolonged effects. Avoid if pre-existing overlay of depression or other psychiatric disorders.

Melarsoprol (Mel B, Arsobal) (CDC)	2.2 mg/kg/day IV x 10 days	**Post-rx encephalopathy (2-10%) with 50% mortality overall, risk of death 2° to rx 8-14%.** Prednisolone 1 mg per kg per day po may ↓ encephalopathy. Other: Heart damage, albuminuria, abdominal pain, vomiting, peripheral neuropathy, Herxheimer-like reaction, pruritus.
		  o Prednisone may prevent/attenuate encephalopathy.
		  o Pretreatment with Suramin (dose as above) is often used in late-stage East African trypanosomiasis to clear the hemolymphatic system of trypanosomes before administration of melarsoprol.

Miltefosine (Impavido) *Med Lett 56:89, 2014* FDA approved in 2014, but no commercialization in US at present	50 mg po bid (wt 33-44 kg); 50 mg po tid (wt ≥45 kg) (max 150 mg/d). Treat for 28 days	**Pregnancy—No;** teratogenic. Side-effects vary: kala-azar pts, vomiting in up to 40%, diarrhea in 17%; "motion sickness", headache & increased creatinine. Metabolized by liver; virtually no urinary excretion.
Nifurtimox (Lampit) *(CDC)* (Manufactured in Germany by Bayer)	8-10 mg/kg per day po div. 4 x per day for 90-120 days for Chaga's. 15 mg/kg/day po, divided q8h x 10 days for West African trypanosomiasis	**Side-effects in 40-70% of pts.** GI: abdominal pain, nausea/vomiting. CNS: polyneuritis (1/3), disorientation, insomnia, twitching, seizures. Skin rash. Hemolysis with G6PD deficiency. Monitor CBC, biochemistry after 4-6 weeks. Monitor for neuropathy. Ref. *CID 2016;63:1056.*
Pentamidine	4 mg/kg IV or IM daily x 7-10 days for African Trypanosomiasis. 300 mg via aerosol q month.	Hypotension, hypocalcemia, hypoglycemia followed by hyperglycemia, pancreatitis. Neutropenia (15%), thrombocytopenia. Nephrotoxicity. Others: nausea/vomiting, ↑ liver tests, rash.
Primaquine phosphate	26.3 mg (<15 mg base). Adult dose is 30 mg of base po daily.	**In G6PD def. pts, can cause hemolytic anemia with methemoglobinuria,** esp. African, Asian peoples. Methemoglobinemia. Rapid G6PD screening tests now readily available. Nausea/abdominal pain if pt. fasting. *(CID 39:1336, 2004).* **Pregnancy: No.**

* For source of drug, see *Table 13D, page 171.*

TABLE 13B (3)

CLASS, AGENT, GENERIC NAME (TRADE NAME)	USUAL ADULT DOSAGE	ADVERSE REACTIONS/COMMENTS
Antiprotozoan Drugs: Non-Intestinal Protozoa/Extraintestinal Parasites: *(continued)*		
Pyrimethamine (Daraprim, Malocide) Also combined with Sulfadoxine as **Fansidar** (25–500 mg)	100 mg, then 25 mg/day. **Very expensive: $75,000 for 100 tabs** (25 mg). Financial assistance may be available 1-877-258-8033. Consider compounding pharmacy (imprimusrx.com).	**Major problem is hematologic**: megaloblastic anemia, ↓ WBC, ↓ platelets. Can give 5 mg folinic acid per day to ↓ bone marrow depression and will not interfere with antitoxoplasmosis effect. If high-dose pyrimethamine, ↑ folinic acid to 10–50 mg/day. Pyrimethamine + sulfadoxine, known to cause mental changes due to carnitine deficiency (*AJM 95:112, 1993*). Other: Rash, vomiting, diarrhea, xerostomia.
Quinidine gluconate Cardiotoxicity ref: *LnID 7-549, 2007*	Loading dose of 10 mg (equiv to 6.2 mg of quinidine base) / kg IV over 1–2 hr, then constant infusion of 0.02 mg of quinidine gluconate / kg per minute. May be available for compassionate use from Lilly.	**Adverse reactions of quinidine/quinine similar**: (1) IV bolus injection can cause fatal hypotension, (2) hyperinsulinemic hypoglycemia, esp. in pregnancy, (3) ↓ rate of infusion of IV quinidine if QT interval ↑ 25% of baseline, (4) reduce dose 30–50% after day 3 due to ↓ renal clearance and ↓ vol. of distribution.
Quinine sulfate (Qualaquin)	324 mg tabs. No IV prep. in US. Oral rx of chloroquine-resistant falciparum malaria: 624 mg po tid x 3 days, then (tetracycline 250 mg po qid or doxy 100 mg bid) x 7 days	Cinchonism; tinnitus, headache, nausea, abdominal pain, blurred vision. Rarely: blood dyscrasias, drug fever, asthma, hypoglycemia. Transient blindness in <1% of 500 pts (*AnIM 136-339, 2002*). **Contraindicated if prolonged QTc, myasthenia gravis, optic neuritis or G6PD deficiency.**
Spiramycin (Rovamycin)	1 gm po q8h (see *Comment*).	GI and allergic reactions have occurred. Available at no cost after consultation with Palo Alto Medical Foundation Toxoplasma Serology Lab: 650-853-4828 or from U.S. FDA 301-796-1600.
Sulfadiazine	1–1.5 gm po q6h.	See *Table 10A, page 117, for sulfonamide side-effects*
Sulfadoxine & Pyrimethamine combination (Fansidar)	Contains 500 mg Sulfadoxine & 25 mg Pyrimethamine	Long half-life of both drugs: Sulfadoxine 169 hrs, pyrimethamine 111 hrs allows weekly dosage. In African, used empirically in pregnancy for intermittent preventative treatment (ITPp) against malaria; dosing at 3 set times during pregnancy. Reduces material and fetal mortality if HIV+. See *Expert Rev Anti Infect Ther 8-589, 2010*. **Fatalities reported due to Stevens-Johnson syndrome and toxic epidermal necrolysis.** Renal excretion—caution if renal impairment.
DRUGS USED TO TREAT NEMATODES, TREMATODES, AND CESTODES		
Albendazole (Albenza)	Doses vary with indication. Take w/th food; fatty meal increases absorption. See *Table 13D for US availability*	FDA Pregnancy Category C due to lack of data but available evidence suggests no difference in congenital abnormalities in 2nd and 3rd trimesters. CDC suggests use of albendazole in 3rd trimester if infection is compromising the pregnancy. Abdominal pain (with prolonged courses), nausea/vomiting, alopecia, ↑ serum transaminase. Rare leukopenia.
Diethylcarbamazine *(CDC)*	Dose varies with species of filaria.	Headache, dizziness, nausea, fever. In Onchocerciasis, host may experience inflammatory reaction to death of microfilariae: fever, urticaria, asthma, GI upset (**Mazzotti reaction). Pregnancy—No.**
Ivermectin (Stromectol, Mectizan) (3 mg tab & topical 0.5% lotion for head lice). Take on empty stomach.	Strongyloidiasis dose: 200 µg/kg/day po x 2 days Onchocerciasis: 150 µg/kg x 1 po Scabies: 200 µg/kg po x 1; if AIDS, wait 14 days & repeat	Mild side-effects: fever, pruritus, rash. In rx of onchocerciasis, can see *tender lymphadenopathy*; headache, bone/joint pain.
Mebendazole (Vermox)	In developing world chewable tablet, 500 mg po once in public health campaigns. 100 mg po twice/day for 3 days is optimal for most intestinal nematodes; 100 mg single dose adequate for pinworm. See Table 13D for US avail/ability	Rarely causes abdominal pain, nausea, diarrhea. FDA Pregnancy Category C due to lack of data but available evidence suggests no difference in congenital abnormalities. WHO allows use of mebendazole in 2nd and 3rd trimesters. CDC suggests consideration in 3rd trimester if infection is compromising the pregnancy.
Praziquantel (Biltricide)	Doses vary with parasite; see *Table 13A*.	Mild: dizziness/drowsiness, N/V, rash, fever. **Only contraindication is ocular cysticercosis.** Potential exacerbation of neurocysticercosis. Metab-induced by anticonvulsants and steroids; can negate effect with cimetidine 400 mg po tid. Reduce dose if advanced liver disease. Praziquantel is pregnancy category B. Available evidence suggests no difference in adverse birth outcomes. WHO encourages the use of praziquantel in any stage of pregnancy. CDC advises individual risk-benefit assessment according to clinical disease in the mother.
Pyrantel pamoate (over-the-counter)	Oral suspension. Dose for all ages: 11 mg/kg (to max. of 1 gm) x 1 dose	Rare GI upset, headache, dizziness, rash

* For source of drug, see *Table 13D, page 171*.

TABLE 13B (4)

CLASS, AGENT, GENERIC NAME (TRADE NAME)	USUAL ADULT DOSAGE	ADVERSE REACTIONS/COMMENTS
DRUGS USED TO TREAT NEMATODES, TREMATODES, AND CESTODES *(continued)*		
Suramin (Germanin) *(CDC)*	Drug powder mixed to 10% solution with 5 mL water and used within 30 min. First give test dose of 0.1 gm IV. Try to avoid during pregnancy.	Does not cross blood-brain barrier; no effect on CNS infection. Side-effects: vomiting, pruritus, urticaria, fever, paresthesias, albuminuria (discontinue drug if casts appear). Do not use if renal/liver disease present. Deaths from vascular collapse reported.
Triclabendazole (Egaten) (CDC)	Used for fasciola hepatica liver fluke infection: 10 mg/kg po x 1 dose. May repeat in 12-24 hrs. 250 mg tabs	AEs ≥10%; sweating and abdominal pain. AEs 1-10%; weakness, chest pain, fever, anorexia, nausea, vomiting. **Note:** use with caution if G6PD def. or impaired liver function.

TABLE 13C - PARASITES THAT CAUSE EOSINOPHILIA (EOSINOPHILIA IN TRAVELERS)

Frequent and Intense (>5000 eos/mcL)	Moderate to Marked Early Infections	During Larval Migration; Absent or Mild During Chronic Infections	Other
Strongyloides (absent in compromised hosts); Lymphatic Filariasis; Toxocara (cutaneous larva migrans); Trichinella	Ascaris; Hookworm; Clonorchis; Paragonimus; Fasciola	Opisthorchis; Baylisascaris	Schistosomiasis; Cysticercosis; Trichuris; Angiostrongylus; Onchocerciasis; echinococcus
			Non-lymphatic filariasis; Gnathostoma; Capillaria; Trichostrongylus

⁎ For source of drug, see *Table 13D, page 171.*

TABLE 13D – SOURCES FOR HARD-TO-FIND ANTIPARASITIC DRUGS

Source	Drugs Available	Contact Information
CDC Drug Service	Artesunate, Benznidazole, Diethylcaramazine (DEC), Eflornithine, Melarsoprol, Nifurtimox, Sodium stibogluconate, Suramin, Triclabendazole	www.cdc.gov/laboratory/drugservice/index.html (+1) 404-639-3670 or drugservice@cdc.gov
WHO	Drugs for treatment of African trypanosomiasis	priottog@who.int; (+41) 794-682-726; (+41) 227-911-345 francoj@who.int; (+41) 796-198-535; (+41) 227-913-313
Compounding Pharmacies, Specialty Distributors, Others		
Expert Compounding Pharmacy	Albendazole, Furazolidone, Iodoquinol, Mebendazole (100 mg tabs), Niclosamide, Paromomycin (oral), Praziquantel, Pyrantel pamoate, Quinacrine, Thiabendazole, Tinidazole	www.expertpharmacy.org 1-800-247-9767; (+1) 818-988-7979
Exeltis, Inc. / Benznidazole	Commercial FDA approved tab for <12 yr olds, may use off-label in adults (expected 2Q 2018)	+1 800-964-9650
Leiter's Pharmacy	Fumagillin	www.leiterx.com 1-800-292-6772; +1-408-292-6772
Profounda, Inc.	Miltefosine (leishmaniasis or free-living ameba)	www.impavido.com; +1 407-270-7790
Victoria Apotheke Zurich will ship worldwide if sent physicians prescription.	Paromomycin (oral and topical), Triclabendazole. Other hard to find anti-parasitic drugs	www.pharmaworld.com. (+41) 43-344-6060
Palo Alto Medical Foundation, Toxoplasma Serology Lab	Spiramycin (consultation required for release)	(+1) 650-853-4828; toxlab@pamf.org
Imprimis (compounding pharmacy)	Pyrimethamine	-1 844-446-6979; www.imprimisrx.com

Note: In the U.S. FDA-approved generic Albendazole (Albenza) and Mebendazole marketed by Amedra is very costly and is difficult for retail pharmacies to access.
    Vermox brand mebendazole 500 mg tablets is FDA-approved but for donation only and not sold in the U.S.

TABLE 14A – ANTIVIRAL THERAPY*

For HIV, see *Table 14C*; For Hepatitis, *see Table 14E* and *Table 14F*. For Antiviral Activity Spectra, *see Table 4C, page 84*

VIRUS/DISEASE	DRUG/DOSAGE	SIDE EFFECTS/COMMENTS
Adenovirus: Cause of RTIs including fatal pneumonia in children & young adults and 60% mortality in transplant pts (*CID 43:331, 2006*). Frequent cause of cystitis in transplant patients. Adenovirus 14 associated with severe pneumonia in otherwise healthy young adults (*MMWR 56(45):1181, 2007*). Findings include: fever, ↑ liver enzymes, leukopenia, thrombocytopenia, diarrhea, pneumonia, or hemorrhagic cystitis. Ref: *Infect Dis Clin N Amer 2017:31-455*.	In severe cases of pneumonia or post HSCT: **Cidofovir** • 5 mg/kg/wk x 2 wks, then q 2 wks + **Probenecid** 1.25 gm/M² given 3 hrs before cidofovir and 3 & 9 hrs after each infusion • Or 1 mg/kg IV 3x/wk. For adenovirus hemorrhagic cystitis (*CID 40:199, 2005; Transplantation 2006; 81:1398*): Intravesical **Cidofovir** (5 mg/kg in 100 mL saline instilled into bladder).	Routine monitoring with HAdV viral load recommended 1- 2 times/wk in high-risk patients: Allo-HSCT with haploidentical donor or unrelated cord blood graft; Severe GVHD; Severe lymphopenia; and/or Rx with alemtuzumab. Monitoring should continue until immune reconstitution. Those with at least 1 risk factor and viremia should be Rx'd with cidofovir. Ribavirin not recommended. Vidarabine and Ganciclovir have in vitro activity against adenovirus; little to no clinical data. **Brincidofovir** (CMX001-Chimerix) oral lipid complex cidofovir prodrug shows no evidence of efficacy in Phase III study. Donor specific T-cells should be reserved for those who have failed antiviral therapy and administered as part of a clinical trial.
Bunyaviridae: Severe fever with thrombocytopenia syndrome virus (SFTSV) Possibly transmitted by *Haemaphysalis longicornis* and *Amblyomma americanum* (lone star) ticks.	No therapy recommended. Ribavirin ineffective. Clinical symptoms: Fever, weakness, myalgias, GI symptoms	Lab: Elevated LDH (>1200) and CPK (>800) associated with higher mortality rates. Initially thought to be an anaplasma infection, but serology showed a new virus.
Coronavirus— **SARS-CoV:** Severe acute respiratory syndrome (*NEJM 348:1953 & 1967, 2003*) **MERS-CoV:** Middle East respiratory syndrome (*NEJM 2017;376:584*)	**SARS:** • Ribavirin—ineffective. • Interferon alfa ± steroids—small case series. • Pegylated IFN-α effective in monkeys. • Low dose steroids alone successful in one Beijing hospital. High dose steroids ↑ serious fungal infections. Inhaled nitric oxide improved oxygenation & improved chest x-ray (*CID 39:1531, 2004*). **MERS:** Increased 14 day survival with Ribavirin po + PEG-IFN 180 mcg/wk sc x 2 wks (*LnID 14:1090, 2014*). Other therapies: *LnID 14:1136, 2014*.	**SARS: Transmission by close contact:** effective infection control practices (**mask changed frequently**), eye protection, gown, gloves) key to stopping transmission. **MERS:** Suspected reservoirs are camels and perhaps other animals. *Review: Clin Micro Rev. 28:465, 2015.*
Enterovirus—Meningitis: most common cause of aseptic meningitis. Rapid CSF PCR test is accurate; reduces costs and hospital stay for infants (*Peds 120:489, 2007*).	**No rx currently recommended.**	No clinical benefit from Pleconaril in double-blind placebo-controlled study in 21 infants with enteroviral aseptic meningitis (*PID 22:335, 2003*).
Hemorrhagic Fever Virus Infections: *Review: LnID 6-203, 2006.* **Congo-Crimean Hemorrhagic Fever** (HF) Tick-borne; symptoms include N/V, fever, headache, myalgias, & stupor (1/3). Signs: *conjunctival injection, hepatomegaly, petechiae (1/3)*. Lab: ↓ platelets, ↓ WBC, ↑ ALT, AST, LDH & CPK (100%).	Oral **ribavirin**, **30 mg/kg** as initial loading dose & 15 mg/kg q6h x 4 days & then 7.5 mg/kg q8h x 6 days (WHO recommendation) (*See Comment*). Reviewed *Antiviral Res 78:125, 2008.*	3/3 healthcare workers in Pakistan had complete recovery (*LN 346:472, 1995*). & 61/69 (89%) with confirmed CCHF given ribavirin survived in Iran (*CID 36:1613, 2003*). Shorter time of hospitalization among ribavirin treated pts (7.7 vs. 10.3 days), but no difference in mortality or transfusion needs in study done in Turkey (*J Infection 52: 207-215, 2006*). Suggested benefit from ribavirin & dexamethasone (281 pts) (*CID 57:1270, 2013*).

¹ HSCT = Hematopoietic stem cell transplant

° *See page 2 for abbreviations. NOTE: All dosage recommendations are for adults (unless otherwise indicated) and assume normal renal function.*

TABLE 14A (2)

VIRUS/DISEASE	DRUG/DOSAGE	SIDE EFFECTS/COMMENTS
Hemorrhagic Fever Virus Infections *(continued)*		
Ebola/Marburg HF (Central Africa) Largest ever documented outbreak of Ebola virus (EVD). West Africa, 2014. Diagnostic testing at U.S. CDC. Within a few days of symptom onset, diagnosis is most commonly made by antigen-capture enzyme linked immunosorbent assay (ELISA), IgM antibody ELISA, NAAT or viral culture. *Updated in http://emergency.cdc.gov/han/han00365.asp.* See also: *http://www.bt.cdc.gov/han/han00364.asp*	**No effective antiviral rx** (*J Virol 77: 9233, 20C3*). Investigational antibody treatment "ZMapp" used as compassionate use in a few selected cases (ZMapp is a 3 monoclonal antibody preparation derived from mice exposed to small fragments of Ebola virus. Use of convalescent serum from pts who have recovered is approved for use in newly infected pts by the WHO (*BMJ 349:g5539, 2014*). GS-5734 (Gilead) active in animal models. BCX-4430 (Biocryst) is under evaluation by the NIH.	**Abrupt onset of symptoms typically 8-10 days after exposure (range 2-21 days).** Nonspecific symptoms, which may include fever, chills, myalgias, and malaise. Fever, anorexia, asthenia/ weakness are the most common signs and symptoms. Patients may develop a diffuse erythematous maculopapular rash (days 5-7) (usually involving the face, neck, trunk, and arms) that can desquamate. EVD can **often be confused with** other more infectious diseases such as malaria, typhoid fever, meningococcemia, and other bacterial infections (e.g., pneumonia). **Gastrointestinal symptoms:** severe watery diarrhea, nausea, vomiting and abdominal pain. **Other:** chest pain, shortness of breath, headache or confusion, may also develop. Patients often have conjunctival injection. Hiccups reported. Seizures may occur, and cerebral edema reported. Bleeding is not universally present but can manifest later in the course as petechiae, ecchymosis/bruising, or oozing from venipuncture sites and mucosal hemorrhage. Frank hemorrhage is less common. Pregnant women may experience spontaneous miscarriages.
With pulmonary syndrome Hantavirus pulmonary syndrome, "sin nombre virus"	**No benefit from ribavirin demonstrated** (*CID 39:1307, 2004*). Early recognition of disease and supportive (usually ICU) care is key to successful outcome.	Acute onset of fever, headache, myalgias, non-productive cough, thrombocytopenia, increased PT and non-cardiogenic pulmonary edema with respiratory insufficiency following exposure to droppings of infected rodents.
With renal syndrome: Lassa, Venezuelan, Korean, HF, Sabia, Argentinian HF, Bolivian HF, Junin, Machupo >90% occur in China (*CID 59:1040, 2014*)	Oral ribavirin, 30 mg/kg as initial loading dose & 15 mg/kg q6h x 4 days & then 7.5 mg/kg x 6 days (WHO recommendation) *(see Comment)*.	Toxicity low, hemolysis reported but recovery when treatment stopped. No significant changes in WBC, platelets, hepatic or renal function. *See CID 36:1254, 2003.* Diagnosis for management of contacts.
Dengue and dengue hemorrhagic fever (DHF) *www.cdc.gov/hcidod/dvbid/dengue/dengue-hcp.htm* Think dengue in traveler to tropics or subtropics (incubation period usually 4-7 days) with fever, bleeding, thrombocytopenia, or hemoconcentration with shock. Dx by viral isolation or serology; serum to CDC (telephone 787-706-2399).	**No data on antiviral rx.** Fluid replacement with careful hemodynamic monitoring critical. Rx of DHF with colloids effective: 6% hydroxyethyl starch preferred in 1 study (*NEJM 353:9, 2005*). Review in *Semin Ped Infect Dis 16: 60-65, 2005.*	Of 77 cases dx at CDC (2001-2004), recent (2-wks) travel to Caribbean island 30%, Asia 17%, Central America 15%, S. America 15% (*MMWR 54:556, June 10, 2005*), 5 pts with severe **DHF** rx with dengue antibody-neg, gamma globulin 500 mg per kg q24h IV for 3-5 days; rapid ↑ in platelet counts (*CID 36:1623, 2003*). Diagnosis: ELISA detects IgM in pts with symptoms c/w Dengue Fever.
West Nile virus (*JAMA 310:308, 2013*) A flavivirus transmitted by mosquitoes, blood transfusions, transplanted organs & breast-feeding. Birds (>200 species) are main host with humans & horses incidental hosts. The US epidemic continues.	**No proven rx.** Supportive care (See www.cdc.gov/ westnile/healthcareproviders/). RCT of IVIG of no benefit (*BMC Infect Dis 2014;14:248*).	Usually nonspecific febrile disease but 1/150 cases develops meningoencephalitis, aseptic meningitis or polio-like paralysis (neuromuscular weakness & psychiatric) common. Diagnosis: increased IgM antibody in serum & CSF or CSF PCR (contact State Health Dept./CDC . Blood supply now tested in U.S.
Yellow fever	**No data on antiviral rx** Guidelines for use of preventative vaccine: (*https://www.cdc.gov/mmwr/preview/mmwrhtml/mm64a23a5.htm?s_cid=mm64a23a5_w*)	Reemergence in Africa & S. Amer. due to urbanization of susceptible population (*Lancet Inf 5:604, 2005*). Vaccination Diagnosis: increased IgM antibody safe and effective in HIV patients, especially in those with suppressed VL and higher CD4 counts (*CID 48:659, 2009*). A purified whole-virus, inactivated, cell-culture-derived vaccine (XRX-001) using the 17D strain proven safe and resulted in neutralizing antibodies after 2 doses in a de-escalation, phase I study (*N Engl J Med 2011 Apr 7; 364:1326*)
Chikungunya fever: brake bone fever A self-limited arbovirus illness spread by Aedes mosquito. High epidemic potential (Caribbean).	**No antiviral therapy.** Fluids, analgesics, anti-pyretics (*NEJM 371:885, 2014*).	Clinical presentation: high fever, severe myalgias & headache, morbilliform rash with occ. thrombocytopenia. Rarely hemorrhagic complications. Dx: mostly clinical; definitive diagnosis by PCR (*NEJM 372:1231, 2015; JCl 12017; 27: 737*).
SFTSV (Severe Fever with thrombocytopenia syndrome virus)	*See Bunyaviridae, page 172*	
Hepatitis Viral Infections	*See Table 14E (Hepatitis A & B), Table 14F (Hepatitis C)*	

^a *See page 2 for abbreviations.* NOTE: *All dosage recommendations are for adults (unless otherwise indicated) and assume normal renal function.*

TABLE 14A (3)

VIRUS/DISEASE	DRUG/DOSAGE	SIDE EFFECTS/COMMENTS
Herpesvirus Infections		
Cytomegalovirus (CMV) At risk pts: HIV/AIDS, cancer chemotherapy, transplant Ref: *Transplantation 96:333, 2013*; *Am J Transplant 13(Suppl 4):93, 2013*	**Primary prophylaxis** not generally recommended except in certain transplant populations (*see Table 15E*). Preemptive therapy in pts with † CMV DNA plasma VL & CD4 <100/mm³. If used: **valganciclovir** 900 mg po q12h (*CID 52: 313, 2011*). Primary prophylaxis in pts with † CMV DNA plasma VL & CD4 <100/mm³. If used: **valganciclovir** 900 mg po q12h (*CID 332: 783, 2001*). Primary prophylaxis may be dc if † resol CD4, 200th † CD4 >100 for 6 mos. (*MMWR 53:98, 2004*).	Risk for developing CMV disease correlates with quantity of CMV DNA in plasma: each log₁₀ † associated with 3.1-fold † in disease (*CID 28:758, 1999*). Resistance demonstrated in 5% of transplant recipients receiving primary prophylaxis (*J Antimicrob Chemother 65:2628, 2010*). Consensus guidelines: *Transplantation 96:333, 2013*. Brincidofovir not effective against CMV in transplant patients. Maribavir effective as primary preventative Rx in transplant patients (approval expected in late 2017).
CMV: Colitis, Esophagitis, Gastritis Symptoms relate to site of disease	**Mild: Valganciclovir** 900 mg po bid with food × 14-21 days **Severe: Ganciclovir** 5 mg/kg IV q12h × 14-21 days OR **Foscarnet** (60 mg/kg IV q8h or 90 mg/kg q12h) × 14-21 days *Post-treatment suppression:* **Valganciclovir** 900 mg po once daily until CD4 >100 × 6 mos	Diagnosis: Elevated whole blood quantitative PCR & histopathology. Severe bouts of Inflammatory Bowel Disease (IBD) colitis may be confused with CMV: Rx of CMV in this setting is recommended (*European J Clin Micro & Inf Dis 34:13, 2015*). Rx of CMV in less severe bouts of IBD colitis is unclear.
CMV: Neurologic disease, Encephalitis Myelitis, polyradiculopathy, peripheral neuropathy Symptoms relate to site of disease	Treat as for colitis, esophagitis, gastritis above	Diagnosis: Elevated whole blood and/or CSF quantitative PCR. NOTE: **Severe or fatal IRIS** has occurred in AIDS pts; suggest delay starting ART for 2 wks after initiation of CMV therapy.
CMV: Pneumonia At risk: 1st 6 months post-transplant & 3 months post-stopping prophylaxis Require evidence of invasive disease. Diagnosis: prefer whole blood quantitative PCR and/or positive lung biopsy histopathology Ref: *Transplantation 96:333, 2013*; *Am J Transplant 13(Suppl 4):93, 2013*	*Viremic but non-mild symptoms:* **Valganciclovir** 900 mg po bid (*Am J Transplant 7:2106, 2007*). *Severe in lung transplant or AIDS pts:* **Ganciclovir** 5 mg/kg IV q12h (adjust for renal insufficiency). Treat until clinical resolution & neg blood PCR; min duration: 2 wks. *If Ganciclovir-resistant:* **Foscarnet** (60 mg/kg q8h or 90 mg/kg q12h) IV (adjust for renal insufficiency). Try to reduce immunosuppression.	*Post-treatment suppression:* Valganciclovir 900 mg once daily × 1-3 months if high risk of relapse. Suspect Ganciclovir resist CMV if treatment failure or relapse. Do genotype resistance testing (*CID 56:1018, 2013*). NOTE: IVIG or CMV specific immunoglobulin did not improve overall or attributable mortality in retrospective study of 421 bone marrow transplant pts (*CID 61:31, 2015*).
CMV: Retinitis Most common ocular complication of HIV/AIDS. Rare in pts on ART with CD4 >200. If not on ART, wait to start until after 2 wks of CMV therapy. Ref: aidsinfo.nih.gov/guidelines **CMV immune recovery retinitis:** new retinitis after starting ART. Do not stop ART or Valganciclovir. No steroids.	*Not sight-threatening:* **Valganciclovir** 900 mg po bid with food × 14-21 days, then 900 mg po once daily until CD4 >100 × 6 months. *Sight-threatening (see Comment):* **Valganciclovir** + intravitreal **Ganciclovir** 2 mg (1-4 doses over 7-10 days).	Sight-threatening: <1500 microns from fovea or next to head of optic nerve. If can't use Valganciclovir, **Ganciclovir** 5 mg/kg IV q12h × 14-21 days, then 5 mg/kg IV once daily. If suspect Ganciclovir resistance: Foscarnet (60 gm/kg q8h or 90 mg/kg q12h) × 14-21 days. Ganciclovir ocular implants no longer available.
CMV in Transplant patients: *See Table 15E for CMV prophylaxis:* CMV disease can manifest as CMV syndrome with or without end-organ disease. **Guidelines for CMV therapy** (*Transplantation, 2013; 96(4):333*; and *Am J Transplant, 2013; 13 Suppl 4:93*). Ganciclovir 5 mg/kg IV q12h OR **Valganciclovir** 900 mg po q12h (*Am J Transplant 7:2106, 2007*) are effective treatment options. Treatment duration should be individualized. Continue treatment until (1) CMV PCR or antigenemia has become undetectable, (2) clinical evidence of disease has resolved, and (3) at least 2-3 weeks of treatment (*Am J Transplant 13(Suppl 4):93, 2013; Blood 113:5711, 2009*). Secondary prophylaxis (**Valganciclovir** in pts with severe CMV disease, or those with >1 episode of CMV disease during drug toxicity. Ganciclovir not effective against CMV in transplant patients. immunosuppression such as lymphocyte depleting antibodies, should be considered for 1-3 month course in patients recently treated with high-dose in similar cases balancing the risk of recurrent infection with drug toxicity. In HSCT recipients, secondary prophylaxis should be considered		
CMV in pregnancy: Hyperimmune globulin 200 IU/kg maternal weight as single dose during pregnancy (early), administered IV reduced complications of CMV in infant at one year of life. (*CID 55: 497, 2012*).		
CMV: Congenital/Neonatal Symptomatic	**Valganciclovir** 16 mg/kg po bid × 6 mos	Better outcome after 6 mos compared to 6 wks with no difference in AEs (*NEJM 372:933, 2015*).

TABLE 14A (4)

VIRUS/DISEASE	DRUG/DOSAGE	SIDE EFFECTS/COMMENTS
Herpesvirus Infections (continued)		
Epstein Barr Virus (EBV) — Mononucleosis	No treatment. Corticosteroids for tonsillar obstruction, CNS complications, or threat of splenic rupture.	Diff dx of atypical lymphocytes: EBV, CMV, Hep A, Hep B, Toxo, measles, mumps, drugs, HHV6, HHV7, HIV & others.
HHV-6—Implicated as cause of roseola (exanthem subitum) & other febrile diseases of childhood (NEJM 352:768, 2005). Fever & rash documented in transplant pts (JID 179:311, 1999). Reactivation in 47% of 110 U.S. hematopoietic stem cell transplant pts assoc. with delayed monocyte & platelet engraftment (CID 40:932, 2005). Recognized in assoc. with meningoencephalitis in immunocompetent adults. Diagnosis made by pos. PCR in CSF. ↓ viral copies in CSF in response to ganciclovir rx (CID 40:890 & 894, 2005). Foscarnet therapy improved thrombotic microangiopathy (Am J Hematol 76:156, 2004). Cidofovir is second line therapy (Bone Marrow Transplantation 2008) 42, 227–240)		
HHV-7—ubiquitous virus (>90% of the population is infected by age 3 yrs). No relationship to human disease. Infects CD4 lymphocytes via CD4 receptor; transmitted via saliva.		
HHV-8—The agent of Kaposi's sarcoma, Castleman's disease, & body cavity lymphoma. Associated with diabetes in sub-Saharan Africa (JAMA 299:2770, 2008).	No antiviral treatment. Effective anti-HIV therapy may help.	Localized lesions: radiotherapy, laser surgery or intralesional chemotherapy. Systemic: chemotherapy. Castleman's disease responded to ganciclovir (Blood 103:1632, 2004) & valganciclovir (Blood 2006).
Herpes simplex virus (HSV Types 1 & 2)		
Bell's palsy H. simplex most common etiology. Other etiologic considerations: VZV, HHV-6, Lyme disease.	As soon as possible after onset of palsy: **Valacyclovir** 1 mg/kg po divided bid x 5 days then taper to 5 mg bid over the next 5 days (total of 10 days of Prednisone). + **Prednisone** 1 mg/	Cochrane Review (2015)/JAMA 2016,316:874) "compared with oral corticosteroids alone, addition of valacyclovir or famciclovir associated with greater number of recoveries at 3–12 mos".
Encephalitis (Excellent reviews: CID 35: 254, 2002). UK experience (EID 9:234, 2003; Eur J Neurol 12:331, 2005; Antiviral Res: 71:141-148, 2006). HSV-1 is most common cause of sporadic encephalitis; Survival & recovery from neurological sequelae are related to mental status at time of initiation of rx. **Early dx and rx imperative** NEJM 371:68, 2014.	**Acyclovir** IV 10 mg/kg IV (infus over 1 hr) q8h x 14-21 days. 20 mg/kg q8h in children <12 yrs. Dose calculation in obese patients uncertain. To lessen risk of nephrotoxicity with larger doses seems reasonable to infuse each dose over more than 1 hour. In morbid obesity, use actual body weight.	Mortality rate reduced from >70% to 19% with acyclovir rx. PCR analysis of CSF for HSV-1 DNA is 100% specific & 75–98% sensitive. 8/33 (25%) CSF samples drawn before day 3 were neg by PCR; neg. PCR assoc. with ↓ protein & <10 WBC per mm³ in CSF (CID day 3 36:335, 2003). All were + after 3 days. Relapse was associated with a lower total dose of initial acyclovir rx (285 ± 82 mg per kg in relapse group vs. 462 ± 149 mg per kg, p <0.03). (CID 30:185, 2000; Neuropediatrics 35:371, 2004). Series in 106 adults J Clin Virol 60:112, 2014
Genital Herpes: Sexually Transmitted Treatment Guidelines MMWR 64(RR-3):1, 2015; NEJM 2016,375:666.		
Primary (initial episode)	**Acyclovir** (Zovirax or generic) 400 mg po tid x 7–10 days OR **Valacyclovir** (Valtrex) 1000 mg po bid x 7-10 days __OR__ **Famciclovir** (Famvir) 250 mg po tid x 7–10 days	↓ by 2 days time to resolution of signs & symptoms, ↓ by 4 days time to healing of lesions, ↓ by 7 days duration of viral shedding. Does not prevent recurrences. For severe cases only: 5 mg per ≥9 IV q8h times 5-7 days. An ester of acyclovir, which is well absorbed, bioavailability 3-5 times greater than acyclovir. Metabolized to penciclovir, which is active component. Side effects and activity similar to acyclovir. **Famciclovir** 250 mg po tid **equal to acyclovir** 200 mg 5 times per day.
Episodic recurrences	**Acyclovir** 800 mg po tid x 2 days or 400 mg po tid x 5 days or **Famciclovir** 1000 mg po bid x 1 day or 125 mg po bid x 5 days or **Valacyclovir** 500 mg po bid x 3 days or 1 gm po once daily x 5 days For HIV patients, see Comment	For episodic recurrences in HIV patients: **Acyclovir** 400 mg po tid x 5–10 days or **Famciclovir** 500 mg po bid x 5–10 days or **Valacyclovir** 1 gm po bid x 5–10 days

TABLE 14A (5)

VIRUS/DISEASE	DRUG/DOSAGE	SIDE EFFECTS/COMMENTS
Herpesvirus Infections/Herpes simplex virus (HSV Types 1 & 2)		
Chronic daily suppression	Suppressive therapy reduces the frequency of genital herpes recurrences by 70–80% among pts who have frequent recurrences (i.e., >6 recurrences per yr) & many report no symptomatic outbreaks. **Acyclovir** 400 mg po bid, **or Famciclovir** 250 mg po bid, **or Valacyclovir** 1 gm po q24h; pts with <9 recurrences per yr could use 500 mg po q24h and then use **Valacyclovir** 1 gm po q24h if breakthrough at 500 mg. For HIV patients, see Comment.	For chronic suppression in HIV patients: (all regimens equally efficacious: *Cochrane Database System Rev 8:CD009036, 2014)* **Acyclovir** 400–800 mg po bid or tid or **Famciclovir** 500 mg po bid or **Valacyclovir** 500 mg po bid
Genital, immunocompetent		
Gingivostomatitis, primary (children)	**Acyclovir** 15 mg/kg po 5x/day x 7 days	Efficacy in randomized double-blind placebo-controlled trial *(BMJ 314:1800, 1997).*
Keratoconjunctivitis and recurrent epithelial keratitis	**Trifluridine** (Viroptic), 1 drop 1% solution q2h (max. 9 drops per day) for max. of 21 days *(See Table 1, page 14)*	In controlled trials, response % > idoxuridine. Suppressive rx with acyclovir (400 mg bid) reduced recurrences of ocular HSV from 32% to 19% *(NEJM 339:300, 1998).*
Mollaret's recurrent "aseptic" meningitis (usually HSV-2)	No controlled trials of antiviral rx & resolves spontaneously. If therapy is to be given, **Acyclovir** (15–30 mg/kg/ day IV) or **Valacyclovir** 1–2 gm po qid should be used.	Pos. PCR for HSV in CSF confirms dx *(E/CMID 23:560, 2004).* In randomized controlled trial, no benefit from valacyclovir suppressive rx *(CID 2012;54:1304).*
Mucocutaneous *(for Genital: see page 175)*		
Oral labial, "fever blisters":	Start rx with prodrome symptoms (tingling/burning) before lesions show.	Penciclovir *(AAC 46: 2848, 2002).* Oral acyclovir 5% cream *(AAC 46:2238, 2002).* Oral famciclovir *(JID 179:303, 1999).* Topical fluocinonide (0.05% Lidex gel) q8h times 5 days in combination with famciclovir ↓ lesion size and pain when compared to famciclovir alone *(JID 181:1906, 2000).* Acyclovir 5% cream + 1% hydrocortisone (Xerese) superior to acyclovir alone *(AAC 58:1273, 2014).*
Normal host: *See Ann Pharmacotherapy 38:705, 2004; JAC 53:703, 2004*	**Drug** **Dose** **Sx Decrease** **Oral:** Valacyclovir 2 gm po q12h x 1 day ↓1 day Famciclovir[2,4a] 500 mg po bid x 7 days ↓2 days Acyclovir[2,4a] 400 mg po 5 x per day (q4h while awake) x 5 days) ↓½ day **Topical:** Penciclovir 1% cream q2h during day x 4 days ↓1 day Acyclovir 5% cream[3] 6x/day (q3h) x 7 days ↓1½ day *See Table 1, page 27*	
Herpes Whitlow		
Oral labial or genital: Immunocompromised (includes pts with AIDS) and critically ill pts in ICU setting/large necrotic ulcers in perineum or face. (See Comment) Primary HSV in pregnancy: increased risk of dissemination, including severe hepatitis. Risk greatest in 3rd trimester *(NEJM 370:2211, 2014).*	**Acyclovir** 5 mg per kg IV (infused over 1 hr) q8h times 7 days (250 mg per M²) or 400 mg po 5 times per day times 14–21 days *(see Comment if suspect acyclovir-resistant)* **OR Famciclovir:** In HIV infected, 500 mg po bid for 7 days for recurrent episodes of genital herpes **OR Valacyclovir[2,4a]:** In HIV-infected, 500 mg po bid for 5–10 days for recurrent episodes of genital herpes or 500 mg po bid for chronic suppressive rx.	**Acyclovir-resistant HSV: IV foscarnet** 90 mg/kg IV q12h x 7 days. Suppressive therapy with famciclovir (500 mg po bid), valacyclovir (500 mg po bid) or acyclovir (400–800 mg po bid) reduces viral shedding and clinical recurrences.

[2] FDA approved only for HIV pts
[3] Approved for immunocompromised pts
[4a] See page 2 for abbreviations.   NOTE: All dosage recommendations are for adults (unless otherwise indicated) and assume normal renal function.

TABLE 14A (6)

VIRUS/DISEASE	DRUG/DOSAGE	SIDE EFFECTS/COMMENTS
Herpesvirus Infections/Herpes Simplex virus (HSV) Types 1 & 2)/Mucocutaneous (continued)		
Pregnancy and genital H. simplex	Acyclovir safe even in first trimester. No proof that acyclovir at delivery reduces risk/severity of neonatal Herpes. In contrast, C-section in women with active lesions reduces risk of transmission. Ref. Obstet Gyn 106:845, 2006.	
Herpes simiae (Herpes B virus); **Monkey bite** CID 35:1191, 2002	**Postexposure prophylaxis: Valacyclovir** 1 gm po q8h times 14 days or acyclovir 800 mg po 5 times per day times 14 days. **Treatment of disease:** (1). CNS symptoms absent: **Acyclovir** 12.5–15 mg per kg IV q8h or ganciclovir 5 mg per kg IV q12h. (2) CNS symptoms present: **Ganciclovir** 5 mg per kg IV q12h	Fatal human cases of myelitis and hemorrhagic encephalitis have been reported following bites, scratches, or eve inoculation of saliva from monkeys. Initial sx include fever, headache, myalgias and diffuse adenopathy. Incubation period of 2–14 days (EID 9:246, 2003). In vitro ACV and ganciclovir less active than other nucleosides (penciclovir or 5-ethyldeoxyuridine may be more active; clinical data needed) (AAC 51:2028, 2007).
Varicella-Zoster Virus (VZV)		
Varicella: Vaccination has markedly ↓ incidence of varicella & morbidity (MMWR 61:609, 2012). Guidelines for VZV vaccine (MMWR 56(RR-4) 2007).		
Normal host (chickenpox)		
Child (2–12 years)	**In general, treatment not recommended.** Might use oral **acyclovir** for healthy persons at ↑ risk for moderate to severe varicella, i.e., >12 yrs of age; chronic cutaneous or pulmonary diseases; chronic salicylate rx (↑ risk of Reye syndrome). **Acyclovir dose:** 20 mg/kg po qid x 5 days (start within 24 hrs of rash) or **Valacyclovir** 20 mg/kg tid x 5 days.	Acyclovir slowed development and ↓ number of new lesions and ↓ duration of disease in children: 9 to 7.6 days (PID 21:739, 2002). Oral dose of acyclovir in children should not exceed 80 mg per kg per day or 3200 mg per day.
Adolescents, young adults	Start within 24 hrs of rash: **Valacyclovir** 1000 mg po tid x 5–7 days or **Famciclovir** 500 mg po tid (probably effective, but data lacking).	↓ duration of fever, time to healing, and symptoms.
Pneumonia or chickenpox in 3rd trimester of pregnancy	**Acyclovir** 800 mg po 5 times per day or 10 mg per kg IV q8h times 5 days. Risks and benefits to fetus and mother still unknown. Many experts recommend rx, especially in 3rd trimester. Some would add VZIG (varicella-zoster immune globulin).	Varicella pneumonia associated with 41% mortality in pregnancy. Acyclovir ↓ incidence and severity (JID 185:422, 2002). If varicella-susceptible mother exposed and respiratory symptoms develop within 10 days after exposure, start acyclovir
Immunocompromised host	**Acyclovir** 10–12 mg per kg (500 mg per M²) IV (infused over 1 hr) q8h times 7 days	Disseminated 19 varicella infection reported during infliximab rx of rheumatoid arthritis (J Rheum. 31:2517, 2004). Continuous infusion of high-dose acyclovir (2 mg per kg per hr) successful in 1 pt with severe hemorrhagic varicella (NEJM 336:732, 1997).
Prevention—Postexposure prophylaxis Varicella deaths still occur in unvaccinated persons (MMWR 56 (RR-4) 1–40, 2007)	**CDC Recommendations for Prevention:** Since <5% of cases of varicella occur in this age group: **1st, varicella vaccine** (VZIG) (125 units/10 kg (22 lbs) body weight IM up to a max of 625 units); minimum dose is 125 units) is recommended for postexposure prophylaxis in susceptible persons at greater risk for complications (immunocompromised such as HIV+, pregnancy, and steroid therapy) as soon as possible after exposure (<96 hrs). If varicella develops, initiate treatment quickly (<24 hr) if rash) with acyclovir. None would receive vaccine. **2nd,** susceptible adults should be evaluated. Check antibody in adults with negative or uncertain hx (presumptively with 80–90% will be Ab+) and vaccinate those who are Ab-neg. **3rd,** susceptible children should receive vaccination. Recommended routinely before age 12–18 mos, but OK at any age.	

See page 2 for abbreviations.   NOTE: All dosage recommendations are for adults (unless otherwise indicated) and assume normal renal function.

TABLE 14A (7)

VIRUS/DISEASE	DRUG/DOSAGE	SIDE EFFECTS/COMMENTS
Herpesvirus Infections (continued)		
Herpes zoster (shingles) (See NEJM 369:255, 2013)		Increasing recognition of risk of stroke during 6 mos after episode of Shingles. Oral antivirals during clinical H. zoster infection may have protective effect (CID 58:1497, 1504, 2014). VZV found in wall of cerebral and temporal arteries of pts with giant cell arteritis. (Neurology 84:1948, 2015; JID 51:537, 2015).
Normal host	[NOTE: Trials showing benefit of therapy: only in pts treated within 3 days of onset of rash]	
• Effective therapy most evident in pts age >50 yrs.	**Valacyclovir** 1000 mg po tid times 7 days (adjust dose for renal failure) (See Table 17A)	
(For treatment of post-herpetic neuralgia, see CID 36: 877, 2003; Ln 374:1252, 2009)	OR.	
• Herpes zoster subunit vaccine (Shingrix) preferred for immunocompetent adults age 50 yrs or older (NEJM 2016;375:1019)	**Famciclovir** 500 mg tid x 7 days. Adjust for renal failure (See Table 17A)	Time to healing more rapid. Reduced incidence of post-herpetic neuralgia (PHN) vs placebo in pts >50 yrs of age. Famciclovir similar to acyclovir in reduction of acute pain and incidence of PHN (J Micro Immunol Inf 37:75, 2004).
• Analgesics for acute pain associated with Herpes zoster (NEJM 369:255, 2013)	OR	A meta-analysis of 4 placebo-controlled trials (691 pts): acyclovir accelerated by approx. 2-fold pain resolution and reduced incidence of post-herpetic neuralgia at 3 & 6 mos (CID 22:341, 1996); med. time to resolution of pain 41 days vs 101 days in those >50 yrs.
	Acyclovir 800 mg po 5 times per day times 7–10 days	In post-herpetic neuralgia, controlled trials demonstrated effectiveness of **gabapentin**, the **lidocaine patch** (5%) & **opioid analgesic** in controlling pain (Drugs 64:937, 2004; J Clin Virol 29:248, 2004). **Nortriptyline & amitriptyline** are equally effective but nortriptyline is better tolerated (CID 36:877, 2003). Role of antiviral drugs in rx of PHN
	Add **Prednisone** in pts over 50 yrs old to decrease discomfort during acute phase of zoster. Does not decrease incidence of post-herpetic neuralgia. Dose: 30 mg po bid days 1–7, 15 mg bid days 8–14 and 7.5 mg bid days 15–21.	unproven (Neurol 64:21, 2005) but 8 of 15 pt improved with IV acyclovir 10 mg/kg q 8 hrs x 14 days followed by oral valacyclovir 1gm 3x a day for 1 month (Arch Neur 63:940, 2006). Review: NEJM 371:1526, 2014; Expert Opin Pharmacotherapy 15-61, 2014
Immunocompromised host		
Not severe	**Acyclovir** 800 mg po 5 times per day times 7 days.	If progression, switch to IV.
	Options: Famciclovir 750 mg po q24h or 500 mg bid or 250 mg 3 times per day times 7 days **OR Valacyclovir** 1000 mg po tid times 7 days, though both are not FDA-approved for this indication]	RA pts on TNF-alpha inhibitors at high risk for VZV. Zoster more severe, but less post-herpetic neuralgia (JAMA 301:737, 2009).
Severe: >1 dermatome, trigeminal nerve or disseminated	**Acyclovir** 10–12 mg per kg IV (infusion over 1 hr) q8h times 7–10 days. In older pts, ↓ to 7.5 mg per kg. If nephrotoxicity and pt improving, ↓ to 5 mg per kg q8h.	A common manifestation of immune reconstitution following HAART in HIV-infected children (J All Clin Immun 113:742, 2004). For Acyclovir-resistant VZV in HIV+ pts previously treated with acyclovir: **Foscarnet** (40 mg per kg IV q8h for 14–26 days).
Progressive Outer Retinal Necrosis (PORN)	**Ganciclovir** 5 mg/kg and/or **Foscarnet** 90 mg/kg IV q12h + **Ganciclovir** 2 mg/0.05 mL and/or **Foscarnet** 1.2 mg/0.05 mL intravitreal twice weekly.	Expert consultation with an ophthalmologist. NB: **Ganciclovir** ocular implants no longer manufactured. If HIV pt, optimize ARV therapy.
Human T-cell Leukotrophic Virus-1 (HTLV-1) Causes illness in only 5% of infected persons. Two are associated with HTLV-1: Adult T-cell leukemia/lymphoma (NEJM 367:552, 2012) and HTLV-1-associated myelopathy (HAM), also known as tropical spastic paraparesis (TSP).	No proven therapy. Some nucleoside antiretroviral therapies used with limited success	Laboratory diagnosis is by blood and CSF. Anti-HTLV-1 antibodies are detected by ELISA antibody testing; Western Blot is used for confirmation (Focus Diagnostics or Quest Diagnostics). HTLV DNA can be detected by PCR in circulating CD4 cells. One tube multiplex qPCR highly specific / sensitive (Retrovirology 11(Suppl): P105, 2014).

ᵃ See page 2 for abbreviations.   NOTE: All dosage recommendations are for adults (unless otherwise indicated) and assume normal renal function.

TABLE 14A (8)

Influenza A & B and novel influenza viruses Refs: *http://www.cdc.gov/flu/professionals/antivirals/index.htm http://www.cdc.gov/flu/weekly/; NEJM 370:789, 2014.*
Vaccine Info (*http://www.cdc.gov/flu/professionals/acip/index.html*); *Med Lett 56:92, 2014; MMWR 63:591, 2014.*

- **Oseltamivir and zanamivir are recommended drugs.** Amantadine and rimantadine should not be used because of widespread resistance.
- Novel influenza HINI (referred to as pandemic HINI, pHINI, HINIpdm and formerly swine flu) emerged in 2009 and now is the dominant HINI strain worldwide. Old distinction from seasonal HINI is still sometimes used but not relevant
- Rapid influenza tests can be falsely negative in 20-50%. PCR is gold standard test.
- Initiate therapy as close to the onset of symptoms as possible, and certainly within 48 hrs of onset of symptoms. Starting therapy after 48 hours of onset of symptoms is associated with reduced therapeutic benefit. However, starting therapy up to 5 days after onset in patients who are hospitalized is associated with improved survival (*Clin Infect Dis 55:1198, 2012*).
- Empiric therapy should be started for all patients who are hospitalized, have severe or progressive influenza or are at higher risk of complications due to age or underlying medical conditions.
- Look for concomitant bacterial pneumonia.
- Other important influenza viruses causing human disease
  o **H3N2v influenza:** 159 cases of influenza A/H3N2v reported over the summer of 2012. Most of the cases of influenza A/H3N2v occurred in children under the age of 10 with direct contact with pigs. This variant is susceptible to the neuraminidase inhibitors, oseltamivir and zanamivir. See *MMWR 61:619, 2012.*
  o **Avian influenza H5N1:** Re-emerged in Asia in 2003 and human cases detected in 15 countries mostly in Asia as well as Egypt, Nigeria and Djibouti. Circulation associated with massive poultry die off. Imported cases rare – one in Canada. As of January 2014, 648 confirmed cases and 384 deaths (59%). Human infection associated with dose contact with poultry; very limited human to human transmission. Mortality associated with high viral load, disseminated replication, and high cytokine activity (*Nature Medicine 12:1203-1207 2006*). Sensitive to oseltamivir but oseltamivir resistance has emerged on therapy (*NEJM 353:2667-272, 2005*). Use oseltamivir and consider IV zanamivir
  o **Avian influenza H7N9:** Emerged in Eastern China in March 2013 and 132 cases documented during Spring 2013 with 44 deaths (33%). Cases appeared again in early winter 2013-2014 and continue to increase. Infection associated with close contact with live bird markets; extremely limited human to: human transmission to date. Mortality highest among older persons and those with medical conditions. Oseltamivir active against most but not all strains. No zanamivir resistance documented to date.

Virus/Disease	Susceptible to (Recommended Drug/Dosage):	Resistant to:	Alternatives/Side Effects/Comments
A/HINI (current seasonal resembles pandemic HINI) **Influenza B** **Influenza A (A/H3N2, A/H3N2v[a], A/H5NI, A/H7N9[a])**	**Oseltamivir** Adult: Oseltamivir 75 mg po bid x 5 days Pediatric (child age 1-12 years): Infant 2 wks-11 months: 3 mg/kg bid x 5 days ≤15 kg: 30 mg bid x 5 days >15 kg to 23 kg: 45 mg bid x 5 days >23 kg to 40 kg: 60 mg bid x 5 days >40 kg: 75 mg bid x 5 days or **Zanamivir** 2 inhalations (5 mg each) bid x 5 days or Peramivir 600 mg IV once daily x 5-10 days For IV Zanamivir, see Comment **Laninamivir** (approved in Japan): Age < 10yrs: 20 mg once daily by inhalation Age > 10 yrs: 40 mg once daily by inhalation	Amantadine and rimantadine (100%) [a] A/H3N2v strain are susceptible [a] A/H7N9 resistant to oseltamivir (rarely)	- **A/HINI:** Higher dose (150 mg bid) more effective for HINI - **Zanamivir** not recommended for children <7 years or those with reactive airway disease - **IV zanamivir** is available under compassionate use IND and clinical trials for hospitalized Influenza patients with suspected or known gastric stasis, gastric malabsorption, gastrointestinal bleeding, or for patients suspected or confirmed with oseltamivir-resistant influenza virus infection. For compassionate use, contact GlaxoSmithKline at (+1) 919-315-5215 or email: gskclinicalsupportHD@GSK.com. - **Influenza B:** One study suggested virologic benefit to higher dose oseltamivir for critically ill patients with influenza B. - **A/H5n1:** Given high mortality, consider obtaining investigational drug, Zanamivir retains activity against most oseltamivir resistant H5N1 - Association between corticosteroid rx & increased mortality (*CID 212:183, 2015*). For now, avoid steroids unless indicated for another reason.

[a] See page 2 for abbreviations.   NOTE: All dosage recommendations are for adults (unless otherwise indicated) and assume normal renal function.

TABLE 14A (9)

VIRUS/DISEASE	DRUG/DOSAGE	SIDE EFFECTS/COMMENTS
Measles Increasing reports of measles in unvaccinated children and adults *(MMWR 63:781, 2014; NEJM 371:358, 2014).*		
Children	No therapy or **vitamin A** 200,000 units po daily times 2 days	**Vitamin A** may ↓ severity of measles.
Adults	No rx or **ribavirin** IV: 20–35 mg per kg per day times 7 days	↓ severity of illness in adults *(CID 20:454, 1994).*
Metapneumovirus (HMPV)		
A paramyxovirus isolated from pts of all ages, with mild bronchiolitis/bronchospasm to pneumonia. Review: *Infect Dis Clin N Amer 2017;31:455.*	**No proven antiviral therapy** (intravenous ribavirin used anecdotally with variable results) Investigational Agents Reviewed *(Clin Vaccine Immunol 22:8 & 858, 2015)*	Human metapneumovirus isolated from 6–21% of children with RTIs *(NEJM 350:443, 2004).* Dual infection with RSV assoc. with severe bronchiolitis *(JID 191:382, 2005).*
Monkeypox (orthopox virus) *(see LnID 4:17, 2004)*		
Outbreak from contact with ill prairie dogs. Source likely imported Gambian giant rats *(CID 58:260, 2014)*	**No proven antiviral therapy.** Cidofovir is active in vitro & in mouse model	Incubation period of 12 days, then fever, headache, cough, adenopathy, & a vesicular papular rash that pustulates, umbilicates, & crusts on the head, trunk, & extremities. Transmission in healthcare setting rare.
Norovirus (Norwalk-like virus, or NLV)		
Vast majority of outbreaks of non-bacterial gastroenteritis *(JID 213(Suppl D):1, 2016).*	**No antiviral therapy.** Replete volume. Transmission by contaminated food, fecal-oral contact with contaminated surfaces, or fomites.	Sudden onset of nausea, vomiting, and/or watery diarrhea lasting 12–60 hours. Ethanol-based hand rubs effective *(J Hosp Inf 60:144, 2005).*
Papillomaviruses: Warts		
External Genital Warts Also look for warts in anal canal *(MMWR 64(3):1, 2015)*	**Patient applied:** **Podofilox** (0.5% solution or gel): apply 2x/day x 3 days, 4ᵗʰ day no therapy, repeat cycle 4x; OR **Imiquimod** 5% cream: apply once daily hs 3x/wk for up to 16 wks. **Sinecatechins:** Apply to external genital warts only 3x/day until effect or adverse effect **Provider administered:** Cryotherapy with liquid nitrogen; repeat q1-2 wks; OR **Trichloroacetic acid** (TCA): repeat weekly as needed; OR surgical removal.	**Podofilox:** Inexpensive and safe (pregnancy safety not established). Mild irritation after treatment; **Imiquimod:** Mild to moderate redness & irritation. Topical imiquimod effective for treatment of vulvar intraepithelial neoplasms *(NEJM 358:1465, 2008).* Safety in pregnancy not established. **Sinecatechins:** Local irritation, redness, pain, and itching **Cryotherapy:** Blistering and skin necrosis common. **Podophyllin resin:** No longer recommended as other less toxic regimens available. **TCA:** Caustic. Can cause severe pain on adjacent normal skin. Neutralize with soap or sodium bicarbonate.
Warts on cervix	Need evaluation for evolving neoplasia	Gynecological consult advised.
Vaginal warts	Cryotherapy with liquid nitrogen or **TCA**	
Urethral warts	Cryotherapy with liquid nitrogen.	
Anal warts	Cryotherapy with liquid nitrogen or **TCA** or surgical removal	Advise anoscopy to look for rectal warts.
Skin papillomas	**Topical α-lactalbumin. Oleic acid** (from human milk) applied 1x/day for 3 wks	↓ lesion size & recurrence vs placebo (p <0.001) *(NEJM 350:2663, 2004).* Further studies warranted.

° *See page 2 for abbreviations.   NOTE: All dosage recommendations are for adults (unless otherwise indicated) and assume normal renal function.*

TABLE 14A (10)

VIRUS/DISEASE	DRUG/DOSAGE	SIDE EFFECTS/COMMENTS
Parvo B19 Virus (Erythrovirus B19). Review: *NEJM 350:586, 2004. Wide range of manifestation. Treatment options for common symptomatic infections:*		
Erythema infectiosum	Symptomatic treatment only.	**Diagnostic tools:** IgM and Igb antibody titers. Perhaps better: blood parvovirus PCR.
Arthritis/arthralgia	Nonsteroidal anti-inflammatory drugs (NSAID)	
Transient aplastic crisis	Transfusions and oxygen	Dose of IVIG not standardized; suggest 400 mg/kg IV of commercial IVIG for 10 days or 1000 mg/kg IV for 3 days.
Fetal hydrops	Intrauterine blood transfusion	Most dramatic anemias in pts with pre-existing hemolytic anemia.
Chronic infection with anemia	**IVIG** and transfusion *(CID 56:968, 2013)* For dose, *see Comment*	Bone marrow shows erythrocyte maturation arrest with giant pronormoblasts. *(Rev Med Virol 25:224, 2015)*
Chronic infection without anemia	Perhaps **IVIG**	
Papovavirus/Polyomavirus		
Progressive multifocal leukoencephalopathy (PML) Serious demyelinating disease due to JC virus in immunocompromised pts	No specific therapy for JC virus. Two general approaches: 1. In HIV pts: HAART. Cidofovir may be effective. 2. Stop or decrease immunosuppressive therapy.	Failure of treatment with interferon alfa-2b, cytarabine and topotecan. Immunosuppressive **Natalizumab** temporarily removed from market due to reported associations with PML. Mixed reports on **cidofovir.** Most likely effective in ART-experienced pts. **Watch for IRIS when starting ARV Rx.** *(CID 49:233, 2009).*
BK virus induced nephropathy in immunocompromised pts and hemorrhagic cystitis	Decrease immunosuppression if possible. Suggested antiviral therapy based on anecdotal data. If progressive renal dysfunction: 1. **Fluoroquinolone** first; 2. **IVIG** 500 mg/kg IV; 3. **Leflunomide** 100 mg po daily x 3 days, then 10-20 mg po daily; 4. **Cidofovir** only if refractory to all of the above *(see Table 14B for dose).*	Use PCR to monitor viral "load" in urine and/or plasma. Report of cidofovir as potentially effective for BK hemorrhagic cystitis *(CID 49:233, 2009).*
Rabies *(see Table 20B, page 243; diagnosis and management: www.cdc.gov/rabies)* Rabid dogs account for 50,000 cases per yr worldwide. Most cases in the U.S. are cryptic, 70% assoc. with 2 rare bat species *(EID 9:151, 2003).* An important concern with early rabies infected 4 recipients (2 kidneys, liver, artery) all died avg. 13 days after transplant *(NEJM 352:1103, 2005).*	**Mortality 100% with only survivors those who receive rabies vaccine before the onset of illness/symptoms** *(CID 36:61, 2003).* A 15-year-old female who developed rabies 1 month post-bat bite survived after drug induction of coma (+ other rx) for 7 days, did not receive immunoprophylaxis *(NEJM 352:2508, 2005).*	Corticosteroids ↑ mortality rate and ↓ incubation time in mice. Therapies that have failed after symptoms develop include rabies vaccine, rabies immuno-globulin, rabies virus neutralizing antibody, ribavirin, alfa interferon, & ketamine. For post-exposure prophylaxis, *see Table 20B, page 243.*
Respiratory Syncytial Virus (RSV) Major cause of morbidity in neonates/infants. Diagnosis: airway swab for RSV PCR Review: *Infect Dis Clin N Amer 2017;31:455.*	All ages: Hydration, O2 as needed. If wheezing, trial of beta-agonist. *Corticosteroids:* children–no; adults–maybe Nebulized **Ribavirin:** for severe RSV in children, adults *Mono RSV antibody + RSV immune globulin:* immunocompromised adults (HSCT) *(CID 56:258, 2013).*	In adults, RSV accounted for 10.6% of hospitalizations for pneumonia, 11.4% of AECB, 7.2% for asthma & 5.4% for CHF in pts >65 yrs of age *(NEJM 352:1749, 2005).* RSV caused 11% of clinically important respiratory illnesses in military recruits *(CID 41:311, 2005).*
Prevention of RSV Inc		
(1) Children <24 mos. old with chronic lung disease or prematurity (formerly broncho-pulmonary dysplasia) requiring supple-mental O₂ or (2) Premature infants (<32 wks gestation) and <6 mos. old at start of RSV season or (3) Children with selected congenital heart diseases	**Palivizumab** (Synagis) 15 mg per kg IM q month Nov.-Apr. See *Pediatrics 126:e16, 2010.*	Expense argues against its use. Guidance from the Academy of Pediatrics recommends use of Palivizumab only in newborn infants born at 29 weeks gestation (or earlier) and in special populations (e.g., those infants with significant heart disease). *(Pediatrics 2014;134:415-420)*

ª See page 2 for abbreviations.   NOTE: All dosage recommendations are for adults (unless otherwise indicated) and assume normal renal function.

TABLE 14A (11)

VIRUS/DISEASE	DRUG/DOSAGE	SIDE EFFECTS/COMMENTS
Respiratory Syncytial Virus (RSV) (continued)		
Rhinovirus (Colds) See Infect Dis Clin N Amer 2017:31:455; Chest 2017;152:1021. Found in 1/2 of children with community-acquired pneumonia; role in pathogenesis unclear (CID 39:681, 2004). High rate of rhinovirus identified in children with significant lower resp tract infections (Ped Inf Dis 28:337, 2009).	No antiviral rx indicated (Ped Ann 34:52, 2005). Symptomatic rx: • **Ipratropium bromide** nasal (2 sprays per nostril tid) • **Clemastine** 1.34 mg 1–2 tab po bid–tid (OTC). Oral zinc preparations reduce duration of symptoms by ~ 1 day; does not reduce severity of symptoms (JAMA 311:1440, 2014) Avoid intranasal zinc products (see Comment).	Sx relief: ipratropium nasal spray ↓ rhinorrhea and sneezing vs placebo (Ann IM 125:89, 1996). Clemastine (an antihistamine) ↓ sneezing, rhinorrhea but associated with dry mouth, mouth & throat in 6–19% (CID 22:656, 1996). **Echinacea** didn't work (CID 38:1367, 2004 & 40:807, 2005)—put it to rest! Public health advisory advising that three over-the-counter cold remedy products containing **zinc** (e.g., Zicam) should not be used because of multiple reports of permanent anosmia (www.fda.gov/Safety/MedWatch/SafetyInformation/SafetyAlertsforHumanMedicalProducts/ucm166996.htm).
Rotavirus: Leading recognized cause of diarrhea-related illness among infants and children world-wide and kills ½ million children annually.	No antiviral rx available: oral hydration life-saving.	**Two live-attenuated vaccines highly effective (85 and 98%)** and safe in preventing rotavirus diarrhea and hospitalization (NEJM 354: 1 & 23, 2006). ACIP recommends either of the two vaccines, RV1 or RV5, for infants (MMWR 58(RR02): 1, 2009).
Smallpox (NEJM 346:1300, 2002)	Smallpox vaccine (if within 4 days of exposure) + cidofovir (dosage uncertain but likely similar to CMV (5 mg/kg IV once weekly for 2 weeks followed by once weekly dosing. Must be used with hydration and Probenecid; contact CDC: 770-488-7100.	
Contact vaccinia (JAMA 288:1901, 2002)	From vaccination: Progressive vaccinia—vaccinia immune globulin may be of benefit, contact CDC: 770-488-7100. (CID 39:759, 776 & 819, 2004)	
West Nile virus: See page 173		
Zika Virus: Mosquito (Aedes sp.) transmitted flavivirus CDC updates at: http://www.cdc.gov/zika/index.html	No treatment available. Symptomatic support (avoid aspirin, NSAIDs until Dengue ruled out. Most serious manifestation of infection is **congenital birth defect(s):** microcephaly and fetal demise. Sexual transmission occurs. For preconception counseling and prevention, see MMWR 65(39):1077, 2016.	3–7 day incubation. Asymptomatic infection most often; when symptoms occur, usually consists of low grade fever, arthralgias, morbilliform rash, and / or conjunctival redness (non-purulent conjunctivitis). Duration of symptoms ranges from a few days to one week. Rare Guillain-Barré syndrome. Hospitalization very infrequent, fatalities are very rare.

TABLE 14B – ANTIVIRAL DRUGS (NON-HIV)

DRUG NAME(S) GENERIC (TRADE)	DOSAGE/ROUTE IN ADULTS*	COMMENTS/ADVERSE EFFECTS
CMV		
Cidofovir (Vistide)	5 mg per kg IV once weekly for 2 weeks, then once every other week. **Properly timed IV prehydration with normal saline & Probenecid must be used with each cidofovir infusion:** 2 gm po 3 hrs before each dose and further 1 gm doses 2 & 8 hrs after completion of the cidofovir infusion. Renal function (serum creatinine and urine protein) must be monitored prior to each dose (*see pkg insert for details*). Contraindicated if creatinine >1.5 mg/dL, CrCl ≤55 mL/min or urine protein ≥100 mg/dL.	**Adverse effects: Nephrotoxicity:** dose-dependent proximal tubular injury (Fanconi-like syndrome): proteinuria, glycosuria, bicarbonaturia, phosphaturia, polyuria (nephrogenic diabetic insipidus, ↑ creatinine. Concomitant saline prehydration, probenecid, extended dosing intervals allow use but still highly nephrotoxic. Other major toxicities: neutropenia (give G-CSF as needed); eye: monthly intra-ocular pressure. Dc cidofovir if pressure decreases 50% or uveitis occurs. **Black Box warning.** Renal impairment can occur after ≤2 doses. Contraindicated in pts receiving concomitant nephrotoxic agents. Monitor for ↓ WBC. In animals, carcinogenic, teratogenic, causes ↓ sperm and ↓ fertility. FDA indication only CMV retinitis in HIV pts. **Comment:** Dose must be reduced or discontinued if changes in renal function occur during rx. For ↑ of 0.3-0.4 mg per dl. in serum creatinine, cidofovir dose must be ↓ from 5 to 3 mg per kg; discontinue cidofovir if ↑ of 0.5 mg per dl. above baseline or 3+ proteinuria develops (for 2+ proteinuria, observe pts carefully and consider dc discontinuation).
Foscarnet (Foscavir)	Induction: 90 mg per kg IV, over 1.5-2 hours, q12h OR 60 mg per kg, over 1 hour, q8h Maintenance: 90 –120 mg per kg IV, over 2 hours, q24h Dosage adjustment with renal dysfunction (*see Table 17A*).	Use infusion pump to control rate of administration. **Adverse effects:** Major toxicity is renal impairment (1/3 of patients). Can cause infusion-related ionized hypocalcemia: manifests as arrhythmia, tetany, paresthesia, changes in mental status. Slow infusion rate and avoid drugs that lower Ca++, e.g., pentamidine. –↑ creatinine, proteinuria, nephrogenic diabetes insipidus, ↓K+, ↓Ca++, ↓ Mg++. Adequate hydration may ↓ toxicity. Other: headache: mild (100%); fatigue (100%), nausea (30%), fever (25%). CNS: seizures. Hematol: ↓ WBC, ↓ Hgb. Hepatic: liver function tests ↑. Neuropathy. Penile and oral ulcers.
Ganciclovir (Cytovene)	IV: 5 mg per kg q12h times 14 days (induction) 5 mg per kg IV q24h or 6 mg per kg 5 times per wk (maintenance) Dosage adjust. with renal dysfunction (*see Table 17A*)	**Adverse effects: Black Box warnings:** cytopenias, carcinogenicity/teratogenicity & aspermia in animals. Absolute neutrophil count: dropped below 500 per mm³ in 15%, thrombocytopenia 21%, anemia 6%. Fever 48%, GI 50%: nausea, vomiting, diarrhea, abdominal pain 19%, rash 10%. Confusion, headache, psychiatric disturbances and seizures. Neutropenia may respond to granulocyte colony stimulating factor (G-CSF or GM-CSF). Severe myelosuppression may be ↑ with coadministration of zidovudine or azathioprine. 32% dc/interrupt rx, principally for neutropenia. Avoid extravasation.
Letermovir (Prevymis)	480 mg po/IV once daily starting between days 0-28 post-transplant & continuing to day 100	**Adverse effects:** N/V, diarrhea, peripheral edema, cough, headache, abdominal pain **Drug interactions:** ↑ concomitant cyclosporine, reduce dose to 240 mg once daily. Avoid if severe hepatic impairment.
Valganciclovir (Valcyte)	450 mg tablets; take with food. Oral solution: 50 mg/mL. Adult dose 900 mg. Treatment (induction): 900 mg po q12h with food. Prophylaxis (maintenance): 900 mg po q24h. Dosage adjustment for renal dysfunction (*See Table 17A*).	A prodrug of ganciclovir with better bioavailability than oral ganciclovir: 60% with food. Preg cat: C (may be teratogenic, contraceptive precaution for females). **Adverse effects:** Similar to ganciclovir. May cause dose limiting neutropenia, anemia, thrombocytopenia. Acute renal failure may occur. Diarrhea (16-41%), nausea (8-30%), vomiting (3-21%). CMV retinitis (sight-threatening lesions): 900 mg po q12h + intravitreal Ganciclovir: 900 mg po q12h x 14-21 days, then 900 mg po q24h for maintenance.
Herpesvirus		
Acyclovir (Zovirax or generic)	Doses: *see Table 14A for various indications* 400 mg or 800 mg tab 200 mg cap Suspension 200 mg per 5 mL Ointment or cream 5% IV injection Dosage adjustment for renal dysfunction	**po:** Generally well-tolerated with occ. diarrhea, vertigo, fatigue, insomnia, fever, menstrual abnormalities, acne, sore throat, muscle cramps, lymphadenopathy. Less frequent rash, arthralgia. With high doses may crystalize in renal tubules → obstructive uropathy (rapid infusion, dehydration, renal insufficiency and ↑ dose ↑ risk). Adequate pre-hydration may prevent such nephrotoxicity. **Hepatic:** ↑ ALT, AST. Uncommon: neutropenia, rash, diaphoresis, hypotension, headache, nausea. **Neurotoxicity:** hallucination, death delusions, involuntary movements. To avoid, lower dose if renal impairment (*AJM 128:692, 2015*). **IV:** Phlebitis, caustic with vesicular lesions with IV infiltration. **IV or po:** Renal (3%): ↑ creatinine, hematuria.

*See page 2 for abbreviations.

NOTE: *All dosage recommendations are for adults (unless otherwise indicated) and assume normal/renal function.*

TABLE 14B (2)

DRUG NAME(S) GENERIC (TRADE)	DOSAGE/ROUTE IN ADULTS[a]	COMMENTS/ADVERSE EFFECTS
Herpesvirus *(continued)*		
Famciclovir (Famvir)	125 mg, 250 mg, 500 mg tabs Dosage depends on indication: *(see label and Table 14A).*	Metabolized to penciclovir. **Adverse effects:** similar to acyclovir; included headache, nausea, diarrhea, and dizziness but incidence does not differ from placebo. May be taken without regard to meals. Dose should be reduced if CrCl <60 mL per min *(see package insert & Table 14A, page 175 & Table 17A, page 235).* May be taken with or without food.
Penciclovir (Denavir)	Topical 1% cream	Apply to area of recurrence of herpes labialis with start of sx, then q2h while awake times 4 days. Well tolerated.
Trifluridine (Viroptic)	Topical 1% solution: 1 drop q2h (max. 9 drops/day) until corneal re-epithelialization, then dose is ↓ for 7 more days (one drop q4h for at least 5 drops/day), not to exceed 21 days total rx.	Mild burning (5%), palpebral edema (3%), punctate keratopathy, stromal edema. For HSV keratoconjunctivitis or recurrent epithelial keratitis.
Valacyclovir (Valtrex)	500 mg, 1 gm tabs Dosage depends on indication and renal function *(see label, Table 14A & Table 17A)*	An ester pro-drug of acyclovir that is well-absorbed, bioavailability 3-5 times greater than acyclovir. **Adverse effects** similar to acyclovir. Thrombotic thrombocytopenic purpura/hemolytic uremic syndrome reported in pts with advanced HIV disease and transplant recipients participating in clinical trials at doses of 8 gm per day. Death delusion with high serum levels.
Valganciclovir (Valcyte)	450 mg tablets; take with food. Oral solution: 50 mg/mL. Adult does 900 mg. Treatment (induction): 900 mg po q12h with food. Prophylaxis (maintenance): 900 mg po q24h. Dosage adjustment for renal dysfunction *(See Table 17A).*	A prodrug of ganciclovir with better bioavailability than oral ganciclovir; 60% with food. Preg cat: C (may be teratogenic, contraceptive precaution for females). **Adverse effects:** Similar to ganciclovir. May cause dose limiting neutropenia, anemia, thrombocytopenia. Acute renal failure may occur. Diarrhea (16-41%), nausea (8-30%), vomiting (3-21%). **CMV retinitis** (sight-threatening lesions): 900 mg po q12h + intravitreal Ganciclovir: 900 mg po q12h x 14-21 days, then 900 mg po q24h for maintenance.
Hepatitis B		
Adefovir dipivoxil (Hepsera)	10 mg po q24h (with normal CrCl) 10 mg tab	It is an acyclic nucleotide analog with activity against hepatitis B (HBV) at 0.2-2.5 mM (IC₅₀). See *Table 9* for Cmax & T½. Active against lamivudine-resistant HBV strains and in vitro vs. entecavir- resistant strains. To minimize resistance, use in combination with lamivudine for lamivudine-resistant HBV strains; consider alternative therapy if viral load remains >1,000 copies/mL with treatment. Primarily renal excretion—adjust dose. No food interactions. Generally few side effects, but **Black Box warning** regarding lactic acidosis/hepatic steatosis with nucleoside analogs. At 10 mg per day potential for delayed nephrotoxicity. Monitor renal function, esp. in pts with pre-existing or other risks for renal impairment. Pregnancy Category C. **Hepatitis may exacerbate when treatment discontinued;** monitor closely. Up to 25% of pts developed ALT ↑ 10 times normal within 12 wks; usually responds to re-treatment or self-limited, but hepatic decompensation has occurred. **Do not use adefovir in HIV infected patients.**
Entecavir (Baraclude)	0.5 mg q24h. If refractory or resistant to lamivudine or telbivudine: 1 mg per day Tabs: 0.5 mg & 1 mg. Oral solution: 0.05 mg/mL. Administer on an empty stomach.	A nucleoside analog active against HBV including lamivudine-resistant mutants. Minimal adverse effects reported; headache, fatigue, dizziness, & nausea reported in 22% of pts. Alopecia, anaphylactoid reactions reported. Potential for lactic acidosis and exacerbation of hepB at discontinuation (**Black Box warning**). Do not use as single anti-retroviral agent in HIV co-infected pts; M184 mutation can emerge *(NEJM 356:2614, 2007).* Adjust dosage in renal impairment *(see Table 17A, page 234).* **Black Box warnings:** caution; dose is lower than HIV dose, so must exclude co-infection with HIV before using this formulation; lactic acidosis/hepatic steatosis; severe exacerbation of liver disease can occur on dc. YMDD-mutants resistant to lamivudine may emerge on treatment.
Lamivudine (3TC) (Epivir-HBV)	HBV dose: 100 mg po q24h Dosage adjustment with renal dysfunction *(see label).* Tabs 100 mg and oral solution 5 mg/mL	**Adverse effects:** See *Table 14D.*

[a] *See page 2 for abbreviations. NOTE: All dosage recommendations are for adults (unless otherwise indicated) and assume normal renal function.*

TABLE 14B (3)

DRUG NAME(S) GENERIC (TRADE)	DOSAGE/ROUTE IN ADULTS*	COMMENTS/ADVERSE EFFECTS
Hepatitis B *(continued)*		
Telbivudine (Tyzeka)	**HBV:** 600 mg orally q24h, without regard to food. Dosage adjustment with renal dysfunction, Ccr <50 mL/min *(see label).* 600 mg tabs; 100 mg per 5 mL solution.	An oral nucleoside analog approved for Rx of Hep B. It has ↑ rates of response and superior viral suppression than lamivudine *(NEJM 357:2576, 2007).* **Black Box warnings** regarding lactic acidosis/hepatic steatosis with nucleosides and potential for severe exacerbation of HepB on dc. Generally well-tolerated with ↑ mitochondrial toxicity, myopathies, and no dose limiting toxicity observed *(Medical Letter 49:11, 2007).* Myalgias, myopathy and rhabdomyolysis reported. Rare peripheral neuropathy. Emtricitabine resistance was 4% by one yr, ↑ to 21.6% by 2 yrs of rx of edge pts. Selects for rtM2OI (YMDD) mutation like lamivudine. Combination with lamivudine was inferior to monotherapy *(Hepatology 45:507, 2007).*
Tenofovir (TDF/TAF)	See page 200	
Hepatitis C - (For all HCV direct acting agents (DAA) a **Black Box warning** exists regarding potential flare of HBV when HCV is cured among those coinfected with HBV and HCV)		
Direct Acting Agents:		
Daclatasvir (Daklinza)	60 mg 1 tab po once daily (dose adjustment when used with CYP 3A4 inhibitors / inducers)	Contraindicated with strong CYP3A inducers, e.g., phenytoin, carbamazepine, Rifampin, St. John's wort. Most common AE: headache and fatigue. Bradycardia when administered in combination with Sofosbuvir and Amiodarone. **Co-administration with Amiodarone not recommended.** If used, cardiac monitoring advised.
Elbasvir + Grazoprevir (Zepatier)	Combination formulation (Elbasvir 50 mg + Grazoprevir 100 mg) 1 tab po once daily	NS5A and NS3-4a PI inhibitors with activity against genotypes 1 and 4. Contraindicated in patients with moderate or severe hepatic impairment (Child-Pugh Class B or C). Also contraindicated with concomitant use of organic ion transporter polypeptide 1B (OATP1B) inhibitors, strong inducers of cytochrome P450 3A (CYP3A), and efavirenz.
Glecaprevir + Pibrentasvir (Mavyret)	Combination formulation (Glecaprevir 100 mg + Pibrentasvir 40 mg) 3 tabs, po once daily with food	Contraindicated if severe hepatic impairment (Child-Pugh C). **Do not co-administer with Atazanavir or Rifampin.** Most common AEs: headache and fatigue.
Ledipasvir + Sofosbuvir (Harvoni);	Combination formulations: (Ledipasvir 90 mg + Sofosbuvir 400 mg) 1 tab po once daily; (Voxilaprevir 100 mg + Sofosbuvir 400 mg) 1 tab po daily; (Velpatasvir 100 mg + Sofosbuvir 400 mg) 1 tab po once daily with food	NS5A/NS5B inhibitor combination for Genotype 1 HCV. First agent for HCV treatment without Ribavirin or Interferon. No adjustment for mile/moderate renal or hepatic impairment. Most common AEs: fatigue (16%), headache (14%), insomnia (7%), nausea (7%), diarrhea (3%). Antacids and H2 blockers interfere with absorption of ledipasvir. The drug solubility decreases as pH increases. Recommended to separate administration of ledipasvir and antacid Rx by at least 4 hours.
Voxilaprevir + Velpatasvir + Sofosbuvir (Vosevi)		
Paritaprevir + Ritonavir + Ombitasvir + Dasabuvir (PrOD) (Viekira Pak);	Ombitasvir 12.5 mg, Paritaprevir 75 mg, and Ritonavir 50 mg co-packaged with tablets of Dasabuvir 250 mg (Viekira Pak); or without Dasabuvir (Technivie)	Do not co-administer with drugs that are highly dependent on CYP3A for clearance; strong inducers of CYP3A and CYP2C8; and strong inhibitors of CYP2C8. Do not use if known hypersensitivity to Ritonavir (e.g., toxic epidermal necrolysis, Stevens-Johnson syndrome). If used with Ribavirin: fatigue, nausea, pruritus, other skin reactions, insomnia and asthenia. When used without Ribavirin: fatigue, nausea, pruritus and insomnia. **Warning: Hepatic decompensation and hepatic failure, including liver transplantation or fatal outcomes, have been reported mostly in patients with advanced cirrhosis.**
Paritaprevir + Ritonavir + Ombitasvir (Technivie)		
Simeprevir (Olysio)	150 mg 1 cap po once daily with food + both Ribavirin and Interferon	NS3/4A inhibitor. Need to screen patients with HCV genotype 1a for the Q80K polymorphism; if present consider alternative therapy. Contraindicated in pregnancy and in men whose female partners are pregnant (risk category C₁, concern is combination with ribavirin (risk category X). No dose adjustment required in patients with mild, moderate or severe renal impairment. No dose adjustment for mild hepatic impairment. Most common AEs (in combination with Ribavirin, Interferon): rash, pruritus, nausea. CYP3A inhibitors affect plasma concentration of Simeprevir.
Sofosbuvir (Sovaldi)	400 mg 1 tab po once daily with food + both Pegylated Interferon and Ribavirin. For combination formulation, see Ledipasvir.	NS5B inhibitor for Genotypes 1, 2, 3, 4 HCV. Efficacy established in patients awaiting liver transplant and in patients with HIV-1/HCV co-infection. No adjustment needed for mild to moderate renal impairment. No dose adjustment for mild, moderate, or severe hepatic impairment. Most common AEs (in combination with Interferon and ribavirin): fatigue, headache, nausea, insomnia, anemia. Rifampin and St. John's wort may alter plasma concentration of Sofosbuvir.

* See page 2 for abbreviations.   NOTE: All dosage recommendations are for adults (unless otherwise indicated) and assume normal renal function.

TABLE 14B (4)

DRUG NAME(S) GENERIC (TRADE)ᵃ	DOSAGE/ROUTE IN ADULTSᵃ	COMMENTS/ADVERSE EFFECTS
Hepatitis C (continued)		
Other:		
Interferon alfa is available as alfa-2a (Roferon-A), alfa-2b (Intron-A)	For HCV combination therapy, usual Roferon-A and Intron-A doses are 3 million international units 3x weekly subQ.	Depending on agent, available in pre-filled syringes, vials of solution, or powder. **Black Box warnings:** can cause/aggravate psychiatric illness, autoimmune disorders, ischemic events, infection. Withdraw therapy if any of these suspected.
PEG interferon alfa-2b (PEG-Intron)	0.5–1.5 mcg/kg subQ q wk	**Adverse effects: Flu-like syndrome** is common, esp. during 1st wk of rx: fever 98%, fatigue 89%, myalgia 73%, headache 71%. GI: anorexia 46%, diarrhea 29%. CNS: dizziness 21%. Hemorrhagic or ischemic stroke. Rash 18%, may progress to Stevens Johnson or exfoliative dermatitis. Alopecia. ↑ TSH, autoimmune thyroid disorders with ↓- or ↑- thyroidism. **Hematol:** ↓ WBC 49%, ↓ platelets 35%. Post-marketing report is of antibody-mediated pure red cell aplasia in patients receiving interferon/ribavirin with erythropoiesis-stimulating agents.
Pegylated-40k interferon alfa-2a (Pegasys)	180 mcg subQ q wk	Acute reversible hearing loss &/or tinnitus in up to 1/3 (Ln 343:1134, 1994). Optic neuropathy (retinal hemorrhage, cotton wool spots, ↓ in color vision) reported (AIDS 18:1805, 2004). Doses may require adjustment (or dc) based on individual response or adverse events, and can vary by product, indication (eg, HCV or HBV) and mode of use (mono- or combination-rx). (Refer to labels of individual products and to ribavirin if used in combination for details of use.)
Ribavirin (Rebetol, Copegus)	For use with an interferon for hepatitis C. Available as 200 mg caps and 40 mg/mL oral solution (Rebetol) or 200 mg and 400 mg tabs (Copegus) (See Comments regarding dosage).	**Black Box warnings:** ribavirin monotherapy of HCV is ineffective; hemolytic anemia may precipitate cardiac events; teratogenic/ embryocidal (**Preg Category X**). Drug may persist for 6 mos, avoid pregnancy for at least 6 mos after end of rx of women or their partners. Only approved for pts with Ccr >50 mL/min. Do not use in pts with severe heart disease or hemoglobinopathies. ARDS reported (Chest 124:406, 2003). **Adverse effects:** hemolytic anemia (may require dose reduction or dc), dental/periodontal disorders, and all adverse effects of concomitant interferon must be used (see above). Postmarketing: retinal detachment, ↓ hearing, hypersensitivity reactions. See Table 14A for specific regimens, but dosing depends on: interferon used, weight, HCV genotype, and is modified (or dc) based on side effects (especially degree of hemolysis), with different criteria in those with/without cardiac disease. **Initial Rebetol dose with Intron A (interferon alfa-2b) is wt-based:** 400 mg am & 600 mg pm for ≤75 kg, and 600 mg am & 600 mg pm for wt >75 kg, but with Pegintron approved dose is 400 mg am & 400 mg pm with meals. Doses and duration of Copegus with peg-interferon alfa-2a are less in pts with genotype 2 or 3 (800 mg per day divided into 2 doses, for 24 wks) than with genotypes 1 or 4 (1000 mg per day [divided into 2 doses for wt <75 kg and 1200 mg per day divided into 2 doses for >75 kg for 48 wks]); in HIV/HCV co-infected pts, dose is 800 mg per day regardless of genotype. (See individual labels for details, including initial dosing and criteria for dose modification in those with/without cardiac disease.)
Influenza A		
Amantadine (Symmetrel) or Rimantadine (Flumadine) Influenza B is intrinsically resistant.	**Amantadine** 100 mg caps, tabs; 50 mg/mL oral solution & syrup. Treatment or prophylaxis: 100 mg bid; or 100 mg daily if age ≥65 y; dose reductions with CrCl starting at ≤50 mL/min. **Rimantadine** 100 mg tabs, 50 mg/5 mL syrup. Treatment or prophylaxis: 100 mg bid, or 100 mg daily in elderly nursing home pts, or severe hepatic disease, or CrCl ≤10 mL/min. For children, rimantadine only approved for prophylaxis.	**Side-effects/toxicity: CNS** (can be mild: nervousness, anxiety, difficulty concentrating, and lightheadedness). Serious: delirium, hallucinations, and seizures—are associated with high plasma drug levels resulting from renal insufficiency, esp. in older pts, those with prior seizure disorders, or psychiatric disorders.

ᵃ See page 2 for abbreviations.   NOTE: All dosage recommendations are for adults (unless otherwise indicated) and assume normal renal function.

TABLE 14B (5)

DRUG NAME(S) GENERIC (TRADE)	DOSAGE/ROUTE IN ADULTS[a]	COMMENTS/ADVERSE EFFECTS
Influenza A and B—For both drugs, initiate within 48 hrs of symptom onset		
Zanamivir (Relenza) For pts ≥ 7 yrs of age (treatment) or ≥5 yrs (prophylaxis)	Powder is inhaled by a specially designed inhalation device. Each blister contains 5 mg zanamivir. **Treatment:** oral inhalation of 2 blisters (10 mg) bid for 5 days. **Prophylaxis:** oral inhalation of 2 blisters (10 mg) once daily for 10 days (household outbreak) to 28 days (community outbreak).	Active by inhalation against neuraminidase of both Influenza A and B and inhibits release of virus from epithelial cells of respiratory tract. Approx. 4–17% of inhaled dose absorbed into plasma. Excreted by kidney but with low absorption, dose reduction not necessary in renal impairment. Minimal side-effects: <3% cough, sinusitis, diarrhea, nausea and vomiting. Reports of respiratory adverse events in pts with or without h/o airways disease, should be avoided in pts with underlying respiratory disease. Allergic reactions and neuropsychiatric events have been reported. **Caution: do not reconstitute zanamivir powder for use in nebulizers or mechanical ventilators** (MedWatch report of death). Zanamivir for IV administration is available for compassionate use through an emergency IND application. Contact GSK (301-796-1500 or 301-796-9900).
Oseltamivir (Tamiflu) For pts ≥1 yr (treatment or prophylaxis)	For adults: **Treatment,** 75 mg po bid for 5 days; 150 mg po bid has been used for morbidly obese patients but this dose is not FDA-recommended. **Prophylaxis,** 75 mg po once daily for 10 days to 6 wks. (See label for pediatric weight-based dosing.) Adjust doses for CCl ≤30 mL/min. 30 mg, 45 mg, 75 mg caps; powder for oral suspension.	Well absorbed (80% bioavailable) from GI tract as ethyl ester of active compound GS-4071. T½ 6–10 hrs; excreted unchanged by kidney. Adverse effects include diarrhea, nausea, vomiting, headache. Rare, severe skin reactions (toxic epidermal necrolysis, Stevens-Johnson syndrome, erythema multiforme). Delirium & abnormal behavior reported (CID 48:1003, 2009). No benefit from higher dose in non-critically ill; not recommended (CID 57:1511, 2013).
Peramivir (Rapivab)	600 mg IV single dose (acute uncomplicated influenza)	FDA indication is for single dose use in acute uncomplicated influenza. No approved dose for hospitalized patients but 200–400 mg IV daily for 5 days used in trial. Flu with H275Y oseltamivir resistance has moderate resistance to peramivir
Respiratory Syncytial Virus (RSV) monoclonal antibody		
Palivizumab (Synagis) Used for prevention of RSV infection in high-risk children	15 mg per kg IM q month throughout RSV season Single dose 100 mg vial	A monoclonal antibody directed against the surface F glycoprotein; **AEs:** uncommon, occ. ↑ ALT. Anaphylaxis <1/10³ pts; acute hypersensitivity reaction <1/1000. Postmarketing reports: URI, otitis media, fever, ↓ pits, injection site reactions. Preferred over polyclonal immune globulin in high risk infants & children.
Warts Regimens are from drug labels specific for external genital and/or perianal condylomata acuminata only *(see specific labels for indications, regimens, age limits).*		
Interferon alfa-2b (Intron A)	Injection of 1 million international units into base of lesion, thrice weekly on alternate days for up to 3 wks. Maximum 5 lesions per course.	Interferons may cause "flu-like" illness and other systemic effects. 88% had at least one adverse effect. **Black box warning:** alpha interferons may cause or aggravate neuropsychiatric, autoimmune, ischemic or infectious disorders.
Interferon alfa-N3 (Alferon N)	Injection of 0.05 mL into base of each wart, up to 0.5 mL total per session, twice weekly for up to 8 weeks.	Contraindicated with allergy to mouse IgG, egg proteins, or neomycin.
Imiquimod (Aldara)	5% cream. Thin layer applied at bedtime, washing off after 6-10 hr, thrice weekly to maximum of 16 wks; 3.75% cream apply qd.	Erythema, itching & burning, erosions. Flu-like syndrome, increased susceptibility to sunburn (avoid UV).
Podofilox (Condylox)	0.5% gel or solution twice daily for 3 days, no therapy for 4 days, can use up to 4 such cycles.	Local reactions—pain, burning, inflammation in 50%. Can ulcerate. Limit surface area treated as per label.
Sinecatechins (Veregen)	15% ointment. Apply 0.5 cm strand to each wart three times per day until healing but not more than 16 weeks.	Application site reactions, which may result in ulcerations, phimosis, meatal stenosis, superinfection.

[a] *See page 2 for abbreviations.   NOTE: All dosage recommendations are for adults (unless otherwise indicated) and assume normal renal function*

TABLE 14C – ANTIRETROVIRAL THERAPY (ART) IN TREATMENT-NAÏVE ADULTS (HIV/AIDS)

Overview
- Antiretroviral therapy (ART) in **treatment-naïve adults** (aidsinfo.nih.gov/guidelines/html/1/adult-and-adolescent-treatment-guidelines/0)
- Guidelines: *www.aidsinfo.nih.gov; iasusa.org; JAMA 316:191, 2016*

When to Start ART
- **All patients with HIV regardless of CD4 count** (*NEJM 373:795, 2015; NEJM 373:808, 2015*)
- Only exceptions are:
  - Patient is not ready to start (for personal reasons or lack of commitment to take medications)
  - Patient is an "Elite Controller", i.e., HIV RNA undetectable for extended period without ART. Controversy exists about treating such patients, though many experts suggest ART owing to inflammation resulting from ongoing de novo HIV replication.
  - Many clinics are adopting a "treat now" policy whereby the ARV regimen is started on the first encounter with the clinic. In such instances, resistance tests are obtained and the regimen(s) adjusted as indicated once the resistance test data return.

What Regimen to Start
- Design a regimen consisting of:

Dual nucleoside / nucleotide reverse transcriptase inhibitor (**NRTI component**) PLUS either a	• Non-nucleoside reverse transcriptase inhibitor (**NNRTI**) **OR** • Protease inhibitor (**PI**) **OR** • Integrase strand-transfer inhibitor (**INST**)

Note: Prefer combination that includes Tenofovir-AF over original Tenofovir-DF

NRTI: e.g., Tenofovir, Abacavir, Emtricitabine, or Lamivudine
NNRTI: e.g., Efavirenz, Rilpivirine, or Etravirine
PI: e.g., Darunavir or Atazanavir (both boosted with either Ritonavir or Cobicistat)
INSTI: e.g., Dolutegravir, Elvitegravir, or Raltegravir

- Selection of components is influenced by many factors, including:
  - Results of viral resistance testing
  - Pregnancy: Efavirenz is now permitted for use in pregnancy; Dolutegravir and TAF not recommended yet for pregnant women owing to higher drug levels in fetus (unclear clinical significance)
  - Potential drug interactions or adverse drug effects; special focus on tolerability (even low grade side effects can profoundly affect adherence)
  - Co-morbidities (e.g., lipid effects of PIs, liver or renal disease, cardiovascular disease risk, chemical dependency, psychiatric disease)
  - Convenience of dosing. Co-formulations increase convenience, but sometimes prescribing the two constituents individually is preferred, as when dose-adjustments are needed for renal disease
  - HLA-B5701 testing required prior to using Abacavir (ABC)

Recommended Regimens

Once daily therapy (all component drugs in single tablet)	• **Genvoya** (Elvitegravir/Cobicistat/Emtricitabine/Tenofovir-AF) 1 tablet once daily **OR** • **Stribild** (Elvitegravir/Cobicistat/Emtricitabine/Tenofovir-DF) 1 tablet once daily **OR** • **Triumeq** (Abacavir/3TC/Dolutegravir) 1 tablet once daily (*See Warnings, below*)
Once or twice daily therapy (component drugs divided into separate tablets)	• **Descovy** (Emtricitabine/Tenofovir-AF) + Dolutegravir 1 tablet of each once daily **OR** • **Descovy** (Emtricitabine/Tenofovir-AF) 1 tablet once daily + Raltegravir 1 tablet twice daily **OR** • **Truvada** (Emtricitabine/Tenofovir-DF) 1 tablet once daily + Raltegravir 1 tablet twice daily **OR** • **Truvada** (Emtricitabine/Tenofovir-DF) + Dolutegravir 1 tablet of each once daily **OR** • **Epzicom/Kivexa** (Abacavir/3TC) + Dolutegravir 1 tablet of each once daily

TABLE 14C (2)

Alternative Regimens

Single tablet combinations	• **Atripla** (Tenofovir-DF/Emtricitabine/Efavirenz) 1 tablet once daily qhs OR • **Complera/Eviplera** (Emtricitabine/Tenofovir-DF/Rilpivirine) 1 tablet once daily with food (avoid when VL >100,000 cells/mL) OR • **Juluca** (Dolutegravir/ Rilpivirine) 1 tablet once daily with food (Two drug FDC used to replace initial standard 3-drug regimen after 6 months of successful suppression < 50c/ml with no evidence of virologic failure and baseline wild-type virus with no resistance mutations) OR • **Odefsey** (Emtricitabine/Tenofovir-AF/Rilpivirine) 1 tablet once daily with food (avoid when VL >100,000 cells/mL).
NNRTI based multi-tablet regimens (select one)	• **Efavirenz** 1 tablet once daily qhs **PLUS** (one from the next column) OR • **Rilpivirine** 1 tablet once daily with food (avoid when VL >100,000 cells/mL) **PLUS** (one from the next column)	• **Descovy** (Tenofovir-AF/Emtricitabine) 1 tablet once daily OR • **Truvada** (Tenofovir-DF/Emtricitabine) 1 tablet once daily OR • **Epzicom/Kivexa** (Abacavir/3TC) 1 tablet each once daily qhs (avoid when VL >100,000 cells/mL.) *(see Warnings below)*
Boosted Protease Inhibitor multi-tablet regimens (select one)	• **Evotaz** (Atazanavir/Cobicistat) 1 tablet each once daily **PLUS** (one from the next column) OR • **Atazanavir/Ritonavir** 1 tablet each once daily **PLUS** (one from the next column) OR • **Prezcobix** (Darunavir/Cobicistat) 1 tablet each once daily **PLUS** (one from the next column) OR • **Darunavir/Ritonavir** 1 tablet each once daily **PLUS** (one from the next column)	

Legend, Warnings and Notes Regarding Regimens

- Legend
  - **NNRTI** = Non-nucleoside reverse transcriptase inhibitor
  - **PI** = Protease inhibitor
  - **INSTI** = Integrase strand-transfer inhibitor
  - **Tenofovir-AF** = Tenofovir alafenamide fumarate
  - **Tenofovir-DF** = Tenofovir disoproxil fumarate
- Warnings
  - Epzicom/Kivexa (Abacavir/3TC) containing regimens: Use only in patients who are HLA-B5701 negative. Use Abacavir with caution in those with HIV RNA <100,000 c/mL
    at baseline (this does not apply when Dolutegravir is the anchor drug of the regimen)
- Notes
  - Co-formulations increase convenience, but sometimes prescribing the two components individually is preferred, as when dose adjustments are needed for renal disease.
  - Rilpivirine is best used for patients with viral load <100,000 C/L.
  - Raltegravir 800 mg once daily is not quite as effective as 400 mg bid. New formulation of Raltegravir as once daily tablet anticipated in 2017.

Other drugs that may be used in selected populations (typically not used as initial therapy)
- FDC Dolutegravir/rilpivirine can be used to simplify 3-drug regimen to 2-drugs when initial regimen successful (< 50c/ml for > 6 months), no baseline pre-Rx resistance mutations, and no virologic failure.
- Etravirine and Rilpivirine are options for some patients who have NNRTI resistance mutations, e.g., K103N, at baseline. Expert consultation is recommended.
- Boosted PIs can be administered once or twice daily.
- Both Ritonavir and Cobicistat are available as PI-boosting agents
- Non-boosted PIs are no longer recommended

Pregnancy Considerations
- Timing of initiation of therapy and drug choice must be individualized
- Viral resistance testing should be performed
- Long-term effects of agents is unknown
- Efavirenz is now a permitted alternative in pregnancy
- If recommended drugs are not available, remember that certain drugs are contraindicated, e.g., Didanosine plus Stavudine

Other Special Populations
- Primary (acute) HIV
- Hepatitis B/C co-infection (See Table 14E & 14F)
- Opportunistic infection

TABLE 14C (3)

Selected Characteristics of Antiretroviral Drugs (¹CPE = CSF penetration effectiveness: 1-4)

1. **Selected Characteristics of Nucleoside or Nucleotide Reverse Transcriptase Inhibitors (NRTIs)**

All agents have Black Box warning: **Risk of lactic acidosis/hepatic steatosis.** Also, risk of fat redistribution/accumulation. For combinations, see warnings for component agents.

¹ **CPE (CNS Penetration Effectiveness) value:** 1= Low Penetration; 2 - 3 = Intermediate Penetration; 4 = Highest Penetration into CNS (AIDS 25:357, 2011)

Generic/ Trade Name	Pharmaceutical Prep.	Usual Adult Dosage & Food Effect	% Absorbed, po	Serum T½ hrs	Intracellular T½ hrs	CPE¹	Elimination	Major Adverse Events/Comments (See Table 14D)
Abacavir (ABC, Ziagen)	300 mg tabs or 20 mg/mL oral solution	300 mg po bid or 600 mg po q24h. Food OK	83	1.5	20	1	Liver metab, renal excretion of metabolites, 82%	**Hypersensitivity reaction:** fever, rash, N/V, malaise, diarrhea, abdominal pain, respiratory symptoms. (Severe reactions may be ↑ with 600 mg dose.) **Do not rechallenge!** Report to 800-270-0425. **Test HLA-B*5701 before use.** **See Comment Table 14D.** Studies raise concerns re ABC/3TC regimens in pts with VL ≥ 100,000 (www.niaid.nih.gov/news/newsreleases/2008/actg5202bulletin.htm). Controversy re increased CV events with use of ABC. Large meta-analysis shows no increased risk (AIDS 61, 441, 2012)
Abacavir/lamivudine (Epzicom or Kivexa)	Film coated tabs ABC 600 + 3TC 300 mg	1 tab once daily (not recommended)						(See for individual components) **Black Box warning**— limited data for VL >100,000 copies/mL. Not recommended as initial therapy because of inferior virologic efficacy.
Abacavir (ABC)/ lamivudine (3TC) + dolutegravir (DTV) (Triumeq)	Film coated tabs: ABC 600 mg + 3TC 300 mg + DTV 50 mg	1 tab po once daily					*(See individual components)*	
Abacavir (ABC)/ lamivudine (3TC)/ zidovudine (AZT) (Trizivir)	Film-coated tabs: ABC 300 mg + 3TC 150 mg + ZDV 300 mg	1 tab po bid (not recommended for wt <40 kg or CrCl <50 mL/min or impaired hepatic function)						
Didanosine (ddI; Videx or Videx EC)	125, 200, 250, 400 enteric-coated caps; 100, 167, 250 mg powder for oral solution;	≥60 kg: Usually 400 mg enteric-coated po q24h 0.5 hr before or 2 hrs after meal. Do not crush. <60 kg: 250 mg EC po q24h. Food ↓ levels. See Comment	30-40	1.6	25-40	2	Renal excretion, 50%	**Pancreatitis**, peripheral neuropathy, lactic acidosis & hepatic steatosis (rare but life-threatening, esp. combined with stavudine in pregnancy). Retinal, optic nerve changes. **The combination ddI + TDF is generally avoided, but if used, reduce dose of ddI-EC from 400 mg to 250 mg EC q24h (or from 250 mg EC to 200 mg EC for adults <60 kg). Monitor for ↑ toxicity & possible ↓ in efficacy of this combination; may result in ↓ CD4.**
Dolutegravir (DTV)/ Rilpivirine (RPV) (Juluca)	Film-coated tabs: DTV 50 + RPV 25 mg	1 tab once daily with meal					*(See individual components)*	Contraindicated if prior hypersensitivity reaction to DTV or RPV; do not co-administer with dofetilide or with drugs that significantly decrease RPV plasma concentrations. Warnings: Severe skin and hypersensitivity reactions (rash) and sometimes liver injury reported with DTV and RPV. **Common AEs:** diarrhea and headache.

TABLE 14C (4)

Selected Characteristics of Antiretroviral Drugs: 1-4)

1. **Selected Characteristics of Nucleoside or Nucleotide Reverse Transcriptase Inhibitors (NRTIs): 1-4)**

Generic/ Trade Name	Pharmaceutical Prep.	Usual Adult Dosage & Food Effect	% Absorbed, po	Serum T½, hrs	Intracellular T½, hrs	CPE*	Elimination	Major Adverse Events/Comments (See Table 14D)
Emtricitabine (FTC, Emtriva)	200 mg caps; 10 mg per mL oral solution.	200 mg po q24h. Food OK	93 (caps), 75 (oral sol'n)	Approx. 10	39	3	Renal excretion 86%	Well tolerated; headache, nausea, vomiting & diarrhea occasionally, skin rarely. Skin hyperpigmentation. Differs only slightly in structure from lamivudine (5-fluoro substitution.) Exacerbation of HepB reported in pts after stopping FTC. Monitor at least several months after stopping FTC in Hep B pts; some may need anti-HBV therapy.
Emtricitabine/ tenofovir disoproxil fumarate (Truvada)	Film-coated tabs: FTC 200 mg + TDF 300 mg	1 tab po q24h for CrCl ≥50 mL/min.	92/25	10/17	—	(See individual components)	Primarily renal/renal	See Comments for individual agents Black Box warning—Exacerbation of HepB after stopping FTC but preferred therapy for those with Hep B/HIV co-Infection.
Emtricitabine/ Tenofovir/Efavirenz (Atripla)	Film-coated tabs: FTC 200 mg + TDF 300 mg + Efavirenz 600 mg	1 tab po q24h on an empty stomach, preferably at bedtime. Do not use if CrCl <50 mL/min						Not recommended for pts <18 yrs. (See warnings for individual components). Exacerbation of Hep B reported in pts discontinuing component drugs; some need anti-HBV therapy (tenofovir preferred). Pregnancy category D- Efavirenz may cause fetal harm. Avoid in pregnancy or in women who may become pregnant.
Emtricitabine/ Tenofovir/ Rilpivirine (Complera/Eviplera)	Film-coated tabs: FTC 200 mg + TDF 300 mg + RPL 25 mg	1 tab po q24h with food		(See individual components)				See individual components. Preferred use in pts with HIV RNA level <100,000 c/mL. Should not be used with PPI agents.
Lamivudine (3TC, Epivir)	150, 300 mg tabs; 10 mg/mL oral solution	150 mg po bid or 300 mg po q24h. Food OK	86	5–7	18	2	Renal excretion, minimal metabolism	Use HIV dose, not Hep B dose. Usually well-tolerated. Risk of exacerbation of Hep B after stopping 3TC. Monitor at least several months after stopping 3TC in Hep B pts; some may need anti-HBV therapy.
Lamivudine/ abacavir (Epzicom)	Film-coated tabs: 3TC 300 mg + abacavir 600 mg	1 tab po q24h. Food OK Not recommended for CrCl <50 mL/min or impaired hepatic function	86/86	5–7/1.5	16/20	(See individual components)	Primarily renal/ metabolism	See Comments for individual agents. Note abacavir hypersensitivity Black Box warnings (severe reactions may be somewhat more frequent with 600 mg dose) and 3TC Hep B warnings. Test HLA-B*5701 before use.
Lamivudine/ zidovudine (Combivir)	Film-coated tabs: 3TC 150 mg + ZDV 300 mg	1 tab po bid. Food OK Not recommended for CrCl <50 mL/min or impaired hepatic function Food OK	86/64	5–7/0.5–3	—	(See individual components)	Primarily renal/ metabolism with renal excretion of glucuronide	See Comments for individual agents Black Box warning—exacerbation of Hep B in pts stopping 3TC

TABLE 14C (5)

Selected Characteristics of Antiretroviral Drugs (*CPE = CSF penetration effectiveness: 1-4)

1. **Selected Characteristics of Nucleoside or Nucleotide Reverse Transcriptase Inhibitors (NRTIs)** *(continued)*

Generic/ Trade Name	Pharmaceutical Prep.	Usual Adult Dosage & Food Effect	% Absorbed, po	Serum T½ hrs	Intracellular T½ hrs	CPE*	Elimination	Major Adverse Events/Comments *(See Table 14D)*
Stavudine (d4T; Zerit)	15, 20, 30, 40 mg capsules; 1 mg per mL oral solution	≥60 kg: 40 mg po bid <60 kg: 30 mg po bid Food OK	86	1.2–1.6	3.5	2	Renal excretion, 40%	Not recommended by DHHS as initial therapy because of adverse reactions. Highest incidence of lipoatrophy, hyperlipidemia, & lactic acidosis of all NRTIs. Pancreatitis. Peripheral neuropathy. *(See Didanosine comments)*.
Tenofovir disoproxil fumarate (TDF; Viread)—a nucleotide	300 mg tabs	CrCl ≥50 mL/min: 300 mg po q24h. Food OK; high-fat meal ↑ absorption	39 (with food)	17	>60	1	Renal excretion	Headache, N/V. Cases of renal dysfunction reported: check renal function before using (dose reductions necessary if CrCl <50 cc/min); avoid concomitant nephrotoxic agents. One study found ↑ renal function at 48-wks in pts receiving TDF with a PI (mostly lopinavir/ritonavir) than with a NNRTI (JID 197:102, 2008). Avoid concomitant ddI. Atazanavir & lopinavir/ritonavir ↑ tenofovir concentrations: monitor for adverse effects. **Black Box warning—exacerbations of Hep B reported after stopping tenofovir.** Monitor liver enzymes if TDF stopped on HBV pts.
Tenofovir alafenamide (TAF)	25 mg (10 mg when used with Cobi or RTV)	CrCl >30 mL/min Food OK; high-fat meal ↑ absorption	25 (fasted)					
Zidovudine (ZDV, AZT; Retrovir)	100 mg caps, 300 mg tabs; 10 mg per mL IV solution; 10 mg/mL oral syrup	300 mg po q12h. Food OK	64	1.1	11	4	Metabolized to glucuronide & excreted in urine	Bone marrow suppression, GI intolerance, headache, insomnia, malaise, myopathy.
2. **Selected Characteristics of Non-Nucleoside Reverse Transcriptase Inhibitors (NNRTIs)**								
Delavirdine (Rescriptor)	100, 200 mg tabs	400 mg po three times daily. Food OK	85	5.8	3		Cytochrome P450 (3A inhibitor). 51% excreted in urine (<5% unchanged)	Rash severe enough to stop drug in 4.3%. ↑ AST/ALT, headaches. **Use of this agent is not recommended.**

TABLE 14C (6)

Selected Characteristics of Antiretroviral Drugs (@CPE = CSF penetration effectiveness: 1-4).

2. Selected Characteristics of Non-Nucleoside Reverse Transcriptase Inhibitors (NNRTIs) (continued)

Generic/Trade Name	Pharmaceutical Prep.	Usual Adult Dosage & Food Effect	% Absorbed, po	Serum T½, hrs	Intracellular T½, hrs	CPE	Elimination	Major Adverse Events/Comments (See Table 14D)
Efavirenz (Sustiva) New Guidelines indicate is OK to use in pregnant women (WHO Guidelines) or continue EFV in women identified as pregnant (HHS Guidelines).	50, 100, 200 mg capsules; 600 mg tablet	600 mg po q24h at bedtime, without food. Food may ↑ serum conc. which can lead to ↑ risk of adverse events.	42	40–55 See Comment	3		Cytochrome P450 2B6 (3A mixed inducer; inhibitor). 14–34% excreted in urine as glucuronidated metabolites, 16–61% in feces	Severe rash in 17%. High frequency of CNS AEs: somnolence, dreams, confusion, agitation. Serious psychiatric symptoms. Certain CYP2B6 polymorphisms may predict exceptionally high plasma levels with standard doses (CID 45:1230, 2007). False-pos. cannabinoid screen. Very long tissue T½: **If rx to be discontinued, stop Efavirenz 1–2 wks before stopping companion drugs.** Otherwise, risk of developing Efavirenz resistance, as after 1–2 days only Efavirenz in blood &/or tissue. Some bridge this gap by adding a PI to the NRTI backbone after Efavirenz is discontinued. (CID 42:401, 2006)
Etravirine (Intelence)	100 mg tabs 200 mg tabs	200 mg twice daily after a meal. May also be given as 400 mg once daily	Unknown (↓ systemic exposure if taken fasting)	41	2		Metabolized by CYP3A4 (inducer) & 2C9, 2C19 (inhibitor). Fecal extraction.	For pts with HIV-1 resistant to NNRTIs & others. Active in vitro against most such isolates. Rash common, but rarely can be severe. Potential for multiple drug interactions. Generally, multiple mutations are required for high-level resistance. See Table 14D, page 200 for specific mutations and effects. Because of interactions, do not use with boosted atazanavir, boosted tipranavir, unboosted PIs, or other NNRTIs.
Nevirapine (Viramune) Viramune XR	200 mg tabs; 50 mg per 5 mL oral suspension; XR 400 mg tabs	200 mg po q24h x 14 days & then 200 mg bid (see comments & Black Box warning) Food OK. If using Viramune XR, Still need the lead in dosing of 200 mg q24h prior to using 400 mg/d	>90	25–30	4		Cytochrome P450 (3A4, 2B6) 80% excreted in urine as glucuronidated metabolites, 10% in feces	**Black Box warning—fatal hepatotoxicity.** Women with CD4 >250 esp. vulnerable, inc. pregnant women. Avoid in this group unless benefit > risks (www.fda.gov/cder/drug/advisory/nevirapine.htm). Intensive monitoring for liver toxicity required. Men with CD4 >400 also at ↑ risk. Severe rash in 7%, **severe or life-threatening skin reactions** in 2%. Do not restart if any suspicion of ↓ skin reactions. 2 wks dose escalation period may ↓ skin reactions. Because of long T½, consider continuing companion agents for several days if nevirapine is discontinued.

TABLE 14C (7)

Selected Characteristics of Antiretroviral Drugs (ᵃCPE = CSF penetration effectiveness: 1-4)

2. Selected Characteristics of Non-Nucleoside Reverse Transcriptase Inhibitors (NNRTIs) *(continued)*

Generic/ Trade Name	Pharmaceutical Prep.	Usual Adult Dosage & Food Effect	% Absorbed, po	Serum T½ hrs	Intracellular T½ hrs	CPE	Elimination	Major Adverse Events/Comments *(See Table 14D)*
Rilpivirine (Edurant)	25 mg tabs	25 mg daily with food	absolute bioavailability unknown; 40% lower Cmax in fasted state	50	unknown		Metabolized by CYP3A4 in liver; 25% excreted unchanged in feces.	QTc prolongation with doses higher than 50 mg per day, Conc AEs: depression, insomnia, headache, and rash. Do not co-administer with carbamazepine, phenobarbital, phenytoin, rifabutin, rifampin, rifapentine, proton pump inhibitors, or multiple doses of dexamethasone. A fixed dose combination of rilpivirine + TDF/FTC (Complera/Eviplera) is approved. **Needs stomach acid for absorption. Do not administer with PPI.**

3. Selected Characteristics of Protease Inhibitors (PIs)

All PIs: Glucose metabolism; new diabetes mellitus or deterioration of glucose control; fat redistribution; hypertriglyceridemia or hypercholesterolemia. Exercise caution re: potential drug interactions & contraindications. QTc prolongation has been reported in a few pts taking PIs; some PIs can block hERG channels in vitro (Lancet 365:682, 2005).

Generic/ Trade Name	Pharmaceutical Prep.	Usual Adult Dosage & Food Effect	% Absorbed, po	Serum T½ hrs	Intracellular T½ hrs	CPEᵃ	Elimination	Major Adverse Events/Comments *(See Table 14D)*
Atazanavir (Reyataz)	100, 150, 200, 300 mg capsules	400 mg po q24h with food. Ritonavir-boosted dose atazanavir 300 mg po q24h + ritonavir 100 mg po q24h) with food, is recommended for ART-experienced pts. Use boosted dose when combined with either Efavirenz 600 mg po q24h or TDF 300 mg po q24h. If used with buffered ddI, take with food 2 hr pre or 1 hr post ddI.	Good oral bioavailability; food enhances bioavailability & pharmacokinetic variability. Absorption ↓ by antacids, H₂-blockers, proton pump inhibitors. Avoid unboosted drug with PPIs/H2-blockers. Boosted drug can be used with or >10 hr after H2-blockers or >12 hr after a PPI, if limited doses of the acid agents are used.	Approx. 7		2	Cytochrome P450 (3A4, 1A2, 2C9 inhibitor?) & UGT1A1 inhibitor, 13% excreted in urine (7% unchanged), 79% excreted in feces (20% unchanged)	Lower potential for ↑ lipids. Asymptomatic unconjugated hyperbilirubinemia common; jaundice especially likely in Gilbert's syndrome (JID 192:1381, 2005). Headache, rash, GI symptoms. Prolongation of PR interval (1st degree AV block) reported. Caution in pre-existing conduction system disease. Efavirenz & Tenofovir ↓ atazanavir exposure: use atazanavir/ritonavir regimen; also, atazanavir + tenofovir concentrations—watch for adverse events. In rx-experienced pts taking TDF and needing H2 blockers, atazanavir 400 mg with ritonavir 100 mg can be given; do not use PPIs. Rare reports of renal stones.
Darunavir (Prezista)	400 mg, 600 mg, 800 mg tablets	[600 mg darunavir + 100 mg ritonavir] po bid, when given with food or [800 mg darunavir + 100 mg ritonavir (two 400 mg tabs or one 800 mg tab) + 100 mg ritonavir] po once daily with food (Preferred regimen in ART naive pts)	82% absorbed (taken with ritonavir). Food ↑ absorption.	Approx 15 hr (with ritonavir)		3	Metabolized by CYP3A and is a CYP3A inhibitor	Contains sulfa moiety. Rash, nausea, headaches seen. Coadmin of certain drugs cleared by CYP3A is contraindicated (see label). Use with caution in pts with hepatic dysfunction. (FDA warning about occasional hepatic dysfunction early in the course of treatment). Monitor carefully, esp. first several months and with pre-existing liver disease. May cause hormonal contraception failure.

TABLE 14C (8)

Selected Characteristics of Antiretroviral Drugs (ᵃCPE = CSF penetration effectiveness: 1-4) *(continued)*

3. Selected Characteristics of Protease Inhibitors (PIs) *(continued)*

Generic/ Trade Name	Pharmaceutical Prep.	Usual Adult Dosage & Food Effect	% Absorbed, po	Serum T½, hrs	CPEᵃ	Elimination	Major Adverse Events/Comments *(See Table 14D)*
Fosamprenavir (Lexiva)	700 mg tablet; 50 mg/mL oral suspension	1400 mg fosamprenavir po bid OR with ritonavir: [1400 mg fosamprenavir (2 tabs) + ritonavir 100 mg or 200 mg] po q24h OR [700 mg fosamprenavir (1 tab) + ritonavir 100 mg] po bid	Bioavailability not established. Food OK	7.7 Amprenavir	3	Hydrolyzed to amprenavir, then acts as cytochrome P450 (3A4 substrate, inhibitor, inducer)	Amprenavir prodrug. Contains sulfa moiety. Potential for serious drug interactions (see label). Rash, including Stevens-Johnson syndrome. Once daily regimens: (1) not recommended for PI-experienced pts; (2) additional ritonavir needed if given with Efavirenz (see label). Boosted twice daily regimen is recommended for PI-experienced pts. Potential for PI cross-resistance with darunavir.
Indinavir (Crixivan)	100, 200, 400 mg capsules Store in original container with desiccant	Two 400 mg caps (800 mg) po q8h, without food or with light meal. Can take with enteric-coated Videx. [If taken with ritonavir (e.g., 800 mg indinavir + 100 mg ritonavir po q12h), no food restrictions]	65	1.2-2	4	Cytochrome P450 (3A4 inhibitor)	Maintain hydration. Nephrolithiasis, nausea, inconsequential ↑ of indirect bilirubin (jaundice in Gilbert syndrome), ↑ AST/ALT, headache, asthenia, blurred vision, metallic taste, hemolysis. ↑ urine WBC (>100/hpf) has been assoc. with nephritis/ medullary calcification, cortical atrophy.
Lopinavir + ritonavir (Kaletra)	(200 mg lopinavir + 50 mg ritonavir) and (100 mg lopinavir + 25 mg ritonavir) tablets. Tabs do not need refrigeration. Oral solution: (80 mg lopinavir + 20 mg ritonavir) per mL. Refrigerate, but can be kept at room temp. (≤77°F) x 2 mos.	(400 mg lopinavir + 100 mg ritonavir)—2 tabs po bid. Higher dose may be needed in non-naïve pts when used with Efavirenz, nevirapine, or unboosted fosamprenavir. [Dose adjustment in concomitant drugs may be necessary, see Table 22b.]	No food effect with tablets.	5-6	3	Cytochrome P450 (3A4 inhibitor)	Nausea/vomiting/diarrhea (worse when administered with zidovudine), ↑ AST/ ALT, pancreatitis. Oral solution 42% alcohol. Lopinavir + ritonavir can be taken as a single daily dose of 4 tabs (total 800 mg lopinavir + 200 mg ritonavir), except in treatment-experienced pts or those taking concomitant Efavirenz, nevirapine, amprenavir, or nelfinavir. Possible PR and QT prolongation. Use with caution in those with cardiac conduction abnormalities or when used with drugs with similar effects.
Nelfinavir (Viracept)	625, 250 mg tabs; 50 mg/gm oral powder	Two 625 mg tabs (1250 mg) po bid, with food	20-80 Food ↑ exposure & ↓ variability	3.5-5	1	Cytochrome P450 (3A4 inhibitor)	Diarrhea. Coadministration of drugs with life-threatening toxicities & which are cleared by CYP3A4 is contraindicated. Not recommended in initial regimens because of inferior efficacy; prior concerns about EMS now resolved. Acceptable choice in pregnant women although it has inferior virologic efficacy than most other ARV drugs.

TABLE 14C (9)

3. Selected Characteristics of Antiretroviral Drugs (°CPE = CSF penetration effectiveness: 1-4)

Selected Characteristics of Protease Inhibitors (PIs). (continued)

Generic/ Trade Name	Pharmaceutical Prep.	Usual Adult Dosage & Food Effect	% Absorbed, po	Serum T½, hrs	CPE°	Elimination	Major Adverse Events/Comments (See Table 14D)
Ritonavir (Norvir)	100 mg capsules; 600 mg per 7.5 mL solution. Refrigerate caps but not solution. Room temperature for 1 mo. is OK.	Full dose not recommended (see comments). With rare exceptions, used exclusively to enhance pharmacokinetics of other PIs, using lower ritonavir doses.	Food ↑ absorption	3-5	1	Cytochrome P450, Potent 3A4 & 2 d6 inhibitor	Nausea/vomiting/diarrhea, extremity & circumoral paresthesias, hepatitis, pancreatitis, taste perversion, CPK & uric acid. Black Box warning—potentially fatal drug interactions. Many drug interactions— see Table 22A-Table 22B.
Saquinavir (Invirase—hard gel caps or tabs) + ritonavir	Saquinavir 200 mg caps, 500 mg film-coated tabs; ritonavir 100 mg caps	[2 tabs saquinavir (1000 mg) + 1 cap ritonavir (100 mg)] po bid with food	Erratic, 4 (saquinavir alone). Much more reliably absorbed when boosted with ritonavir.	1-2	1	Cytochrome P450 (3A4 inhibitor)	Nausea, diarrhea, headache, ↑ AST/ALT. Avoid rifampin with saquinavir + ritonavir; ↑ hepatitis risk. Black Box warning—Invirase to be used only with ritonavir. Possible QT prolongation. Use with caution in those with cardiac conduction abnormalities or when used with drugs with similar effects.
Tipranavir (Aptivus)	250 mg caps. Refrigerate unopened bottles. Use opened bottles within 2 mo. 100 mg/mL solution	[500 mg (two 250 mg caps) + ritonavir 200 mg] po bid with food.	Absorption low, ↑ with high fat meal, ↓ with Al⁺⁺ & Mg⁺⁺ antacids.	5.5-6	1	Cytochrome 3A4 but with ritonavir, most of drug is eliminated in feces.	Contains sulfa moiety. Black Box warning—reports of fatal/nonfatal intracranial hemorrhage, hepatitis, fetal hepatic failure. Use cautiously in liver disease, esp. hepB, hepC; contraindicated in Child-Pugh class B-C. Monitor LFTs. Coadministration of certain drugs contraindicated (see label). For highly ART-experienced pts or for multiple-PI resistant virus. Do not use tipranavir and etravirine together owing to 76% reduction in etravirine levels.

4. Selected Characteristics of Fusion Inhibitors

Generic/ Trade Name	Pharmaceutical Prep.	Usual Adult Dosage	% Absorbed	Serum T½, hrs	CPE°	Elimination	Major Adverse Events/Comments (See Table 14D)
Enfuvirtide (T20, Fuzeon)	Single-use vials of 90 mg/mL when reconstituted. Vials should be stored at room temperature. Reconstituted vials can be refrigerated for 24 hrs only.	90 mg (1 mL) subcut. bid. Rotate injection sites, avoiding those currently inflamed.	84	3.8	1	Catabolism to its constituent amino acids with subsequent recycling of the amino acids in the body pool. Elimination pathway(s) have not been performed in humans. Does not alter the metabolism of CYP3A4, CYP2 d6, CYP1A2, CYP2C9 or CYP2E1 substrates.	Local reaction site reactions 98%, 4% discontinue; erythema/induration ~80-90%, nodules/cysts ~80%. Hypersensitivity reactions reported (fever, rash, chills, N/V, ↓ BP, &/or ↑ AST/ALT)—do not restart if occur. Including background regimens, peripheral neuropathy 8.9%, insomnia 11.3%, ↓ appetite 6.3%, myalgia 5%, lymphadenopathy 2.3%, eosinophilia ~10%; ↑ incidence of bacterial pneumonias.

TABLE 14C (10)

Selected Characteristics of Antiretroviral Drugs: 1-4) (^CPE = CSF penetration effectiveness: 1-4)

Generic/ Trade Name	Pharmaceutical Prep.	Usual Adult Dosage & Food Effect	% Absorbed	Serum T½ hrs	CPE	Elimination	Major Adverse Events/Comments (See Table 14D)
5. Selected Characteristics of CCR-5 Co-receptor Antagonists							
Maraviroc (Selzentry)	150 mg, 300 mg film-coated tabs	Without regard to food: -150 mg bid if concomitant meds include CYP3A inhibitors including PIs (except tipranavir/ritonavir) and delavirdine (with/ without CYP3A inducers) -300 mg bid without significantly interacting meds including NRTIs, tipranavir/ritonavir, nevirapine -600 mg bid if concomitant meds include CYP3A inducers, including Efavirenz (without strong CYP3A inhibitors)	Est. 33% with 300 mg dosage	14-18	3	CYP3A and P-glycoprotein substrate. Metabolites (via CYP3A) excreted feces > urine	**Black Box: Warning–Hepatotoxicity, may be preceded by rash, ↑ eos or IgE. NB: no hepatotoxicity was noted in MVC trials. Black box inserted owing to concern about potential CCR5 class effect.** Data lacking in hepatic/renal insufficiency; ↑ concern with either could ↑ risk of LFT. Currently for treatment-experienced patients with multi-resistant strains. **Document CCR-5-tropic virus before use, as treatment failures assoc. with appearance of CXCR-4 or mixed-tropic virus.**
6. Selected Characteristics of Integrase Strand Transfer Inhibitors (INSTI)							
Raltegravir (Isentress)	400 mg film-coated tabs	400 mg po bid without regard to food	Unknown	~ 9	3	Glucuronidation via UGT1A1, with excretion into feces and urine. (Therefore does NOT require ritoavir boosting)	For naïve patients and treatment experienced pts with multiply-resistant virus. Well-tolerated. Nausea, diarrhea, headache, fever similar to placebo. CK↑ & rhabdomyolysis reported; unclear relationship. Increased depression in those with a history of depression. Low genetic barrier to resistance. Increase in CPK, myositis, rhabdomyolysis have been reported. Rare Stevens Johnson Syndrome. Better oral absorption if chewed (CID 57-480, 2013).
Elvitegravir/ cobicistat (Stribild)	150 mg - 150 mg	150 mg-150 mg once daily with or without food	<10%	12.9 (Cobi), 3.5 (ELV)	U-known	The majority of elvitegravir metabolism is mediated by CYP3A enzymes. Elvitegravir also undergoes glucuronidation via UGT1A1/3 enzymes. Cobicistat is metabolized by CYP3A and to a minor extent by CYP2D6	For both treatment naïve patients and treatment experienced pts with multiply-resistant virus. Generally well-tolerated. Use of cobicistat increases serum creatinine by ~ 0.1 mg/dl via inhibition of proximal tubular enzyme; this does not result in reduction in true GFR but will result in erroneous apparent reduction in eGFR by MDRD or Cockcroft Gault calculations. Usual AEs are similar to those observed with ritonavir (cobi) and tenofovir/FTC.

TABLE 14C (11)

Generic/ Trade Name	Pharmaceutical Prep.	Usual Adult Dosage & Food Effect	% Absorbed	Serum T½, hrs	CPE	Elimination	Major Adverse Events/Comments (See Table 14D)

6. **Selected Characteristics of Strand Transfer Integrase Inhibitors** *(continued)*

| Dolutegravir (Tivicay) | 50 mg | 50 mg po once daily 50 mg po bid (if STI resistance present or if co-admin with EFV, FOS, TIP, or RIF | Unknown | 14 | 4 | Glucuronidation via UGT1A1 (therefore does not require ritonavir or cobicistat boosting) | Hypersensitivity (rare); Most common: insomnia (3%) headache (2%), N/V (1%), rash (<1%). Watch for IRIS; Watch for elevated LFTs in those with HCV |

Other Considerations in Selection of Therapy

Caution: Initiation of ART may result in immune reconstitution syndrome with significant clinical consequences. *See Table 11B, of Sanford Guide to HIV/AIDS Therapy (AIDS Reader 16:199, 2006).*

1. Resistance testing: Given current rates of resistance, resistance testing is recommended in all patients prior to initiation of therapy, including those with acute infection syndrome (may initiate therapy while waiting for test results, and adjusting Rx once results return), at time of change of therapy owing to antiretroviral failure, when suboptimal virologic response is observed, and in pregnant women. **Resistance testing NOT recommended if pt is off ART for >4 weeks or if HIV RNA is <1000 c/mL.** *See Table 6F of SANFORD GUIDE TO HIV/AIDS THERAPY.*

2. Drug-induced disturbances of glucose & lipid metabolism *(see Table 14D)*
3. Drug-induced lactic acidosis & other FDA "box warnings" *(see Table 14D)*
4. Drug-drug interactions *(see Table 22B)*
5. Risk in pregnancy *(see Table 8)*
6. Use in women & children *(see Table 14C)*
7. Dosing in patients with renal or hepatic dysfunction *(see Table 17A & Table 17B)*

* **CPE (CNS Penetration Effectiveness) value:** 1= Low Penetration; 2 - 3 = Intermediate Penetration; 4 = Highest Penetration into CNS *(AIDS 25:357, 2011)*

TABLE 14D - ANTIRETROVIRAL DRUGS & ADVERSE EFFECTS
(www.aidsinfo.nih.gov)

DRUG NAME(S): GENERIC (TRADE)	MOST COMMON ADVERSE EFFECTS	MOST SIGNIFICANT ADVERSE EFFECTS
Nucleoside Reverse Transcriptase Inhibitors (NRTI) Black Box warning for all nucleoside/nucleotide RTIs: lactic acidosis/hepatic steatosis, potentially fatal. Also carry Warnings that fat redistribution and immune reconstitution syndromes (including autoimmune syndromes with delayed onset) have been observed		
Abacavir (Ziagen)	Headache 7–13%, nausea 7–19%, diarrhea 7%, malaise 7–12%	**Black Box warning–Hypersensitivity reaction (HR)** in 8% with malaise, fever, GI upset, rash, lethargy & respiratory symptoms most commonly reported; myalgia, arthralgia, edema, paresthesia less common. **Discontinue immediately if HR suspected. Rechallenge contraindicated; may be life-threatening.** Severe HR may be more common with once-daily dosing. **HLA-B*5701 allele** predicts ↑ risk of HR in Caucasian pop.; excluding pts with B*5701 markedly ↓↑ HR incidence *(NEJM 358:568, 2008)*; DHHS guidelines recommend testing for B*5701 and use of abacavir only if HLA-B*5701 negative; Vigilance essential in all groups. Possible increased risk of MI with use of abacavir had been suggested *(JID 201:318, 2010)*. Other studies found no increased risk of MI *(CID 52: 929, 2011)*. A meta-analysis of randomized trials by FDA also did not show increased risk of MI *(www.fda.gov/drugs/drugsafety/ucm245164.htm)*. Nevertheless, care is advised to optimize potentially modifiable risk factors when abacavir is used.
Didanosine (ddl) (Videx)	Diarrhea 28%, nausea 6%, rash 9%, headache 7%, fever 12%, hyperuricemia 2%	**Pancreatitis 1–9%. Black Box warning–Cases of fatal & nonfatal pancreatitis** have occurred in pts receiving ddl, especially when used in combination with ddl or d4T + hydroxyurea. Fatal lactic acidosis in pregnancy with ddl + d4T. Peripheral neuropathy in 20%, 12% required dose reduction. ↑ toxicity if used with ribavirin. Use with TDF generally avoided (but would require dose reduction of ddl) because of ↑ toxicity and possible ↓ efficacy; may result in ↓ CD4. Rarely, retinal changes or optic neuropathy. Diabetes mellitus and rhabdomyolysis reported in post-marketing surveillance. Possible liver toxicity *(www.fda.gov/ODER.../ucm/CDER/.../201378, 2010)*. Non-cirrhotic portal hypertension with ascites, varices, splenomegaly reported in post-marketing surveillance. See also *Clin Infect Dis 49:626, 2009; Amer J Gastroenterol 104:1707, 2009.*
Emtricitabine (FTC) (Emtriva)	Well tolerated. Headache, diarrhea, nausea, rash, skin hyperpigmentation	Potential for lactic acidosis (as with other NRTIs). Also in Black Box—severe exacerbation of hepatitis B on stopping drug reported—monitor clinical/labs for several months after stopping in pts with hepB. Anti-HBV rx may be warranted if FTC stopped.
Lamivudine (3TC) (Epivir)	Well tolerated. Headache 35%, nausea 33%, diarrhea 18%, abdominal pain 9%, insomnia 11% (all in combination with ZDV). Pancreatitis more common in pediatrics.	**Black Box warning.** Make sure to stop HIV dosage, not Hep B dosage. Exacerbation of hepatitis B on stopping drug. **Patients with hepB who stop lamivudine require close clinical/lab monitoring for several months.** Anti-HBV rx may be warranted if 3TC stopped.
Stavudine (d4T) (Zerit)	Diarrhea, nausea, vomiting, headache	**Peripheral neuropathy** 15–20%. Pancreatitis 1%. Appears to produce lactic acidosis, hepatic steatosis and lipatrophy/lipodystrophy more commonly than other NRTIs. **Black Box warning—Fatal & nonfatal pancreatitis with d4T + ddl.** Use with TDF generally avoided (but would require dose reduction of ddl) because of ↑ toxicity and possible ↓ efficacy, may result in ↓ CD4. Rarely, retinal changes or optic neuropathy. Diabetes mellitus and rhabdomyolysis reported in post-marketing surveillance. Fatal lactic acidosis in **pregnant women receiving d4T + ddl.** Fatal and non-fatal lactic acidosis and severe hepatic steatosis can occur in others receiving d4T. Use with particular caution on patients with risk factors for liver disease, but lactic acidosis can occur even in those without known risk factors. Possible ↑ toxicity if used with ribavirin. Motor weakness in the setting of lactic acidosis mimicking the clinical presentation of Guillain-Barré syndrome (including respiratory failure) (rare).
Zidovudine (ZDV, AZT) (Retrovir)	Nausea 50%, anorexia 20%, vomiting 17%, headache 62%. Also reported; asthenia, insomnia, myalgias, nail pigmentation. Macrocytosis expected with all dosage regimens.	**Black Box warning—hematologic toxicity, myopathy. Anemia** (<8 gm, 1.1%), granulocytopenia (<750, 1.8%). Anemia may respond to epoetin alfa if endogenous serum erythropoietin levels are ≤500 milliUnits/mL. Possible ↑ toxicity if used with ribavirin. Co-administration with Ribavirin not advised. Hepatic decompensation may occur in HIV/HCV co-infected patients receiving zidovudine with interferon alfa ± ribavirin.

TABLE 14D (2)

DRUG NAME(S): GENERIC (TRADE)	MOST COMMON ADVERSE EFFECTS	MOST SIGNIFICANT ADVERSE EFFECTS
Nucleotide Reverse Transcriptase Inhibitor (NtRTI) Black Box warning for all nucleoside/nucleotide RTIs: lactic acidosis/hepatic steatosis, potentially fatal. Also carry Warnings that fat redistribution and immune reconstitution syndromes (including autoimmune syndromes with delayed onset) have been observed *(continued)*		
Tenofovir disoproxil fumarate (TDF) (Viread) ; Tenofovir alafenamide (TAF)	Diarrhea 11%, nausea 8%, vomiting 5%, flatulence 4% (generally well tolerated)	**Black Box warning—Severe exacerbations of hepatitis B may occur in pts who stop tenofovir.** Monitor carefully if drug is stopped; anti-HBV rx may be warranted if TDF stopped. Reports of renal injury from TDF, including Fanconi syndrome *(CID 37:e174, 2003; J AIDS 35:269,204; CID 42:283, 2006)*. Fanconi syndrome and diabetes insipidus reported with TDF + ddI *(AIDS Reader 19:114, 2009)*. Modest decline in renal function appears greater with TDF than with NtRTIs *(CID 51:296, 2010)* or TAF and may be greater in those receiving TDF with a PI instead of an NNRTI *(CID 197:102, 2008; AIDS 26:567, 2012)*. In a VA study that followed >10,000 HIV-infected individuals, TDF exposure was significantly associated with increased risk of proteinuria, a more rapid decline in renal function and chronic kidney disease *(AIDS 26:867, 2012)*. Monitor Ccr, serum phosphate and urinalysis, especially carefully in those with pre-existing renal dysfunction, or report otoxic medications. TDF, but not TAF, also appears to be associated with increased risk of bone loss. In a substudy of an ACTG comparative treatment trial, those randomized to TDF-FTC experienced greater decreases in spine and hip bone mineral density (BMD) at 96 weeks compared with those treated with ABC-3TC *(JID 203:1791, 2011)*. Consider monitoring BMD in those with history of pathologic fractures, or who have risks for osteoporosis or bone loss.
Non-Nucleoside Reverse Transcriptase Inhibitors (NNRTI). Labels caution that fat redistribution and immune reconstitution can occur with ART.		
Delavirdine (Rescriptor)	Skin rash has occurred in 18%; can continue or restart drug in most cases. Stevens-Johnson syndrome & erythema multiforme have been reported rarely. ↑ in liver enzymes in <5% of patients.	Stevens-Johnson syndrome and erythema multiforme reported in post-marketing surveillance.
Efavirenz (Sustiva)	**CNS side effects 52%:** vertigo, impaired concentration, insomnia, somnolence, impaired concentration, psychiatric, & abnormal dreams; symptoms are worse after 1st or 2nd dose & improve over 2–4 weeks; discontinuation rate 2.6%. Rash 26% (vs. 17% in comparators); often improves with oral antihistamines; discontinuation rate 1.7%. Can cause false-positive urine test results for cannabinoid with CEDIA DAU multi-level THC assay. Metabolite can cause false-positive urine screening test for benzodiazepines *(CID 48:1787, 2009)*.	**Caution:** CNS effects may impair driving and other hazardous activities. Serious neuropsychiatric symptoms reported, including severe depression (2.4%) & suicidal ideation (0.7%). Elevations in liver enzymes. Fulminant hepatitis, failure reported rarely *(see FDA alert)*. **Teratogenic in primates; pregnancy category D**—may cause fetal harm; avoid in pregnant women or those who might become pregnant. NOTE: No single method of contraception is 100% reliable. Barrier + 2nd method of contraception advised, continued 12 weeks after stopping Efavirenz. Contraindicated with certain drugs metabolized by CYP3A4. Slow metabolism in those homozygous for the CYP-2B6 G516T allele can result in exaggerated toxicity and intolerance. This allele much more common in blacks and whites *(CID 42:408, 2006)*.
Etravirine (Intelence)	Rash 9%, generally mild to moderate and spontaneously resolving; 2% dc clinical trials for rash. More common in women. Nausea 5%.	Severe rash (erythema multiforme, toxic epidermal necrolysis, Stevens-Johnson syndrome) has been reported. Hypersensitivity reactions can occur with rash, constitutional symptoms and organ dysfunction, including hepatic failure *(see FDA label)*. Potential for CYP450-mediated drug interactions. Rhabdomyolysis has been reported in post-marketing surveillance.
Nevirapine (Viramune)	Rash 37%: usually occurs during 1st 6 wks of therapy. Follow recommendations for 14-day lead-in period to ↓ risk of severe rash *(see Table 14C)*. Women experience 7-fold ↑ in risk of severe rash *(CID 32:124, 2001)*. 50% resolve within 1 month. 6.7% discontinuation rate.	**Black Box warning—Severe life-threatening skin reactions reported.** Stevens-Johnson syndrome, toxic epidermal necrolysis, & hypersensitivity reaction or drug rash with eosinophilia & systemic symptoms (DRESS) *(ARIM 161:2501, 2001)*. For severe rashes, dc drug immediately & do not restart. In a clinical trial, the use of prednisone ↑ the risk of rash. **Black Box warning—Life-threatening hepatotoxicity reported**, 2/3 during the first 12 wks of rx. Overall 1% develop hepatitis. Pts with pre-existing ↑ in ALT or AST &/or history of chronic Hep B or C ↑ susceptible *(Hepatol 35:182, 2002)*. Women with CD4 >250, including pregnant women, at ↑ risk. Avoid in this group unless no other options. Men with CD4 >400 also at ↑ risk. Monitor pts intensively (clinical & LFTs), esp. during the first 12 wks of rx. If clinical hepatotoxicity, severe skin or hypersensitivity reactions occur, dc drug & never rechallenge.

TABLE 14D (3)

DRUG NAME(S): GENERIC (TRADE)	MOST COMMON ADVERSE EFFECTS	MOST SIGNIFICANT ADVERSE EFFECTS
Non-Nucleoside Reverse Transcriptase Inhibitors (NNRTI) *(cont/nued)*		
Rilpivirine (Edurant)	Headache (3%), rash (3%; led to discontinuation in 0.1%), insomnia (3%), depressive disorders (4%). Psychiatric disorders led to discontinuation in 1%. Increased liver enzymes observed.	Drugs that induce CYP3A or increase gastric pH may decrease plasma concentration of rilpivirine and co-administration with rilpivirine should be avoided. Among these are certain anticonvulsants, rifamycins, PPIs, dexamethasone and St. John's wort. At supra-therapeutic doses, rilpivirine can increase QTc interval; use with caution with other drugs known to increase QTc. May cause depressive disorder, including suicide attempts or suicidal ideation. Overall, appears to cause fewer neuropsychiatric side effects than Efavirenz. *(JAIDS 60-33, 2012)*.

Protease Inhibitors (PI)
Diarrhea is common AE (**crofelemer** 125 mg bid may help, but expensive). Abnormalities in glucose metabolism, dyslipidemias, fat redistribution syndromes are potential problems. Pts taking PI may be at increased risk for developing osteopenia/osteoporosis. Spontaneous bleeding episodes have been reported in +IV+ pts with hemophilia being treated with PI. Rheumatoid complications have been reported *(An Rheum Dis 61:82, 2002)*. Potential for QTc prolongation *(Lancet 365:682, 2005)*. Caution **for all PIs**—Coadministration with drugs dependent on CYP3A or other enzymes for elimination & for which ↑ levels can cause serious toxicity may be contraindicated. ART may result in immune reconstitution syndromes, which may include early or late presentations of autoimmune syndromes. Increased premature births among women receiving ritonavir-boosted PIs as compared with those receiving other antiretroviral therapy, even after accounting for other potential risk factors *(CID 54: 1348, 2012)*.

Atazanavir (Reyataz)	Asymptomatic unconjugated hyperbilirubinemia in up to 60% of pts, jaundice in 7–9% (especially with Gilbert syndrome *(JID 192: 1381, 2005)*). Moderate to severe events: Diarrhea 1–3%, nausea 6–14%, abdominal pain 4%, headache 6%, rash 20%.	Prolongation of PR interval (1st degree AV block in 5–6%) reported; rarely 2° AV block. QTc increase and torsades reported *(CID 44:e67, 2007)*. Acute interstitial nephritis *(Am J Kid Dis 44:E81, 2004)* and urolithiasis (atazanavir stones) reported *(AIDC 20:2131, 2006; NEJM 355:2158, 2006)*. Potential ↑ transaminases in pts co-infected with HBV or HCV. Severe skin eruptions (Stevens-Johnson syndrome, erythema multiforme, and toxic eruptions, or DRESS syndrome) have been reported.
Darunavir (Prezista)	With background regimens, headache 15%, nausea 18%, diarrhea 20%, ↑ amylase 17%. Rash in 10% of treated; 0.5% discontinuation.	Hepatitis in 0.5%, some with fatal outcome. Use caution in pts with HBV or HCV co-infections or other hepatic dysfunction. Monitor for clinical symptoms and LFTs. Stevens-Johnson syndrome, toxic epidermal necrolysis, erythema multiforme. Contains sulfa moiety. Potential for major drug interactions. May cause failure of hormonal contraceptives.
Fosamprenavir (Lexiva)	Skin rash – 20% (moderate or worse in 3–8%), nausea, headache, diarrhea.	Rarely Stevens-Johnson syndrome, hemolytic anemia. Pro-drug of amprenavir. Contains sulfa moiety. Angioedema and nephrolithiasis reported in post-marketing experience. Potential increased risk of MI *(see FDA label)*. Nausea, oral paresthesias, myocardial infarction and nephrolithiasis reported in post-marketing experience. Elevated LFTs seen with higher than recommended doses; increased risk in those with pre-existing liver abnormalities. Acute hemolytic anemia reported with amprenavir.
Indinavir (Crixivan)	↑ in indirect bilirubin 10–15% (≥2.5 mg/dl, with overt jaundice especially likely in those with Gilbert syndrome *(JID 192: 1381, 2005)*. Nausea 12%, vomiting 4%, diarrhea 5%. Metallic taste. Paronychia and ingrown toenails reported *(CID 32:140, 2001)*.	**Kidney stones.** Due to indinavir crystals in collecting system. Nephrolithiasis in 12% of adults, higher in pediatrics. Minimize risk with good hydration (at least 48 oz. water/day) *(AAC 42:332, 1998)*. Tubulointerstitial nephritis may rarely occur asymptomatically reported in association with asymptomatic ↑ urine WBC. Severe hepatitis reported in 3 cases *(AIDS 349:924, 1997)*. Hemolytic anemia reported.
Lopinavir/Ritonavir (Kaletra)	GI: **diarrhea** 14–24%, nausea 2–16%. More diarrhea with q24h dosing.	Lipid abnormalities in up to 20–40%. Possible increased risk of MI with cumulative exposure *(JID 201:318, 2010)*. ↑ PR interval, 2° or 3° heart block described. Post-marketing reports of ↑ QTc and torsades: avoid use in congenital QTc prolongation or in other circumstances that prolong QTc or increase susceptibility to torsades. Hepatitis, with hepatic decompensation especially in those with pre-existing liver disease. Pancreatitis. Inflammatory edema of legs *(AIDS 16:673, 2002)*. Stevens-Johnson syndrome & erythema multiforme reported. Note high drug concentration in oral solution (contains ethanol and propylene glycol) in neonates. Toxic potential of oral soIution (contains ethanol and propylene glycol).
Nelfinavir (Viracept)	Mild to moderate **diarrhea** 20%. Oat bran tabs, calcium, or oral anti-diarrheal agents (e.g., loperamide, diphenoxylate/atropine sulfate) can be used to manage diarrhea.	Potential for drug interactions. Powder contains phenylalanine.

TABLE 14D (4)

DRUG NAME(S): GENERIC (TRADE)	MOST COMMON ADVERSE EFFECTS	MOST SIGNIFICANT ADVERSE EFFECTS
Protease inhibitors (PI) (continued)		
Ritonavir (Norvir) (Currently, primary use is to enhance levels of other anti-retrovirals, because of ↑ toxicity/interactions with full-dose ritonavir)	GI: bitter aftertaste ↓ by taking with chocolate milk, Ensure, or Advera; nausea 23%, ↓ by initial dose esc (titration) regimen; vomiting 13%, diarrhea 15%. Circumoral paresthesias 5–6%. Dose >100 mg bid assoc. with ↑ GI side effects & ↑ in lipid abnormalities.	**Black Box** warning relates to many important drug-drug interactions—inhibits P450 CYP3A & CYP2 D6 system—may be life-threatening (see Table 22A). Several cases of iatrogenic Cushing's syndrome reported with concomitant use of ritonavir and corticosteroids, most notably during the latter by inhalation, epidural injection or a single IM injection. Rarely severe reactions, including toxic epidermal necrolysis anaphylaxis. Primary A-v block (and higher) and pancreatitis have been reported. Hepatic reactions, including fatalities. Monitor LFTs carefully during therapy, especially in those with pre-existing liver disease, including HBV and HCV.
Saquinavir (Invirase: hard cap, tablet)	Diarrhea, abdominal discomfort, nausea, headache	**Warning—Use Invirase only with Ritonavir.** Avoid garlic capsules (may reduce SQV levels) and use cautiously with proton-pump inhibitors (increased SQV levels). Use of saquinavir/ritonavir can prolong QTc interval or may rarely cause 2° or 3° heart block. Torsades reported. Contraindicated in patients with prolonged QTc or those taking drugs or who have other conditions (e.g., low K+ or Mg++) that pose a risk with prolonged QTc (http://www.fda.gov/drugs/DrugSafety/ucm230096.htm, accessed May 25, 2011). Contraindicated in patients with complete AV block, or those at risk, who do not have pacemaker. Hepatic toxicity encountered in patients with pre-existing liver disease or in individuals receiving concomitant rifampin. Rarely, Stevens Johnson syndrome.
Tipranavir (Aptivus)	Nausea & vomiting, diarrhea, abdominal pain. Rash in 8–14%, more common in women, & 33% in women taking ethinyl estradiol. Major lipid effects.	**Black Box Warning—associated with hepatitis & fatal hepatic failure.** Risk of hepatotoxicity increased in hepB or hepC co-infection. Possible photosensitivity skin reactions. Contraindicated in Child-Pugh Class B or C hepatic impairment. **Associated with fatal/nonfatal intracranial hemorrhage (can inhibit platelet aggregation).** Caution in those with bleeding risks. Potential for major drug interactions. Contains sulfa moiety and vitamin E.
Fusion Inhibitor		
Enfuvirtide (T20, Fuzeon)	Local injection site reactions (98% at least ↑ local ISR, 4% dc because of ISR (pain & discomfort, induration, erythema, nodules & cysts, pruritus, & ecchymosis). Diarrhea 32%, nausea 23%, fatigue 20%.	↑ Rate of bacterial pneumonia (3.2 pneumonia events/100 pt yrs). **hypersensitivity reactions** ≤1% (rash, fever, nausea & vomiting, chills, rigors, hypotension, & ↑ serum liver transaminases); can occur with reexposure. Cutaneous amyloid deposits containing enfuvirtide reported in skin plaques persisting after discontinuation of drug (J Cutan Pathol 39:220, 2012).
CCR5 Co-receptor Antagonists		
Maraviroc (Selzentry)	With ARV background: Cough 13%, fever 12%, rash 10%, abdominal pain 8%. Also, dizziness, myalgia, arthralgias. ↑ Risk of URI, HSV infection.	**Black box warning–Hepatotoxicity.** May be preceded by allergic features (rash, ↑eosinophils or ↑IgE levels). Use with caution in pt with HepB or C. Cardiac ischemia/infarction in 1.3%. May cause ↓BP, orthostatic syncope, especially in patients with renal dysfunction. Significant interactions with CYP3A inducers/inhibitors. Long-term risk of malignancy unknown. Stevens-Johnson syndrome reported post-marketing. Generally favorable safety profile during trial of ART-naive individuals (CID 254: 803, 2010).
Integrase Inhibitors		
Raltegravir (Isentress)	Diarrhea, headache, insomnia, nausea. LFT ↑ may be more common in pts co-infected with HBV or HCV.	Hypersensitivity reactions can occur. Rash, Stevens-Johnson syndrome, toxic epidermal necrolysis reported. Hepatic failure reported. ↑CK, myopathy and rhabdomyolysis reported (AIDS 22:1382, 2008). ↑ hadomyolysis reported depression in 4 pts; all could continue raltegravir after adjustment of psych. meds (AIDS 22:1890, 2008). Chewable tablets contain phenylalanine.
Elvitegravir+ Cobicistat (Stribild), Elvitegravir (Vitekta)	Nausea and the two most common AEs. Increased serum creatinine 0.1-0.15 mg/dL due to inhibition of prox. tubular enzymes by cobicistat with no decrease in GFR.	**Same Black Box warning as ritonavir and tenofovir (TDF and TAF).** Rare lactic acidosis syndrome. Owing to renal toxicity, should not initiate Rx when pre-Rx eGFR is <70 cc/min. Follow serial serum creatinine and urinary protein and glucose. Discontinue drug if serum Cr rises >0.4 mg/dl above baseline value.
Dolutegravir (Tivicay)	Insomnia and headache (2-4%)	Rash, liver injury reported. Increased ALT/AST in 20%. Competition with creatinine for tubular secretion increased serum creatinine by a mean of 0.1 mg/dL with no change in GFR.

TABLE 14E – HEPATITIS A & HBV TREATMENT
For HBV Activity Spectra, *see Table 4C, page 84*

Hepatitis A Virus (HAV)

1. **Drug/Dosage:** No therapy recommended. If within 2 wks of exposure, prophylactic IVIG 0.02 mL per kg IM times 1 protective. Hep A vaccine equally effective as IVIG in randomized trial and is emerging as preferred Rx *(NEJM 357:1685, 2007).*

2. **HAV Superinfection:** 40% of pts with chronic Hepatitis C virus (HCV) infection who developed superinfection with HAV developed fulminant hepatic failure *(NEJM 338:286, 1998).* Similar data in pts with chronic Hepatitis B virus (HBV) infection that suffer acute HAV *(Ann Trop Med Parasitol 93:745, 1999).* Hence, need to vaccinate all HBV and HCV pts with HAV vaccine.

Hepatitis B Virus (HBV): Treatment

	ALT	HBV DNA	HBe Ag	Recommendation
Immune-Tolerant Phase	Normal	>1x106 IU/mL	Positive	**Monitor:** ALT levels be tested at least every 6 months for adults with immune tolerant CHB to monitor for potential transition to immune-active or - inactive CHB. **NB: For those over 40 years of age + liver fibrosis, TREAT as Immune Active (below)**
HBeAg+ Immune Active Phase	Elevated	>20,000 IU/mL	Positive	**TREAT (Duration of therapy+):** Tenofovir (indefinitely; esp. if fibrosis) OR Entecavir (indefinitely; esp. if fibrosis) OR Peg-IFN++ (48 weeks of Rx)
Inactive CHB Phase	Normal	<2,000 IU/mL	Negative	**Monitor:** ALT levels at least once / year
HBeAg-neg Immune Reactivation Phase	Elevated	>2,000 IU/mL	Negative	**TREAT (Duration of therapy+):** Tenofovir (indefinitely; esp. if fibrosis) OR Entecavir (indefinitely; esp. if fibrosis) OR Peg-IFN++ (48 weeks of Rx)

+ Duration of therapy largely unknown; most experts favor indefinite Rx, esp. among those with moderate to advanced fibrosis or inflammation (liver biopsy)
++ Peg-INF contraindicated in patients with decompensated cirrhosis, autoimmune disease, uncontrolled psychiatric disease, cytopenias, severe cardiac disease, and uncontrolled seizures

For details of therapy, especially in special populations (e.g., pregnant women, children) *see updated AASLD Guidelines (Hepatology), 2015 Nov 13. doi: 10.1002/hep.2)*

HBV Treatment Regimens. Single drug therapy is usually sufficient; combination therapy recommended for HIV co-infection.

	Drug/Dose	Comments
Preferred Regimens	**Pegylated-Interferon-alpha 2a** 180 μg sc once weekly OR **Entecavir** 0.5 mg po once daily OR **Tenofovir alafenamide (TAF/Vemlidy)** 25 mg po once daily	PEG-IFN: Treat for 48 weeks Entecavir: Do not use Entecavir if Lamivudine resistance present. Entecavir/Tenofovir: Treat for at least 24-48 weeks after seroconversion from HBeAg to anti-HBe (if no mod-adv fibrosis present). Indefinite chronic therapy for HBeAg negative patients. Renal impairment dose adjustments necessary.
Alternative Regimens	**Lamivudine** 100 mg po once daily OR **Telbivudine** 600 mg po once daily OR **Emtricitabine** 200 mg po once daily (Investigational) OR **Adefovir** 10 mg po once daily OR **Tenofovir disoproxil (TDF)** 300 mg po once daily	These alternative agents are rarely used except in combination. When used, restrict to short term therapy owing to high rates of development of resistance. Not recommended as first-line therapy. Use of Adefovir has mostly been replaced by Tenofovir.
Preferred Regimen for HIV-HBV Co-Infected Patient	**Truvada (Tenofovir 300 mg + Emtricitabine 200 mg)** po once daily + another anti-HIV drug	ALL patients if possible as part of a fully suppressive anti-HIV/anti-HBV regimen. Continue therapy indefinitely.

TABLE 14F – HCV TREATMENT REGIMENS AND RESPONSE
For HCV Activity Spectra, see Table 4C, page 84

1. **Indications for Treatment.** Treatment is indicated for **all patients** with chronic HCV. Rx should be initiated urgently for those with more advanced fibrosis (F3 / F4) and those with underlying co-morbid conditions due to HCV. Type and duration of Rx is based on genotype and stage of fibrosis. Pegylated interferon (Peg-IFN) is no longer a recommended regimen; all DAA regimens with or without ribavirin are the preferred choice.

2. **Definitions of Response to Therapy.**

End of Treatment Response (ETR)	Undetectable at end of treatment.
Relapse	Undetectable at end of therapy (ETR) but rebound (detectable) virus within 12 weeks after therapy stopped.
Sustained Virologic Response (SVR)	CURE! Still undetectable at end of therapy and beyond 12 weeks after therapy is stopped.

3. **HCV Treatment Regimens**

- Biopsy is a 'gold standard' for staging HCV infection and is helpful in some settings to determine the ideal timing of HCV treatment. When bx not obtained, "non-invasive" tests are often employed to assess the relative probability of advanced fibrosis or cirrhosis. Fibroscan (elastography) is now approved in the US and most of the world as a means of assessing liver fibrosis. Elastography values of >10 kPa (Kilopascals) correlates with significant fibrosis (F3 or F4 disease).

- Resistance tests: Genotypic resistance assays are available that can determine polymorphisms associated with reduction in susceptibility to some DAAs (Direct Acting Agents, e.g., protease inhibitors). **However, resistance tests are recommended only for those who have failed treatment with a prior NS5A or protease inhibitor regimen.**

- Patients with decompensated cirrhosis should only be treated by hepatologists owing to the risk of rapid clinical deterioration while receiving treatment for HCV.

- **IMPORTANT NOTE REGARDING TREATMENT DECISION-MAKING:** Newer drugs are in development and options for Rx are changing rapidly (i.e., several times per year). Monitor updates at webedition.sanfordguide.com or hcvguidelines.org.

- **Black Box Warning for ALL Direct Acting Agents (DAA):** Cases of HBV reactivation, occasionally fulminant, during or after DAA therapy have been reported in HBV/HCV coinfected patients who were not already on HBV suppressive therapy. See U.S. FDA Drug Safety Announcement, Oct 4, 2016. **For HCV/HBV coinfected patients who are HBsAg+ and are not already on HBV suppressive therapy, monitoring HBV DNA levels during and immediately after DAA therapy for HCV is recommended and antiviral treatment for HBV should be given if treatment criteria for HBV are met.** See HBV treatment.

CURRENT DRUGS FOR INITIAL TREATMENT FOR PATIENTS WITH CHRONIC HCV

- Drugs and regimens are evolving. For updates go to: webedition.sanfordguide.com and www.hcvguidelines.org

Agents/Abbreviation	Tradename	Formulation/Dosing Specifics
Daclatasvir (DCV)	Daklinza	60 mg tab po once daily. Note: decrease dose to 30 mg/d when co-administered with a strong CYP3A inhibitor, e.g., several ARV drugs; increase dose to 90 mg/d when co-administered with a mild-moderate CYP3A inducer. Contraindicated when co-administered with a strong CYP3A inducer.
Elbasvir + Grazoprevir	Zepatier	Fixed dose combination (Elbasvir 50 mg + Grazoprevir 100 mg) 1 tab po once daily
Glecaprevir + Pibrentasvir	Mavyret	Fixed dose combination (Glecaprevir 100 mg + Pibrentasvir 40 mg) 3 tabs once daily with food
Paritaprevir/ritonavir + Ombitasvir (PrO)	Technivie	Fixed dose combination (Paritaprevir 150 mg/ritonavir 100 mg + Ombitasvir 25 mg) 1 tab po once daily
Paritaprevir/ritonavir + Ombitasvir + Dasabuvir (PrOD)	Viekira Pak	Fixed dose combination [(Paritaprevir 150 mg/ritonavir 100 mg + Ombitasvir 25 mg) 1 tab po once daily + Dasabuvir 250 mg] 1 tab twice daily with food
	Viekira XR	Extended release fixed dose combination [(Dasabuvir 200 mg + Paritaprevir 50 mg/ritonavir 33.3 mg + Ombitasvir 8.33 mg) 3 tabs once daily with food
Simeprevir (SMV)	Olysio	150 mg tab po once daily with food
Sofosbuvir (SOF)	Solvadi	400 mg tab po once daily
Sofosbuvir + Ledipasvir	Harvoni	Fixed dose combination (Sofosbuvir 400 mg + Ledipasvir 90 mg) 1 tab po once daily
Sofosbuvir + Velpatasvir	Epclusa	Fixed dose combination (Sofosbuvir 400 mg + Velpatasvir 100 mg): 1 tab po once daily
Sofosbuvir + Velpatasvir + Voxilaprevir	Vosevi	Fixed dose combination (Sofosbuvir 400 mg + Velpatasvir 100 mg + Voxilaprevir 100 mg): 1 tab po once daily with food
Ribavirin	Ribavirin, Copegus	Weight-based daily dosing: 1000 mg (Wt <75 kg) or 1200 mg (Wt >75 kg). Low dose: 600 mg/day. Taken with food.
Pegylated interferon (alfa 2a)	Roferon, Intron-A, Peg-Intron, Pegasys	180 mcg sc per week

TABLE 14F (2)

HCV RECOMMENDED TREATMENT REGIMENS
(P = Primary regimen, A = Alternative regimen, Regimens from prior page)

HCV Mono Infection

Genotype	P/A	Regimen	Cirrhosis	Duration	Comments
1-6	P	Epclusa 1 tab po once daily	With or without	12 weeks	Pan-genotypic DAAs
	P	Mavyret 3 tabs po once daily	Without	8 weeks	
			With	12 weeks	
1a	P	Epclusa 1 tab po once daily	With or without	12 weeks	
	P	Harvoni 1 tab po once daily	Without*	8 weeks	* If patient is non-black, HIV-uninfected, non-cirrhotic, and HCV RNA <6 million c/mL
			With**	12 weeks	** If patient is black, HIV-co-infected, compensated cirrhosis, or HCV RNA >6 million c/mL
	P	Mavyret 3 tabs po once daily	Without	8 weeks	
			With	12 weeks	
	P	Zepatier 1 tab po once daily	With or without	12 weeks	If no baseline high-fold NS5A resistance associated mutations
	A	Viekira Pak (as directed) + RBV	Without only	12 weeks	RBV dosing is wt-based
	A	(DCV + SOF) po once daily	Without only	12 weeks	
	A	(SOF + SMV ± RBV) po divided twice daily	Without only	12 weeks	RBV dosing is wt-based
1b	P	Epclusa 1 tab po once daily	With or without	12 weeks	
	P	Harvoni 1 tab po once daily	Without*	8 weeks	* If patient is non-black, HIV-uninfected, non-cirrhotic, and HCV RNA <6 million c/mL
			With**	12 weeks	** If patient is black, HIV-co-infected, compensated cirrhosis, or HCV RNA >6 million c/mL
	P	Mavyret 3 tabs po once daily	Without	8 weeks	
			With	12 weeks	
	P	Zepatier 1 tab po once daily	With or without	12 weeks	
	A	Viekira Pak (as directed)	With or without	12 weeks	
	A	(DCV + SOF) po once daily	Without only	12 weeks	
	A	(SOF + SMV ± RBV) po divided twice daily	Without only	12 weeks	RBV dosing is wt-based
2	P	Epclusa 1 tab po once daily	With or without	12 weeks	
	P	Mavyret 3 tabs po once daily	Without	8 weeks	
			With	12 weeks	
	A	(DCV + SOF) po once daily	Without	12 weeks	
			With	16-24 weeks	
3	P	Epclusa 1 tab po once daily	With or without	12 weeks	Do not use in cirrhosis if RAV Y93H is present
	P	Mavyret 3 tabs po once daily	Without	8 weeks	
			With	12 weeks	
	A	Vosevi 1 tab po once daily	With	12 weeks	RAS Y93H is present
	A	(DCV + SOF) po once daily	Without	12 weeks	
			With	16-24 weeks	

TABLE 14F (3)

HCV Mono Infection *(continued)*

Genotype	P/A	Regimen	Cirrhosis	Duration	Comments
4	P	**Epclusa** 1 tab po once daily	With or without	12 weeks	
	P	**Harvoni** 1 tab po once daily	Without*	8 weeks	* If patient is non-black, HIV-uninfected, non-cirrhotic, and HCV RNA <6 million c/mL.
			With**	12 weeks	** If patient is black, HIV-co-infected, compensated cirrhosis, or HCV RNA >6 million c/mL.
	P	**Mavyret** 3 tabs po once daily	Without	8 weeks	
			With	12 weeks	
	P	**Zepatier** 1 tab po once daily	With or without	12 weeks	
	A	**Technivie** once daily	Without	12 weeks	
	A	**Technivie** once daily + RBV twice daily	With	12 weeks	RBV dosing is wt-based
5 & 6	P	**Epclusa** 1 tab po once daily	With or without	12 weeks	
	P	**Harvoni** 1 tab po once daily	Without*	8 weeks	* If patient is non-black, HIV-uninfected, non-cirrhotic, and HCV RNA <6 million c/mL.
			With**	12 weeks	** If patient is black, HIV-co-infected, compensated cirrhosis, or HCV RNA >6 million c/mL.
	P	**Mavyret** 3 tabs po once daily	Without	8 weeks	
			With	12 weeks	

HCV-HIV Co-Infection

Genotype	P/A	Regimen	Cirrhosis	Duration	Comments
1a & 1b	P/A	Same as for HCV Mono Infection		8-12 weeks✧	Watch for drug-drug interactions. ✧ 8 weeks ONLY in HCV Rx naive co-infected patients receiving **Mavyret**; otherwise, minimum 12 weeks with any other regimen
2	P/A	Same as for HCV Mono Infection		8-12 weeks✧	Watch for drug-drug interactions. ✧ 8 weeks ONLY in HCV Rx naive co-infected patients receiving **Mavyret**; otherwise, minimum 12 weeks with any other regimen
3	P/A	Same as for HCV Mono Infection			Watch for drug-drug interactions.
4, 5, 6		Not enough experience; if treatment required, use same as for HCV Mono Infection			

Decompensated Cirrhosis

Genotype	P/A	Regimen	Cirrhosis	Duration	Comments
1, 4, 5, 6	P	**Epclusa** 1 tab po once daily + RBV		12 weeks	RBV dosing is wt-based. If RBV-intolerant, treat without RBV for 24 weeks. If prior SOF or NS5A treatment experience, RBV alone for 24 weeks.
	P	**Harvoni** 1 tab po once daily + low dose RBV		12 weeks	If RBV-intolerant, treat without RBV for 24 weeks. If prior SOF or NS5A treatment experience, RBV alone for 24 weeks.
1, 4	P	(DCV + SOF) po once daily + low dose RBV		12 weeks	24 weeks if RBV intolerant
2, 3	P	**Epclusa** 1 tab po once daily + RBV		12 weeks	RBV dosing is wt-based. If RBV-intolerant, treat without RBV for 24 weeks. If prior SOF or NS5A treatment experience, RBV alone for 24 weeks.
	P	(DCV + SOF) po once daily + low dose RBV		12 weeks	24 weeks if RBV intolerant

TABLE 14F (4)

Post-Liver Transplant

Genotype	P/A	Regimen	Cirrhosis	Duration	Comments
1, 4, 5, 6	P	**Mavyret** 3 tabs po once daily	Without	12 weeks	Alternative if compensated cirrhosis
	P	**Harvoni** 1 tab po once daily + RBV	With or without	12 weeks	RBV dosing is wt-based. Dose as tolerated.
	A	**(DCV + SOF)** po once daily + low dose RBV	Without	12 weeks	
1, 4	A	**(SOF + SMV ± RBV)** po divided twice daily	Without	12 weeks	RBV dosing is wt-based.
2, 3	P	**Mavyret** 3 tabs po once daily	Without	12 weeks	Alternative if compensated cirrhosis
	P	**(DCV + SOF)** po once daily + low dose RBV	With	12 weeks	Compensated or decompensated
	A	**Epclusa** 1 tab po once daily + RBV	With	12 weeks	Compensated or decompensated. RBV dosing is wt-based
	A	**SOF + RBV** po daily		24 weeks	RBV initial dose 600 mg/day, increased monthly by 200 mg/day as tolerated up to max wt-based dose

TABLE 15A – ANTIMICROBIAL PROPHYLAXIS FOR SELECTED BACTERIAL INFECTIONS*

CLASS OF ETIOLOGIC AGENT/DISEASE/CONDITION	PROPHYLAXIS AGENT/DOSE/ROUTE/DURATION	COMMENTS
Group B streptococcal disease (GBS), neonatal: Approaches to management (CDC Guidelines, *MMWR 59 (RR-10):1, 2010; CID 2017;65(S2):S143*)		

Pregnant women—intrapartum antimicrobial prophylaxis procedures:
1. Screen all pregnant women with vaginal & rectal swab for GBS at 35–37 wks gestation (unless other indications for prophylaxis exist: GBS bacteriuria during this pregnancy or previously delivered infant with invasive GBS disease; even then cultures may be useful for susceptibility testing). Use transport medium; GBS survive at room temp. up to 96 hrs. **Rx during labor if swab culture positive.**
2. Rx during labor if previously delivered infant with invasive GBS infection, or if any GBS bacteriuria during this pregnancy.
3. Rx if GBS status unknown but, if any of the following are present: (a) delivery at <37 wks gestation (see *MMWR 59 (RR-10):1, 2010*) algorithms for preterm premature rupture of membranes]; or (b) duration of ruptured membranes ≥18 hrs; or (c) intrapartum temp ≥100.4°F (≥38.0°C). If amnionitis suspected, broad-spectrum antibiotic coverage should include an agent active vs. group B streptococci.
4. Rx if positive intra-partum NAAT for GBS.
5. Unless other conditions exist, Rx not indicated if: negative vaginal/rectal cultures at 35–37 wks gestation or C-section performed before onset of labor with intact amniotic membranes (use standard surgical prophylaxis).
	Regimens for prophylaxis against early-onset group B streptococcal disease in neonate used during labor:
	Penicillin G 5 million Units IV (initial dose) then 2.5 to 3 million Units IV q4h until delivery
	Alternative: **Ampicillin** 2 gm IV (initial dose) then 1 gm IV q4h until delivery
	Penicillin-allergic patients:
	• Patient not at high risk for anaphylaxis: **Cefazolin** 2 gm IV (initial dose) then 1 gm IV q8h until delivery
	• Patient at high risk for anaphylaxis from β-lactams:
	  ○ If organism is both clindamycin- and erythromycin-susceptible, **or** is erythromycin-resistant, but clindamycin-susceptible confirmed by D-zone test (or equivalent) showing lack of inducible resistance: **Clindamycin** 900 mg IV q8h until delivery
	  ○ If susceptibility of organism unknown, lack of inducible resistance to clindamycin has not been excluded, or patient is allergic to clindamycin: **Vancomycin** 1 gm IV q12h until delivery	

Neonate (of mother given prophylaxis).	*See detailed algorithm in MMWR 59 (RR-10):1, 2010.*	
Preterm, premature rupture of the membranes: Grp B strep-negative women Cochrane Database Rev 12:CD000-1058, 2013; Obstet Gyn 124:515-2014; Am J Ob-Gyn 207:475, 2012.	(**AMP** 2 gm IV q6h + **Erythro** 250 mg IV q6h) x 48 hrs, then (**Amox** 250 mg po q8h + **Erythro base** 333 mg po q8h) x 5 days (*ACOG Practice Bulletin; Obstet Gynecol 127: e39, 2016*).	
Post-splenectomy bacteremia. Usually encapsulated bacteria: pneumococci, meningococci, H. flu type B; bacteremia: Enterobacter, S. aureus, Capnocytophaga, P. aeruginosa. Also at risk for fatal malaria, severe babesiosis. Asplenia review (*Chest 2016;150:1394*)	Protein conjugate and polysaccharide vaccines at age appropriate intervals (Adults: *www.cdc.gov/vaccines/schedules/downloads/adult/adult-combined-schedule.pdf*; Children: *www.cdc.gov/vaccines/schedules/downloads/child/0-18yrs-child-combined-schedule.pdf*). Daily Prophylaxis in asplenic child (daily until age 5 yrs or minimum of 1 yr rx): **Amox** 125 mg po bid (age 2mo-3yr); **Amox** 250 mg po bid (age >3yr-5 yr). If allergic, e.g. rash only: **Cephalexin** 250 mg po bid. Fever in Children & Adults: **AM-CL** 875/125 po bid (adult), 90 mg/kg/day po bid (child). Alternative: (**Levo** 750 mg po or **Moxi** 400 mg po) once daily. Seek immediate medical care. Some recommend **Amox** 2 gm po before sinus or airway procedures.	

TABLE 15A (2)

CLASS OF ETIOLOGIC AGENT/DISEASE/CONDITION	PROPHYLAXIS AGENT/DOSE/ROUTE/DURATION	COMMENTS
Sexual Exposure		
Sexual assault: survivor [likely agents and risks, see CDC Guidelines at *MMWR 64(RR-3):1, 2015].* For review of overall care: *NEJM 365:834, 2011.*	[**Ceftriaxone** 250 mg IM + **Azithro** 1gm po once + (**Metro** 2 gm po once or **Tinidazole** 2 gm po once)]. Can delay Metro/Tinidazole if alcohol was recently ingested.	• Obtain expert individualized advice re: forensic exam and specimens, pregnancy (incl. emergency contraception), physical trauma, psychological support • Test for chlamydia and gonococci at sites of penetration or attempted penetration by NAATs. Obtain molecular tests for trichomonas and check vaginal secretions for BV and candidiasis. • Serological evaluation for syphilis, HIV, HBV, HCV • Initiate post-exposure protocols for HBV vaccine, HIV post-exposure prophylaxis as appropriate • HPV vaccine recommended for females 9-26 or males 9-21, if not already immunized • Follow-up in 1 week to review results, repeat negative tests in 1-2 weeks to detect infections not detected previously, repeat syphilis testing 4-6 weeks and 3 months, repeat HIV testing 6 weeks and 3-6 months. • Check for anogenital warts at 1-2 months. Notes: If ceftriaxone not available, can use cefixime 400 mg po once in its place for prevention of gonorrhea, but the latter is less effective for pharyngeal infection and against strains with reduced susceptibility to cephalosporins. For non-pregnant individuals who cannot receive cephalosporins, treatment with (Gemifloxacin 320 mg po once + azithro 2 gm po once) or (Gentamicin 240 mg IM once + azithro 2 gm po once) can be substituted for ceftriaxone/azithro.
Contact with specific sexually transmitted diseases	*See comprehensive guidelines for specific pathogens in MMWR 64(RR-3):1, 2015.*	
Syphilis exposure		Presumptive rx for exposure within 3 mos., as tests may be negative. *See Table 1, page 24.* If exposure occurred >90 days prior, establish dx or treat empirically.
Sickle-cell disease. Likely agent: S. pneumoniae (See *post-splenectomy,* above) Ref.: *NEJM 376:1561, 2017*	Children <5 yrs: **Penicillin V** 62.5 to 125 mg po bid ≥5 yrs: **Penicillin V** 250 mg po bid. (Alternative in children: Amoxicillin 20 mg per kg per day)	Start prophylaxis by 2 mos. *(Pediatrics 106:367, 2000)*; continue until at least age 5. When to d/c must be individualized. Age-appropriate vaccines, including pneumococcal, Hib, influenza, meningococcal. Treating infections, consider possibility of penicillin non-susceptible pneumococci. May need malaria prophylaxis entire life.

TABLE 15B - ANTIBIOTIC PROPHYLAXIS TO PREVENT SURGICAL INFECTIONS IN ADULTS[a]
2013 Guidelines: Am J Health Syst Pharm 70:195, 2013; Med Lett 58:63, 2016

General Comments:
- To be optimally effective, antibiotics must be started within 60 minutes of the surgical incision. Vancomycin and FQs may require 1-2 hr infusion time, so start dose 2 hrs before the surgical incision.
- Most applications employ a single preoperative dose or continuation for less than 24 hrs.
- For procedures lasting >2 half-lives of prophylactic agent, intraoperative supplementary dose(s) may be required.
- Dose adjustments may be desirable in pts with BMI >30.
- Prophylaxis does carry risk: e.g., C. difficile colitis, allergic reactions
- Active S. aureus screening, decolonization & customized antimicrobial prophylaxis demonstrated efficacious in decreasing infections after hip, knee & cardiac surgery *(JAMA 313:2137, & 2162, 2015)*.
- See additional details for prevention of surgical site infections by CDC *(JAMA Surg 152: 784, 2017)* and Am Coll Surg/Surg Infect Soc *(J Am Coll Surg 224: 59, 2016)*. Both support no further antibiotics once surgical wound is closed, although latter includes possible exceptions: breast reconstruction, joint arthroplasty, and cardiac procedures.

Use of Vancomycin:
- For many common prophylaxis indications, vancomycin is considered an alternative to β-lactams in pts allergic to or intolerant of the latter.
- Vancomycin use may be justifiable in centers where rates of post-operative infection with methicillin-resistant staphylococci are high or in pts at high risk for these.
- Unlike β-lactams in common use, vancomycin has no activity against gram-negative organisms. **When gram-negative bacteria are a concern following specific procedures, it may be necessary or desirable to add a second agent with appropriate in vitro activity.** This can be done using cefazolin with vancomycin in the non-allergic pt, or in pts intolerant of β-lactams using vancomycin with another ram-negative agent (e.g., aminoglycoside, fluoroquinolone, possibly aztreonam, if pt not allergic; local resistance patterns and pt factors would influence choice).
- Infusion of vancomycin, especially too rapidly, may result in hypotension or other manifestations of histamine release (red person syndrome). Does not indicate an allergy to vancomycin.

TYPE OF SURGERY	PROPHYLAXIS	COMMENTS
Cardiovascular Surgery		
Antibiotic prophylaxis in cardiovascular surgery has been proven beneficial in the following procedures: - Reconstruction of abdominal aorta - Procedures on the leg that involve a groin incision - Any vascular procedure that inserts prosthesis/foreign body - Lower extremity amputation for ischemia - Cardiac surgery - Permanent Pacemakers *(Circulation 121:458, 2010)* - Implanted cardiac defibrillators	**Cefazolin** 1–2 gm (Wt <120 kg) or 3 gm (Wt >120 kg) IV as a single dose or q8h for 1-2 days or **Cefuroxime** 1.5 gm IV as a single dose or q12h for total of 6 gm or **Vanco** 1 gm IV as a single dose or q12h for 1-2 days. For pts weighing >90 kg, use vanco 1.5 gm IV as a single dose or q12h for 1-2 days. Re-dose cefazolin q4h if CrCl>30 mL/min or q8h if CrCl ≤30 mL/min. Consider **intranasal Mupirocin** evening before, day of surgery & bid for 5 days post-op in pts with pos. nasal culture for S. aureus. Mupirocin resistance has been encountered.	**Timing & duration:** Single infusion just before surgery as effective as multiple doses. No prophylaxis needed for cardiac catheterization. For prosthetic heart valves, customary to stop prophylaxis either after removal of retrosternal drainage catheters or just a 2nd dose after coming off bypass. **Vanco** may be preferable in hospitals with ↑ freq of MRSA, in high-risk pts, those colonized with MRSA or for Pen-allergic pt. Clindamycin 900 mg IV is another alternative for Pen-allergic pt. For insertion of ventricular assist devices, prophylaxis same as for cardiac surgery (e.g., cefazolin ± vancomycin) *(CID 64: 222, 2017)*.
Gastroduodenal/Biliary		
Gastroduodenal and Colonic Surgery		
Gastroduodenal, includes percutaneous endoscopic gastrostomy (high risk only), pancreaticoduodenectomy (Whipple procedure)	**Cefazolin** (1-2 gm IV) or **Cefoxitin** (1-2 gm IV) or **Cefotetan** (1-2 gm IV) or **Ceftriaxone** (2 gm IV) as a single dose (some give additional doses q12h for 2-3 days). See Comment	Gastroduodenal (PEG placement): High-risk is marked obesity, obstruction, ↓ gastric acid or ↓ motility. Re-dose Cefazolin q4h and Cefoxitin q2h if CrCl >30 mL/min; q8h and q4h, respectively, if CrCl ≤30 mL/min
Biliary, includes laparoscopic cholecystectomy	Low risk, laparoscopic: No prophylaxis Open cholecystectomy: **Cefazolin, Cefoxitin, Cefotetan, Ampicillin-sulbactam**	Biliary high-risk or open procedure age >70, acute cholecystitis, non-functioning gallbladder, obstructive jaundice or common duct stones. With cholangitis, treat as infection, not prophylaxis.
Endoscopic retrograde cholangiopancreatography	No rx without obstruction; **Cefazolin.** If obstruction: **CIP** 500-750 mg po or 400 mg IV 2 hrs prior to procedure or **PIP-TZ** 4.5 gm IV 1 hr prior to procedure	Most studies show that achieving adequate drainage will prevent post-procedural cholangitis or sepsis and no further benefit from prophylactic antibiotics; greatest benefit likely when complete drainage cannot be achieved. *See Gastroint Endosc 81: 81, 2015 for American Society of Gastrointestinal Endoscopy recommendations for ERCP; Gut 58:868, 2009.*

TABLE 15B (2)

TYPE OF SURGERY	PROPHYLAXIS	COMMENTS
Gastric, Biliary and Colonic Surgery *(continued)*		
Colorectal Recommend combination of: • Mechanical bowel prep (*See Comment*) • po antibiotic (*See Comment*) • IV antibiotic Mechanical bowel prep + po antibiotics recommended for all elective colectomies (*J Am Coll Surg 224:59, 2016*).	**Parenteral regimens** (emergency or elective): [Cefazolin 2 gm IV + Metro 0.5 gm IV] (*see Comment*) or **Cefoxitin** or **Cefotetan** 1-2 gm IV (if available) or **Ceftriaxone** 2 gm IV + **Metro** 0.5 gm IV or **ERTA** 1 gm IV. Beta-lactam allergy, see Comment	**Oral regimens: Neomycin + Erythro.** Pre-op day: (1) 10 am 4L polyethylene glycol electrolyte soluton (Colyte, GoLYTELY) po over 2 hr. (2) Clear liquid diet only. (3) 1 pm, 2 pm & 11 pm, Neomycin 1 gm + Erythro base 1 gm po. (4) NPO after midnight. Alternative regimens have been less well studied; GoLYTELY 1-6 pm, then Neomycin 2 gm po + Metronidazole 2 gm po at 7 pm & 11 pm. Oral regimen as effective as parenteral; parenteral in addition to oral not required but often used (*Am J Surg 189:395, 2005*). Study found **Ertapenem** more effective than cefotetan, but associated with non-significant ↑ risk of C. difficile (*NEJM 355:2640, 2006*). **Beta-lactam allergy: Clinda** 900 mg IV + (**Gent** 5 mg/kg **or Aztreonam** 2 gm IV or **CIP** 400 mg IV).
Ruptured viscus: See Peritoneum/Peritonitis, Secondary, Table 1, page 48.		
Head and Neck Surgery	**Cefazolin** 2 gm IV (Single dose) (some add **Metro** 500 mg IV) OR **Clinda** 600-900 mg IV (single dose) ± **Gent** 5 mg/kg IV (single dose) (*See Table 10D for weight-based dose calculation*).	Antimicrobial prophylaxis in head & neck surg appears efficacious only for procedures involving oral/ pharyngeal mucosa (e.g., laryngeal or pharyngeal tumor) but even with prophylaxis, wound infection rate can be high. **Clean, uncontaminated head & neck surg does not require prophylaxis.** Re-dose cefazolin q4h if CrCl>30 mL/min or q8h if CrCl ≤30 mL/min
Neurosurgical Procedures Clean, non-implant; e.g., elective craniotomy	**Cefazolin** 1-2 gm IV once. Alternative: **Vanco** 1 gm IV once; for pts weighing >90 kg, use vanco 1.5 gm IV as single dose.	**Clindamycin** 900 mg IV is alternative for vanco-allergic or beta-lactam allergic pt. Re-dose cefazolin q4h if CrCl>30 mL/min or q8h if CrCl ≤30 mL/min
Clean, contaminated (cross sinuses, or naso/oropharynx)	**Clindamycin** 900 mg IV (single dose)	British recommend **Amoxicillin-Clavulanate** 1.2 gm IV[NUS] or ((**Cefuroxime** 1.5 gm IV + Metronidazole 0.5 gm IV).
CSF shunt surgery, intrathecal pumps:	**Cefazolin** 1-2 gm (Wt <120 kg) or 3 gm (Wt ≥120 kg) IV once. Alternative: **Vanco** 1 gm IV once; for pts weighing >90 kg, use vanco 1.5 gm IV as single dose OR **Clindamycin** 900 mg IV.	Randomized study in a hospital with high prevalence of infection due to methicillin-resistant staphylococci showed Vancomycin was more effective than cefazolin in preventing CSF shunt infections (*J Hosp Infect 69:337, 2008*). Re-dose cefazolin q4h if CrCl >30 mL/min or q8h if CrCl ≤30 mL/min
Obstetric/Gynecologic Surgery Vaginal or abdominal hysterectomy	**Cefazolin** 1-2 gm IV or **Cefoxitin** 1-2 gm or **Cefotetan** 1-2 gm IV or **Ampicillin-sulbactam** 3 gm IV 30 min. before surgery.	Alternative: (**Clindamycin** 900 mg IV or **Vancomycin** 1 gm IV) + (**Gentamicin** 5 mg/kg IV x 1 dose or **Aztreonam** 2 gm IV or **Ciprofloxacin** 400 mg IV) OR (**Metronidazole** 500 mg IV + **Ciprofloxacin** 400 mg IV).
Cesarean section for premature rupture of membranes or active labor	**Cefazolin** 1-2 gm IV x 1 dose before surgery. Alternative: **Clindamycin** 900 mg IV – (**Gentamicin** 5 mg/kg IV or **Tobramycin** 5 mg/kg IV) x 1 dose. **Note:** If not elective or obese pt., see Comment.	Administering prophylaxis before the skin incision reduces surgical site infections. In non-elective C-section, addition of Azithro 500 mg IV in addition to standard antibiotics significantly decreased endometritis and SSIs (*NEJM 375:1231, 2016*). In obesity, give standard cefazolin dose; for pts >120 kg, then ((Cephalexin 500 mg po q8h + Metro 500 mg po q8h) x 18 hrs (*JAMA 207:2318:1012.6, 1026*). Meta-analysis showed benefit of antibiotic prophylaxis in all risk groups.
Surgical Abortion (1st trimester)	1st trimester: **Doxycycline** 300 mg po: 100 mg 1 hr before procedure & 200 mg post-procedure.	
Ophthalmic Surgery	(Neomycin-Gentamicin-Polymyxin B or Gati or Moxi) eye drops, 1 drop q5-15 min x 5 doses	Some add Cefazolin 100 mg under conjunctival at end of surgery.

TABLE 15B (3)

TYPE OF SURGERY	PROPHYLAXIS	COMMENTS
Orthopedic Surgery		
Hip arthroplasty, spinal fusion	Same as cardiac surgery	Customarily stopped after "Hemovac" removed. 2013 Guidelines recommend stopping prophylaxis within 24 hrs of surgery (*Am J Health Syst Pharm 70:195, 2013*).
Total joint replacement (other than hip)	**Cefazolin** 1–2 gm IV pre-op (± 2nd dose) or **Vanco** 1 gm IV. For pts weighing >90 kg, use vanco 1.5 gm IV as single dose or **Clinda** 900 mg IV.	2013 Guidelines recommends stopping prophylaxis within 24 hrs of surgery (*Am J Health Syst Pharm 70:195, 2013*). Usual to administer before tourniquet inflation. Intranasal mupirocin if colonized with S. aureus.
Open reduction of closed fracture with internal fixation	**Ceftriaxone** 2 gm IV once	3.6% (ceftriaxone) vs 8.3% (for placebo) infection found in Dutch trauma trial (*Ln 347:1133, 1996*). In general, alternative antimicrobials can ↓ risk of infection
Prophylaxis to protect prosthetic joints from hematogenous infection related to distant procedures (patients with plates, pins and screws only are not considered to be at risk)		• A prospective, case-control study concluded that antibiotic prophylaxis did not decrease the risk of hip or knee prosthesis infection (*Clin Infect Dis 50:8, 2010*). (*Cochrane Database Syst Rev 2010; CD004440*). • An expert panel of the American Dental Association concluded that, in general, prophylactic antibiotics are not recommended prior to dental procedures to prevent prosthetic joint infection (*J Amer Dental Assoc 146: 11, 2015*). • Individual circumstances should be considered; when there is planned manipulation of tissues thought to be actively infected, antimicrobial therapy for the infection is likely to be appropriate.
Peritoneal Dialysis Catheter Placement	**Vanco** single 1 gm IV dose 12 hrs prior to procedure	Effectively reduced peritonitis during 14 days post-placement in 221 pts: Vanco 1%, Cefazolin 7%, placebo 12% (p=0.02) (*Am J Kidney Dis 36:1014, 2000*).
Urologic Surgery/Procedures • See Best Practice Policy Statement of Amer. Urological Assoc. (AUA) (*J Urol 179:1379, 2008*) and 2013 Guidelines (*Am J Health Syst Pharm 70:195, 2013*). • Selection of agents targeting urinary pathogens may require modification based on local resistance patterns; † TMP-SMX and/or fluoroquinolone (FQ) resistance among enteric gram-negative bacteria is a concern.		
Cystoscopy	• Prophylaxis generally not necessary if urine is sterile (however, AUA recommends FQ or TMP-SMX for those with several potentially adverse host factors (e.g., advanced age, immunocompromised state, anatomic abnormalities, etc.) • Treat patients with UTI prior to procedure using an antimicrobial active against pathogens isolated	
Cystoscopy with manipulation	**Ciprofloxacin** 500 mg po (TMP-SMX 1 DS tablet po may be an alternative in populations with low rates of resistance).	Procedures mentioned include ureteroscopy, biopsy, fulguration, TURP, etc. Treat UTI with targeted therapy before procedure if possible.
Transrectal prostate biopsy	**Ciprofloxacin** 500 mg po 12 hrs prior to biopsy and repeated 12 hrs after 1st dose. See Comment.	Bacteremia 7% with **CIP** vs 37% with **Gentamicin** (*JAC 39:115, 1997*). **Levofloxacin** 500 mg 30-60 min before procedure was effective in low risk pts; additional doses were given before 2nd risk (*J Urol 168:1021, 2002*). Serious bacteremias due to FQ-resistant organisms have been encountered in patients receiving FQ prophylaxis. Screening stool cultures pre-procedure for colonization with FQ-resistant organisms is increasingly utilized to inform choice of prophylaxis (*Clin Infect Dis 60: 979, 2015*). One study showed non-significant decrease in risk of infection with culture-directed antimicrobial prophylaxis (*Urology 146: 71, 2015*). Pre-operative prophylaxis should be determined on an institutional basis based on susceptibility profiles of prevailing organisms. Although 2nd or 3rd generation Cephalosporins or addition of single-dose gentamicin has been suggested, infections due to ESBL-producing and gent-resistant organisms have been encountered (*Urol 74:332, 2009*).
Other		
Breast surgery, herniorrhaphy, thoracotomy	**Cefazolin** 1–2 gm IV x 1 dose or **AM-SB** 3 gm IV x 1 dose or **Clinda** 900 mg IV x 1 dose or **Vanco** 1 gm IV x 1 dose (1.5 gm if wt >90 kg)	*Am J Health Syst Pharm 70:195, 2013*.
Vascular surgery: aneurysm repair, revascularization	**Cefazolin** 2 gm IV x 1 dose	

TABLE 15C – ANTIMICROBIAL PROPHYLAXIS FOR THE PREVENTION OF BACTERIAL ENDOCARDITIS IN PATIENTS WITH UNDERLYING CARDIAC CONDITIONS*

In 2007, the American Heart Association guidelines for the prevention of bacterial endocarditis were updated. The resulting document (*Circulation 2007; 116:1736-1754 and http://circ.ahajournals.org/cgi/reprint/116/15/1736*), which was also endorsed by the Infectious Diseases Society of America, represents a significant departure from earlier recommendations.

- Antibiotic prophylaxis for dental procedures is now directed at individuals who are likely to suffer the most devastating consequences should they develop endocarditis.
- Prophylaxis to prevent endocarditis is no longer specified for gastrointestinal or genitourinary procedures. The following is adapted from and reflects the new AHA recommendations. *See original publication for explanation and precise details.*

SELECTION OF PATIENTS FOR ENDOCARDITIS PROPHYLAXIS

FOR PATIENTS WITH ANY OF THESE HIGH-RISK CARDIAC CONDITIONS ASSOCIATED WITH ENDOCARDITIS:	WHO UNDERGO DENTAL PROCEDURES INVOLVING:	WHO UNDERGO INVASIVE RESPIRATORY PROCEDURES INVOLVING:	WHO UNDERGO INVASIVE PROCEDURES OF THE GI OR GU TRACTS:	WHO UNDERGO PROCEDURES INVOLVING INFECTED SKIN AND SOFT TISSUES:
Prosthetic heart valves Previous infective endocarditis Congenital heart disease with any of the following: • Completely repaired cardiac defect using prosthetic material (Only for 1st 6 months) • Partially corrected but with residual defect near prosthetic material • Uncorrected cyanotic congenital heart disease • Surgically constructed shunts and conduits Valvulopathy following heart transplant [Benefit unclear in pt with ventricular assist device (*CID 64: 222, 2017*).]	Any manipulation of gingival tissue, dental periapical regions, or perforating the oral mucosa. **PROPHYLAXIS RECOMMENDED‡** (*see Dental Procedures Regimens table below*) (Prophylaxis is *not* recommended for routine anesthetic injections (unless through infected area), dental x-rays, shedding of primary teeth, adjustment of orthodontic appliances or removable orthodontic brackets or removable appliances.)	Incision of respiratory tract mucosa **CONSIDER PROPHYLAXIS** (*see Dental Procedures Regimens table*) OR For treatment of established infection **PROPHYLAXIS RECOMMENDED** (*see Dental Procedures Regimens table for oral flora, but include anti-staphylococcal coverage when S. aureus is of concern*)	PROPHYLAXIS is no longer recommended solely to prevent endocarditis, **but the following approach is reasonable:** For patients with enterococcal UTIs • treat before elective GU procedures • include enterococcal coverage in perioperative regimen for non-elective procedures For patients with existing GU or GI infections or those who receive perioperative antibiotics to prevent surgical site infections or sepsis • it is reasonable to include agents with anti-enterococcal activity in perioperative coverage¹	Include coverage against staphylococci and β-hemolytic streptococci in treatment regimens

¹ Agents with anti-enterococcal activity include penicillin, ampicillin, amoxicillin, vancomycin and others. Check susceptibility if available. (*See Table 5 for highly resistant organisms.*)
‡ 2008 AHA/ACC focused update of guidelines on valvular heart disease use term "is reasonable" to reflect level of evidence (*Circulation 118:887, 2008*).

PROPHYLACTIC REGIMENS FOR DENTAL PROCEDURES

SITUATION	AGENT	REGIMEN¹
Usual oral prophylaxis	Amoxicillin	Adults 2 gm, children 50 mg per kg; orally, 1 hour before procedure
Unable to take oral medications	Ampicillin²	Adults 2 gm, children 50 mg per kg; IV or IM, within 30 min before procedure.
Allergic to penicillins	Cephalexin² OR	Adults 2 gm, children 50 mg per kg; orally, 1 hour before procedure.
	Clindamycin OR	Adults 600 mg, children 20 mg per kg; orally, 1 hour before procedure
	Azithromycin or clarithromycin	Adults 500 mg, children 15 mg per kg; orally, 1 hour before procedure
Allergic to penicillins and unable to take oral medications	Cefazolin² OR	Adults 1 gm children 50 mg per kg; IV or IM, within 30 min before procedure
	Clindamycin	Adults 600 mg, children 20 mg per kg; IV or IM, within 30 min before procedure

¹ Children's dose should not exceed adult dose. AHA document lists all doses as 30-60 min before procedure.
² AHA lists Cefazolin or Ceftriaxone (at appropriate doses) as alternatives here.
³ Cephalosporins should not be used in individuals with immediate-type hypersensitivity reaction (urticaria, angioedema, or anaphylaxis) to penicillins or other β-lactams. AHA proposes ceftriaxone as potential alternative to cefazolin; and other 1st or 2nd generation cephalosporin in equivalent doses as potential alternatives to cephalexin.

TABLE 15D – MANAGEMENT OF EXPOSURE TO HIV-1 AND HEPATITIS B AND C[a]

OCCUPATIONAL EXPOSURE TO BLOOD, PENILE/VAGINAL SECRETIONS OR OTHER POTENTIALLY INFECTIOUS BODY FLUIDS OR TISSUES WITH RISK OF TRANSMISSION OF HEPATITIS B/C AND/OR HIV-1 (E.G., NEEDLESTICK INJURY)

Free consultation for occupational exposures, call (PEPline) 1-888-448-4911. *(Information also available at www.aidsinfo.nih.gov)*

General steps in management:

1. Wash clean wounds/flush mucous membranes immediately (use of caustic agents or squeezing the wound is discouraged; data lacking regarding antiseptics).
2. Assess risk by doing the following: (a) Characterize exposure; (b) Determine/evaluate source of exposure by medical history, risk behavior, & testing for hepatitis B/C, HIV;
   (c) Evaluate and test exposed individual for hepatitis B/C & HIV.

Hepatitis B Occupational Exposure Prophylaxis *(MMWR 62(RR-10):1-19, 2013)*

Exposed Person Vaccine Status	Exposure Source		
	HBs Ag+	HBs Ag–	Status Unknown or Unavailable for Testing[f]
Unvaccinated	Give HBIG 0.06 mL per kg IM & initiate HB vaccine	Initiate HB vaccine	Initiate HB vaccine
Vaccinated (antibody status unknown)	Do anti-HBs on exposed person: If titer ≥10 milli-international units per mL, no rx If titer <10 milli-international units per mL, give HBIG + 1 dose HB vaccine**	No rx necessary	Do anti-HBs on exposed person: If titer ≥10 milli-international units per mL, no rx § If titer <10 milli-international units per mL, give 1 dose of HB vaccine**

§ Persons previously infected with HBV are immune to reinfection and do not require postexposure prophylaxis.

For known vaccine series responder (titer ≥10 milli-international units per mL), monitoring of levels or booster doses not currently recommended. Known non-responder (<10 milli-international units per mL) to 1º series HB vaccine & exposed to either HBsAg+ source or suspected high-risk source—rx with HBIG & re-initiate vaccine series or give 2 doses HBIG 1 month apart. For non-responders after a 2nd vaccine series, 2 doses HBIG 1 month apart is preferred approach to new exposure.

If known high risk source, treat as if source were HBsAG positive

** Follow-up to assess vaccine response or address completion of vaccine series.

Hepatitis B Non-Occupational Exposure & Reactivation of Latent Hepatitis B

Non-Occupational Exposure *(MMWR 59(RR-10):1, 2010)*

- Exposure to blood or sexual secretion of HBsAg-positive person
  - Percutaneous (bite, needlestick)
  - Sexual assault
- Initiate immunoprophylaxis within 24 hrs or sexual exposure & no more than 7 days after parenteral exposure
- Use Guidelines for occupational exposure for use of HBIG and HBV vaccine

Reactivation of Latent HBV *(AnIM 164:30 & 64, 2016)*

- Patients requiring administration of anti-CD 20 monoclonal antibodies as part of treatment selected malignancies, rheumatoid arthritis and vasculitis are at risk for reactivation of latent HBV
- Use of two FDA-approved anti-CD 20 drugs: ofatumumab (Azerra) & rituximab (Rituxan) put patients at risk
- Prior to starting anti-CD 20 drug, test for latent HBV with test for HBsAg and Anti IgG HB core antibody and/or Anti IgG HBc AB = occult Hepatitis B
- If pt has latent (occult) HBV & anti-CD 20 treatment is necessary, treatment should include an effective anti-HBV drug

Hepatitis C Exposure

Determine antibody to hepatitis C for both exposed person &, if possible, exposure source. If source + or unknown and exposed person negative, follow-up for HCV RNA (detectable in blood in 1-3 weeks) and HCV antibody (90% who seroconvert will do so by 3 months). Immune serum globulin, immune serum globulin not effective. No recommended postexposure prophylaxis; as therapy may ↓ risk of progression to chronic hepatitis. Persons who remain viremic 8-12 weeks after exposure should be treated with a course of pegylated interferon *(Gastro 130:632, 2006 and HoLV. Apr 43-923, 2006)*. See Table 14F. Case-control study suggested risk factors for occupational HCV transmission include percutaneous exposure to needle that had been in artery or vein, deep injury, male sex of HCW, & was more likely when source VL >6 log10 copies/mL.

TABLE 15D (2)

HIV: Occupational exposure management [*Adapted from CDC recommendations, Infect Control Hosp Epi 34: 875, 2C14*]

- The decision to initiate postexposure prophylaxis (PEP) for HIV is a clinical judgment that should be made in concert with the exposed healthcare worker (HCW). It is based on:
  1. Likelihood of the source patient having HIV infection: Patient with history of high-risk activity—injection drug use, sexual activity with known HIV+ person, unprotected sex with multiple partners (either hetero- or homosexual), receipt of blood products 1978–1985, ↑ with clinical symptoms suggestive of advanced HIV (unexplained wasting, night sweats, thrush, seborrheic dermatitis, etc.).
  2. Type of exposure (approx. 1 in 300–400 needlesticks from infected source will transmit HIV).
  3. Limited data regarding efficacy of PEP (*Cochrane Database Syst Rev, Jan 24; (1):CD002835, 2007*).
  4. Significant adverse effects of PEP drugs & potential for drug interactions.

     Substances considered potentially infectious include: blood, tissues, semen, vaginal secretions, CSF, synovial, pleural, peritoneal, pericardial and amniotic fluids; and other visibly bloody fluids.

     Fluids normally considered low risk for transmission, unless visibly bloody, include: urine, vomitus, stool, sweat, saliva, nasal secretions, tears and sputum.

- If source person is **known positive** for HIV or **likely to be infected** and status of exposure warrants PEP, antiretroviral drugs should be started **immediately**. If source person is HIV antibody negative, drugs can be stopped or not be started at all. In this situation, the HCW should be re-tested at **3–4 weeks, 3 & 6 months** whether PEP is used or not (the vast majority of seroconversions will occur by 3 months; delayed seroconversion after 6 months are exceedingly rare). Tests for HIV RaA should not be used for dx of HIV infection in HCW because of false-positives (esp. at low titers) & these tests are only approved for established HIV infection [a possible exception is if pt develops signs of acute HIV (mononucleosis-like) syndrome within the 1st 4–6 wks of exposure when antibody tests might still be negative.]

- PEP for HIV is usually given for **4 wks** and monitoring of adverse effects recommended: baseline complete blood count, renal and hepatic panel to be repeated at **2 weeks**, 50–75% of HCW on PEP demonstrates mild side-effects (nausea, diarrhea, myalgias, headache, etc.) but in up to ½ severe enough to discontinue PEP. Consultation with infectious diseases/ HIV specialist is valuable when questions regarding PEP arise. **Seek expert help in special situations, such as pregnancy, renal impairment, treatment-experienced source.**

3 Steps to HIV Postexposure Prophylaxis (PEP) After Occupational Exposure: [*Latest CDC recommendations available at www.aidsinfo.nih.gov*]

Step 1: Determine the exposure code (EC)

Is source material blood, bloody fluid, semen/vaginal fluid or other normally sterile fluid or tissue (see above)?

Yes → What type of exposure occurred?

No → No PEP

What type of exposure occurred?

Mucous membrane or skin integrity compromised (e.g. dermatitis, open wound)
- Volume
  - Small: Few drops → EC1
  - Large: Major splash &/or long duration → EC2

Intact skin → No PEP*

Percutaneous exposure
- Severity
  - Less severe: Solid needle, scratch → EC2
  - More severe: Large-bore hollow needle, deep puncture, visible blood, needle used in blood vessel of source → EC3

No → No PEP

Exceptions can be considered when there has been prolonged, high-volume contact.

TABLE 15D (3)

3 Steps to HIV Postexposure Prophylaxis (PEP) After Occupational Exposure (continued)

Step 2: Determine the HIV Status Code (HIV SC)

What is the HIV status of the exposure source?

HIV negative	HIV positive		Status unknown	Source unknown
→	→	→	→	→
No PEP	Low titer exposure: asymptomatic & high CD4 count, low VL (<1500 copies per mL)	High titer exposure: advanced AIDS, primary HIV, high viral load or low CD4 count	HIV SC unknown	HIV SC unknown
	↓	↓		
	HIV SC 1	HIV SC 2		

Regimens: (Treat for 4 weeks; monitor for drug side-effects every 2 weeks)
Basic regimen: Descovy (TAF+ FTC) or **Truvada** (TDF+ FTC)+ either **Raltegravir** 1200 mg (2 600 mg tabs) po OR **Dolutegravir** 50 mg po, all meds taken once daily.
For pregnant women, or women of unknown pregnancy status, use TDF+ FTC + raltegravir at doses indicated above.
[**Do not use nevirapine:** serious adverse reactions including hepatic necrosis reported in healthcare workers.] **Note:** Descovy preferred over Truvada because lower potential for renal injury, ability to be used in individuals with some degree of renal impairment (CrCl ≥30mL/min), and lower potential osteomalacia for TAF compared to TDF.
Other regimens can be designed. If possible, use antiretroviral drugs for which resistance is unlikely based on susceptibility data or treatment history of source pt (if known). Seek expert consultation if ART-experienced source or in pregnancy or potential for pregnancy.

Step 3: Determine Postexposure Prophylaxis (PEP) Recommendation

EC	HIV SC	PEP
1	1	Consider basic regimen*
2	1	Recommend basic regimen*
1	2	Recommend basic regimen
2	2	Recommend basic regimen
3	1 or 2	Recommend basic regimen
1, 2, 3	Unknown	If exposure setting suggests risks of HIV exposure, consider basic regimen

* Based on estimates of ↓ risk of infection after mucous membrane exposure in occupational setting compared with needlestick.

Around the clock, urgent expert consultation available from: National Clinicians' Postexposure Prophylaxis Hotline (PEPline) at 1-888-448-4911 (1-888-HIV-4911) and on-line at http://www.ucsf.edu/hivcntr

POSTEXPOSURE PROPHYLAXIS FOR NON-OCCUPATIONAL EXPOSURES TO HIV-1
(Adapted from CDC recommendations, MMWR 54 (RR2), 2005, available at www.cdc.gov/mmwr/indrr_2005.html)

Because the risk of transmission of HIV via sexual contact or sharing needles may reach or exceed that of occupational needlestick exposure, it is reasonable to consider PEP in persons who have had a non-occupational exposure to blood or other potentially infected fluids (e.g. genital/rectal secretions, breast milk) from an HIV+ source. Risk of HIV acquisition per exposure varies with the act (for needle sharing and receptive anal intercourse, ≥0.5%; approximately 10-fold lower with insertive vaginal and anal intercourse, 0.05–0.07%). Overt or occult traumatic lesions may ↑ risk in survivors of sexual assault.

For pts at risk of HIV acquisition through non-occupational exposure to HIV+ source material having occurred ≤72 hours before evaluation, DHHS recommendation is to treat for 28 days with an antiretroviral **basic regimen.** Failures of prophylaxis have been reported, and may be associated with longer interval from exposure to start of PEP; this supports prompt initiation of PEP if it is to be used.

Areas of uncertainty: (1) while PEP not recommended for exposures >72 hours before evaluation, it may possibly be effective in some cases, (2) when HIV status of source patient is unknown, decision to treat and regimen selection must be individualized based on assessment of specific circumstances (see Table 15A) and treat as indicated.

Evaluate for exposures to Hep B, Hep C (see Occupational PEP above), and bacterial sexually-transmitted diseases as indicated.

TABLE 15E – PREVENTION OF SELECTED OPPORTUNISTIC INFECTIONS IN HUMAN HEMATOPOIETIC CELL TRANSPLANTATION (HCT)
OR SOLID ORGAN TRANSPLANTATION (SOT) IN ADULTS WITH NORMAL RENAL FUNCTION.

General comments: Medical centers performing transplants will have detailed protocols for the prevention of opportunistic infections which are appropriate to the infections encountered, patients represented and resources available at those sites. Regimens continue to evolve and protocols adopted by an institution may differ from those at other centers. Care of transplant patients should be guided by physicians with expertise in this area.

References:
For HCT: Expert guidelines endorsed by the IDSA, updating earlier guidelines (*MMWR 49 (RR-10):1, 2000*) In: *Biol Blood Marrow Transpl 15:1143, 2009.* These guidelines provide recommendations for prevention of additional infections not discussed in this table and provide more detailed information on the infections included here.
For SOT: Recommendations of an expert panel of The Transplantation Society for management of CMV is solid organ transplant recipients in: *Transplantation 89:779, 2010.* Timeline of infections following SOT in: *Amer J Transpl 9 (Suppl 4):S3, 2009.*

OPPORTUNISTIC INFECTION	TYPE OF TRANSPLANT	PROPHYLACTIC REGIMENS
CMV (Recipient + or Donor +/Recipient –) Ganciclovir resistance: risk, detection, management (*CID 56:1018, 2013*)	SOT	**Prophylaxis: Valganciclovir** 900 mg po q24h Alternatives include **Ganciclovir** 1000 mg po 3 x/day, **Valacyclovir** 2 gm po 4 x/day (*kidney only, see comment*), CMV IVIG or IVIG. **Also consider preemptive therapy** (monitor weekly for CMV viremia by PCR (or antigenemia) for 3-6 months post transplant. If viremia detected, start **Valganciclovir** 900 mg po bid or **Ganciclovir** 5 mg/kg IV q12h until clearance of viremia. CMV IVIG is as adjunct to prophylaxis in high-risk lung, heart/lung, heart, or pancreas organ transplant recipients. Dosing: 150 mg/kg within 72 hrs of transplant and at 2, 4, 6 and 8 weeks; then 100 mg/kg at weeks 12 and 16. *CID 58:785, 2014.*
	HCT	**Preemptive Strategy:** Monitor weekly for CMV viremia by PCR (or antigenemia) for 3-6 months post transplant with consideration for more prolonged monitoring in patients at risk for late-onset CMV disease (chronic GVHD, requiring systemic treatment, patients receiving high-dose steroids, T-cell depleted or cord blood transplant recipients, and CD4 <100 cells/mL). Start treatment with identification of CMV viremia or antigenemia as above. Consider prophylaxis (beginning post-engraftment with **Valganciclovir** 900 mg po q24h or **Ganciclovir** 5 mg/kg IV q24h or **Letermovir** 480 mg po/IV once daily. *National Comprehensive Cancer Network Guidelines on Prevention and Treatment of Cancer-Related Infections, Version 1.2013, Blood 113:5711, 2009, and Biol Blood Marrow Transpl 15:1143, 2009.*
Hepatitis B	SOT	For anti-viral agents with activity against HBV, see Table 14B, page 194. For discussion of prevention of HBV re-infection after transplantation and prevention of donor-derived infection see *Am. J Transplant 9: S116, 2013.*
	HCT	Patients who are anti-HBC positive and anti-HBs positive, but without evidence of active viral replication, can be monitored for ↑LFTs and presence of ++HBV-DNA, and given pre-emptive therapy at that time. Alternatively, prophylactic anti-viral therapy can be given, commencing before transplant. (*See guidelines for other specific situations: Biol Blood Marrow Transpl 15:1143, 2009.*) These guidelines recommend Lamivudine 100 mg po q24h as an anti-viral.
Herpes simplex	SOT	**Acyclovir** 400 mg po bid, starting early post-transplant (*Clin Microbiol Rev 10:86, 1992*).
	HCT	**Acyclovir** 250 mg per meter-squared iv q12h **or Acyclovir** 400 to 800 mg po bid, from conditioning to engraftment or resolution of mucositis. For those requiring prolonged suppression of HSV, the higher dose (Acyclovir 800 mg po bid) is recommended to minimize the risk of emerging resistance.

* See page 2 for abbreviations

TABLE 15E (2)

OPPORTUNISTIC INFECTION	TYPE OF TRANSPLANT	PROPHYLACTIC REGIMENS
Aspergillus spp.	SOT	Lung and heart/lung transplant: Inhaled **Amphotericin B** and/or a mold active oral azole are commonly used, but optimal regimen not defined. Aerosolized **Amphotericin B** 6 mg q8h (or 25 mg/day) OR aerosolized **LAB** 25 mg/day OR **Voriconazole** 200 mg po bid OR **Itraconazole** 200 mg po bid. 59% centers employ universal prophylaxis for 6 months in lung transplant recipients with 97% targeting Aspergillus. Most use Voriconazole alone or in combination with inhaled Amphotericin B (*Am J Transplant 11:361, 2011*). Consider restarting prophylaxis during periods of intensified immune suppression. Liver transplant: Consider only in high-risk, re-transplant and/or those requiring renal-replacement therapy. Recommendations on aspergillus prophylaxis in SOT can be found at (*Am J Transplant 13:228, 2013*).
	HCT/Heme malignancy	Indications for prophylaxis against aspergillus include AML and MDS with neutropenia and HCT with GVHD. Posaconazole 200 mg po tid approved for this indication (*NEJM 356:335, 2007 and NEJM 356:348,2007*). Posaconazole ER tablets, also approved for prophylaxis (300 mg po BID x 1 day, then 300 daily). Retrospective analysis suggests that Voriconazole would have efficacy in steroid-treated patients with GVHD (*Bone Marrow Transpl 45:662, 2010*), but is not approved for this indication. Amphotericin B and echinocandins are alternatives as well.
Candida spp.	SOT	Consider in select, high risk patients (liver, small bowel, pancreas): Consider in select, high-risk patients (re-transplants, dialysis). **Fluconazole** 400 mg daily for 4 weeks post-transplant (*Amer J Transpl 13:200, 2013*).
	HCT	Recipient with positive serology, no active infection at time of transplant: **Fluconazole** 400 mg once daily x 1 year; then 200 mg once daily indefinitely. Recipient of organ from donor with positive serology, no active infection: ◦ Lung transplant recipients: **Fluconazole** 400 mg once daily, indefinitely. ◦ Other organ recipients: **Fluconazole** 400 mg once daily x 1 year, then 200 mg once daily indefinitely. Recipient residing in an endemic area who underwent an organ transplant (primary prevention): **Fluconazole** 200 mg once daily x 6-12 months post transplantation (*Clin Infect Dis 63:e112, 2016*).
Coccidioides immitis	Any	**Fluconazole** 200–400 mg po q24h (*Transpl Inf Dis 5:3, 2003; Am J Transpl 6:340, 2006*). See *CDID 21:45, 2008* for approach at one center in endemic area; e.g., for positive serology without evidence of active infection, Fluconazole 400 mg q24h for first year post-transplant, then 200 mg q24h thereafter.
Pneumocystis jiroveci	SOT	**TMP-SMX:** 1 single-strength tab po once daily for 3 to 7 days per week. Duration: kidney: 6 mos to 1 year (*Amer J Transpl 9 (Suppl 3): S59, 2009)*; heart, lung, liver: ≥ 1 year to life-long (*Amer J Transpl 4 (Suppl 10): 135, 2004*).
	HCT	**TMP-SMX:** 1 single-strength tab po once daily or once a day for 3 days per week, from engraftment to ≥ 6 mos post transplant.
Toxoplasma gondii	SOT	**TMP-SMX** (1 SS tab po q24h or 1 DS tab po once daily) x 3-7 days/wk for 6 mos post-transplant. (See *Clin Micro Infect 14:1089, 2008*).
	HCT	**TMP-SMX:** 1 single-strength tab po q24h or 1 double-strength tab po once daily or once a day for 3 days per week, from engraftment to ≥ 6 mos post transplant for seropositive allogeneic transplant recipients.
Trypanosoma cruzi	Heart	May be transmitted from organs or transfusions (*CID 48:1534, 2009*). Inspect peripheral blood of suspected cases for parasites (*MMWR 55:798, 2006*). Risk of reactivation during immunosuppression is variable (*JAMA 298:2171, 2007; JAMA 299:1134, 2008; J Cardiac Fail 15:249, 2009*). If known Chagas disease in donor or recipient, contact CDC for treatment options (*phone 770-488-7775 or in emergency 770-488-7100*), *Am J Transplant 11:672, 2011.*

See page 2 for abbreviations

TABLE 16 – PEDIATRIC DOSING (AGE >28 DAYS)

Editorial Note
There is limited data on when to switch adolescents to adult dosing. In general, pediatric weight based dosing is appropriate through mid puberty (Tanner 3) if no maximum dose is specified. Some change to adult dosing at 40 kg. If in doubt, when treating serious infections in peri-pubertal adolescents with drugs that have large margins of safety (e.g. Beta lactams and carbapenems) it may be safer to err on the side of higher doses.

DRUG	DOSE (AGE >28 DAYS) (Daily maximum dose shown, when applicable)
ANTIBACTERIALS	
Aminoglycosides	
Amikacin	15-20 mg/kg q24h; 5-7.5 mg/kg q8h
Gentamicin	5-7 mg/kg q24h; 2.5 mg/kg q8h
Tobramycin	5-7 mg/kg q24h; 2.5 mg/kg q8h.
Beta-Lactams	
Carbapenems	
Ertapenem	30 mg/kg/day (divided q12h). Max per day: 1 gm
Imipenem	60-100 mg/kg/day (divided q6-8h). Max per day: 2-4 gm
Meropenem	60 mg/kg/day (divided q8h); Meningitis: 120 mg/kg/day (divided q8h). Max per day: 2-4 gm
Cephalosporins (po)	
Cefaclor	20-40 mg/kg/day (divided q8-12h). Max per day: 1 gm
Cefadroxil	30 mg/kg/day (divided q12h). Max per day: 2 gm
Cefdinir	14 mg/kg/day (divided q12-24h)
Cefixime	8 mg/kg/day (divided q12-24h)
Cefpodoxime	10 mg/kg/day (divided q12h). Max per day: 400 mg
Cefprozil	15-30 mg/kg/day (divided q12h) -- use 30 for AOM
Ceftibuten	9 mg/kg/day (divided q12-24h). Max per day: 1 gm
Cefuroxime axetil	20-30 mg/kg/day (divided q12h) -- use 30 for AOM. Max per day: 1 gm
Cephalexin	25-100 mg/kg/day (divided q6h). Max per day: 4 gm
Loracarbef	15-30 mg/kg/day (divided q12h). Max per day: 800 mg
Cephalosporins (IV)	
Cefazolin	50-150 mg/kg/day (divided q6-8h). Max per day: 6 gm
Cefepime (non-Pseudomonal)	100 mg/kg/day (divided q8h)
Cefepime (Pseudomonal)	150 mg/kg/day (divided q8h)
Cefotaxime	150-200 mg/kg/day (divided q6-8h). Meningitis: 300 mg/kg/day (divided q6h)
Cefotetan	60-100 mg/kg/day (divided q12h). Max per day: 6 gm
Cefoxitin	80-160 mg/kg/day (divided q6-8h)
Ceftaroline	2 mon to <2 yrs: 8 mg/kg q8h ≥2 yrs to <18 yrs, ≤33 kg: 12 mg/kg q8h ≥2 yrs to <18 yrs, >33 kg: 400 mg q8h or 600 mg q12h
Ceftazidime	150-200 mg/kg/day (divided q8h) CF: 300 mg/kg/day (divided q8h)
Ceftizoxime	150-200 mg/kg/day (divided q6-8h)
Ceftriaxone	50-100 mg/kg q24h; Meningitis: 50 mg/kg q12h
Cefuroxime	150 mg/kg/day (divided q8h); Meningitis: 80 mg/kg q8h
Penicillins	
Amoxicillin	25-50 mg/kg/day (divided q8h)
Amoxicillin (AOM, pneumonia)	80-100 mg/kg/day (divided q8-12h; q12h for AOM)
Amoxicillin-clavulanate 7:1 formulation	45 mg/kg/day (divided q12h)
Amoxicillin-clavulanate 14:1 (AOM)	90 mg/kg/day (divided q12h) for wt <40 kg
Ampicillin (IV)	200 mg/kg/day (divided q6h); Meningitis: 300-400 mg/kg/day (divided q6h)
Ampicillin-sulbactam	100-300 mg/kg/day (divided q6h)
Cloxacillin (po)	If <20 kg: 25-50 mg/kg/day (divided q6h); Otherwise dose as adult
Dicloxacillin (mild - moderate)	12.5-25 mg/kg/day (divided q6h)
Dicloxacillin (osteo articular infection)	100 mg/kg/day (divided q 6h)
Flucloxacillin	Age 2-10: 50% of adult dose; Age<2: 25% of adult dose
Nafcillin	150-200 mg/kg/day (divided q6h)
Oxacillin	150-200 mg/kg/day (divided q6h)
Penicillin G	150,000-300,000 units/kg/day (divided q4-6h). Max per day: 12-20 million units
Penicillin VK	25-75 mg/kg/day (divided q6-8h)
Piperacillin-tazobactam	300 mg/kg/day (divided q6h)
Temocillin	25 mg/kg q12h
Fluoroquinolones * Approved only for CF, anthrax, and complicated UTI	
Ciprofloxacin (po)	20-40 mg/kg/day (divided q12h) *. Max per day: 1.5 gm
Ciprofloxacin (IV)	20-30 mg/kg/day (divided q12h) *. Max per day: 1.2 gm
Levofloxacin (IV/po)	16-20 mg/kg/day (divided q12h) *. Max per day: 750 mg

TABLE 16 (2)

DRUG	DOSE (AGE >28 DAYS) (Daily maximum dose shown, when applicable)
ANTIBACTERIALS *(continued)*	
Lincosamides	
Clindamycin (po)	30-40 mg/kg/day (divided q6-8h)
Clindamycin (IV)	20-40 mg/kg/day (divided q6-8h)
Lincomycin	10-20 mg/kg/day (divided q8-12h)
Lipopeptides	
Daptomycin	6-10 mg/kg/day (once daily)
Macrolides	
Azithromycin (po)	5-12 mg/kg/day (once daily)
Azithromycin (IV)	10 mg/kg/day (once daily)
Clarithromycin	15 mg/kg/day (divided q12h). Max per day: 1 gm
Erythromycin (po, IV)	40-50 mg/kg/day (divided q6h)
Monobactams	
Aztreonam	90-120 mg/kg/day (divided q8h). Max per day: 8 gm
Tetracyclines	
Doxycycline (po/IV, age >8 yrs)	2-4 mg/kg/day (divided q12h). Max per day: 200 mg
Fosfomycin (po)	2 gm once
Fusidic acid (po)	Age 1-5: 250 mg q8h Age 6-12: 250-500 mg q8h
Minocycline (po, age >8)	4 mg/kg/day (divided q12h)
Tetracycline	Age >8: 25-50 mg/kg/day (divided q6h). Max per day: 2 gm
Other	
Chloramphenicol (IV)	50-100 mg/kg/day (divided q6h). Max per day: 2-4 gm
Colistin	2.5-5 mg/kg/day (divided q6-12h) CF: 3-8 mg/kg/day (divided q8h)
Linezolid (up to age 12 yrs)	30 mg/kg/day IV/po (divided q8h)
Methenamine hippurate (age 6-12)	500-1000 mg q12h
Methenamine mandelate	Age >2 to 6: 50-75 mg/kg/day (divided q6-8h) Age 6-12: 500 mg q6h
Metronidazole (po)	30-40 mg/kg/day (divided q6h)
Metronidazole (IV)	22.5-40 mg/kg/day (divided q6h)
Nitrofurantoin (po Cystitis)	5-7 mg/kg/day (divided q 6h)
Nitrofurantoin (po UTI prophylaxis)	1-2 mg/kg/day (once daily)
Polymyxin B (age 2 and older)	2.5 mg/kg (load), then 1.5 mg/kg q12h
Rifampin (meningococcal prophylaxis)	10 mg/kg q12h x2 days
Tinidazole (age >3 for Giardia, amebiasis)	50 mg/kg q24h x1-5 days. Max per day: 2 gm
Sulfadiazine	120-150 mg/kg/day (divided q4-6h). Max per day: 6 gm
TMP-SMX (UTI and other)	8-12 mg TMP/kg/day (divided q12h)
TMP-SMX (PCP)	15-20 mg TMP/kg/day (divided q12h)
Trimethoprim	4 mg/kg/day (divided q12h)
Vancomycin (IV)	40-60 mg/kg/day (divided q6-8h) (Use serum concentration to target trough 10-15 mcg/mL; 60 mg/kg/day most likely to achieve target)
Vancomycin (po for C. difficile)	40 mg/kg/day (divided q6h)
ANTIMYCOBACTERIALS	
Capreomycin	15-30 mg/kg/day (divided q12-24h). Max per day: 1 gm
Cycloserine	10-15 mg/kg/day (divided q12h). Max per day: 1 gm
Ethambutol	15-25 mg/kg/day (once daily). Max per day: 2.5 gm
Ethionamide	15-20 mg/kg/day (divided q12h). Max per day: 1 gm
Isoniazid (daily dosing)	10-15 mg/kg/day (once daily). Max per day: 300 mg
Isoniazid (2 x/week)	20-30 mg/kg twice weekly. Max per day: 900 mg
Kanamycin	15 -30 mg/kg/day (divided q12-24h). Max per day: 1 gm
Para-aminosalicylic acid	200-300 mg/kg/day (divided q6-12h)
Pyrazinamide (daily)	15-30 mg/kg/day (once daily). Max per day: 2 gm
Pyrazinamide (2 x/week)	50 mg/kg/day (2 days/week). Max per day: 2 gm
Rifabutin (MAC prophylaxis)	5 mg/kg/day (once daily). Max per day: 300 mg
Rifabutin (active TB)	10-20 mg/kg/day (once daily). Max per day: 300 mg
Rifampin	10-20 mg/kg/day (divided q12-24h). Max per day: 600 mg
Streptomycin (age 2 and older)	20-40 mg/kg/day (once daily). Max per day: 1 gm
ANTIFUNGALS	
Amphotericin B deoxycholate	0.5-1 mg/kg/day (once daily)
Amphotericin B lipid complex	5 mg/kg/day (once daily)
Anidulafungin	1.5-3 mg/kg loading dose then .75-1.5 mg/kg/day (once daily)
Caspofungin	70 mg/m2 loading dose then 50 mg/m2 (once daily)

TABLE 16 (3)

DRUG	DOSE (AGE >28 DAYS) (Daily maximum dose shown, when applicable)
ANTIFUNGALS *(continued)*	
Fluconazole	6 mg/kg/day for oral/esophageal Candida; 12 mg/kg/day for invasive disease
Isavuconazonium sulfate (prodrug of Isavuconazole)	Not known; adult dose 372 mg q8h x 3 doses loading dose then 744 mg/day (divided q12h)
Itraconazole	5-10 mg/kg/day (divided q12h)
Ketoconazole	3.3-6.6 mg/kg/day (once daily)
Micafungin	Age >4 mon: 2 mg/kg q24h (max 100 mg) for candidiasis; for EC use 3 mg/kg q24h if <30 kg, 2.5 mg/kg q24h (max 150 mg) if >30 kg
Posaconazole	Not known; adult dose 300 mg bid loading dose then 300 mg/day (extended release)
Terbinafine	<20 kg 67.5 mg/day; 20-40 kg 125 mg/day; >40 kg 250 mg/day (adult dose)
Voriconazole	12-20 mg/kg/day (divided q12h) (Variable bioavailability and metabolism. Adjust to trough level 1-6 mcg/mL)
ANTIRETROVIRALS	
Abacavir (ABC)	Oral soln, age ≥3 mon: 8 mg/kg q12h or 16 mg/kg q24h (start soln q12h). Tabs, wt-based: 14 to <20 kg: 150 mg q12h; ≥20 to <25 kg: 150 mg qAM, 300 mg qPM; ≥25 kg: 300 mg q12h (OK to start tabs q24h). Adolescent: 300 mg q12h or 600 mg q24h
Atazanavir (ATV)	Neonates: not recommended. Age ≥3 mon, oral powder: 5 to <15 kg: ATV 200 mg + RTV 80 mg q24h; 15 to <25 kg: ATV 250 mg + RTV 80 mg q24h; ≥25 kg: ATV 300 mg + RTV 100 mg q24h. Age >6 yrs, capsules: 15 to <20 kg: ATV 150 mg + RTV 100 mg q24h; 20 to <32 kg: ATV 200 mg + RTV 100 mg q24h; 32 to <39 kg: ATV 250 mg + RTV 100 mg q24h; ≥39 kg: ATV 300 mg + RTV 100 mg q24h. Adolescents: 400 mg q24h, or 300 mg + RTV 100 mg q24h
Darunavir (DRV)	Neonate: not approved. Age <3 or wt <10 kg: avoid use. Age ≥3 yr, tx naive or exp ± one or more DRV mut: 10 to <11 kg: 200 mg (+ RTV 32 mg) q12h; 11 to <12 kg: 220 mg (+ RTV 32 mg) q12h; 12 to <13 kg: 240 mg (+ RTV 40 mg) q12h; 13 to <14 kg: 260 mg (+ RTV 40 mg) q12h; 14 to <15 kg: 280 mg (+ RTV 48 mg) q12h; 15 to <30 kg: 375 mg (+ RTV 48 mg) q12h; 30 to <40 kg: 450 mg (+ RTV 100 mg) q12h; ≥40 kg: 600 mg (+ RTV 100 mg) q12h. Adolescent: ≥30 to <40 kg, tx exp, ≥1 DRV mut: 450 mg (+ RTV 100 mg) q12h; ≥40 kg, tx naive/exp, no DRV mut: 800 mg (+ RTV 100 mg) q24h; ≥40 kg, tx exp, ≥1 DRV mut: 600 mg (+ RTV 100 mg) q12h
Delavirdine (DLV)	Safety/efficacy in patients ≤16 years not established
Didanosine (ddI)	Age 2 wk to 3 mon: 50 mg/m2 q12h. Age ≥3 mon to 8 mon: 100 mg/m2 q12h. Age >8 mon: 120 mg/m2 q12h (240 mg/m2 q24h if age 3-21 yr and tx naive). EC caps (age 6-18 yr): 20 to <25 kg, 200 mg q24h; 25 to <60 kg, 250 mg q24h; ≥60 kg, 400 mg q24h
Dolutegravir (DTG)	Wt 30 to <40 kg: 35 mg q24h; Wt ≥40 kg: 50 mg q24h; ↑ to q12h if given w/EFV, FPV/r, TPV/r, CBZ, rifampin
Efavirenz (EFV)	Neonates: not approved for use. Age ≥3 yr: 10 to <15 kg, 200 mg q24h; 15 to <20 kg, 250 mg q24h; 20 to <25 kg, 300 mg q24h; 25 to <32.5 kg, 350 mg q24h; 32.5 to <40 kg, 400 mg q24h; ≥40 kg, 600 mg q24h. Age 3 mon to <3 yr: not recommended
Elvitegravir (EVG)	As Vitekta, not for use in children age <18 yrs
Emtricitabine (FTC)	Oral soln: 0 to ≤3 mon, 3 mg/kg q24h. 3 mon to 17 yr: 6 mg/kg (max 240 mg) q24h. ≥18 yr, 240 mg q24h. Caps, wt >33 kg: 200 mg q24h
Enfuvirtide (T-20)	Age <6 yrs: not approved for use. Age 6-16 yr: 2 mg/kg (max 90 mg) sc q12h. Age >16 yr: 90 mg sc q12h
Etravirine (ETR)	Age 6-18 yr: 16 to <20 kg, 100 mg q12h; 20 to <25 kg, 125 mg q12h; 25 to <30 kg, 150 mg q12h; ≥30 kg, 200 mg q12h
Fosamprenavir (FPV)	Neonate: use not recommended. Age 2-5 yrs (ARV naive): 30 mg/kg q12h (not recommended). Age 6 mon to 18 yrs (ARV naive or experienced): <11 kg: 45 mg/kg q12h (+ RTV 7 mg/kg q12h); 11 to <15 kg: 30 mg/kg q12h (+ RTV 3 mg/kg q12h); 15 to <20 kg: 23 mg/kg q12h (+ RTV 3 mg/kg q12h); ≥20 kg: 18 mg/kg q12h (+ RTV 3 mg/kg q12h). Adolescent, ARV naive: 700 mg q12h (+ RTV 100 mg q12h), or; 1400 mg q24h (+ RTV 100-200 mg q24h). Adolescent, ARV exp: 700 mg q12h (+ RTV 100 mg q12h)
Indinavir (IDV)	Neonate/infant: not approved for use. Children: not approved for use. Adolescent: 800 mg q12h (+ RTV 100-200 mg q12h)
Lamivudine (3TC)	Oral solution: Age <4 wks: 2 mg/kg q12h; Age ≥4 wks: 4 mg/kg (max 150 mg) q12h. Tabs: 14 to <20 kg: 75 mg q12h; ≥20 to <25 kg: 75 mg qam + 150 mg qpm; ≥25 kg: 150 mg q12h
Maraviroc (MVC)	Age ≥2 yrs, w/3A4 inhibitor: 10 to <20 kg: 50 mg q12h (tab or soln); 20 to <30 kg: 80 mg soln q12h or 75 mg tab q12h; 30 to <40 kg: 100 mg q12h (tab or soln); ≥40 kg: 150 mg q12h (tab or soln). Age ≥2 yrs, no interacting meds: <30 kg: not recommended; ≥30 kg: 300 mg q12h (tab or soln). Age ≥2 yrs, w/3A4 inducer: not recommended
Nelfinavir (NFV)	Neonate (NICHD/HPTN 040/PACTG 1043): Wt 1.5 to 2 kg: 100 mg q12h; Wt >2 to 3 kg: 150 mg q12h; Wt >3 kg: 200 mg q12h. Age 2-13 yrs: 45-55 mg/kg q12h (8th CROI 2001, #250). Adolescent: 1250 mg q12h

TABLE 16 (4)

DRUG	DOSE (AGE >28 DAYS) (Daily maximum dose shown, when applicable)
ANTIRETROVIRALS *(continued)*	
Nevirapine (NVP)	Neonate, 34-37 wk EGA: 4 mg/kg q12h (no lead-in); increase to 6 mg/kg q12h after one week; Neonate, ≥37 wk EGA to <1 mon: 6 mg/kg q12h (no lead-in); Neo prophylaxis: 2 mg/kg at birth, 48 hr after dose 1, 96 hr after dose 2; 1 mon to <8 yr: 7 mg/kg or 200 mg/m2 q12h; ≥8 yr: 4 mg/kg or 120-150 mg/m2 q12h; Adolescent dose: 200 mg q24h x14 days then 200 mg q12h.
Raltegravir (RAL)	Oral susp, age ≥4 weeks: 3 to <4 kg, 20 mg q12h; 4 to <6 kg, 30 mg q12h; 6 to <8 kg, 40 mg q12h; 8 to <11 kg, 60 mg q12h; 11 to <14 kg, 80 mg q12h; 14 to <20 kg, 100 mg q12h. Chew tab, 2 to <12 yr: 11 to <14 kg, 75 mg q12h; 14 to <20 kg, 100 mg q12h; 20 to <28 kg, 150 mg q12h; 28 to <40, 200 mg q12h; ≥40 kg, 300 mg q12h. Film-coated tab: ≥25 kg: 400 mg q12h; ≥40 kg, tx-naive or suppr on 400 mg q12h: 1200 mg q24h. Neonates (invest), ≥37 wks gestation, wt ≥2 kg; Birth to 7 days: 1.5 mg/kg q24h; 8 days to 28 days: 3 mg/kg q12h; ≥4 weeks: 6 mg/kg q12h (see above)
Rilpivirine (RPV)	Adolescent ≥12 yrs, ≥35 kg: 25 mg q24h
Ritonavir (RTV)	Neonates: dose not established. Peds dose: 350-400 mg/m2 q12h (not recommended). Used as pharmacologic enhancer
Saquinavir (SQV)	Neonate/infant: not approved for use. Age <2 yrs: dose not determined. Age ≥2 yrs: Wt 5 to <15 kg: 50 mg/kg q12h (+RTV 3 mg/kg q12h); Wt 15 to <40 kg: 50 mg/kg q12h (+RTV 2.5 mg/kg q12h); Wt ≥40 kg: 50 mg/kg q12h (+RTV 100 mg q12h). Adolescent (age ≥16 yrs): 1 gm q12h (+RTV 100 mg q12h).
Stavudine (d4T)	Age 0-13 days: 0.5 mg/kg q12h. Age ≥14 days, <30 kg: 1 mg/kg q12h; ≥30 kg: 30 mg q12h
Tenofovir alafenamide (TAF)	≥12 yrs, wt ≥35 kg: 10 mg q24h (part of Genvoya); 25 mg q24h (part of Descovy, Odefsey). Vemlidy not approved for patients <18 yrs of age
Tenofovir (TDF)	Age 2 to <12 yr: 8 mg/kg powder (max 300 mg) q24h [1 scoop=40 mg]. Tablets, weight-based: 17 to <22 kg: 150 mg q24h; 22 to <28 kg: 200 mg q24h; 28 to <35 kg: 250 mg q24h; ≥35 kg: 300 mg q24h
Tipranavir (TPV)	Age <2 yrs: use not approved. Age ≥2 to 18 yrs: by BSA: 375 mg/m2 q12h (+RTV 150 mg/m2 q12h); by wt: 14 mg/kg q12h (+RTV 6 mg/kg q12h) (not recommended for tx naive pts). Adolescent: 500 mg q12h (+RTV 200 mg q12h) (not recommended for tx naive pts)
Zidovudine (ZDV)	Neonate, EGA <30 wks: age 0-4 weeks: 2 mg/kg po q12h or 1.5 mg/kg IV q12h; (increase to 3 mg/kg po q12h at age 4 weeks); Neonate, EGA ≥30 to <35 wks: age 0-2 weeks: 2 mg/kg po q12h or 1.5 mg/kg IV q12h; (increase to 3 mg/kg po q12h at age 2 weeks); EGA ≥35 wks, age 0-4 wks: 4 mg/kg q12h or 1.5 mg/kg IV q6h. Infant/child (EGA ≥35 wks, age ≥4 wks): 4 to <9 kg: 12 mg/kg po q12h; 9 to <30 kg: 9 mg/kg po q12h; ≥30 kg: 300 mg q12h; Dosing by BSA: 180-240 mg/m2 po q12h. Adolescent: 300 mg q12h
Antiretroviral combination products	
Atripla (EFV/FTC/TDF)	Age ≥12 yr, wt ≥40 kg: one tab q24h
Combivir (3TC/AZT)	Age ≥12 yr, wt ≥30 kg: one tab q12h
Complera (RPV/FTC/TDF)	Age ≥12 yr, wt ≥35 kg: one tab q24h
Descovy (FTC/TAF)	Age ≥12 yr, wt ≥35 kg: one tab q24h
Epzicom (ABC/3TC)	Wt ≥25 kg: one tab q24h
Evotaz (ATV/cobi)	Age <18: not recommended
Genvoya (EVG/cobi/FTC/TAF)	Age ≥12 yr, wt ≥35 kg: one tab q24h
Kaletra (LPV/RTV)	Age <14 days: avoid use. Age 14 days to 12 mon: 300 mg/75 mg per m2 q12h. Age >12 mon to 18 yrs: 300 mg/75 mg per m2 q12h (tx-experienced); 230 mg/57.5 mg per m2 q12h (tx-naive)
Odefsey (RPV/FTC/TAF)	Age ≥12 yr, wt ≥35 kg: one tab q24h
Prezcobix (DRV/cobi)	Age <18: not recommended
Stribild (EVG/cobi/FTC/TDF)	Age ≥12 yr, wt ≥35 kg: one tab q24h
Triumeq (DTG/ABC/3TC)	Wt ≥40 kg: one tab q24h
Trizivir (ABC/3TC/ZDV)	Wt ≥40 kg: one tab q12h
Truvada (FTC/TDF)	Wt 17 to <22 kg: 100 mg/150 mg q24h; Wt 22 to <28 kg: 133 mg/200 mg q24h; Wt 28 to <35 kg: 167 mg/250 mg q24h; Wt ≥35 kg: 200 mg/300 mg q24h
ANTIVIRALS	
Acyclovir (IV) neonatal herpes simplex	60 mg/kg/day (divided q8h)
Acyclovir (IV) HSV encephalitis >3 months	30-45 mg/kg/day (divided q8h)
Acyclovir (IV) varicella immunocompromised	<1 year: 30 mg/kg/day (divided q8h); >1 year: 30 mg/kg/day or 1500 mg/m2/day (divided q8h)
Acyclovir (IV) HSV immunocompromised	30 mg/kg/day (divided q8h)
Cidofovir	Induction 5 mg/kg once weekly. Suppressive therapy 3 mg/kg once weekly (all with hydration + probenecid)
Entecavir (treatment-naive)	Wt 10-11 kg, 0.15 mg q24h; >11 to 14 kg, 0.2 mg q24h; >14 to 17 kg, 0.25 mg q24h; >17 to 20 kg, 0.3 mg q24h; >20 to 23 kg, 0.35 mg q24h; >23 to 26 kg, 0.4 mg q24h; >26 to 30 kg, 0.45 mg q24h; >30 kg, 0.5 mg q24h

TABLE 16 (5)

DRUG	DOSE (AGE >28 DAYS) (Daily maximum dose shown, when applicable)
ANTIVIRALS *(continued)*	
Entecavir (lamivudine-experienced)	Wt 10-11 kg, 0.3 mg q24h; >11 to 14 kg, 0.4 mg q24h; >14 to 17 kg, 0.5 mg q24h; >17 to 20 kg, 0.6 mg q24h; >20 to 23 kg, 0.7 mg q24h; >23 to 26 kg, 0.8 mg q24h; >26 to 30 kg, 0.9 mg q24h; >30 kg, 1 mg q24h
Foscarnet	120-180 mg/kg/day (divided q8-12h)
Ganciclovir	Symptomatic congenital CMV 12 mg/kg/day (divided q12h). CMV tx or first 2 weeks after SOT: 10 mg/kg/day (divided q12h). Suppressive tx or prophylaxis 5 mg/kg/day (divided q24h)
Glecaprevir/pibrentasvir (Mavyret)	Age <18: safety and effectiveness not established
Ledipasvir/sofosbuvir (Harvoni)	Age ≥12 yrs or ≥35 kg: 1 tab q24h; Geno 1, tx-naive, no cirr or comp: 12 wks; Geno 1, tx-exp, no cirr=12 wks; Geno 1, tx-exp with comp=24 wks; Geno 4/5/6, tx-naive/exp, no cirr or comp=12 wks
Oseltamivir <1 year old	6 mg/kg/day (divided q12h)
Oseltamivir ≥1 year old	<15 kg: 30 mg bid; >15 to 23 kg: 45 mg bid; >23 to 40 kg: 60 mg bid; >40 kg: 75 mg bid (adult dose)
Peramivir	Not studied
Ribavirin (with sofosbuvir)	Wt <47 kg: 15 mg/kg/day; 47-49 kg: 600 mg/day; 50-65 kg: 800 mg/day; 66-80 kg: 1000 mg/day; >80 kg: 1200 mg/day (all doses divided bid)
Sofosbuvir	Age ≥12 yrs or ≥35 kg: 400 mg (1 tab) q24h; Geno 2, tx-naive/exp, no cirr or comp=12 wks (with ribavirin); Geno 3, tx-naive/exp, no cirr or comp=24 wks (with ribavirin).
Valacyclovir (Varicella or Herpes Zoster)	60 mg/kg/day (divided q8h)
Valganciclovir	Symptomatic congenital CMV: 32 mg/kg/day (divided q12h); Prevention of CMV after SOT: 7 mg x BSA x CrCl; (once daily; use Schwartz formula for CrCl).
Zanamivir (age >7 years)	10 mg (two 5-mg inhalations) q12h

TABLE 17A - DOSAGE OF ANTIMICROBIAL DRUGS IN ADULT PATIENTS WITH RENAL IMPAIRMENT

- For listing of drugs with NO need for adjustment for renal failure, see Table 17B.
- Adjustments for renal failure are based on an estimate of creatinine clearance (CrCl) which reflects the glomerular filtration rate.
- **Different methods for calculating estimated CrCl are suggested for non-obese and obese patients.**
  - Calculations for ideal body weight (IBW) in kg:
    - Men: 50 kg plus 2.3 kg/inch over 60 inches height.
    - Women: 45 kg plus 2.3 kg/inch over 60 inches height.
  - Obese is defined as 20% over ideal body weight or body mass index (BMI) >30

- Calculations of estimated CrCl (References, see (NEJM 354:2473, 2006 (non-obese), AJM 84:1053, 1988 (obese))
  - **Non-obese patient—**
    - Calculate ideal body weight (IBW) in kg (as above)–
    - Use the following formula to determine estimated CrCl

$$\frac{(140 \text{ minus age})(\text{IBW in kg})}{72 \times \text{serum creatinine}} = \begin{array}{l} \text{CrCl in mL/min for men.} \\ \text{Multiply answer by 0.85} \\ \text{for women (estimated)} \end{array}$$

  - **Obese patient—**
    - Weight ≥20% over IBW or BMI >30
    - Use the following formulas to determine estimated CrCl

$$\frac{(137 \text{ minus age}) \times [(0.285 \times \text{wt in kg}) + (12.1 \times \text{ht in meters}^2)]}{51 \times \text{serum creatinine}} = \text{CrCl (obese male)}$$

$$\frac{(146 \text{ minus age}) \times [(0.287 \times \text{wt in kg}) + (9.74 \times \text{ht in meters}^2)]}{60 \times \text{serum creatinine}} = \text{CrCl (obese female)}$$

- If estimated CrCl ≥90 mL/min, see Tables 10A and 10D for dosing.
- What weight should be used to calculate dosage on a mg/kg basis?
  - If less than 20% over IBW, use the patient's actual weight for all drugs.
  - **For obese patients (≥20% over IBW or BMI >30):**
    - **Aminoglycosides:** (IBW plus 0.4(actual weight minus IBW) = adjusted weight.
    - **Vancomycin:** actual body weight whether non-obese or obese.
    - **All other drugs:** insufficient data (Pharmacotherapy 27:1081, 2007).

- For slow or sustained extended daily dialysis **(SLEDD)** over 6-12 hours, adjust does as for CRRT. For details, see CID 49:433, 2009; CCM 39:560, 2011.
- General reference: Drug Prescribing in Renal Failure, 5th ed., Aronoff, et al. (eds) (Amer College Physicians, 2007 and drug package inserts).

TABLE 17A (2)

ANTIMICROBIAL	Half-life, hrs (renal function normal)	Half-life, hrs (ESRD)	Dose (renal function normal)	CrCl >50-90	CrCl 10-50	CrCl <10	Hemodialysis	CAPD	CRRT
ANTIBACTERIAL ANTIBIOTICS									
AMINOGLYCOSIDES, MDD									
Amikacin[1,2]	2-3	30-70	7.5 mg/kg IM/IV q12h (once-daily dosing below)	7.5 mg/kg q12h	7.5 mg/kg q24h	7.5 mg/kg q24h	7.5 mg/kg q48h (+ extra 3.75 mg/kg AD)	15-20 mg lost per L of dialysate/day	7.5 mg/kg q24h
Gentamicin, Netilimicin[NUS], Tobramycin[1,2]	2-3	30-70	1.7-2.0 mg/kg IM/IV q8h	1.7-2.0 mg/kg q8h	1.7-2.0 mg/kg q12-24h	1.7-2.0 mg/kg q48h	1.7-2.0 mg/kg q48h (+ extra 0.85-1.0 mg/kg AD)	3-4 mg lost per L of dialysate/day	1.7-2.0 mg/kg q24h
AMINOGLYCOSIDES, ODD (see Table 10D)			Dose for CrCl >80 (mg/kg q24h)	CrCl 60-80 (mg/kg q24h)	CrCl 40-60 (mg/kg q24h)	CrCl 30-40 (mg/kg q24h)	CrCl 20-30 (mg/kg q48h)	CrCl 10-20 (mg/kg q48h)	CrCl 0-10 (mg/kg q72h and AD)
Gentamicin, Tobramycin	2-3	30-70	5.1	4	3.5	2.5	4	3	2
Amikacin, Kanamycin, Streptomycin	2-3	30-70	15	½	7.5	4	7.5	4	3
Isepamicin[NUS]	2-3	30-70	8	8	8	8 mg/kg q48h	8	8 mg/kg q72h	8 mg/kg q96h
Netilmicin[NUS]	2-3	30-70	6.5	5	4	2	3	2.5	2
BETA-LACTAMS									
Carbapenems									
Doripenem	1	18	500 mg IV q8h	500 mg q8h	CrCl 30-50: 250 mg q8h; CrCl 10-30: 250 mg q12h	No data	No data	No data	500 mg q8h (JAC 69:2508, 2014)
Ertapenem	4	>4	1 gm IV q24h	1 gm q24h	CrCl <30: 0.5 gm q24h	0.5 gm q24h	0.5 gm q24h	0.5 gm q24h	0.5-1 gm q24h
Imipenem	1	4	500 mg IV q6h	250-500 mg q6-8h	250 mg q8-12h	125-250 mg q12h	125-250 mg q12h (give one of the dialysis day doses AD)	125-250 mg q12h	0.5-1 gm q12h (AAC 49:2421, 2005)
Meropenem	1	10	1 gm IV q8h	1 gm q8h	CrCl 25-50: 1 gm q12h; CrCl 10-25: 0.5 gm q12h	0.5 gm q24h	0.5 gm q24h (give dialysis day dose AD)	0.5 gm q24h	1 gm q12h
Meropenem-vaborbactam	Mer 1.2 Vab 1.7	Mer 10 Vab ND	2 gm/2 gm IV q8h	eGFR ≥50: 2 gm/2 gm q8h	eGFR 30-49: 1 gm/1 gm q8h; 15-29: 1 gm/1 gm q12h	eGFR <15: 0.5 gm/0.5 gm q12h	0.5 gm/0.5 gm q12h (AD)	No data	No data

TABLE 17A (3)

ANTIMICROBIAL	Half-life, hrs (renal function normal)	Half-life, hrs (ESRD)	Dose (renal function normal)	CrCl >50-90	CrCl 10-50	CrCl <10	Hemodialysis	CAPD	CRRT
Cephalosporins, IV, 1st gen									
Cefazolin	1.9	40-70	1-2 gm IV q8h	1-2 gm q8h	1-2 g q12h	1-2 gm q24-48h	1-2 gm q24-48h (+ extra 0.5-1 gm AD)	0.5 gm IV q12h	1-2 gm q12h
Cephalosporins, IV, 2nd gen									
Cefotetan	4	13-25	1-2 gm IV q12h	1-2 gm q12h	1-2 gm q24h	1-2 gm q48h	1-2 gm q24h (+ extra 1 gm AD)	1 gm q24h	750 mg q12h
Cefoxitin[4]	0.8	13-23	2 gm IV q8h	2 gm q8h	2 gm q8-12h	2 gm q24-48h	2 gm q24-48h (+ extra 1 gm AD)	1 gm q24h	2 gm q8-12h
Cefuroxime	1.5	17	0.75-1.5 gm IV q8h	0.75-1.5 gm q8h	0.75-1.5 gm q8-12h	0.75-1.5 gm q24h	0.75-1.5 gm q24h (give dialysis day dose AD)	0.75-1.5 gm q24h	0.75-1.5 gm q8-12h
Cephalosporins, IV, 3rd gen, non-antipseudomonal									
Cefotaxime[5]	1.5	15-35	2 gm IV q8h	2 gm q8-12h	2 gm q12-24h	2 gm q24h	2 gm q24h (+ extra 1 gm AD)	0.5-1 gm q24h	2 gm q12-24h
Ceftizoxime	1.7	15-35	2 gm IV q8h	2 gm q8-12h	2 gm q12-24h	2 gm q24h	2 gm q24h (+ extra 1 gm AD)	0.5-1 gm q24h	2 gm q12-24h
Ceftriaxone[5]	8	Unchanged	1-2 gm IV q12-24h	1-2 gm q12-24h	1-2 gm q12-24h	1-2 gm q12-24h	1-2 gm q12-24h	1-2 gm q12-24h	1-2 gm q12-24h
Cephalosporins, IV, antipseudomonal									
Cefepime	2	18	2 gm IV q8h	>60: 2 gm q8-12h	30-60: 2 gm q12h; 11-29: 2 gm q24h	1 gm q24h	1 gm q24h (+ extra 1 gm AD)	1-2 gm q48h	2 gm q12-24h
Ceftazidime	1.9	13-25	2 gm IV q8h	2 gm q8-12h	2 gm q12-24h	2 gm q24-48h	2 gm q24-48h (+ extra 1 gm AD)	No data	1-2 gm q12-24h (depends on flow rate)
Ceftazidime/ avibactam	ceftaz 2.8, avi 2.7	ceftaz 13-25	2.5 gm IV q8h	2.5 gm q8h	30-50: 1.25 gm q8h; 10-30: 0.94 gm q12h	0.94 gm q48h	0.94 gm q48h (give dialysis day dose AD)	No data	1.25 mg q8h (AAC 2017;61:e00464-17)
Ceftolozane/ tazobactam	ceftolozane 3.1	ceftolozane 40	1.5 gm IV q8h	1.5 gm q8h	30-50: 750 mg q8h 15-30: 375 mg q8h	<15: see HD	750 mg x1, then 150 mg q8h (give doses AD)	No data	No data
Cephalosporins, IV, anti-MRSA									
Ceftaroline	2.7	No data	600 mg IV (over 5-60 min) q12h	600 mg q12h	30-50: 400 mg q12h; 15-30: 300 mg q12h	<15: 200 mg q12h	200 mg q12h	No data	No data
Ceftobiprole[NUS]	2.9-3.3	21	500 mg IV q8-12h	500 mg q8-12h	30-50: 500 mg q12h over 2 hr; 10-30: 250 mg q12h over 2 hr	No data	No data	No data	No data

TABLE 17A (4)

ANTIMICROBIAL	Half-life, hrs (renal function normal)	Half-life, hrs (ESRD)	Dose (renal function normal)	CrCl >50-90	CrCl 10-50	CrCl <10	Hemodialysis	CAPD	CRRT
Cephalosporins, oral, 1st gen									
Cefadroxil	1.5	20	1 gm po q12h	1 gm q12h	1 gm, then 500 mg q12-24h	1 gm, then 500 mg q36h	1 gm, then 1 gm AD	500 mg q24h	No data
Cephalexin	1	20	500 mg po q6h	500 mg q6h	500 mg q12h	250 mg q12h	250 mg q12h (give one of the dialysis day doses AD)	500 mg q12h	No data
Cephalosporins, oral, 2nd gen									
Cefaclor	0.8	3	500 mg po q8h	500 mg q8h	500 mg q8h	500 mg q12h	500 mg q12h (give one of the dialysis day doses AD)	500 mg q12h	No data
Cefprozil	1.5	5-6	500 mg po q12h	500 mg q12h	500 mg q24h	250 mg q12h	250 mg q12h (give one of the dialysis day doses AD)	250 mg q24h	No data
Cefuroxime axetil	1.5	17	500 mg po q8h	500 mg q8h	500 mg q12h	500 mg q24h	500 mg q24h (give extra 250 mg AD)	500 mg q24h	No data
Cephalosporins, oral, 3rd gen									
Cefdinir	1.7	16	300 mg po q12h	300 mg q12h	300 mg q12h	300 mg q24h	300 mg q24h (dose AD on dialysis days)	300 mg q24h	No data
Cefditoren pivoxil	1.6	5	400 mg po q12h	400 mg q12h	200 mg q12h	200 mg q24h	200 mg q24h (dose AD on dialysis days)	200 mg q24h	No data
Cefixime	3	12	400 mg po q24h	400 mg q24h	300 mg q24h	200 mg q24h	200 mg q24h (dose AD on dialysis days)	200 mg q24h	No data
Cefpodoxime proxetil	2.3	10	200 mg po q12h	200 mg q12h	200 mg q12h	200 mg q24h	200 mg q24h (dose AD on dialysis days)	200 mg q24h	No data
Ceftibuten	2.5	13	400 mg po q24h	400 mg q24h	200 mg q24h	100 mg q24h	100 mg q24h (dose AD on dialysis days)	100 mg q24h	No data
Monobactams									
Aztreonam	2	6-8	2 gm IV q8h	2 gm q8h	1-1.5 gm q8h	500 mg q8h	500 mg q8h (give additional 250 mg AD)	500 mg q8h	1-1.5 gm q8h
Penicillins (natural)									
Penicillin G	0.5	6-20	0.5-4 million U IV q4h	0.5-4 million U q4h	0.5-4 million U q8h	0.5-4 million U q12h	0.5-4 million U q12h (give one of the dialysis day doses AD)	0.5-4 million U q12h	1-4 million U q6-8h
Penicillin V	0.5	4.1	250-500 mg po q6-8h	250-500 mg q6-8h	250-500 mg q6-8h	250-500 mg q6-8h	250-500 mg q6-8h (give one or more doses AD)	250-500 mg q6-8h	No data

TABLE 17A (5)

ANTIMICROBIAL	Half-life, hrs (renal function normal)	Half-life, hrs (ESRD)	Dose (renal function normal)	CrCl >50-90	CrCl 10-50	CrCl <10	Hemodialysis	CAPD	CRRT
Penicillins (amino)									
Amoxicillin	1.2	5-20	250-500 mg po q8h	250-500 mg q8h	250-500 mg q8-12h	250-500 mg q24h	250-500 mg q24h (give dialysis day dose AD)	250 mg q12h	250-500 mg q8-12h
Amoxicillin ER	1.2-1.5	?	775 mg po q24h	775 mg q24h	30: No data, avoid usage	No data, avoid usage	No data	No data	No data
Amoxicillin/Clavulanate[a]	amox 1.4, clav 1	amox 5-20, clav 4	500/125 mg po q8h	500/125 mg q8h	250-500 mg (amox component) q12h	250-500 mg (amox) q24h	250-500 mg (amox) q24h (give an extra dose AD on dialysis days)	No data	No data
Ampicillin	1.2	7-20	1-2 gm IV q4-6h	1-2 gm q4-6h	30-50: 1-2 gm q6-8h; 10-30: 1-2 gm q8-12h	1-2 gm q12h	1-2 gm q12h (give one of the dialysis day doses AD)	500 mg - 1 gm q12h	1-2 gm q8-12h
Ampicillin/Sulbactam	amp 1.4, sulb 1.7	amp 7-20, sulb 10	3 gm IV q6h	3 gm q6h	3 gm q8-12h	3 gm q24h	3 gm q24h (give AD on dialysis day)	3 gm q24h	3 gm q12h
Penicillins (penicillinase-resistant)									
Dicloxacillin	0.7	No change	125-500 mg po q6h	125-500 mg q6h	125-500 mg q6h	125-500 mg q6h			
Temocillin	4	No data	1-2 gm IV q12h	1-2 gm q12h	1-2 gm q24h	1 gm q48h	1 gm q48h (give AD on dialysis days)	1 gm q48h	No data
Penicillins (antipseudomonal)									
Piperacillin/Tazobactam (non-Pseudomonas dose)	pip 1, Tazo 1	pip 3-5, Tazo 2.8	3.375 gm IV q6h (over 30 min)	>40: 3.375 gm q6h	20-40: 2.25 gm q6h; <20: 2.25 gm q8h	2.25 gm q8h	2.25 gm q12h (+ extra 0.75 gm AD)	2.25 gm q12h	2.25 gm q6h
Piperacillin/Tazobactam (Pseudomonas dose)	pip 1, Tazo 1	pip 3-5, Tazo 2.8	4.5 gm IV q6h (over 30 min)	>40: 4.5 gm q6h	20-40: 3.375 gm q6h; <20: 2.25 gm q6h	2.25 gm q6h	2.25 gm q8h (+ extra 0.75 gm AD)	2.25 gm q8h	MIC ≤16: 3.375 gm (over 30 min) q6h; MIC >16 to 64: 4.5 gm (over 4 hr) q8h (*Pharmacother 35:600, 2015*)
FLUOROQUINOLONES									
Ciprofloxacin po (not XR)	4	6-9	500-750 mg po q12h	500-750 mg q12h	250-500 mg q12h	500 mg q12h	500 mg q24h (dose AD on dialysis days)	500 mg q24h	250-500 mg q12h
Ciprofloxacin XR po	5-7	6-9	500-1000 mg po q24h	500-1000 mg q24h	30-50: 500-1000 mg q24h; 10-30: 500 mg q24h	500 mg q24h	500 mg q24h (dose AD on dialysis days)	500 mg q24h	No data

TABLE T7A (6)

ANTIMICROBIAL	Half-life, hrs (renal function normal)	Half-life, hrs (ESRD)	Dose (renal function normal)	CrCl >50-90	CrCl 10-50	CrCl <10	Hemodialysis	CAPD	CRRT
FLUOROQUINOLONES (continued)									
Ciprofloxacin IV	4	6-9	400 mg IV q12h	400 mg q12h	400 mg q24h	400 mg q24h	400 mg q24h (dose AD on dialysis days)	400 mg q24h	200-400 mg q12h
Delafloxacin IV	4.2-8.5	No data	300 mg IV q12h	300 mg q12h	eGFR 30-50: 300 mg q12h; 15-29: 200 mg q12h	eGFR-15: No data	No data	No data	No data
Delafloxacin po	4.2-8.5	No data	450 mg po q12h	450 mg q12h	eGFR 15-50: 450 mg q12h	eGFR-15: No data	No data	No data	No data
Gatifloxacin[NUS]	7-8	11-40	400 mg po/IV q24h	400 mg q24h	400 mg, then 200 mg q24h	400 mg, then 200 mg q24h	200 mg q24h (give dialysis day dose AD)	200 mg q24h	400 mg, then 200 mg q24h
Gemifloxacin	7	>7	320 mg po q24h	320 mg q24h	160 mg q24h	160 mg q24h	160 mg q24h (give dialysis day dose AD)	160 mg q24h	No data
Levofloxacin	7	76	750 mg po/IV q24h	750 mg q24h	20-49: 750 mg q48h	<20: 750 mg x1, then 500 mg q48h	750 mg x1, then 500 mg q48h	750 mg x1, then 500 mg q48h	750 mg x1, then 500 mg q48h
Norfloxacin	3-4	8	400 mg po q12h	400 mg q12h	30-49: 400 mg q12h; 10-30: 400 mg q24h	400 mg q24h	400 mg q24h	400 mg q24h	Not applicable
Ofloxacin	7	28-37	200-400 mg po q12h	200-400 mg q12h	200-400 mg q24h	200 mg q24h	200 mg q24h (give dialysis day dose AD)	200 mg q24h	200-400 mg q24h
Prulifloxacin[NUS]	10.6-12.1	No data	600 mg po q12h	No data	No data	No data	No data	No data	No data
GLYCOPEPTIDES, LIPOGLYCOPEPTIDES, LIPOPEPTIDES									
Dalbavancin	147-258 (terminal)	No data	1 gm IV x1, then 500 mg IV in 7 days	1 gm x1, then 500 mg in 7 days	30-49: 1 gm x1, then 500 mg in 7 days; <30, non-regular HD: 750 mg x1, then 375 mg in 7 days	30-49: 1 gm x1, then 500 mg in 7 days; <30: 750 mg x1, then 375 mg in 7 days	Regularly scheduled HD: 1 gm x1, then 500 mg in 7 days	No data	No data
Daptomycin	8-9	30	4-6 mg/kg IV q24h	4-6 mg/kg q24h	30-49: 4-6 mg/kg q24h; <30: 6 mg/kg q48h	No data	6 mg/kg q48h (during or after q48h dialysis); if next planned dialysis is 72 hrs away, give 9 mg/kg (JAC 57:864, 2013; JAC 69:200, 2014)	6 mg/kg q48h	6 mg/kg q48h
Oritavancin	245 (terminal)	No data	1200 mg IV x1	1200 mg IV x1	<30: No data	No data	Not removed by hemodialysis	No data	No data

TABLE 17A (7)

ANTIMICROBIAL	Half-life, hrs (renal function normal)	Half-life, hrs (ESRD)	Dose (renal function normal)	CrCl >50-90	CrCl 10-50	CrCl <10	Hemodialysis	CAPD	CRRT
GLYCOPEPTIDES, LIPOGLYCOPEPTIDES, LIPOPEPTIDES *(continued)*									
Teicoplanin[NUS]	70-100	up to 230	12 mg/kg IV q12h x3 doses (load), then 12 mg/kg q24h	12 mg/kg q24h (after load)	12 mg/kg q48h (after load)	12 mg/kg q72h (after load)	12 mg/kg q72h (after load). Give AD on dialysis day	12 mg/kg q72h	12 mg/kg q48h
Telavancin	8.1	17.9	10 mg/kg IV q24h	10 mg/kg IV q24h	30-50: 7.5mg/kg q24h; 10-30: 10 mg/kg q48h	10 mg/kg q48h	No data	No data	No data
Vancomycin[7]	4-6	200-250	15-30 mg/kg IV q12h	15-30 mg/kg q12h	15 mg/kg q24-96h	7.5 mg/kg q2-3 days	For trough conc of 15-20, give 15 mg/kg if next dialysis in 1 day; give 25 mg/kg if next dialysis in 2 days; give 35 mg/kg if next dialysis in 3 days (CID 53:124, 2011)	7.5 mg/kg q2-3 days	CAVH/CVVH: 500 mg q24-48h
MACROLIDES, AZALIDES, LINCOSAMIDES, KETOLIDES									
Azithromycin	68	Unchanged	250-500 mg IV/po q24h	250-500 mg q24h	250-500 mg q24h	250-500 mg q24h	250-500 mg q24h	250-500 mg q24h	250-500 mg q24h
Clarithromycin (not ER)	5-7	22	500 mg po q12h	500 mg q12h	500 mg q12-24h	500 mg q24h	500 mg q24h (dose AD on dialysis days)	500 mg q24h	500 mg q12-24h
Telithromycin[9]	10	15	800 mg po q24h	800 mg q24h	30-50: 800 mg 10-30: 600 mg q24h	600 mg q24h	600 mg q24h (give AD on dialysis days)	No data	No data
MISCELLANEOUS ANTIBACTERIALS									
Chloramphenicol[5]	4.1	Unchanged	50-100 mg/kg/day po/IV (divided q6h)	50-100 mg/kg/ day (divided q6h)	50-100 mg/kg/day (divided q6h)	50-100 mg/kg/day (divided q6h)	50-100 mg/kg/day (divided q6h)	50-100 mg/kg/day (divided q6h)	50-100 mg/kg/day (divided q6h)
Fosfomycin po	5.7	50	3 gm po x1		Do not use (low urine concentrations)				
Fusidic acid[NUS]	8.9-11	8.9-11	250-750 mg po q8-12h	250-750 mg q8-12h	250-750 mg q8-12h	250-750 mg q8-12h	250-750 mg q8-12h	250-750 mg q8-12h	250-750 mg q8-12h
Metronidazole[8]	6-14	7-21	7.5 mg/kg IV/po q6h	7.5 mg/kg q6h	7.5 mg/kg q6h	7.5 mg/kg q6h	7.5 mg/kg q12h (give one of the dialysis doses AD)	7.5 mg/kg q12h	7.5 mg/kg q6h
Nitrofurantoin	1	-	100 mg po q12h (Macrobid)	100 mg q12h (Macrobid)	Avoid use	Avoid use	Avoid use	Avoid use	Avoid use

TABLE 17A (8)

ANTIMICROBIAL	Half-life, hrs (renal function normal)	Half-life, hrs (ESRD)	Dose (renal function normal)	CrCl >90-90	CrCl 10-50	CrCl <10	Hemodialysis	CAPD	CRRT
MISCELLANEOUS ANTIBACTERIALS (continued)									
Tinidazole	13	No data	2 gm po q24h x i-5 days	2 gm q24h x1-5 days	2 gm q24h x1-5 days	2 gm q24h x1-5 days	2 gm q24h x1-5 days (+ extra 1 gm AD)	No data	No data
Trimethoprim	8-15	20-49	100-200 mg po q12h	100-200 mg q12h	>30: 100-200 mg q12h; 10-30: 100-200 mg q18h	>30: 100-200 mg q24h	100-200 mg q24h (give dialysis day dose AD)	100-200 mg q24h	100-200 mg q18h
TMP/SMX (treatment)	TMP 8-15, SMX 10	TMP 20-49, SMX 20-50	5-20 mg/kg/day po/IV (div q6-12h) base on TMP	5-20 mg/kg/ day (divided q6-12h)	30-50: 5-20 mg/kg/day (div q6-12h); 10-29: 5-10 mg/kg/day (div q12h)	Not recommended (but if used: 5-10 mg/kg q24h)	Not recommended (but if used: 5-10 mg/ kg q24h; give dialysis day dose AD)	Not recommended (but if used: 5-10 mg/kg q24h)	5 mg/kg q8h
TMP/SMX (prophylaxis)	as above	as above	1 DS tab po q24h or 3x/week	1 DS tab q24h or 3x/week	1 DS tab q24h or 3x/week	1 DS tab q24h or 3x/week			
OXAZOLIDINONES									
Linezolid	5	6-8	600 mg po/IV q12h	600 mg q12h	600 mg q12h	600 mg q12h	600 mg q12h (give one of the dialysis day doses AD)	600 mg q12h	600 mg q12h
Tedizolid		Unchanged	200 mg po/IV q24h	200 mg q24h	200 mg q24h	200 mg q24h	200 mg q24h	200 mg q24h	200 mg q24h
POLYMYXINS									
Colistin (polymyxin E) See Table 10A All doses refer to colistin base in mg	6.3-12	≥48	Load: (2.0) x (2) x (pt wt in kg) Use lower of ideal or actual wt Max loading dose 300 mg Start maintenance 12 hrs later (see formula)	Daily maintenance dose = 2.0 x [(1.5 x CrClin) + 30] Divide and give q8-12h. CrClin = CrCl x (pt BSA in m² divided by 1.73)	Daily maintenance dose = 2.0 x [(1.5 x CrClin) + 30] Divide and give q8-12h.	Daily maintenance dose = 2.0 x [(1.5 x CrClin) + 30] Divide and give q8-12h.	130 mg/day divided q12h on non-dialysis days; on dialysis days, 175 mg for first dose after end of dialysis	160 mg q24h	For Css of 2.0 μg/mL, total daily dose is 480 mg divided q12h). This dose is necessarily high due to drug removal by the dialysis membrane. See AAC 55:3284, 2011
TETRACYCLINES, GLYCYLCYCLINES									
Tetracycline	6-12	57-108	250-500 mg po q6h	250-500 mg q8-12h	250-500 mg q12-24h	250-500 mg q24h	250-500 mg q24h	250-500 mg q24h	250-500 mg q12-24h
ANTIMETABOLITES									
Flucytosine*	3-5	75-200	25 mg/kg po q6h	25 mg/kg q6h	25 mg/kg q12h	25 mg/kg q24h	25 mg/kg q24h (give dialysis day dose AD)	0.5-1 gm q24h	25 mg/kg q12h

TABLE 17A (9)

ANTIMICROBIAL	Half-life, hrs (renal function normal)	Half-life, hrs (ESRD)	Dose (renal function normal)	CrCl >50-90	CrCl 10-50	CrCl <10	Hemodialysis	CAPD	CRRT
ALLYLAMINES, AZOLES									
Fluconazole	20-50	100	100-400 mg po/IV q24h	100-400 mg q24h	50-200 mg q24h	50-200 mg q24h	100-400 mg q24h (give dialysis day dose AD)	50-200 mg q24h	200-400 mg q24h
Itraconazole (IV)[§]	35-40	Unchanged	200 mg IV q12h	200 mg IV q12h	Do not use IV itraconazole if CrCl<30 due to accumulation of cyclodextrin vehicle				
Itraconazole (oral solution)[§]	35-40	Unchanged	100-200 mg po q12h	100-200 mg q12h	100-200 mg q12h	50-100 mg q12h	100 mg q12-24h	100 mg q12-24h	100-200 mg q12h
Terbinafine	36	No data	250 mg po q24h	250 mg q24h	Avoid use	Avoid use	Avoid use	Avoid use	Avoid use
Voriconazole (IV)[§]	dose-dependent	dose-dependent	6 mg/kg IV q12h x2 doses, then 4 mg/kg IV q12h	6 mg/kg q12h x2 doses, then 4 mg/kg q12h	If CrCl<50, IV vehicle (cyclodextrin) accumulates. Use oral or discontinue.	If CrCl<50, IV vehicle (cyclodextrin) accumulates.	Avoid use	Avoid use	Avoid use
ANTIMYCOBACTERIALS **First line, tuberculosis**									
Ethambutol[§]	4	7-15	15-25 mg/kg po q24h	15-25 mg/kg q24h	CrCl 30-50: 15-25 mg/kg q24-36h; CrCl 10-30: 15-25 mg/kg q36-48h	15 mg/kg q48h	15 mg/kg q48h (administer AD on dialysis days)	15 mg/kg q48h	15-25 mg/kg q24h
Isoniazid (INH)[§]	0.7-4	8-17	5 mg/kg po q24h	5 mg/kg q24h	5 mg/kg q24h	5 mg/kg q24h	5 mg/kg q24h (administer AD on dialysis days)	5 mg/kg q24h	5 mg/kg q24h
Pyrazinamide	10-16	26	25 mg/kg (max 2.5 gm) po q24h	25 mg/kg q24h	CrCl 21-50: 25 mg/kg q24h; CrCl 10-20: 25 mg/kg q48h	25 mg/kg q48h	25 mg/kg q48h (administer AD on dialysis days)	25 mg/kg q24h	25 mg/kg q24h
Rifabutin[§]	32-67	Unchanged	300 mg po q24h	300 mg q24h	150 mg q24h	150 mg q24h	No data	No data	No data
Rifampin[§]	1.5-5	up to 11	600 mg po q24h	600 mg q24h	300-600 mg q24h	300-600 mg q24h	300-600 mg q24h	300-600 mg q24h	300-600 mg q24h
Rifapentine	13.2-14.1	Unchanged	600 mg po 1-2x/wk	600 mg po 1-2x/wk	600 mg 1-2x/wk	600 mg 1-2x/wk	600 mg 1-2x/wk	600 mg 1-2x/wk	600 mg 1-2x/wk
Streptomycin[§,2]	2-3	30-70	15 mg/kg (max 1 gm) IM q24h	15 mg/kg q24h	15 mg/kg q24-72h	15 mg/kg q72-96h	15 mg/kg q72-96h (+ extra 7.5 mg/kg AD)	20-40 mg lost per L of dialysate/day	15 mg/kg q24-72h

TABLE 17A (10)

ANTIMICROBIAL	Half-life, hrs (renal function normal)	Half-life, hrs (ESRD)	Dose (renal function normal)	CrCl >50-90	CrCl 10-50	CrCl <10	Hemodialysis	CAPD	CRRT
ANTIMYCOBACTERIALS *(continued)*									
Second line, tuberculosis									
Bedaquiline	24-30 (terminal 4-5 mo)	No data	400 mg po q24h x2 wks, then 200 mg po 3x/wk x22 wks	400 mg q24h x2 wk, then 200 mg 3x/wks x22 wks	400 mg q24h x2 wks, then 200 mg 3x/wks x22 wks	Use with caution	Use with caution	Use with caution	Use with caution
Capreomycin	2-5	No data	15 mg/kg IM/IV q24h	15 mg/kg q24h	15 mg/kg q24h	15 mg/kg 3x/wk	15 mg/kg 3x/wk (give AD on dialysis days)	No data	No data
Cycloserine[NB]	10	No data	250-500 mg po q12h	250-500 mg q12h	250-500 mg q12h-24h (dosing interval poorly defined)	500 mg q48h (or 3x/wk)	500 mg 3x/wk (give AD on dialysis days)	No data	No data
Ethionamide	2	9	500 mg po q12h	500 mg q12h	500 mg q12h	250 mg q12h	250 mg q12h	250 mg q12h	500 mg q12h
Kanamycin[12]	2-3	30-70	7.5 mg/kg IM/IV q12h	7.5 mg/kg q12h	7.5 mg/kg q24h	7.5 mg/kg q48h	7.5 mg/kg q48h (+ extra 3.25 mg/kg AD)	15-20 mg lost per L of dialysate/day	7.5 mg/kg q24h
Para-aminosalicylic acid (PAS)	0.75-1.0	23	4 gm po q12h	4 gm q12h	2-3 gm q12h	2 gm q12h	2 gm q12h (dose AD on dialysis days)	No data	No data
ANTIPARASITICS: ANTIMALARIALS									
Artemether/ lumefantrine (20 mg/120 mg)	art, DHA 1.6-2.2, lum 101-119	No data	4 tabs x1, 4 tabs in 8 hr, then 4 tabs q12h x2 days	4 tabs x1, 4 tabs in 8 hr, then 4 tabs q12h x2 days	4 tabs x1, 4 tabs in 8 hr, then 4 tabs q12h x2 days	4 tabs x1, 4 tabs in 8 hr, then 4 tabs q12h x2 days	No data	No data	No data
Atovaquone	67	No data	750 mg po q12h	750 mg q12h	CrCl 30-50: 750 mg q12h; CrCl 10-30: use with caution	Use with caution	No data	No data	No data
Atovaquone/ Proguanil (250 mg/100 mg)	atov 67, pro 12-21	No data	4 tabs po q24h x3 days	4 tabs q24h x3 days	CrCl <30: use with caution	Use with caution	No data	No data	No data
Chloroquine phosphate	45-55 days (terminal)	No data	2.5 gm po over 3 days	2.5 gm over 3 days	2.5 gm over 3 days	2.5 gm over 3 days (consider reducing dose 50%)	2.5 gm over 3 days (consider reducing dose 50%)	No data	No data

TABLE 17A (11)

ANTIMICROBIAL	Half-life, hrs (renal function normal)	Half-life, hrs (ESRD)	Dose (renal function normal)	CrCl >50-90	CrCl 10-50	CrCl <10	Hemodialysis	CAPD	CRRT
ANTIPARASITICS, ANTIMALARIALS *(continued)*									
Mefloquine	13-24 days	No data	750 mg po, then 500 mg po in 6-8 hrs	750 mg, then 500 mg in 6-8 hrs	750 mg, then 500 mg in 6-8 hrs	750 mg, then 500 mg in 6-8 hrs	No data	No data	No data
Quinine	9.7-12.5	up to 16	648 mg po q8h	648 mg q8h	648 mg q8-12h	648 mg q24h	648 mg q24h (give dialysis day dose AD)	648 mg q24h	648 mg q8-12h
OTHER									
Albendazole	8-12	No data	400 mg po q12-24h	400 mg q12-24h	400 mg q12-24h	400 mg q12-24h	No data	No data	No data
Dapsone	10-50	No data	100 mg po q24h	No data	No data	No data	No data	No data	No data
Ivermectin	20	No data	200 µg/kg/day x1-2 days	200 µg/kg/day x1-2 days	200 µg/kg/day x1-2 days	200 µg/kg/day x1-2 days	No data	No data	No data
Miltefosine	7-31 days	No data	50 mg po q8h	No data	No data	No data	No data	No data	No data
Nitazoxanide	tizoxanide 1.3-1.8	No data	500 mg po q12h	No data	No data	No data	No data	No data	No data
Pentamidine	3-12	73-118	4 mg/kg IM/IV q24h	4 mg/kg q24h	4 mg/kg q24h	4 mg/kg q24-36h	4 mg/kg q48h (give dialysis day dose AD)	4 mg/kg q24-36h	4 mg/kg q24h
ANTIVIRALS HEPATITIS B									
Adefovir	7.5	15	10 mg po q24h	10 mg q24h	10 mg q48-72h	10 mg q72h	10 mg weekly (dose AD on dialysis days)	No data	No data
Entecavir	128-149	?	0.5 mg po q24h	0.5 mg q24h	0.15-0.25 mg q24h	0.05 mg q24h	0.05 mg q24h (dose AD on dialysis days)	0.05 mg q24h	No data
Telbivudine	40-49	No data	600 mg po q24h	600 mg q24h	30-49: 600 mg q48h; 10-30: 600 mg q72h	600 mg q96h	600 mg q96h (dose AD on dialysis days)	No data	No data
HEPATITIS C (SINGLE AGENTS)									
Daclatasvir	12-15	No data	60 mg po q24h	60 mg q24h	60 mg q24h	60 mg q24h	No data	No data	No data
Ribavirin	44	No data	Depends on indication	No dosage adjustment	Use with caution	Use with caution	No data	No data	No data
Simeprevir	41	Unchanged	150 mg po q24h	150 mg q24h	Use with caution (no data for use in patients with CrCl<30)			No data	No data
Sofosbuvir	sofosbuvir 0.5-0.75	Unchanged	400 mg po q24h	400 mg q24h	Use with caution (no data for use in patients with CrCl<30)			No data	No data

TABLE 17A (12)

ANTIMICROBIAL	Half-life, hrs (renal function normal)	Half-life, hrs (ESRD)	Dose (renal function normal)	CrCl >50-90	CrCl 10-50	CrCl <10	Hemodialysis	CAPD	CRRT
HEPATITIS C (FIXED-DOSE COMBINATIONS)									
Epclusa (Velpatasvir, Sofosbuvir)	velpat 15, sofos 0.5	No data	1 tab po q24h	1 tab po q24h	Use with caution (no data for use in patients with CrCl<30)		No data	No data	No data
Harvoni (Ledipasvir, Sofosbuvir)	ledipasvir 47	No data	1 tab po q24h	1 tab po q24h	Use with caution (no data for use in patients with CrCl<30)		No data	No data	No data
Technivie (Ombitasvir, Paritaprevir, RTV)	ombit 28-34, parita 5.8	No data	2 tabs po q24h	2 tabs q24h	2 tabs q24h	2 tabs q24h	No data	No data	No data
Viekira Pak (Dasabuvir, Ombitasvir, Paritaprevir, RTV)	dasabuvir 5-8	No data	2 Ombit/Parita/RTV tabs q24h, Dasa 250 mg q12h	2 Ombit/Parita/RTV tabs q24h, Dasa 250 mg q12h	2 Ombit/Parita/RTV tabs q24h, Dasa 250 mg q12h	2 Ombit/Parita/RTV tabs q24h, Dasa 250 mg q12h	No data	No data	No data
Zepatier (Ebasvir, Grazoprevir)	efba 24, grazo 31	No data	1 tab po q24h	1 tab po q24h	1 tab po q24h	1 tab po q24h	1 tab po q24h	No data	No data
HERPESVIRUS									
Acyclovir (IV)[1]	2.5-3.5	20	5-12.5 mg/kg IV q8h	5-12.5 mg/kg q8h	5-12.5 mg/kg q12-24h	2.5-6.25 mg/kg q24h	2.5-6.25 mg/kg q24h (dose AD on dialysis days)	2.5-6.25 mg/kg q24h	5-10 mg/kg q24h
Cidofovir (induction)	2.6	No data	5 mg/kg IV q-week x2 weeks	CrCl>55: 5 mg/kg q-week x2 weeks	Contraindicated in patients with CrCl of 55 mL/min or less		Contraindicated	Contraindicated	Contraindicated
Cidofovir (maintenance)	2.6	No data	5 mg/kg IV every 2 weeks	CrCl>55: 5 mg/kg every 2 weeks	Contraindicated in patients with CrCl of 55 mL/min or less		Contraindicated	Contraindicated	Contraindicated
Famciclovir	penciclovir 2-3	10-22	500 mg po q8h (VZV)	500 mg po q8h	500 mg q12-24h	250 mg q24h	250 mg q24h (dose AD on dialysis days)	No data	No data
Ganciclovir (IV induction)	3.5	30	5 mg/kg IV q12h	CrCl 70-90, 5 mg/kg q12h; CrCl 50-69, 2.5 mg/kg q12h	CrCl 25-49, 2.5 mg/kg q24h; CrCl 10-24, 1.25 mg/kg q24h	1.25 mg/kg 3x/week	1.25 mg/kg 3x/week (dose AD on dialysis days)	1.25 mg/kg 3x/week	CVVHF: 2.5 mg/kg q24h (AAC 58:94, 2014)
Ganciclovir (IV maintenance)	3.5	30	5 mg/kg IV q24h	2.5-5 mg/kg q24h	0.625-1.25 mg/kg q24h	0.625 mg/kg 3x/week	0.625 mg/kg 3x/week (dose AD on dialysis days)	0.625 mg/kg 3x/week	No data
Ganciclovir (oral)	3.5	30	1 gm po q8h	0.5-1 gm q8h	0.5-1 gm q24h	0.5 gm 3x/week	0.5 gm 3x/week (dose AD on dialysis days)	No data	No data
Letermovir	12	ND	480 mg po/IV q24h	480 mg q24h	480 mg q24h	No data	No data	No data	No data

TABLE 17A (13)

ANTIMICROBIAL	Half-life, hrs (renal function normal)	Half-life, hrs (ESRD)	Dose (renal function normal)	CrCl >50-90	CrCl 10-50	CrCl <10	Hemodialysis	CAPD	CRRT
HERPESVIRUS (continued)									
Valacyclovir	3	14	1 gm po q8h (VZV)	1 gm q8h	1 gm q12-24h	0.5 gm q24h	0.5 gm q24h (dose AD on dialysis days)	0.5 gm q24h	1 gm q12-24h
Valganciclovir	ganciclovir 4	ganciclovir 67	900 mg po q12h	900 mg q12h	450 mg q24-48h	Do not use	*See prescribing information*	No data	No data
			CrCl above 1.4 mL/min/kg (foscarnet only)	CrCl >1 to 1.4 mL/min/kg (foscarnet only)	CrCl >0.8 to 1.0 mL/min/kg (foscarnet only)	CrCl >0.6 to 0.8 mL/min/kg (foscarnet only)	CrCl >0.5 to 0.6 mL/min/kg (foscarnet only)	CrCl 0.4 to 0.5 mL/min/kg (foscarnet only)	CrCl <0.4 mL/min/kg (foscarnet only)
Foscarnet (induction) special dosing scale	3 (terminal 18-88)	Very long	60 mg/kg IV q8h	45 mg/kg q8h	50 mg/kg q12h	40 mg/kg q12h	60 mg/kg q24h	50 mg/kg q24h	Not recommended
Foscarnet (maintenance) special dosing scale	3 (terminal 18-88)	Very long	90-120 mg/kg IV q24h	70-90 mg/kg q24h	50-65 mg/kg q24h	80-105 mg/kg q48h	60-80 mg/kg q48h	50-65 mg/kg q48h	Not recommended
INFLUENZA									
Amantadine	14.8	500	100 mg po q12h	100 mg q12h	100 mg q24-48h	100 mg weekly	100 mg weekly (give AD on dialysis days)	100 mg weekly	100 mg q24-48h
Oseltamivir	carboxylate 6-10	carboxylate >20	75 mg po q12h	CrCl >60: 75 mg q12h	CrCl 31-60: 30 mg q12h; CrCl 10-30: 30 mg q24h	No recommendation unless HD	30 mg after each dialysis, no drug on non-HD days (see comments)	30 mg after a dialysis exchange	No data
Peramivir	20	No data	600 mg IV q24h	600 mg q24h	CrCl 31-49: 200 mg q24h; CrCl 10-30: 100 mg q24h	100 mg x1, then 15 mg q24h	100 mg x1, then 100 mg 2 hrs AD on dialysis days only	No data	No data
Rimantadine[§]	24-36	prolonged	100 mg po q12h	100 mg q12h	100 mg q12-24h	100 mg q24h	No data	No data	Use with caution
ANTIRETROVIRALS (NRTIs)									
Abacavir (ABC)[§]	1.5	No data	600 mg po q24h	600 mg q24h	600 mg q24h	600 mg q24h	No data	No data	No data
Didanosine enteric coated (ddI)	1.6	4.5	400 mg EC po q24h	400 mg EC q24h	CrCl 30-49: 125-200 mg q24h; CrCl 15-29: 200 mg q24h	Do not use	No data	No data	No data
Emtricitabine capsules (FTC)	10	>10	200 mg po q24h	200 mg q24h	CrCl 30-49: 200 mg q48h; CrCl 15-29: 200 mg q72h	CrCl <15: 200 mg q96h	200 mg q96h	No data	No data
Emtricitabine oral solution (FTC)	10	>10	240 mg po q24h	240 mg q24h	CrCl 30-49: 120 mg q24h; CrCl 15-29: 80 mg q24h	CrCl <15: 60 mg q24h	60 mg q24h	No data	No data

TABLE 17A (14)

ANTIMICROBIAL	Half-life, hrs (renal function normal)	Half-life, hrs (ESRD)	Dose (renal function normal)	CrCl >50-90	CrCl 10-50	CrCl <10	Hemodialysis	CAPD	CRRT
ANTIRETROVIRALS (NRTIs) *(continued)*									
Lamivudine (3TC)	5-7	15-35	300 mg po q24h (HIV dose)	300 mg q24h (HIV)	50-150 mg q24h (HIV)	25-50 mg q24h (HIV)	25-50 mg q24h (dose AD on dialysis days) (HIV)	25-50 mg po q24h (HIV)	100 mg first day, then 50 mg q24h (HIV)
Stavudine (d4T)	1.2-1.6	5.5-8	30-40 mg po q12h	30-40 mg q12h	15-20 mg q12h	≥60 kg: 20 mg q24h; <60 kg: 15 mg q24h	≥60 kg: 20 mg q24h; <60 kg: 15 mg q24h (dose AD on dialysis days)	No data	30-40 mg q12h
Tenofovir (TDF)	17	Prolonged	300 mg q24h	300 mg q24h	CrCl 30-49: 300 mg q48h; CrCl 10-29: 300 mg q72-96h	No data	300 mg after every 3rd dialysis, or q7 days if no dialysis	No data	No data
Zidovudine (ZDV)	0.5-3	1.3-3	300 mg q12h	300 mg q12h	300 mg q12h	100 mg q8h	100 mg q8h (dose AD on dialysis days)	No data	300 mg q12h
FUSION/ENTRY INHIBITORS									
Enfuvirtide (ENF, T20)*	3.8	Unchanged	90 mg sc q12h	90 mg q12h	Not studied in patients with CrCl<35; DO NOT USE		Avoid use	Avoid use	Avoid use
Maraviroc (MVC)	14-18	No data	300 mg po q12h	300 mg q12h	No data	No data	No data	No data	No data
FIXED-DOSE COMBINATIONS									
Atripla (EFV/FTC/TDF)	*See components*	*See components*	1 tab po q24h	1 tab q24h	Do not use	Do not use	Do not use	Do not use	Do not use
Combivir (3TC/ZDV)	*See components*	*See components*	1 tab po q12h	1 tab q12h	Do not use	Do not use	Do not use	Do not use	Do not use
Complera, Eviplera (RPV/FTC/TDF)	*See components*	*See components*	1 tab po q24h	1 tab q24h	Do not use	Do not use	Do not use	Do not use	Do not use
Dutrebis (3TC/RAL)	*See components*	*See components*	1 tab po q12h	1 tab q12h	Do not use	Do not use	Do not use	Do not use	Do not use
Epzicom, Kivexa (ABC/3TC)	*See components*	*See components*	1 tab po q24h	1 tab q24h	Do not use	Do not use	Do not use	Do not use	Do not use
Evotaz (ATV/cobi)[B]	*See components*	*See components*	1 tab po q24h	1 tab q24h	1 tab q24h	1 tab q24h	Do not use	No data	No data
Genvoya (EVG/FTC/TAF/cobi)	*See components*	*See components*	1 tab po q24h	1 tab po q24h	CrCl 30-49: 1 tab po q24h; do not use if CrCl <30	Do not use	Do not use	Do not use	Do not use

TABLE 17A (15)

ANTIMICROBIAL	Half-life, hrs (renal function normal)	Half-life, hrs (ESRD)	Dose (renal function normal)	CrCl >50-90	CrCl 10-50	CrCl <10	Hemodialysis	CAPD	CRRT
FIXED-DOSE COMBINATIONS (continued)[13]									
Prezcobix (DRV/cobi)[13]	See components	See components	1 tab po q24h	1 tab q24h	1 tab q24h	1 tab q24h	1 tab q24h	1 tab q24h	1 tab q24h
Stribild (EVG/FTC/TDF/cobi)	See components	See components	1 tab po q24h	Do not use if CrCl <70	Do not use	Do not use	Do not use	Do not use	Do not use
Triumeq (DTG/ABC/3TC)	See components	See components	1 tab po q24h	1 tab q24h	Do not use	Do not use	Do not use	Do not use	Do not use
Trizivir (ABC/3TC/ZDV)	See components	See components	1 tab po q12h	1 tab q12h	Do not use	Do not use	Do not use	Do not use	Do not use
Truvada (FTC/TDF)	See components	See components	1 tab po q24h	1 tab q24h	CrCl 30-49: 1 tab q48h; do not use if CrCl <30	Do not use	Do not use	Do not use	Do not use

1 High flux HD membranes lead to unpredictable drug Cl; measure post-dialysis drug levels.
2 Check levels with CAPD, PK likely variable. Usual method w/CAPD: 2 L dialysis fluid replaced qid (Example amikacin; give 8 L x 20 mg lost/L = 160 mg amikacin IV supplement daily).
3 Gentamicin SLEDD dose: 6 mg/kg IV q48h beginning 30 min before start of SLEDD (AAC 54:3635, 2010).
4 May falsely increase Scr by interference with assay.
5 Dosage adjustment may be required in hepatic disease.
6 Clav cleared by liver; thus as dose of combination is decreased, a clav deficiency may occur (JAMA 285:386, 2001). If CrCl≤30, do not use 875/125 or 1000/62.5.
7 New hemodialysis membranes increase Vancomycin clearance; check levels.
8 Goal peak serum concentration: 25-100 μg/mL.
9 Monitor serum concentrations if possible in dialysis patients.
10 Goal peak serum concentration: 20-35 μg/mL.
11 Rapid infusion can increase SCr.
12 Dosing for age >1 yr (dose after each hemodialysis): ≤15 kg, 7.5 mg; 16-23 kg, 10 mg; 24-40 kg, 15 mg; >40 kg, 30 mg (CID 50:t27, 2010).
13 Do not use with Tenofovir if CrCl <70.

TABLE 17B – NO DOSAGE ADJUSTMENT WITH RENAL INSUFFICIENCY BY CATEGORY

Antibacterials		Antifungals	Anti-TBc	Antivirals		Antiparasitics
Azithromycin	Minocycline	Amphotericin B	Bedaquiline	Abacavir	Mavyret	Albendazole
Ceftriaxone	Moxifloxacin	Anidulafungin	Ethionamide	Atazanavir	Nelfinavir	Artesunate
Chloramphenicol	Nafcillin	Caspofungin	Isoniazid	Daclatasvir	Nevirapine	Ivermectin
Clindamycin	Oritavancin	Isavuconazonium	Rifampin	Darunavir	Raltegravir	Mefloquine
Dicloxacillin	Polymyxin B	sulfate	Rifabutin	Delavirdine	Rilpivirine	Praziquantel
Doxycycline	Rifaximin	Itraconazole oral	Rifapentine	Dolutegravir	Ritonavir	Primaquine
Fidaxomicin	Secnidazole	solution		Efavirenz	Saquinavir	Pyrimethamine
Fusidic acid	Tedizolid	Ketoconazole		Elvitegravir	Simeprevir[2]	
Linezolid[3]	Tigecycline	Micafungin		Enfuvirtide[1]	Sofosbuvir[2]	
Quinupristin-Dalfopristin		Posaconazole, **po only**		Epclusa[2]	Technivie	
		Voriconazole, **po only**		Etravirine	Tipranavir	
				Fosamprenavir	Viekira Pak	
				Harvoni[2]	Viekira XR	
				Indinavir	Zepatier	
				Letermovir		
				Lopinavir		

[1] Enfuvirtide: Not studied in patients with CrCl <35 mL/min. DO NOT USE.
[2] No data for CrCl <30 mL/min
[3] Increased risk of bone marrow toxicity

TABLE 17C – ANTIMICROBIAL DOSING IN OBESITY

The number of obese patients is increasing. Intuitively, the standard doses of some drugs may not achieve effective serum concentrations. Pertinent data on anti-infective dosing in the obese patient is gradually emerging. Though some of the data needs further validation, the following table reflects what is currently known. **Obesity is defined as ≥20% over Ideal Body Weight (Ideal BW) or Body Mass Index (BMI) >30. Dose =** suggested body weight (BW) for dose calculation in obese patient, or specific dose if applicable. In general, the absence of a drug in the table indicates a lack of pertinent information in the published literature.

Drug	Dose	Comments
Acyclovir	Use **Adjusted BW** (see Comments) Example: for HSV encephalitis, give 10 mg/kg of Adjusted BW q8h	Unpublished data from 7 obese volunteers (Davis, et al., ICAAC abstract, 1991) suggested ideal BW, but newer and more convincing PK data suggest that adjusted BW better approximates drug exposure in normals (AAC 60:1830, 2016).
Aminoglycosides	Use **Adjusted BW** Example: Critically ill patient, Gent or Tobra (not Amikacin) 7 mg/kg of Adjusted BW IV q24h (See Comment)	Adjusted BW = Ideal BW + 0.4(Actual BW – Ideal BW). Ref: Pharmacother 27:1081, 2007 Follow levels so as to lower dose once hemodynamics stabilize.
Cefazolin (surgical prophylaxis)	No dose adjustment may be required: 2 gm x 1 dose (repeat in 3 hours?) See Comments	Conflicting data; unclear whether dose should be repeated, or if an even higher dose is required. Patients with BMI 40-80 studied. PK: 2-4 gm given to obese pts before c-section yielded inadequate conc in myometrium and subcutaneous adipose tissue despite adequate plasma conc. Refs: Surg 136:738, 2004; Eur J Clin Pharmacol 67:985, 2011; Surg Infect 13:33, 2012; Pharmacother 37:1415, 2017.
Cefepime	Modest dose increase: 2 gm IV q8h instead of the usual q12h	Data from 10 patients (mean BMI 48) undergoing bariatric surgery; regimen yields free T > MIC of 60% for MIC of 8 μg/mL. Ref: Obes Surg 22:465, 2012.
Cefoxitin	Larger dose possibly required but data insufficient for a firm recommendation; see comments	Single 40 mg/kg pre-op dose in obese pts (based on actual BW; range 4-7.5 gm) resulted in suboptimal achievement of pharmacodynamic targets in serum and tissue, although performance was better than a simulated 2 gm dose (AAC 60:5885, 2016).
Clindamycin	Possibly use **Actual BW** (see Comments)	Combined PK modeling data from three prospective trials in children suggests actual BW to be most appropriate; no clinical outcome data available (AAC 61:e02014, 2017).
Daptomycin	Use **Actual BW** Example: 4-12 mg/kg of Actual BW IV q24h	Data from a single-dose PK study in 7 obese volunteers. Ref: Antimicrob Ag Chemother 51:2741, 2007. New data suggest similar outcomes with ideal BW and actual BW (AAC 58:88, 2014).
Fluconazole	Larger dose possibly required but data insufficient for a firm recommendation; see comments	Case reports suggest larger dose required in critically ill obese pts. Recent paper suggests that wt-based dosing (12 mg/kg load then 6 mg/kg/day using total BW) reaches desired PK/PD targets more reliably than fixed dosing; clinical validation required (Pharmacother 17:1023, 1997; AAC 60:6550, 2016).
Flucytosine	Use **Ideal BW** Example: Crypto meningitis, give 25 mg/kg of Ideal BW po q6h	Date from one obese patient with cryptococcal disease. Ref: Pharmacother 15:251, 1995.

Drug	Dose	Comments
Levofloxacin	**No dose adjustment may be required** Example: 750 mg po/IV q24h *See comments*	Data from 13 obese patients; variability in study findings renders conclusion uncertain. Refs: *AAC 55:3240, 2011; JAC 66:1653, 2011*. A recent PK study (requiring clinical validation) in patients with BMI of 40 or more suggests that higher doses may be necessary to achieve adequate drug exposure *(Clin Pharmacokin 53:753, 2014).*
Linezolid	**No dose adjustment may be required** Example: 600 mg po/IV q12h *See Comments*	Data from 20 obese volunteers up to 150 kg body weight suggest standard doses provide AUC values similar to nonobese subjects. In a recent case report, standard dosing in a 265 kg male with MRSA pneumonia seemed to have reduced clinical effectiveness. Refs: *Antimicrob Ag Chemother 57:1144, 2013; Ann Pharmacother 47: e25, 2013.*
Oseltamivir	**No dose adjustment may be required** Example: 75 mg po q12h *See Comments*	Data from 10 obese volunteers, unclear if applicable to patients >250 kg (OK to give 150 mg po q12h). Ref: *J Antimicrob Chemother 66:2083, 2011*. Newer data consistent *(AAC 58:1616, 2014).*
Piperacillin-tazobactam	6.75 gm IV over 4 hours and dosed every 8 hours. No data for pt with impaired renal function	Data need confirmation. Based on 14 obese patients with actual BW >130 kg and BMI >40 kg/m². Ref: *Int J Antimicrob Ag 41:52, 2013*. High dose required to ensure adequate conc of both pip and tazo for pathogens with MIC ≤16 mcg/mL, and enhanced bleeding risk is a concern particularly in renal dysfunction.
Telavancin	If weight is 30% or more over ideal BW, dose using adjusted BW as for aminoglycosides.	The correct dosing weight to use for Telavancin is unclear. Actual BW may overdose and increase nephrotoxicity, ideal BW may underdose *(JAC 67:723, 2012; JAC 67:1300, 2012)*. Problematic because serum levels are not routinely available.
Vancomycin	Use **Actual BW** Example: in critically ill patient give 25-30 mg/kg of Actual BW IV load, then 15-20 mg/kg of Actual BW IV q8h-12h (infuse over 1.5-2 hr). No single dose over 2 gm. Check trough levels.	Data from 24 obese patients; Vancomycin half-life appears to decrease with little change in Vd. Ref: *Eur J Clin Pharmacol 54:621, 1998.*
Voriconazole po	**No dose adjustment required** (use **Ideal BW**) *See Comments* Example: 400 mg po q12h x2 doses then 200 mg po q12h. Check trough concentrations (underdosing common with Voriconazole).	Data from a 2-way crossover study of oral Voriconazole in 8 volunteers suggest no adjustment, but other data support use of adjusted BW. Best for now to use ideal BW and check serum concentrations *(AAC 55:2601, 2011; CID 53:745, 2011; CID 63:286, 2016).*

TABLE 17D – NO DOSING ADJUSTMENT REQUIRED IN OBESITY

The pharmacokinetics of antibacterials in obese patients is emerging, but only selected drugs have been evaluated. Those drugs where data justifies a dose adjustment in the obese are summarized in *Table 17C*. Those drugs where data indicates **NO NEED** for dose adjustment are listed below.

Drug	Drug
Ceftaroline	Imipenem/cilastatin
Ceftazidime/avibactam	Meropenem
Ceftolozane/tazobactam	Moxifloxacin
Dalbavancin	Oritavancin
Doripenem	Tedizolid
Ertapenem	Tigecycline

Ref: *Pharmacotherapy 37:1415, 2017*

TABLE 18 – ANTIMICROBIALS AND HEPATIC DISEASE: DOSAGE ADJUSTMENT*

The following alphabetical list indicates antibacterials excreted/metabolized by the liver **wherein a dosage adjustment may be indicated** in the presence of hepatic disease. Space precludes details; consult the PDR or package inserts for details. List is **not** all-inclusive:

Antibacterials		Antifungals	Antiparasitics	Antivirals⁶	
Ceftriaxone	Nafcillin	Caspofungin	Antimony, pentavalent	Abacavir	Indinavir
Chloramphenicol	Rifabutin	Itraconazole	Benznidazole	Atazanavir	Lopinavir/Ritonavir
Clindamycin	Rifampin	Voriconazole	Nifurtimox	Darunavir	Nelfinavir
Fusidic acid	Synercid**		Praziquantel	Delavirdine	Nevirapine
Isoniazid	Telithromycin**			Efavirenz	Ritonavir
Metronidazole	Tigecycline			Enfuvirtide	
	Tinidazole			Fosamprenavir	

⁶ Ref. on antiretrovirals: *CID 40:174, 2005* ** Quinupristin-Dalfopristin ** Telithro: reduce dose in renal & hepatic failure

TABLE 19 – TREATMENT OF CAPD PERITONITIS IN ADULTS
(Adapted from Guidelines – Int'l Soc Peritoneal Dialysis, *Periton Dialysis Intl 2016, 36:481*)

Principles: Empiric antibiotic therapy
- Initiate antibiotics asap after collection of peritoneal fluid & blood for culture
- Empiric regimens must be guided by local susceptibilities
  - Possible gram-positive infection: suggest either Cefazolin or Vanco
  - Possible gram-negative infection: suggest either Cefepime or aminoglycoside, e.g. Gentamicin
- No need to adjust intraperitoneal (IP) dose for residual renal function
- Can treat by IP route or systemic IV therapy, but Guidelines favor IP therapy

Intraperitoneal (IP) therapy
- Can be either continuous (drugs in each exchange) or intermittent (once daily)
- If intermittent, need antibiotic-containing dialysis fluid to dwell for minimum 6 hrs
- Vanco, aminoglycosides, cephalosporins can be combined in same dialysis bag; penicillins and aminoglycosides **cannot be combined**

Specific recommendations

IP Antibiotic Dosing Recommendations for Treatment of Peritonitis		
	Intermittent (1 exchange daily)	**Continuous** (all exchanges)
Aminoglycosides:		
Amikacin	2 mg/kg daily	LD 25 mg/L, MD 12 mg/L
Gentamicin	0.6 mg/kg daily	LD 8 mg/L, MD 4 mg/L
Tobramycin	0.6 mg/kg daily	LD 3 mg/kg, MD 0.3 mg/kg
Cephalosporins:		
Cefazolin	15-20 mg/kg daily	LD 500 mg/L, MD 125 mg/L
Cefepime	1000 mg daily	LD 250-500 mg/L, MD 100-125 mg/L
Ceftazidime	1000-1500 mg daily	LD 500 mg/L, MD 125 mg/L
Ceftriaxone	1000 mg daily	No data
Penicillins:		
Penicillin G	No data	LD 50,000 unit/L, MD 25,000 unit/L
Amoxicillin	No data	MD 150 mg/L
Ampicillin	No data	MD 125 mg/l
Amp/sulb	2 gm/1 gm q12h	LD 750-100 mg/L, MD 100 mg/L
Pip/tazo	No data	LD 4 gm/0.5 gm, MD 1 gm/0.125 gm
Others:		
Aztreonam	2 gm daily	LD 1000 mg/L, MD 250 mg/L
Ciprofloxacin	No data	MD 50 mg/L
Clindamycin	No data	MD 600 mg/bag
Daptomycin	No data	LD 100 mg/L, MD 20 mg/L
Imipenem	500 mg in alternate exch	LD 250 mg/L, MD 50 mg/L
Polymyxin B	No data	MD 300,000 unit (30 mg)/bag
Meropenem	1 gm daily	No data
Teicoplanin	15 mg/kg every 5 days	LD 400 mg/bag, MD 20 mg/bag
Vancomycin	15-30 mg/kg every 5-7 days	LD 30 mg/kg, MD 1.5 mg/kg/bag
Antifungals:		
Fluconazole	IP 200 mg q24-48 hrs	No data
Voriconazole	IP 2.5 mg/kg daily	No data

LD = loading dose in mg; MD = maintenance dose in mg; IP = intraperitoneal
Ref: *Periton Dialysis Intl 2016;36:481*

Systemic dosing recommendations for treatment of CAPD peritonitis
- In general, IP dosing leads to high IP drug levels and, hence, IP is preferable to IV antibiotic administration
- See individual systemic drugs for dose recommendations for patients with end stage renal disease (ESRD)
- Do not co-administer the same drug IP and systemically (either po or IV)

Indications for removal of CAPD catheter
- Relapse with same organism within one month
- No clinical response within 5 days (failure)
- Infection at catheter exit site and/or catheter subcutaneous tunnel
- Fungal peritonitis
- Fecal flora peritonitis; sign of bowel wall erosion & perforation

TABLE 20A – ANTI-TETANUS PROPHYLAXIS, WOUND CLASSIFICATION, IMMUNIZATION

WOUND CLASSIFICATION		
Clinical Features	Tetanus Prone	Non-Tetanus Prone
Age of wound	>6 hours	≤6 hours
Configuration	Stellate, avulsion	Linear
Depth	>1 cm	≤1 cm
Mechanism of injury	Missile, crush, burn, frostbite	Sharp surface (glass, knife)
Devitalized tissue	Present	Absent
Contaminants (dirt, saliva, etc.)	Present	Absent

IMMUNIZATION SCHEDULE				
History of Tetanus Immunization	Dirty, Tetanus-Prone Wound		Clean, non-Tetanus-Prone Wound	
	Td[1,2]	Tetanus Immune Globulin	Td[1,2]	Tetanus Immune Globulin
Unknown or <3 doses[3]	Yes	Yes	Yes	No
3 or more doses	No[4]	No	No[5]	No

Ref: MMWR 60:13, 2011; MMWR 61:468, 2012; MMWR 62:131, 2013 (pregnancy)

[1] Td = Tetanus & diphtheria toxoids, adsorbed (adult). For adult who has not received Tdap previously, substitute one dose of Tdap for Td when immunization is indicated (MMWR 61:468, 2012).
[2] For children <7 years, use DTaP unless contraindicated; for persons ≥7 years, Td is preferred to tetanus toxoid alone, but single dose of Tdap can be used if required for catch-up series.
[3] Individuals who have not completed vaccine series should do so.
[4] Yes, if >5 years since last booster.
[5] Yes, if >10 years since last booster.

All wounds should be cleaned immediately & thoroughly with soap & water.
This has been shown to protect 90% of experimental animals![1]

Exposure to animal saliva or nervous system tissue through a bite, scratch, or contamination of open wounds or mucous membranes (*www.cdc.gov/rabies/exposure/type.html*) or when such exposure cannot be reliably excluded (e.g., bat found in room of sleeping person).

Animal Type	Evaluation & Disposition of Animal	Recommendations for Prophylaxis
Dogs, cats, ferrets	Healthy & available for 10-day observation	Don't start unless animal develops sx, then immediately begin HRIG + vaccine
	Rabid or suspected rabid	Immediate HRIG + vaccine
	Unknown (escaped)	Consult public health officials
Skunks, raccoons, *bats, foxes, coyotes, most carnivores	Regard as rabid	Immediate prophylaxis unless brain of animal tests negative for rabies virus
Livestock, horses, rodents, rabbits; includes hares, squirrels, hamsters, guinea pigs, gerbils, chipmunks, rats, mice, woodchucks	Consider case-by-case	Consult public health officials. Bites of squirrels, hamsters, guinea pigs, gerbils, chipmunks, rats, mice, other small rodents, rabbits, and hares **almost never** require rabies post-exposure prophylaxis.

* Most recent cases of human rabies in U.S. due to contact (not bites) with silver-haired bats or rarely big brown bats but risk of acquiring rabies from non-contact bat exposure is exceedingly low (*CID 48:1493, 2009*). For more detail, see *CID 30:4, 2000; JAVMA 219:1687, 2001; CID 37:96, 2003 (travel medicine advisory); Ln 363:959, 2004; EID 11:1921, 2005; MMWR 55 (RR-5), 2006.*

Postexposure Rabies Immunization Schedule

IF NOT PREVIOUSLY VACCINATED

Treatment	Regimen[2]
Local wound cleaning	**All postexposure treatment should begin with immediate, thorough cleaning of all wounds with soap & water.** Then irrigate with a virucidal agent such as povidone-iodine solution if available.
Human rabies immune globulin (HRIG)	20 IU per kg body weight given once on day 0. If anatomically feasible, the full dose should be infiltrated around the wound(s), the rest should be administered IM in the gluteal area. If the calculated dose of HRIG is insufficient to inject all the wounds, it should be diluted with normal saline to allow infiltration around additional wound areas. HRIG should **not** be administered in the **same syringe, or** into the **same anatomical site** as vaccine, or more than 7 days after the initiation of vaccine. Because HRIG may partially suppress active production of antibody, no more than the recommended dose should be given.[3]
Vaccine	Human diploid cell vaccine (HDCV), rabies vaccine adsorbed (RVA), or purified chick embryo cell vaccine (PCECV) 1 mL **IM (deltoid area[4])**, one each days 0, 3, 7, 14[5].

IF PREVIOUSLY VACCINATED[6]

Treatment	Regimen[2]
Local wound cleaning	All postexposure treatment should begin with immediate, thorough cleaning of all wounds with soap & water. Then irrigate with a virucidal agent such as povidone-iodine solution if available.
HRIG	HRIG should **not** be administered
Vaccine	HDCV or PCEC, 1 mL **IM (deltoid area[4])**, one each on days 0 & 3

CORRECT VACCINE ADMINISTRATION SITES

Age Group	Administration Site
Children & adults	**DELTOID[4]** only (**NEVER** in gluteus)
Infants & young children	Outer aspect of thigh (anterolateral thigh) may be used (**NEVER** in gluteus)

[1] From *MMWR 48:RR-1, 1999; CID 30:4, 2000;* B. T. Matyas, Mass. Dept. of Public Health. *MMWR 57:1, 2008*
[2] These regimens are applicable for all age groups, including children.
[3] In most reported post-exposure treatment failures, only identified deficiency was failure to infiltrate wound(s) with HRIG (*CID 22:228, 1996*). However, several failures reported from SE Asia in patients in whom WHO protocol followed (*CID 28:143, 1999*).
[4] The **deltoid** area is the **only** acceptable site of vaccination for adults & older children. For infants & young children, outer aspect of the thigh (anterolateral thigh) may be used. Vaccine should **NEVER** be administered in gluteal area.
[5] Note that this is a change from previous recommendation of 5 doses (days 0, 3, 7, 14 & 28) based on new data & recommendations from ACIP. Note that the number of doses for persons with altered immunocompetence remains unchanged (5 doses on days 0, 3, 7, 14 & 28) and recommendations for pre-exposure prophylaxis remain 3 doses administered on days 0, 7 and 21 or 28 (*MMWR 59 (RR-2), 2010*).
[6] Any person with a history of pre-exposure vaccination with HDCV, RVA, PCECV; prior post-exposure prophylaxis with HDCV, PCEC or rabies vaccine adsorbed (RVA); or previous vaccination with any other type of rabies vaccine & a documented history of antibody response to the prior vaccination.

TABLE 21 - SELECTED DIRECTORY OF RESOURCES

ORGANIZATION	PHONE/FAX	WEBSITE(S)

ANTIPARASITIC DRUGS & PARASITOLOGY INFORMATION

CDC Drug Line	Weekdays: 404-639-3670	http://www.cdc.gov/ncidod/srp/drugs/drug-service.html
	Evenings, weekends, holidays: 404-639-2888	
DPDx: Lab ID of parasites		www.dpd.cdc.gov/dpdx/default.htm
Malaria	daytime: 770-488-7788	www.cdc.gov/malaria
	other: 770-488-7100	
	US toll free: 855-856-4713	
Expert Compound. Pharm.	800-247-9767/Fax: 818-787-7256	www.expertpharmacy.org
World Health Organization (WHO)		www.who.int
Parasites & Health		www.dpd.cdc.gov/dpdx/HTML/Para_Health.htm

BIOTERRORISM

Centers for Disease Control & Prevention	770-488-7100	www.bt.cdc.gov
Infectious Diseases Society of America	703-299-0200	www.idsociety.org
Johns Hopkins Center Civilian Biodefense		www.jhsph.edu
Center for Biosecurity of the Univ. of Pittsburgh Med. Center		www.upmc-biosecurity.org
US Army Medical Research Institute of Inf. Dis.		www.usamriid.army.mil

HEPATITIS B

Hepatitis B Foundation		www.hepb.org, www.natap

HEPATITIS C

CDC		www.cdc.gov/ncidod/diseases/hepatitis/C
Individual		http://hepatitis-central.com
		www.natap.org
HCV Guidelines		www.hcvguidelines.org

HIV

General		
HIV InSite		http://hivinsite.ucsf.edu
		www.natap.org
Drug Interactions		
Liverpool HIV Pharm. Group		www.hiv-druginteractions.org
Other		http://AIDS.medscape.com
Prophylaxis/Treatment of Opportunistic Infections; HIV Treatment		www.aidsinfo.nih.gov

IMMUNIZATIONS

CDC, Natl. Immunization Program	404-639-8200	www.cdc.gov/vaccines/
FDA, Vaccine Adverse Events	800-822-7967	www.fda.gov/cber/vaers/vaers.htm
National Network Immunization Info.	877-341-6644	www.immunizationinfo.org
Influenza vaccine, CDC	404-639-8200	www.cdc.gov/vaccines/
Institute for Vaccine Safety		www.vaccinesafety.edu
Immunization, "Ask the experts"		www.immunize.org/asktheexperts

OCCUPATIONAL EXPOSURE, BLOOD-BORNE PATHOGENS (HIV, HEPATITIS B & C)

Clinicians Consultation Center	888-448-4911	www.ucsf.edu/hivcntr
PEPline (exposed clinicians)		
WARMline (clinicians of HIV pts)		
Perinatal HIV Hotline	888-448-8765	www.ucsf.edu/hivcntr

Q-T$_c$ INTERVAL PROLONGATION BY DRUGS

		www.qtdrugs.org; www.crediblemeds.org

TRAVELERS' INFO: Immunizations, Malaria Prophylaxis, More

Amer. Soc. Trop. Med. & Hyg.		www.astmh.org
CDC, general	877-394-8747	http://www.cdc.gov/travel/default.asp
CDC, Malaria:		www.cdc.gov/malaria
Prophylaxis		http://www.cdc.gov/travel/default.asp
Medical Considerations Before Int'l Travel		N Engl J Med 2016;375:247
Pan American Health Organization		www.paho.org
World Health Organization (WHO)		www.who.int/home-page

Importance: ± = theory/anecdotal; + = of probable importance; ++ = of definite importance

This table is intended as a starting point for interactions with anti-infective drugs. *See also, Hansten & Horn, Top 100 Drug Interactions* and many websites, including *http://www.drugs.com/drug_interactions.html; http://www.healthline.com/druginteractions; www.medscape.com*

ANTI-INFECTIVE AGENT (A)	OTHER DRUG (B)	EFFECT	IMPORT
Abacavir	Methadone	↓ levels of B	++
Amantadine (Symmetrel)	Alcohol	↑ CNS effects	+
	Anticholinergic and anti-Parkinson agents (ex. Artane, scopolamine)	↑ effect of B: dry mouth, ataxia, blurred vision, slurred speech, toxic psychosis	+
	Trimethoprim	↑ levels of A & B	+
	Digoxin	↑ levels of B	±
Aminoglycosides–parenteral (Amikacin, Gentamicin, Kanamycin, Netilmicin, Sisomicin, Streptomycin, Tobramycin)	Amphotericin B	↑ nephrotoxicity	++
	Cis platinum (Platinol)	↑ nephro & ototoxicity	+
	Cyclosporine	↑ nephrotoxicity	+
	Neuromuscular blocking agents	↑ apnea or respiratory paralysis	+
	Loop diuretics (e.g., furosemide)	↑ ototoxicity	++
	NSAIDs	↑ nephrotoxicity	+
	Non-polarizing muscle relaxants	↑ apnea	+
	Radiographic contrast	↑ nephrotoxicity	+
	Vancomycin	↑ nephrotoxicity	+
Aminoglycosides–oral (kanamycin, neomycin)	Warfarin	↑ prothrombin time	+
Amphotericin B and Ampho B lipid formulations	Antineoplastic drugs	↑ nephrotoxicity risk	+
	Digitalis	↑ toxicity of B if K⁺ ↓	+
	Nephrotoxic drugs: aminoglycosides, Cidofovir, Cyclosporine, Foscarnet, Pentamidine	↑ nephrotoxicity of A	++
Ampicillin, amoxicillin	Allopurinol	↑ frequency of rash	++
Artemether-Lumefantrine	CYP3A inhibitors: Amiodarone, Atazanavir, Itraconazole, Ritonavir, Voriconazole	↑ levels of A; QTc interval	++
	CYP2D6 substrates: Flecainide, Imipramine, Amitriptyline	↑ levels of B; QTc interval	++
Atazanavir	*See protease inhibitors and Table 22B*		
Atovaquone	Rifampin (perhaps Rifabutin)	↓ serum levels of A; ↑ levels of B	+
	Metoclopramide	↓ levels of A	+
	Tetracycline	↓ levels of A	++

Azole Antifungal Agents [Flu = Fluconazole; Itr = Itraconazole; Ket = Ketoconazole; Posa = posaconazole Vor = Voriconazole; Isa = Isavuconazole + = occurs; **blank space** = either studied & no interaction OR no data found (may be in pharm. co. databases)]

Flu	Itr	Ket	Posa	Vor	Isa			
+	+					Amitriptyline	↑ levels of B	+
					+	Bupropion	↓ levels of B	++
+	+	+		+		Calcium channel blockers	↑ levels of B	++
	+			+		Carbamazepine (Vori contra-indicated)	↓ levels of A	++
+	+	+	+	+	+	Cyclosporine	↑ levels of B, ↑ risk of nephrotoxicity	+
	+	+				Didanosine	↓ absorption of A	+
					+	Digoxin	↑ levels of B	++
	+	+	+	+		Efavirenz	↓ levels of A, ↑ levels of B	++ (avoid)
	+	+	+			H₂ blockers, antacids, sucralfate	↓ absorption of A	+
+	+	+	+	+		Hydantoins (phenytoin, Dilantin)	↑ levels of B, ↓ levels of A	++
	+	+				Isoniazid	↓ levels of A	+
				+		Letermovir	↓ levels of A	+
+	+	+	+	+	+	Lovastatin/simvastatin, atorvastatin	Rhabdomyolysis reported; ↑ levels of B	++
				+		Methadone	↑ levels of B	+
					+	Mycophenolate	↑ levels of B	++
+	+	+	+	+		Midazolam/triazolam, po	↑ levels of B	++
+	+			+		Warfarin	↑ effect of B	++
+	+					Oral hypoglycemics	↑ levels of B	++
		+	+			Pimozide	↑ levels of B–**avoid**	++
	+	+		+	+	Protease inhibitors, e.g., LPV	↑ levels of B	++
+	+	+	+			Proton pump inhibitors	↓ levels of A, ↑ levels of B	++
+	+	+	+	+	+	Rifampin/Rifabutin (Vori contra-indicated)	↑ levels of B, ↓ serum levels of A	++
	+					Rituximab	Inhibits action of B	++
			+	+	+	Sirolimus (Vori and Posa contraindicated)	↑ levels of B	++
+		+	+	+	+	Tacrolimus	↑ levels of B with toxicity	++
+		+				Theophyllines	↑ levels of B	+
		+				Trazodone	↑ levels of B	++
+						Zidovudine	↑ levels of B	+

ANTI-INFECTIVE AGENT (A)	OTHER DRUG (B)	EFFECT	IMPORT
Bedaquiline	Rifampin	↓ levels of A	++
	Ketoconazole	↑ levels of A	
Caspofungin	Cyclosporine	↑ levels of A	++
	Tacrolimus	↓ levels of B	++
	Carbamazepine, Dexamethasone, EFZ, Nevirapine, Phenytoin, Rifamycin	↓ levels of A; ↑ dose of caspofungin to 70 mg/d	++
Chloramphenicol	Hydantoins	↑ toxicity of B, nystagmus, ataxia	++
	Iron salts, Vitamin B12	↓ response to B	++
	Protease inhibitors–HIV	↑ levels of A & B	++
Clindamycin (Cleocin)	Kaolin	↓ absorption of A	++
	Muscle relaxants, e.g., Atracurium, Baclofen, Diazepam	↑ frequency/duration of respiratory paralysis	++
	St John's wort	↓ levels of A	++
Cobicistat	See Integrase Strand Transfer Inhibitors		
Cycloserine	Ethanol	↑ frequency of seizures	+
	INH, ethionamide	↑ frequency of drowsiness/dizziness	+
Dapsone	Atazanavir	↑ levels of A - Avoid	++
	Didanosine	↓ absorption of A	+
	Oral contraceptives	↓ effectiveness of B	+
	Pyrimethamine	↑ in marrow toxicity	+
	Rifampin/Rifabutin	↓ serum levels of A	+
	Trimethoprim	↑ levels of A & B (methemoglobinemia)	+
	Zidovudine	May ↑ marrow toxicity	+
Daptomycin	HMG-CoA inhibitors (statins)	Consider DC statin while on dapto	++
Delavirdine (Rescriptor)	See Non-nucleoside reverse transcriptase inhibitors (NNRTIs) and Table 22B		
Didanosine (ddI) (Videx)	Allopurinol	↑ levels of A–avoid	++
	Cisplatin, Dapsone, INH, Metro, NF, Stavudine, Vincristine, Zalcitabine	↑ risk of peripheral neuropathy	+
	Ethanol, Lamivudine, Pentamidine	↑ risk of pancreatitis	+
	Fluoroquinolones	↓ absorption 2° to chelation	+
	Drugs that need low pH for absorption: Dapsone, Indinavir, Itra/ Ketoconazole, Pyrimethamine, Rifampin, Trimethoprim	↓ absorption	+
	Methadone	↓ levels of A	++
	Ribavirin	↑ levels ddI metabolite–avoid	++
	Tenofovir	↑ levels of A (reduce dose of A)	++
Dolutegravir	See Integrase Strand Transfer Inhibitors		
Doripenem	Probenecid	↑ levels of A	++
	Valproic acid	↓ levels of B	++
Doxycycline	Aluminum, bismuth, iron, Mg**	↓ absorption of A	+
	Barbiturates, hydantoins	↓ serum t/2 of A	+
	Carbamazepine (Tegretol)	↓ serum t/2 of A	+
	Digoxin	↑ serum levels of B	+
	Warfarin	↑ activity of B	++
Efavirenz (Sustiva)	See non-nucleoside reverse transcriptase inhibitors (NNRTIs) and Table 22B		
Elvitegravir	See Integrase Strand Transfer Inhibitors		
Ertapenem (Invanz)	Probenecid	↑ levels of A	++
	Valproic acid	↓ levels of B	++
Ethambutol (Myambutol)	Aluminum salts (includes didanosine buffer)	↓ levels of A & B	+
Etravirine	See non-nucleoside reverse transcriptase inhibitors (NNRTIs) and Table 22B		

Fluoroquinolones (**CIP** = Ciprofloxacin; **Gati** = Gatifloxacin; **Gemi** = Gemifloxacin; **Levo** = Levofloxacin; **Moxi** = Moxifloxacin; **Oflox** = Ofloxacin)

NOTE: Blank space = *either studied and no interaction OR no data found*

CIP	Dela	Gati	Gemi	Levo	Moxi	Oflox			
		+		+	+	+	Antiarrhythmics (procainamide, amiodarone)	↑ Q-T interval (torsade)	++
+		+		+	+	+	Insulin, oral hypoglycemics	↑ & ↓ blood sugar	++
+							Caffeine	↑ levels of B	
+							Cimetidine	↑ levels of A	+
+						+	Cyclosporine	↑ levels of A	±
+	+	+		+	+	+	Didanosine	↓ absorption of A	++
+	+	+	+	+	+	+	Cations: Al+++, Ca++, Fe++, Mg++, Zn++ (antacids, vitamins, dairy products), citrate/citric acid	↓ absorption of A (some variability between drugs)	++
+							Methadone	↑ levels of B	++
+				+		+	NSAIDs	↑ risk CNS stimulation/seizures	++
+							Phenytoin	↑ or ↓ levels of B	+

ANTI-INFECTIVE AGENT (A)							OTHER DRUG (B)	EFFECT	IMPORT
Fluoroquinolones *(continued)*									
CIP	Dela	Gati	Gemi	Levo	Moxi	Oflox	NOTE: Blank space = either studied and no interaction OR no data found		
+		+	+			+	Probenecid	↓ renal clearance of A	+
+							Rasagiline	↑ levels of B	++
					+		Rifampin	↓ levels of A *(CID 45:1001, 2007)*	++
+		+	+	+		+	Sucralfate	↓ absorption of A	++
+							Theophylline	↑ levels of B	++
+							Thyroid hormone	↓ levels of B	++
+							Tizanidine	↑ levels of B	++
+			+	+	+	+	Warfarin	↑ prothrombin time	+
Ganciclovir (Cytovene) &							Imipenem	↑ risk of seizures reported	+
Valganciclovir (Valcyte)							Probenecid	↑ levels of A	+
							Zidovudine	↓ levels of A, ↑ levels of B	+
Gentamicin							*See Aminoglycosides-parenteral*		
Imipenem & Meropenem							BCG	↓ effectiveness of B-avoid combination	++
							Divalproex	↓ levels of B	++
							Ganciclovir	↑ seizure risk	++
							Probenecid	↑ levels of A	++
							Valproic acid	↓ levels of B	++
Indinavir							*See protease inhibitors and Table 22B*		

Integrase Strand Transfer Inhibitors (INSTI): Dolutegravir (**DTG**), Raltegravir (**RAL**), Elvitegravir (**ELV**)

DTG	RAL	Stribild (ELV)	NOTE: interactions involving Stribild (Elvitegravir + Cobicistat + Emtricitabine + Tenofovir) reflect one or more of its components (the specifics may not be known).		
x	x	x	Antacids (polyvalent cations)	↓ levels of A-space dosing	++
		x	Antiarrhythmics, digoxin	↑ levels of B-monitor	+
	x		Atazanavir/RTV	↑ levels of A-monitor	±
		x	Atorvastatin	↑ levels of B-monitor	+
		x	Benzodiazepines	↑ levels of B-monitor	+
		x	Beta-blockers	↑ levels of B-monitor	+
		x	Bosentan	↑ levels of B-adjust dose or avoid	++
		x	Buprenorphine	↑ levels of B-monitor	+
		x	Buspirone	↑ levels of B-monitor	+
		x	Calcium channel blockers	↑ levels of B-monitor	+
x			Carbamazepine	↓ levels of A-avoid	++
		x		↓ levels of A, ↑ levels of B-avoid	++
		x	Clarithromycin	↑ levels of A and B-monitor	+
		x	Clonazepam	↑ levels of B-monitor	+
		x	Colchicine	↑ levels of B-adjust dose	+
		x	Cyclosporine	↑ levels of B-monitor	+
		x	Dexamethasone	↓ levels of A-avoid	++
x			Dofetilide	↑ levels of B-avoid	++
x			Efavirenz	↓ levels of A-adjust dose	++
	x			↓ levels of A-monitor	+
		x	Ethosuximide	↑ levels of B-monitor	+
x			Etravirine	↓ levels of A-avoid	++
	x			↓ levels of A-monitor	+
		x	Fluticasone	↑ levels of B-avoid	++
x			Fosamprenavir/RTV	↓ levels of A-adjust dose or avoid	++
x		x	Fosphenytoin/phenytoin	↓ levels of A-avoid	++
		x	Fluconazole	↑ levels of A-monitor	++
		x	Itraconazole	↑ levels of A and B-adjust dose or avoid	++
		x	Ketoconazole	↑ levels of A and B-adjust dose or avoid	++
x			Metformin	↑ levels of B-monitor	++
x			Nevirapine	↓ levels of A-avoid	++
	x		Omeprazole	↑ levels of A-monitor	±
		x	Oral contraceptives	↑ or ↓ levels of B-avoid	++
x		x	Oxcarbazepine	↓ levels of A-avoid	++
x		x	Phenobarbital	↓ levels of A-avoid	++
		x	Phenothiazines	↑ levels of B-monitor	+

ANTI-INFECTIVE AGENT (A)	OTHER DRUG (B)	EFFECT	IMPORT

Integrase Strand Transfer Inhibitors (INSTI) *(continued)*

DTG	RAL	Stribild (ELV)			
			NOTE: Interactions involving Stribild (Elvitegravir + Cobicistat + Emtricitabine + Tenofovir) reflect one or more of its components (the specifics may not be known).		
		x	Phosphodiesterase-5 inhibitors	↑ levels of B-adjust dose or avoid	++
x		x	Primidone	↓ levels of A-avoid	++
x	x	x	Rifampin, rifabutin, rifapentine	↓ levels of A-adjust dose or avoid	++
		x	Risperidone	↑ levels of B-monitor	+
		x	Salmeterol	↑ levels of B-avoid	++
		x	Sirolimus	↑ levels of B-monitor	+
x		x	St. John's wort	↓ levels of A-avoid	++
		x	SSRIs	↑ levels of B-monitor	+
x	x	x	Sucralfate	↓ levels of A-space dosing	++
		x	Tacrolimus	↑ levels of B-monitor	++
x			Tipranavir/RTV	↓ levels of A-adjust dose or avoid	++
	x			↓ levels of A-monitor	±
		x	Trazodone	↑ levels of B-monitor	+
		x	Tricyclic antidepressants	↑ levels of B-monitor	+
		x	Voriconazole	↑ levels of A and B-adjust dose or avoid	++
		x	Warfarin	↑ or ↓ levels of B-monitor	+
		x	Zolpidem ("Z" drugs)	↑ levels of B-monitor	+
Isoniazid			Alcohol, rifampin	↑ risk of hepatic injury	++
			Aluminum salts	↓ absorption (take fasting)	++
			Carbamazepine, phenytoin	↑ levels of B with nausea, vomiting, nystagmus, ataxia	++
			Itraconazole, ketoconazole	↓ levels of B	+
			Oral hypoglycemics	↓ effects of B	+
Lamivudine			Zalcitabine	Mutual interference–do not combine	++
Linezolid (Zyvox)			Adrenergic agents	Risk of hypertension	++
			Aged, fermented, pickled or smoked foods –↑ tyramine	Risk of hypertension	+
			Clarithromycin	↑ levels of A	++
			Meperidine	Risk of serotonin syndrome	++
			Rasagiline (MAO inhibitor)	Risk of serotonin syndrome	+
			Rifampin	↓ levels of A	++
			Serotonergic drugs (SSRIs)	Risk of serotonin syndrome	++
Letermovir			Atorvastatin	↑ conc of B	+
			Cyclosporine	↑ conc of both	+
			Ergot alkaloids	↑ conc of B	++ (Avoid)
			Pimozide	↑ conc of B	++ (Avoid)
			Pitavastatin	↑ conc of B	++ ↓ Avoid w/cyclo-sporine)
			Sirolimus	↑ conc of B	+
			Simvastatin	↑ conc of B	++ (Avoid w/cyclo-sporine)
			Tacrolimus	↑ conc of B	+
			Voriconazole	↓ conc of B	+
Lopinavir			*See protease inhibitors*		

Macrolides [Ery = Erythromycin; Azi = Azithromycin; Clr = Clarithromycin; + = occurs; blank space = either studied and no interaction OR no data]

Ery	Azi	Clr			
	+		Calcium channel blockers	↑ serum levels of B	++
+		+	Carbamazepine	↑ serum levels of B, nystagmus, nausea, vomiting, ataxia	++ (avoid w/erythro)
+		+	Cimetidine, Ritonavir	↑ levels of B	+
+			Clozapine	↑ serum levels of B, CNS toxicity	+
		+	Colchicine	↑ levels of B (potent, fatal)	++ (avoid)
+			Corticosteroids	↑ effects of B	+
+	+	+	Cyclosporine	↑ serum levels of B with toxicity	+
+	+	+	Digoxin, Digitoxin	↑ serum levels of B (10% of cases)	+
		+	Efavirenz	↓ levels of A	++
+		+	Ergot alkaloids	↑ levels of B	++
		+	Linezolid	↑ levels of B	++
−		+	Lovastatin/Simvastatin	↑ levels of B; rhabdomyolysis	++
+			Midazolam, Triazolam	↑ levels of B, ↑ sedative effects	+

ANTI-INFECTIVE AGENT (A)			OTHER DRUG (B)	EFFECT	IMPORT
Macrolides (continued)					

Ery	Azi	Clr			
+		+	Phenytoin	↑ levels of B	+
+	+	+	Pimozide	↑ Q-T interval	++
+		+	Rifampin, Rifabutin	↓ levels of A	+
+		+	Tacrolimus	↑ levels of B	++
+		+	Theophylline	↑ serum levels of B with nausea, vomiting, seizures, apnea	++
+		+	Valproic acid	↑ levels of B	+
+		+	Warfarin	May ↑ prothrombin time	+
		+	Zidovudine	↓ levels of B	+

ANTI-INFECTIVE AGENT (A)	OTHER DRUG (B)	EFFECT	IMPORT
Maraviroc	Clarithromycin	↑ serum levels of A	++
	Delavirdine	↑ levels of A	++
	Itraconazole/Ketoconazole	↑ levels of A	++
	Nefazodone	↑ levels of A	++
	Protease inhibitors (not Tipranavir/Ritonavir)	↑ levels of A	++
	Anticonvulsants: Carbamazepine, Phenobarbital, Phenytoin	↓ levels of A	++
	Efavirenz	↓ levels of A	++
	Rifampin	↓ levels of A	++
Mefloquine	ß-adrenergic blockers, calcium channel blockers, quinidine, quinine	↑ arrhythmias	+
	Divalproex, valproic acid	↓ level of B with seizures	++
	Halofantrine	Q-T prolongation	++ (avoid)
	Calcineurin inhibitors	Q-T prolongation (avoid)	++
Meropenem	See Imipenem		
Meropenem-vaborbactam	Valproic acid	↓ concentration of B	(avoid)
	Probenecid	↑ concentration of A	+
Methenamine mandelate or hippurate	Acetazolamide, sodium bicarbonate, thiazide diuretics	↓ antibacterial effect 2° to ↑ urine pH	++
Metronidazole/Tinidazole	Alcohol	Disulfiram-like reaction	+
	Cyclosporin	↑ levels of B	++
	Disulfiram (Antabuse)	Acute toxic psychosis	+
	Lithium	↑ levels of B	++
	Warfarin	↑ anticoagulant effect	++
	Phenobarbital, hydantoins	↑ levels of B	++
Micafungin	Nifedipine	↑ levels of B	+
	Sirolimus	↑ levels of B	+
Nafcillin	Warfarin	↓ Warfarin effect	++
Nelfinavir	See protease inhibitors and Table 22B		
Nevirapine (Viramune)	See non-nucleoside reverse transcriptase inhibitors (NNRTIs) and Table 22B		
Nitrofurantoin	Antacids	↓ absorption of A	+

Non-nucleoside reverse transcriptase inhibitors (NNRTIs): For interactions with protease inhibitors, *see Table 22B.*
Del = Delavirdine; **Efa** = Efavirenz; **Etr** = Etravirine; **Nev** = Nevirapine

Del	Efa	Etr	Nev	Co-administration contraindicated *(See package insert):*		
+		+		Anticonvulsants: Carbamazepine, Phenobarbital, Phenytoin		++
+	+			Antimycobacterials: Rifabutin, Rifampin		++
+		+		Antipsychotics: Pimozide		++
+	+	+		Benzodiazepines: Alprazolam, Midazolam, Triazolam		++
+	+			Ergotamine		++
+	+	+		HMG-CoA inhibitors (statins): Lovastatin, Simvastatin, Atorvastatin, Pravastatin		++
+		+		St. John's wort		++
				Dose change needed:		
+				Amphetamines	↑ levels of B–**caution**	++
+		+	+	Antiarrhythmics: Amiodarone, Lidocaine, others	↓ or ↑ levels of B–**caution**	++
+	+	+	+	Anticonvulsants: Carbamazepine, Phenobarbital, Phenytoin	↓ levels of A and/or B	++
+	+	+	+	Antifungals: Itraconazole, Ketoconazole, Voriconazole, Posaconazole	Potential ↓ levels of B, ↑ levels of A	++ (avoid)
+			+	Antirejection drugs: Cyclosporine, Rapamycin, Sirolimus, Tacrolimus	↑ levels of B	++
			+	Calcium channel blockers	↑ levels of B	++
+	+	+	+	Clarithromycin	↑ levels of B metabolite, ↑ levels of A	++
+	+	+		Cyclosporine	↑ levels of B	++
+		+		Dexamethasone	↓ levels of A	++
+	+	+	+	Sildenafil, Vardenafil, Tadalafil	↑ levels of B	++
+			+	Fentanyl, Methadone	↑ levels of B	++
+				Gastric acid suppression: antacids, H-2 blockers, proton pump inhibitors	↓ levels of A	++

ANTI-INFECTIVE AGENT (A)				OTHER DRUG (B)	EFFECT	IMPORT
Non-nucleoside reverse transcriptase inhibitors (NNRTIs) *(continued)*						
Del	**Efa**	**Etr**	**Nev**	Co-administration contraindicated *(See package insert):*		
+				Gastric acid suppression: antacids, H-2 blockers, proton pump inhibitors	↓ levels of A	++
	+		+	Mefloquine	↓ levels of B	++
	+	+	+	Methadone, Fentanyl	↓ levels of B	++
	+		+	Oral contraceptives	↑ or ↓ levels of B	++
+	+	+	+	Protease inhibitors–see Table 22B		
+	+	+	+	**Rifabutin, rifampin**	↑ or ↓ levels of rifabutin; ↓ levels of A–caution	++
	+	+	+	St. John's wort	↓ levels of B	
+		+		Warfarin	↑ levels of B	++
Oritavancin				Warfarin	↑ levels of B	++
Pentamidine, IV				Amphotericin B	↑ risk of nephrotoxicity	+
				Pancreatitis-assoc drugs, eg, alcohol, valproic acid	↑ risk of pancreatitis	+
PIP-TZ				Methotrexate	↑ levels of B	++
Polymyxin B				Curare paralytics	Avoid: neuromuscular blockade	++
Polymyxin E (Colistin)				Curare paralytics	Avoid: neuromuscular blockade	++
				Aminoglycosides, Ampho B, Vanco	↑ nephrotoxicity risk	++
Primaquine				Chloroquine, Dapsone, INH, Probenecid, Quinine, sulfonamides, TMP/SMX, others	↑ risk of hemolysis in G6PD-deficient patients	++

Protease Inhibitors–Anti-HIV Drugs. *(Atazan = Atazanavir; Darun = Darunavir; Fosampren = Fosamprenavir; Indin = Indinavir; Lopin = Lopinavir; Nelfin = Nelfinavir; Saquin = Saquinavir; Tipran = Tipranavir).* For interactions with antiretrovirals, *see Table 22B.* Only a partial list–check package insert

Also see *http://aidsinfo.nih.gov*
To check for interactions between more than 2 drugs, *see:*
http://www.drugs.com/drug_interactions.html and
http://www.healthline.com/druginteractions

Atazan	Darun	Fosampren	Indin	Lopin	Nelfin	Saquin	Tipran		EFFECT	IMPORT
								Analgesics:		
							+	1. Alfentanil, Fentanyl, Hydrocodone, Tramadol	↑ levels of B	+
	+			+		+	+	2. Codeine, Hydromorphone, Morphine, Methadone	↓ levels of B *(JAIDS 41:563, 2006)*	+
+	+	+	+	+	+		+	**Anti-arrhythmics: Amiodarone, Lidocaine, Mexiletine, Flecainide**	↑ levels of B; do not co-administer or use caution *(See package insert)*	++
	+		+	+	+	+		**Anticonvulsants: Carbamazepine, Clonazepam, Phenobarbital**	↓ levels of A, ↑ levels of B	++
+		+					+	Antidepressants, all tricyclic	↑ levels of B	++
+	+						+	Antidepressants, all other	↑ levels of B; do not use pimozide	++
+								Antidepressants: SSRIs	↓ levels of B–avoid	++
							+	Antihistamines	Do not use	++
+	+	+					+	Benzodiazepines, e.g., Diazepam, Midazolam, Triazolam	↑ levels of B–do not use	++
+		+		+				Boceprevir	↓ levels of A & B	++
+	+	+	+	+	+	+	+	Calcium channel blockers (all)	↑ levels of B	++
+	+				+	+	+	Clarith, Erythro	↑ levels of B if renal impairment	+
+	+				+	+	+	Contraceptives, oral	↓ levels of A & B	++
	+	+				+		Corticosteroids: prednisone, dexamethasone	↓ levels of A, ↑ levels of B	+
+	+	+	+	+	+	+	+	Cyclosporine	↑ levels of B, monitor levels	+
							+	Digoxin	↑ levels of B	++
+	+	+	+	+	+	+	+	Ergot derivatives	↑ levels of B–do not use	++
		+	+			+	+	Erythromycin, Clarithromycin	↑ levels of A & B	+
			+	+		+		Grapefruit juice (>200 mL/day)	↓ indinavir & ↑ saquinavir levels	++
+	+	+	+	+	+	+	+	H2 receptor antagonists	↓ levels of A	++
+	+	+	+	+	+	+	+	HMG-CoA reductase inhibitors (statins): Lovastatin, Simvastatin	↑ levels of B–do not use	++
+								Irinotecan	↑ levels of B–do not use	++
	+	+	+	+	+	+	+	Ketoconazole, Itraconazole, ? Vori.	↑ levels of A, ↑ levels of B	+
+	+	+	+	+	+	+	+	Posaconazole	↑ levels of A, no effect on B	++
						+		Metronidazole	Poss. disulfiram reaction, alcohol	+
						+		Phenytoin *(JAIDS 36:1034, 2004)*	↑ levels of A & B	++
+	+	+	+	+	+	+	+	Pimozide	↑ levels of B–do not use	++
+	+	+	+	+	+	+	+	Proton pump inhibitors	↓ levels of A	++
+	+	+	+	+	+	+	+	Rifampin, Rifabutin	↓ levels of A, ↑ levels of B **(avoid)**	++
+	+	+	+	+	+	+	+	Sildenafil (Viagra), Tadalafil, Vardenafil	Varies, some ↑ & some ↓ levels of B	++

ANTI-INFECTIVE AGENT (A)								OTHER DRUG (B)	EFFECT	IMPORT
Atazan	Darun	Fosampren	Indin	Lopin	Nelfin	Saquin	Tipran	Also see http://aidsinfo.nih.gov To check for interactions between more than 2 drugs, see: http://www.drugs.com/drug_interactions.html and http://www.healthline.com/druginteractions		

Protease Inhibitors *(continued)*

Atazan	Darun	Fosampren	Indin	Lopin	Nelfin	Saquin	Tipran	OTHER DRUG (B)	EFFECT	IMPORT
+	+	+	+	+	+	+	+	St. John's wort	↓ levels of A–do not use	++
+	+	+	+	+	+	+	+	Sirolimus, Tracrolimus	↑ levels of B	++
+								Tenofovir	↓ levels of A–add ritonavir	++
	+		+	+				Theophylline	↓ levels of B	+
+		+		+			+	Warfarin	↑ levels of B	+
								INH, rifampin	May ↑ risk of hepatotoxicity	±
Pyrimethamine								Lorazepam	↑ risk of hepatotoxicity	+
								Sulfonamides, TMP/SMX	↑ risk of marrow suppression	+
								Zidovudine	↑ risk of marrow suppression	+
Quinine								Digoxin	↑ digoxin levels; ↑ toxicity	++
								Mefloquine	↑ arrhythmias	+
								Warfarin	↑ prothrombin time	++
Quinupristin-Dalfopristin (Synercid)								Anti-HIV drugs: NNRTIs & PIs	↑ levels of B	++
								Antineoplastic: Vincristine, Docetaxel, Paclitaxel	↑ levels of B	++
								Calcium channel blockers	↑ levels of B	++
								Carbamazepine	↑ levels of B	++
								Cyclosporine, Tacrolimus	↑ levels of B	++
								Lidocaine	↑ levels of B	++
								Methylprednisolone	↑ levels of B	++
								Midazolam, Diazepam	↑ levels of B	++
								Statins	↑ levels of B	++
Raltegravir								*See Integrase Strand Transfer Inhibitors*		
Ribavirin								Didanosine	↑ levels of B → toxicity–avoid	++
								Stavudine	↓ levels of B	++
								Zidovudine	↓ levels of B	++
Rifamycins (Rifampin, Rifabutin) Ref.: *AnIM 162:985, 2002* The following is a partial list of drugs with rifampin-induced ↑ metabolism and hence lower than anticipated serum levels: ACE inhibitors, Dapsone, Diazepam, Digoxin, Diltiazem, Doxycycline, Fluconazole, Fluvastatin, Haloperidol, Moxifloxacin, Nifedipine, Progestins, Triazolam, Tricyclics, Voriconazole, Zidovudine *(Clin Pharmacokinetic 42:819, 2003).*								Al OH, Ketoconazole, PZA	↓ levels of A	+
								Atovaquone	↑ levels of A, ↓ levels of B	+
								Beta adrenergic blockers (metoprolol, propranolol)	↓ effect of B	+
								Caspofungin	↓ levels of B–increase dose	++
								Clarithromycin	↑ levels of A, ↓ levels of B	++
								Corticosteroids	↑ replacement requirement of B	++
								Cyclosporine	↓ effect of B	++
								Delavirdine	↑ levels of A, ↓ levels of B–avoid	++
								Digoxin	↓ levels of B	++
								Disopyramide	↓ levels of B	+
								Fluconazole	↑ levels of A	+
								Amprenavir, Indinavir, Nelfinavir, Ritonavir	↑ levels of A (↓ dose of A), ↓ levels of B	++
								INH	Converts INH to toxic hydrazine	++
								Itraconazole, Ketoconazole	↓ levels of B, ↑ levels of A	++
								Linezolid	↓ levels of B	++
								Methadone	↓ serum levels (withdrawal)	+
								Nevirapine	↓ levels of B–avoid	++
								Warfarin	Suboptimal anticoagulation	++
								Oral contraceptives	↓ effectiveness; spotting, pregnancy	+
								Phenytoin	↓ levels of B	+
								Protease inhibitors	↓ levels of A, ↑ levels of B–CAUTION	++
								Quinidine	↓ effect of B	+
								Raltegravir	↓ levels of B	++
								Sulfonylureas	↓ hypoglycemic effect	+
								Tacrolimus	↓ levels of B	++
								Theophylline	↑ levels of B	+
								TMP/SMX	↓ levels of A	+
								Tocainide	↓ effect of B	+
Rimantadine								*See Amantadine*		
Ritonavir								*See protease inhibitors and Table 22B*		
Saquinavir								*See protease inhibitors and Table 22B*		
Stavudine								Ribavirin	↓ levels of A–avoid	++
								Zidovudine	Mutual interference–do not combine	++

TABLE 22A (8)

ANTI-INFECTIVE AGENT (A)	OTHER DRUG (B)	EFFECT	IMPORT
Strand Transfer Integrase Inhibitors (INSTI)	*See Integrase Strand Transfer Inhibitors*		
Sulfonamides	Beta blockers	↑ levels of B	++
	Cyclosporine	↓ cyclosporine levels	+
	Methotrexate	↑ antifolate activity	+
	Warfarin	↑ prothrombin time; bleeding	+
	Phenobarbital, rifampin	↓ levels of A	+
	Phenytoin	↑ levels of B; nystagmus, ataxia	+
	Sulfonylureas	↑ hypoglycemic effect	+
Telithromycin (Ketek)	Carbamazine	↓ levels of A	++
	Digoxin	↑ levels of B–do digoxin levels	++
	Ergot alkaloids	**↑ levels of B–avoid**	++
	Itraconazole; ketoconazole	↑ levels of A; no dose change	+
	Metoprolol	↑ levels of B	++
	Midazolam	↑ levels of B	++
	Warfarin	↑ prothrombin time	+
	Phenobarbital, phenytoin	↓ levels of A	++
	Pimozide	**↑ levels of B; QT prolongation–avoid**	++
	Rifampin	**↓ levels of A–avoid**	++
	Simvastatin & other "statins"	↑ levels of B (↑ risk of myopathy)	++
	Sotalol	↓ levels of B	++
	Theophylline	↑ levels of B	++
Tenofovir	Atazanavir	↓ levels of B–add ritonavir	++
	Didanosine (ddI)	**↑ levels of B (reduce dose)**	++
Terbinafine	Cimetidine	↑ levels of A	+
	Phenobarbital, rifampin	↓ levels of A	+
Tetracyclines	*See Doxycycline, plus:*		
	Atovaquone	↓ levels of B	+
	Digoxin	↑ toxicity of B (may persist several months–up to 10% pts)	++
	Methoxyflurane	↑ toxicity; polyuria, renal failure	+
	Sucralfate	↓ absorption of A (separate by ≥2 hrs)	+
Thiabendazole	Theophyllines	↑ serum theophylline, nausea	+
Tigecycline	Oral contraceptives	↓ levels of B	++
Tinidazole (Tindamax)	*See Metronidazole–similar entity, expect similar interactions*		
Tobramycin	*See Aminoglycosides*		
Trimethoprim	Amantadine, Dapsone, Digoxin, Methotrexate, Procainamide, Zidovudine	↑ serum levels of B	++
	Potassium-sparing diuretics	↑ serum K⁺	++
	Repaglinide	↑ levels of B (hypoglycemia)	++
	Thiazide diuretics	↓ serum Na⁺	+
Trimethoprim-Sulfamethoxazole	Ace inhibitors	↑ serum K+	++
	Amantadine	↑ levels of B (toxicity)	++
	Azathioprine	Reports of leukopenia	+
	Cyclosporine	↓ levels of B, ↑ serum creatinine	+
	Loperamide	↑ levels of B	+
	Methotrexate	Enhanced marrow suppression	++
	Oral contraceptives, Pimozide, and 6-mercaptopurine	↓ effect of B	+
	Phenytoin	↑ levels of B	+
	Rifampin	↑ levels of B	+
	Spironolactone, Sulfonylureas	↑ levels K+	++
	Warfarin	↑ activity of B	+
Valganciclovir (Valcyte)	*See Ganciclovir*		
Vancomycin	Aminoglycosides	↑ frequency of nephrotoxicity	++
Zalcitabine (ddC) (HIVID)	Valproic acid, Pentamidine (IV), alcohol, Lamivudine	↑ pancreatitis risk	+
	Cisplatin, INH, Metronidazole, Vincristine, Nitrofurantoin, d4T, Dapsone	↑ risk of peripheral neuropathy	+
Zidovudine (ZDV) (Retrovir)	Atovaquone, Fluconazole, Methadone	↑ levels of A	+
	Clarithromycin	↓ levels of A	±
	Indomethacin	↑ levels of ZDV toxic metabolite	+
	Nelfinavir	↓ levels of A	++
	Probenecid, TMP/SMX	↑ levels of A	+
	Rifampin/rifabutin	↓ levels of A	++
	Stavudine	**Interference–DO NOT COMBINE!**	++
	Valproic Acid	↑ levels of A	++

TABLE 22B – DRUG-DRUG INTERACTIONS BETWEEN NON-NUCLEOSIDE REVERSE TRANSCRIPTASE INHIBITORS (NNRTIS) AND PROTEASE INHIBITORS
(Adapted from Guidelines for the Use of Antiretroviral Agents in HIV-Infected Adults & Adolescents; see www.aidsinfo.nih.gov)

NAME (Abbreviation, Trade Name)	Atazanavir (ATV, Reyataz)	Darunavir (DRV, Prezista)	Fosamprenavir (FOS-APV, Lexiva)	Indinavir (IDV, Crixivan)	Lopinavir/Ritonavir (LP/R, Kaletra)	Nelfinavir (NFV, Viracept)	Saquinavir (SQV, Invirase)	Tipranavir (TPV)
Delavirdine (DLV, Rescriptor)	No data	No data	Co-administration not recommended	IDV levels ↑ 40%. Dose: IDV 600 mg q8h, DLV standard	Expect LP levels to ↑. No dose data	NFV levels ↑ 2X; DLV levels ↓ 50%. Dose: No data	SQV levels ↑ 5X. Dose: SQV 800 mg q8h, DLV standard	No data
Efavirenz (EFZ, Sustiva)	ATV AUC ↓ 74%. Dose: EFZ standard; ATV/RTV 300/100 mg q24h with food	Standard doses of both drugs	FOS-APV levels ↓. Dose: EFZ standard; FOS-APV 1400 mg + RTV 300 mg q24h or 700 mg FOS-APV + 100 mg RTV q12h	Levels: IDV ↓ 31%. Dose: IDV 1000 mg q8h, EFZ standard	Level of LP ↓ 40%. Dose: LP/R 533/133 mg q12h, EFZ standard	Standard doses	Level: SQV ↓ 62%. Dose: SQV 400 mg + RTV 400 mg q12h	No dose change necessary
Etravirine (ETR, Intelence)	↑ ATV & ↑ ETR levels.	Standard doses of both drugs	↑ levels of FOS-APV.	↓ level of IDV.	↑ levels of ETR, ↓ levels of LP/R.	↑ levels of NFV.	↓ ETR levels 33%; SQV/R no change. Standard dose of both drugs.	↓ levels of ETR, ↑ levels of TPV & RTV. **Avoid combination.**
Nevirapine (NVP, Viramune)	Avoid combination. ATZ increases NVP concentrations >25%; NVP decreases ATZ AUC by 42%.	Standard doses of both drugs	Use with caution. NVP AUC increased 14% (700/100 Fos/rit; NVP AUC inc 29% (Fos 1400 mg bid).	IDV levels ↓ 28%. Dose: IDV 1000 mg q8h or combine with RTV; NVP standard	LP levels ↓ 53%. Dose: LP/R 533/133 mg q12h; NVP standard	Standard doses	Dose: SQV + RTV 400/400 mg, both q12h	Standard doses

TABLE 23 – LIST OF GENERIC AND COMMON TRADE NAMES

GENERIC NAME: TRADE NAMES	GENERIC NAME: TRADE NAMES	GENERIC NAME: TRADE NAMES
Abacavir: Ziagen	Efavirenz: Sustiva	Nystatin: Mycostatin
Abacavir + Lamivudine: Epzicom	Efavirenz + Emtricitabine + Tenofovir: Atripla	Ofloxacin: Floxin
Abacavir + Lamivudine + Dolutegravir: Triumeq	Elbasvir + Grazoprevir: Zepatier	Olysio: Simeprevir
		Oritavancin: Orbactiv
Abacavir + Lamivudine + Zidovudine: Trizivir	Elvitegravir: Vitekta	Oseltamivir: Tamiflu
Acyclovir: Zovirax	Elvitegravir + Cobicistat + Emtricitabine + Tenofovir: Stribild	Oxacillin: Prostaphlin
Adefovir: Hepsera		Palivizumab: Synagis
Albendazole: Albenza	Elvitegravir + Cobicistat + Emtricitabine + Tenofovir AF: Genvoya	Paritaprevir + Ritonavir + Ombitasvir: Technivie
Amantadine: Symmetrel	Emtricitabine: Emtriva	Paritaprevir + Ritonavir + Ombitasvir + Dasabuvir: Viekira Pak
Amikacin: Amikin	Emtricitabine + Tenofovir: Truvada	Paromomycin: Humatin
Amoxicillin: Amoxil, Polymox	Emtricitabine + Tenofovir + Rilpivirine: Complera	Pentamidine: NebuPent, Pentam 300
Amoxicillin extended release: Moxatag	Enfuvirtide (T-20): Fuzeon	Peramivir: Rapivab
Amox./clav.: Augmentin, Augmentin ES-600; Augmentin XR	Entecavir: Baraclude	Piperacillin + Tazobactam: Zosyn, Tazocin
	Ertapenem: Invanz	Piperazine: Antepar
Amphotericin B: Fungizone	Etravirine: Intelence	Podophyllotoxin: Condylox
Ampho B-liposomal: AmBisome	Erythromycin(s): Ilotycin	Polymyxin B: Poly-Rx
Ampho B-lipid complex: Abelcet	*Ethyl succinate:* Pediamycin	Posaconazole: Noxafil
Ampicillin: Omnipen, Polycillin	*Glucoheptonate:* Erythrocin	Praziquantel: Biltricide
Ampicillin + Sulbactam: Unasyn	*Estolate:* Ilosone	Primaquine: Primachine
Artemether + Lumefantrine: Coartem	Erythro + Sulfisoxazole: Pediazole	Proguanil: Paludrine
Atazanavir: Reyataz	Ethambutol: Myambutol	Prulifloxacin: Sword
Atovaquone: Mepron	Ethionamide: Trecator	Pyrantel pamoate: Antiminth
Atovaquone + Proguanil: Malarone	Famciclovir: Famvir	Pyrimethamine: Daraprim
Azithromycin: Zithromax	Fidaxomicin: Dificid	Pyrimethamine + Sulfadoxine: Fansidar
Azithromycin ER: Zmax	Fluconazole: Diflucan	Quinupristin + Dalfopristin: Synercid
Aztreonam: Azactam, Cayston	Flucytosine: Ancobon	Raltegravir: Isentress
Bedaquiline: Sirturo	Fosamprenavir: Lexiva	Retapamulin: Altabax
Benznidazole: Exeltis, Abarax	Foscarnet: Foscavir	Ribavirin: Virazole, Rebetol
Bezlotoxumab: Zinplava	Fosfomycin: Monurol	Rifabutin: Mycobutin
Boceprevir: Victrelis	Fusidic acid: Taksta	Rifampin: Rifadin, Rimactane
Caspofungin: Cancidas	Ganciclovir: Cytovene	Rifapentine: Priftin
Cefaclor: Ceclor, Ceclor CD	Gatifloxacin: Tequin	Rifaximin: Xifaxan
Cefadroxil: Duricef	Gemifloxacin: Factive	Rilpivirine: Edurant
Cefazolin: Ancef, Kefzol	Gentamicin: Garamycin	Rimantadine: Flumadine
Cefdinir: Omnicef	Grazoprevir + Elbasvir: Zepatier	Ritonavir: Norvir
Cefditoren pivoxil: Spectracef	Griseofulvin: Fulvicin	Saquinavir: Invirase
Cefepime: Maxipime	Halofantrine: Halfan	Secnidazole: Solosec
Cefixime^NUS: Suprax	Idoxuridine: Dendrid, Stoxil	Spectinomycin: Trobicin
Cefoperazone + Sulbactam: Sulperazon^NUS	INH + RIF: Rifamate	Stavudine: Zerit
	INH + RIF + PZA: Rifater	Stiboglucomate: Pentostam
Cefonicid: Monocid	Interferon alfa: Intron A	Silver sulfadiazine: Silvadene
Cefotaxime: Claforan	Interferon, pegylated: PEG-Intron, Pegasys	Simeprevir: Olysio
Cefotetan: Cefotan		Sofosbuvir: Sovaldi
Cefoxitin: Mefoxin	Interferon + Ribavirin: Rebetron	Sulfamethoxazole: Gantanol
Cefpodoxime proxetil: Vantin	Imipenem + Cilastatin: Primaxin, Tienam	Sulfasalazine: Azulfidine
Cefprozil: Cefzil	Imiquimod: Aldara	Sulfisoxazole: Gantrisin
Ceftaroline: Teflaro	Indinavir: Crixivan	Tedizolid: Sivextro
Ceftazidime: Fortaz, Tazicef, Tazidime	Isavuconazonium sulfate: Cresemba	Telaprevir: Incivek
Ceftazidime + Avibactam: Avycaz	Itraconazole: Sporanox	Telavancin: Vibativ
Ceftibuten: Cedax	Iodoquinol: Yodoxin	Telbivudine: Tyzeka
Ceftizoxime: Cefizox	Ivermectin: Stromectol, Sklice	Telithromycin: Ketek
Ceftobiprole: Zeftera	Ketoconazole: Nizoral	Temocillin: Negaban, Temopen
Ceftolozane + Tazobactam: Zerbaxa	Lamivudine: Epivir, Epivir-HBV	Tenofovir AF-FTC: Descovy
Ceftriaxone: Rocephin	Lamivudine + Abacavir: Epzicom	Tenofovir alafenamide: Vemlidy
Cefuroxime: Zinacef, Ceftin	Ledipasvir + Sofosbuvir: Harvoni	Tenofovir DF: Viread
Cephalexin: Keflex	Letermovir: Prevymis	Terbinafine: Lamisil
Cephradine: Anspor, Velosef	Levofloxacin: Levaquin	Thalidomide: Thalomid
Chloroquine: Aralen	Linezolid: Zyvox	Thiabendazole: Mintezol
Cidofovir: Vistide	Lomefloxacin: Maxaquin	Tigecycline: Tygacil
Ciprofloxacin: Cipro, Cipro XR	Lopinavir + Ritonavir: Kaletra	Tinidazole: Tindamax
Clarithromycin: Biaxin, Biaxin XL	Loracarbef: Lorabid	Tipranavir: Aptivus
Clindamycin: Cleocin	Mafenide: Sulfamylon	Tobramycin: Nebcin
Clofazimine: Lamprene	Maraviroc: Selzentry	Tretinoin: Retin A
Clotrimazole: Lotrimin, Mycelex	Mebendazole: Vermox	Trifluridine: Viroptic
Cloxacillin: Tegopen	Mefloquine: Lariam	Trimethoprim: Primsol
Colistimethate: Coly-Mycin M	Meropenem: Merrem	Trimethoprim + Sulfamethoxazole: Bactrim, Septra
Cycloserine: Seromycin	Meropenem + vaborbactam: Vabomere	
Daclatasvir: Daklinza	Mesalamine: Asacol, Pentasa	Valacyclovir: Valtrex
Daptomycin: Cubicin	Methenamine: Hiprex, Mandelamine	Valganciclovir: Valcyte
Dalbavancin: Dalvance	Metronidazole: Flagyl	Vancomycin: Vancocin
Darunavir: Prezista	Micafungin: Mycamine	Velpatasvir + Sofosbuvir: Epclusa
Delafloxacin: Baxdela	Minocycline: Minocin	Voriconazole: Vfend
Delavirdine: Rescriptor	Moxifloxacin: Avelox	Zalcitabine: HIVID
Dicloxacillin: Dynapen	Mupirocin: Bactroban	Zanamivir: Relenza
Didanosine: Videx	Nafcillin: Unipen	Zidovudine (ZDV): Retrovir
Diethylcarbamazine: Hetrazan	Nelfinavir: Viracept	Zidovudine + 3TC: Combivir
Diloxanide furoate: Furamide	Nevirapine: Viramune	Zidovudine + 3TC + Abacavir: Trizivir
Dolutegravir: Tivicay	Nitazoxanide: Alinia	
Doripenem: Doribax	Nitrofurantoin: Macrobid, Macrodantin	
Doxycycline: Vibramycin		

TABLE 23 (2)
LIST OF COMMON TRADE AND GENERIC NAMES

TRADE NAMES: GENERIC NAME	TRADE NAMES: GENERIC NAME	TRADE NAMES: GENERIC NAME
Abelcet: Ampho B-lipid complex	Halfan: Halofantrine	Septra: Trimethoprim + Sulfamethoxazole
Albenza: Albendazole	Harvoni: Ledipasvir + Sofosbuvir	Seromycin: Cycloserine
Aldara: Imiquimod	Hepsera: Adefovir	Silvadene: Silver sulfadiazine
Alinia: Nitazoxanide	Herplex: Idoxuridine	Sirturo: Bedaquiline
Altabax: Retapamulin	Hiprex: Methenamine hippurate	Sivextro: Tedizolid
AmBisome: Ampho B-liposomal	HIVID: Zalcitabine	Sklice: Ivermectin lotion
Amikin: Amikacin	Humatin: Paromomycin	Solosec: Secnidazole
Amoxil: Amoxicillin	Ilosone: Erythromycin estolate	Sovaldi: Sofosbuvir
Ancef: Cefazolin	Ilotycin: Erythromycin	Spectracef: Cefditoren pivoxil
Ancobon: Flucytosine	Incivek: Telaprevir	Sporanox: Itraconazole
Anspor: Cephradine	Intelence: Etravirine	Stoxil: Idoxuridine
Antepar: Piperazine	Intron A: Interferon alfa	Stribild: Elvitegravir + Cobicistat +
Antiminth: Pyrantel pamoate	Invanz: Ertapenem	Emtricitabine + Tenofovir
Aptivus: Tipranavir	Invirase: Saquinavir	Stromectol: Ivermectin
Aralen: Chloroquine	Isentress: Raltegravir	Sulfamylon: Mafenide
Asacol: Mesalamine	Kantrex: Kanamycin	Sulperazon^NUS: Cefoperazone +
Atripla: Efavirenz + Emtricitabine +	Kaletra: Lopinavir + Ritonavir	Sulbactam
Tenofovir	Keflex: Cephalexin	Suprax: Cefixime^NUS
Augmentin, Augmentin ES-600	Ketek: Telithromycin	Sustiva: Efavirenz
Augmentin XR: Amox./clav.	Lamisil: Terbinafine	Symmetrel: Amantadine
Avelox: Moxifloxacin	Lamprene: Clofazimine	Synagis: Palivizumab
Avycaz: Ceftazidime +	Lariam: Mefloquine	Synercid: Quinupristin + Dalfopristin
AvibactamAzactam: Aztreonam	Levaquin: Levofloxacin	Taksta: Fusidic acid
Azulfidine: Sulfasalazine	Lexiva: Fosamprenavir	Tamiflu: Oseltamivir
Bactroban: Mupirocin	Lorabid: Loracarbef	Tazicef: Ceftazidime
Bactrim: Trimethoprim + SMX	Macrodantin, Macrobid: Nitrofurantoin	Technivie: Paritaprevir + Ritonavir +
Baraclude: Entecavir	Malarone: Atovaquone + Proguanil	Ombitasvir
Baxdela: Delafloxacin	Mandelamine: Methenamine	Teflaro: Ceftaroline
Biaxin, Biaxin XL: Clarithromycin	mandelate	Tegopen: Cloxacillin
Biltricide: Praziquantel	Maxaquin: Lomefloxacin	Tequin: Gatifloxacin
Cancidas: Caspofungin	Maxipime: Cefepime	Thalomid: Thalidomide
Cayston: Aztreonam (inhaled)	Mefoxin: Cefoxitin	Tienam: Imipenem
Ceclor, Ceclor CD: Cefaclor	Mepron: Atovaquone	Tinactin: Tolnaftate
Cedax: Ceftibuten	Merrem: Meropenem	Tindamax: Tinidazole
Cefizox: Ceftizoxime	Minocin: Minocycline	Tivicay: Dolutegravir
Cefotan: Cefotetan	Mintezol: Thiabendazole	Trecator SC: Ethionamide
Ceftin: Cefuroxime axetil	Monocid: Cefonicid	Triumeq: Abacavir + Lamivudine +
Cefzil: Cefprozil	Monurol: Fosfomycin	Dolutegravir
Cipro, Cipro XR: Ciprofloxacin	Moxatag: Amoxicillin extended release:	Trizivir: Zidovudine + 3TC + Abacavir
& extended release	Myambutol: Ethambutol	Trobicin: Spectinomycin
Claforan: Cefotaxime	Mycamine: Micafungin	Truvada: Emtricitabine + Tenofovir
Coartem: Artemether + Lumefantrine	Mycobutin: Rifabutin	Tygacil: Tigecycline
Coly-Mycin M: Colistimethate	Mycostatin: Nystatin	Tyzeka: Telbivudine
Combivir: Zidovudine + 3TC	Nafcil: Nafcillin	Unasyn: Ampicillin/sulbactam
Complera: Emtricitabine + Tenofovir +	Nebcin: Tobramycin	Unipen: Nafcillin
Rilpivirine	NebuPent: Pentamidine	Vabomere: Meropenem + vaborbactam
Cresemba: Isavuconazonium sulfate	Nizoral: Ketoconazole	Valcyte: Valganciclovir
Crixivan: Indinavir	Norvir: Ritonavir	Valtrex: Valacyclovir
Cubicin: Daptomycin	Noxafil: Posaconazole	Vancocin: Vancomycin
Cytovene: Ganciclovir	Olysio: Simeprevir	Vantin: Cefpodoxime proxetil
Daklinza: Daclatasvir	Omnicef: Cefdinir	Velosef: Cephradine
Dalvance: Dalbavancin	Omnipen: Ampicillin	Vemlidy: Tenofovir alafenamide
Daraprim: Pyrimethamine	Orbactiv: Oritavancin	Vermox: Mebendazole
Descovy: Tenofovir AF-FTC	Pediamycin: Erythro. ethyl succinate	Vfend: Voriconazole
Dificid: Fidaxomicin	Pediazole: Erythro. ethyl succinate +	Vibativ: Telavancin
Diflucan: Fluconazole	sulfisoxazole	Vibramycin: Doxycycline
Doribax: Doripenem	Pegasys, PEG-Intron: Interferon,	Victrelis: Boceprevir
Duricef: Cefadroxil	pegylated	Videx: Didanosine
Dynapen: Dicloxacillin	Pentam 300: Pentamidine	Viekira Pak: Paritaprevir + Ritonavir +
Edurant: Rilpivirine	Pentasa: Mesalamine	Ombitasvir + Dasabuvir
Emtriva: Emtricitabine	Polycillin: Ampicillin	Viracept: Nelfinavir
Epclusa: Velpatasvir + Sofosbuvir	Polymox: Amoxicillin	Viramune: Nevirapine
Epivir, Epivir-HBV: Lamivudine	Poly-Rx: Polymyxin B	Virazole: Ribavirin
Epzicom: Lamivudine + Abacavir	Prezista: Darunavir	Viread: Tenofovir
Exeltis: Benznidazole	Priftin: Rifapentine	Vistide: Cidofovir
Factive: Gemifloxacin	Primaxin: Imipenem + Cilastatin	Vitekta: Elvitegravir
Famvir: Famciclovir	Primsol: Trimethoprim	Xifaxan: Rifaximin
Fansidar: Pyrimethamine + Sulfadoxine	Prostaphlin: Oxacillin	Yodoxin: Iodoquinol
Flagyl: Metronidazole	Rapivab: Peramivir	Zerit: Stavudine
Floxin: Ofloxacin	Rebetol: Ribavirin	Zeftera: Ceftobiprole
Flumadine: Rimantadine	Rebetron: Interferon + Ribavirin	Zepatier: Elbasvir + Grazoprevir
Foscavir: Foscarnet	Relenza: Zanamivir	Zerbaxa: Ceftolozane + Tazobactam
Fortaz: Ceftazidime	Rescriptor: Delavirdine	Ziagen: Abacavir
Fulvicin: Griseofulvin	Retin A: Tretinoin	Zinacef: Cefuroxime
Fungizone: Amphotericin B	Retrovir: Zidovudine (ZDV)	Zinplava: Bezlotoxumab
Furadantin: Nitrofurantoin	Reyataz: Atazanavir	Zithromax: Azithromycin
Fuzeon: Enfuvirtide (T-20)	Rifadin: Rifampin	Zmax: Azithromycin ER
Gantanol: Sulfamethoxazole	Rifamate: INH + RIF	Zovirax: Acyclovir
Gantrisin: Sulfisoxazole	Rifater: INH + RIF + PZA	Zosyn: Piperacillin + Tazobactam
Garamycin: Gentamicin	Rimactane: Rifampin	Zyvox: Linezolid
Genvoya: Elvitegravir + Cobicistat +	Rocephin: Ceftriaxone	
Emtricitabine + Tenofovir AF	Selzentry: Maraviroc	